MEDIA, FEMINISM, CULTURAL STUDIES

Stepping Forward: Essays, Lectures and Interviews
by Wolfgang Iser

Wild Zones: Pornography, Art and Feminism
by Kelly Ives

Global Media Warning: Explorations of Radio, Television and the Press
by Oliver Whitehorne

'Cosmo Woman': The World of Women's Magazines
by Oliver Whitehorne

Andrea Dworkin
by Jeremy Mark Robinson

Cixous, Irigaray, Kristeva: The Jouissance of French Feminism
by Kelly Ives

Sex in Art: Pornography and Pleasure in Painting and Sculpture
by Cassidy Hughes

The Erotic Object: Sexuality in Sculpture
From Prehistory to the Present Day
by Susan Quinnell

Women in Pop Music
by Helen Challis

Detonation Britain: Nuclear War In the UK
by Jeremy Mark Robinson

Julia Kristeva: Art, Love, Melancholy, Philosophy, Semiotics
by Kelly Ives

Luce Irigaray: Lips, Kissing, and the Politics of Sexual Difference
by Kelly Ives

Helene Cixous I Love You: The Jouissance of Writing
by Kelly Ives

The Poetry of Cinema
by John Madden

The Sacred Cinema of Andrei Tarkovsky
by Jeremy Mark Robinson

Feminism and Shakespeare
by B.D. Barnacle

The Cinema of Richard Linklater
by Thomas A. Christie

Walerian Borowczyk
by Jeremy Mark Robinson

The Cinema of Hayao Miyazaki
Jeremy Mark Robinson

Liv Tyler
by Thomas A. Christie

EROTIC ART
In the Early 20th Century

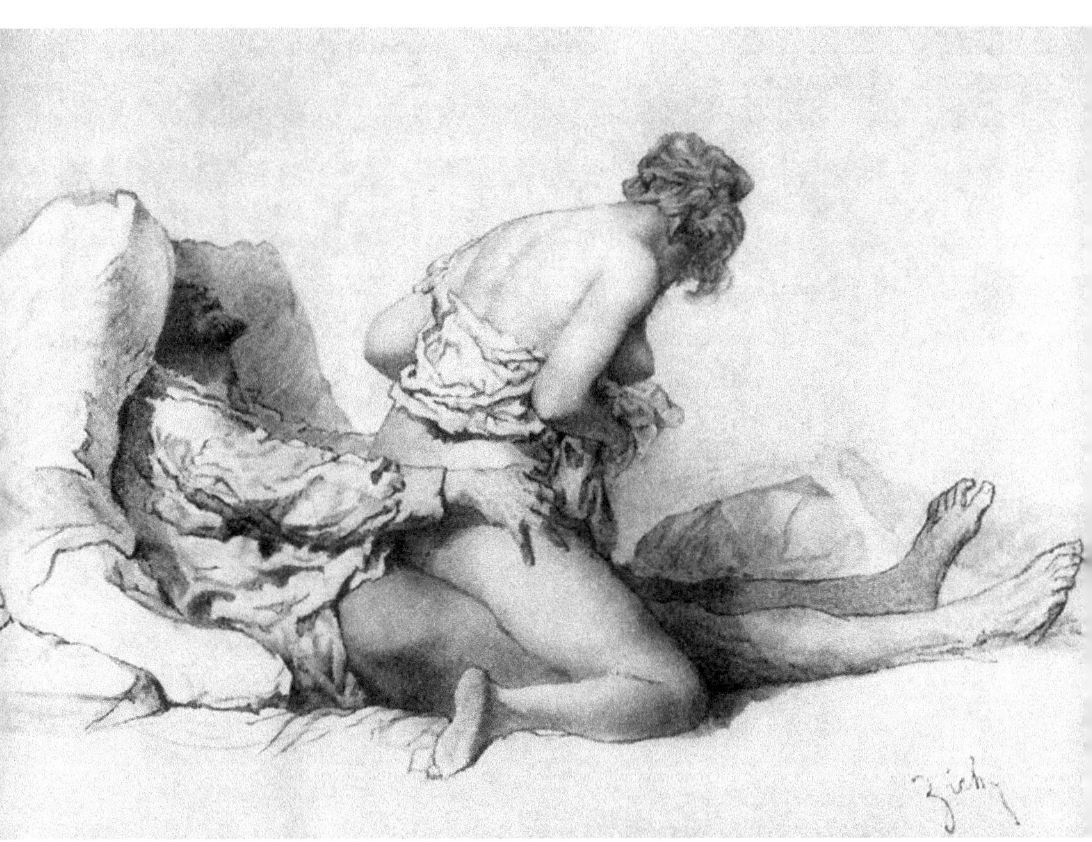

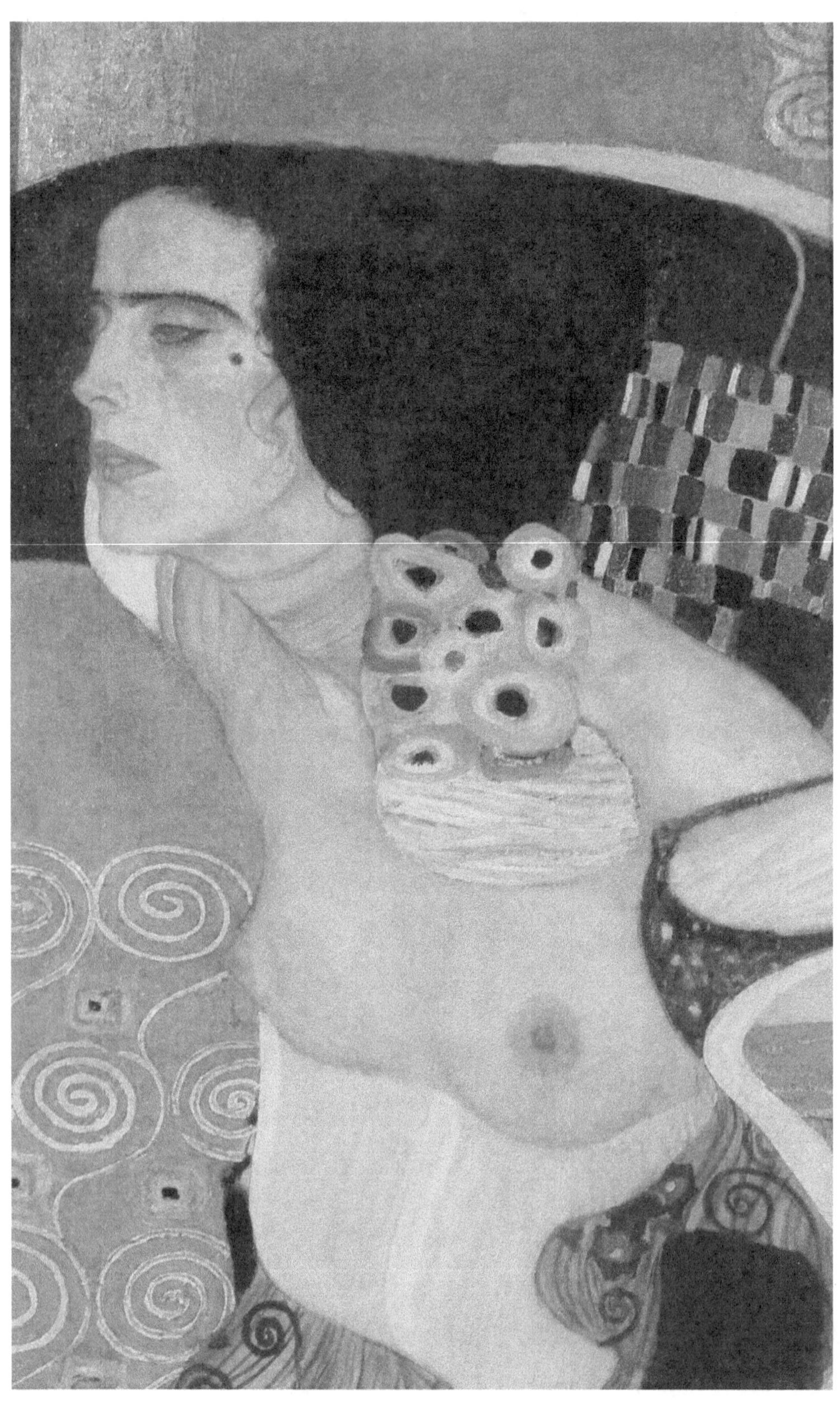

Gustav Klimt in Venice (detail)

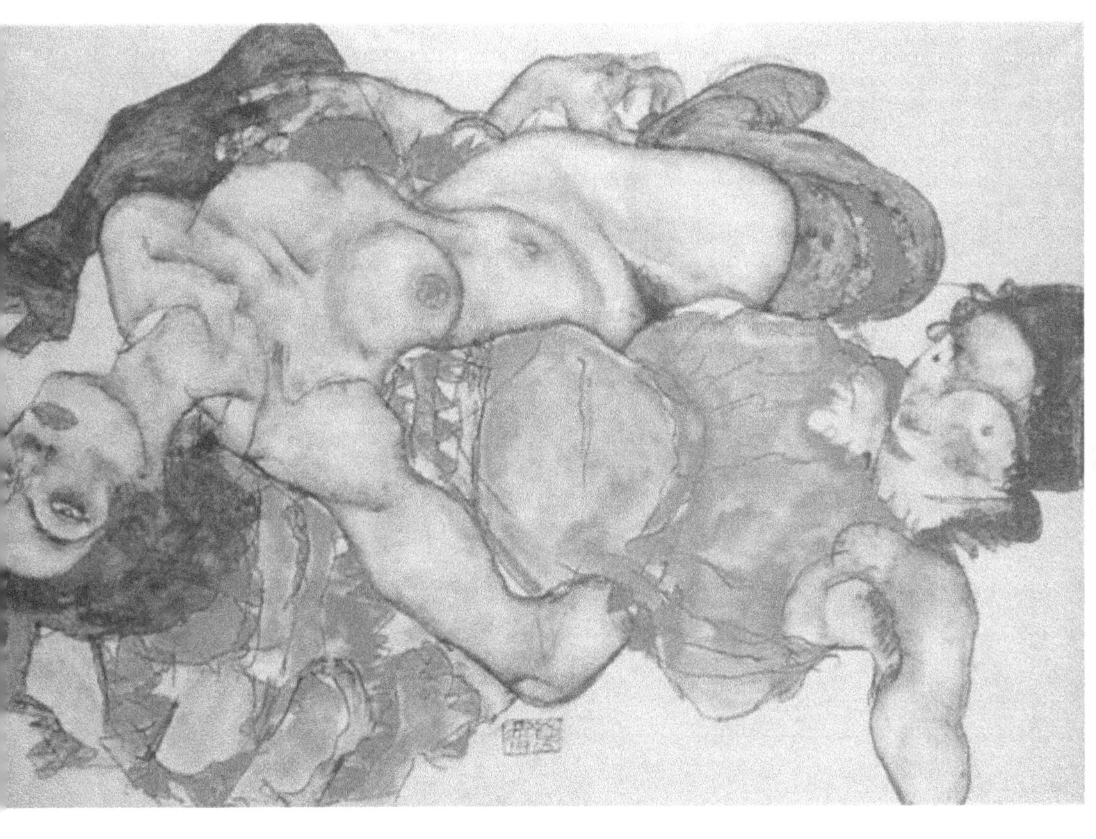

EROTIC ART
In the Early 20th Century

Cassidy Hughes

Crescent Moon

First published 2024.

Set in Book Antiqua 10 on 14pt.
Designed by Radiance Graphics.

Thanks to the authors and publishers quoted.

British Library Cataloguing in Publication data

Hughes, Cassidy
Erotic Art In the Early 20th Century
I. Title
704.9

ISBN-13 9781861711816

CRESCENT MOON PUBLISHING
P.O. Box 1312, Maidstone, Kent, ME14 5XU
Great Britain, www.crmoon.com

CONTENTS

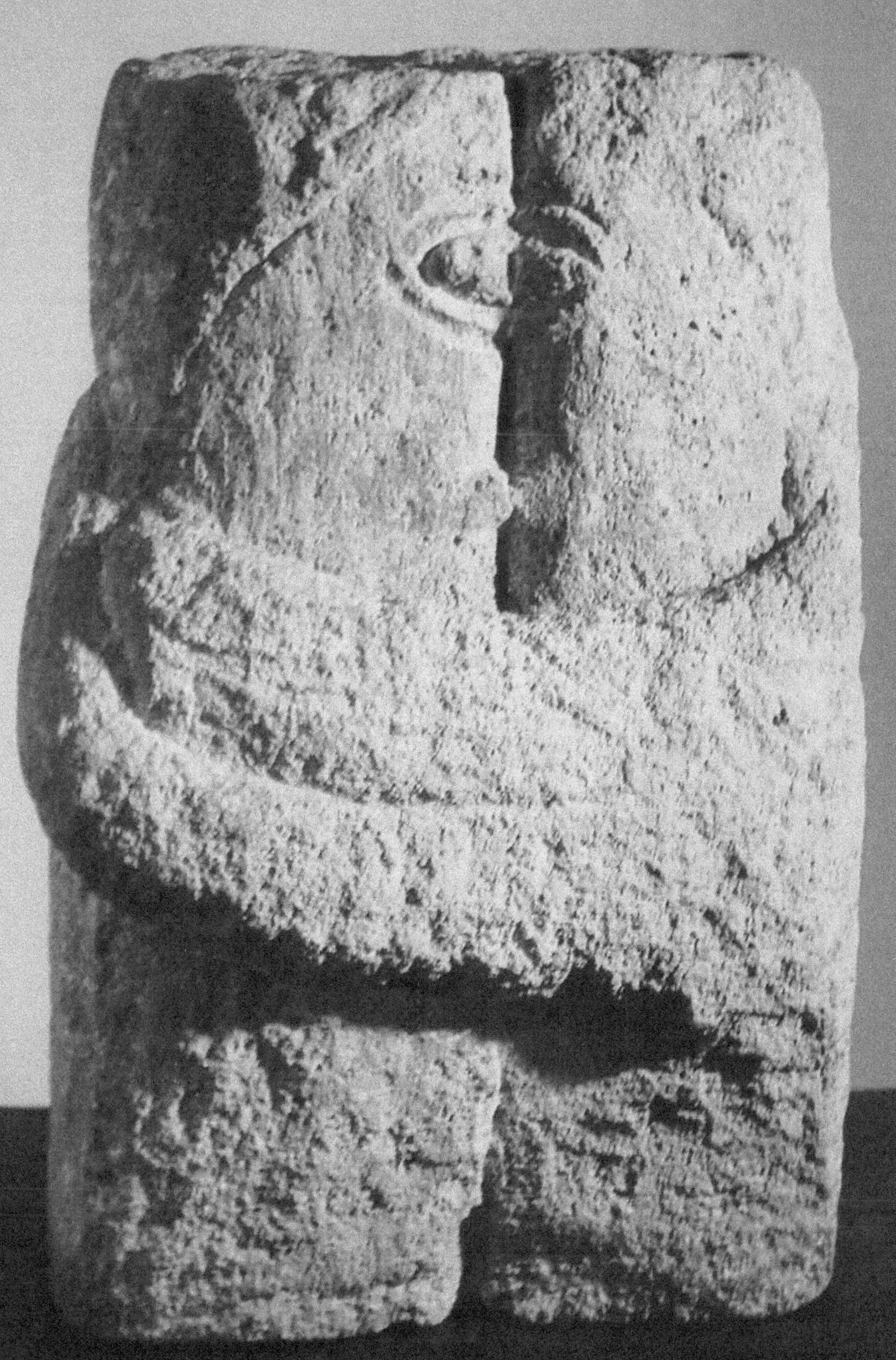

Constantin Brancusi, The Kiss

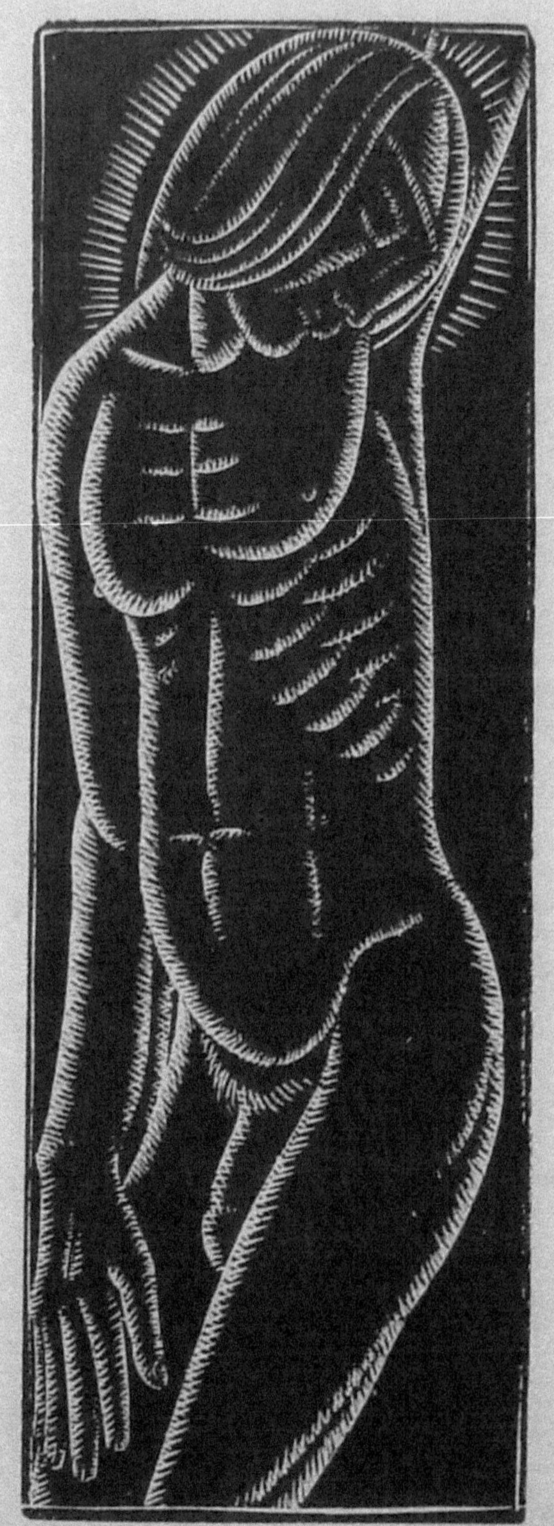

Eric Gill,Deposition,
1924

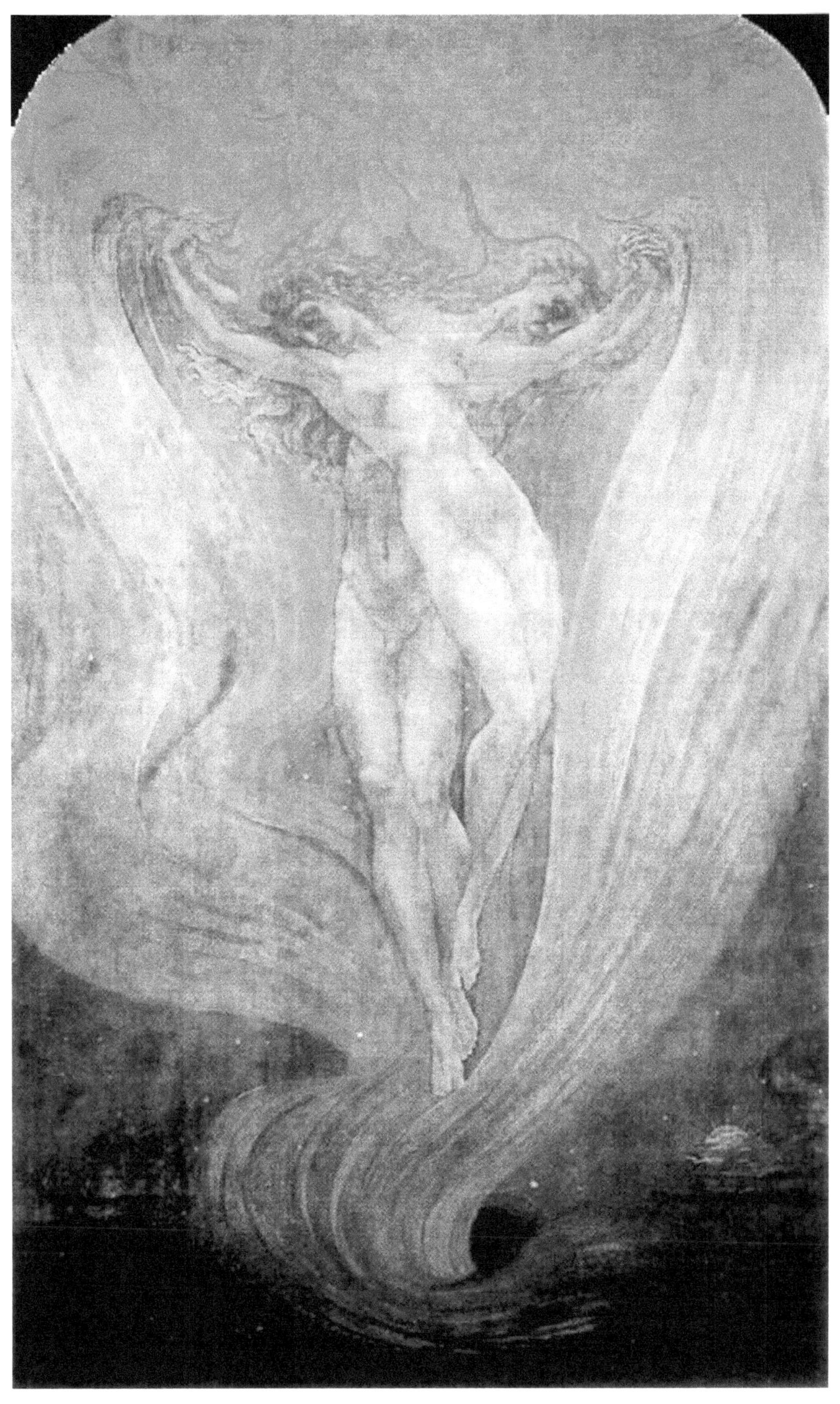

Jean Delville, The Love of Souls, 1900, Brussels

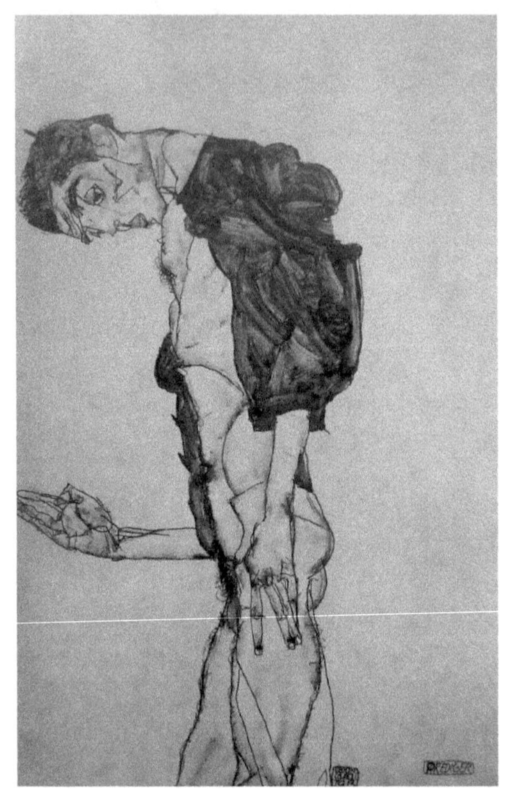

Two Egon Schiele figures:
Preacher, 1913, above.
And Standing Nude Girl With Stockings, 1914, below.

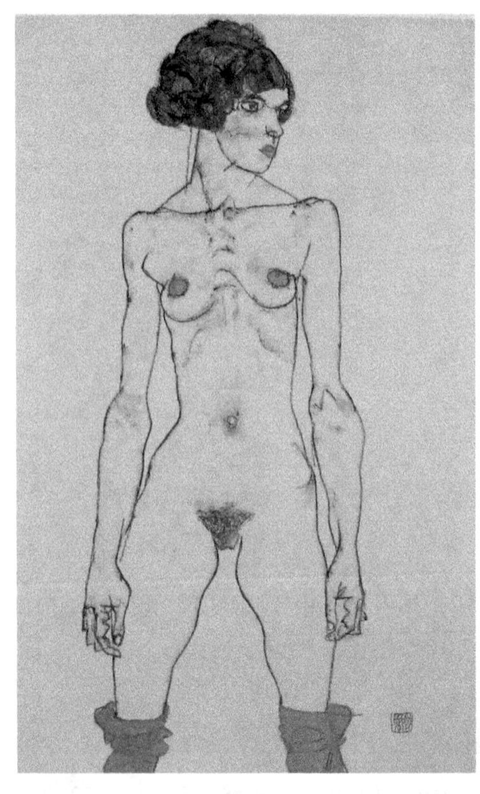

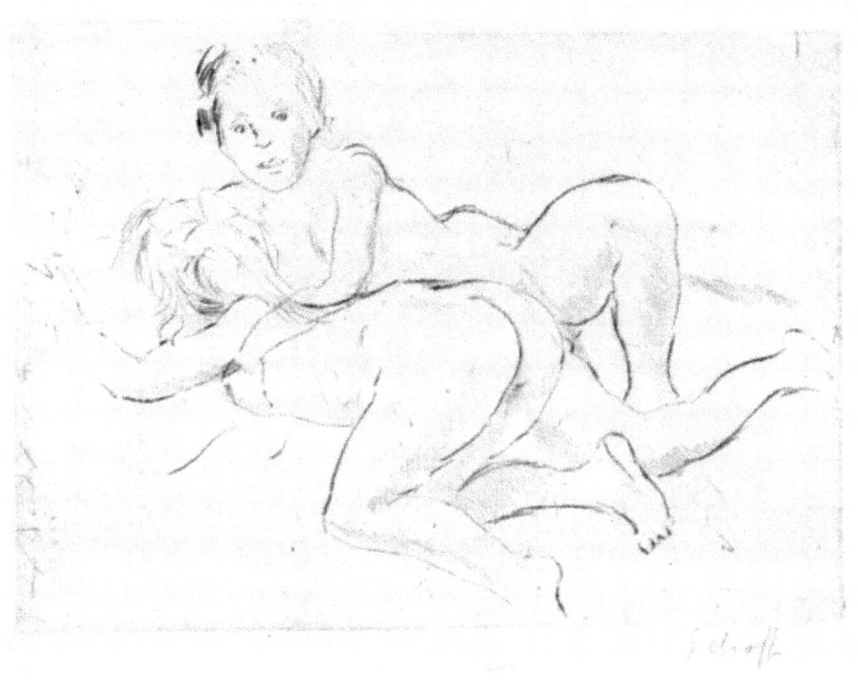

Otto Schoff

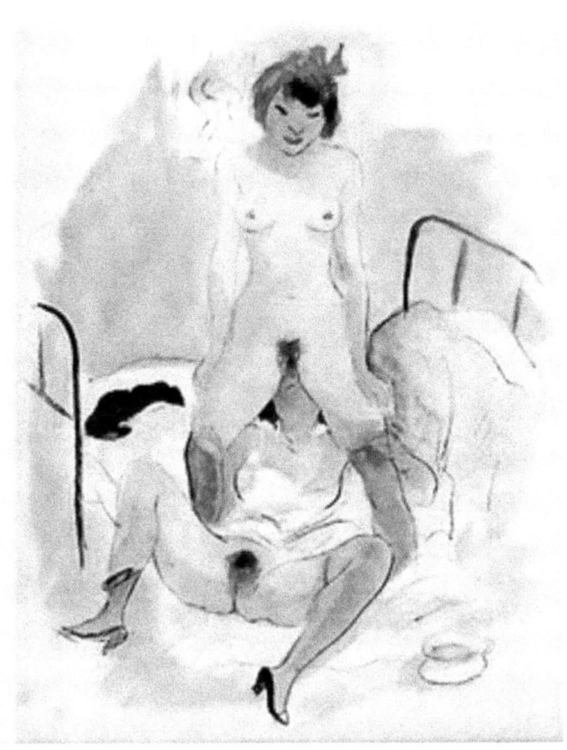

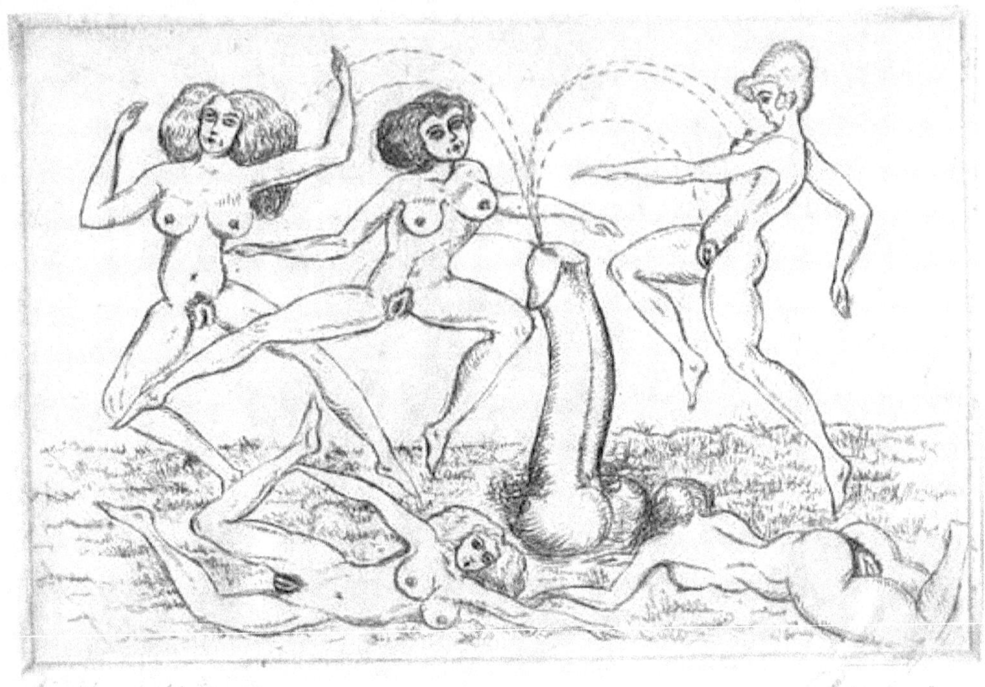

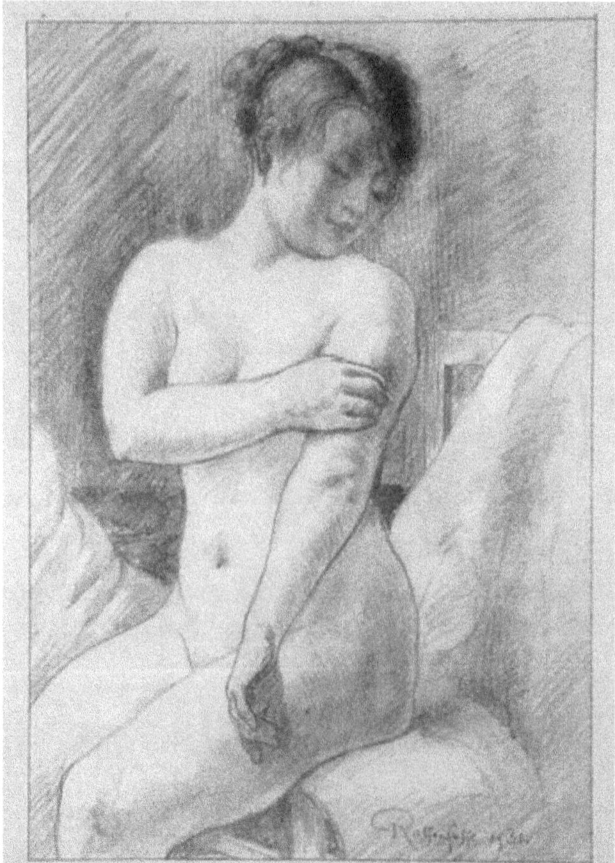

Armand Rassenfosse
(1862-1934)

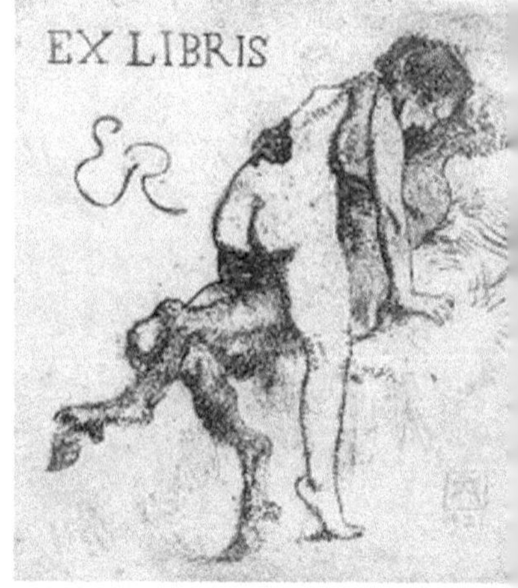

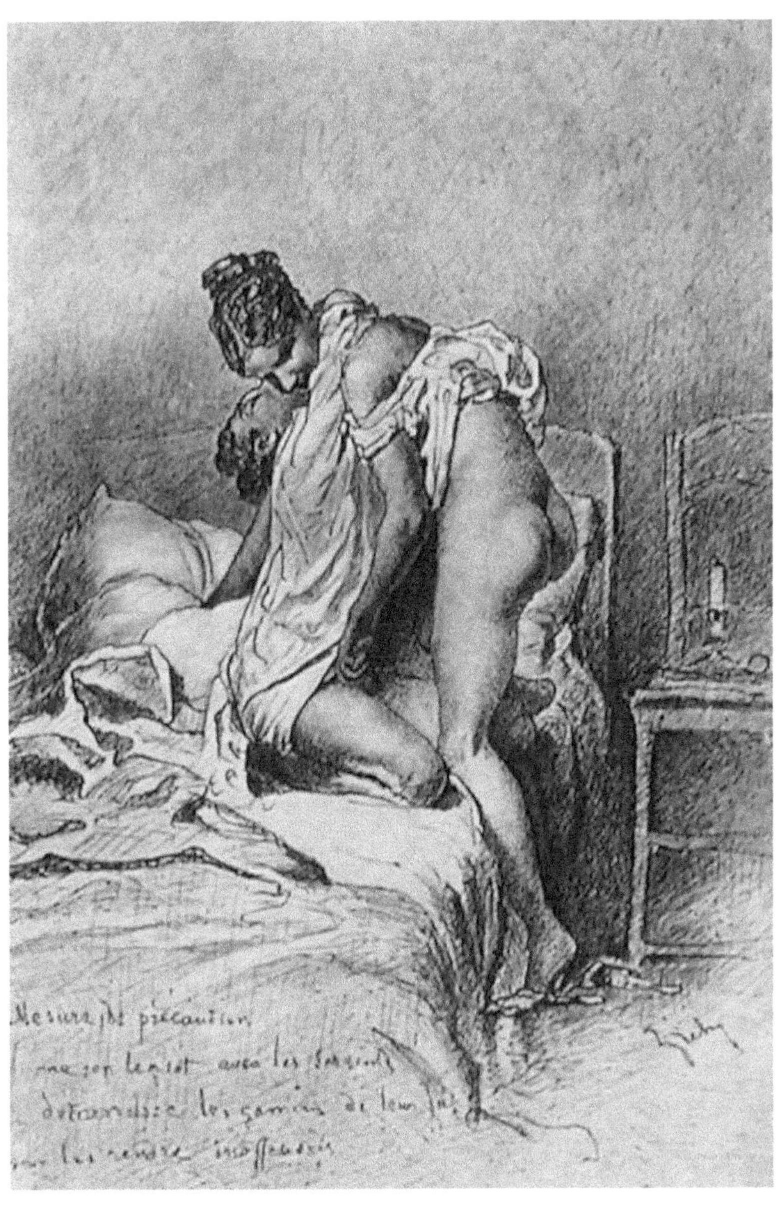

Mihály Zichy, from Liebe, 1911.

The first part of this book on early 20th century erotic art uses short entries about aspects of erotic art (with examples from the whole history of erotic art).

The bulk of the second part of the book focusses on the celebrated artists of the 20th century whose work is considered erotic, as well as many anonymous works.

Part One

Issues In Erotic Art

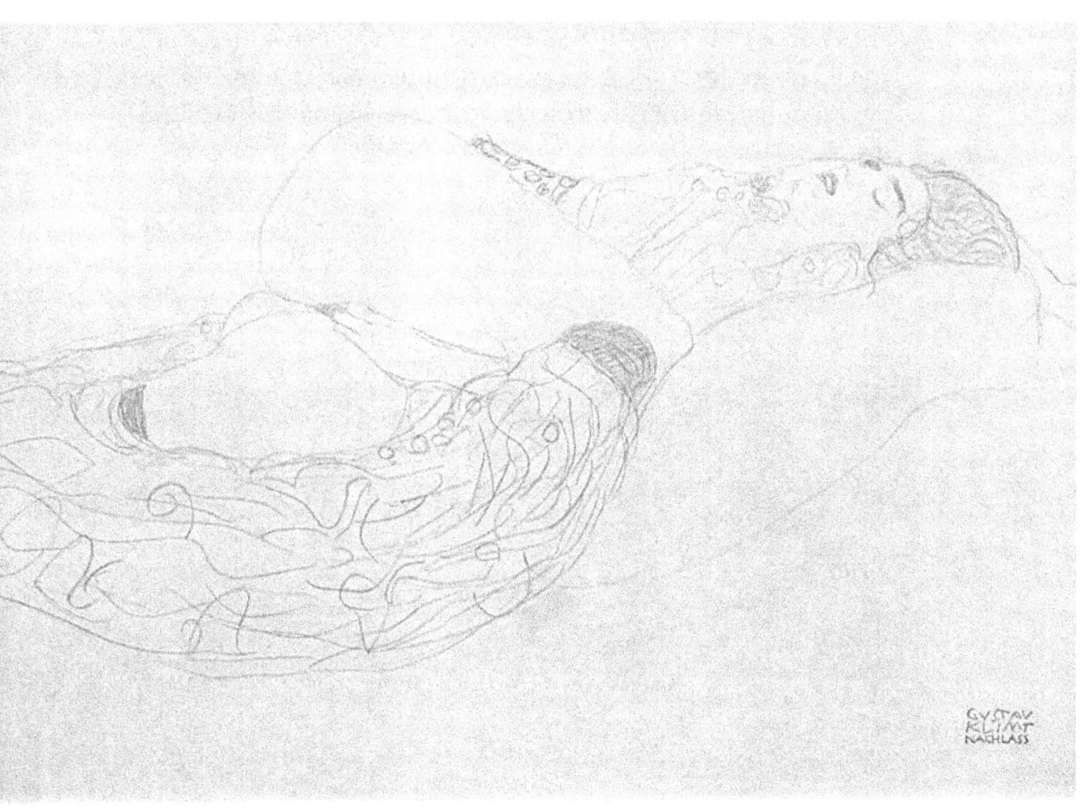

EROTIC ART AND PORNOGRAPHY

The establishment art historical view of erotic art and pornography is that true erotic or high art engenders quiet contemplation, a detached ravishing of the senses, a meditation on Platonic, Aristotlean and Kantian ideas of 'beauty' and æsthetics. 'High art', which is legitimate art, art which justifies itself by its 'genius' or obvious 'greatness', is about distance and disinterested pleasure. The high art nude, in painting or sculpture, in the patriarchal view, justifies its existence by the brilliance of its production, the sumptuousness of its colour and form, the marvel of its human touches, the grandeur of its design, the loftiness of its ambition, the dynamism of its structures, and so on. As that producer of exquisite bodies, French Neo-Classical artist J.A.D. Ingres, wrote:

> There are not two arts, there is only one: it is the one which has as its foundation the beautiful, which is eternal and natural.[1]

1 J.A.D. Ingres, quoted in R. Goldwater, 216

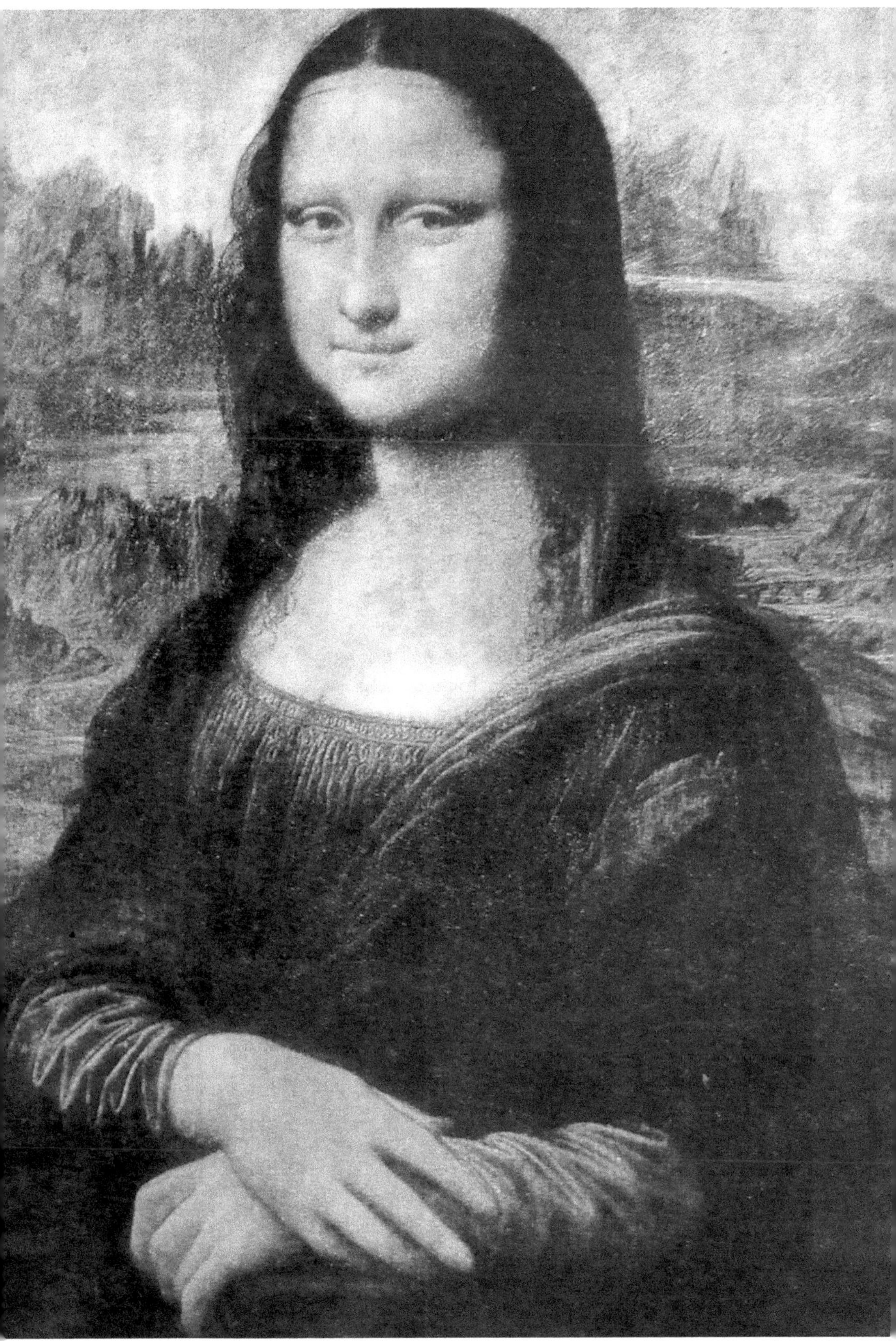

EROTIC ART VERSUS PORNOGRAPHY

We know the male/ patriarchal view of the art versus pornography debate. Eroticism is justified and good because it is 'high art', it is superbly crafted, it is a 'work of art'. Thus the Kronhausens, the organizers of a major exhibition of 'erotic art' (of 1968),[1] write:

> one can perhaps distinguish between pornography and art. The criterion would be that the more a picture contains evidence of interpretative, creative elaboration, the closer it is to art.[2]

For the Kronhausens, as for so many artists and philosophers and intellectuals, erotic art is art because it is done well. Pornography is simply bad art.

Many guardians of æsthetics, many professors of art history and dons of 'the beautiful' go along with this view. Kenneth Clark is a typical establishment critic who puts forward the patriarchal view: nudes are OK provided they are æsthetically pleasing, provided they remain 'in the realm of contemplation' as he put it.[3]

---

1 The 'first international exhibition of erotic art' was at the Museum of Art, Lund, Sweden, and Aarhus, Denmark, in 1968

2 Phyllis & Eberhard Kronhausen: *Erotic Art: A survey of erotic fact and fancy in the fine arts*, W.H. Allen, 1971, 3

3 Quoted in Lord Longford: *Pornography: The Longford Report*, Coronet, 1972, 99f

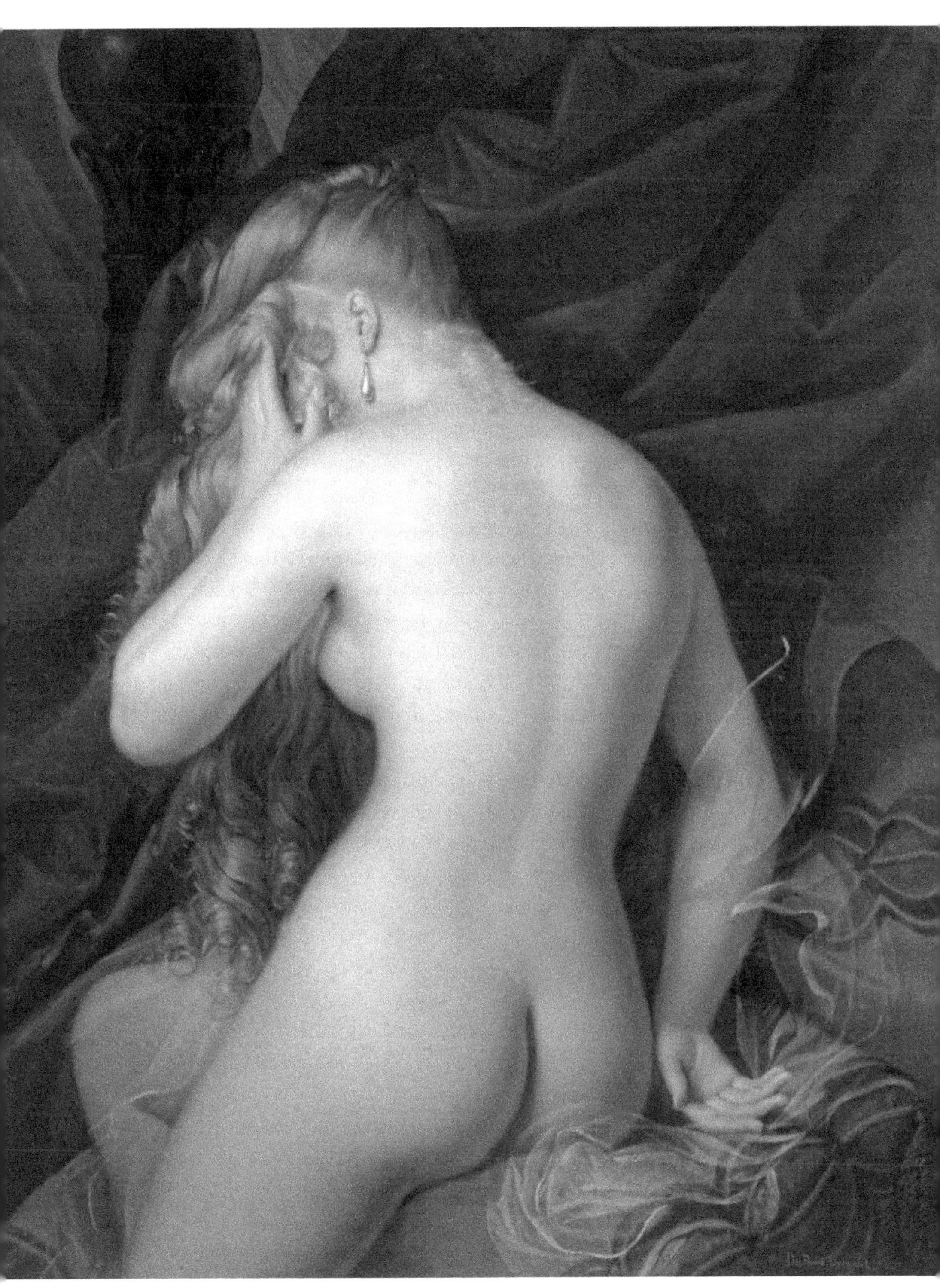

Alexandre-Jean Dubois-Drahonet,
Female Nude, 19th century

THE FEMALE NUDE

The 'sublime' qualities of high art, to use one popular adjective of art criticism, are crucial to its success, as Carol M. Armstrong notes in her essay on Edgar Degas:

> One of the things any painted object does is to resist signification at some level because of its very objecthood. And the female nude – because of *its* objecthood may be seen as almost emblematic of that level of resistance. In fact, the female nude has been linked to that stratum of painting most in tension with the work of signification – the stratum we connect to what we call, inadequately, "abstraction"; facture, the handling of paint per se, foregrounded as an obvious fact of the painting. Femaleness and facture, facture and the female nude, they go together somehow. One need only think of Titian, the first great painter of the female nude in the Western tradition.[1]

Much as worshippers properly gaze at an icon or an image of a deity with wonder, the art critic and historian kneels before 'great art' and worships it.[2] The female nude is the highest form of non-religious art, and it confers a religious awe in its æsthete consumers. The emphasis is on Neoplatonic terms such as 'purity', 'beauty', 'form' and 'symmetry'. As Aristotle puts it: '[t]he chief forms of beauty are order and symmetry and definiteness.'[3]

1 Carol M. Armstrong; "Edgar Degas and the Representation of the Female Body", in S. Suleiman, 223

2 See Pierre Bourdieu: *Distinction: A Social Critique of the Judgment of Taste*, tr Richard Nice, Routledge & Kegan Paul, New York 1984

3 Aristotle: *Metaphysics*, book XIII, in Albert Hofstadter & Richard Kuhns, eds: *Philosophies of Art and Beauty: Selected Readings in Aesthetics From Plato to Heidegger*, Random House, New York 1964, 96

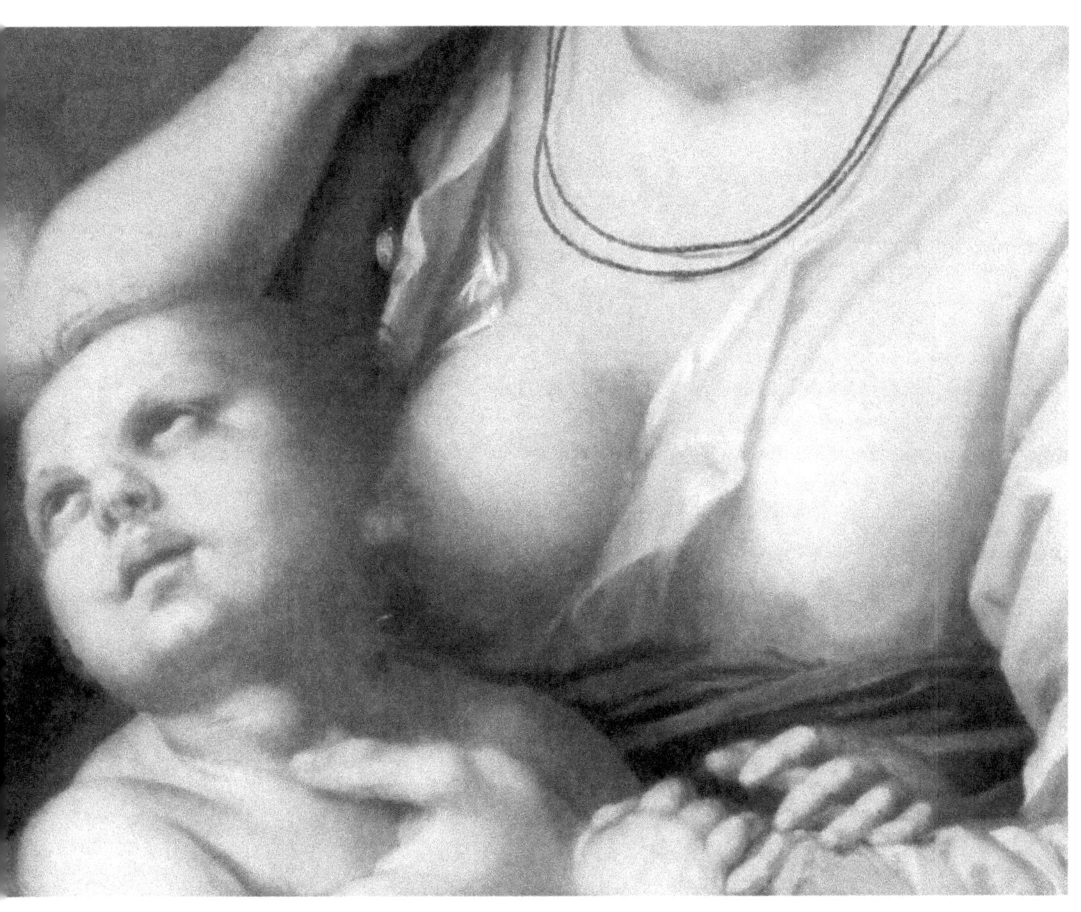

Andrea del Sarto, Madonna and Child, detail

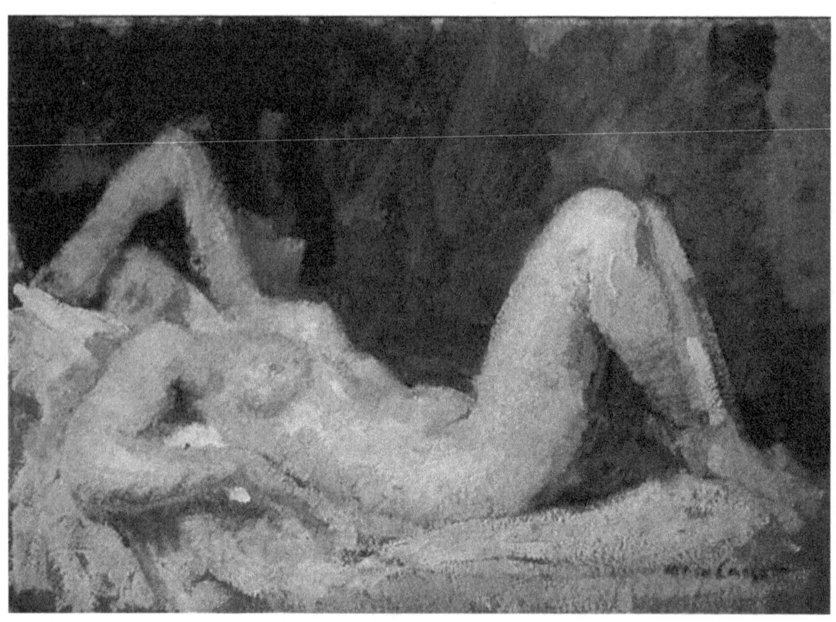

Mary Cassatt, Reclining Nude

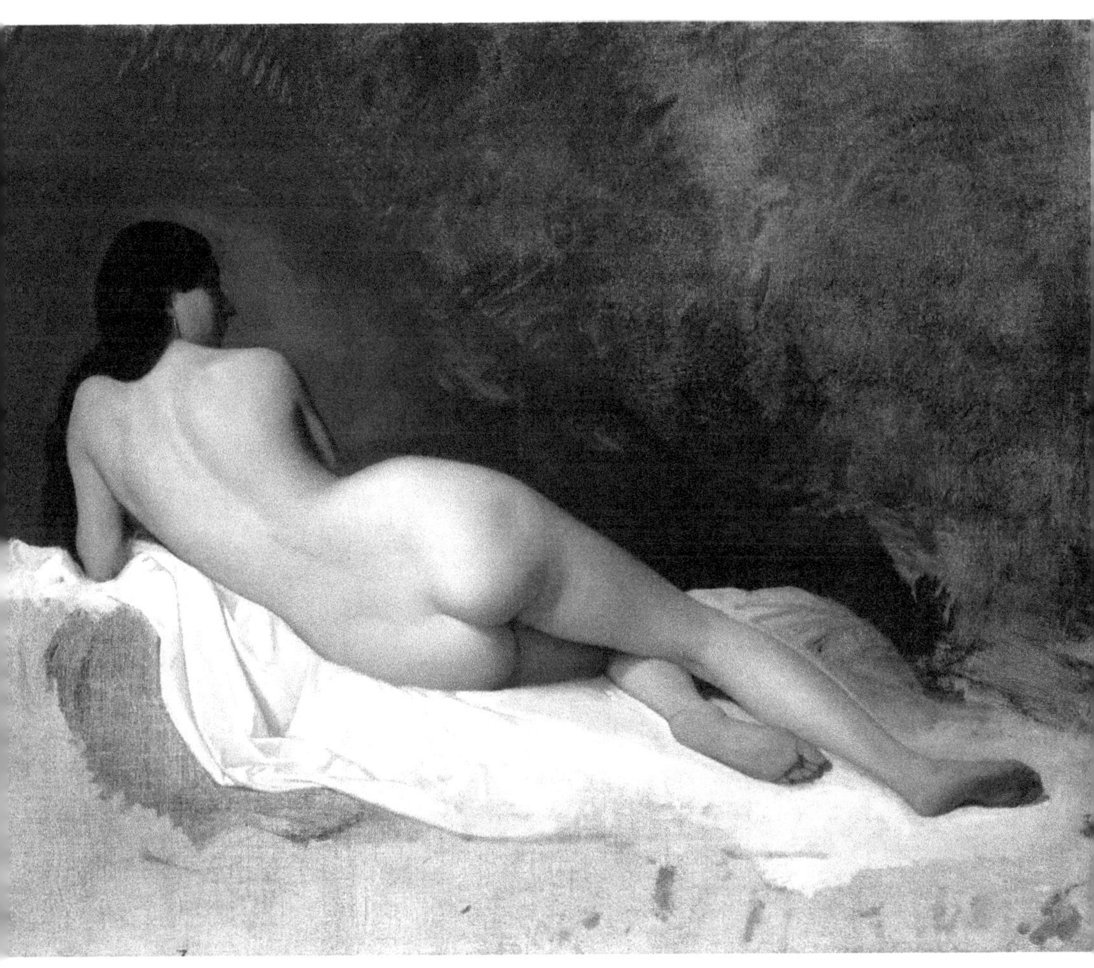

Isidore Pils, Nude Woman, c. 1841

THE FEMALE NUDE

Depictions of the female nude and of erotic gestures or acts can be problematic. The female body, for instance, is already 'objectified' even before it is painted or represented. Once painted, it becomes a cultural artifact, a mass of codes, meanings, signs and values, none of them fixed, all of them dependent on the context of consumption, dependent on the socio-political make-up of the viewer, and so on. None of this, however, has prevented erotic nudes and female nudes from being produced.

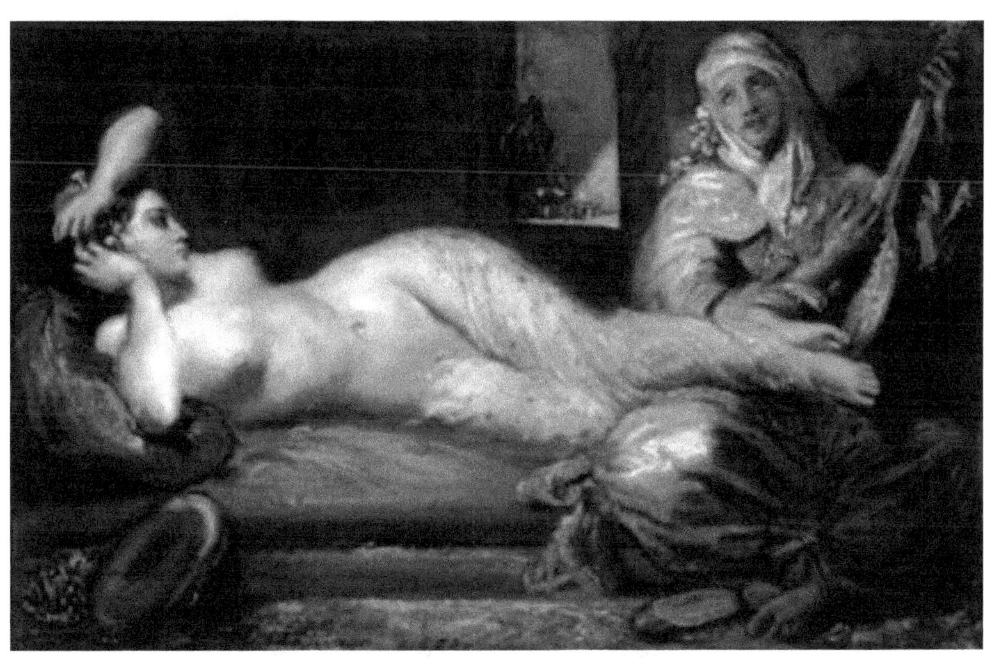

Théodore Chasséreau (1819-56)

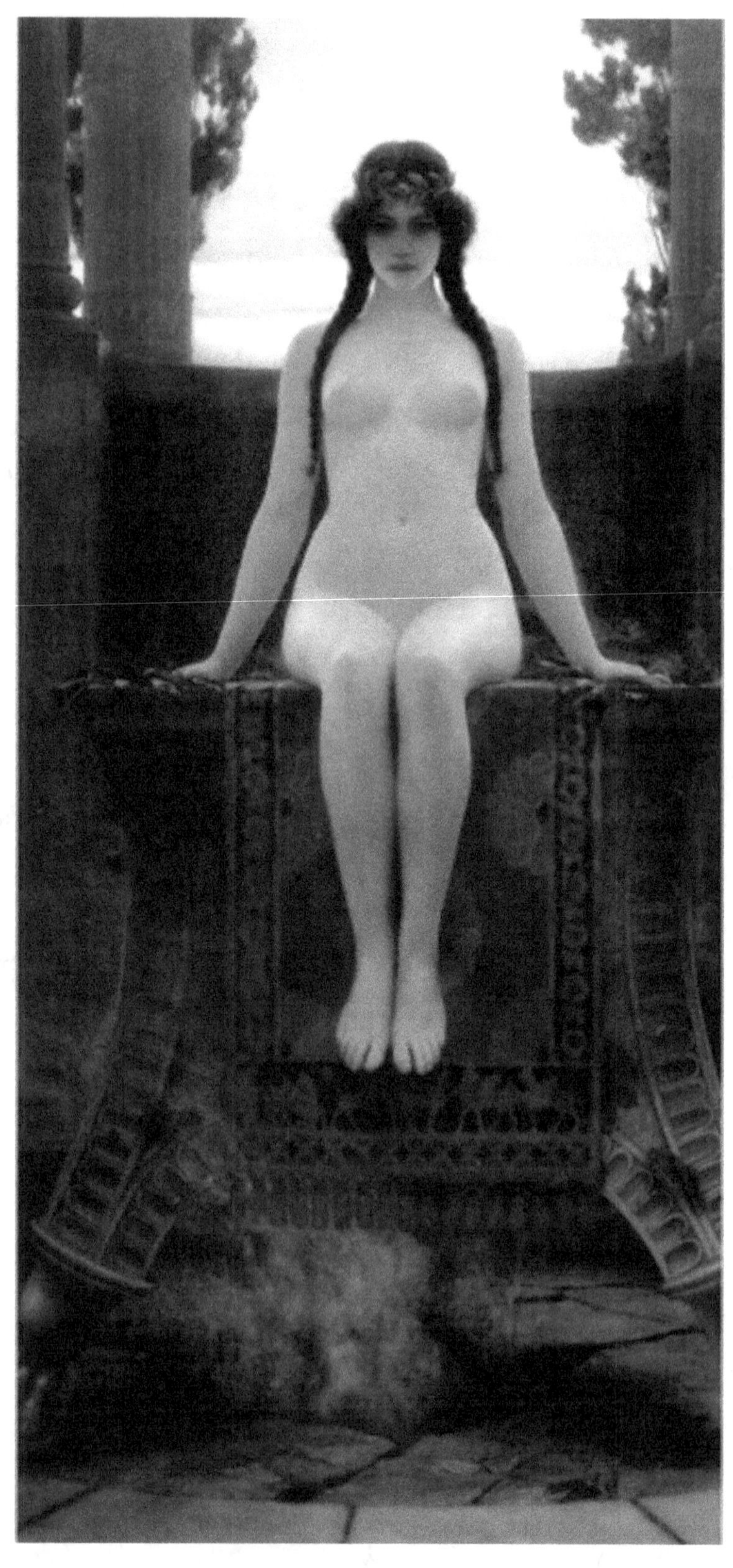

John Godward, The Delphic Oracle, 1899

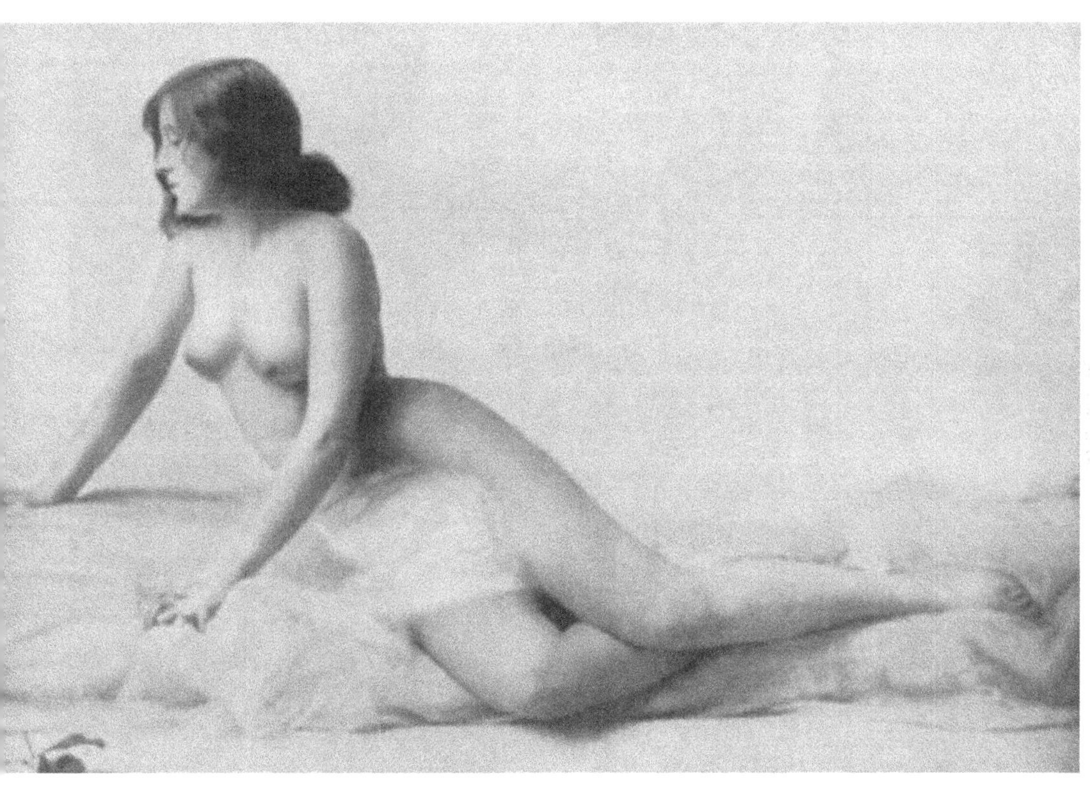

Frederick Armstrong, Greek Slave,
1909, drawn from Lord Leighton

William Bouguereau,
The Birth of Venus,
above

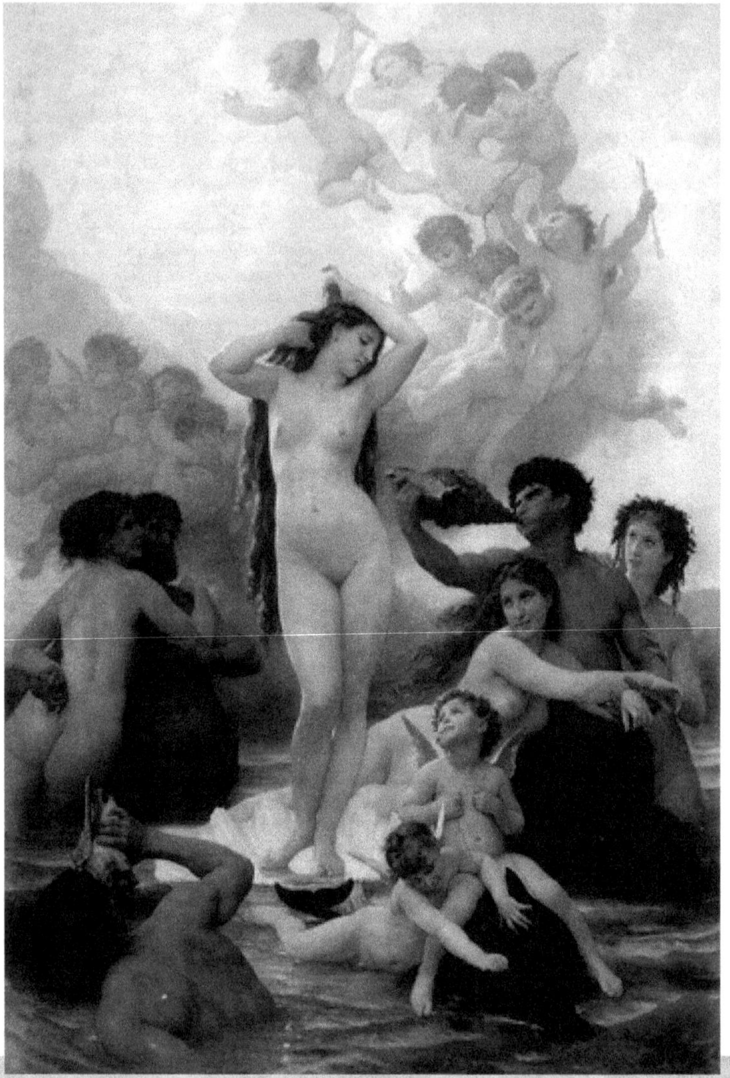

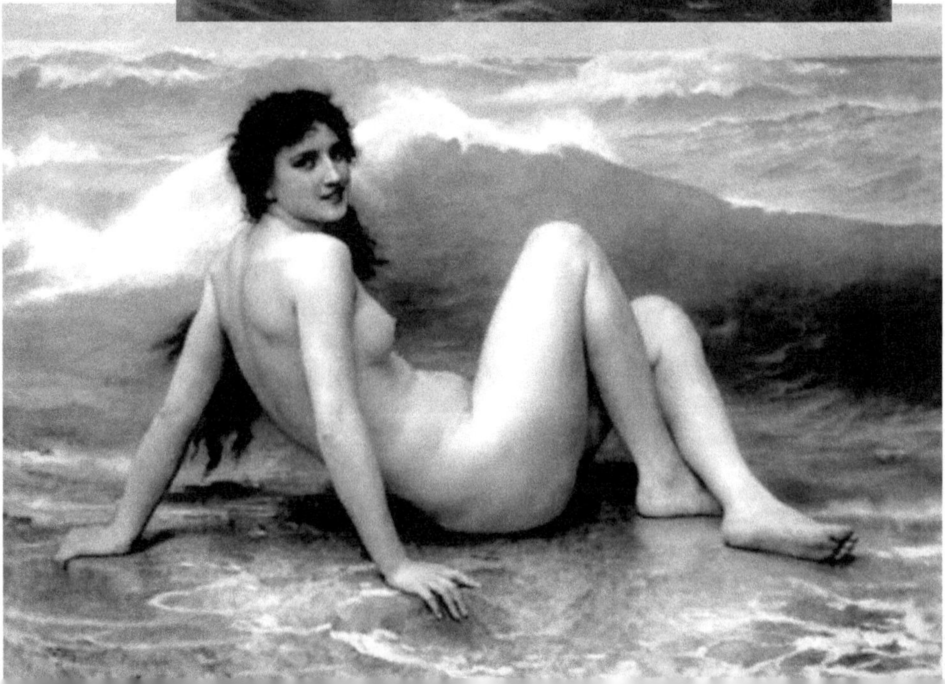

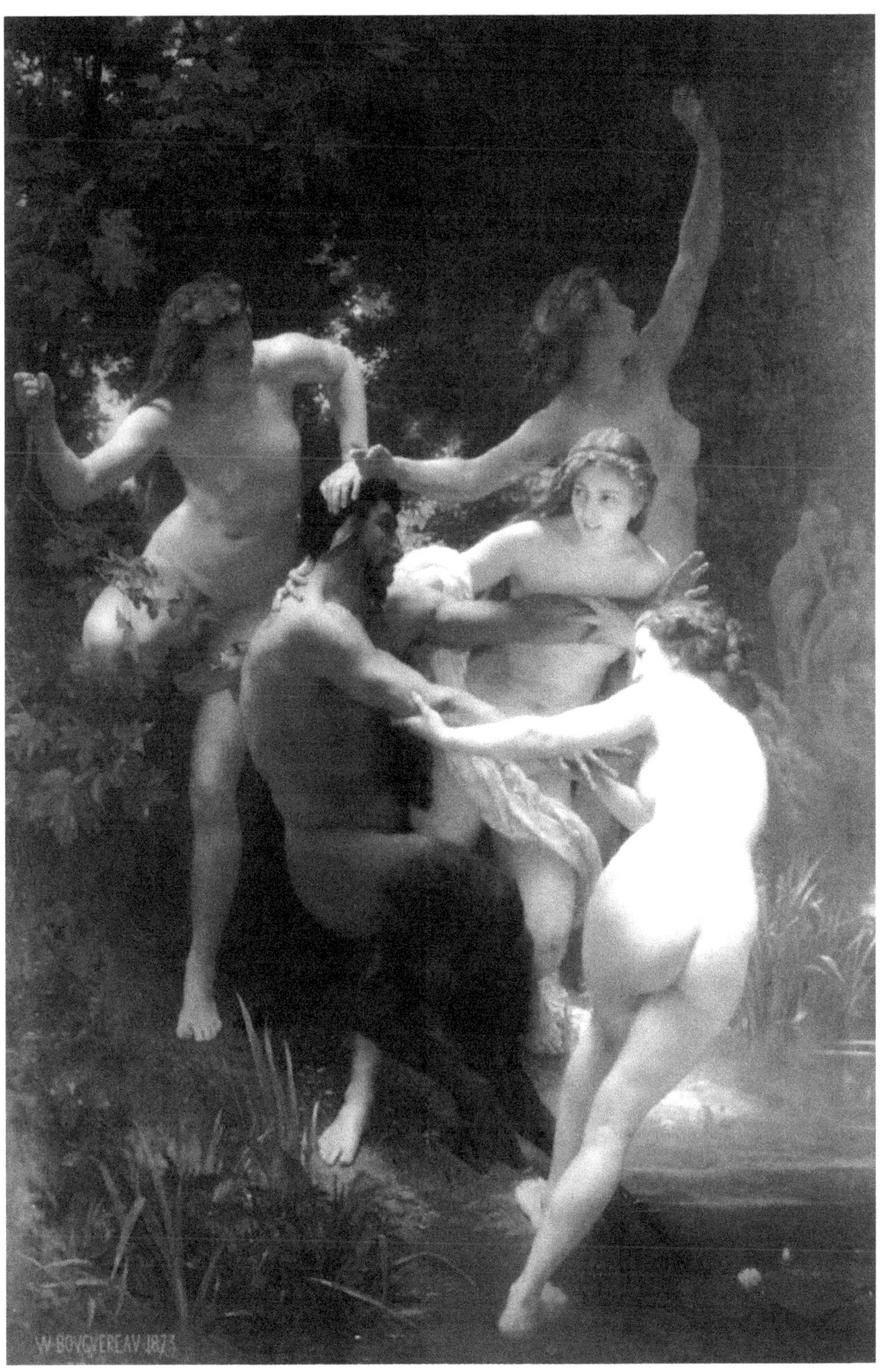

William Bouguereau, Nymphs and Satyr

THE FEMALE NUDE

Context is crucial in matters of eroticism. An image that is seen as 'erotic' in one context can easily be seen as 'pornographic' in another context. Take an image out of context, and soon a new, often ironic set of meanings are set in motion. Jacques Derrida has shown that a text may have many contexts, and is not fixed in one context forever.[1] Feminist artists have explored meanings and contexts, by placing traditional images in new contexts. Meanings are constantly in a state of flux. Nothing is fixed anymore. As Catherine Belsey writes: 'meanings circulate between text, ideology and reader' (144). Roland Barthes wrote that '[a]ll images are polysemous...they imply, underlying their signifiers, a floating chain of signifieds'. The consumer has the ability to 'choose some and ignore others'.[2] The cultural environment, socialization, economy, power relations, education, any number of factors can influence the meanings drawn from an image. With the female nude, in painting or erotica, the meanings are contextualized as erotic. As Anne Hollander notes, the nude always has a sexual dimension to it.

For instance, men can 'possess' and yet never 'possess' a female nude painting. It remains an image. The 'possession' or consumption is of a cerebral order, which is why critics and professors such as Kenneth Clark, Bernard Berenson, Jacob Burckhardt, Walter Pater, John Ruskin, Aby Warburg, Roger Fry, Ernst Gombrich and other art critics emphasize the *intellectual* nature of enjoying art. Art for the head, not the body, art for the eyes, not the full five senses.

1 Jacques Derrida: *Eperons. Les styles de Nietzsche*, Flammarion, Paris 1978, 103f
2 Roland Barthes: *Image-Music-Text*, Hill & Wang, New York 1977, 39

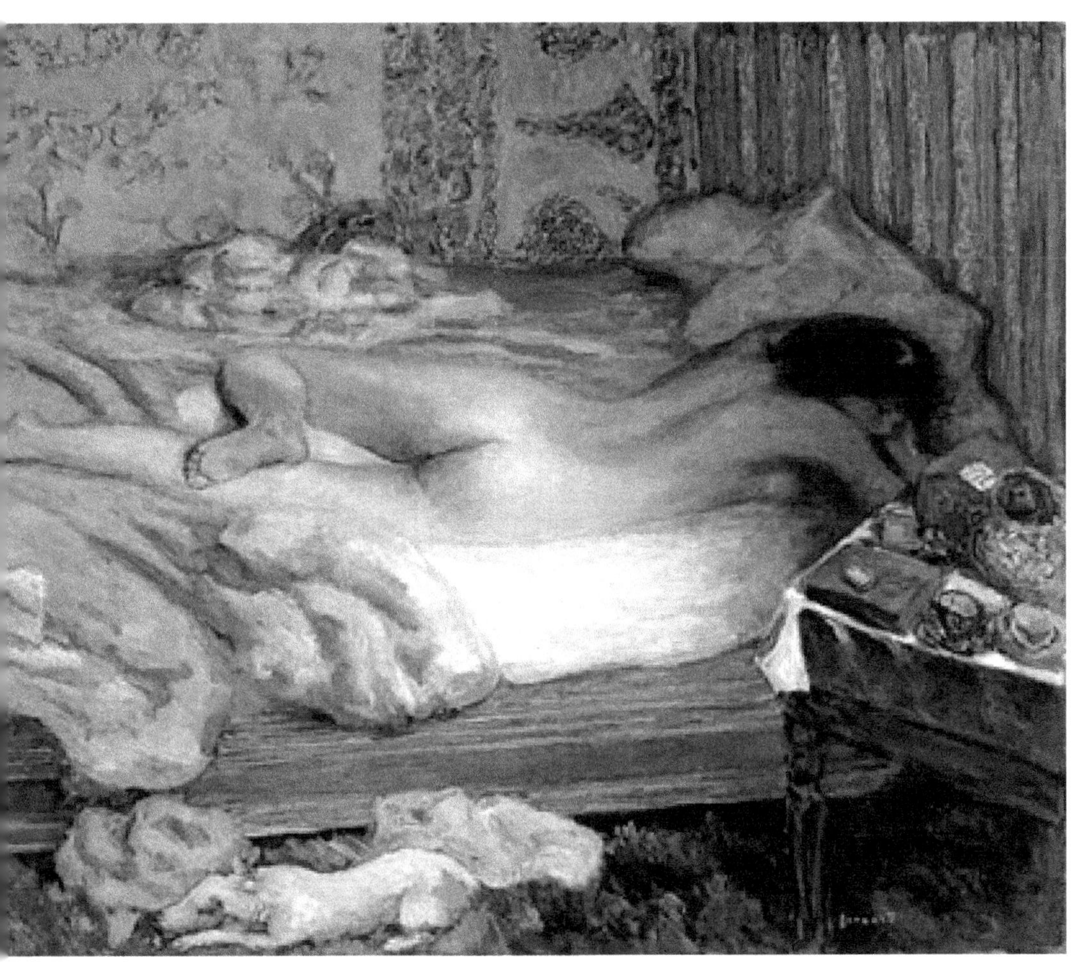

Pierre Bonnard

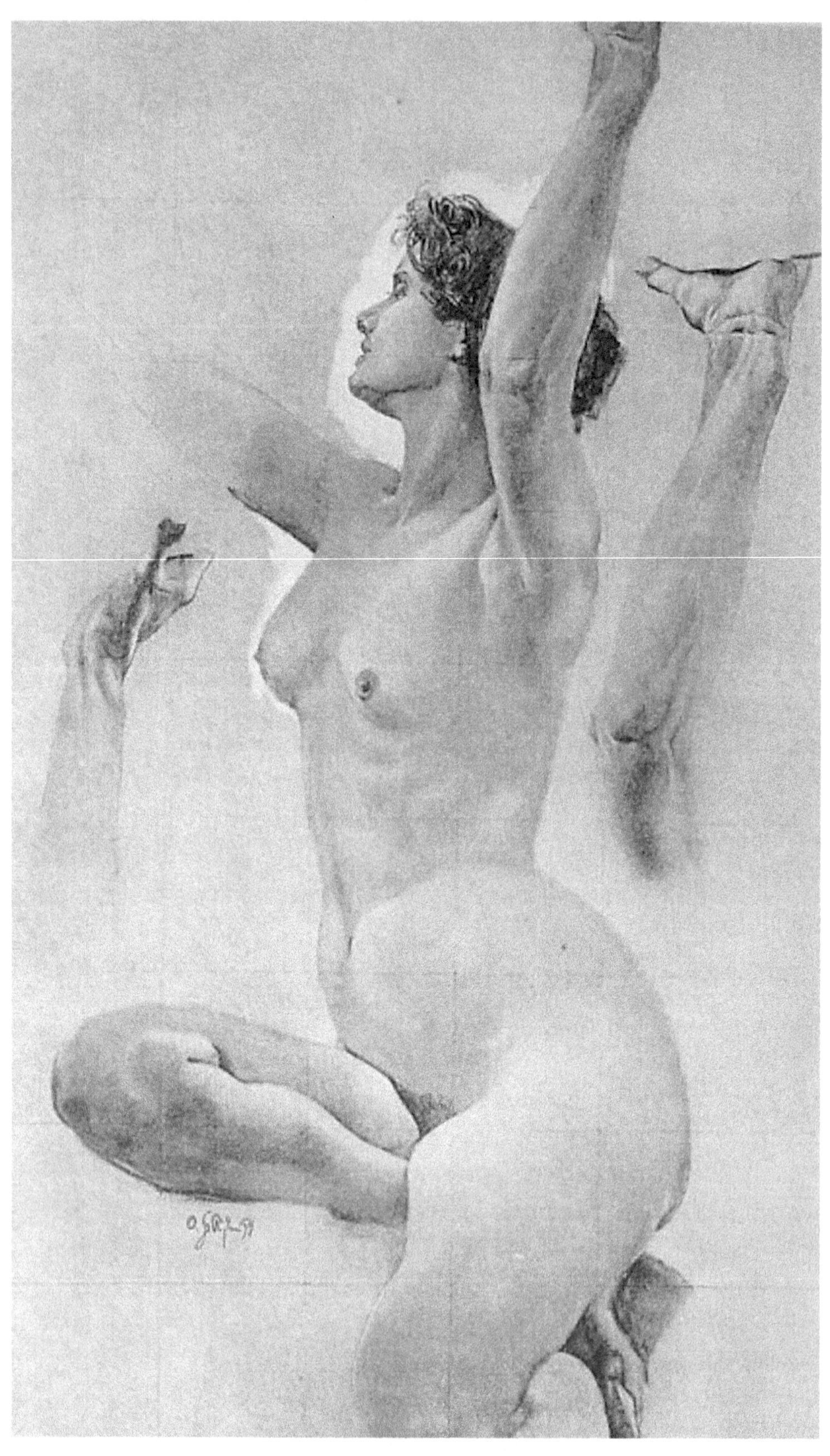

Otto Grenier, Study For Odysseus, 1912-33

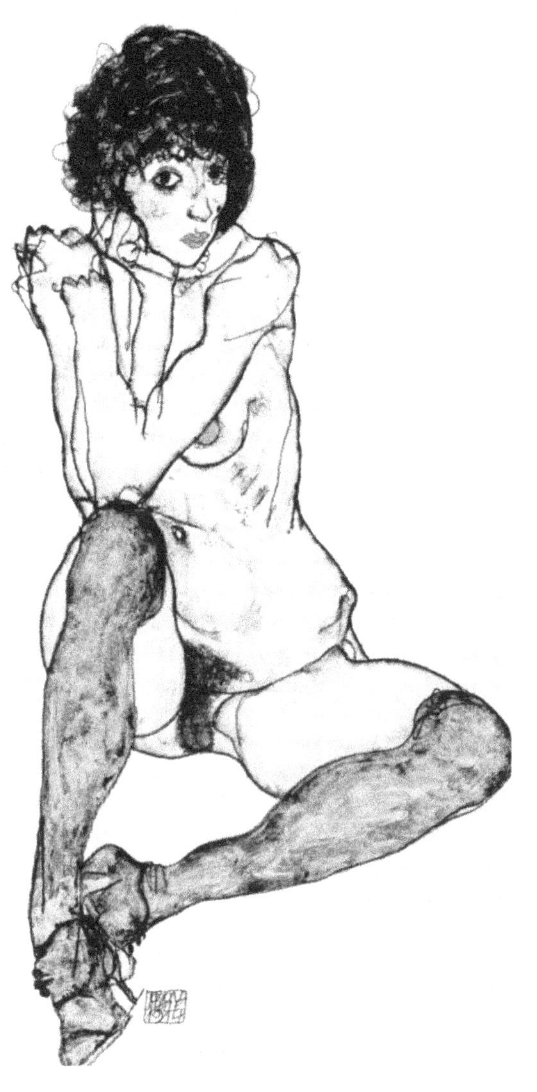

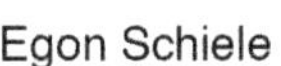

Egon Schiele

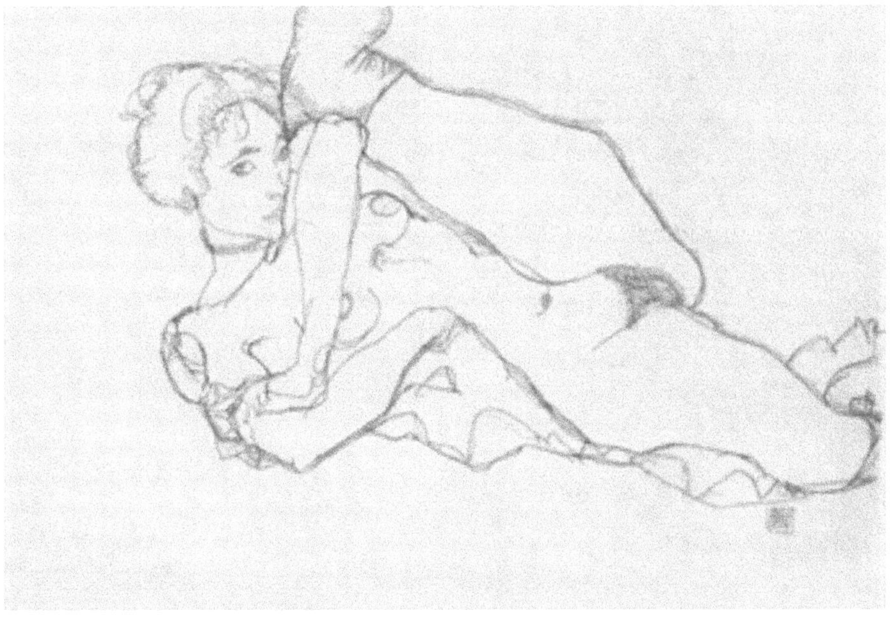

THE FEMALE NUDE

The high art nude, then, is a site of political and economic manipulation, an expression of the power relations between patron and painter, between connoisseur, artist and model. In the trinity of people linked by the painting - patron, painter and model - the model is clearly at the bottom of the pile. She is dependent on both painter and patron. She has to please both of them to be successful. The relation of artist to model thus is another manifestation, like that of husband and wife, of male power, of patriarchal culture in action, of the sexual economics which are at work everywhere in the world, and everywhere in history.

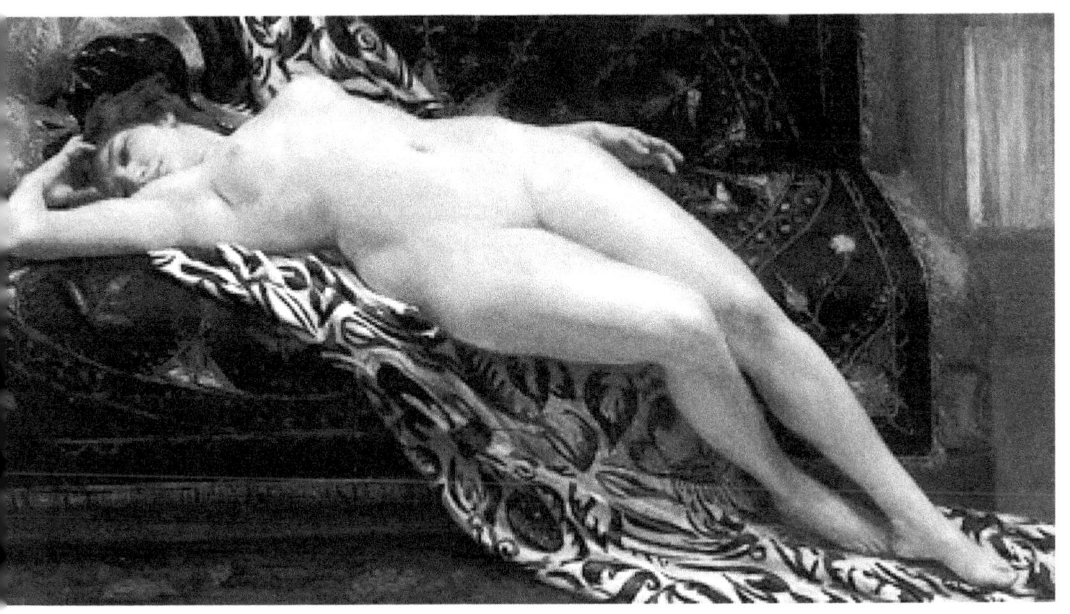

Guillaume Seignac, L'Abandon (above).
The Wave (below).

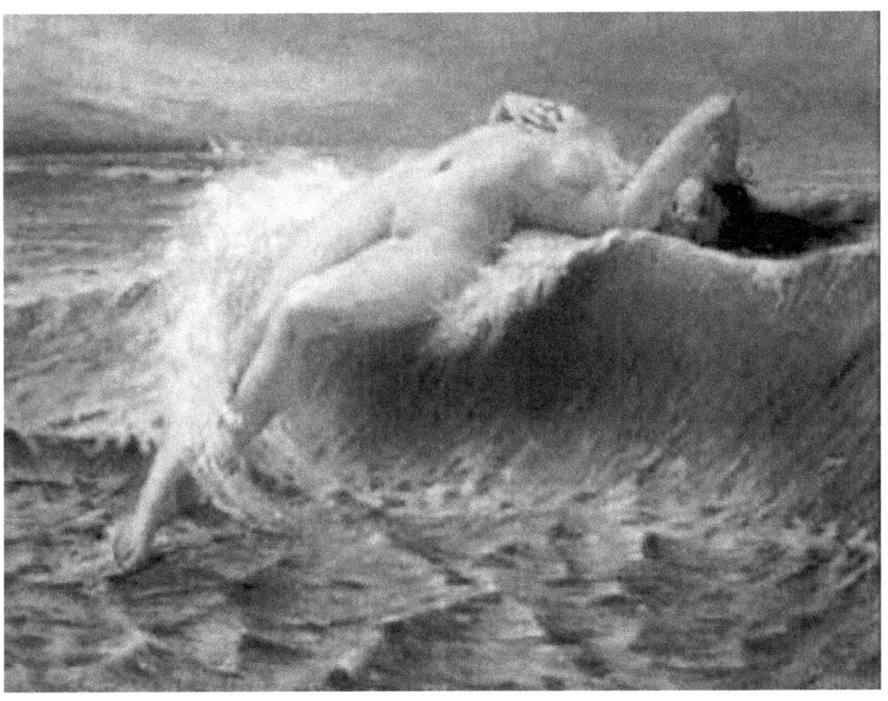

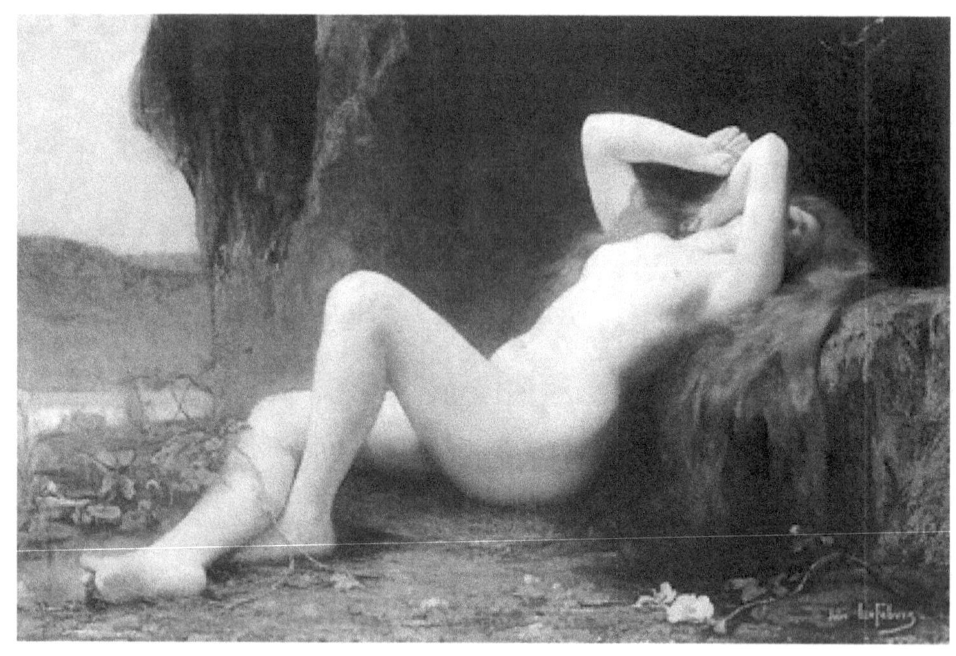

Jules Lefebvre, Nude, 1876 (above).
Odalisque, 1874 (below).

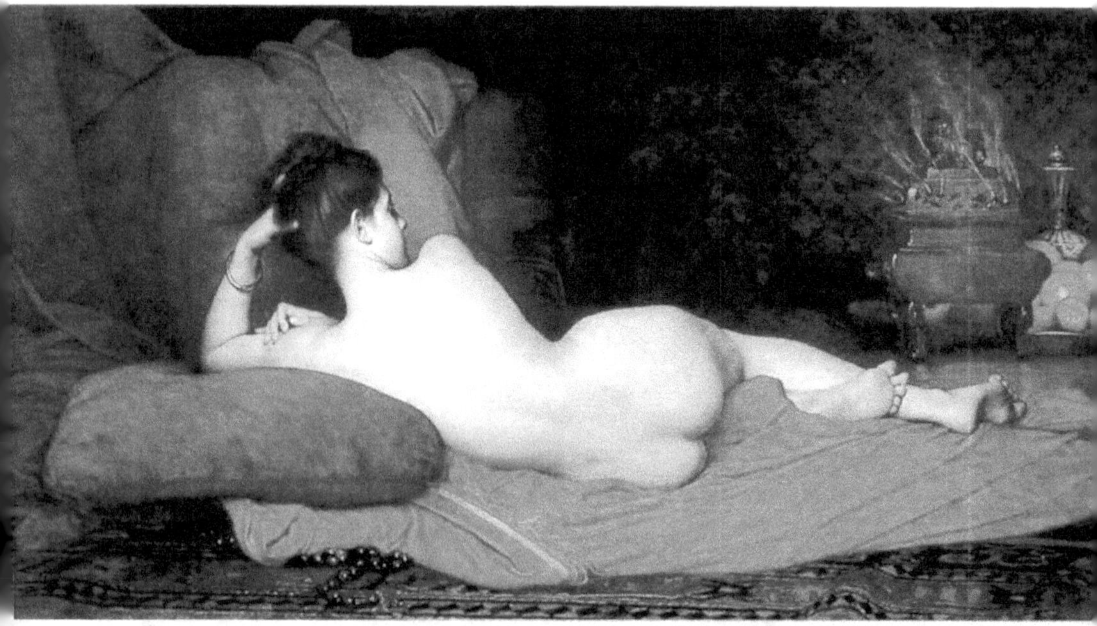

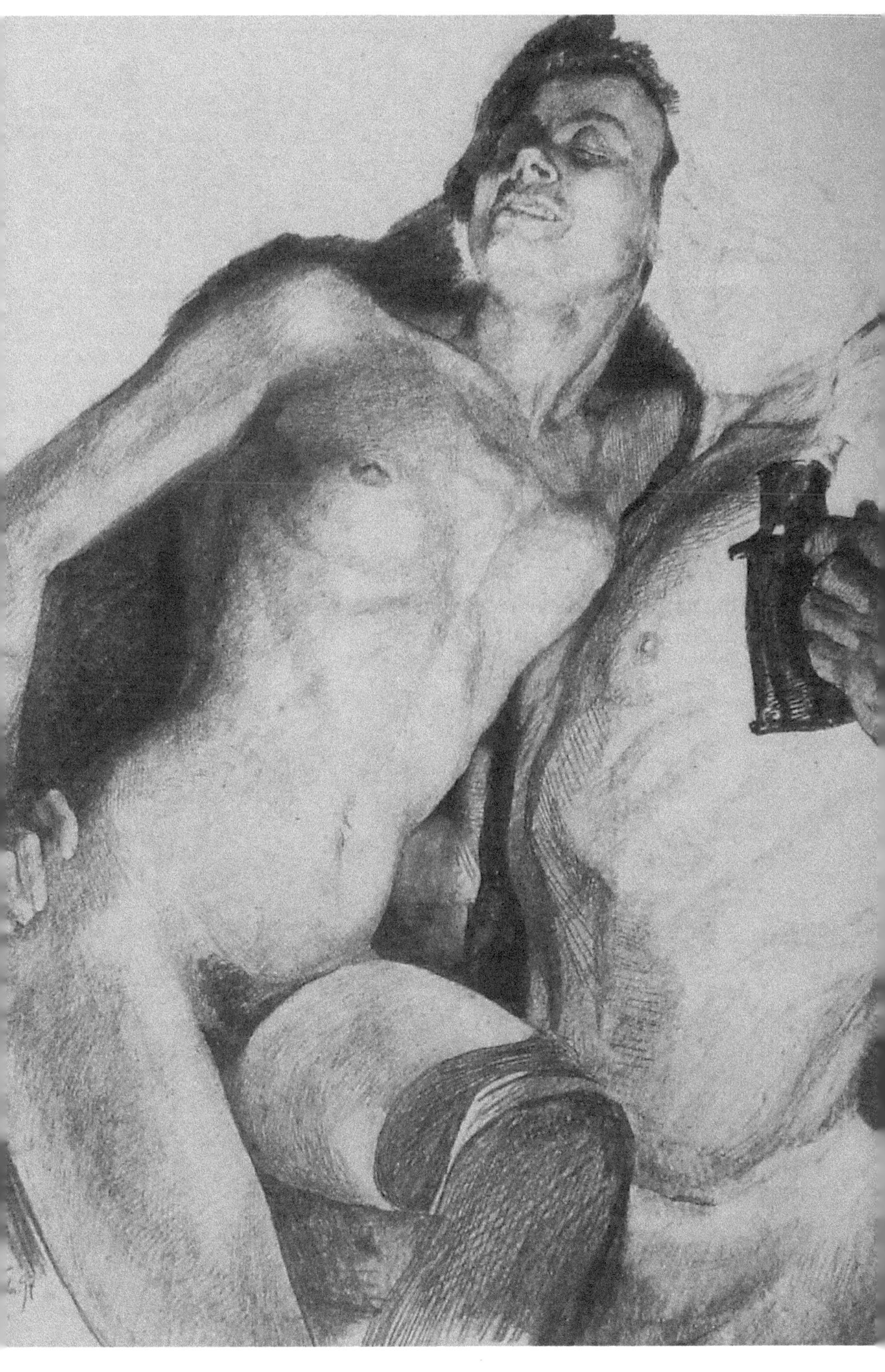

Otto Grenier's truly extraordinary The Devil Showing Woman To the People, 1897

MALE NUDES

The male nude can be seen as a phallus, as Gill Saunders pointed out:

> The male body, while not constructed as the site of sexual pleasure, is often symbolic of phallic power. The whole body, muscular, potent, active, may come to represent the phallus.[1]

The penis isn't a phallus, so, to make up for the disappointing insufficiency of the penis, macho masculinity is demonstrated by bulging muscles, clenched fists, sturdy poses. The male nude poses with a body of 'rippling muscles', bizarrely exaggerated, or gripping a gun, or standing next to a motorcycle, a car, a machine, something that can connote phallic power.

1 G. Saunders: *The Nude*, 26.

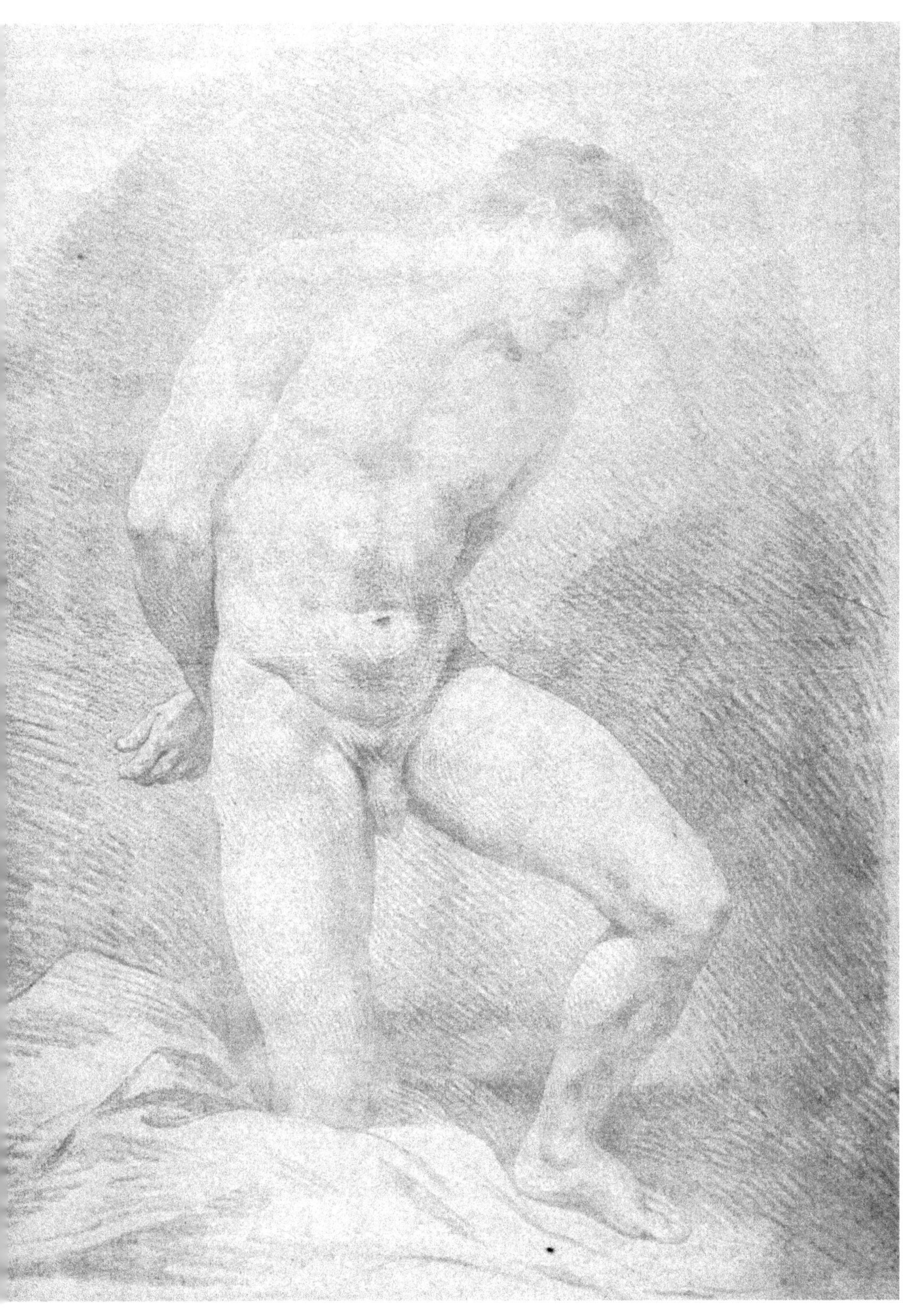

Male Nude, 19th century

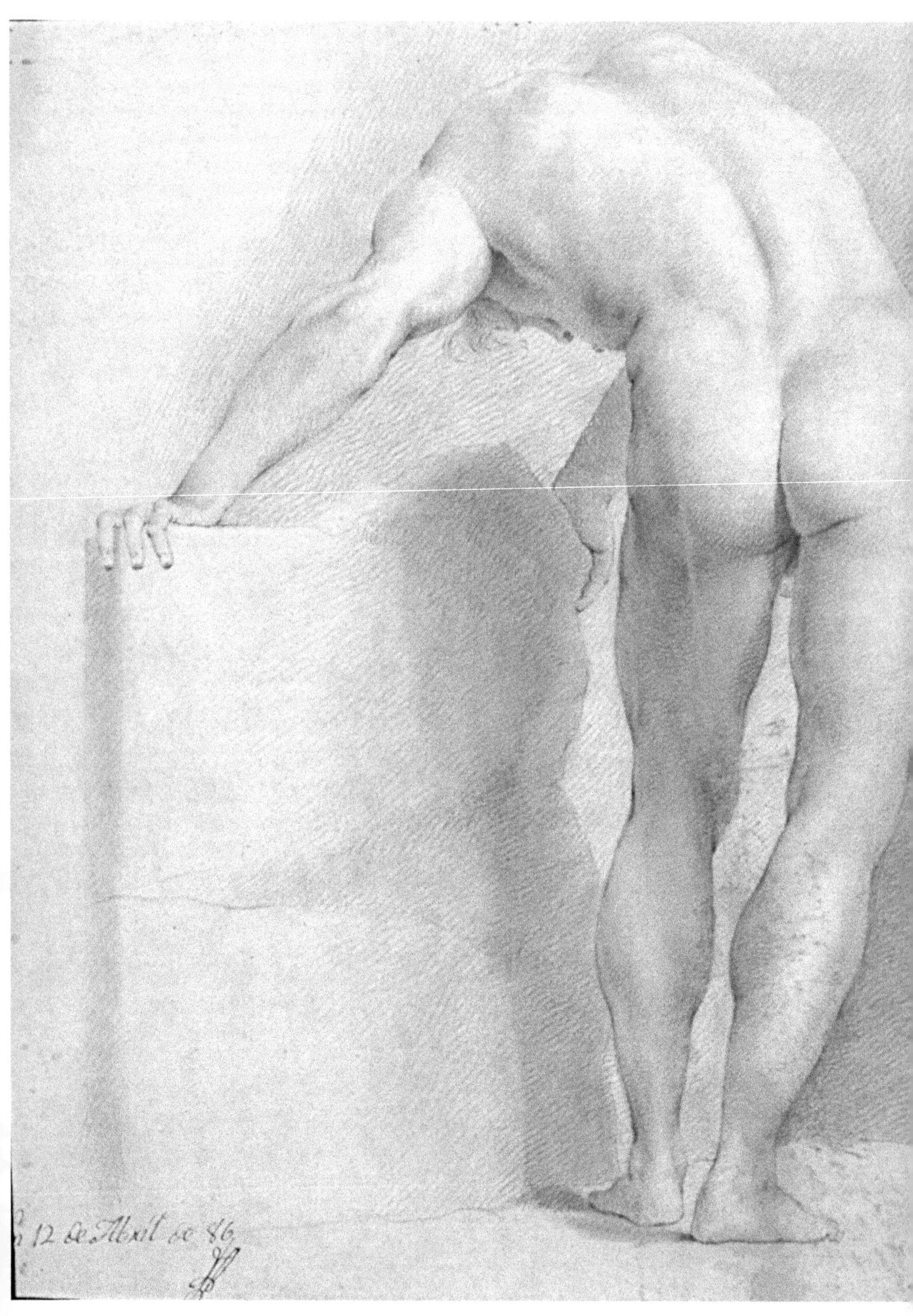

Mariano Amare, Male Nude, 1786.

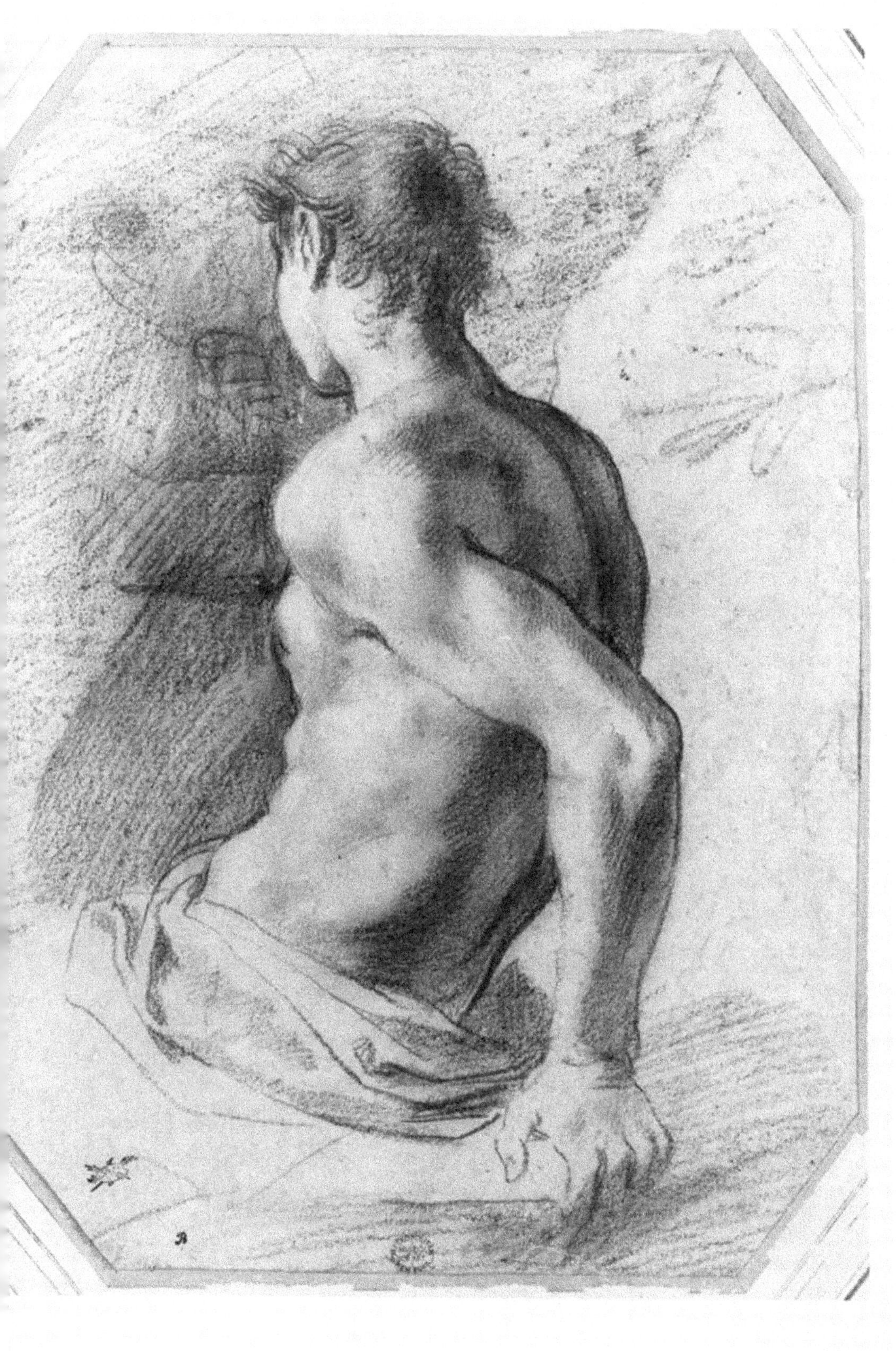

Annibale Carracci, Male Nude, Half-Figure, 16th century

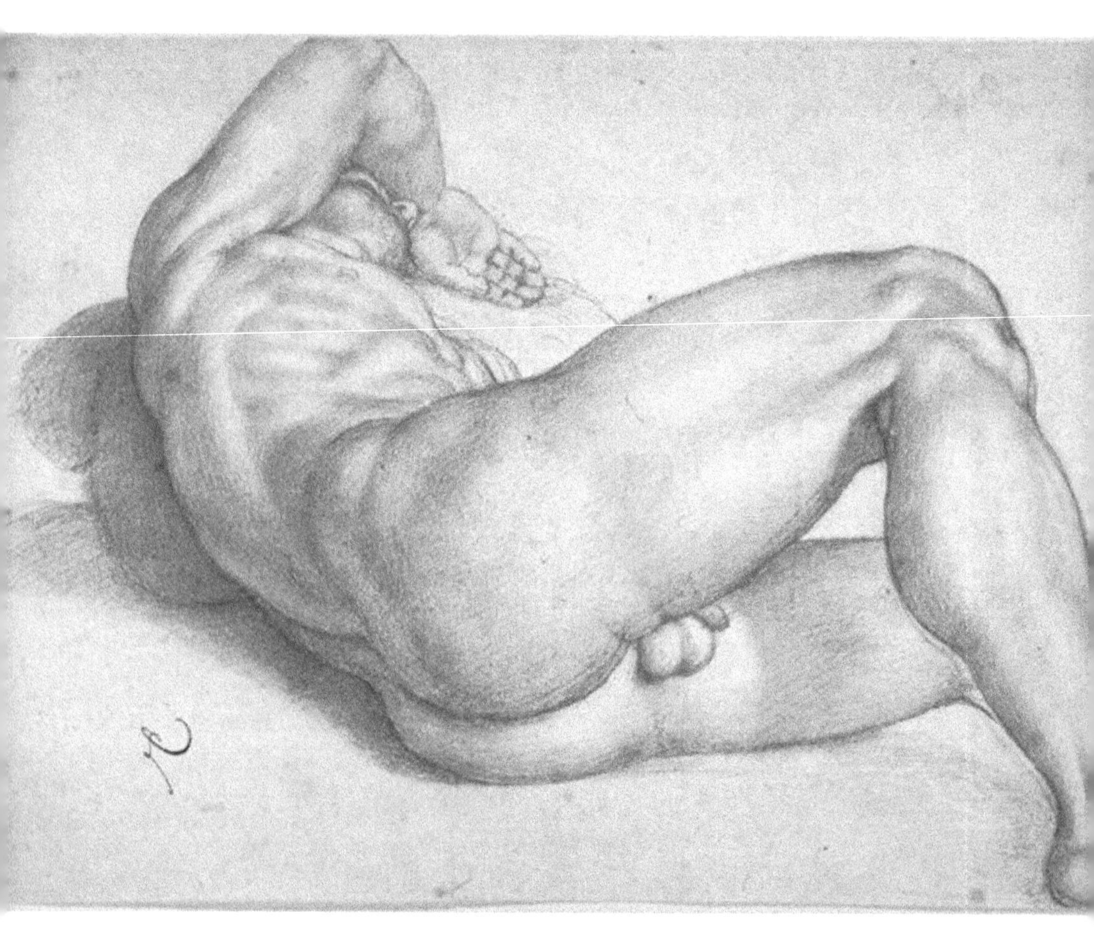

Agnolo di Cosimo (Il Bronzino),
Naked Man Lying On His Back, 16th century

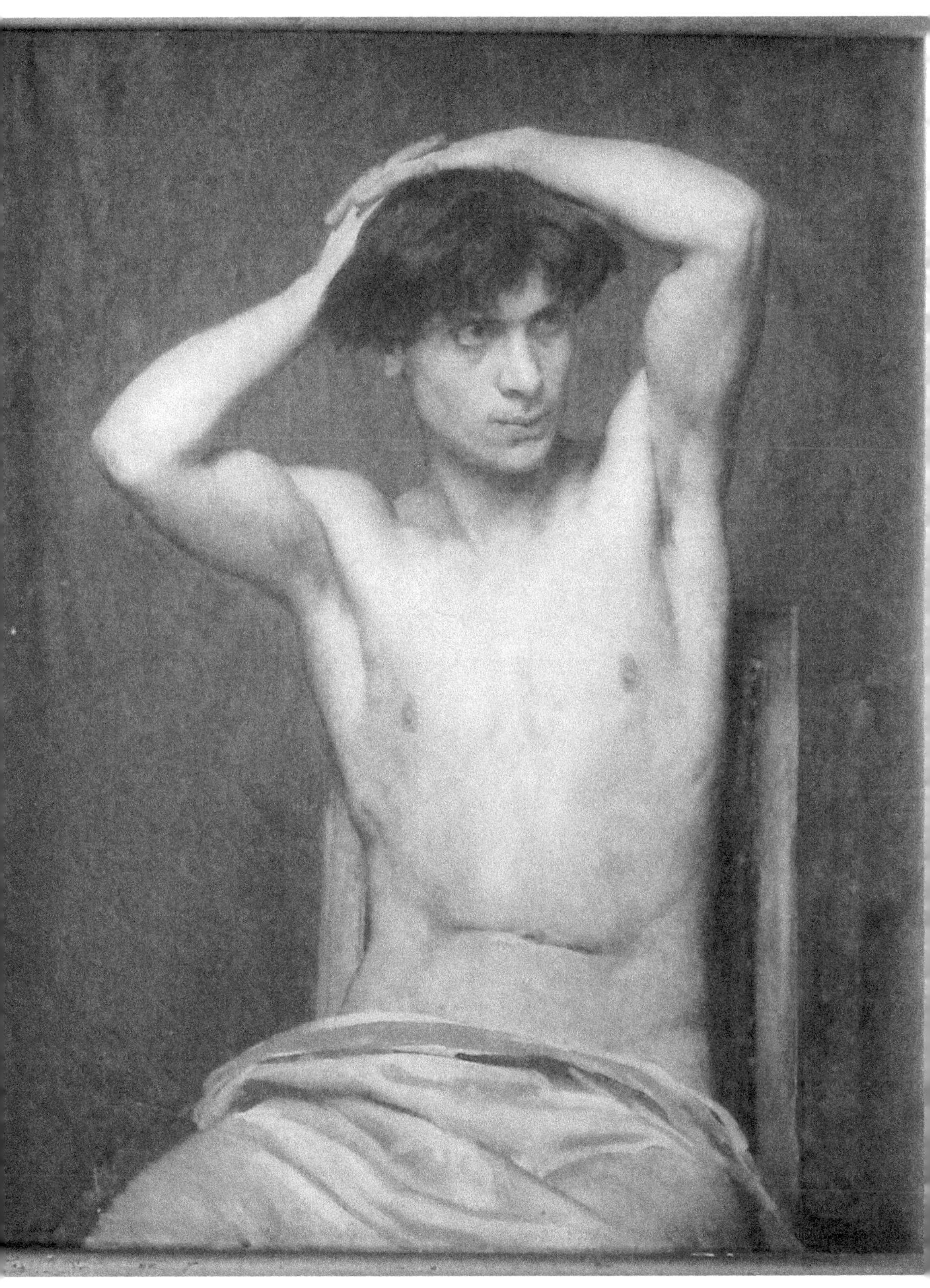

Henri-Lucien Doucet, Half-Nude Figure, 1879

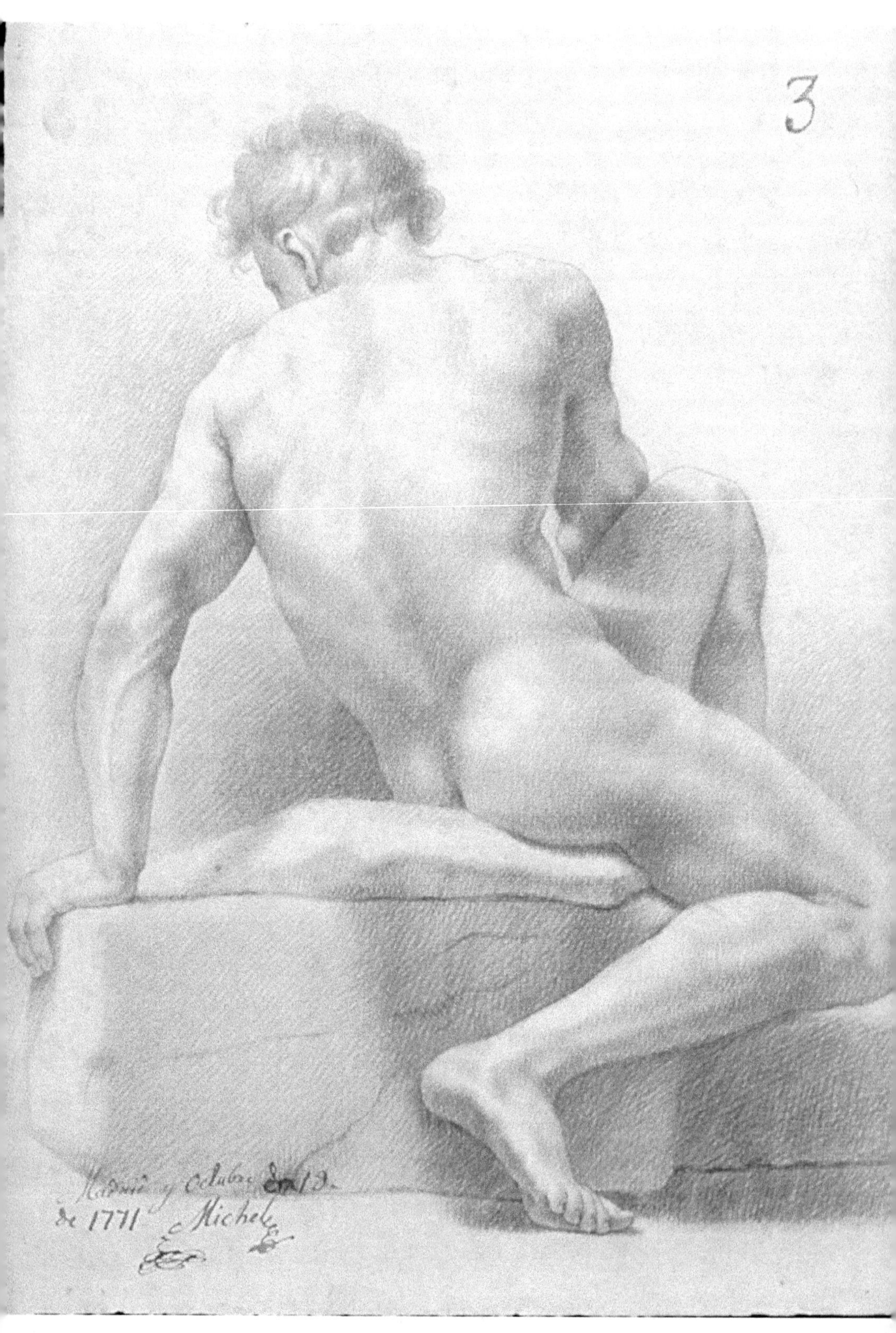

Pedro Pascual Munoz, Seated Male Nude, 1771

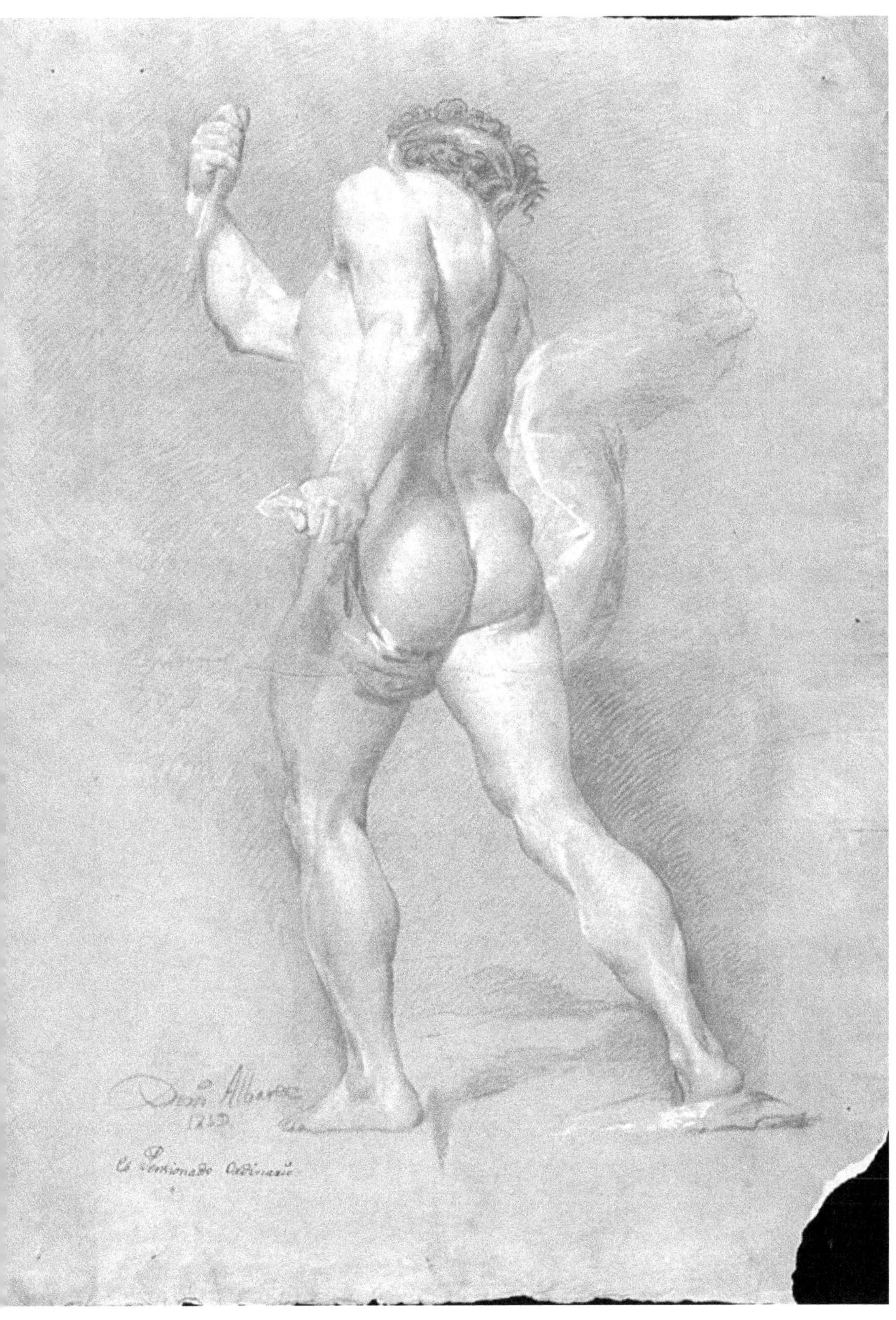

Domingo Alvarez Enciso, Male Nude, 1759

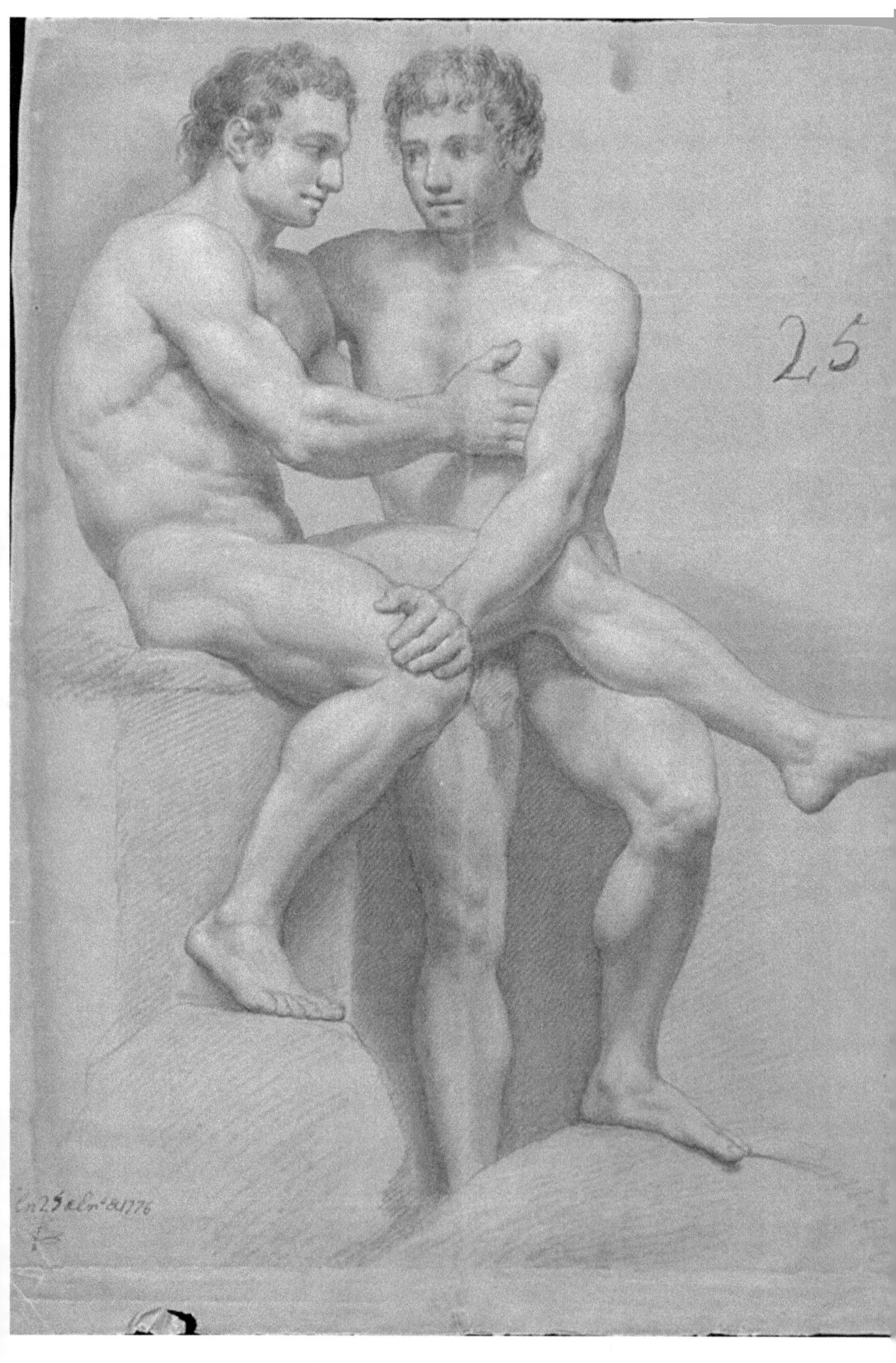

Gustin Esteve Marques, Two Male Nudes, 1776

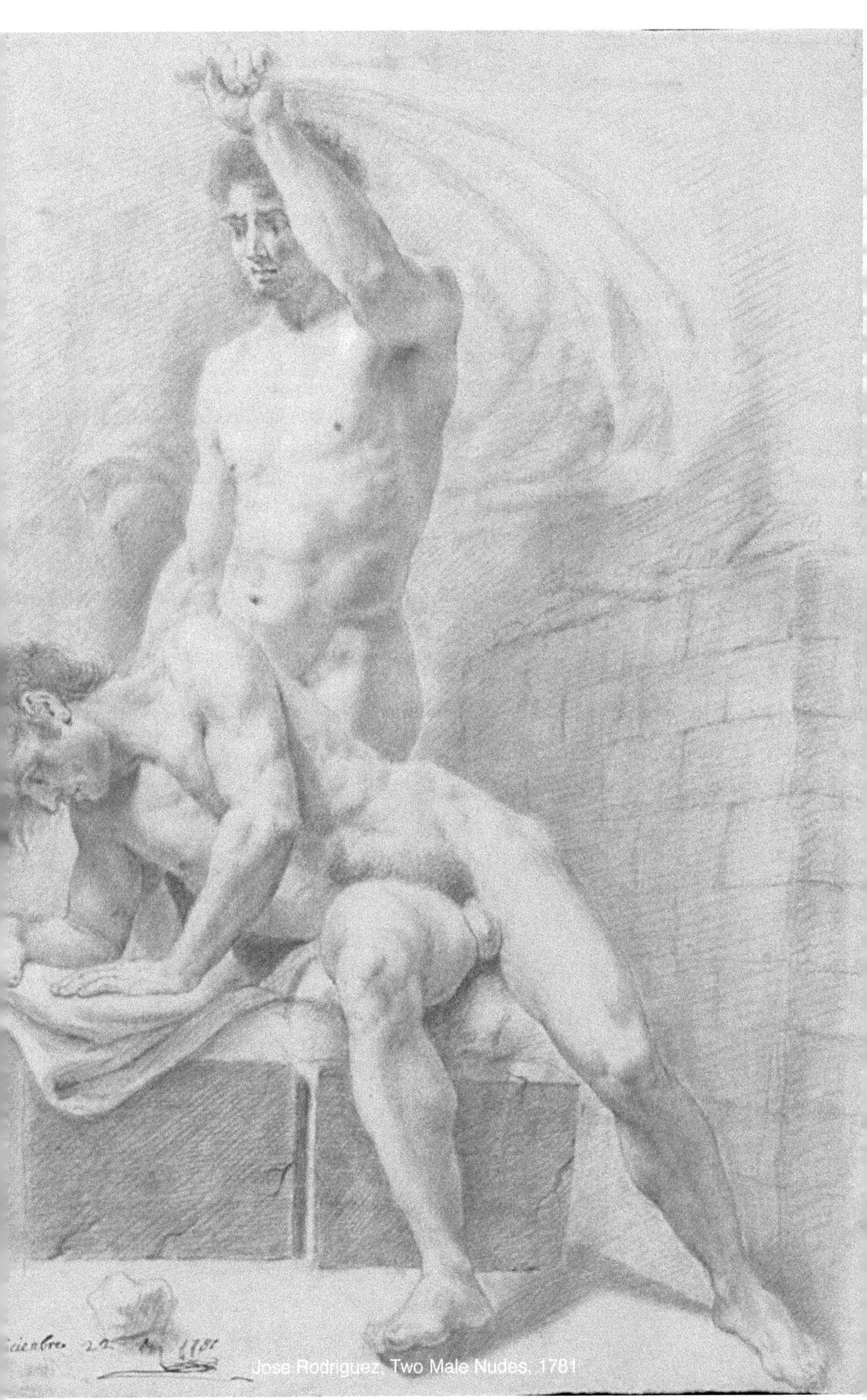

Jose Rodriguez, Two Male Nudes, 1781

MALE NUDES

The male nude can be appear uncomfortable. He doesn't like his photograph or painting or sculpture to be looked at like female nudes. He is used to being the one doing the looking. When the roles are reversed, ambiguity and confusion seeps in. The male nude is set up as spectacle, and as a passive object. To counter the awkwardness of this passivity, the male nude is shown *doing* something. Running, throwing a spear, fighting, etc. It tries to engage a position of activity, because to be the 'looked-at' one, the passive sex object, is very disquieting. Further, the activity of the male nude, which's seen everywhere – in photographs by Eadweard Muybridge,[1] in sculptures by Michelangelo Buonarroti, in movies, in gay porn – aims at portraying phallic power. 'Even in an apparently relaxed, supine pose,' Richard Dyer in 1983,

> the model tightens and tautens his body so that the muscles are emphasized, hence drawing attention to the body's potential for action. More often, the male pin-up is not supine anyhow, but standing taut ready for action.[2]

1 See L. Williams: "Film Body, an implantation of perversions", *Cinétracts*, vol. 3, no.4, Winter 1981, 19-25.
2 Richard Dyer: 'Don't Look Now", *Screen*, vol. 23, 3/ 4, 1983, 20, and in Angela McRobbie, 206

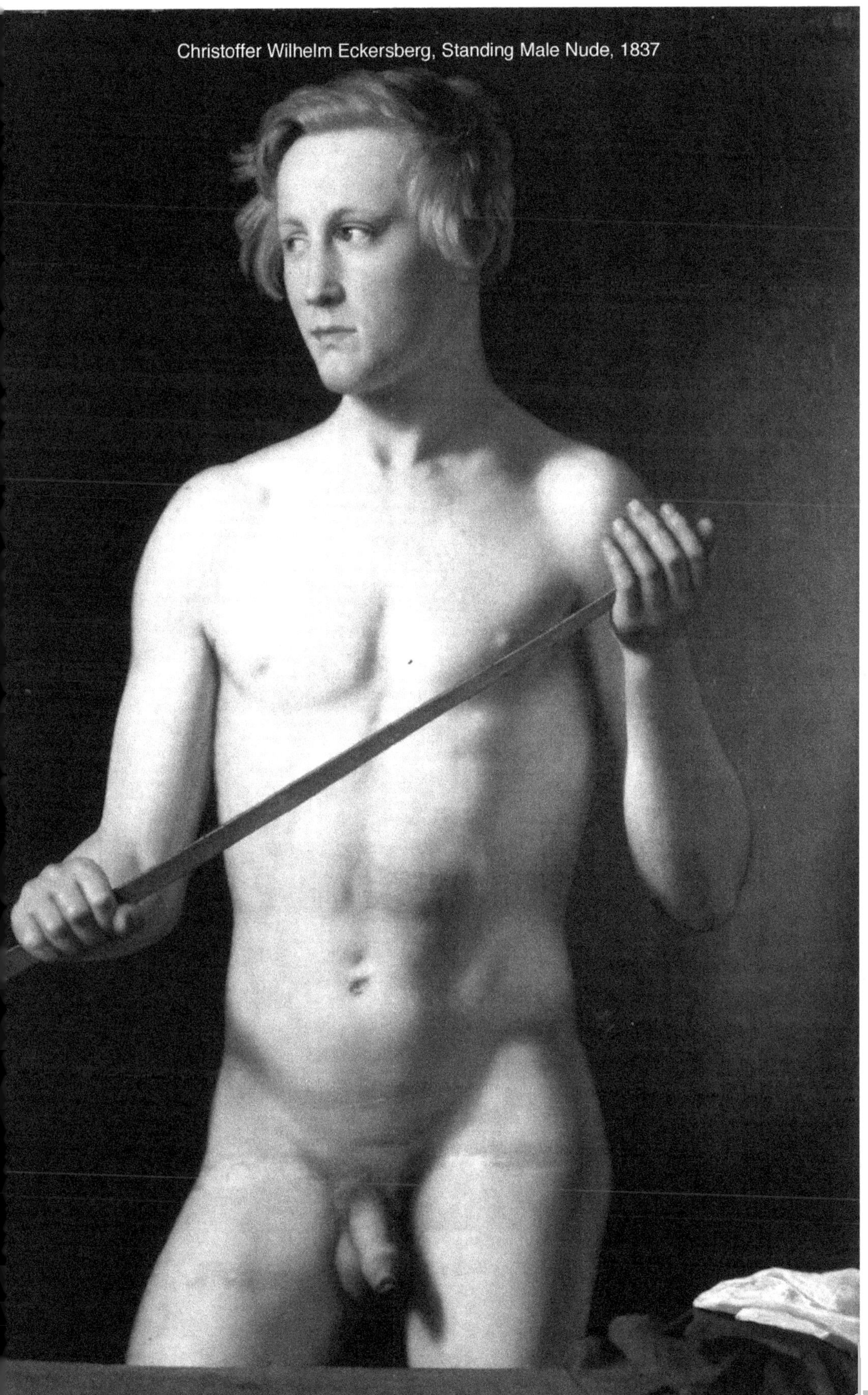
Christoffer Wilhelm Eckersberg, Standing Male Nude, 1837

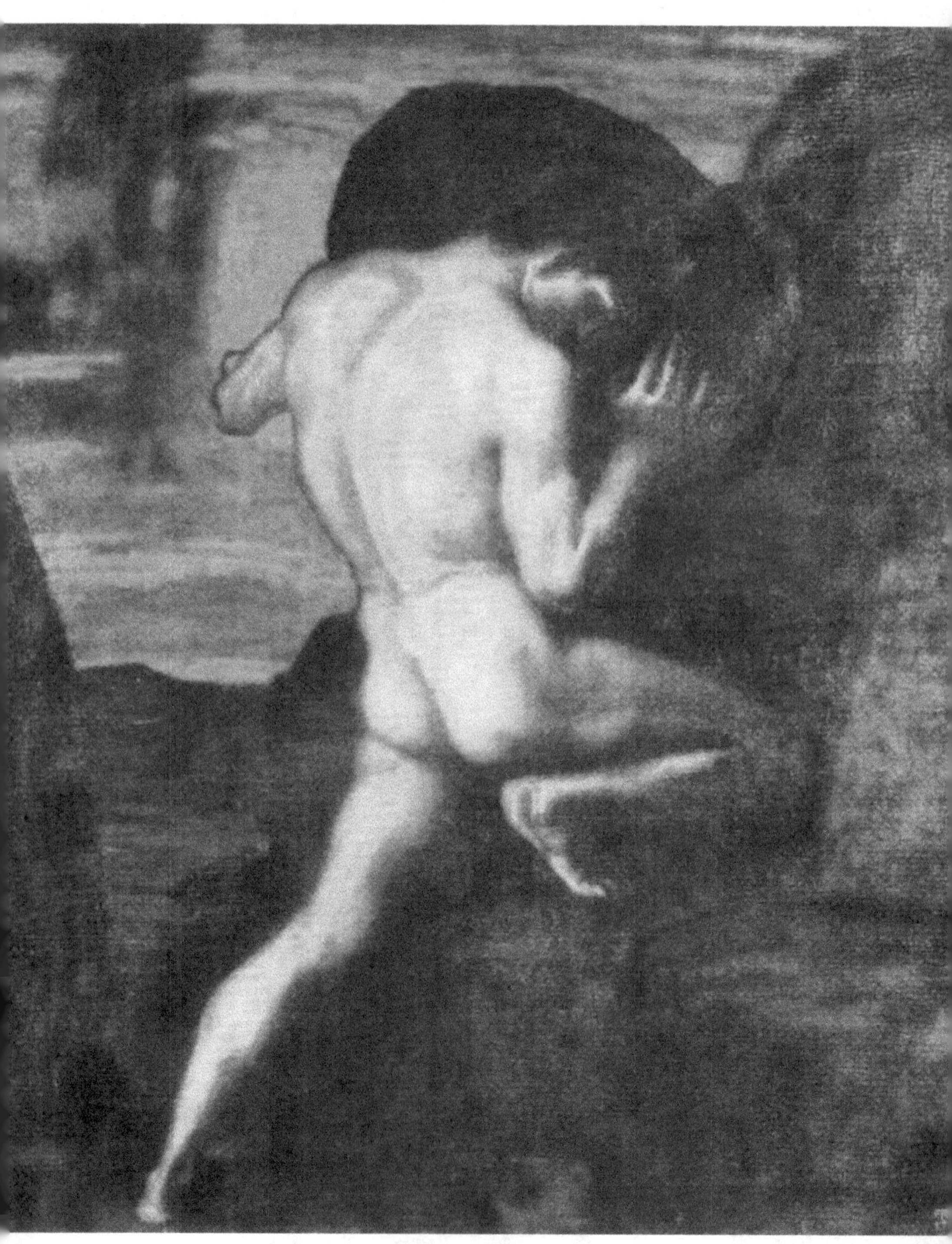

Franz von Stuck, Sisyphus

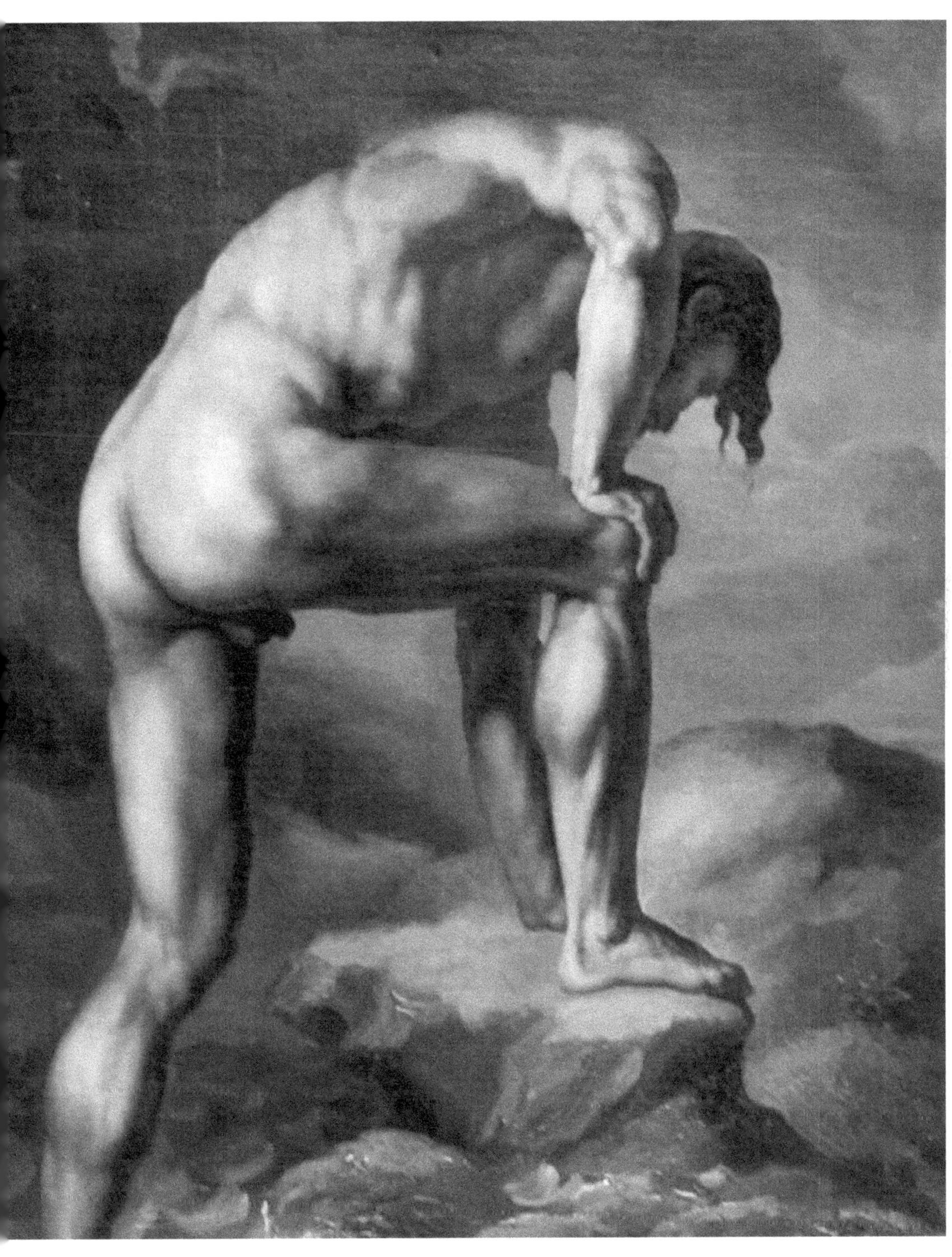

Jean-Louis Andre Theodore Géricault, A Shipwreck, c. 1819

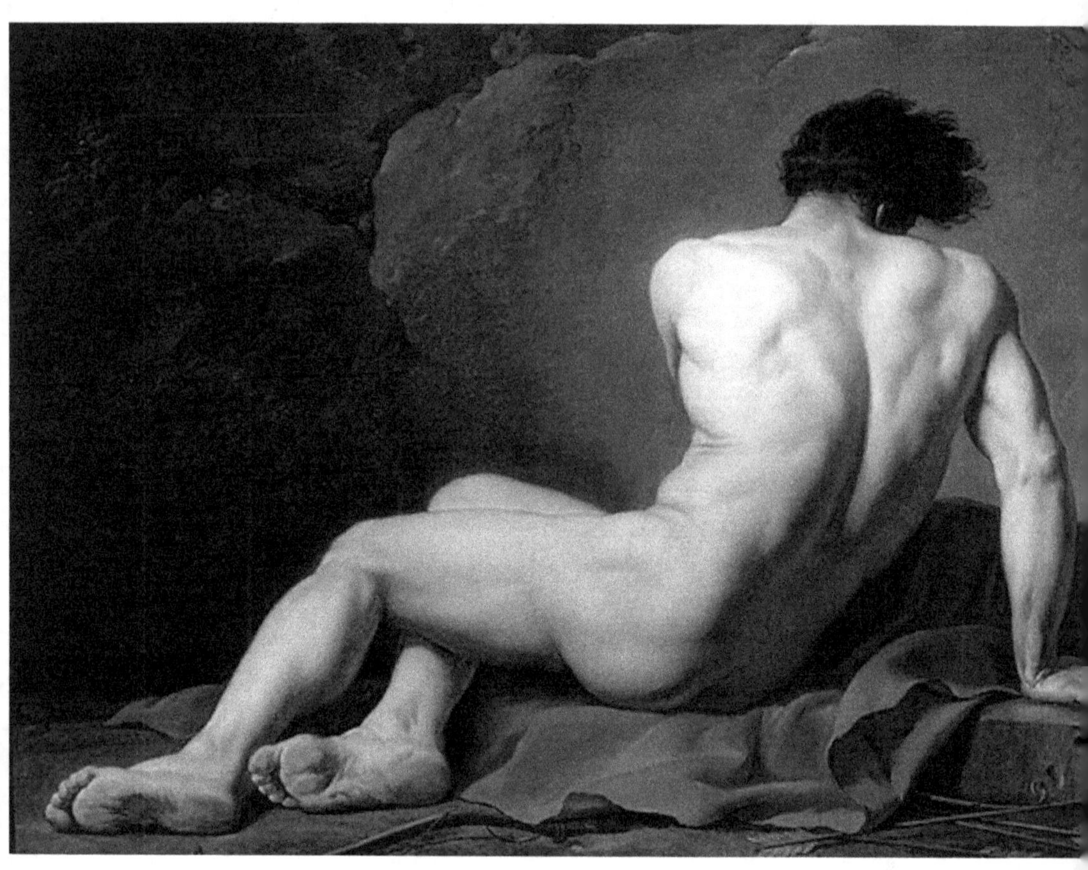

A classical French male nude painting
by Jacques-Louis David (known as Patrocles)

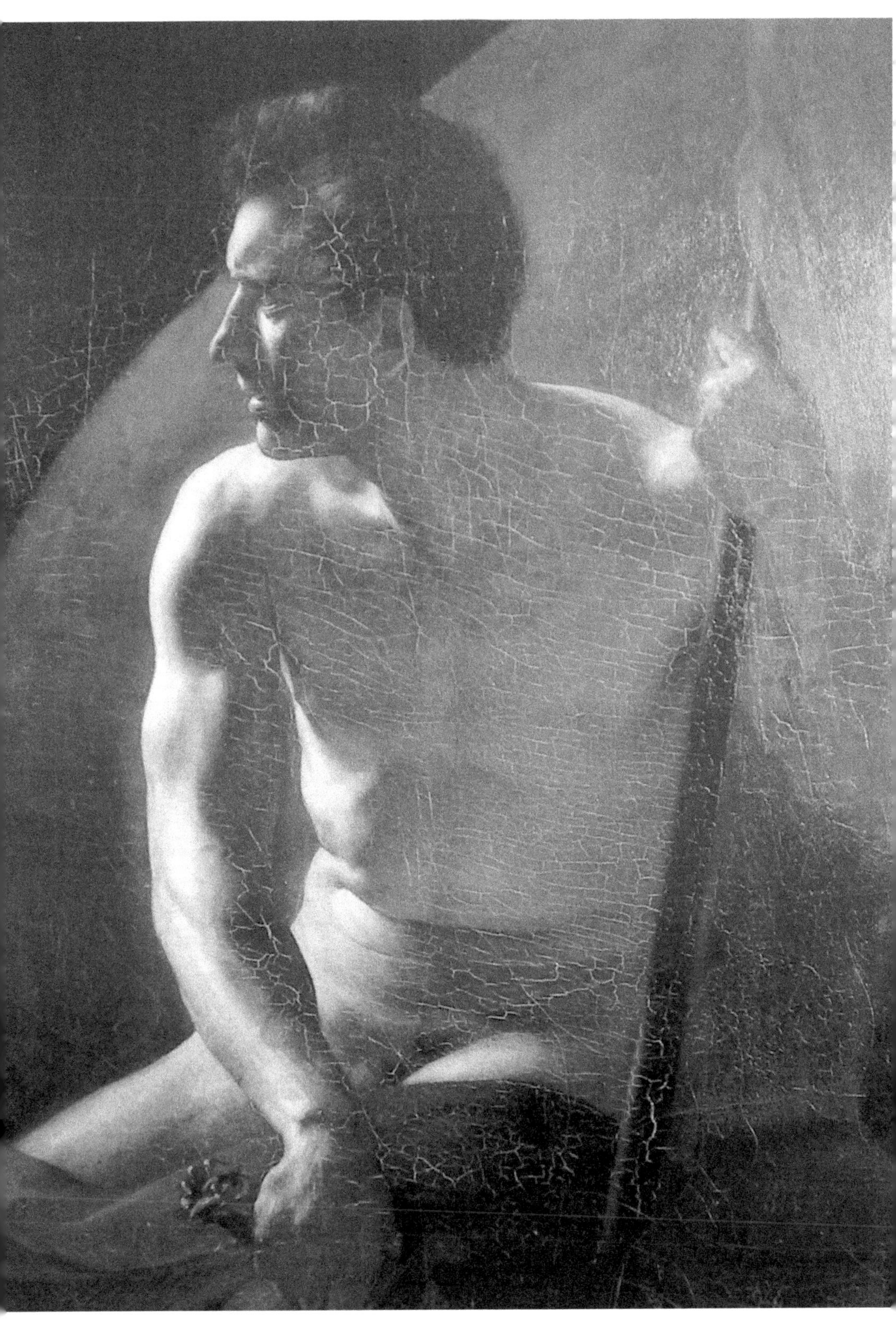

Hippolyte Dominique Holfeld, Half-Nude Figure, 1831

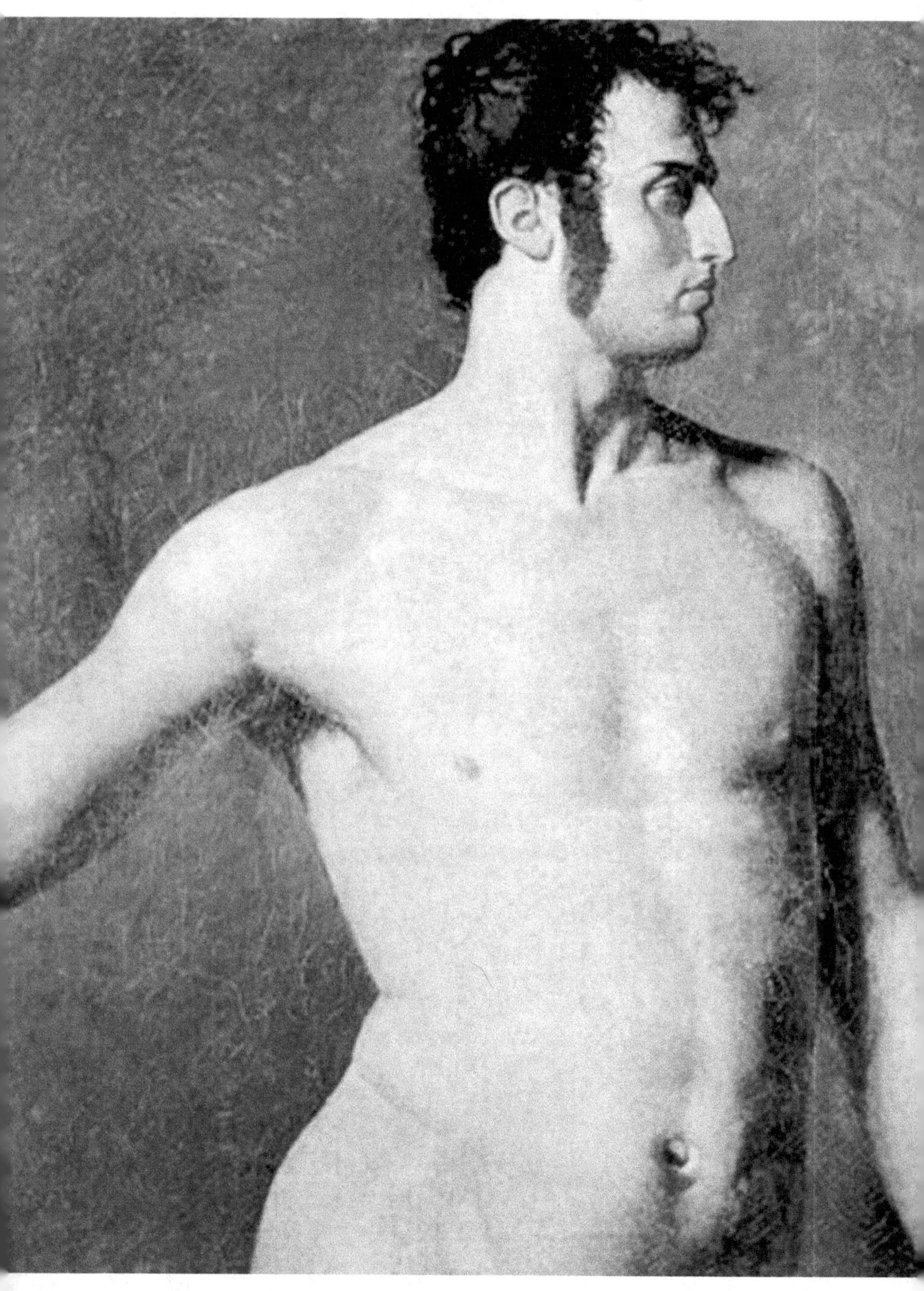

J.A.D. Ingres, Male Torso, 1801, Musée Ingres

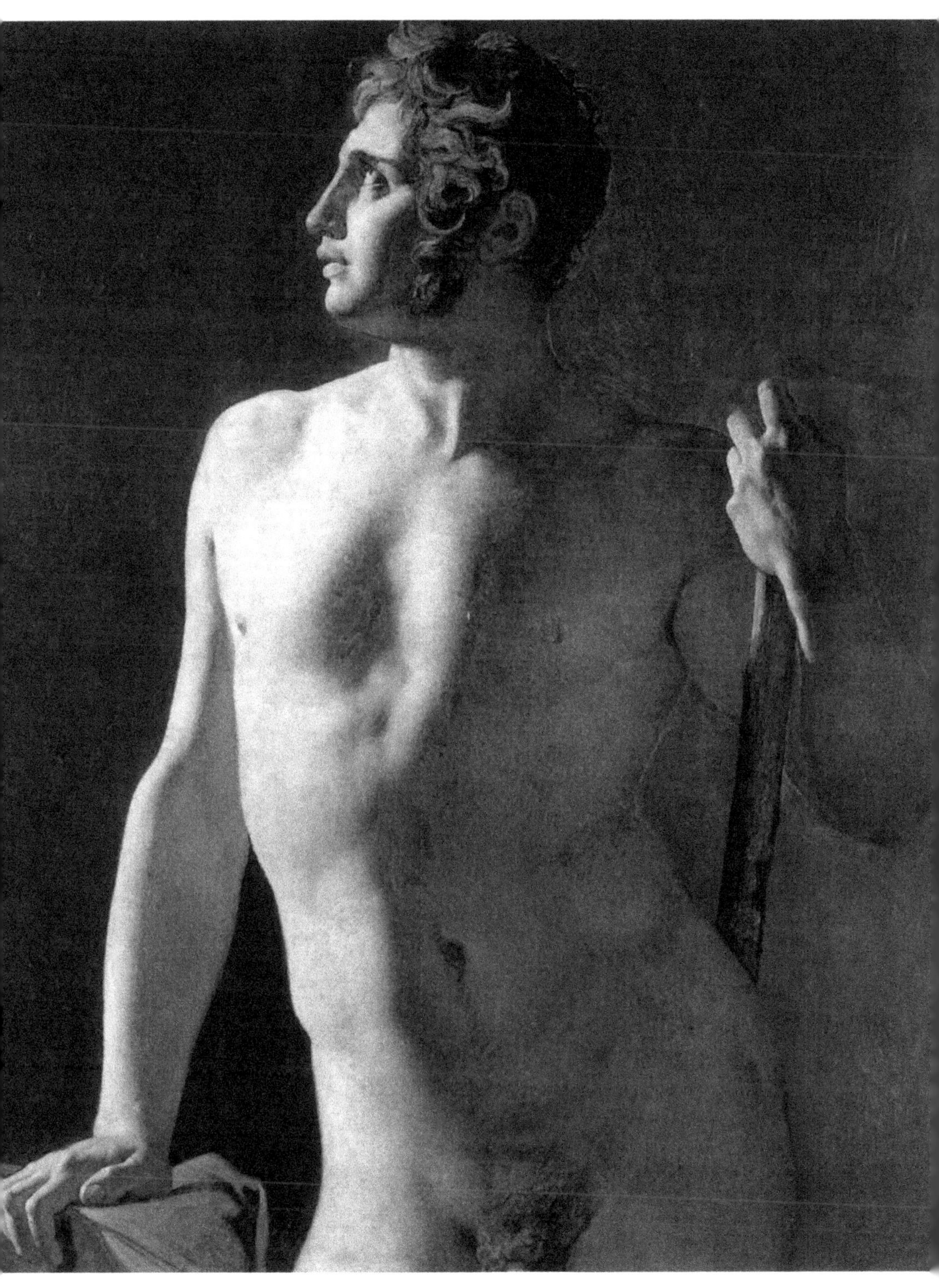

J.A.D. Ingres, Study of a Male Nude, 1801

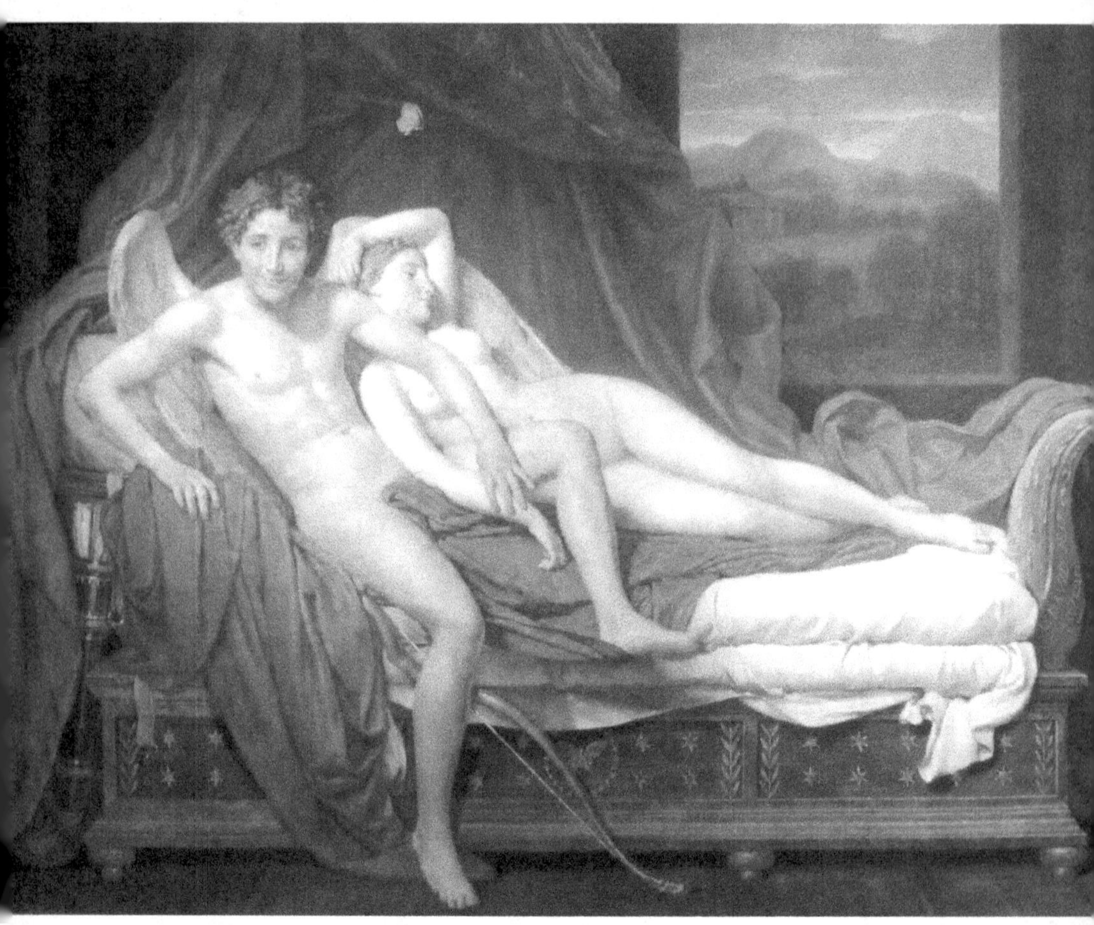

Jacques-Louis David, Cupid and Psyche, 1817,
Cleveland Museum of Art

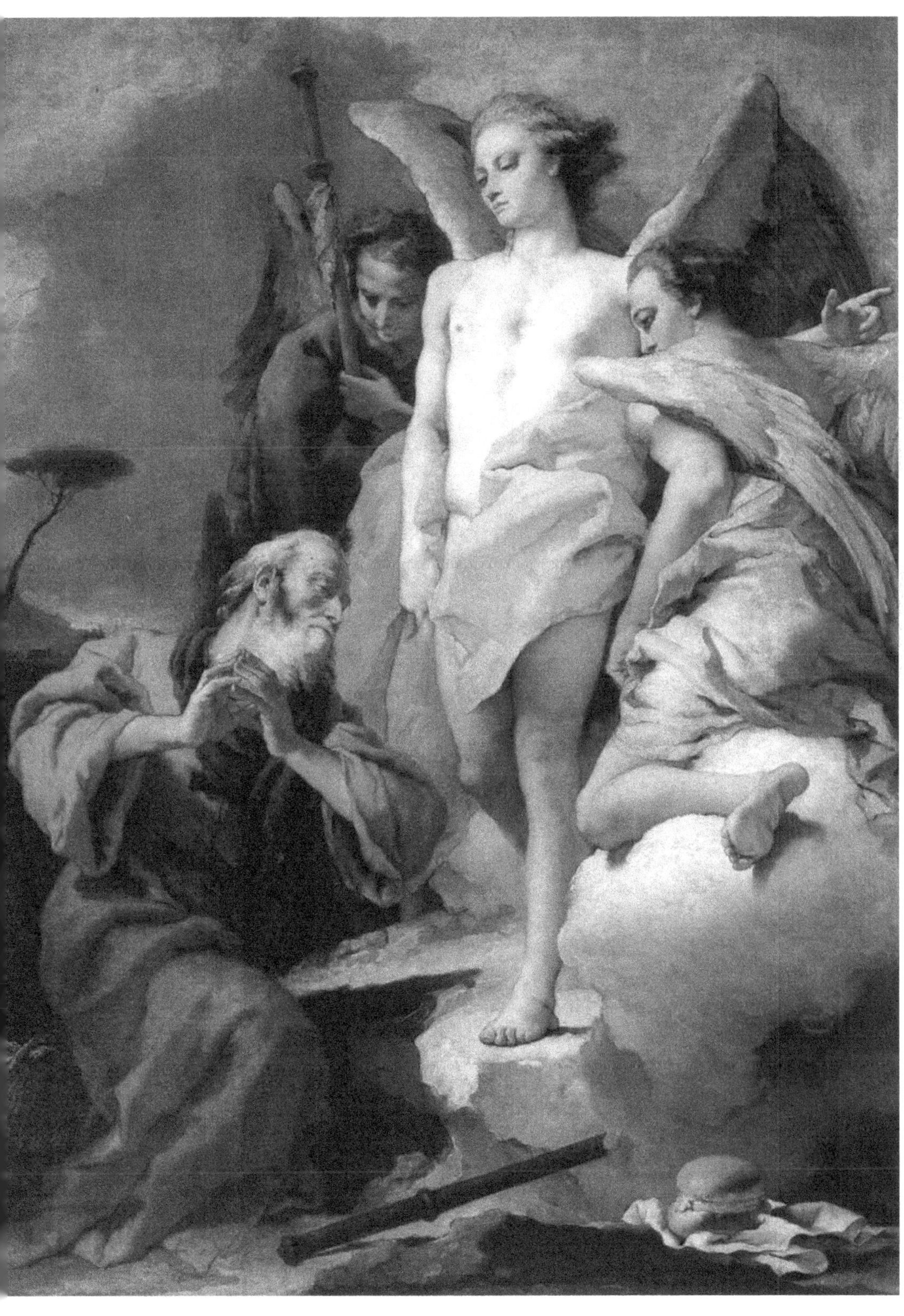

Giovanni Battista Tiepolo, Abraham and Three Angels, c. 1770

MALE NUDES

The male nude image is subject to the same changes in culture as anything else: if you look at the nudes included here, you'll see the changes in fashion and style, at the superficial level, as well as the developments in the politics and society of the time, reflected in the nude images. Even though the body is nude, there are still numerous marks of culture upon it.

In the advanced capitalist, technological world, the body is not a 'natural' form any more, as Elizabeth Grosz explains in *Volatile Bodies*: clothing, exercise, jewellery, lifestyle, habits, negotiations of the cultural and social as well as the physical environment, and all sorts of activities alter it, inscribe it, turn it into something definitely not 'natural':

> Makeup, stilettos, bras, hair sprays, clothing, underclothing mark women's bodies, whether black or white, in ways in which hair styles, professional training, personal grooming, gait, posture, body building, and sports may mark men's. There is nothing natural or ahistorical about these modes of corporeal inscriptions. Through then, bodies are made amenable to the prevailing exigencies of power. They make the flesh into a particular type of body – pagan, primitive, medieval, capitalist, Italian, American, Australian. (142)

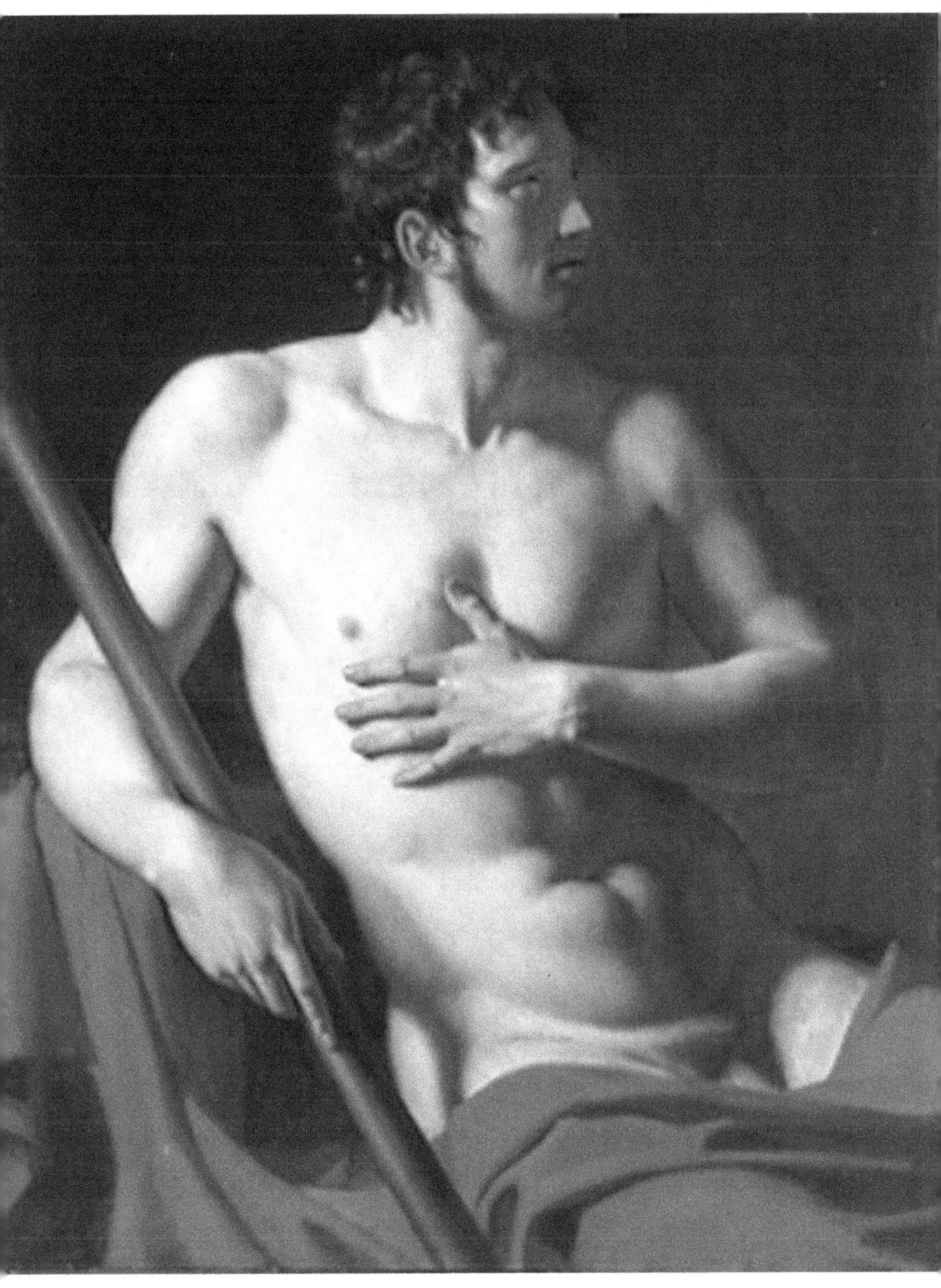

Auguste-Alphonse Gaudar de la Verdine, Male Nude, 1799

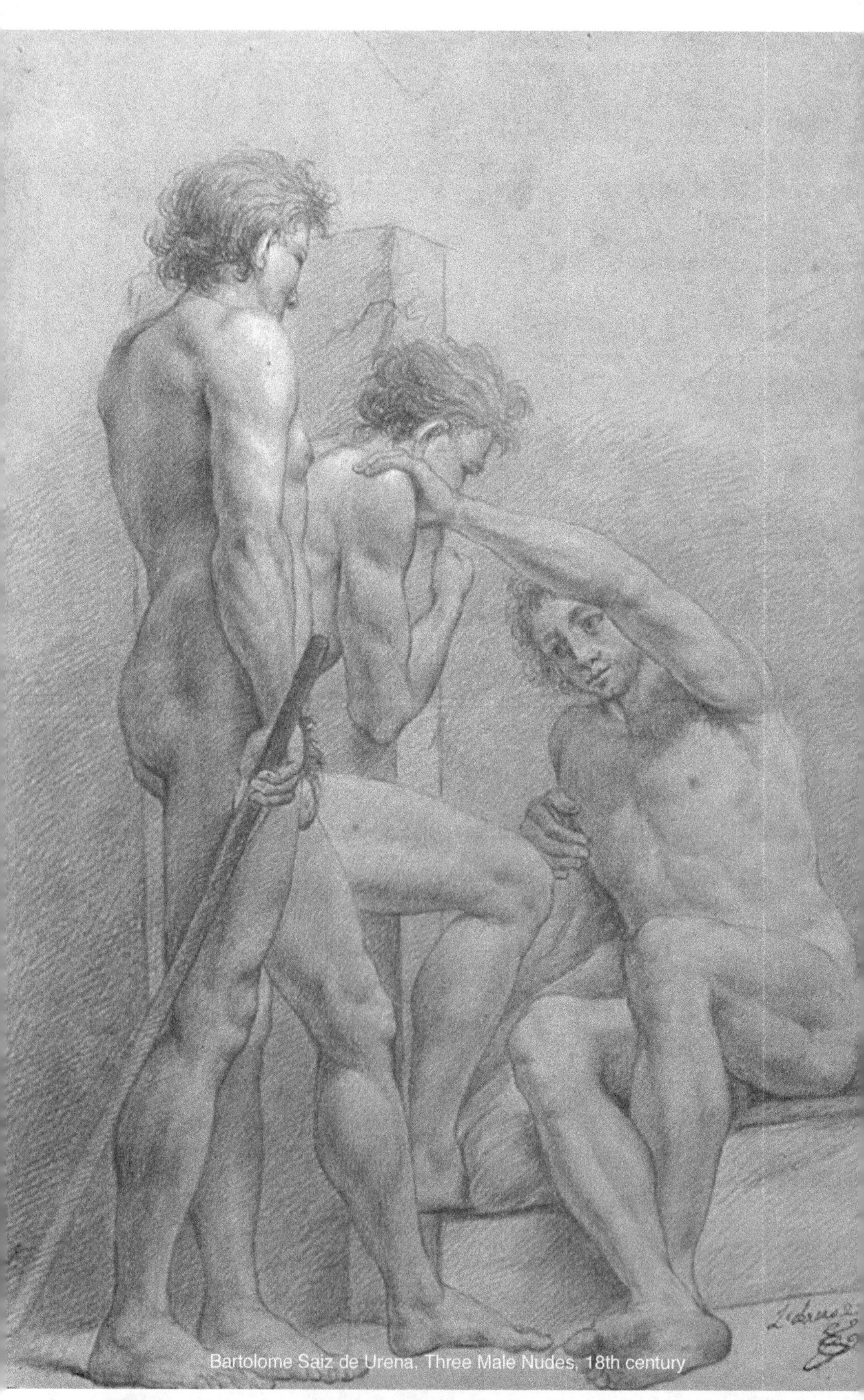

Bartolome Saiz de Urena. Three Male Nudes, 18th century

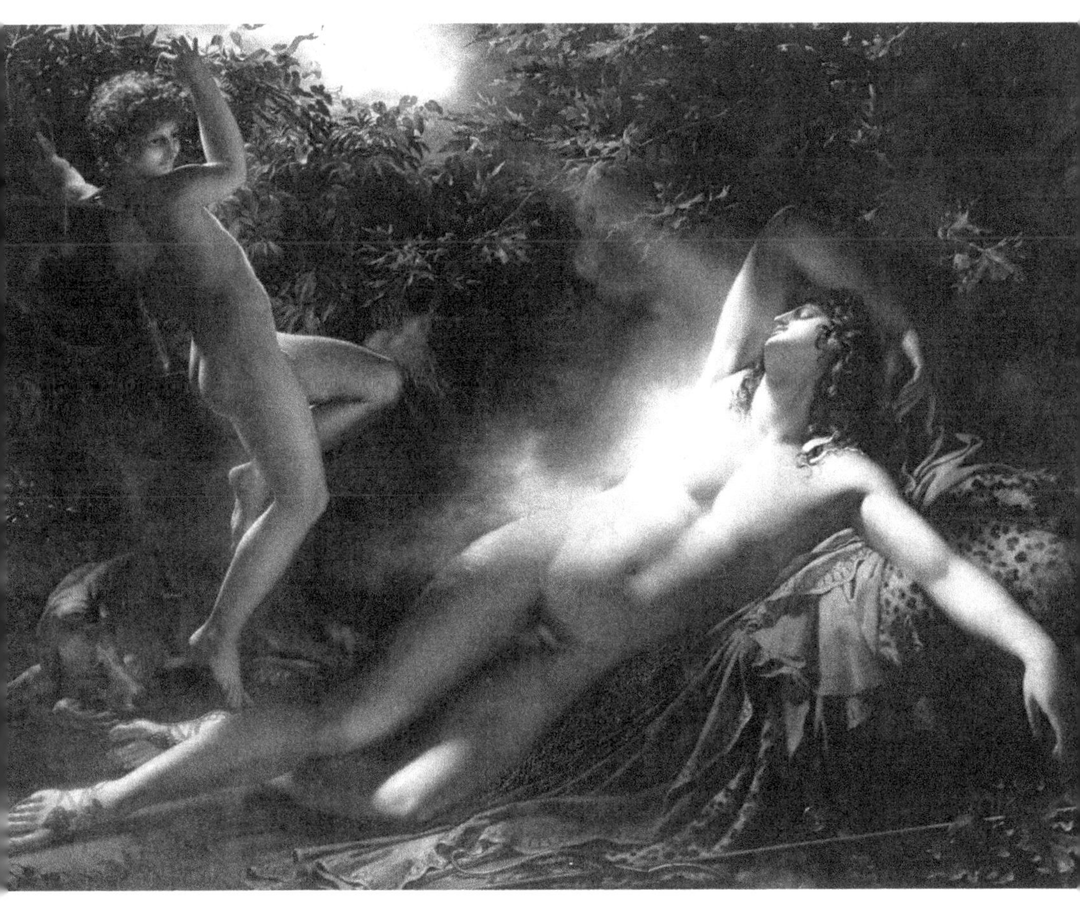

Anne-Louis Girodet-Trioson, Endymion, 1793

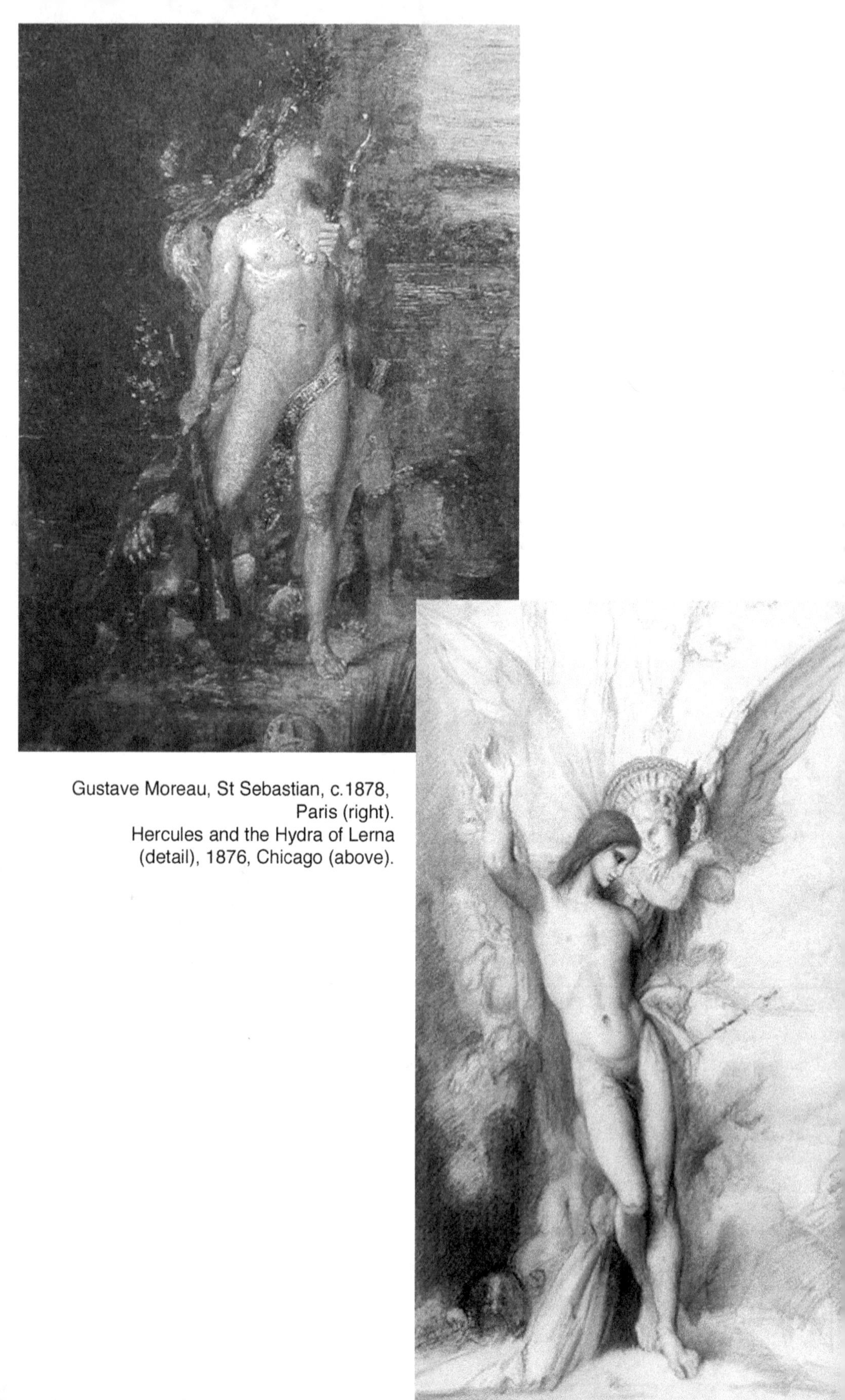

Gustave Moreau, St Sebastian, c.1878, Paris (right).
Hercules and the Hydra of Lerna (detail), 1876, Chicago (above).

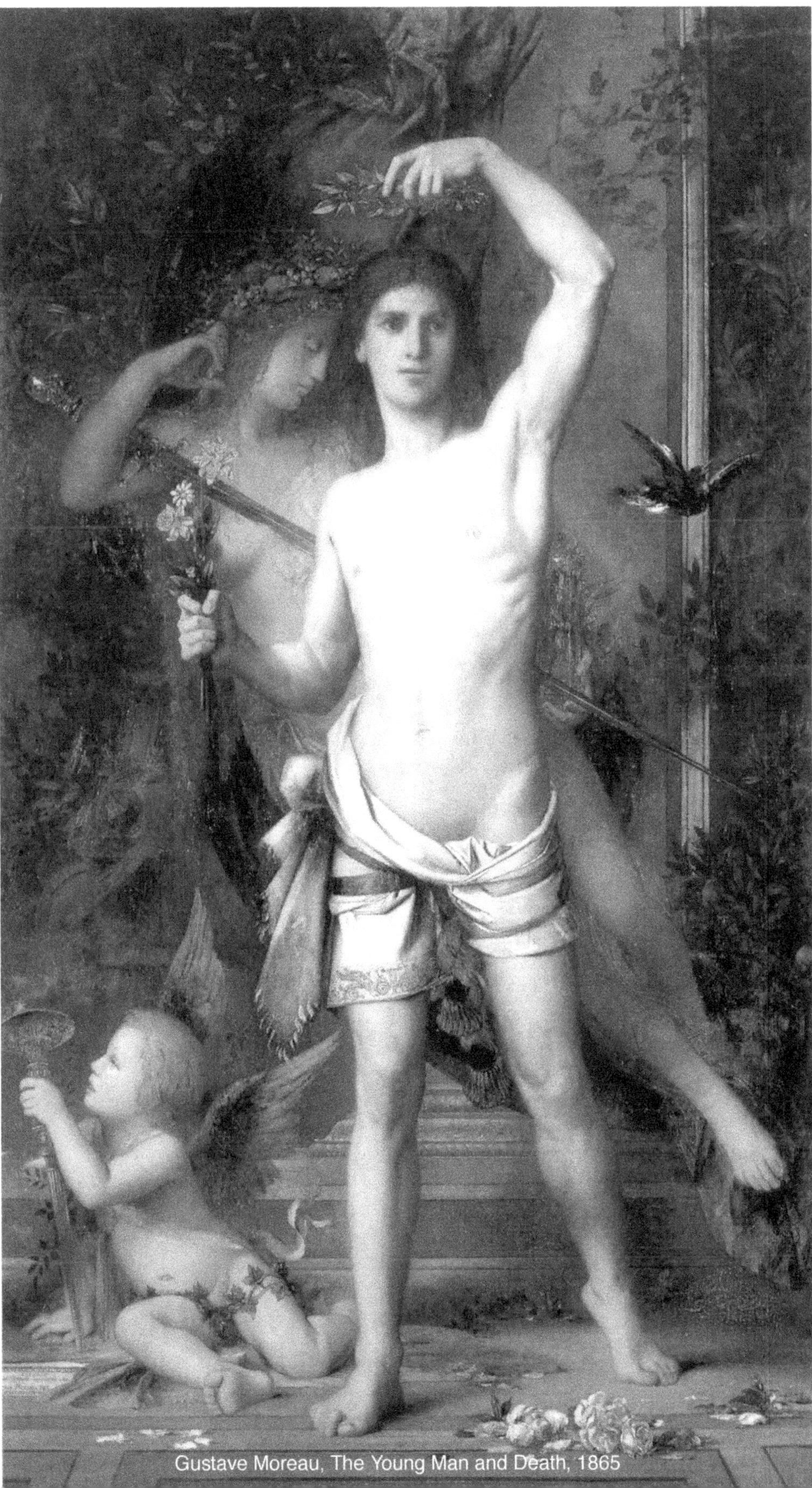

Gustave Moreau, The Young Man and Death, 1865

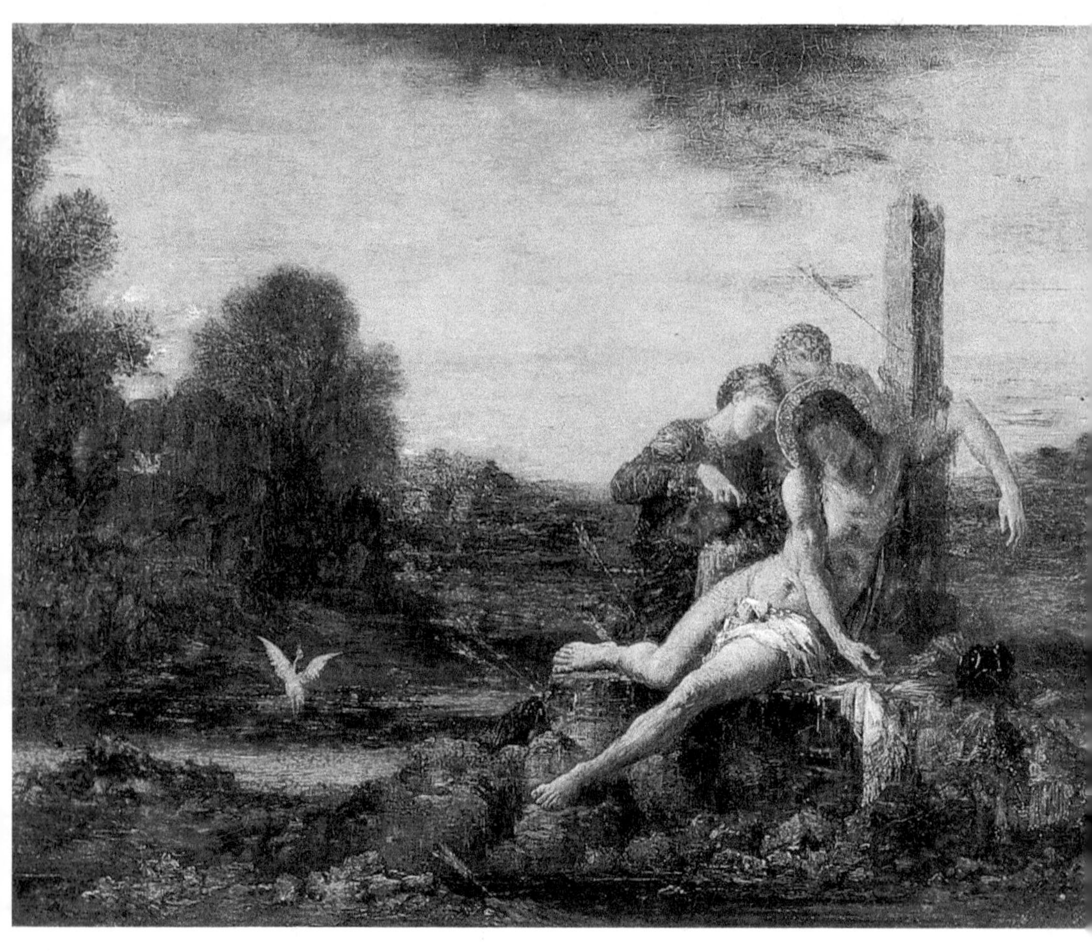

Gustave Moreau, St Sebastian, 1869

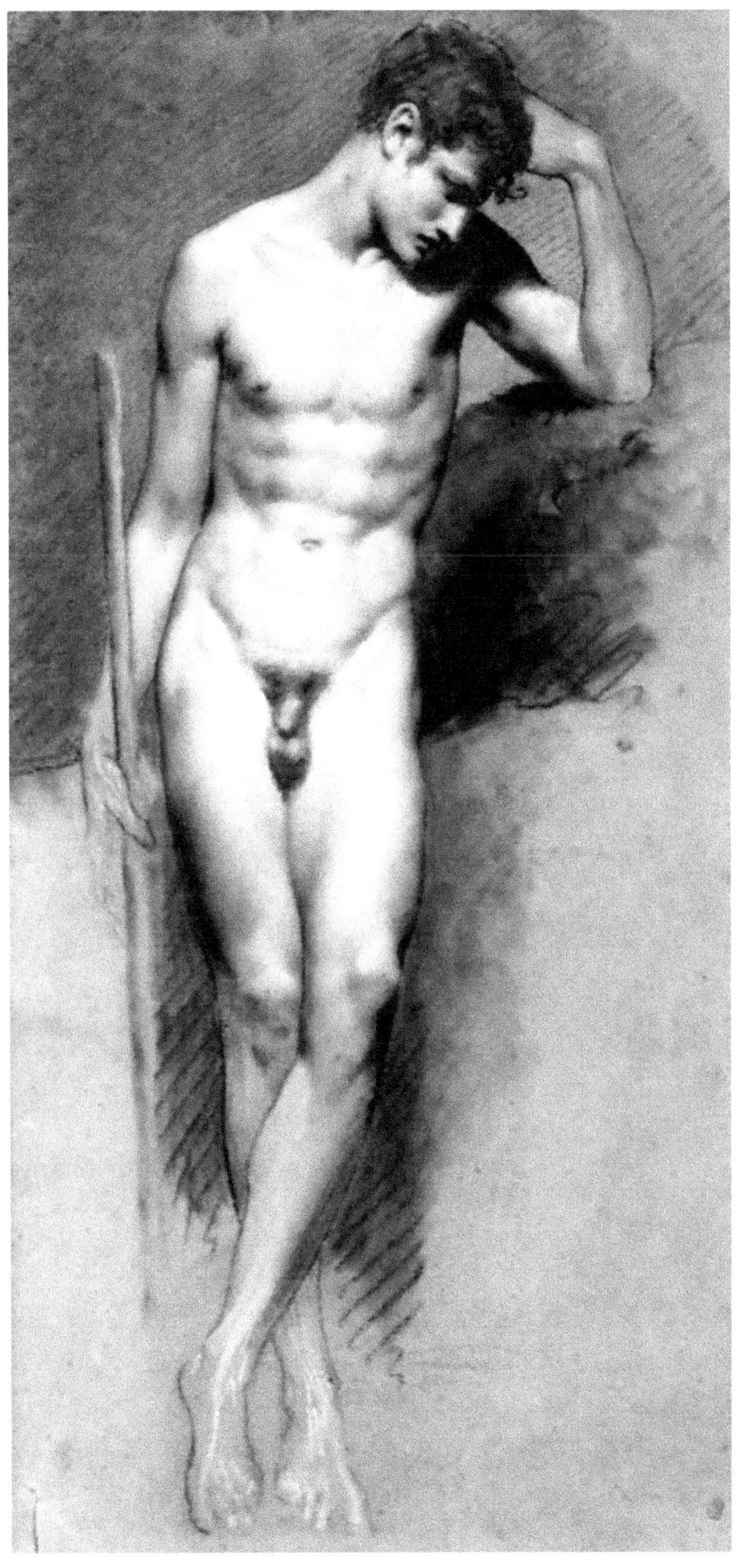

Pierre-Paul Prud'hon (1758-1823), Male Nude Standing

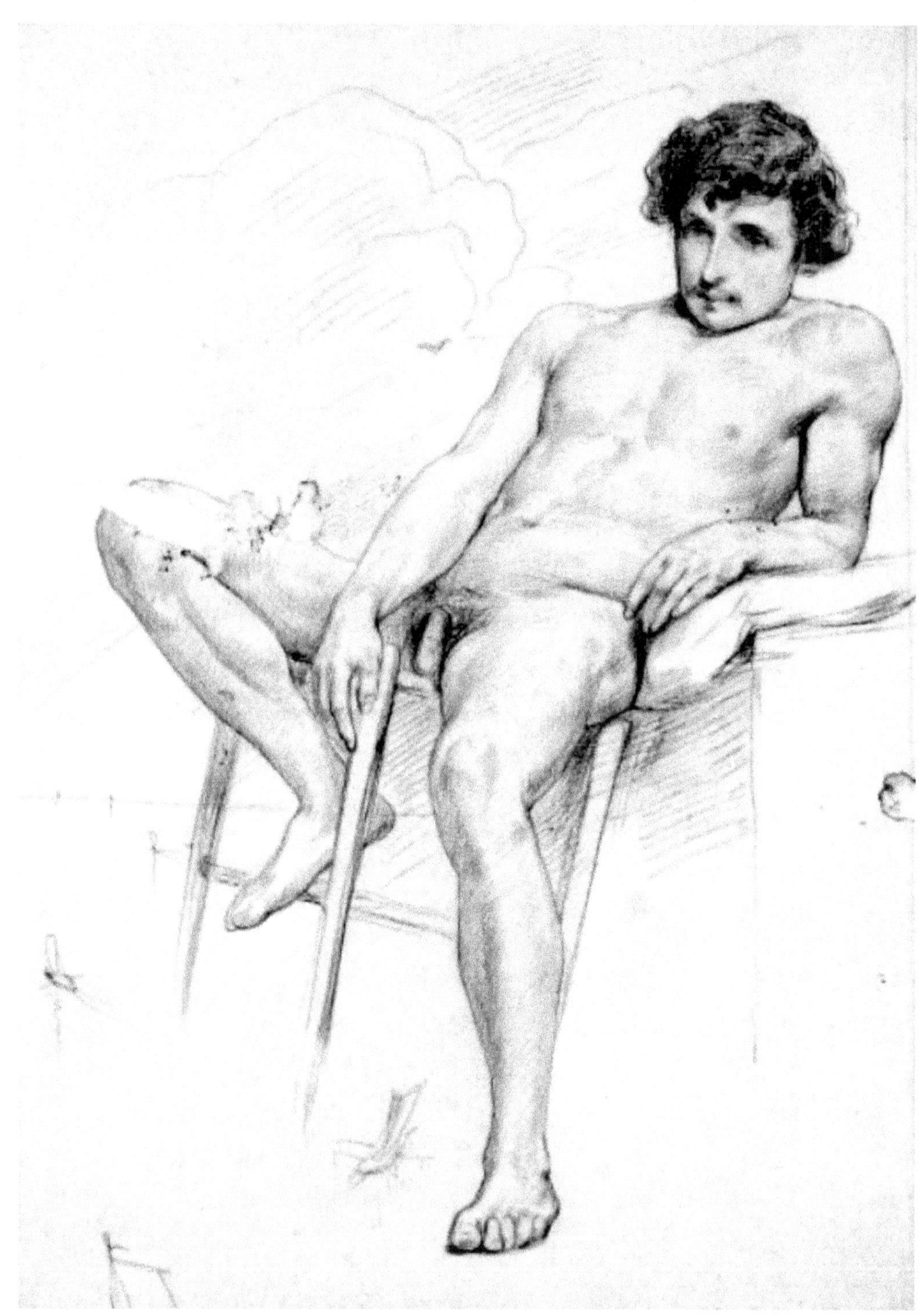

Lord Leighton, life drawing

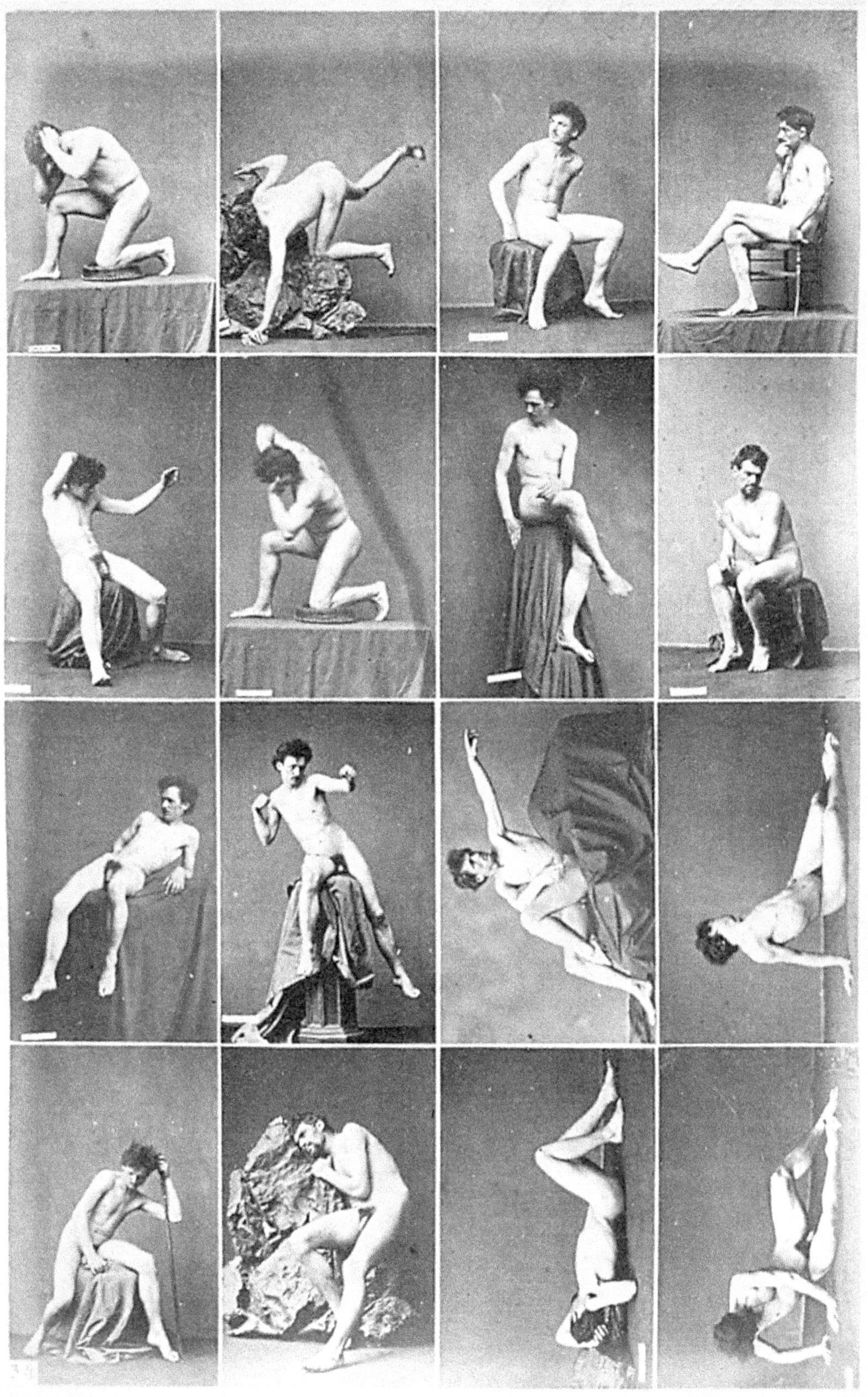

Ignout, Male Nude Studies, 1875

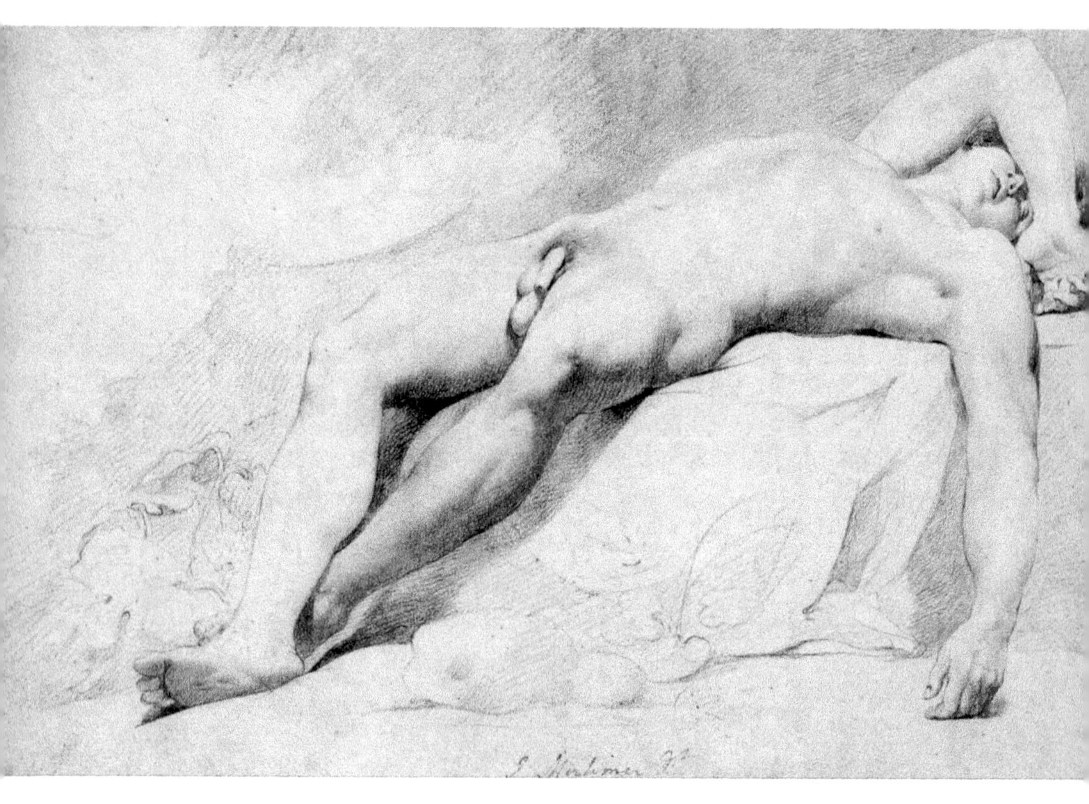

John Hamilton Mortimer, Recumbent Male Nude, c. 1773

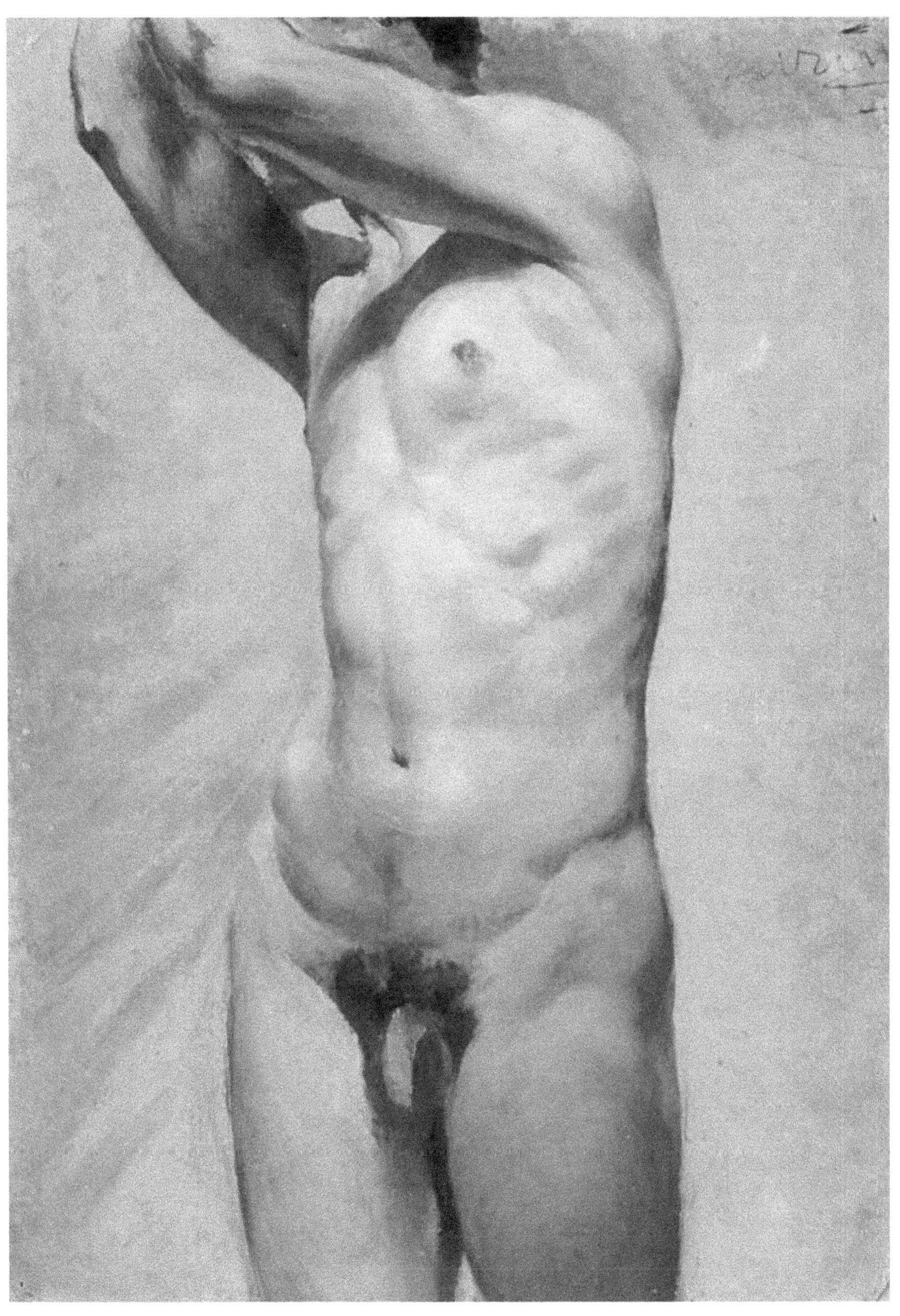

French school, c. 1890

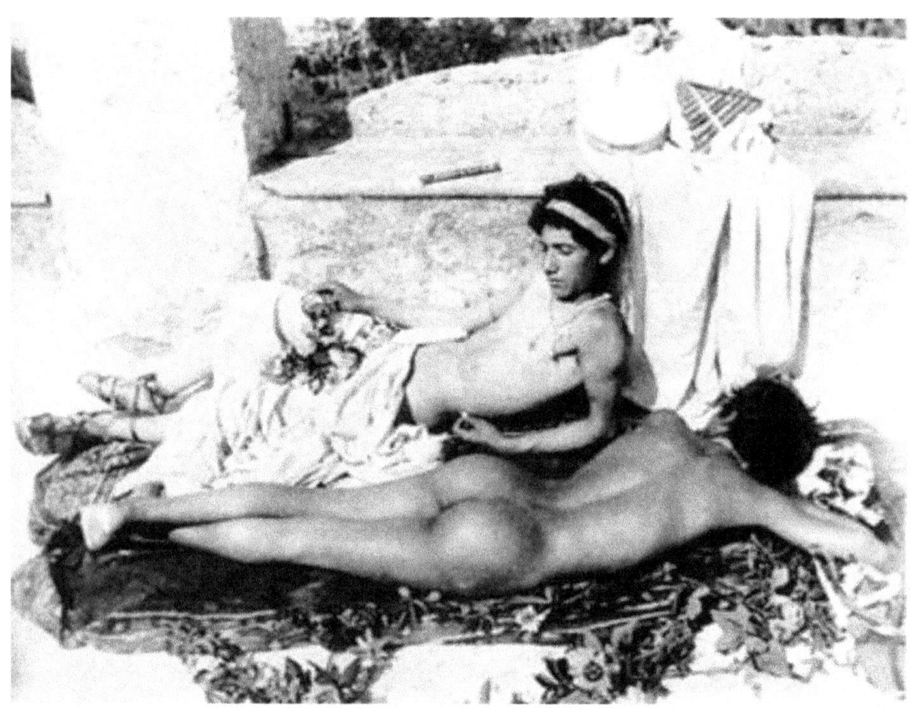

Wilhelm von Gloeden, c. 1900

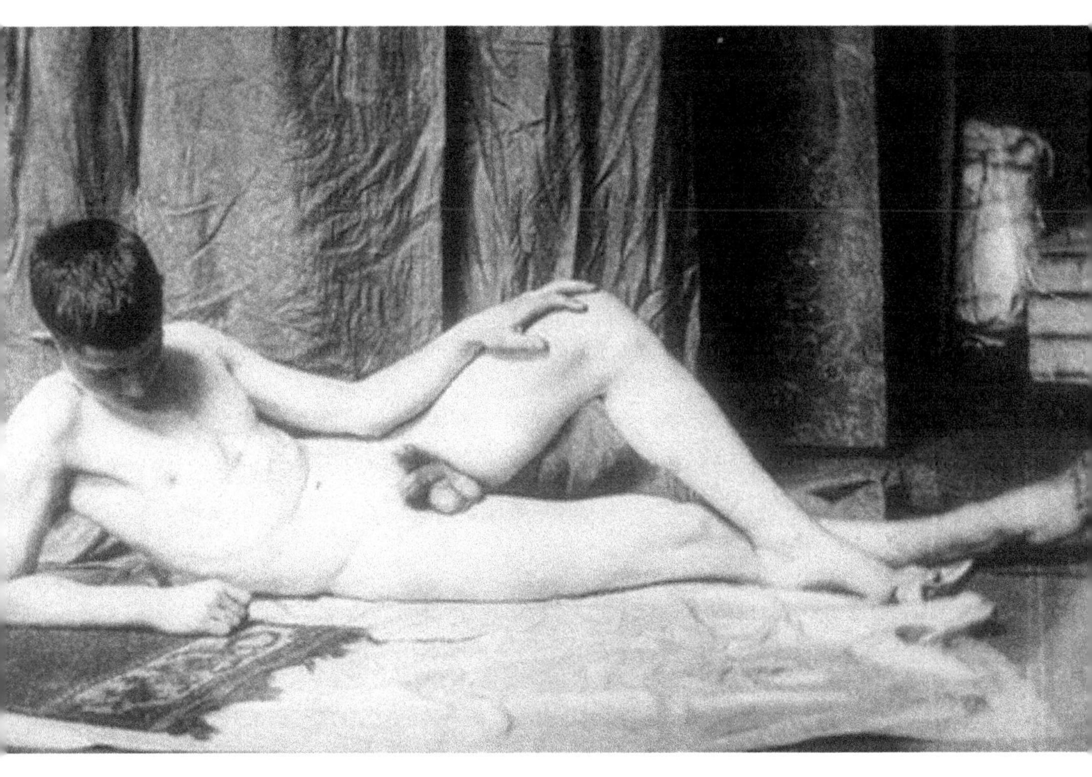

Reclining Male Nude, 1887–92,
Thomas Eakins, platinum print

PORNOGRAPHY

There are many different kinds of pornography, as there are many different kinds of art or feminism. Seen through cultural or postmodern or deconstructionist or semiological theory, pornography can be viewed as a realm of codes, meanings, contexts, signifiers, values, experiences and attitudes, which are politically controlled, manufactured by social, economic and political needs and demands. Pornography is thus the *representation* of... something; maybe certain kinds of sexuality, maybe somebody's thoughts on certain kinds of sexuality. Pornography is not *sexuality in itself*, it is mediation, representation, communication, a relic, a trace.

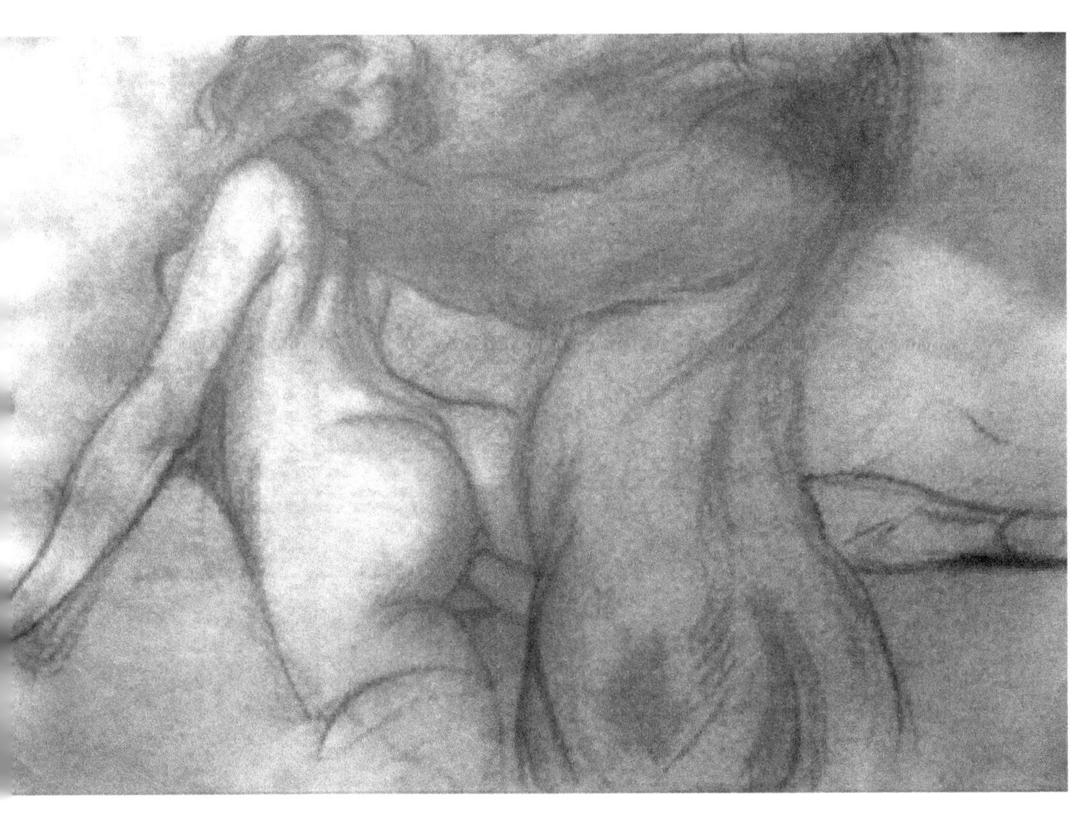

Aroldo Bonzagni

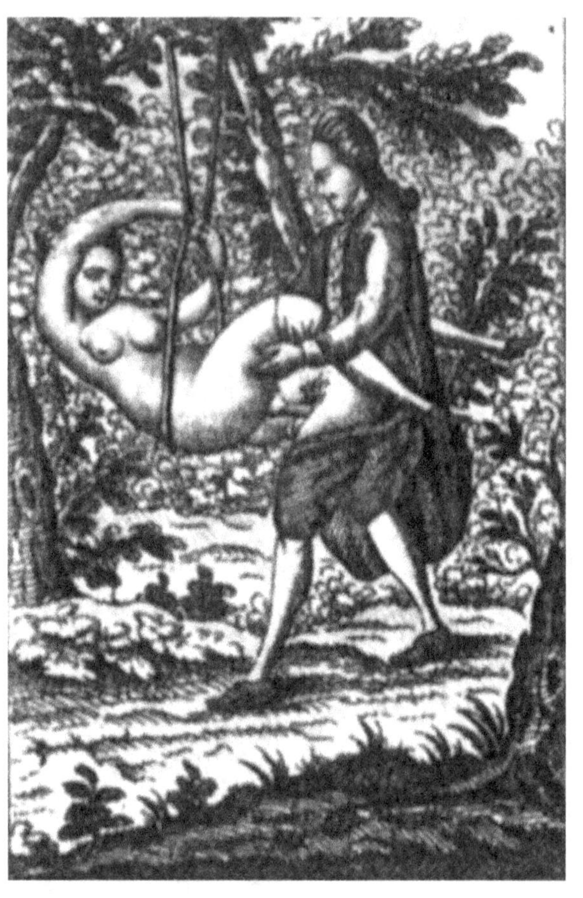

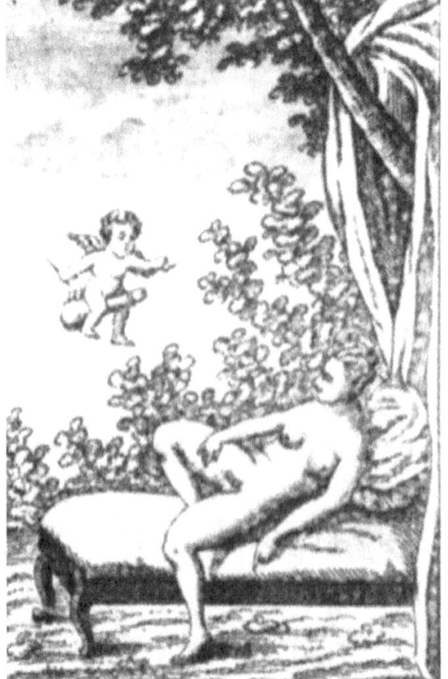

Anonymous,
Memoires du Suzon

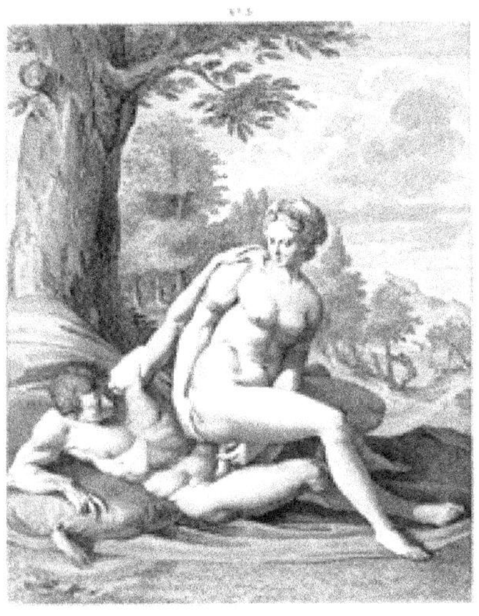

ANGELIQUE ET MEDOR.

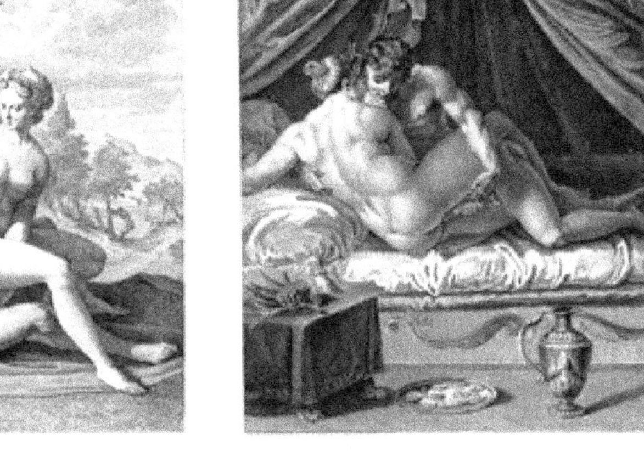

ANTOINE ET CLEOPATRE

Jacques Joseph Coiny, after Agostino Caracci,
I Modi, 1524, and Pietro Aretino

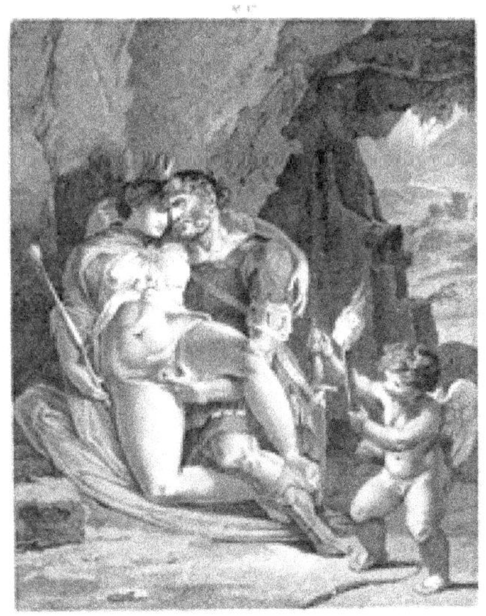

ENEE ET DIDON

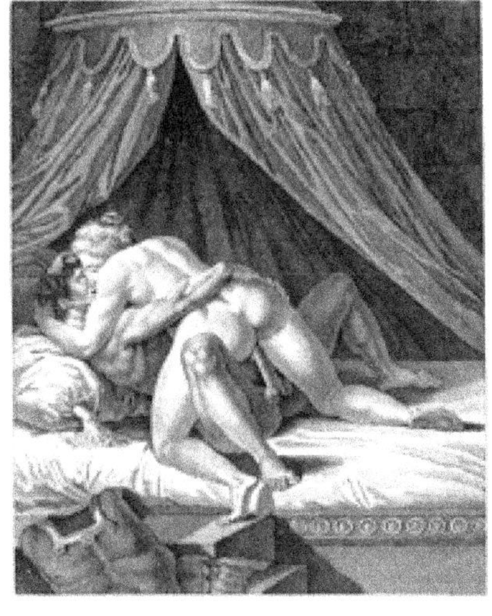

MARS ET VENUS

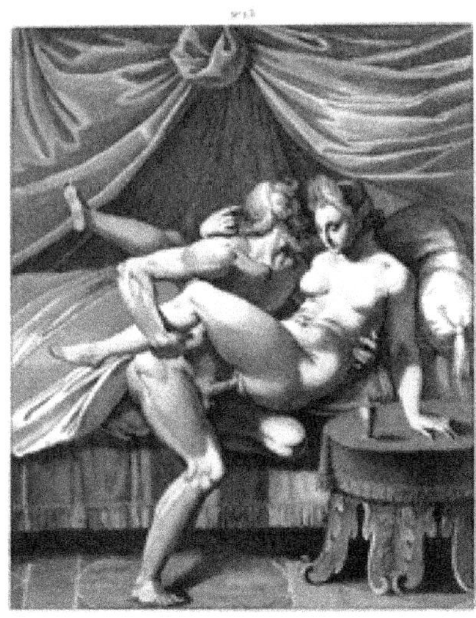

JUPITER ET JUNON

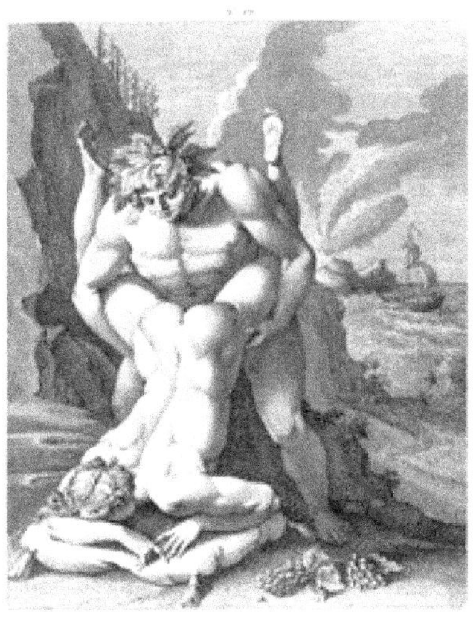

BACHUS ET ARIANE

Pornography has its own 'genres' of sub-categories: there is S/M, hardcore, lesbian, gay porn, soft core, and pornography geared to any number of fetishes; rubber, leather, boots, large breasts, bondage, etc.[1] What's your fetish? Porn will have something for you!

The history of art too has its categories and forms of erotic art, with the reclining (female) nude as perhaps the most well-known, and the most celebrated in art criticism. Other forms include humans and deities, humans and animals (often gods in beast-form), sexual positions, religious subjects, mythological subjects, Venus and Cupid, etc.

1 These sub-genres are institutions in themselves, with their own codes and structures, but their institutionalized sexual images do not express the real eroticism that people experience (they suggest it, perhaps, or reflect parts of it).

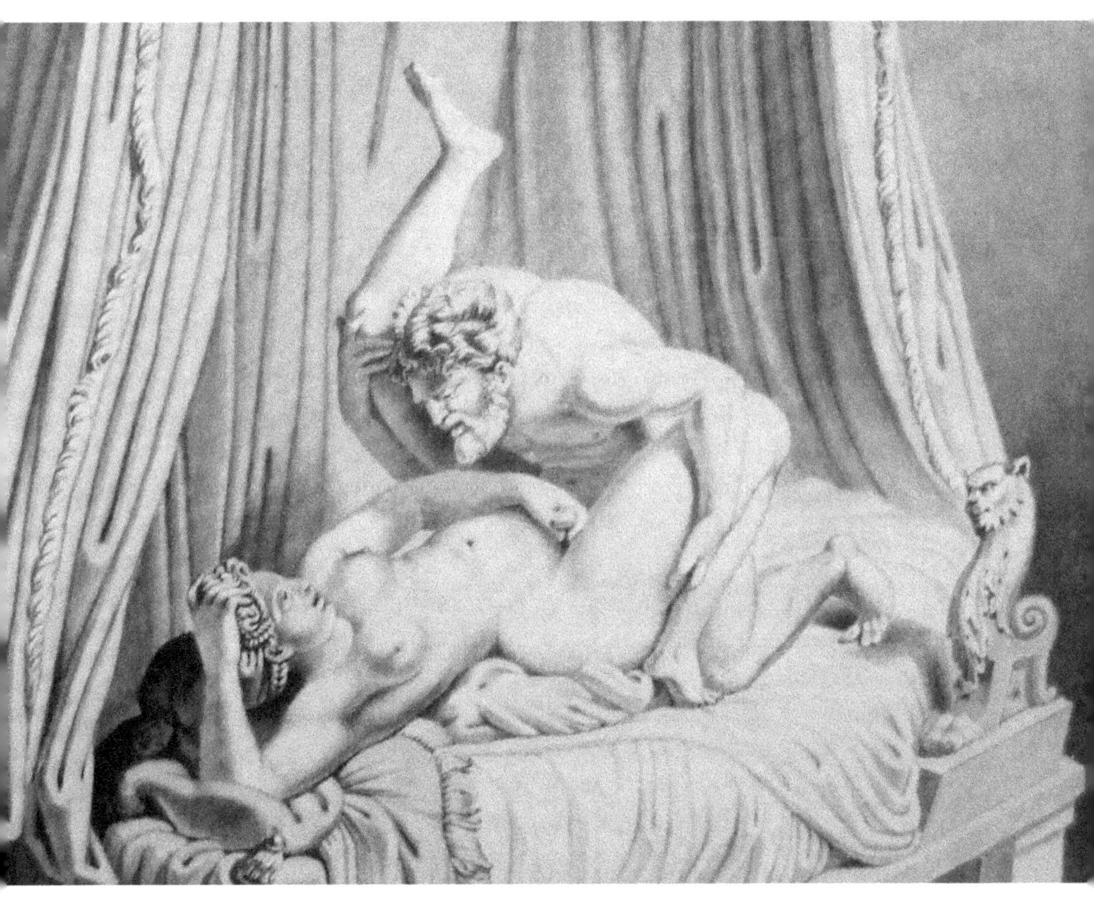

Friedrich von Waldeck, from Postures, c. 1858
(This page and following pages)

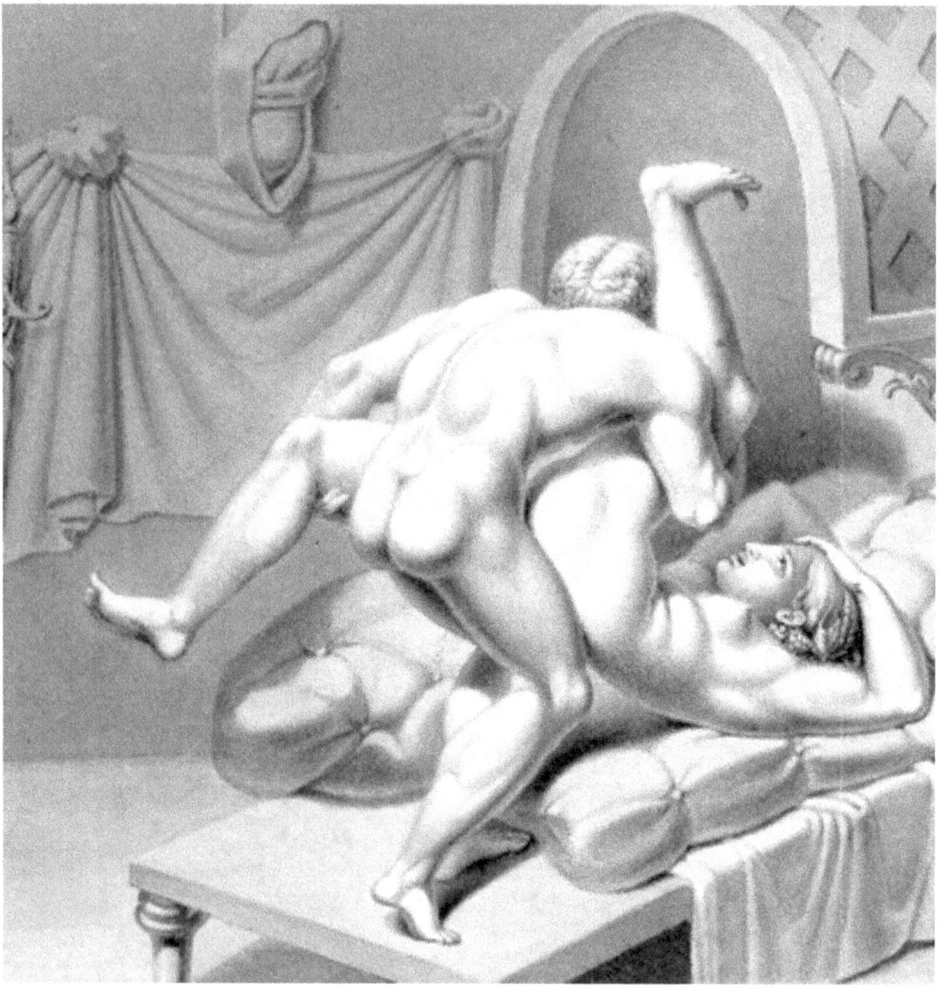

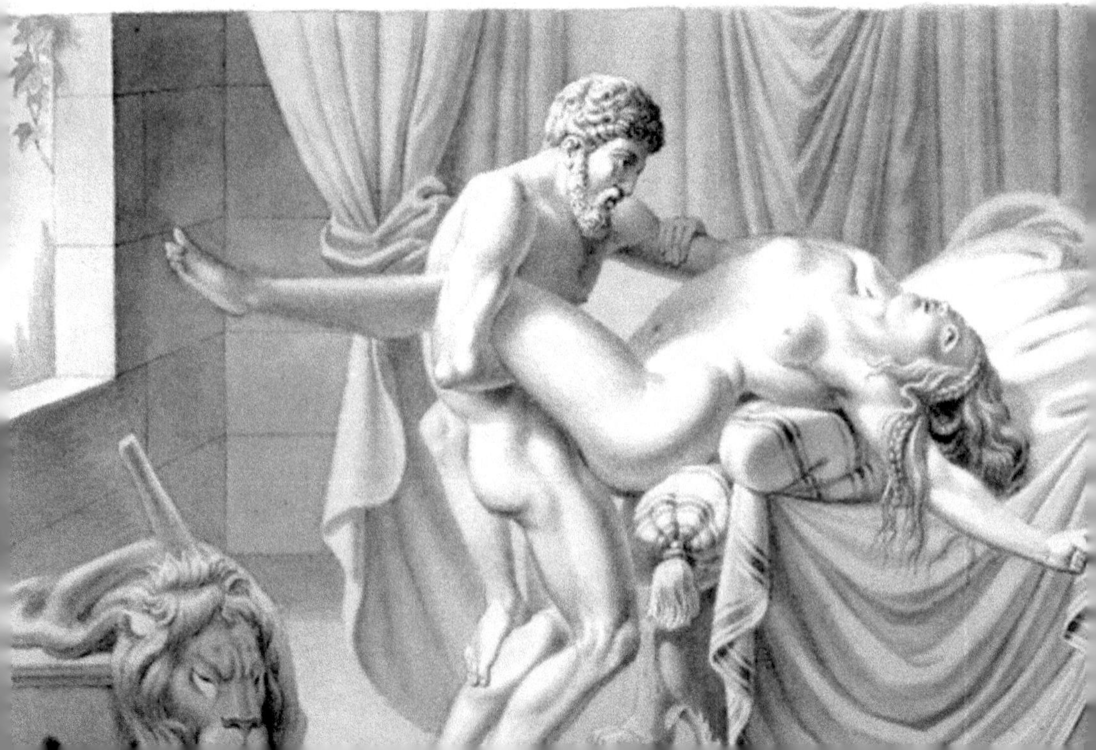

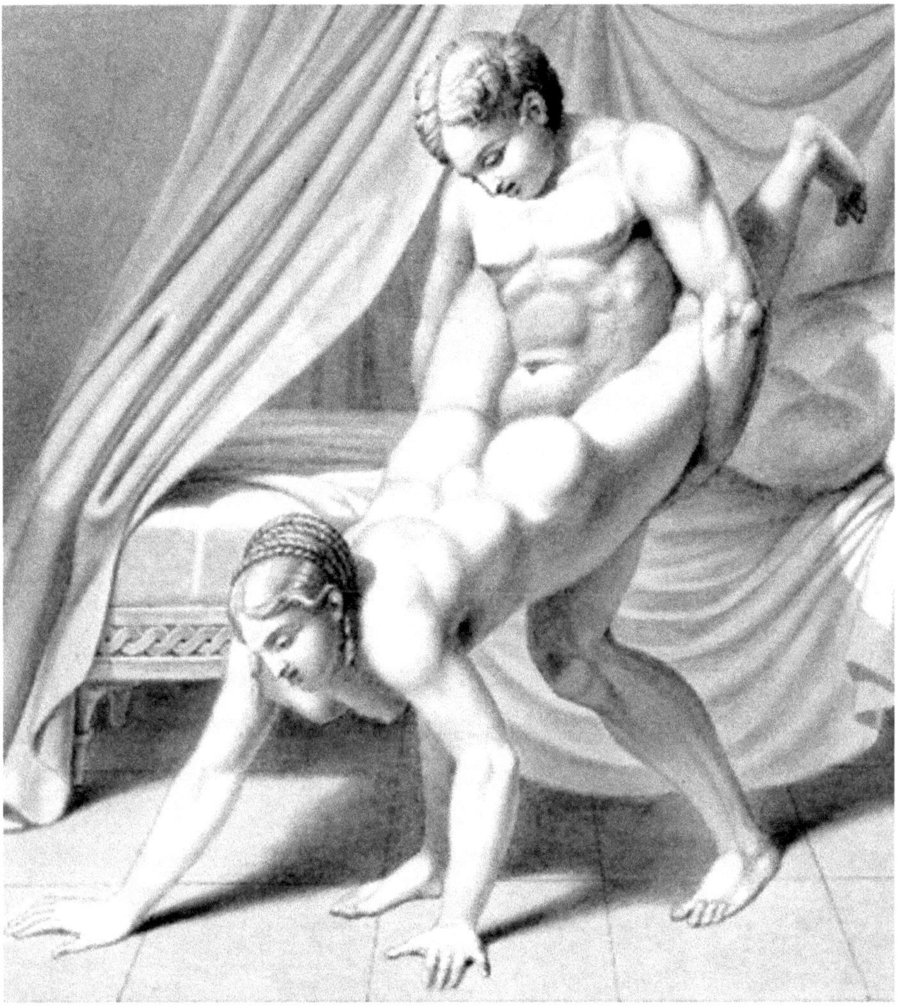

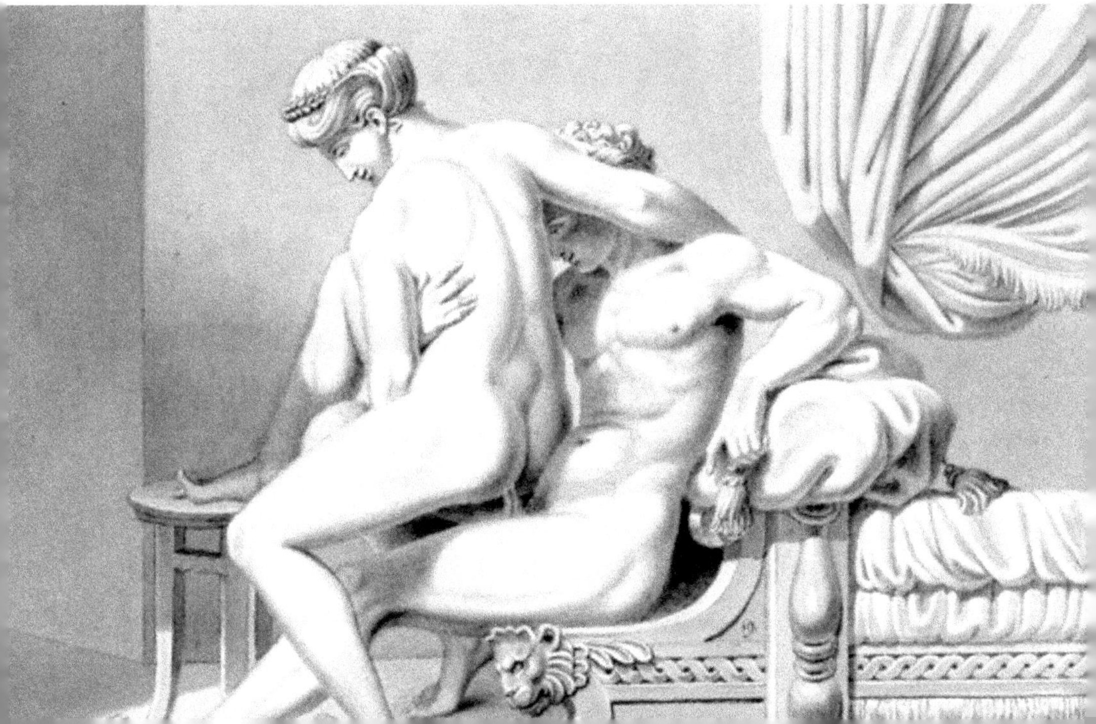

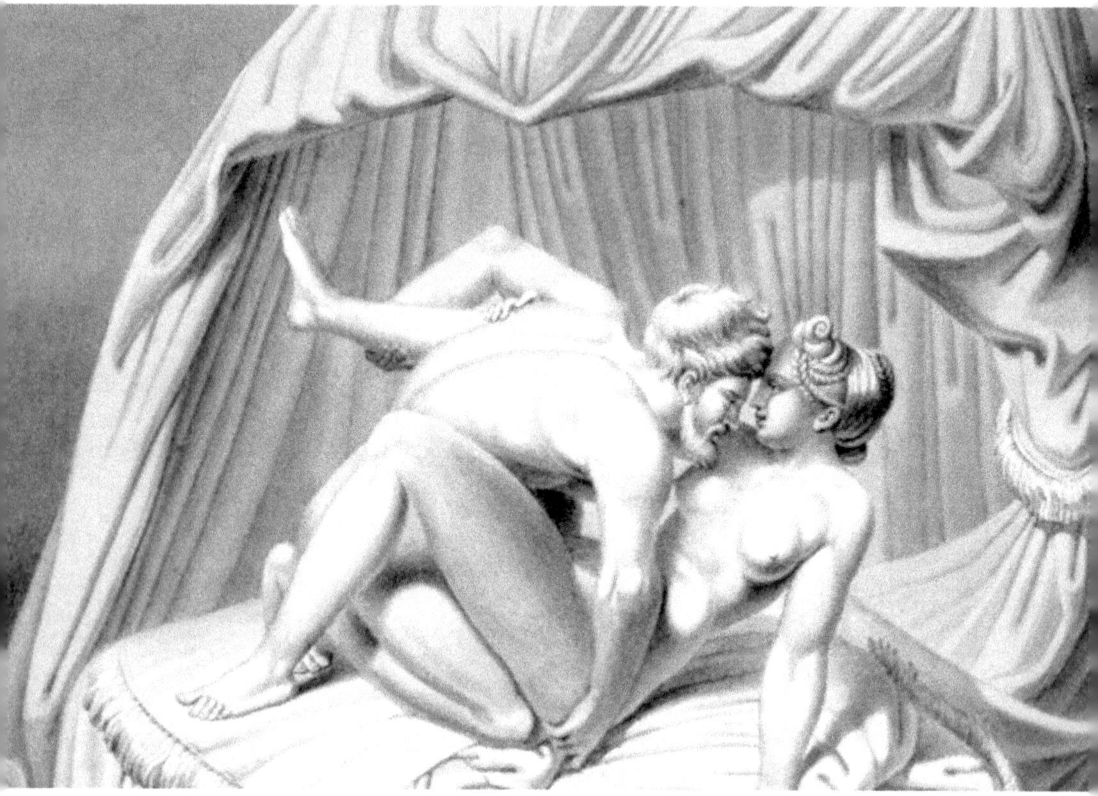

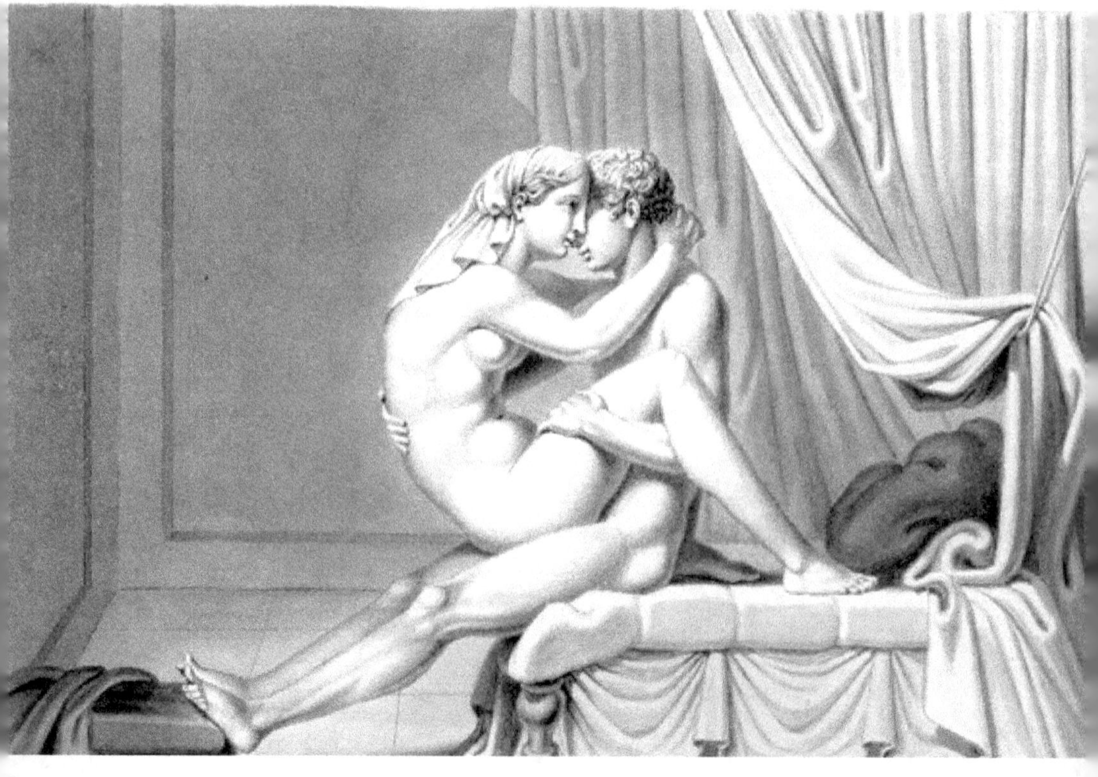

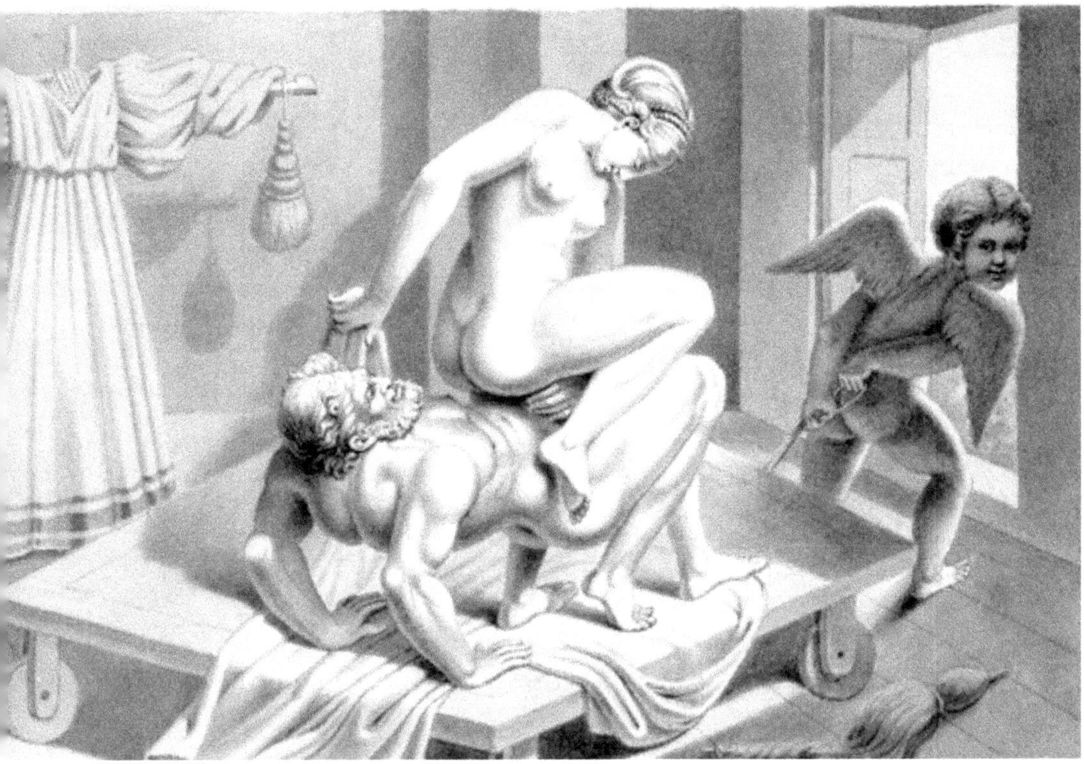

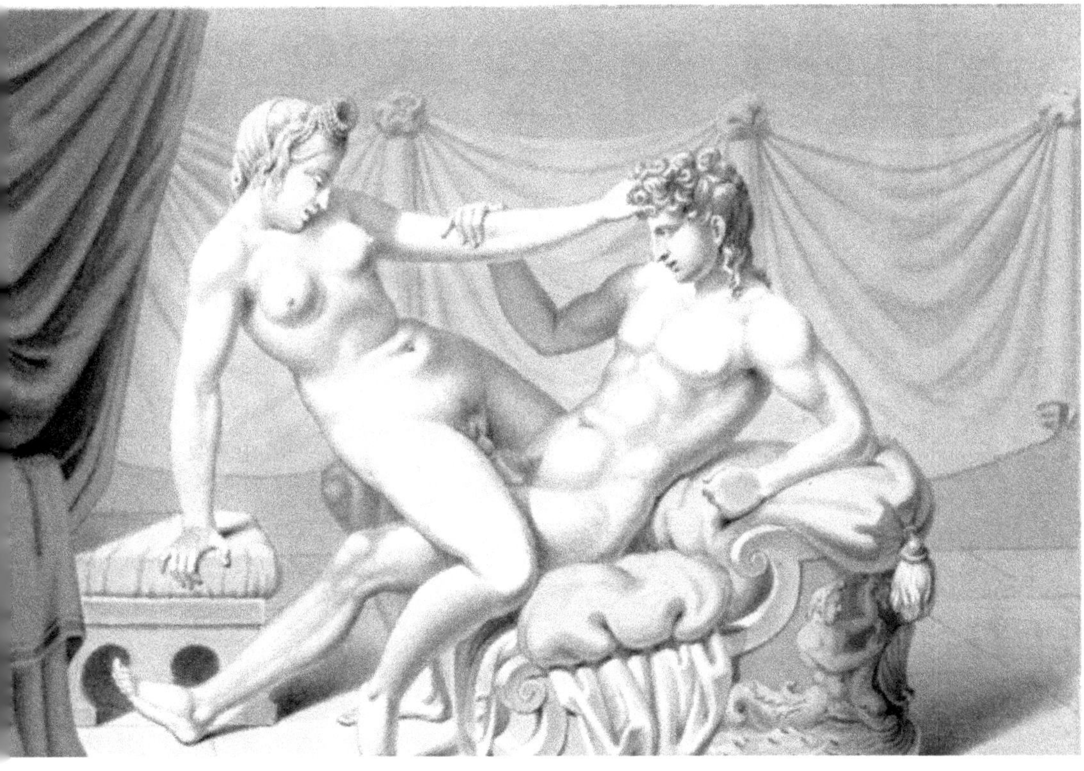

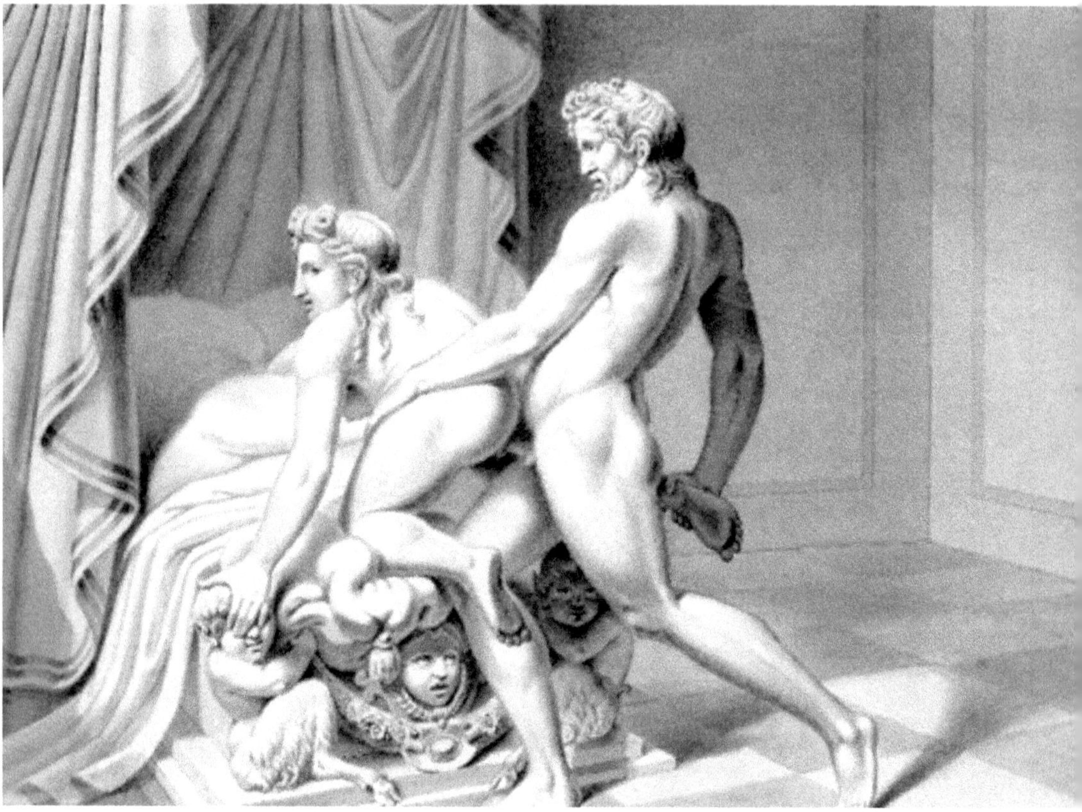

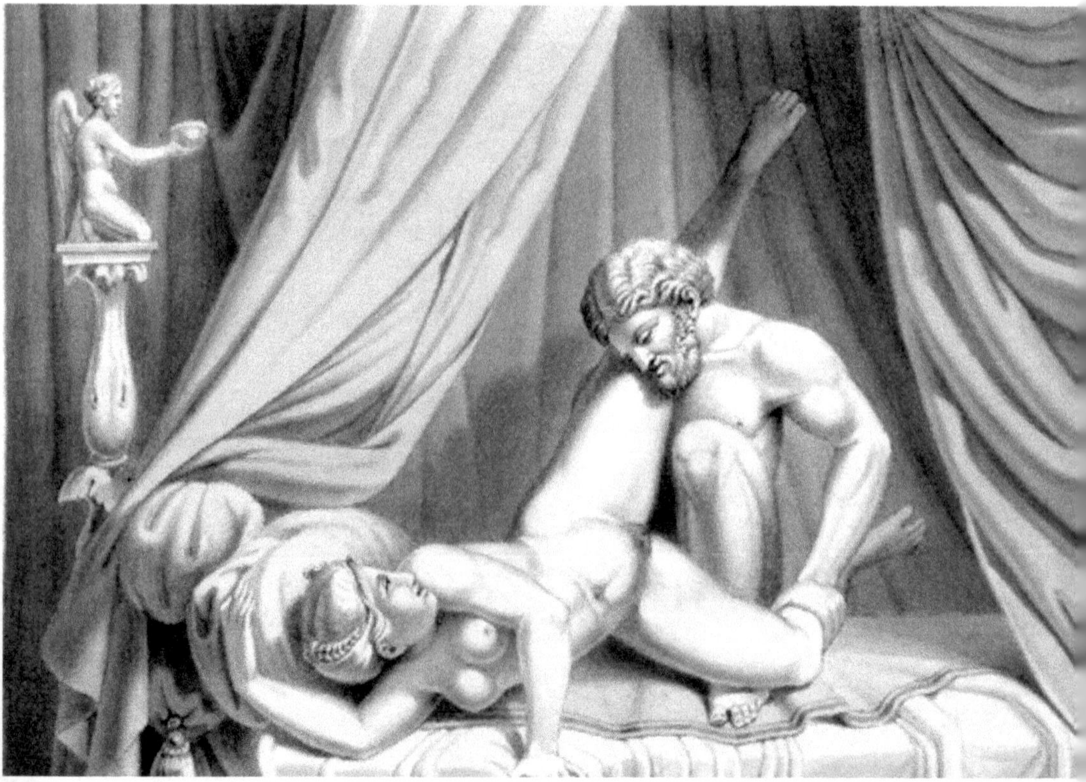

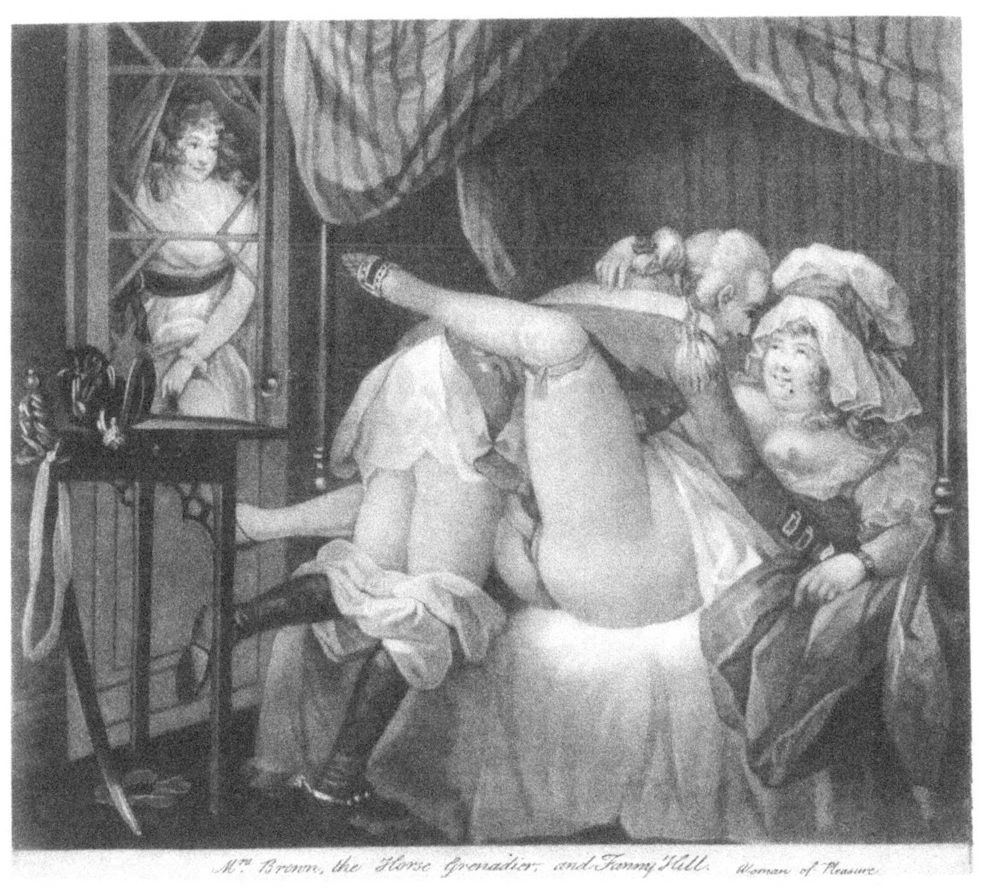

Mrs Brown, the Horse Grenadier, and Fanny Hill, 1750-1800.

What occurs in most Western art, from Greek and Roman sculpture through the glories of the Renaissance to the latest pornography are male representations of female eroticism. Feminists say that there are no real depictions of female *jouissance* in art or literature. 'In my opinion,' wrote Marguerite Duras, 'women have never expressed themselves.'[1] What she means, perhaps, is that women have expressed themselves thus far in the terms and means and social structures defined by men. There is no 'feminine' or 'women's' writing, according to some feminists. Hélène Cixous reckons she's found only three 'inscriptions of femininity' this century: Colette, Marguerite Duras and Jean Genet.[2] In art, there are many women artists who have tackled erotic issues, but in the history of art, going back to, say, the Renaissance, the number of women artists who have survived are far fewer.

1 Duras, interview in *Signs*, Winter 1975, in E. Marks, 175.
2 H. Cixous: "The Laugh of the Medusa", *Signs*, summer 1976, in E. E. Marks, 249.

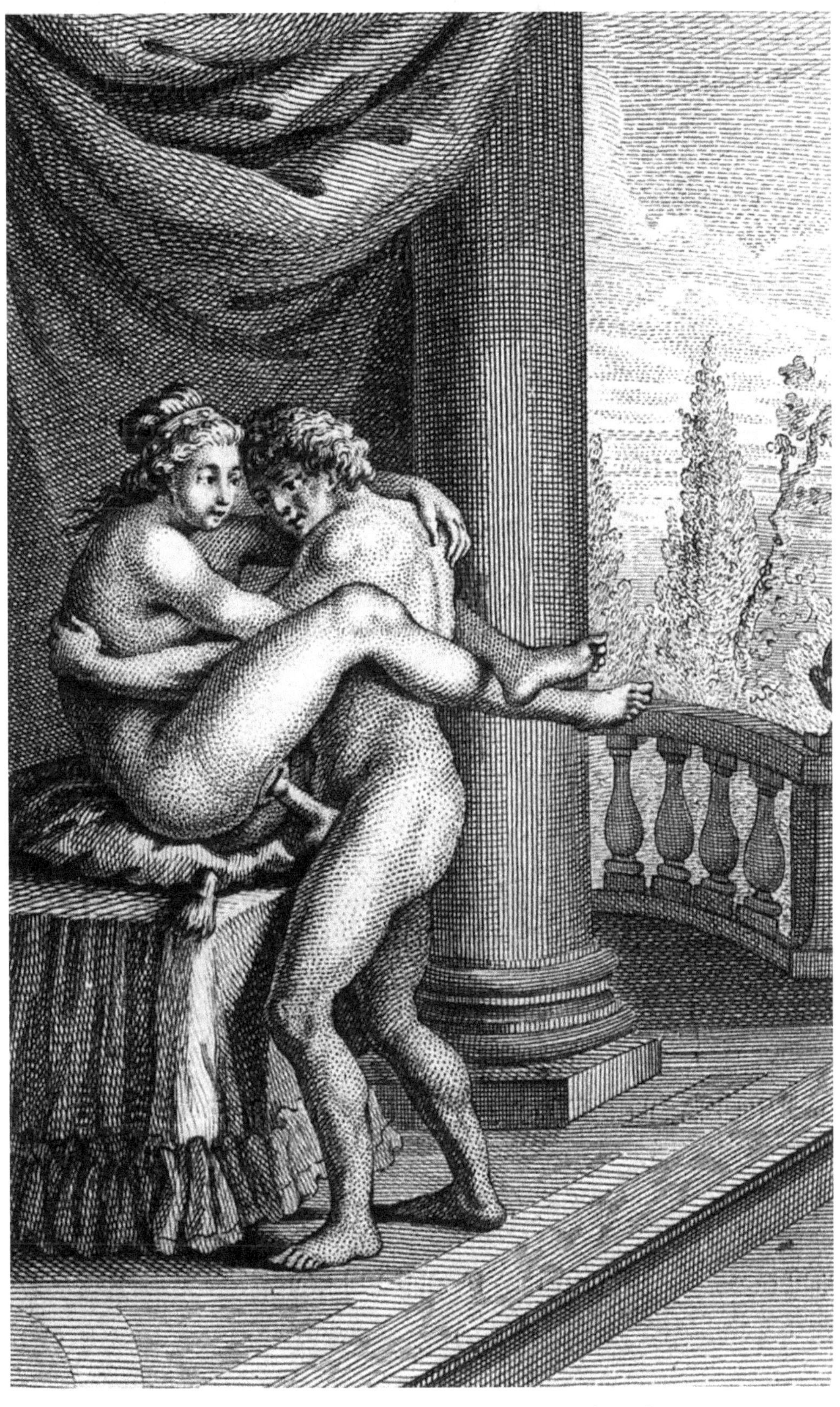

From L'Aretin Francais, engravings after paintings by Giulio Romano,
illustrating the Sonnets of Pietro Aretino
(this page and following pages)

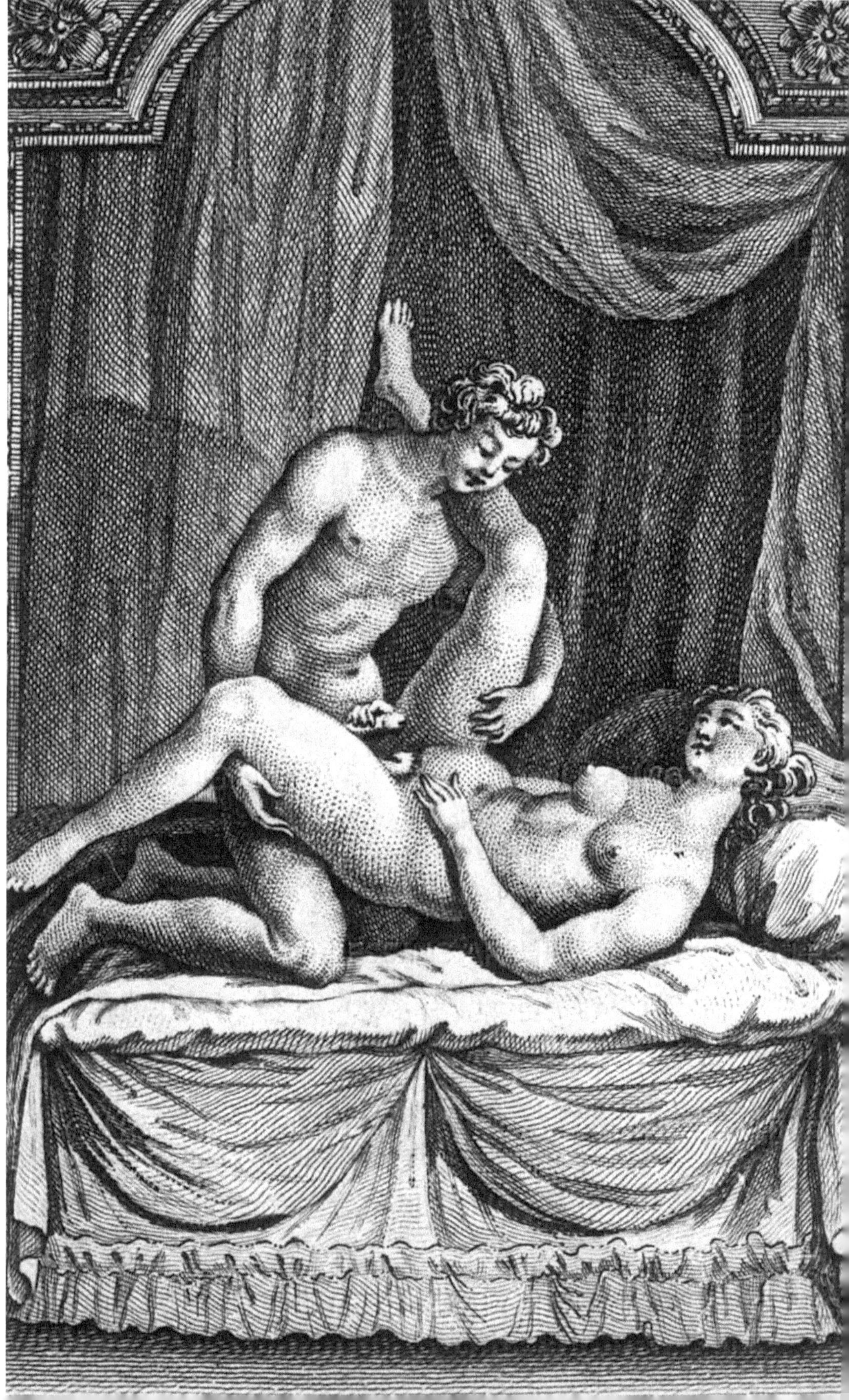

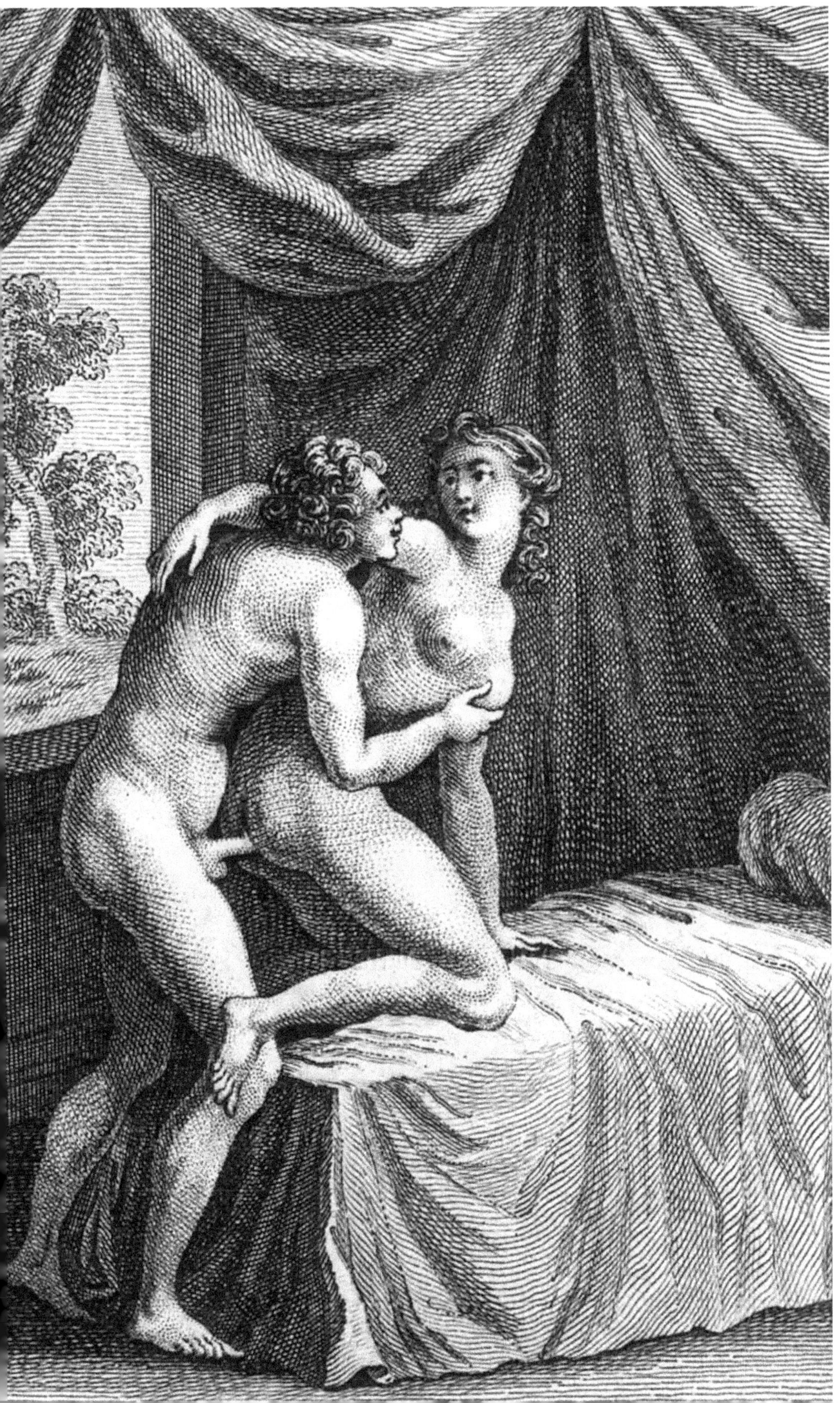

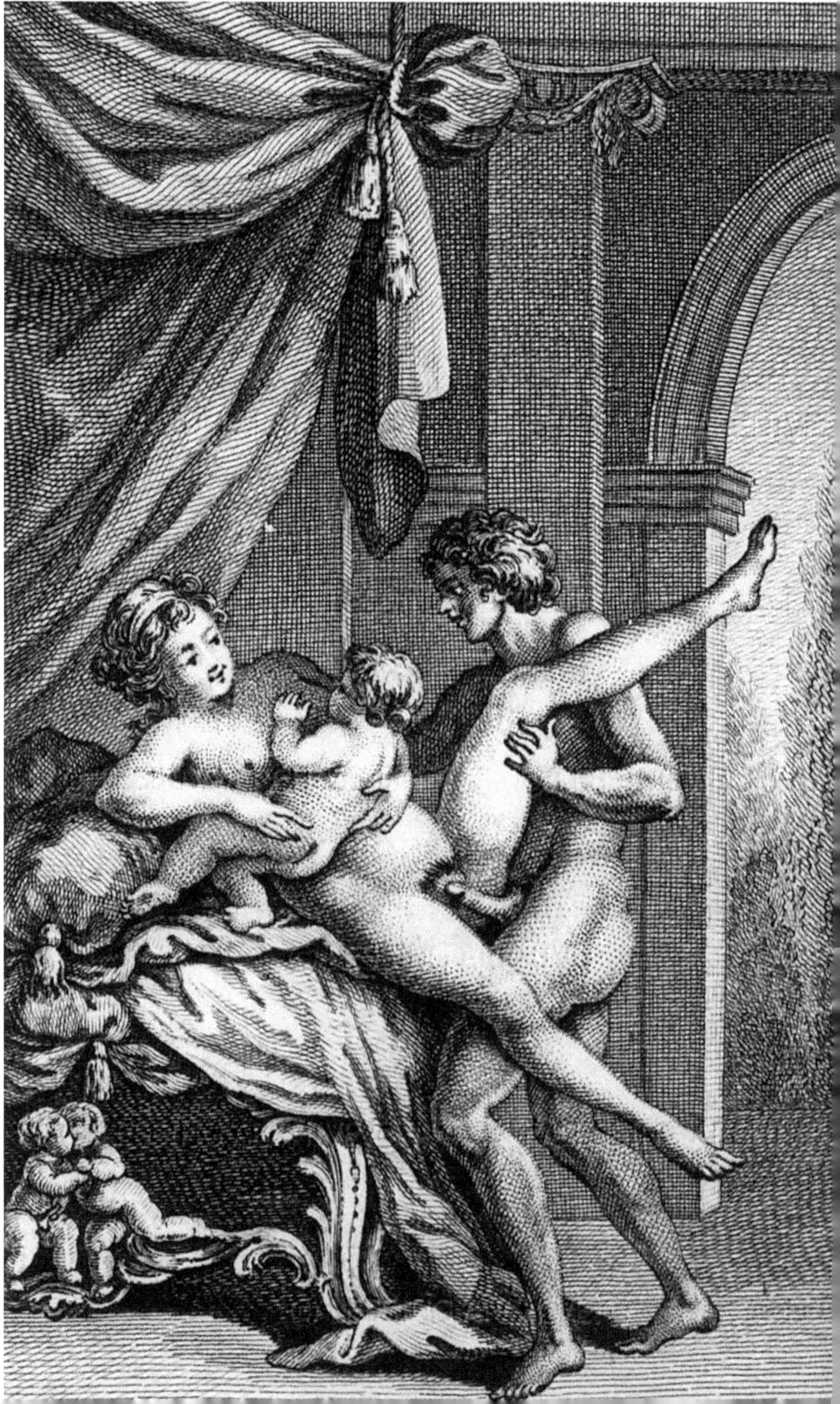

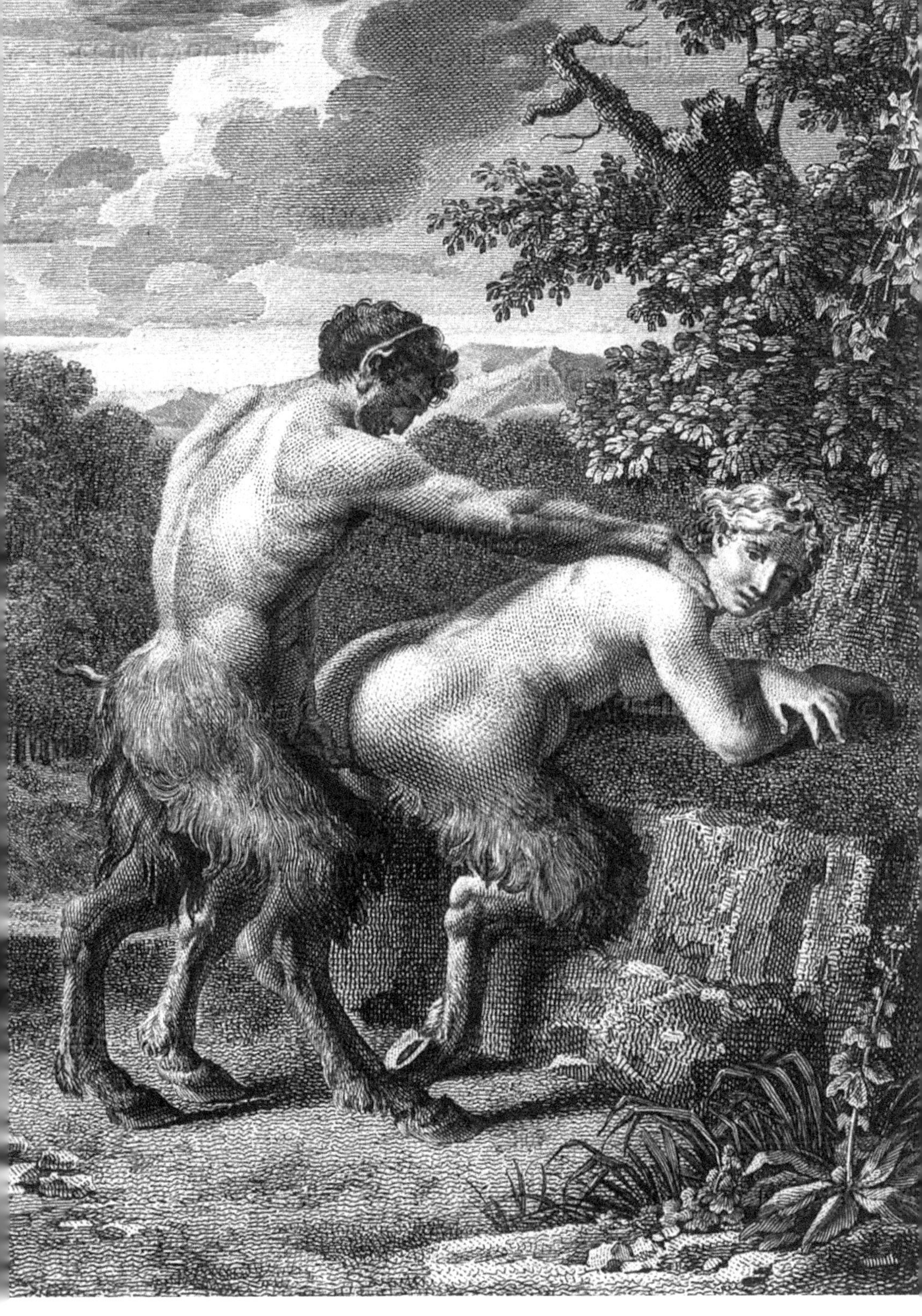

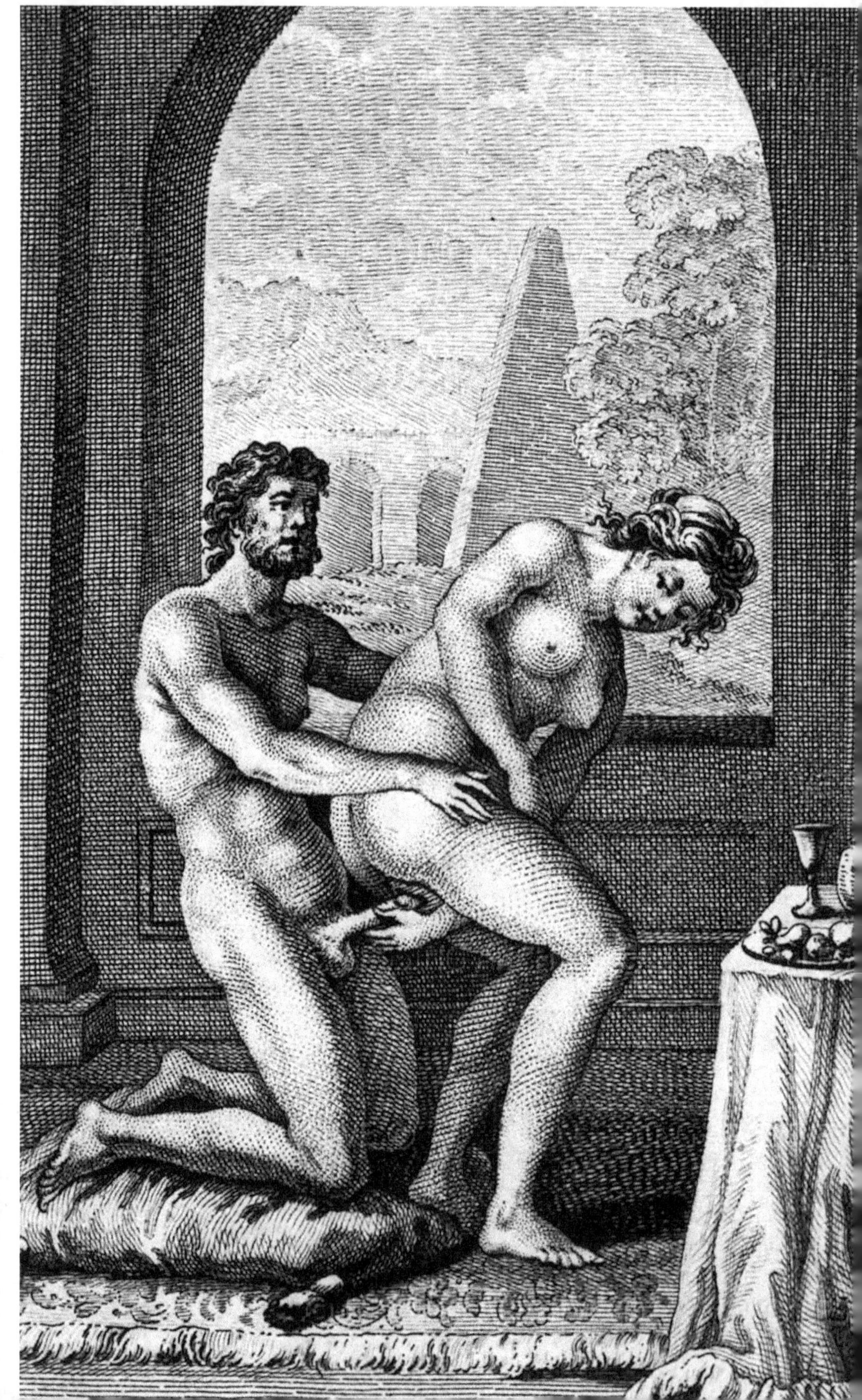

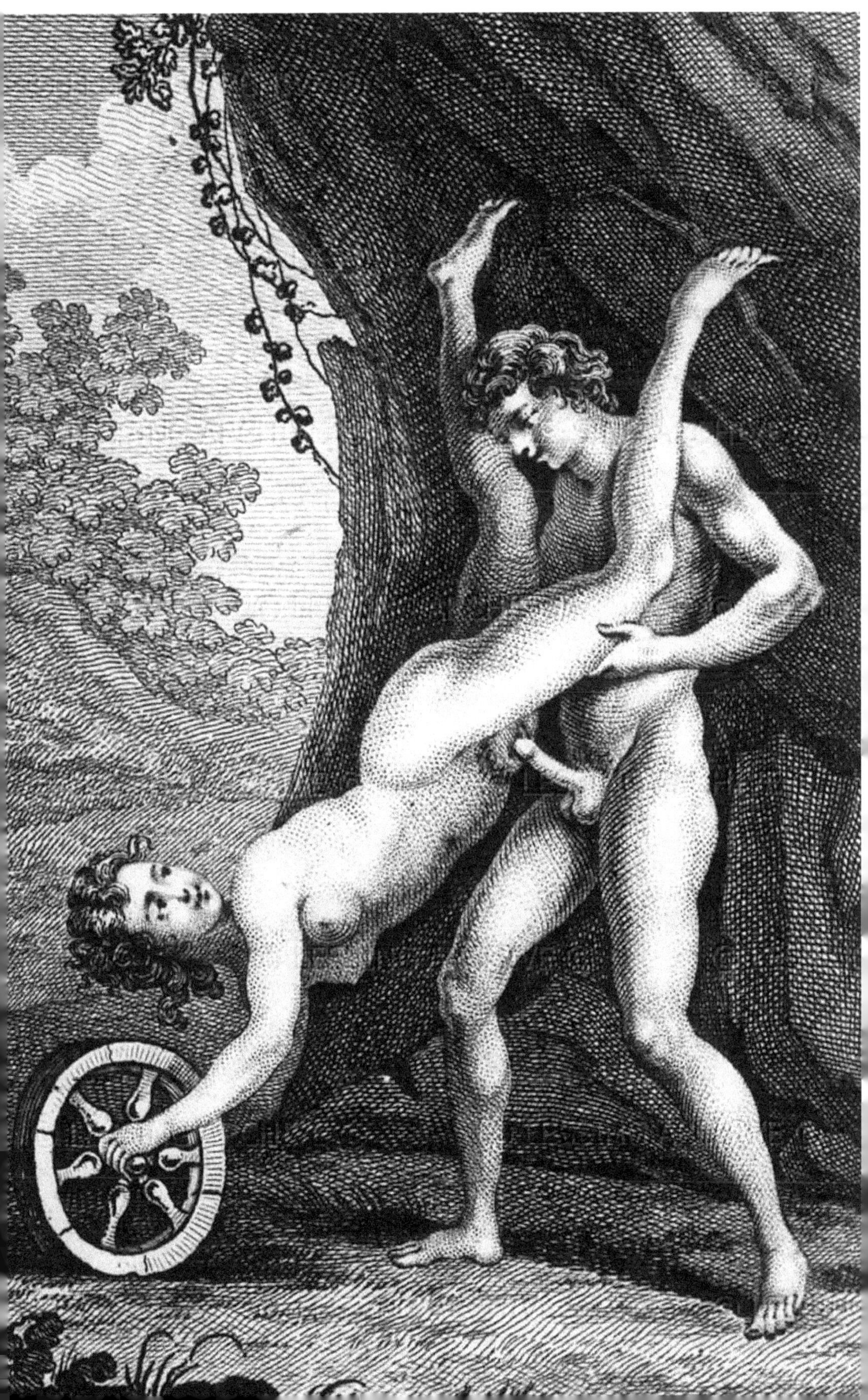

For law-abiding citizens, it seems, the 'line' has to be drawn somewhere. Somewhere between public and private, between sex and love, between visible and invisible, between freedom and control, between secrecy and publicity, between availability and censorship. Indeed, Walter Kendrick said the only definition of pornography is in terms of its forbidden or secret nature.[1]

Pornography brings the secret life of people out into the open. What the Western world holds most dear – the primacy and holiness of the individual, and the primacy and holiness of (heterosexual) love, of marriage, of the family – is cast into doubt by pornography.

Hardcore pornography, in particular, tries to make everything as clear and as visible as possible, and is thus disruptive and unsettling for the establishment. There are, thus, many close-ups of genitals in hard core pornography. Sex is ecstatic, so hard core pornography has to show this ecstasy. It does this by focussing on the genitals.

1 W. Kendrick: *The Secret Museum: Pornography in Modern Culture*, Viking, New York, NY, 1987.

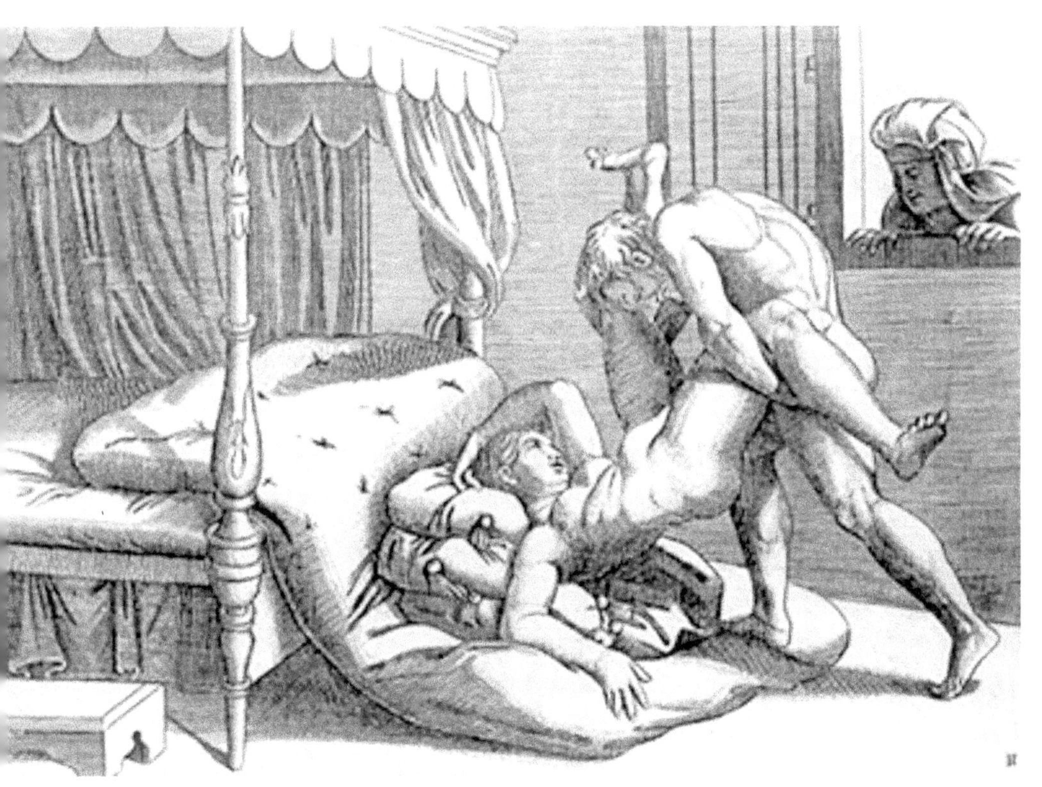

I Modi, by Pietro Aretino, illustrated by Giulio Romano, 16th century

N° 10

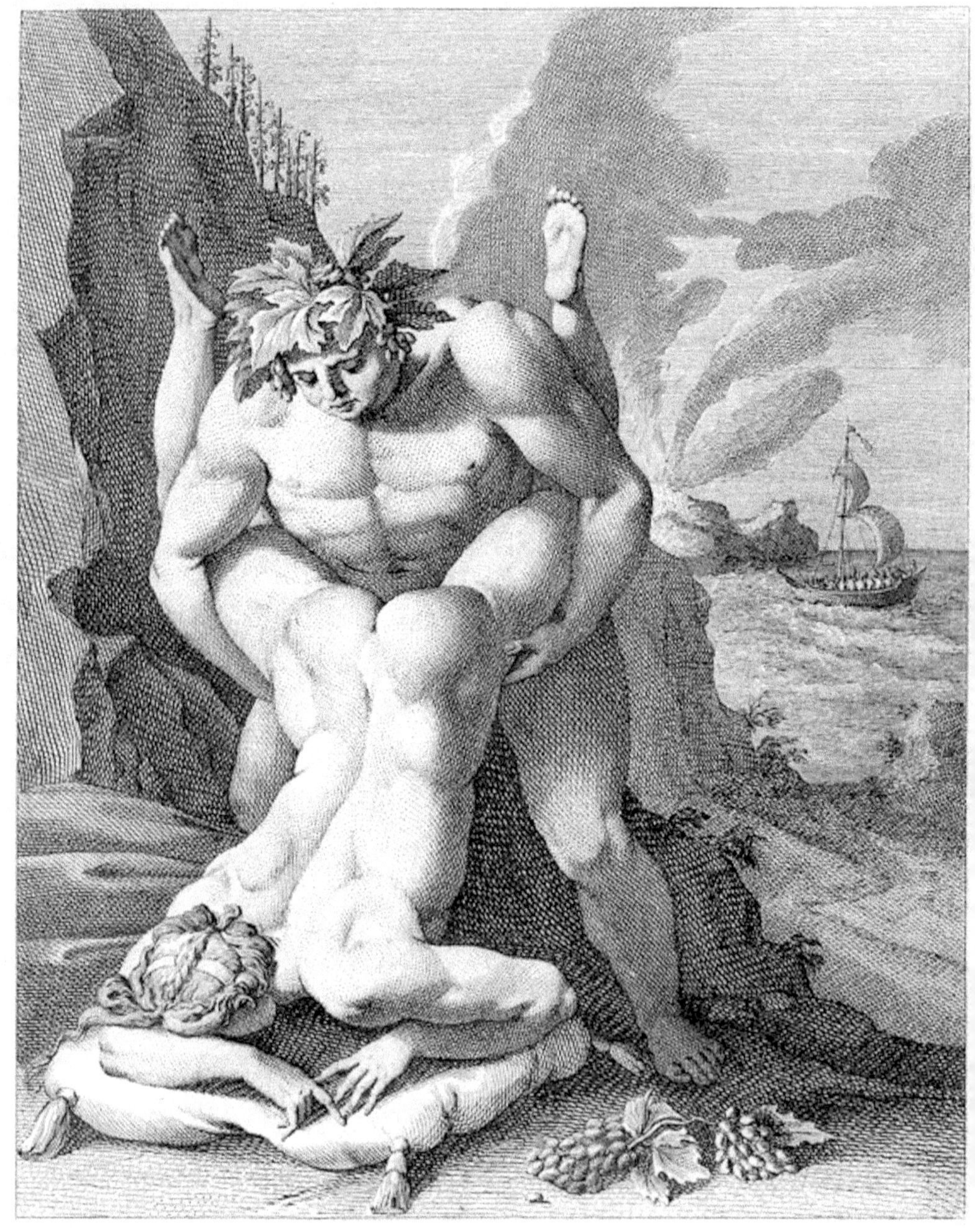

BACHUS ET ARIANE.

After Agostino Caracci, from I Modi

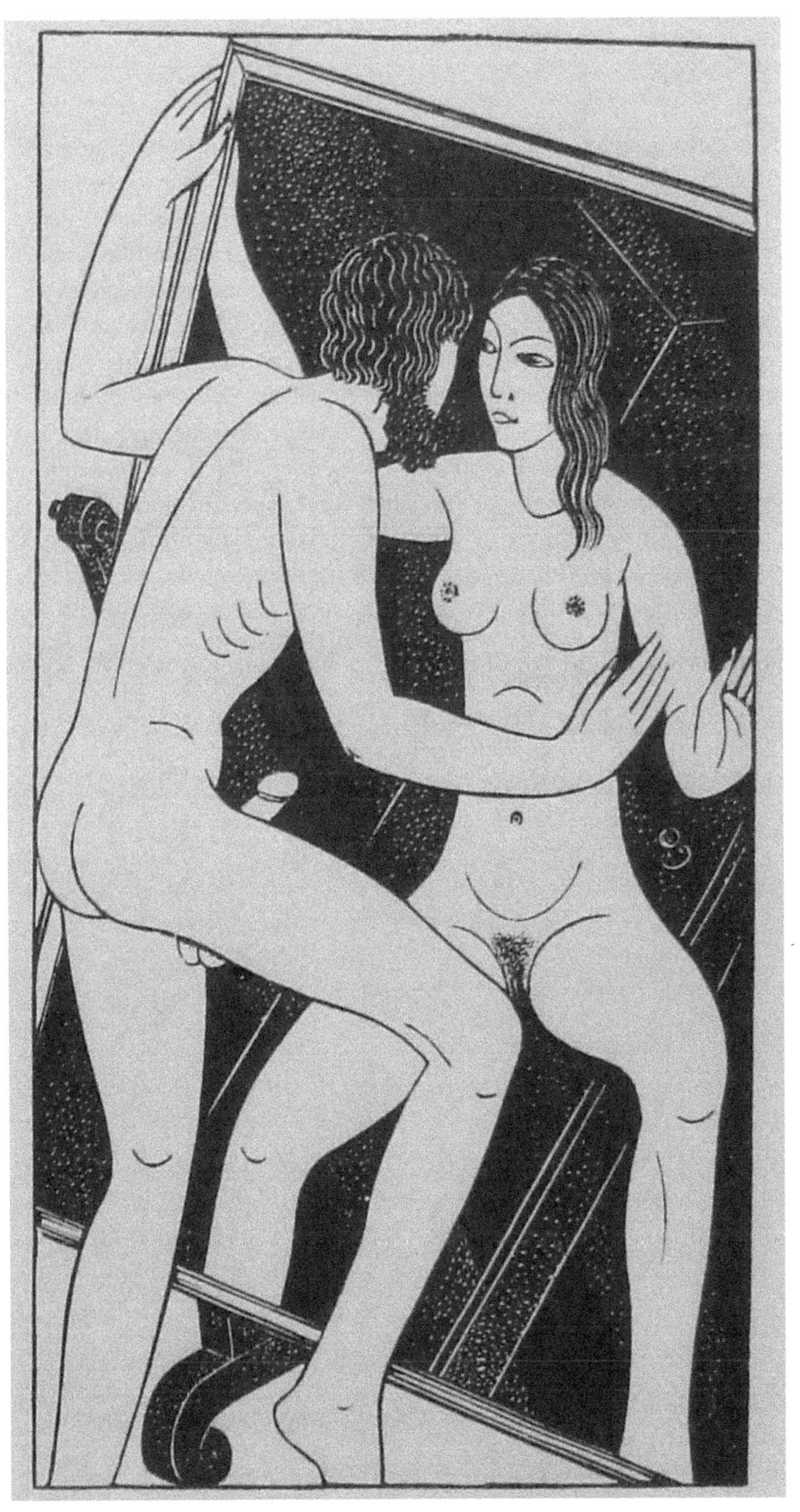

Eric Gill, Artist and Mirror, 1932

Pornography is the culture of eroticism in the West. There is sex on TV, in fiction, in blockbuster films, in theatre, in pop music, but it is in pornography that erotic feelings are most frequently communicated. Yet pornography is commodified sex, materialist sex, sex manufactured into particular types, genres, roles and modes. There are standard pornographic encounters, standard pornographic camera angles, standard pornographic orgasms. Eroticism, as Freud knew, is powerful, whether emotionally, psychologically, culturally or politically. Pornography, then, deals with really wild eroticism by categorizing it, putting into particular genres or narratives. The visual aspect of pornography helps to deal with the wildness and passion of erotic feeling. Pornography produces images and representations, which are easier to deal with than the real thing. Jane Gallop wrote that the 'visual mode produces representations as a way of mastering what is otherwise too intense'.[1] Experiences such as orgasm and erotic desire can be too overwhelming to be communicated in words. Putting these experiences into visual representations enables them to be controlled, packaged, commodified.

1 J. Gallop: *The Daughter's Seduction: Feminism and Psychoanalysis*, Cornell University Press, New York, NY, 1982, 35.

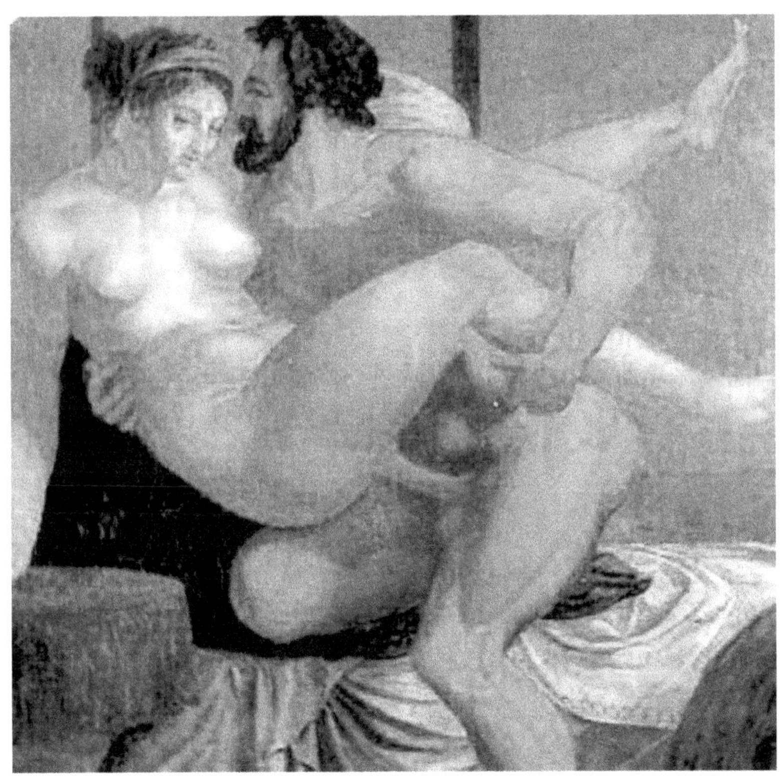

French school, late 18th century

Pornography is *fantasy,* as well as genre, product, system, and materialism. Pornography does not offer the consumer real people, but images, narratives, ideas, suggestions. The visual dimension of pornography helps to create certain kinds of representations of erotic feelings which the consumer can deal with, because they are communicated in recognizable forms. So now we're in an S/M narrative - masters, mistresses and slaves Or, over here we're in the narrative where a sexually frustrated male picks up a female hitchhiker. Or, here we are in the 'bored housewife' scenario: sex-starved, she humps the plumber over the washing machine. The consumer always knows where she or he is with pornography.

Pornography delivers the goods.

It delivers the goods: which's why it's bigger than the movie or pop music industries.

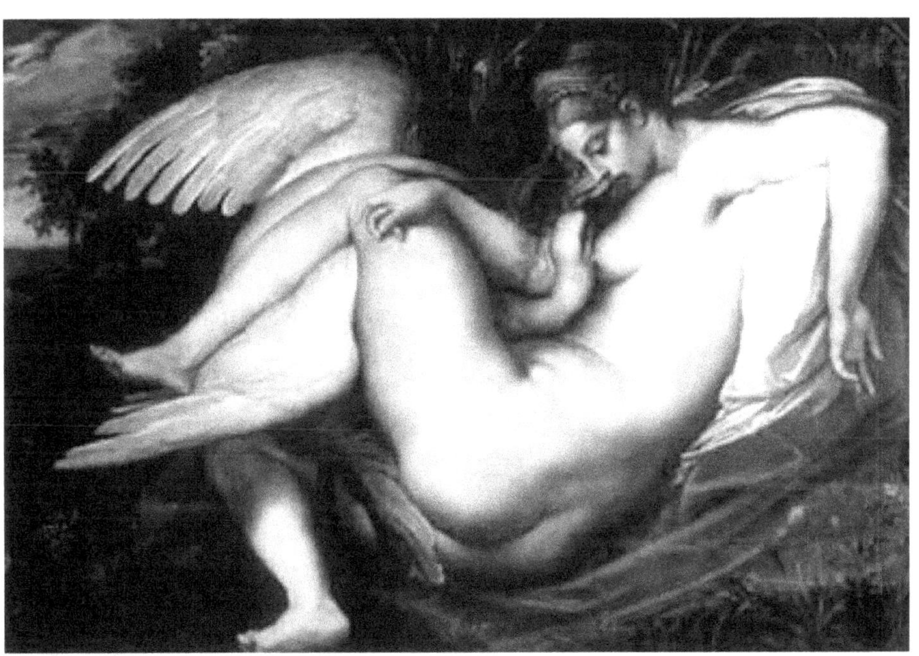

Peter Paul Rubens, Leda and the Swan

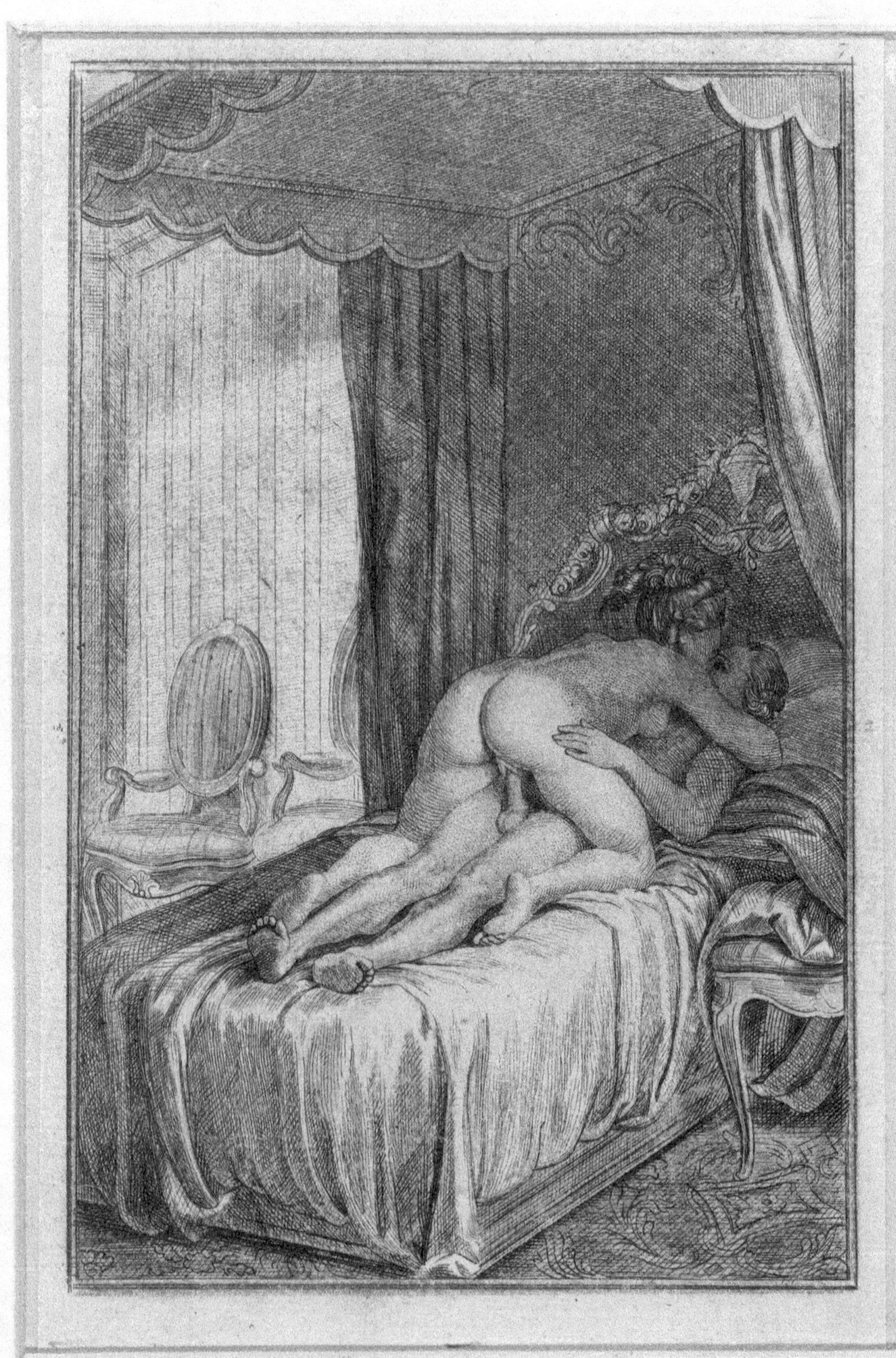

Anonymous, 18th century.

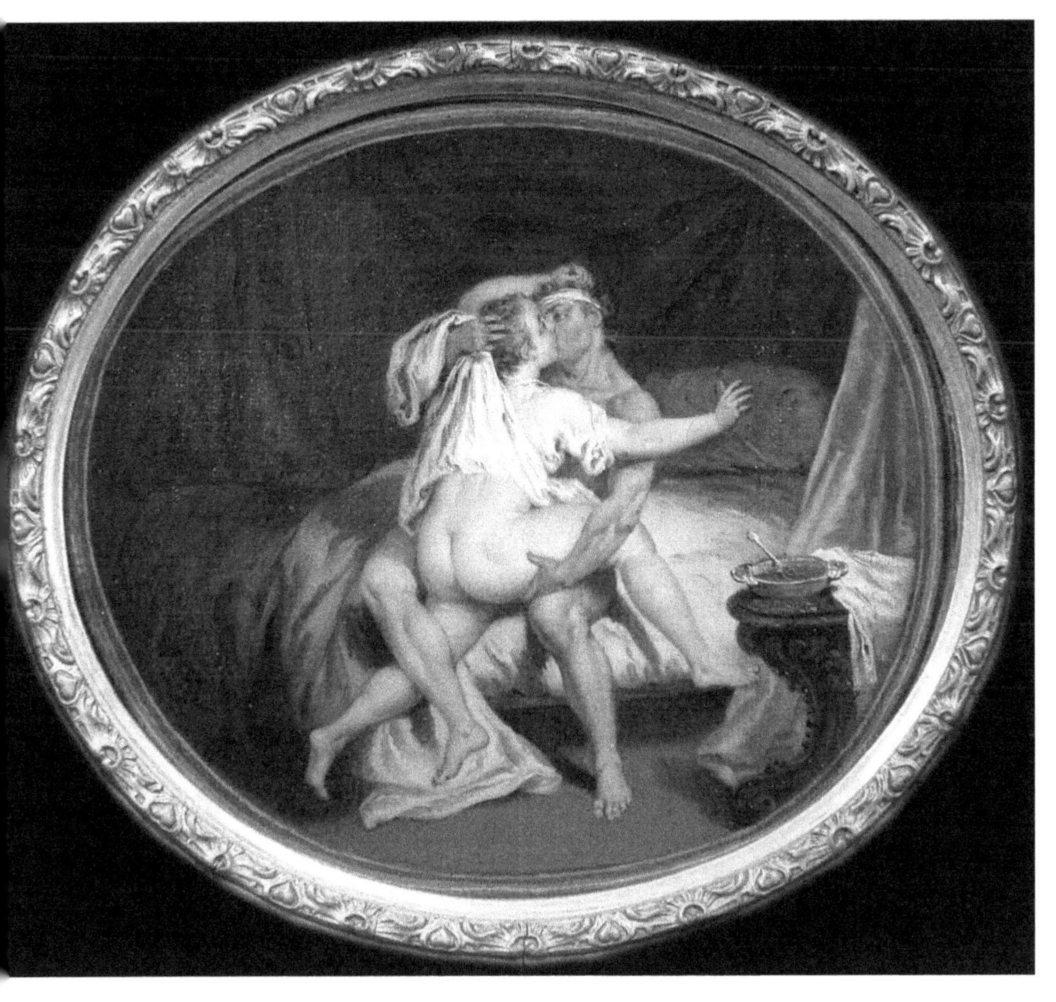

Nicolas Lancret, Scène galante dans une alcôve

If some work is erotic – a scene on TV, a photo, a sculpture, a dance – it's because, in the opinion of some people, you don't 'see' everything. Something is hidden. The 'erotic' in art is about anticipation, waiting, yearning. It's about potential and possibility, hidden but not hidden, partially clothed. As the photographer Grace Lau, who has made many pictures of fetishism, wrote: 'I prefer images that conceal, rather than those that reveal all.'[1]

Pornography, meanwhile, has people doing it now. They undress, and start attacking each other immediately. There's nothing to get in the way, not contraception, not fear, not aversions, not menstruation, not impotence, not interruptions, not anything. In short: it's *fantasy.*

Pornography turns 'what if?' into a reality. What if somebody took their clothes off in this train carriage and started having sex? is a typical question that erotic art suggests but pornography answers. What if this woman at home turns out to be a nymphomaniac and this plumber turns out to be a superstud? What if the wedding guest who just smiled at you turns out to be the fuck of a lifetime? In pornography, people *do* rip their clothes and start mashing each other up.

Pornography presents as a normal, everyday occurrence what is hidden away, what is desired but unspoken. Pornography is the ultimate in fantasy, for in the fairy tale world of pornography, every dream comes true. And it is not only 'true', it is 'real'.

1 Grace Lau: "Confessions of a Complete Scopophiliac", in Gibbons, 195

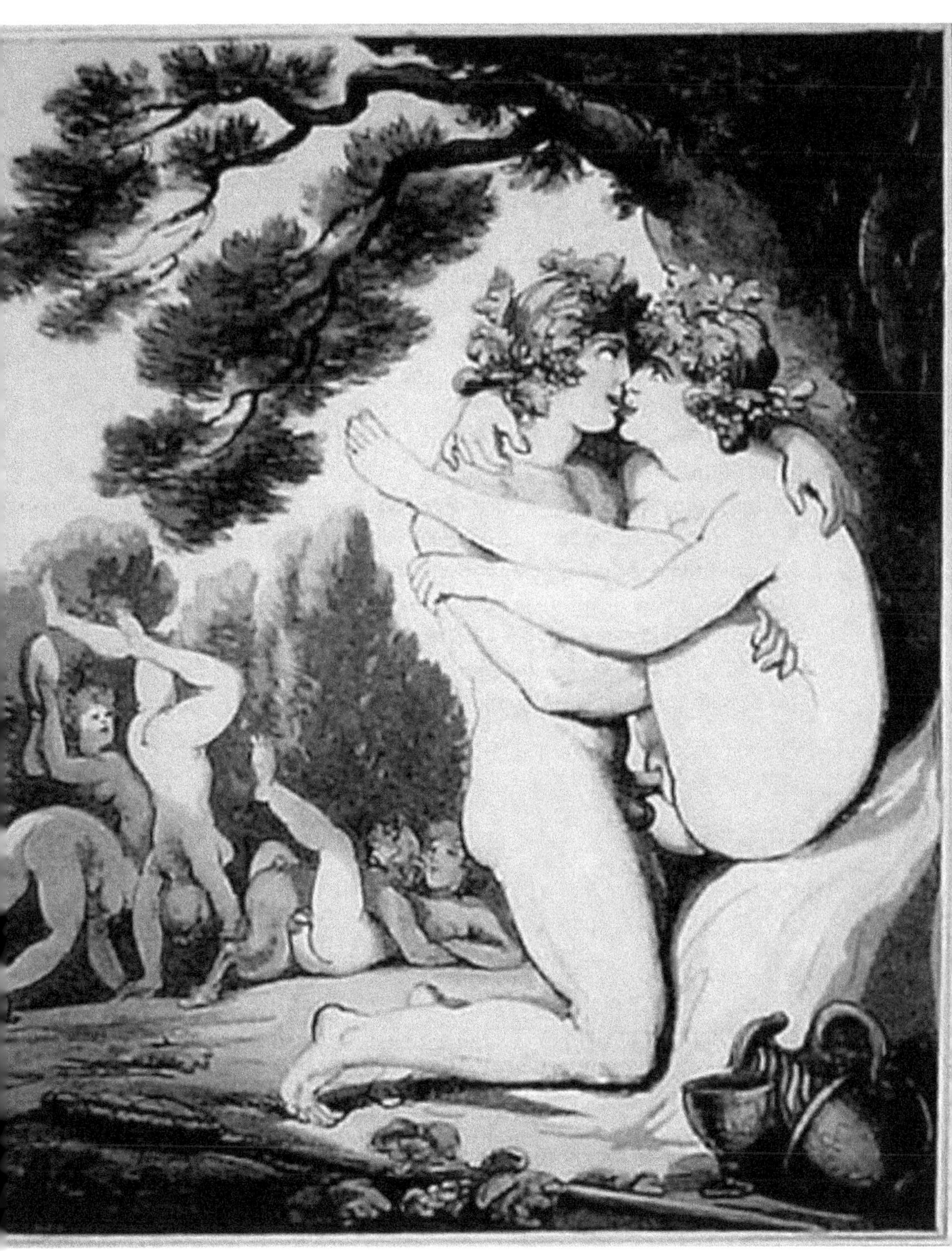

Thomas Rowlandson

CENSORSHIP

One of the most contentious and fiercely debated aspects of erotic art and pornography is the issue of obscenity, taste and censorship. Throughout the history of art and pornography, different individuals or groups of people have sought to defend certain territories, whether moral, psychological, emotional, spiritual, religious, philosophical, political or ideological. There is always some line between the 'acceptable' and the 'obscene'.

The history of censorship is long and complex. In the 20th century there were many confrontations between artists and the establishment: with D.H. Lawrence's *Lady Chatterley's Lover*, with *Ulysses*, with films such as *Last Tango in Paris, Kids, Natural Born Killers, The Killing of Sister George, Performance, Trash, A Clockwork Orange* and countless others, with the *Oz* trials, with Senator Jesse Helms trying to stop NEA tax payers' money funding 'obscene' work, with reference to the photographer Robert Mapplethorpe (whose photos have created much 'controversy'),[1] with internet porn, with punk rock and gangsta rap, and so on.[2]

1 See M. Schoofs: "Robert Mapplethorpe: Exquisite Subversions", *Windy City Times*, 16 Mch, 1989; H. Kramer: "Mapplethorpe Show at the Whitney: A Big, Glossy, Offensive Exhibit", *The New York Observer*, 22 Aug, 1988; A.C. Danto: *Encounters & Reflections*, Farrar Straus Giroux, New York 1990; E. Kastor & Carla Hall: "Mapplethorpe Aftermath", *Washington Post*, 23 June 1989; T.A. Yasui: "The Mapplethorpe Bonanza", *Washington Post*, 21 Aug, 1989; P. Schjeldhal: "The Mainstreaming of Mapplethorpe: Taste and Hunger", *7 Days*, 10 Aug, 1988; R. Rooney: "The unambiguous stare of Mapplethorpe's lens", *Australian*, 25 Feb, 1986.
2 More Mapplethorpe articles: D. Dominick: "Robert Mapplethorpe's Proud Finale", *Vanity Fair*, Feb, 1989; "Robert Mapplethorpe: Aestheticizing the Perverse", *Artscribe International*, Nov/Dec 1988; J. Ribalta: "Decorative Heroism, The death of Mapplethorpe", *Lapiz*, Apl, 1989.

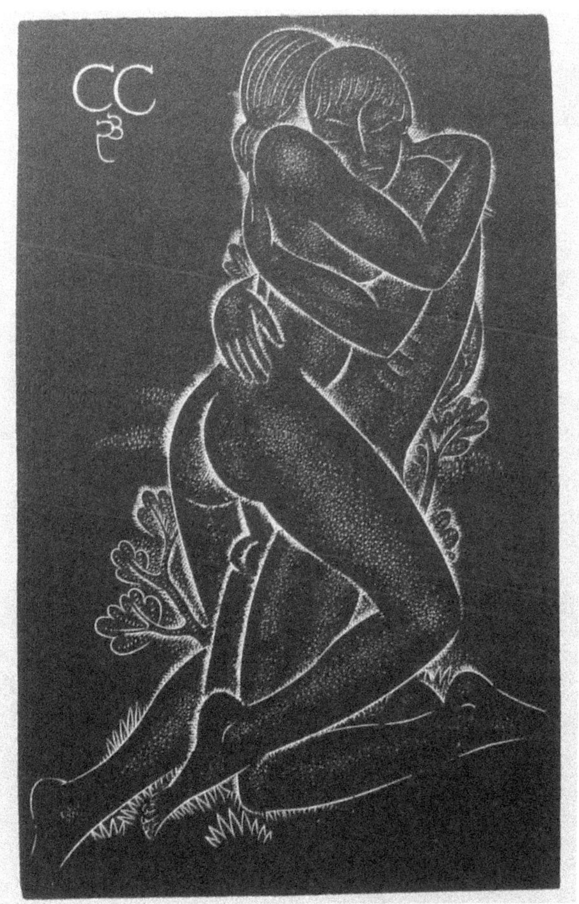

Fucking a flame into being: one of
Eric Gill's illustrations for D.H. Lawrence's book

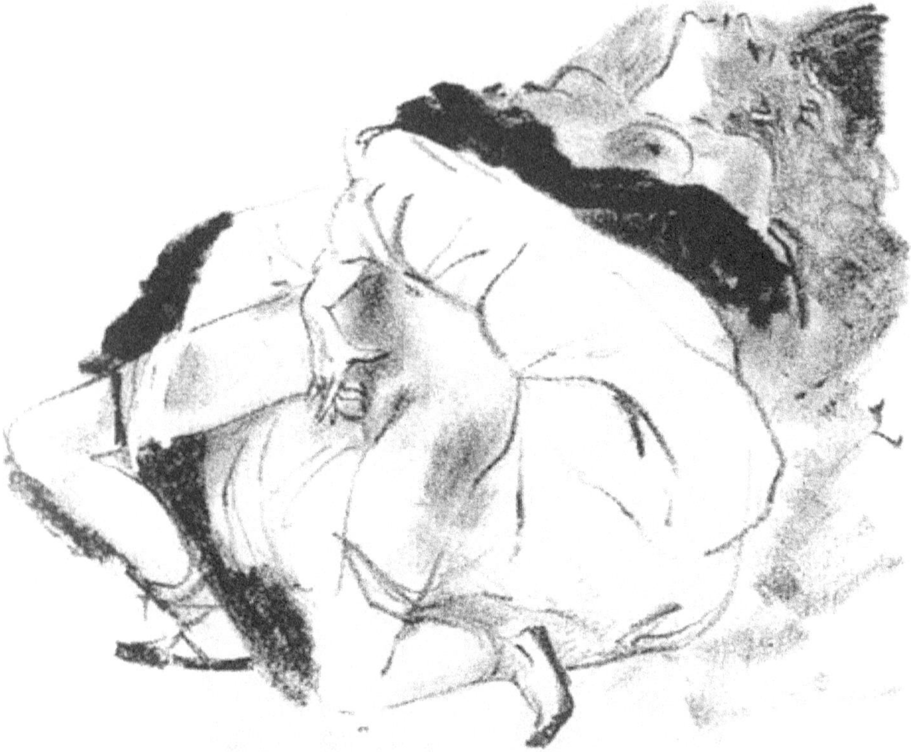

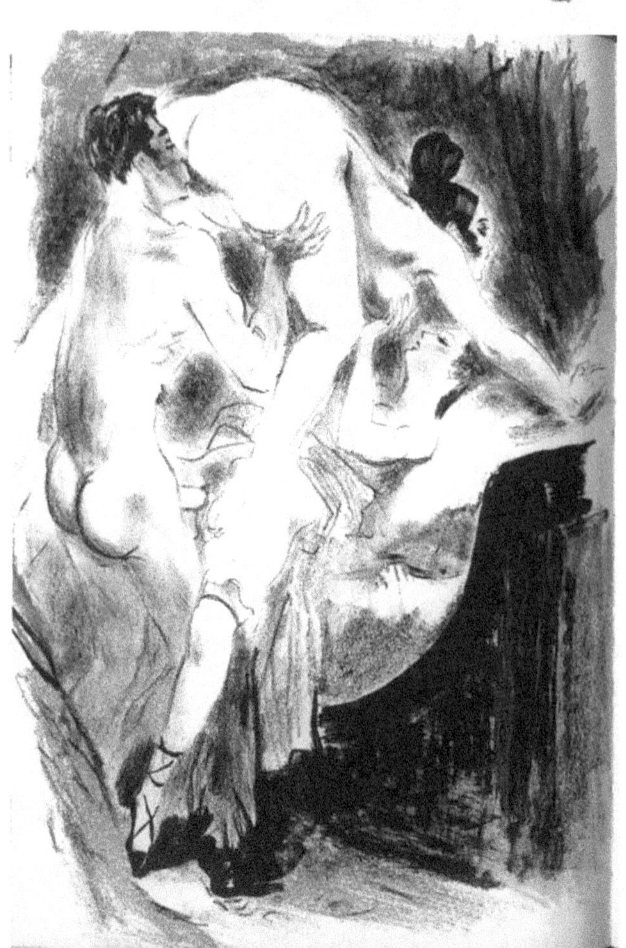

Louis-André Berthomme Saint-André, Gamiani ou Deux Nu d'Excés, by Alfred de Musset

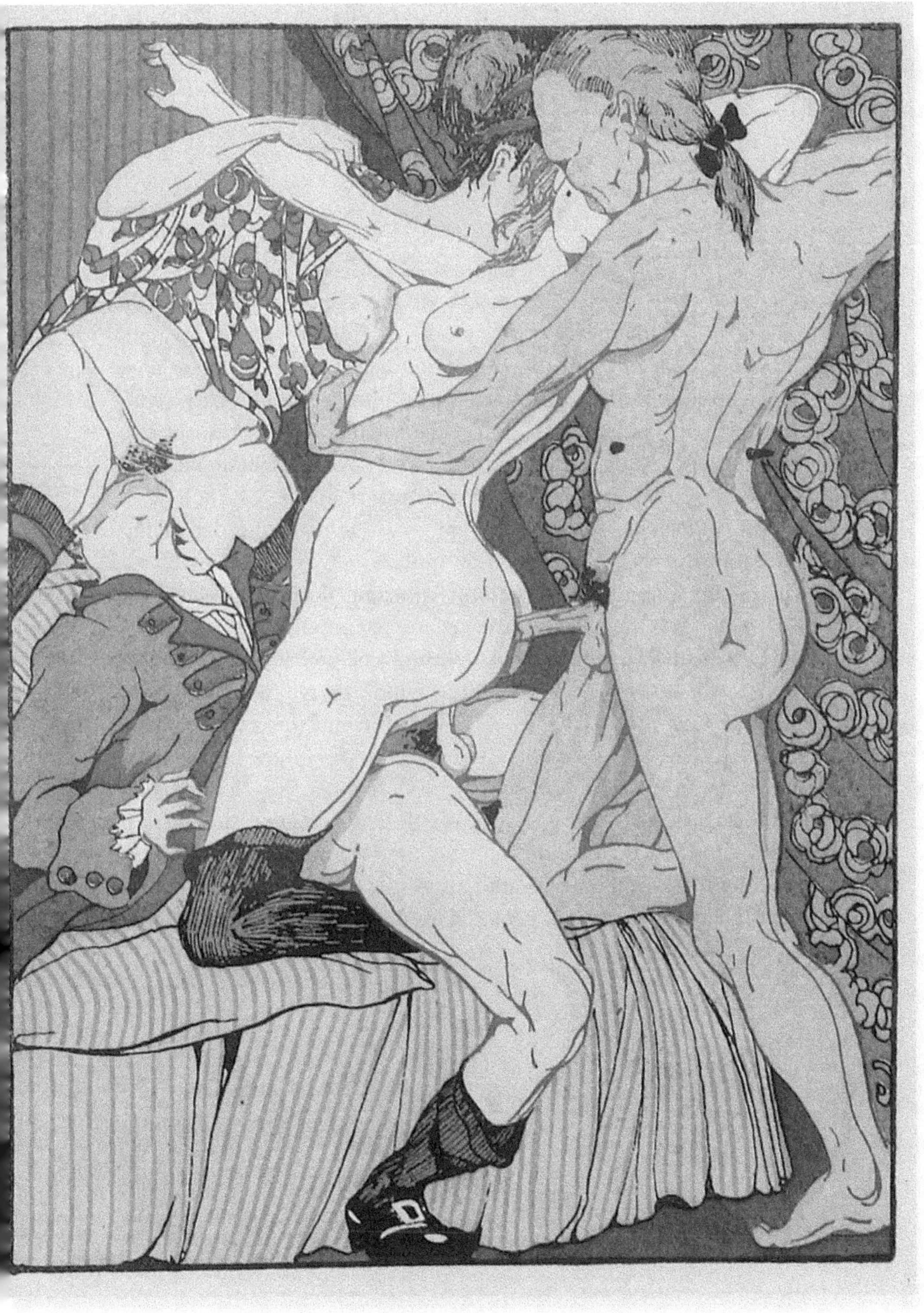

Illustration for the Marquis de Sade,
Le Bordel de Venise, 1921,
by Couperyn (a.k.a. George A. Drains), Paris

CENSORSHIP

The many debates concerning several Obscene Publications Acts and bills, the First Amendment of the American constitution, different regulatory groups, pressure groups, media organizations, publishers, and all manner of intellectuals and artists, have been intense, complex, protracted, and often a shambles. The confusions and ambiguities are at the centre of Western society. Pornography debates produce, very quickly, all manner of confusions and hypocrisies, of a moral, religious, psychological, social and ideological nature.[1] For some, though, the censorship debate is 'in fact, a little internal quibble between sections of the bourgeois community' (according to Suzanne Kappeler).

Pornography goes to the heart of what people hold dear: their identities, their feelings, their philosophical, spiritual and political views, their view of the 'quality of life'. Pornography unsettles these notions and structures. The fervour and uncertainty of the many attempts at legislation and policing show how problematic pornography is. In a case of recent years, five 'homosexual sadomasochists' were convicted in 1990 of inflicting 'injuries on each another's genitals during ritual sex' which involved 'cutting each other's genitals with surgical scalpels, sandpapering scrotums and pushing hooks into penises'. Their appeal was rejected by the courts.[2]

---

1 See *Art in America*, May 1990; C.H. Rolph: *The Trial of Lady Chatterley*, Penguin, London, 1961; G. Robertson: *Obscenity: an Account of Censorship Laws and Their Enforcements in England and Wales*, Weidenfeld & Nicolson, London, 1979; *The Attorney General's Commission on Pornography – the Meese Commission – Final Report*, US Government Printing Office, Washington DC, 1986; L. Lederer, ed, op. cit.

2 I. MacKinnon: "Lords reject appeals by sado-masochists", *The Independent*, 12 Mch, 1993.

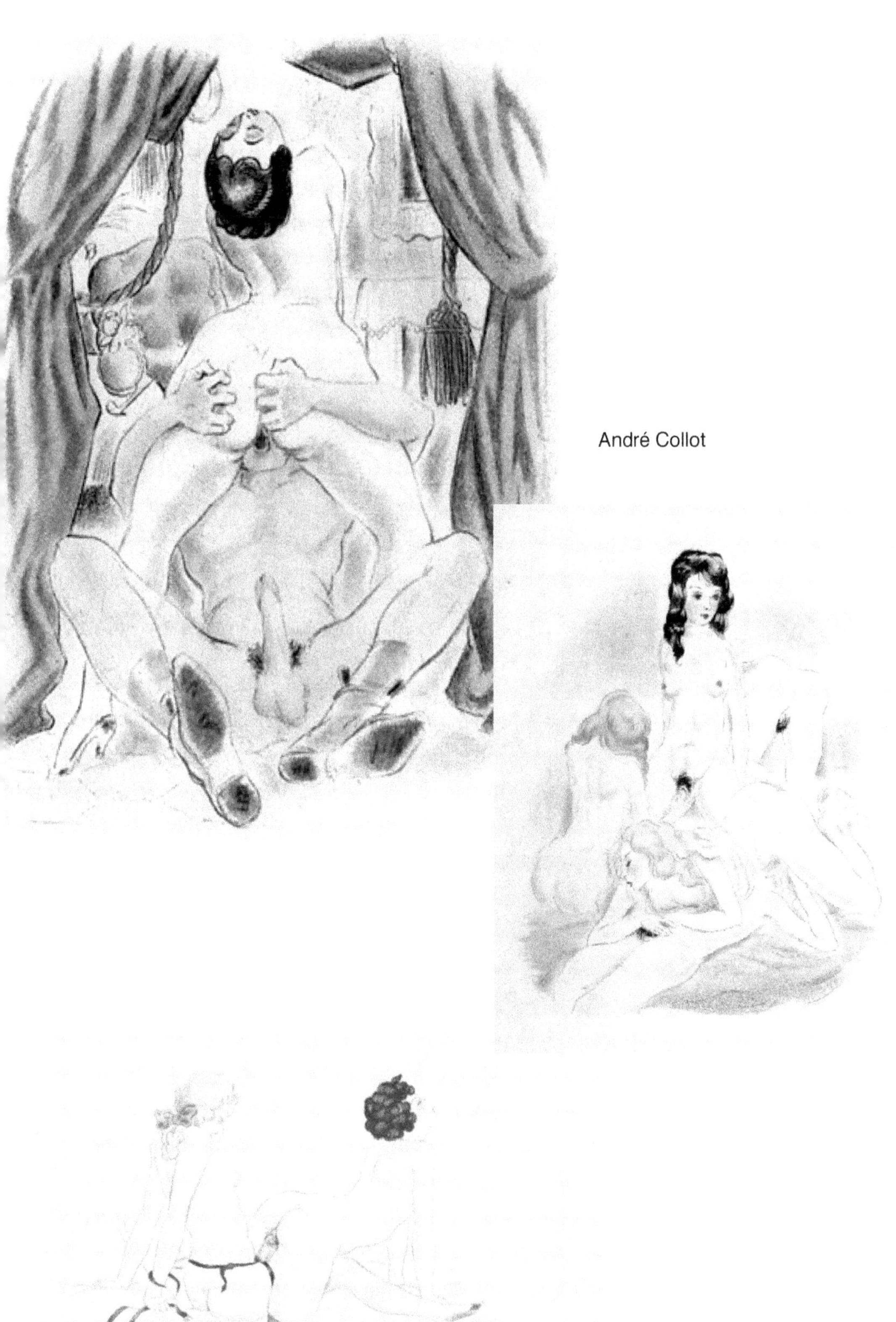

André Collot

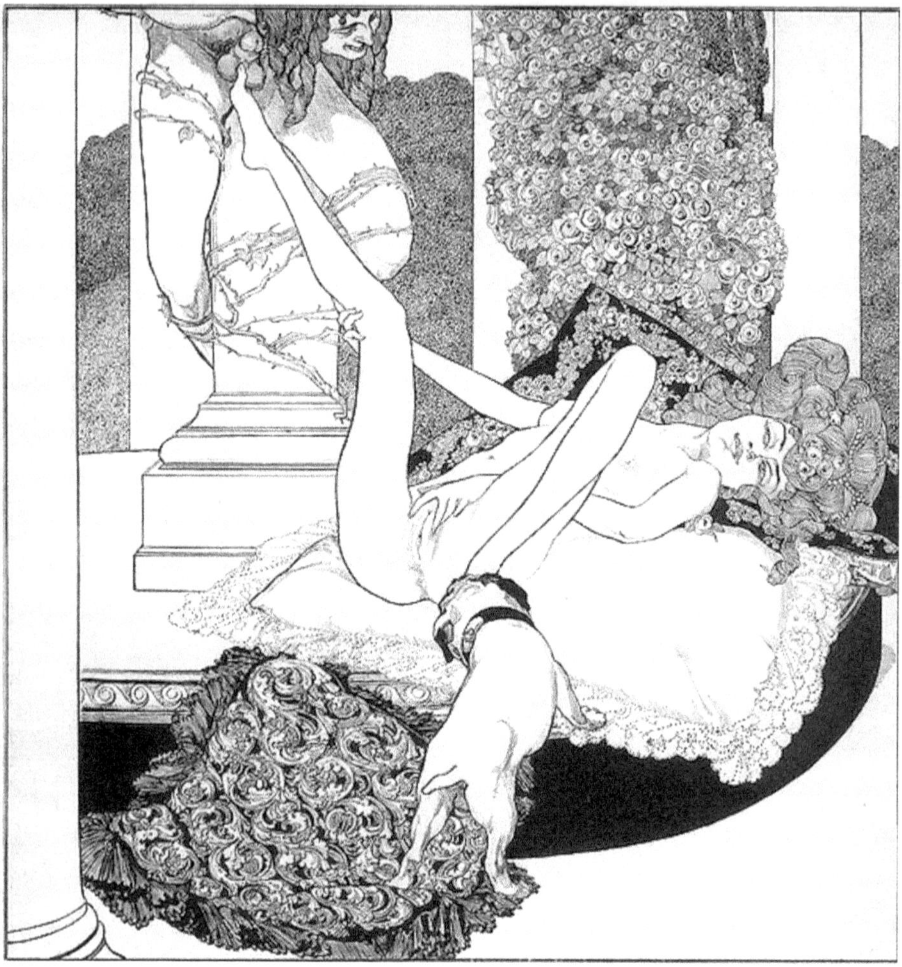

Franz von Bayros (1866-1924),
Der Toilettentisch, Tantalus, 1908

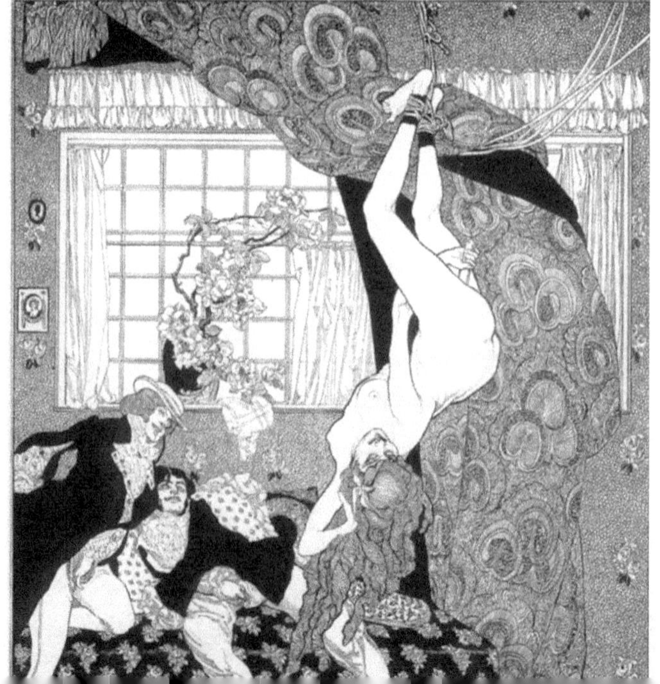

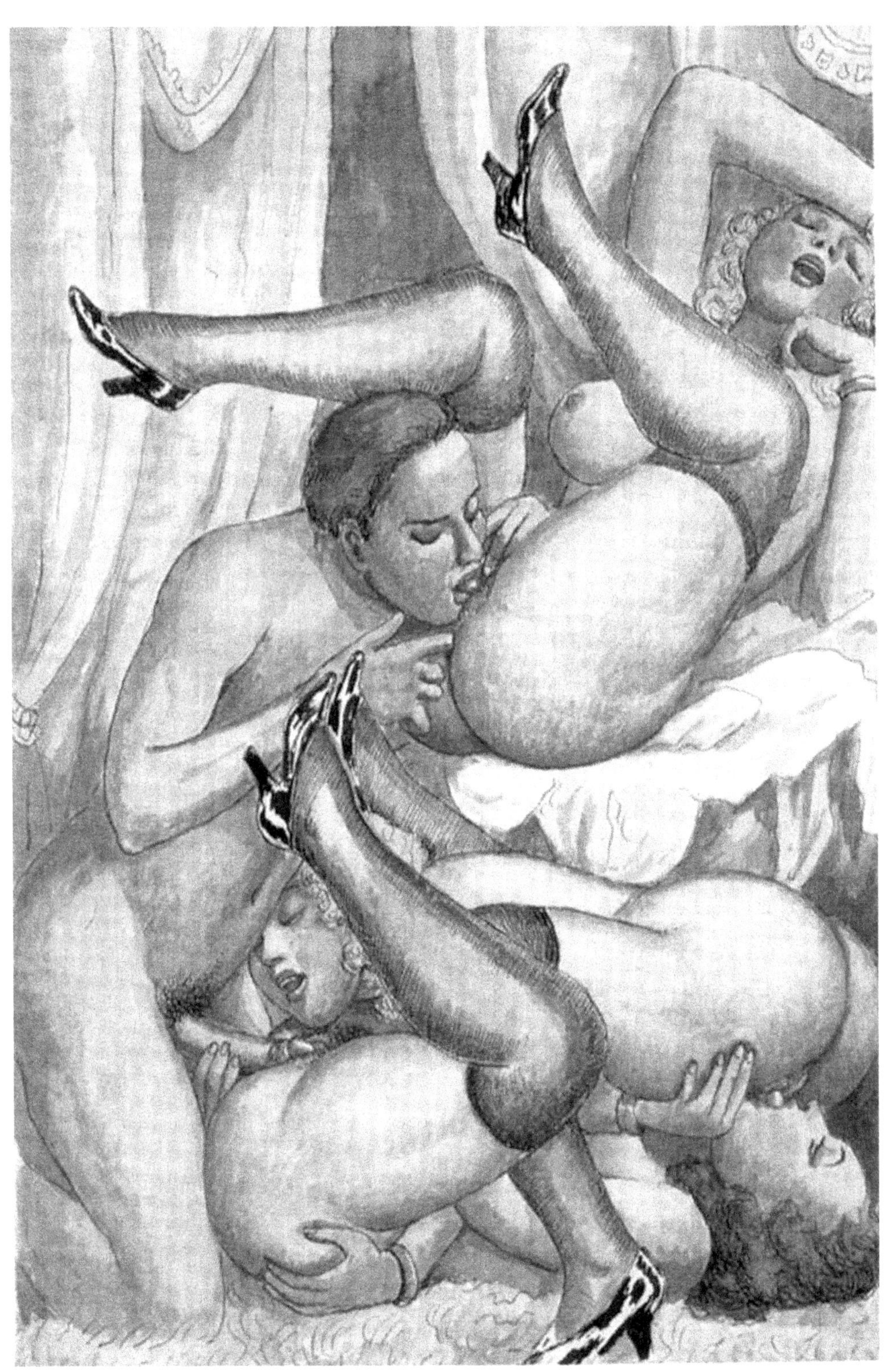

Anonymous, early 20th century

FEMALE ORGASM

The female orgasm is 'anatomically invisible', as far as erotica is concerned. So the history of erotica and porn, for some commentators, 'is the history of visual strategies to overcome the anatomical invisibility of the female orgasm'.[1] In erotica, female orgasm is regarded with confusion and ambivalence. What actually is it? eroticists ask, what does it feel like? (Note that most eroticists throughout history have been men, forever excluded from directly experiencing the female orgasm). Thus the controversy over clitoral and vaginal orgasm, over female 'ejaculation', over 'multiple' orgasms. Female 'ejaculation' is 'visible evidence' of orgasm, yet it is censored by pornographers themselves at times.[2]

1 L. Nead, 98; see also L. Williams, 1990.
2 See S. Bell: "Feminist Ejaculations", in Arthur and Marilouise Kroker, eds: *The Hysterical Male: New Feminist Theory*, St Martin's Press, New York, 155-169; also C. Straayer: "The Seduction of Boundaries: Feminist Fluidity in Annie Sprinkle's Art/Education/Sex", in P. Gibson, ed, 168f

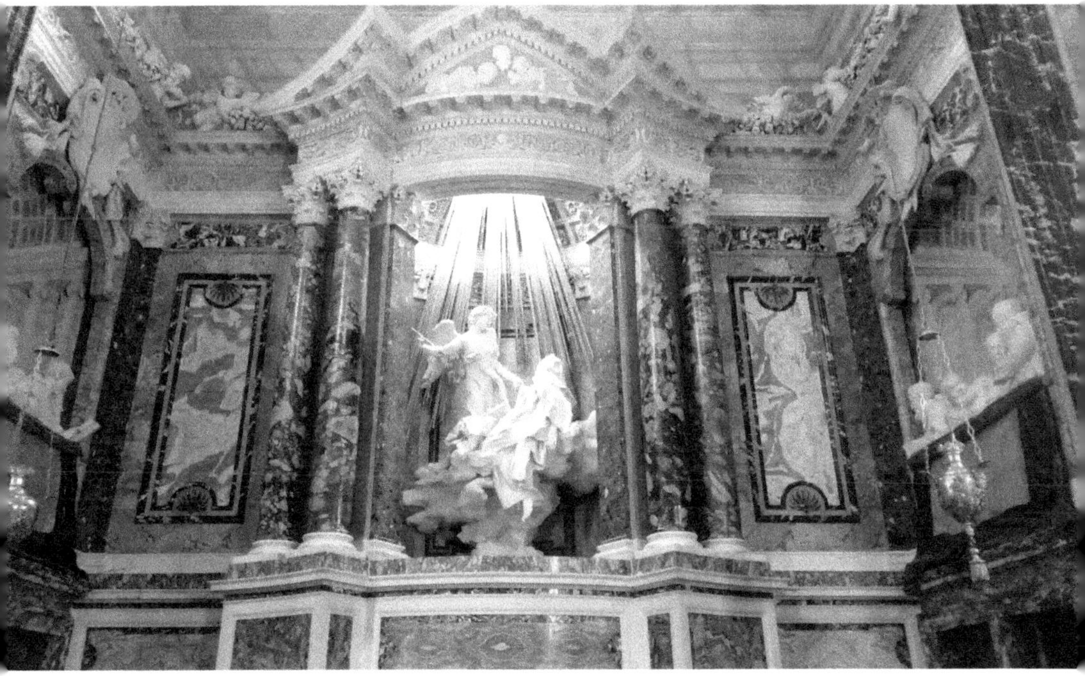

Gianlorenzo Bernini, St Theresa, 1652, Rome.

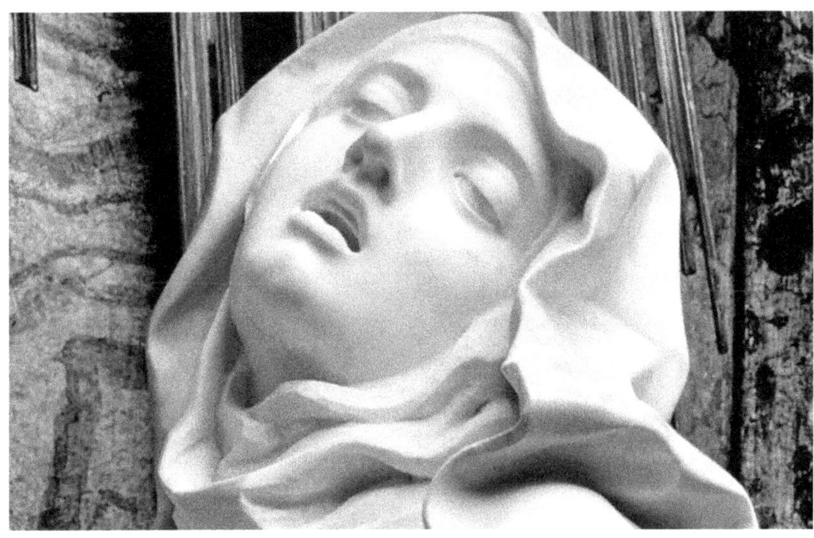

ORGASM

Sexuality is not what you *are,* but what you *do.* It is not *who* is fucking *whom,* but *how.*[1] The question is *how is this fucking being done?* Never *why,* always *how.*

For patriarchal people, of either or any sex, it seems it is essential to know *who* is speaking about sex. Is the author male or female (or some other gender)? What is her/ his sexual identity? Patriarchal people are disturbed when their expectations of gender are disrupted. When, say, a male author writes of lesbian sexuality as if from the 'inside', as if in the 'character' of a lesbian. For example, who is the speaker and who is the subject of this poem:

> First, I want to make
> kiss you...
> I want to make you come
> in my mouth like a storm.[2]

It seems the speaker (Marilyn Hacker) is female and she is describing lesbian sex. But the words could just as apply hetero-sexual or homosexual eroticism. Only when parts of the body are mentioned - clitoris, nipples, penis, breasts - is it possible to decipher the gender of speaker, text or subject, and sometimes not even then.

1 see Valerie Traub, in V. Wayne, 83

2 Marilyn Hacker: 'Noces', from *Love, Death and the Changing of the Seasons,* Arbor House 1986

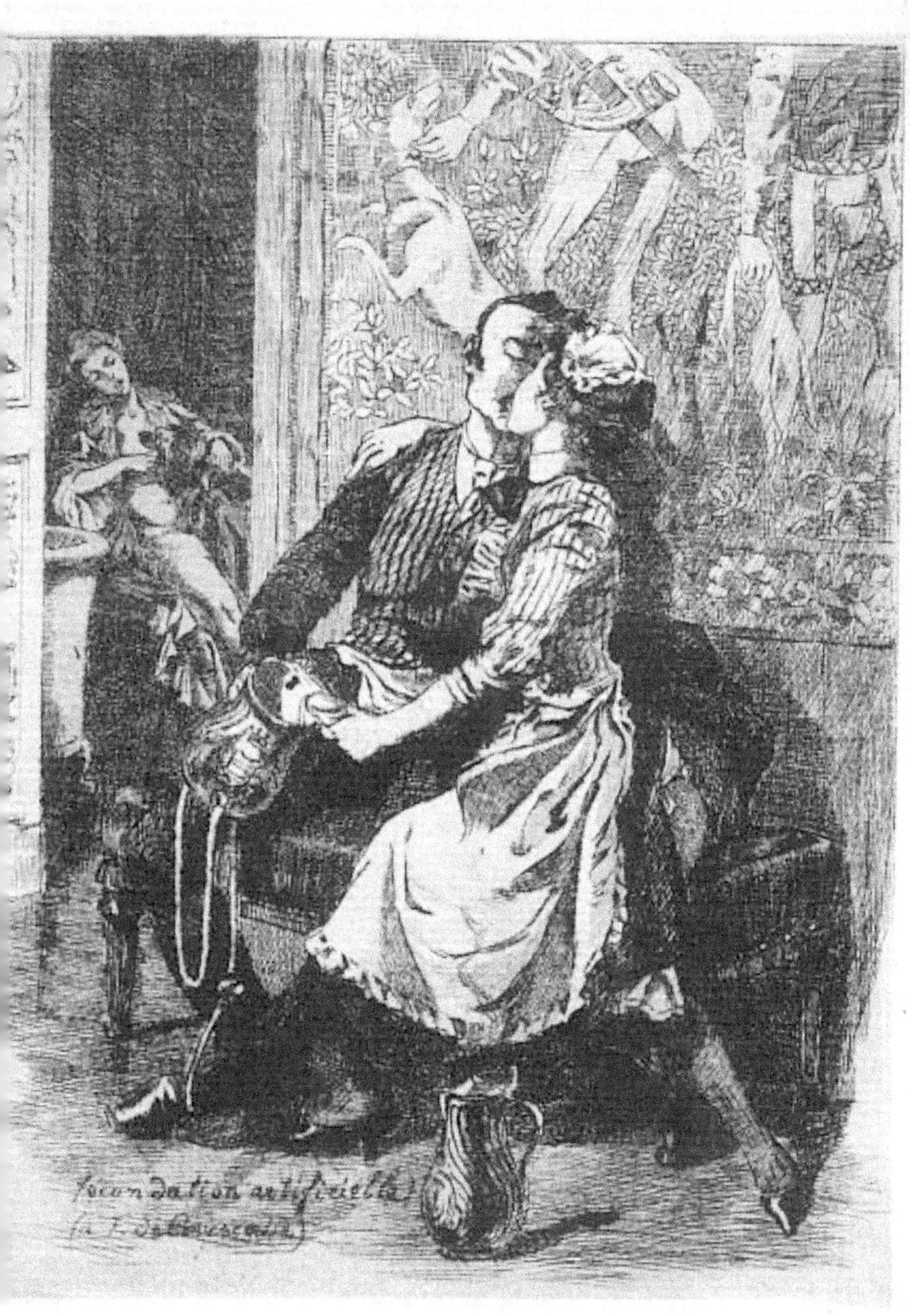

Martin van Maele

THE PHALLUS

In pornography, the great signifier is the phallus, while the site of pleasure is the woman's body. Reclining on a million couches in artists' studios, the female nude offers itself up as a country to be colonized. It is both a pleasure machine and a fantasy. The orchestrator of pleasure in this pornographic scenario is that little slip of flesh, the penis. The phallus is good, whole, true, unifying, as opposed to the bad, fragmented, impure, chaotic vagina.[1] The phallus is the emblem of male power, as many commentators, not only feminists, note: '[t]he supreme power is the power that prevails over mortality', and this power is 'reasonably equated with the phallus'.[2] For feminists, the West is a phallic/ phallocentric/ phallogocentric society, where the phallus, the sublime signifier, the most censored image in the West, is the beginning and the end of sexual pleasure. For Madeleine Gagnon, the phallus is an emblem of male narcissism:

> The phallus... represents repressive capitalist ownership, the exploiting bourgeois... The phallus means everything sets itself up as a mirror. Everything that erects itself as perfection.[3]

1 See T. Moi: *Sexual/ Textual Politics*, 66f; S.M. Gilbert & S. Gubar: *The Madwoman in the Attic: The Woman Writer and the Nineteenth Century Literary Imagination*, Yale University Press, New Haven, CT, 1979.
2 L. Steinberg: *The Sexuality of Christ in Renaissance Art and in Modern Oblivion*, Pantheon, New York, 1984, 90.
3 M. Gagnon: "Corps I", *La venue à l'écriture*, UGE, 10/18, Paris 1977; in E. Marks, 180.

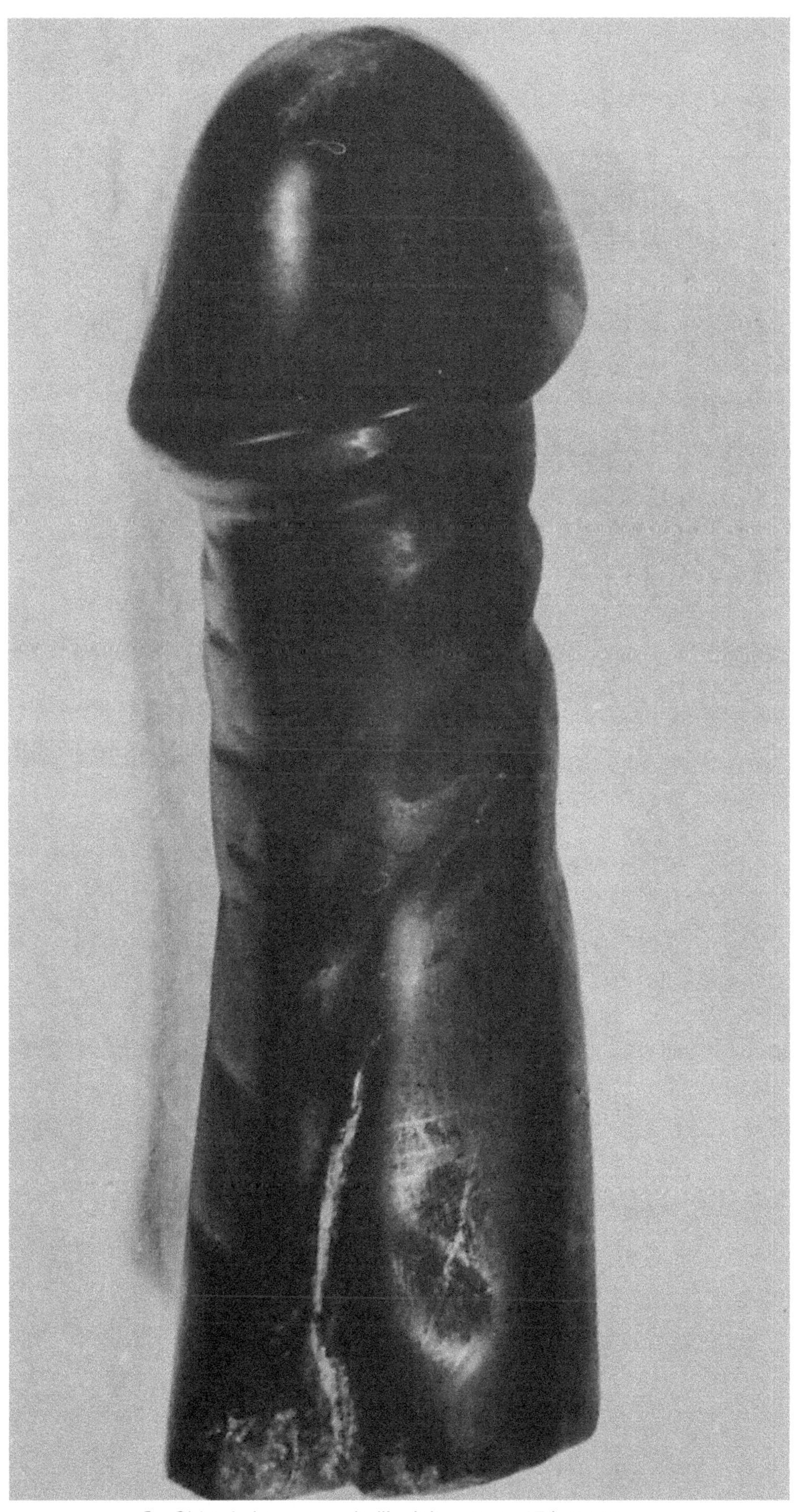

Go-Shintai, Japanese phallic deity, stone, 17th century

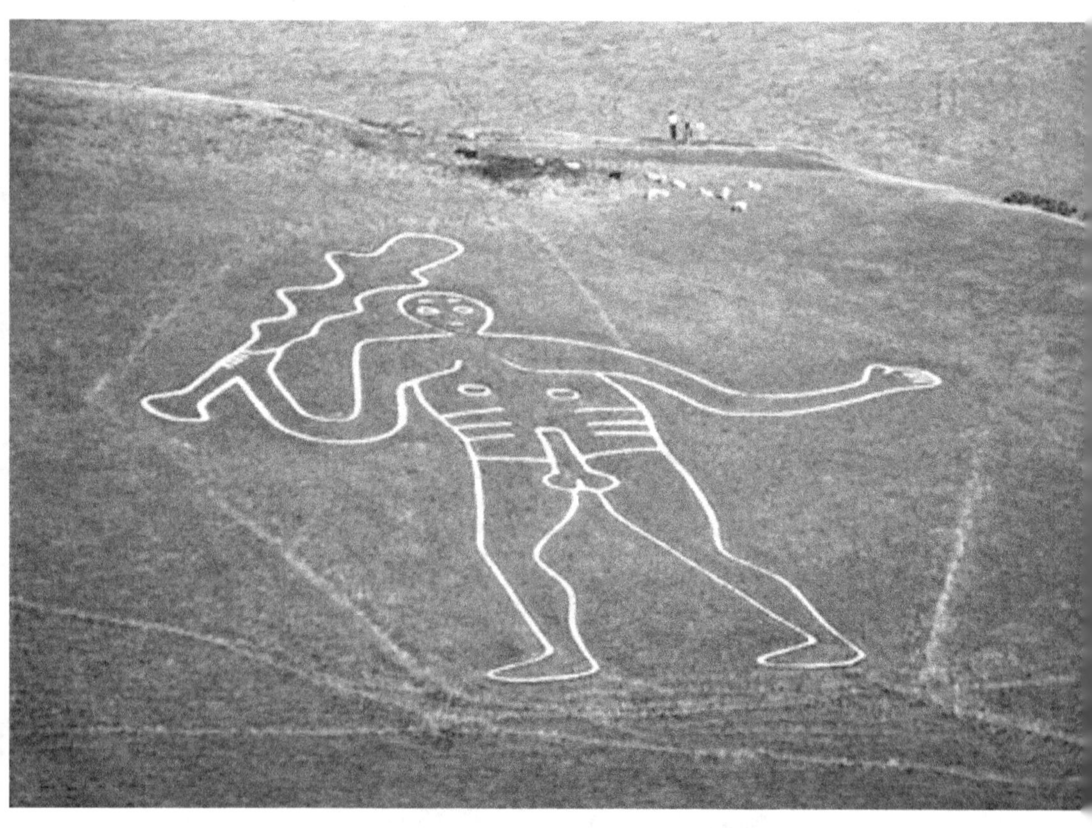

Cerne Giant, Dorset, England

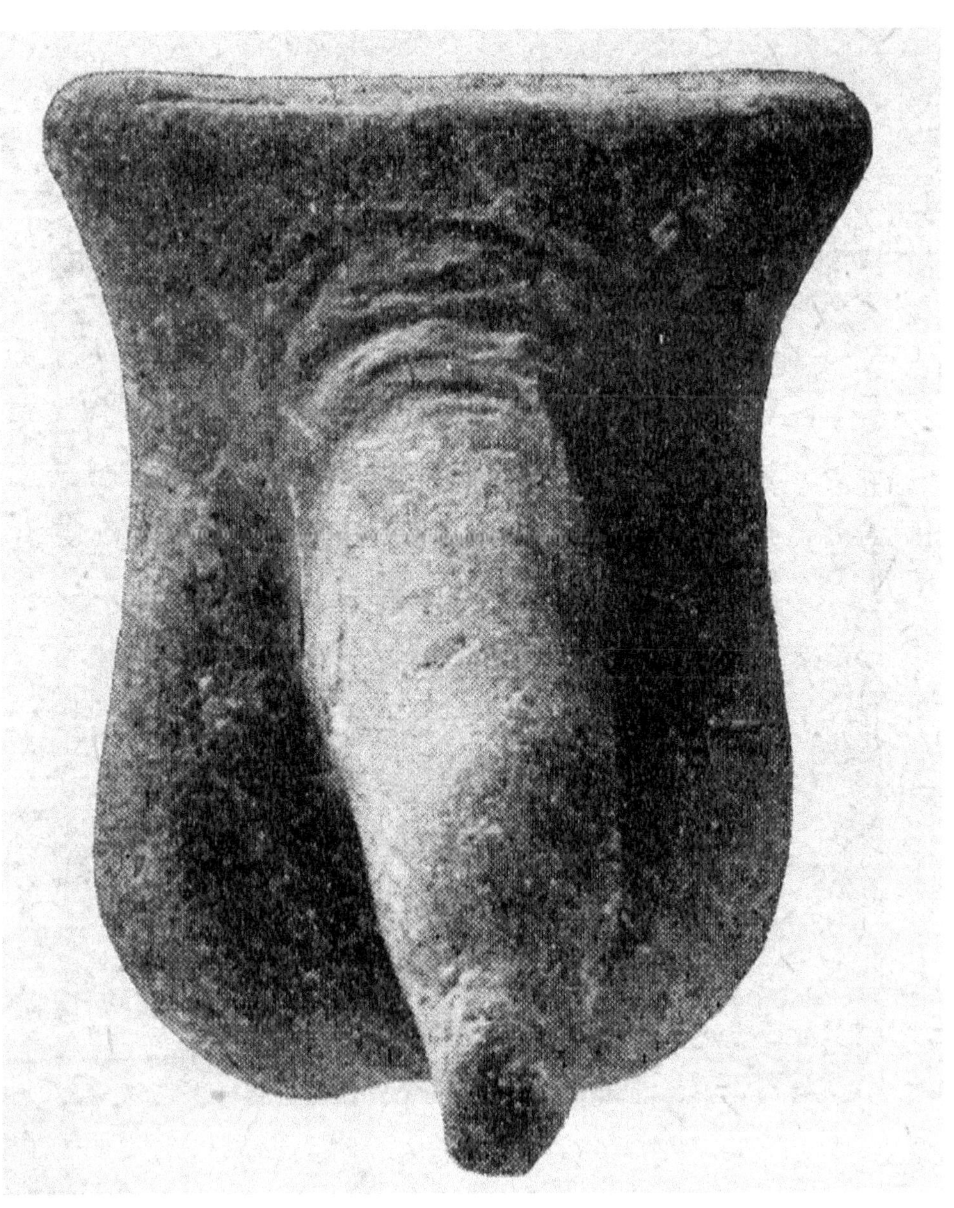

Ancient Votive Phallus, from Albert Moll, Handbuch der Sexualwissenschaften, Verlag Von F.C. Vogel, Leipzig, 1921

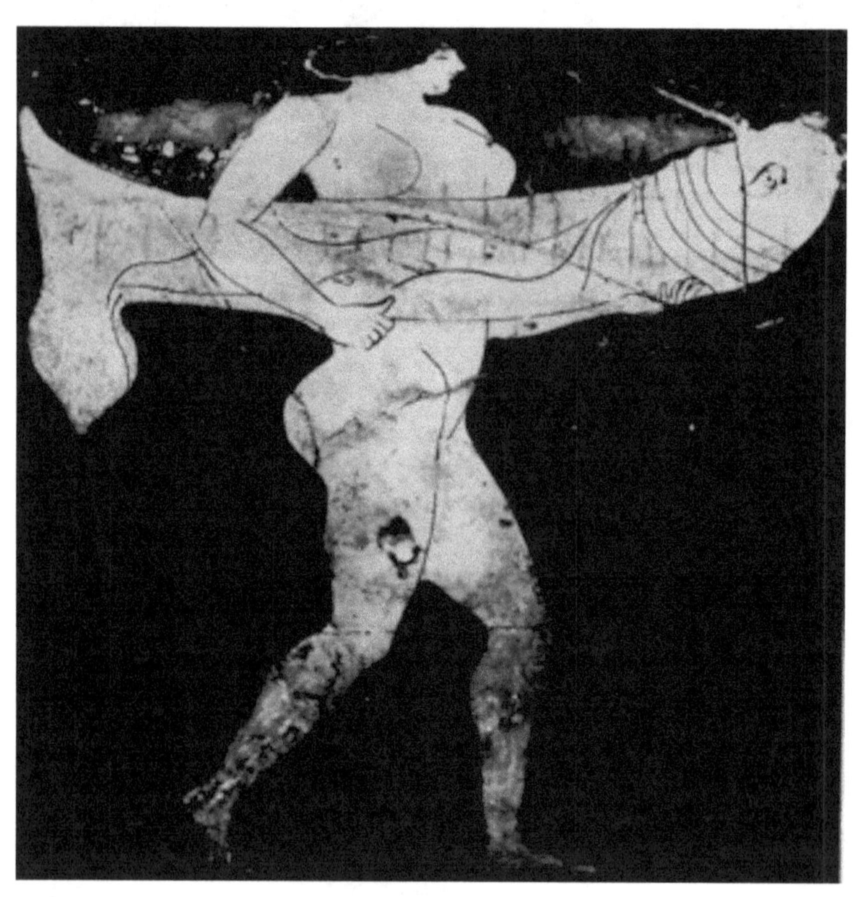

Vase, Ancient Greek

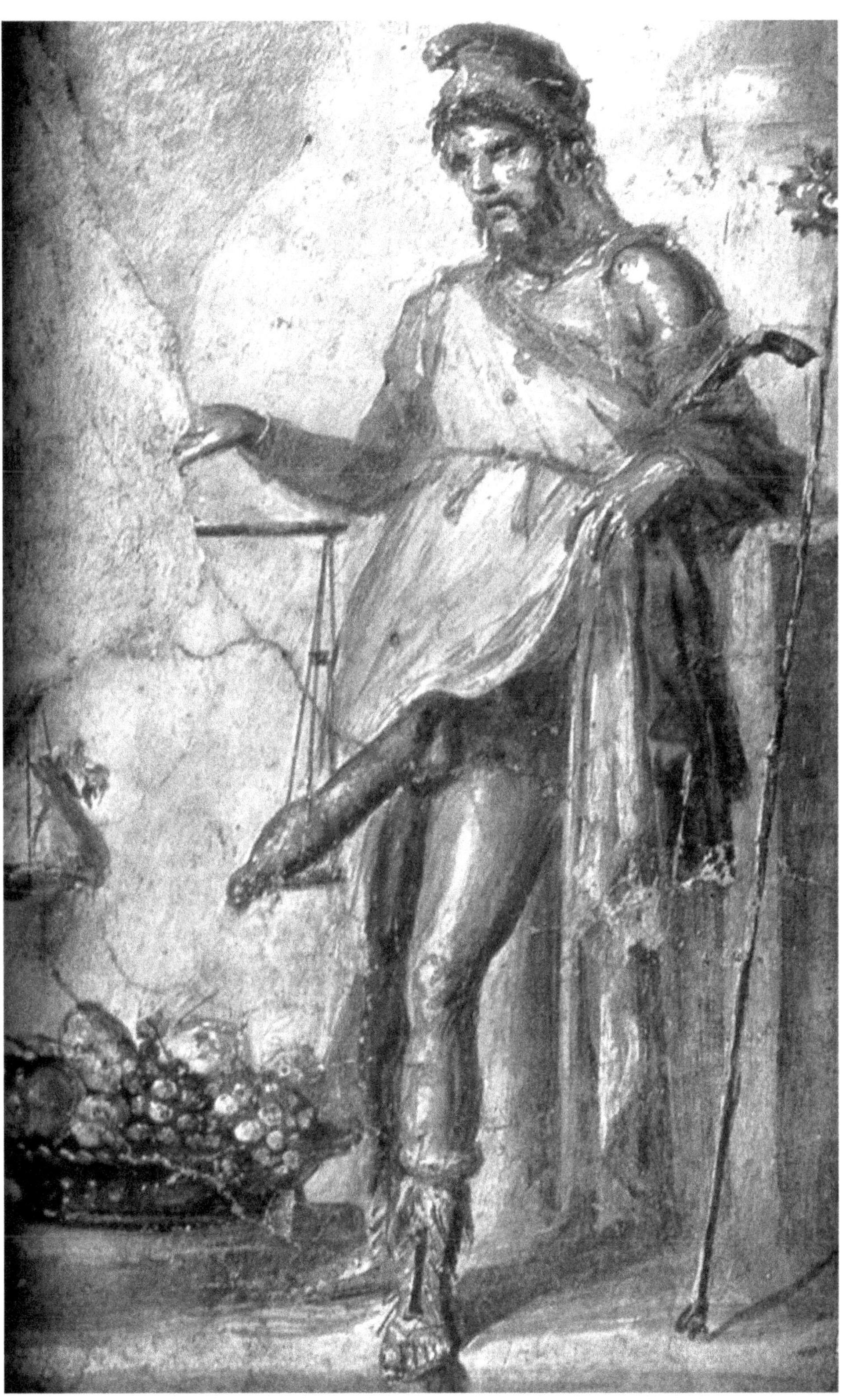

Fresco, Ancient Roman

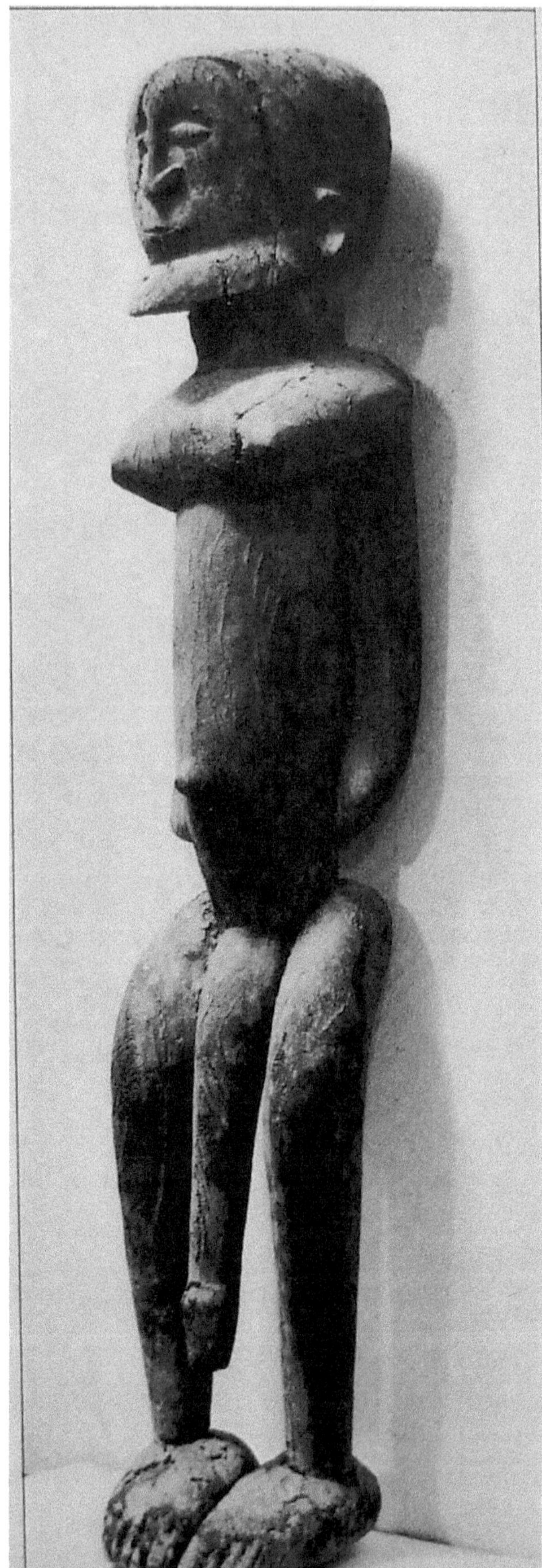

Wood figure, Ivory Coast

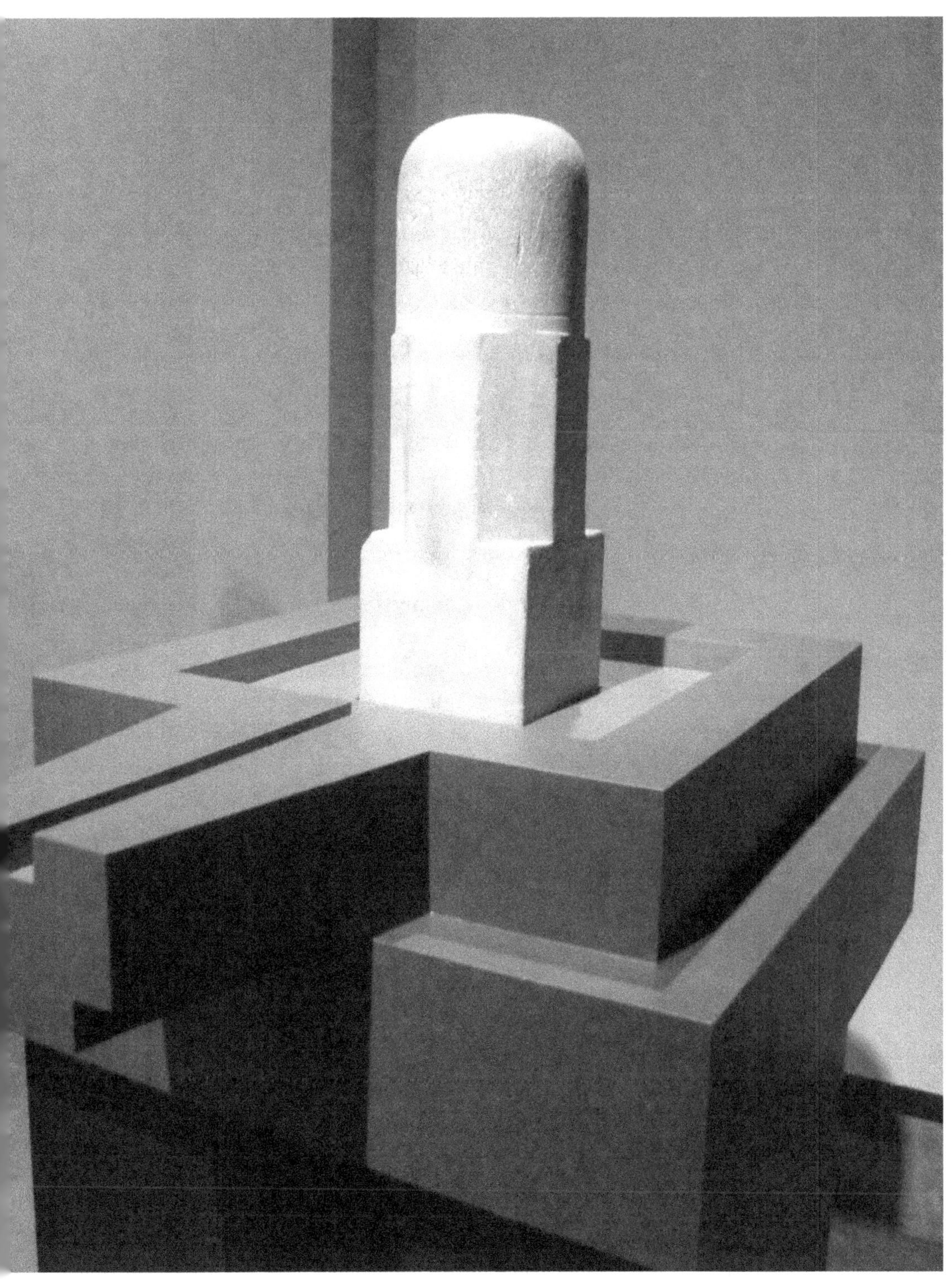

Lingam and Yoni, Cambodian, Norton Simon Museum, Pasadena, CA

THE PHALLUS

Whole philosophic systems are based on the phallus, yet, as Juliet Mitchell remarked in "Feminine Sexuality':

> It's extraordinary what happens when you get rid of the centrality of the concept of the phallus. I mean, you get rid of the unconscious, get rid of sexuality, get rid of the original psychoanalytic point.[1]

If men reduce people to their sexual identities, as some feminists claim, then at the heart of this is the penis. Women are reduced to 'cunt', as Kate Millet put it, while men are all phallus. There are certainly no shortage of phallic symbols and artifacts about. The real thing, the real penis, is censored, carefully guarded – it's not much to look at anyway – so men displace their phallic sexuality onto thrusting cars, lorries, missiles, bombs, towers, cameras, computers, guitars, cigarettes, telephones, swords, guns, eyes, etc. These things abound in (patriarchal) art, and throughout the history of art (and pornography adds a million further fetishes). The trouble is that the penis ain't much of a thing, after all. As Richard Dyer commented: 'the fact is that the penis isn't a patch on the phallus. The penis can never live up to the mystique implied by the phallus'.[2]

1 J. Mitchell: "Feminine Sexuality: Interview with Juliet Mitchell and Jacqueline Rose", *m/f*, 8 (1983), 15.
2 R. Dyer: 'Don't Look Now", *Screen*, vol. 23, 3/4, 1983, and in A. McRobbie, 206.

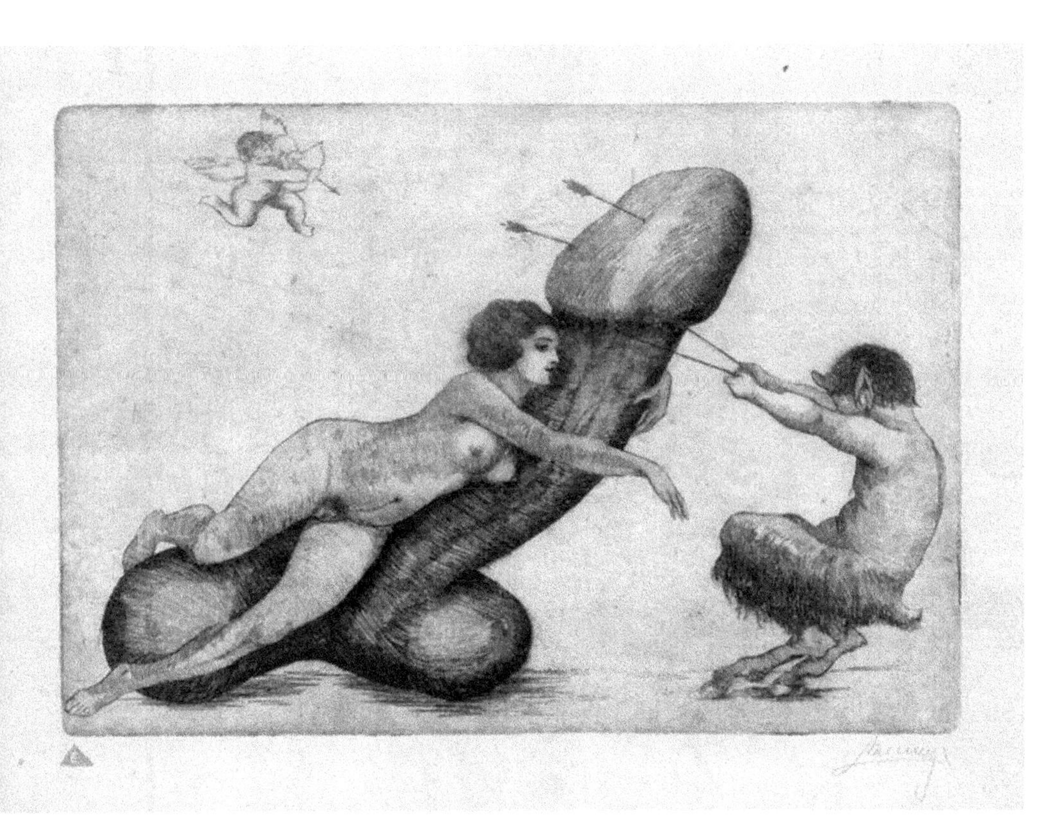

After Max Klinger (1857-1920)

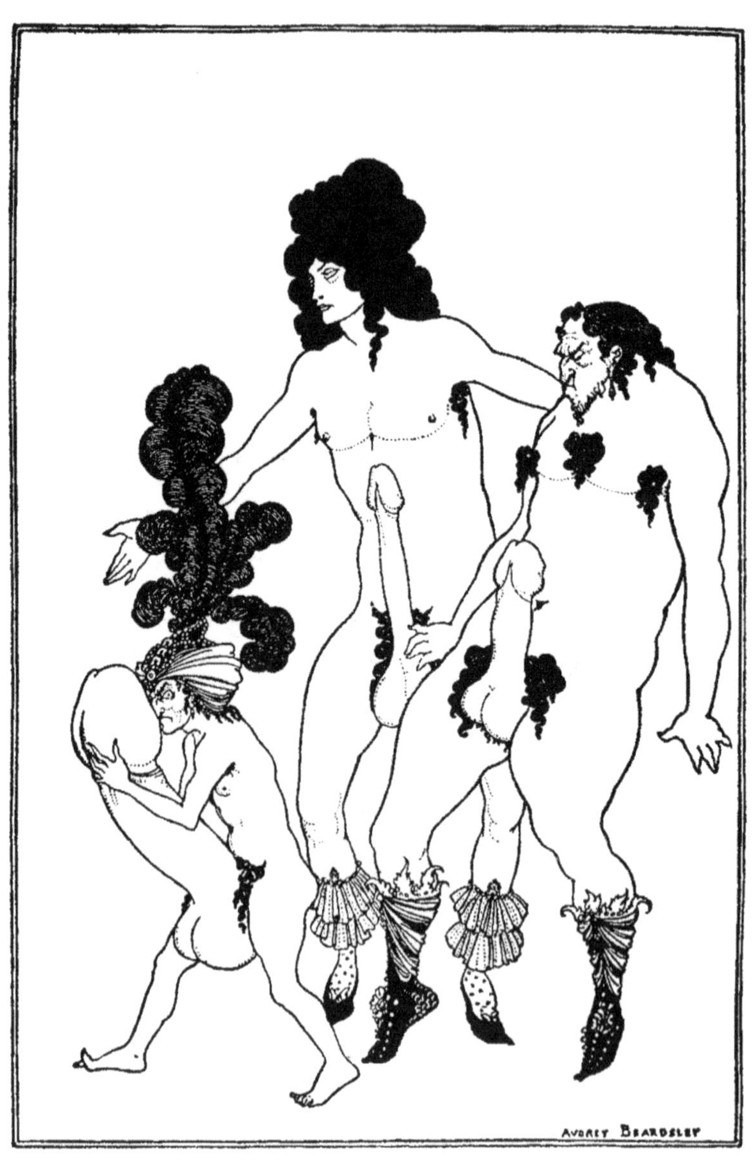

Aubrey Beardsley, Aristophanes, Lysistrata, 1896

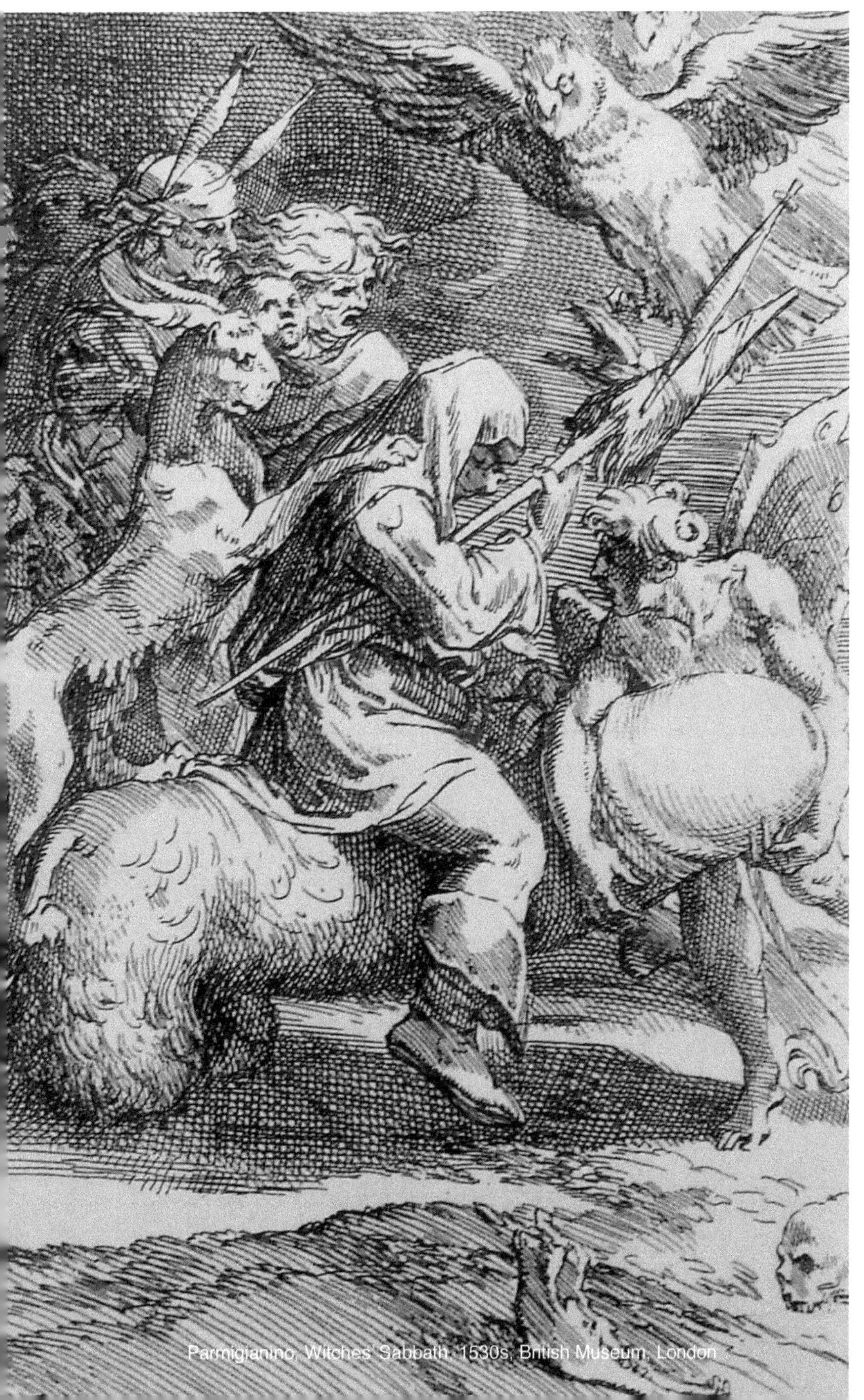

Parmigianino, Witches' Sabbath, 1530s, British Museum, London

In the (second wave) feminist view, the pornographer creates with his penis – the paintbrush, camera, computer or pen – these things are called 'tools', a common euphemism for the penis (there are thousands of other phallic control devices, such as game consoles, TVs, digital cameras, hi-fis, factory machinery, aeroplanes, etc). The quill, stylus or 'sharp projective' is a crucial element in the male's manufacture of art and pornography.[1] When Pierre Renoir was asked how he painted when he hands were crippled by arthritis he replied, '[w]ith my prick'.[2]

In pornography, the eye becomes the phallus, and looking is equated with caressing the obscure object of desire with the phallus (in the Lacanian system). Throughout Western art the phallus has been that visually absent but psychologically and ideologically present object. It is central in erotic art. Look at the Western art nudes – by Titian, Picasso, Ingres, Boucher: the phallus is there even though one doesn't see it. It's the same in any number of books, poems, sculptures, plays, operas, installations.

1 See J. Derrida: *Spurs: Nietzsche's Styles*, tr. B. Harlow, University of Chicago Press, Chicago 1979, 37-9; on the penis as a paintbrush, see Carol Duncan: "The Esthetics of Power in Modern Erotic Art", *Heresies*, 1, 1977, 46-50.
2 In J. Hobhouse, 135.

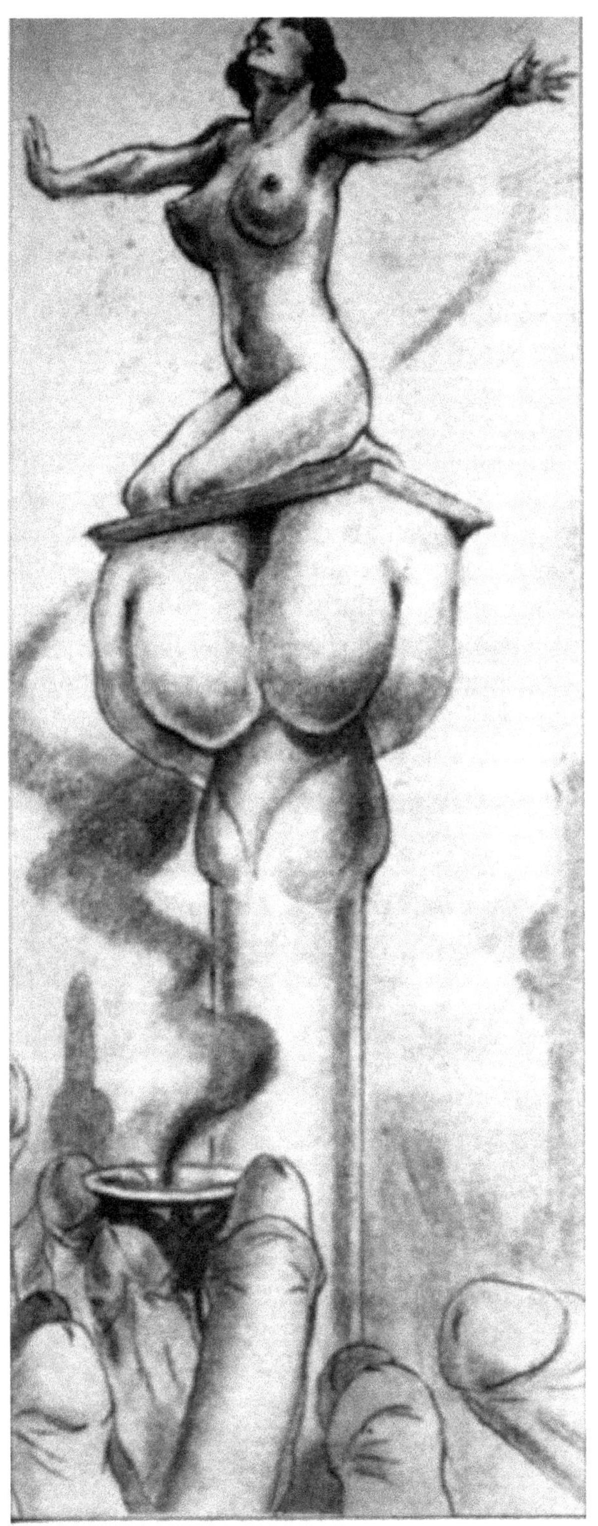

Anonymous, 19th century

LESBIAN EROTICA

In heterosexual pornography, lesbian eroticism is often introduced, but always controlled by a patriarchal force. Typically, in a soft porn scenario, two bisexual women cavort on a bed overseen by a male ('I've always wanted to see ya with another woman' drools the man to his wife/ girlfriend; or, frequently, 'I got back from work an' saw my wife and her best friend writhin' on the bed'). Towards the end of the scene, the man makes love to both women. Why? Because they needed the phallus, they needed a man to be fulfilled. Variations on this scenario occur endlessly in pornography. The male presence (the phallus) is seen as necessary for the true satisfaction for women (for valorization, for authenticity: i.e., it's not *true* sex without the phallus).

Lesbian or women's pornography, made by women for women, disappoints some feminists. Elizabeth Carola, who called herself as a 'radical feminist lesbian', described magazines such as *On Our Backs, Bad Attitude, OW! – Outrageous Women: A Journal of Woman-to-Woman SM, Yellow Silk, The Power Exchange*:

> Like all porn, this new 'woman's' porn is neither about nor for women. Like all porn it is, in a most basic sense, *against* women and *about* male fantasy – the basic male fantasy of Woman as Wholly Sexual Object whose Purpose is To Be Fucked – which feeds men's egos, fuels their violence...

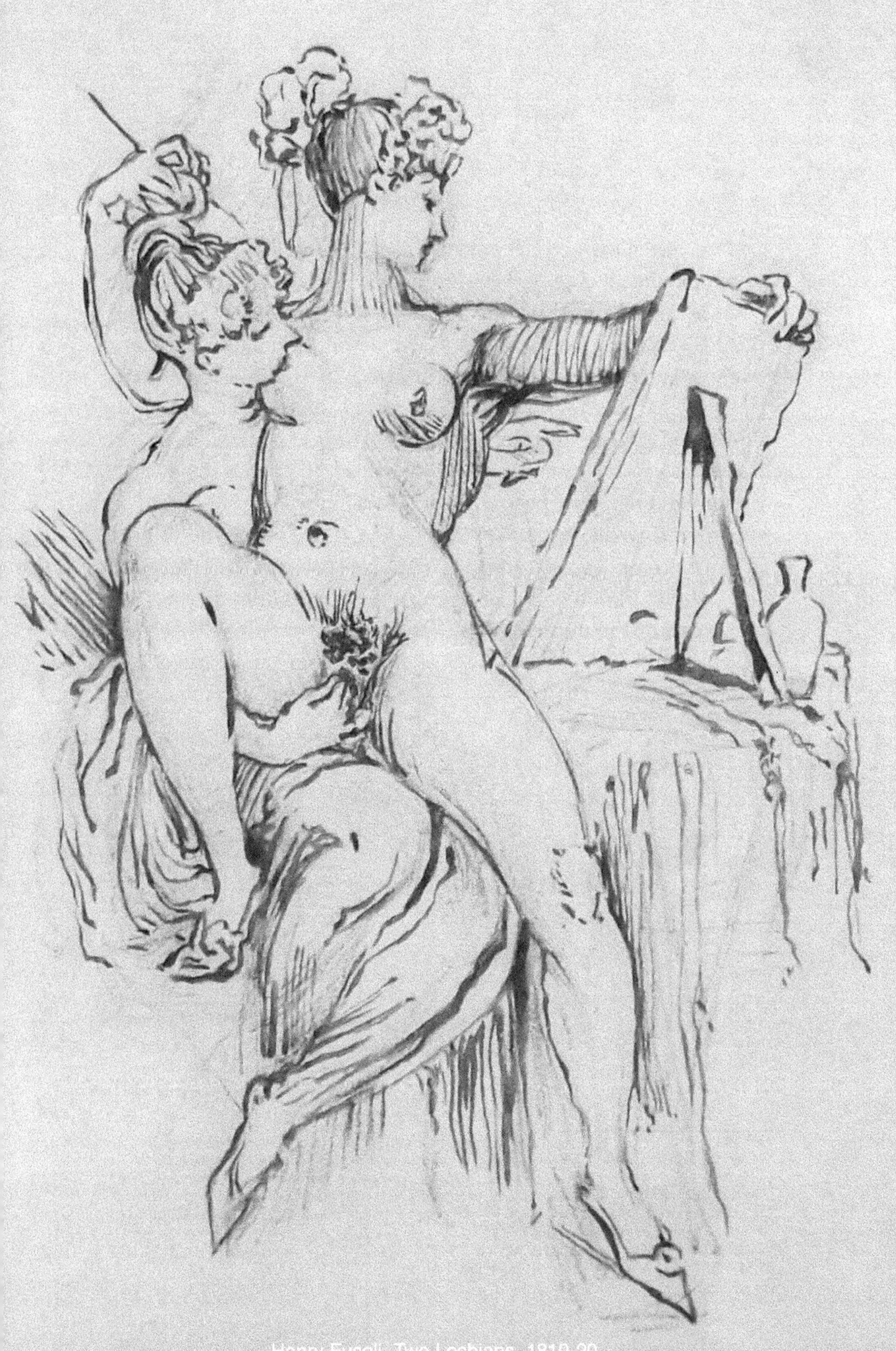

Henry Fuseli, Two Lesbians, 1810-20,
private collection

LESBIAN EROTICISM

Lesbian sex is marked in contemporary cultural theory by the *lack* of the phallus. Hence, lesbian eroticism must always be 'deviant', because it departs from the patriarchal norms which exalt the phallus. Lesbianism must always be 'other', sexually, and many feminists note that the otherness of lesbian sexuality is one of the reasons that men and their patriarchal institutions are very threatened by lesbianism.[1] Lesbian attacks patriarchy at its powerbase. Men cannot control lesbians: '[l]esbians, by loving women and not men, pose a direct threat to the very basis of male supremacy', write Alice, Gordon, Debbie and Mary.[2] The lesbian is crucial, argued Monique Wittig, because she 'is the only concept that I know of which is beyond the categories of sex (man and woman)'.[3] Wittig moved towards a view of culture that goes beyond gender, beyond 'biological dimorphism', and biology.

1 T. Atkinson: *Amazon Odyssey*, Links Books, New York 1974; Alice, Gordon, Debbie and Mary: "Separatism", in S.L. Hoagland & J. Penelope, eds: *For Lesbians Only: A separatist anthology*, Onlywomen Press 1988, 31-40; A. Rich: "Towards a woman-centred university", in *On Lies, Secrets and Silence*, Novotny, New York 1979; J. Johnston: *Lesbian Nation: The Feminist Solution*, Simon & Shuster, New York 1974; S. Rowbotham: *Beyond the Fragments: Feminism and the making of Socialism*, Merlin 1979.

2 Alice, Gordon, Debbie and Mary, op. cit., 31-40.

3 M. Wittig: "One is not born a woman", in S. Hoagland, op. cit., 446-7.

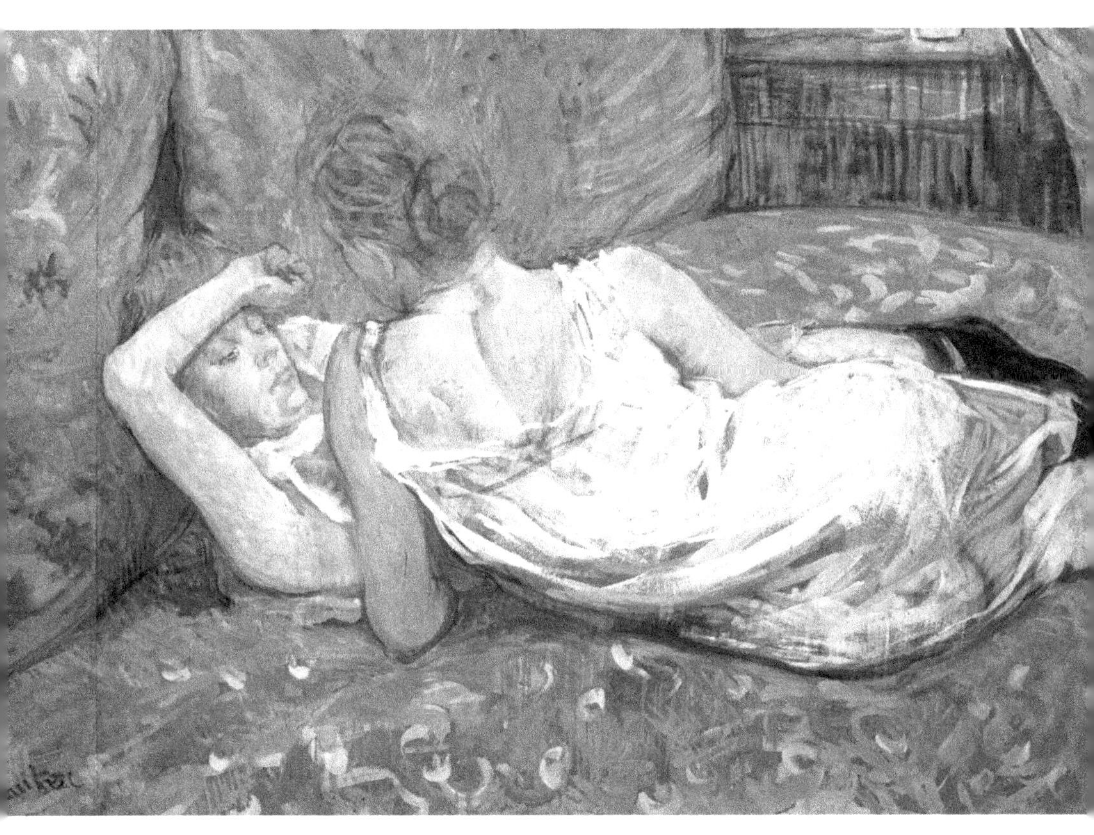

Henri de Toulouse-Lautrec (1864-1901), Two Friends

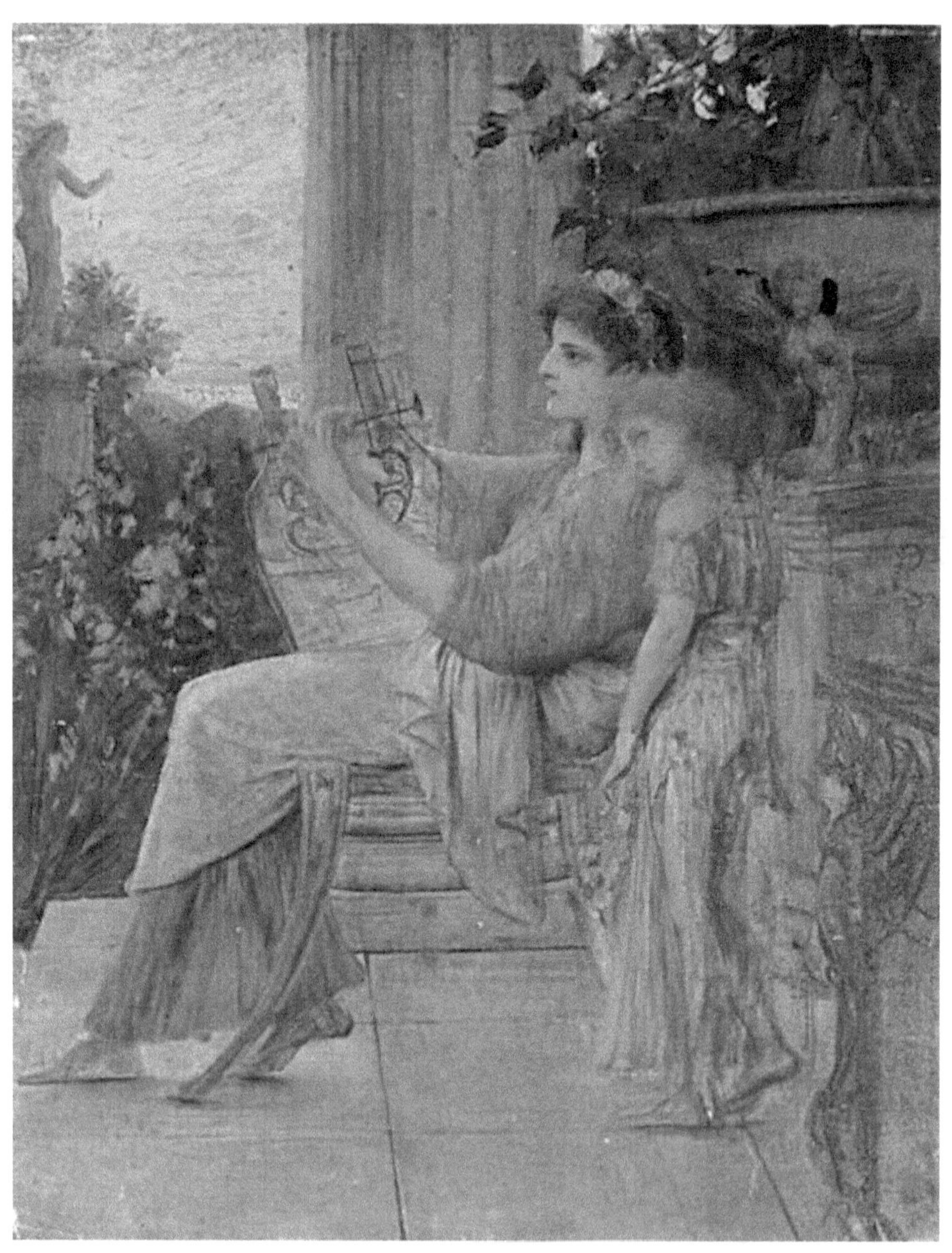

Gustav Klimt, Sappho, 1888-90

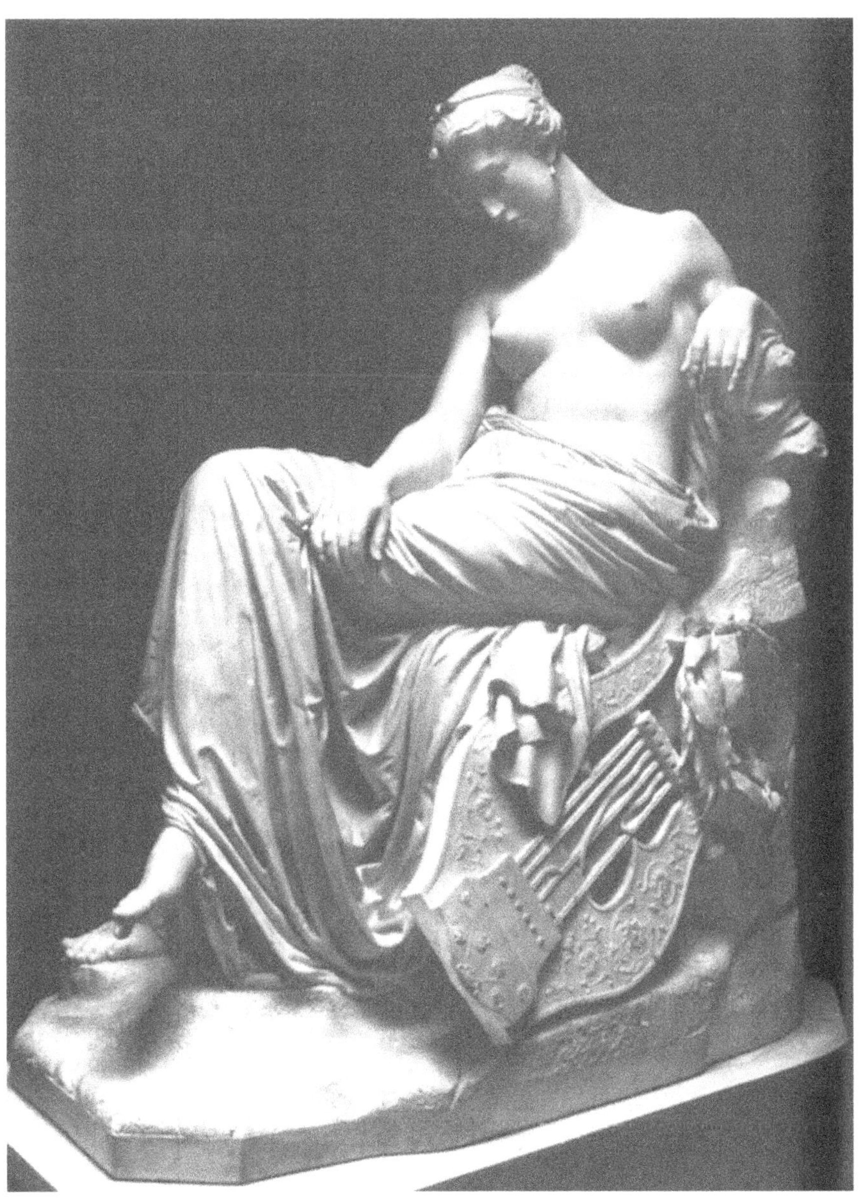

Giovanni Dupré, Sappho, 1857, Rome

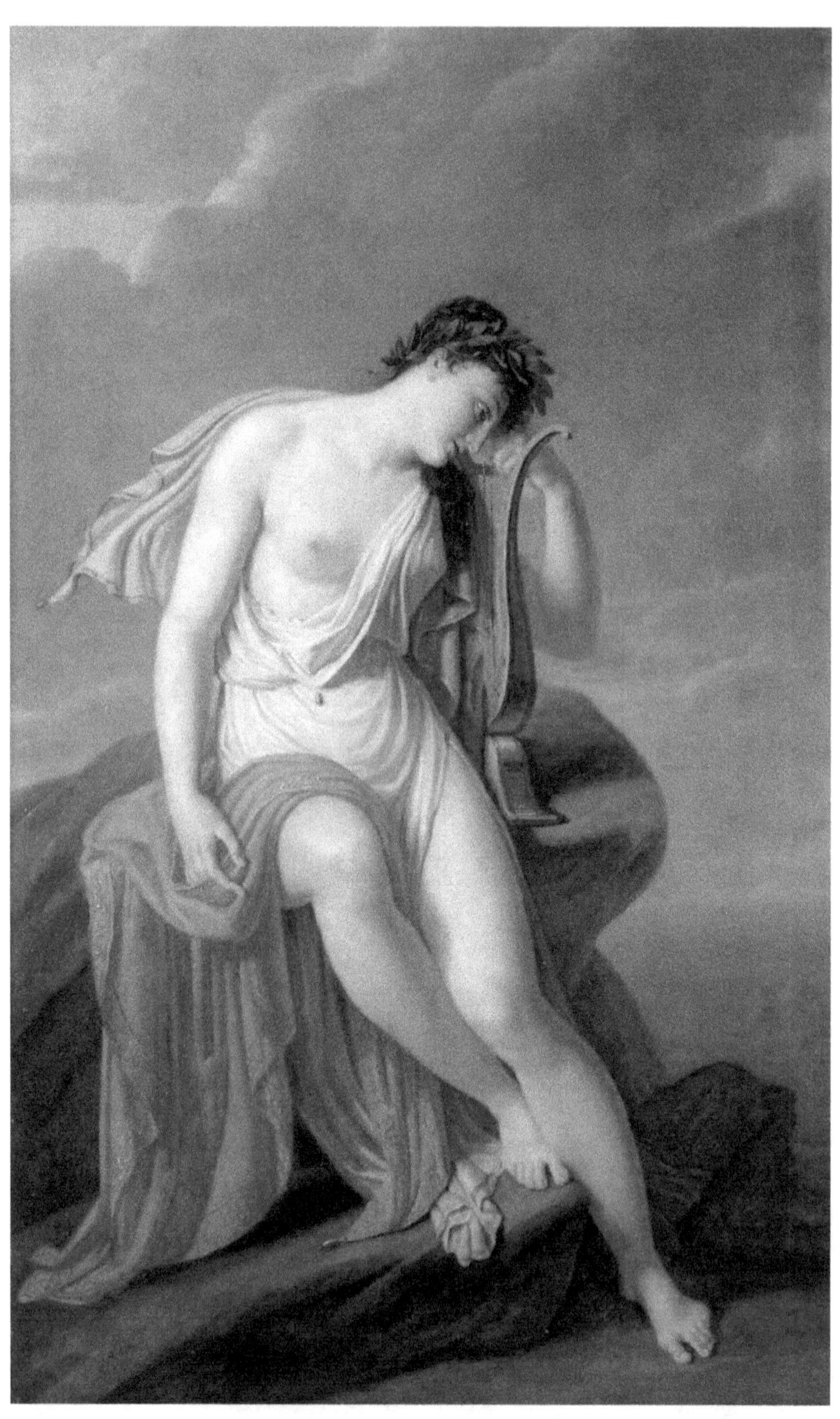

Pierre-Narcisse Guérin, Sappho On the Leucadian Cliff, 1800

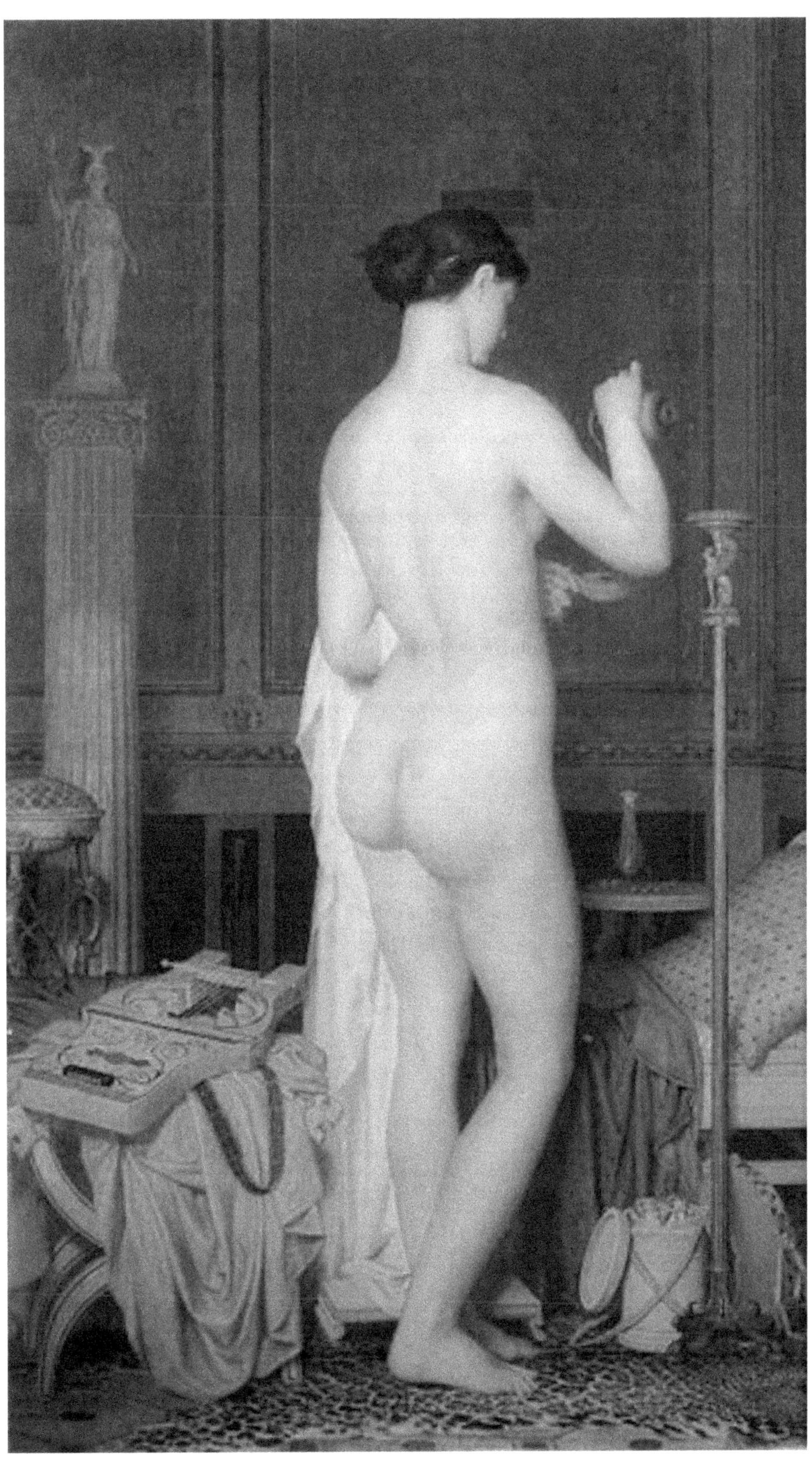

Marc-Charles-Gabriel Gleyre, Le Coucher de Sappho, 1867, Lausanne

LESBIAN EROTICA

According to Elizabeth Carola, lesbian pornographic magazines are full of images and themes usually associated with male pornography:

> *On Our Backs*, in particular, is full of adverts for phalluses and endless verbiage about (and imagery of) extremely masculine 'Butches' introducing large objects - fists, bottles, phalluses - into the bodies of 'Femmes'... *On Our Backs* represents the 'middle range' of lesbian porn. The harder core publications like *The Power Exchange* feature half page adverts for surgical scalpels for 'unparalleled cutting and piercing' interspersed with litanies of young women being violently fist fucked, whipped and pierced and, of course, gratefully licking their 'mistresses' boots in return.[1]

If pornography is a contentious issue among feminists, then lesbian or 'women's' pornography is extremely controversial, and feminists are very divided about it.[2] As Sue George noted: '[f]or a feminist, therefore, to enjoy pornography is to feel doubly guilty.'[3] Writers such as Pat Califa, Lisa Henderson and Sheila Jeffreys argue that sadomasochistic pornography operating inside lesbian practice can be enriching.[4] For men it is clearly threatening, because it excludes them; it is made by women, for women.

---

1 E. Carola: "Women, Erotica, Pornography: - Learning to Play the Game", in G. Chester, 169-171; see S. Jeffreys: "Butch and femme: now and then", *Gossip*, 5, 1987.

2 See the essays in S. Munt's book; A. Koedt: *Radical Feminism*, Quadrangle, New York, NY, 1973.

3 S. George, in G. Chester, op. cit., 111.

4 P. Califa: "Feminism and Sadomasochism", *Heresies*, 12, 1981, *The Lesbian S/M Safety Manual*, Alyson, Boston, 1990, and "Unravelling the Sexual Fringe: A Secret Side of Lesbian Sexuality", *The Advocate*, 27 Dec, 1979; also: L. Henderson: "Lesbian Pornography: Cultural Transgression and Sexual Demystification", in S. Munt, 173-191; S. Jeffreys: "Sadomasochism: the erotic cult of fascism", in *Lesbian Ethics*, 2, 1, 65-82; M. Sulter: "Reviewing lesbian erotica", *Spare Rib*, 219, 1990-1, 42-4; see also, on sadomasochism: R.R. Linden *et al*, 1982; J. Jones: "Why I liked screwing? Or, is heterosexual enjoyment based on sexual violence?", in Onlywomen; K. Davis *et al*, 1983.

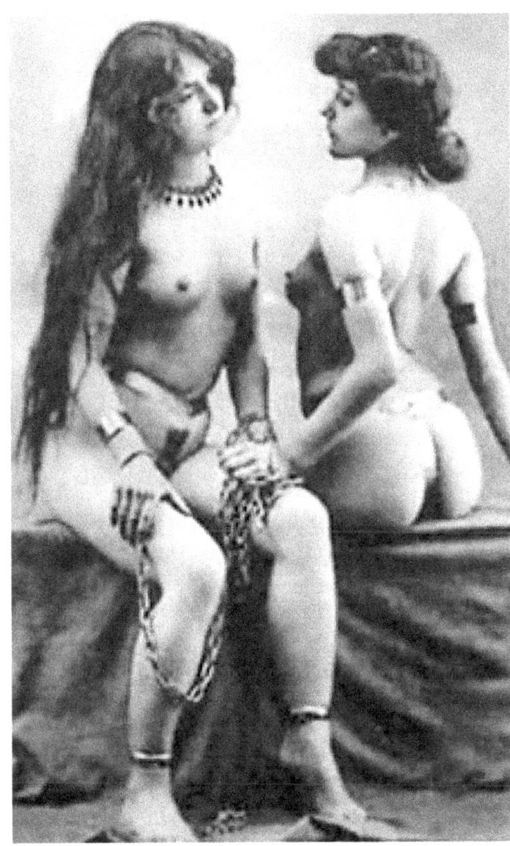

Anonymous, lesbian photograhs,
19th century

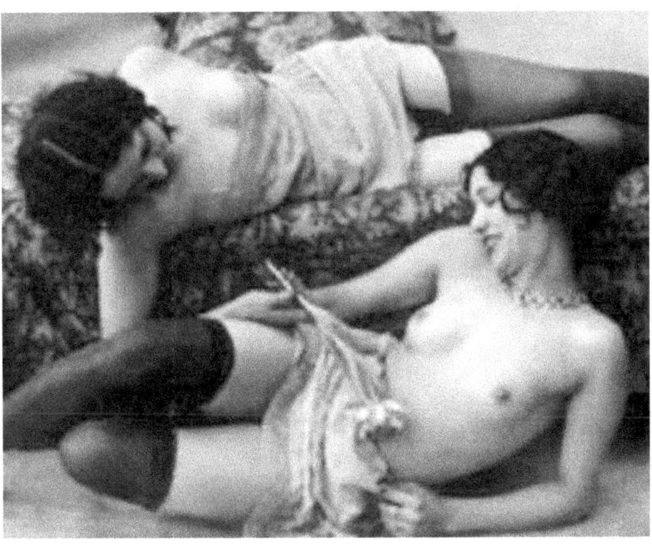

LESBIAN EROTICISM

Not all feminists agree about the revolutionary potential of lesbianism, if it is a lesbianism that keeps defining itself in terms of patriarchy. Elizabeth Mees reckoned that 'lesbianism, as an attack on hetero-relations, takes (its) place within the structure of the institution of heterosexuality. The lesbian is born of/ in it.'[1] There is no escape, it seems, from patriarchal and heterosexuality: the world is permeated with these ancient structures. As Sheila Jeffreys wrote: '[e]very woman grows up in a heteropatriarchal world',[2] while Ann Barr Snitow remarked in "Mass Market Romance':

> One of our culture's most intense myths, the ideal of an individual who is brave and complete in isolation, is for men only. Women are grounded, enmeshed in civilization, in social connection, in family and in love (a condition a feminist culture might well define as desirable) while all our culture's rich myths of individualism are essentially closed to them.[3]

1 E. Mees, in K. Jay & J. Glasgow: *Lesbian Text and Contexts: Radical Revisions*, New York University Press, New York, NY, 1990, 82.
2 S. Jeffreys: "The Censoring of Revolutionary Feminism", in G. Chester, 139.
3 A. Snitow: "Mass Market Romance: Pornography for Women Is Different", *Radical History Review*, no. 20, Spring/Summer, 1979.

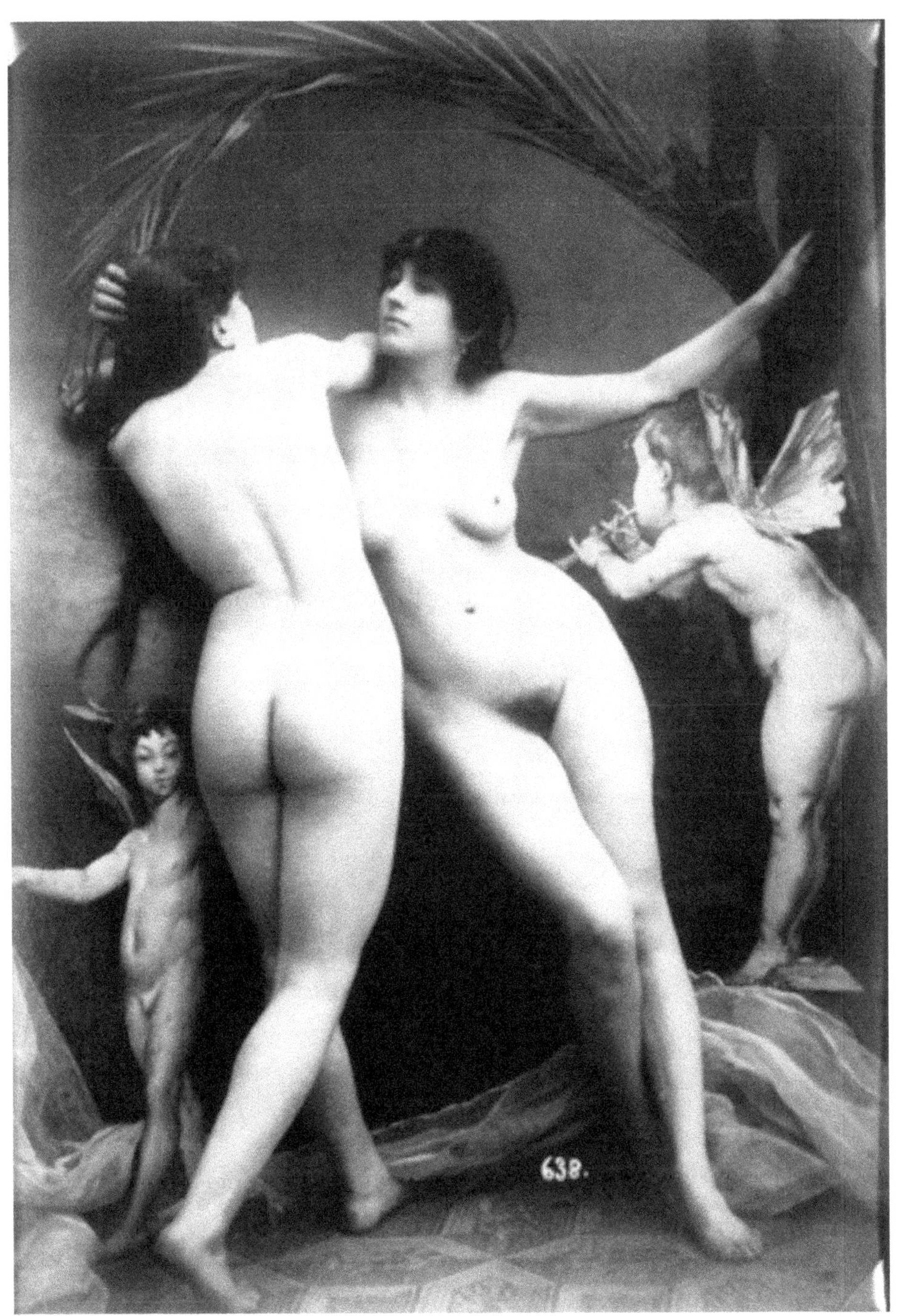

Gaudenzio Marconi (1841-85), Nudes and Angels, 1880s

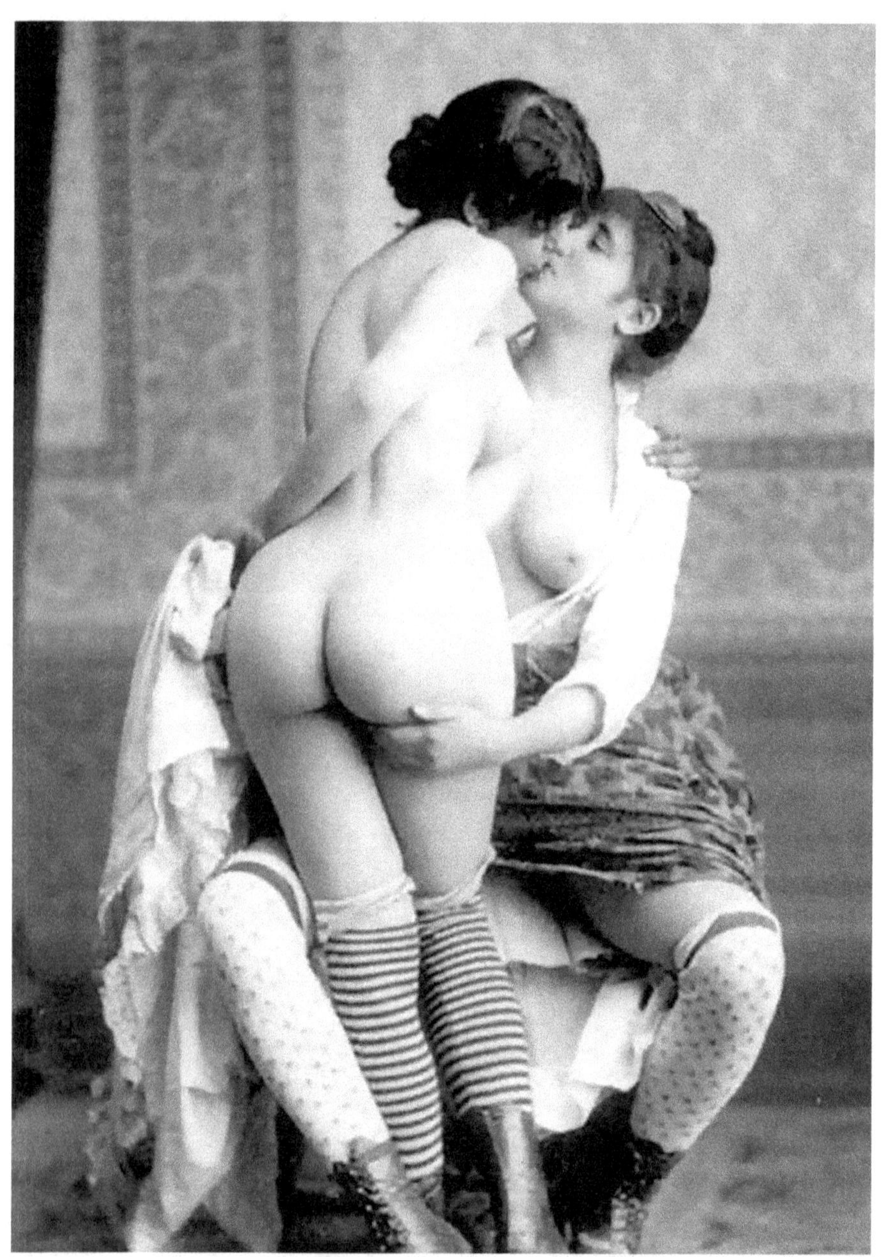

French Postcard, early 20th century

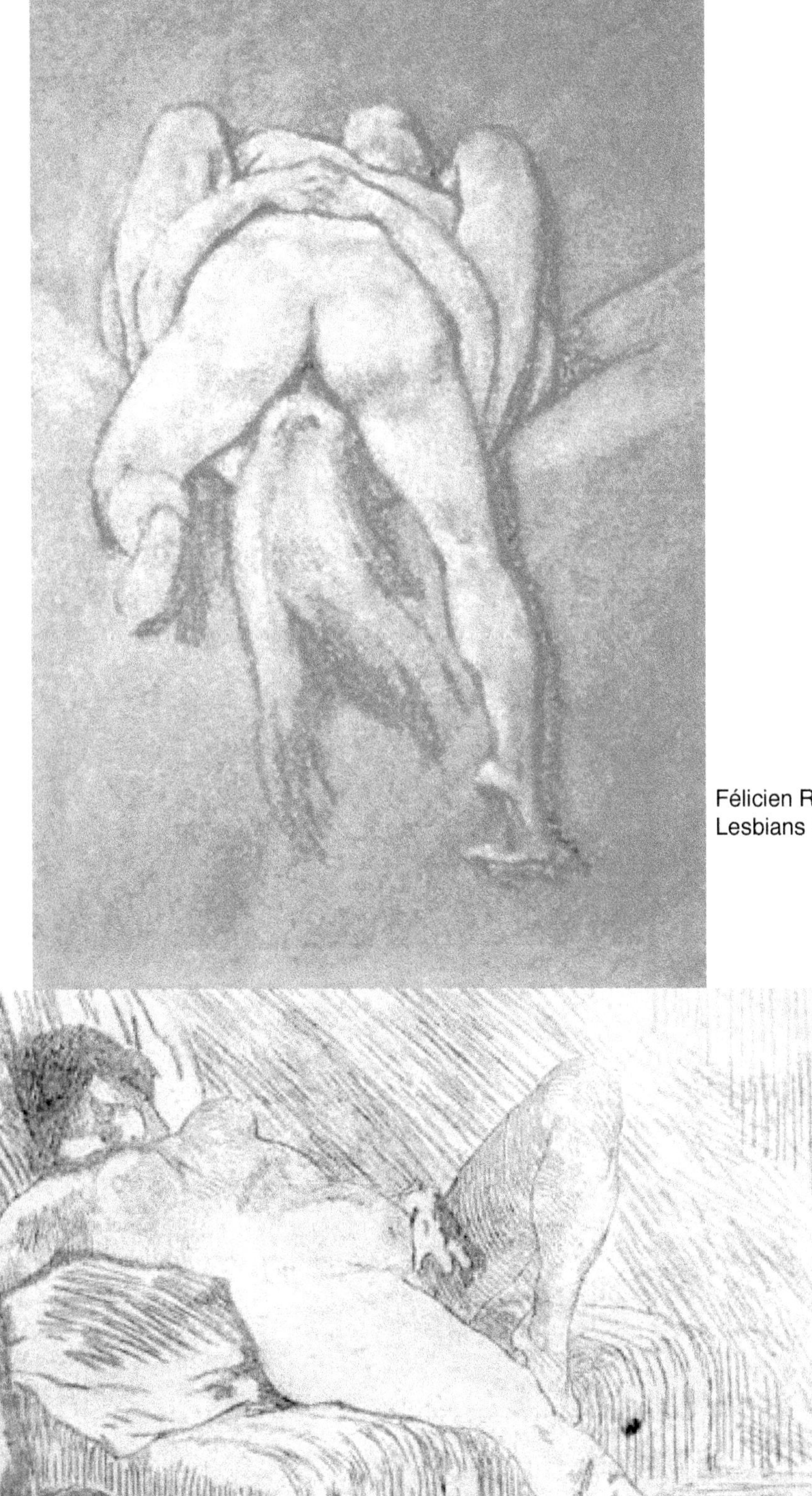

Félicien Rops,
Lesbians (left).

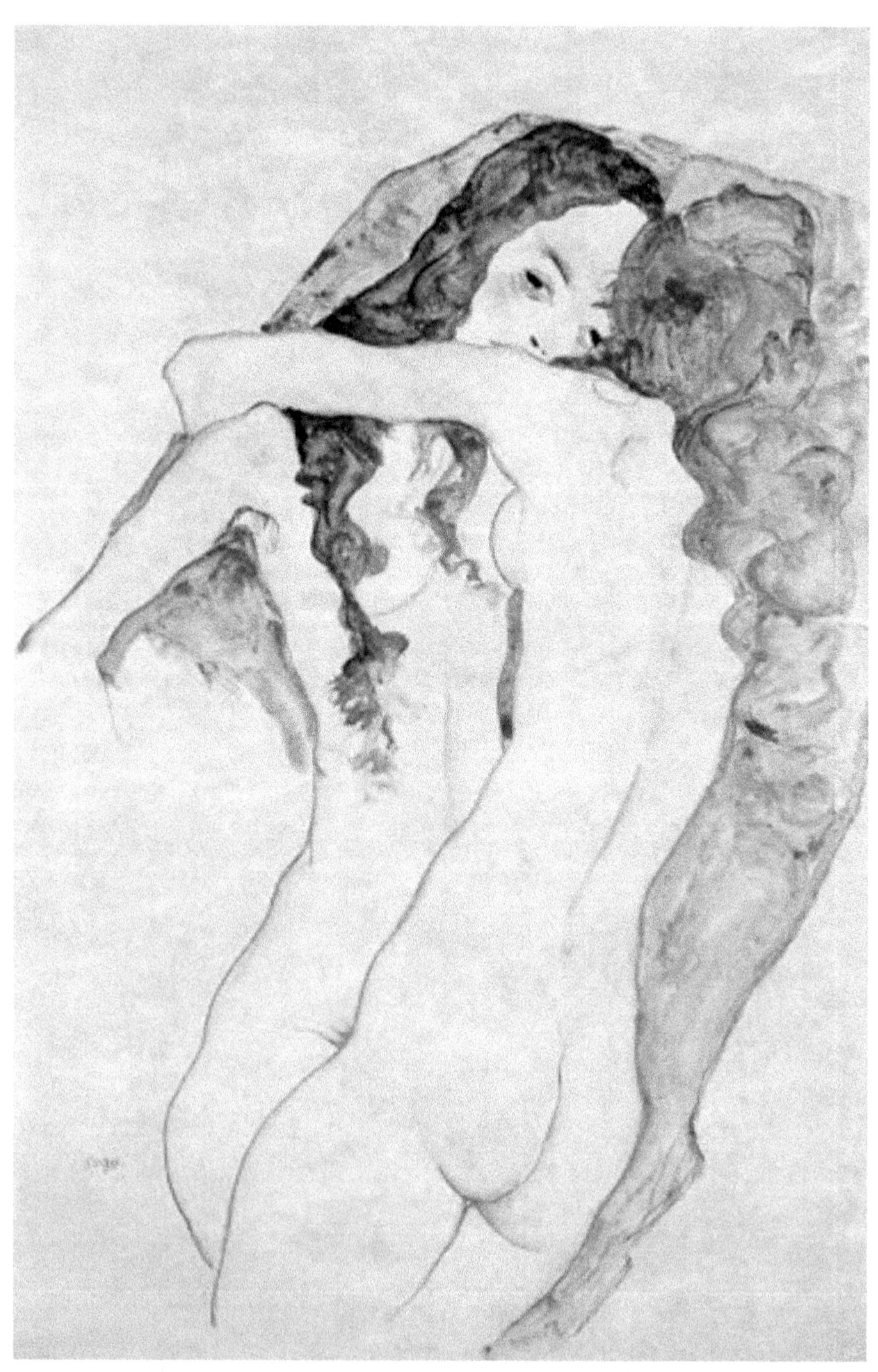

Egon Schiele, Two Women Embracing

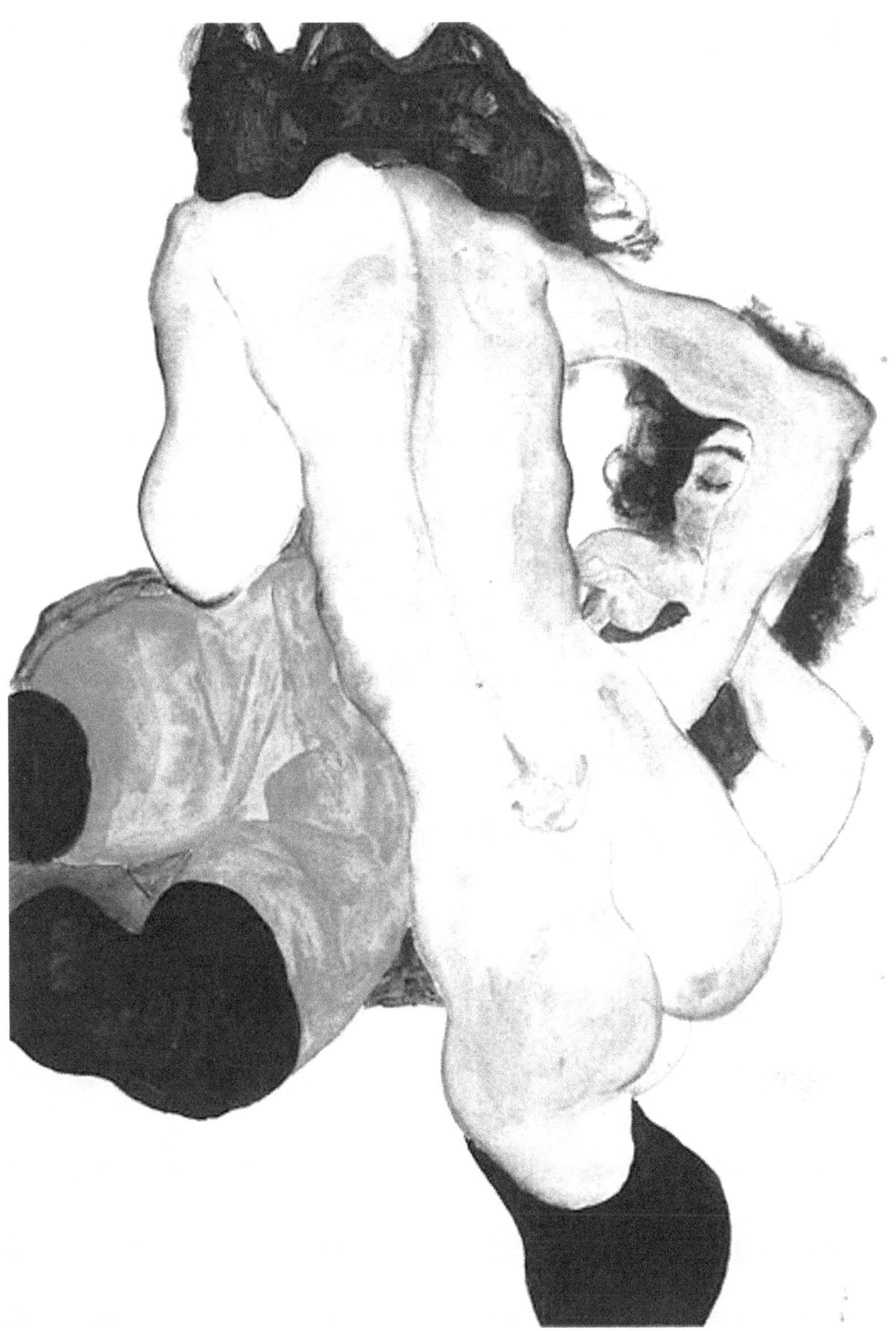

Egon Schiele, Two Lovers

VOYEURISM

The Lacanian Look emphasizes eroticism. Seeing is erotic, the eye becomes a kind of phallus, caressing the obscure object of desire, which it can never 'possess'. As the poet Rainer Maria Rilke wrote '[g]azing is a wonderful thing.'[1] The act of looking eroticizes the object. Jack Zipes describes it thus in *Don't Bet On the Prince*:

> For him [Lacan], seeing is desire, and the eye functions as a kind of phallus. However, the eye cannot clearly see its object of desire, and in the case of male desire, the female object of desire is an illusion created by the male unconscious. Or, in other words, the male desire for woman expressed in the gaze is auto-erotic and involves the male's desire to have his own identity reconfirmed in a mirror image.[2]

The look is an assertion of male power and sexuality. For the gaze is male, and feminists have grappled with the notion of a 'female' gaze, whether there can be such a thing as a 'female' or 'feminine' gaze.[3]

---

1 R. Rilke, letter to Clara Rilke, 8 March 1907, in *Gesammalte Briefe 1892-1926*, Insel Verlag, Leipzig 1940, II, 279f

2 Jack Zipes: *Don't Bet on the Prince: Contemporary Feminist Fairy Tales in North America and England*, Gower, Aldershot 1986, 258

3 Maggie Humm: "Is the gaze feminist? Pornography, film and feminism", *Perspectives on Pornography*, eds G.Day & C. Bloom, Macmillan 1988; Lorraine Gamran & Margaret Marshment, eds: *The Female Gaze*, Women's Press 1988; E.D. Pribram, ed: *Female Spectators: looking at film and television*, Verso, 1988

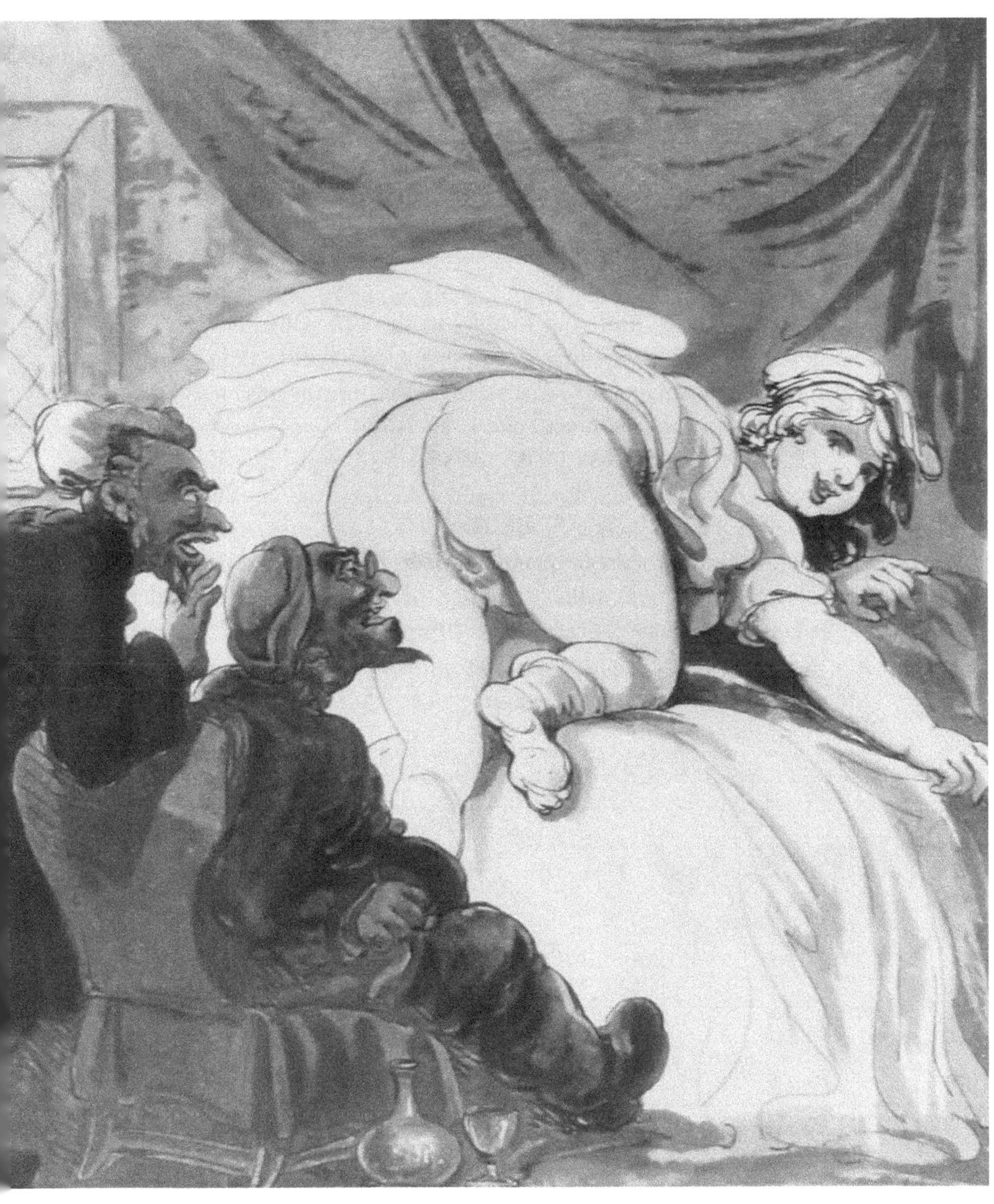

Thomas Rowlandson, Susannah and the Elders, 1820, London

SEX AND DEATH

Pain is good, because it means you are fully alive. This is the Existential view of patriarchal culture. 'Sensual pleasure is agony in the strictest meaning of the word', says C. Mauclair in a Freudian tone.[1] Suffering is holy, in the Christian tradition. The journey from martyrdom to sainthood and beatification is swift. The West exalts pain. Christ *suffered*, say theologians, so he must have been right, he must have lived hard, because he died hard. Death becomes heroic. Death transfigures people. Suicide is even better, if you can manage it. Hence Marilyn Monroe, Vincent van Gogh, Johann Wolfgang von Goethe's Werther, Virginia Woolf. Die young, and become famous (many artists have followed this equation: Egon Schiele, Frédéric Chopin, Wolfgang Amadeus Mozart, Georges Seurat, James Dean, Paula Modersohn-Becker, D.H. Lawrence, Jimmy Hendrix, Jim Morrison, Arthur Rimbaud, Raphael, John Keats, Percy Shelley, and Novalis.

1 C. Mauclair: *Magie de l'amour*, 145, quoted in Julius Evola, 84

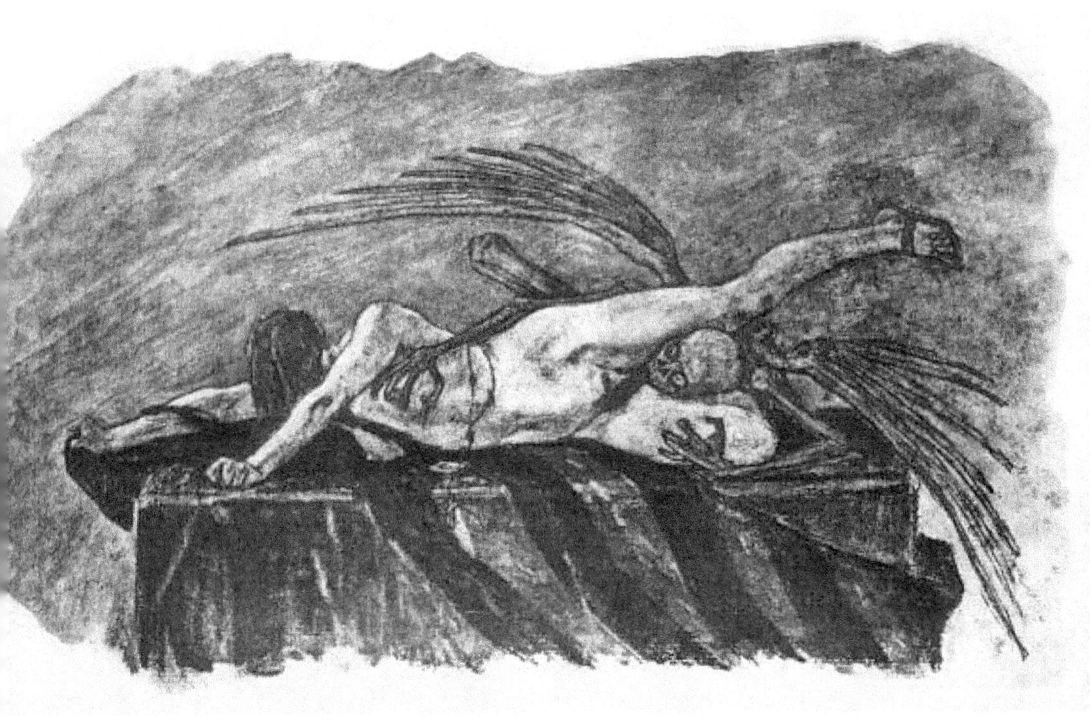

Félicien Rops

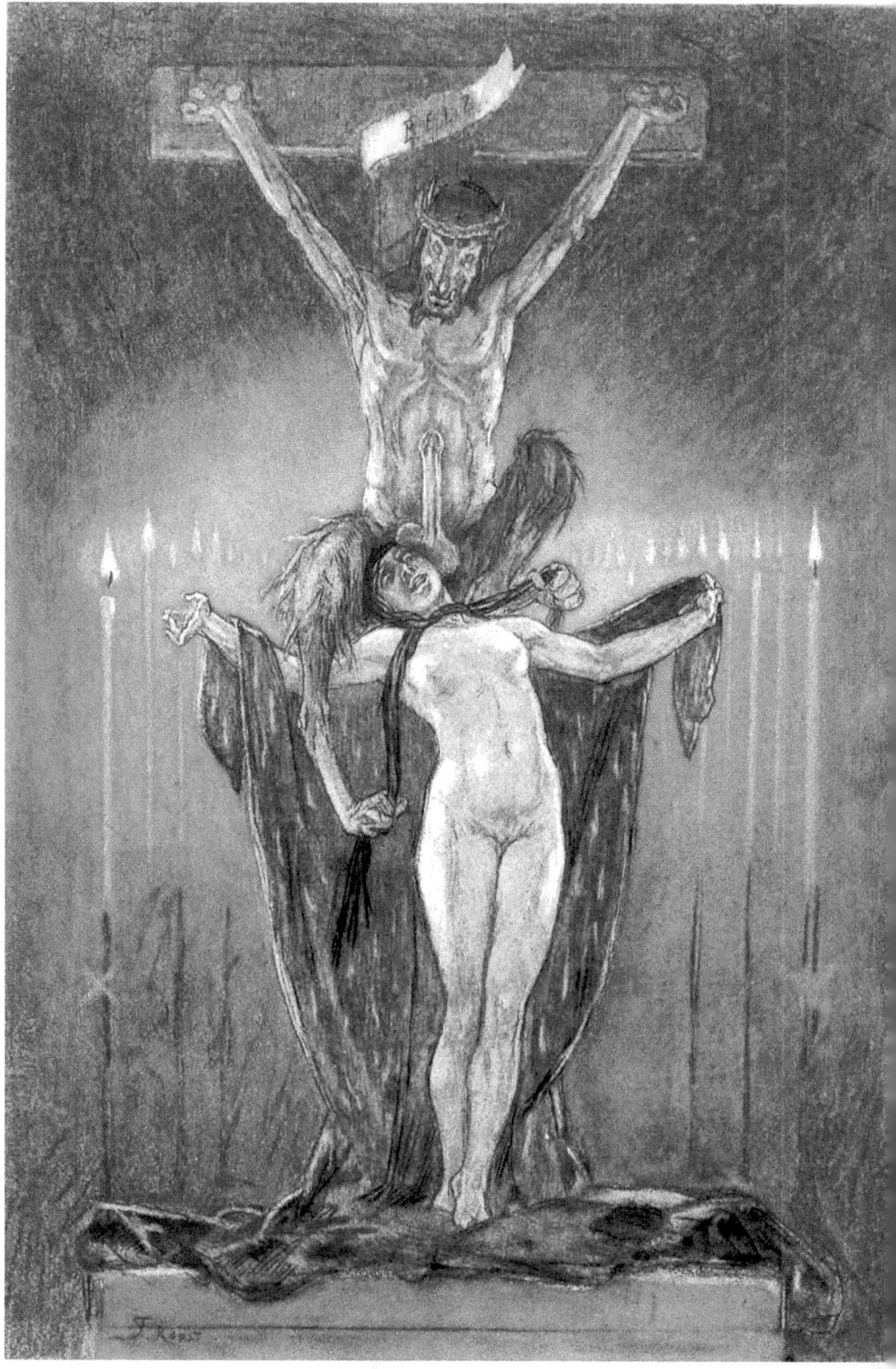

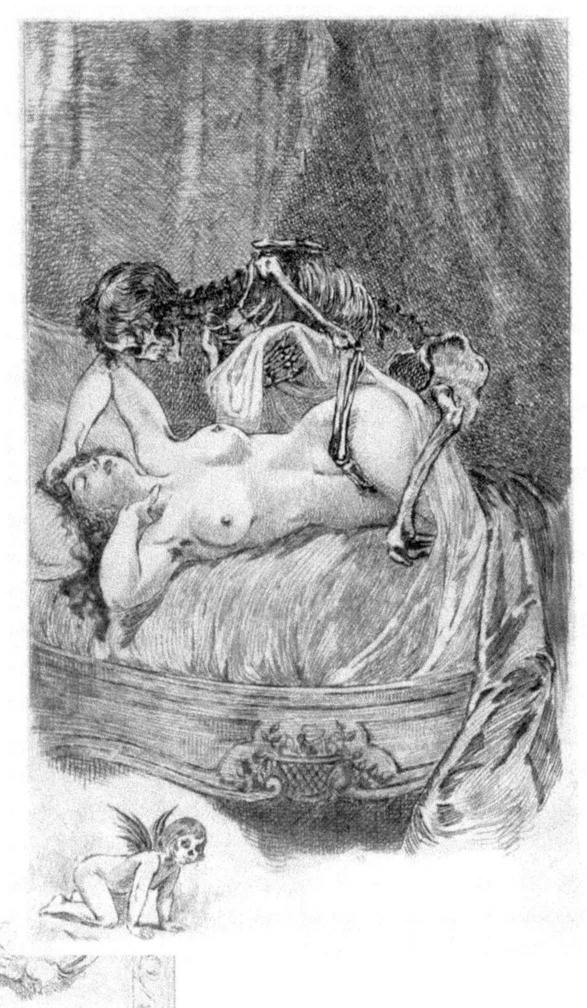

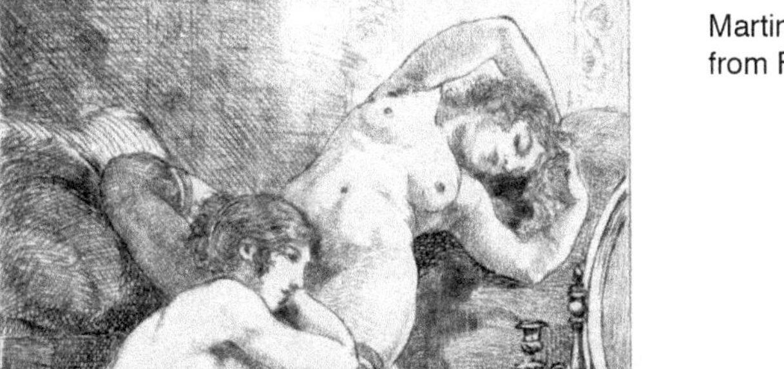

Martin van Maele,
from Fleurs du mal, 1917

Part Two

Erotic Art In the Early 20th Centry

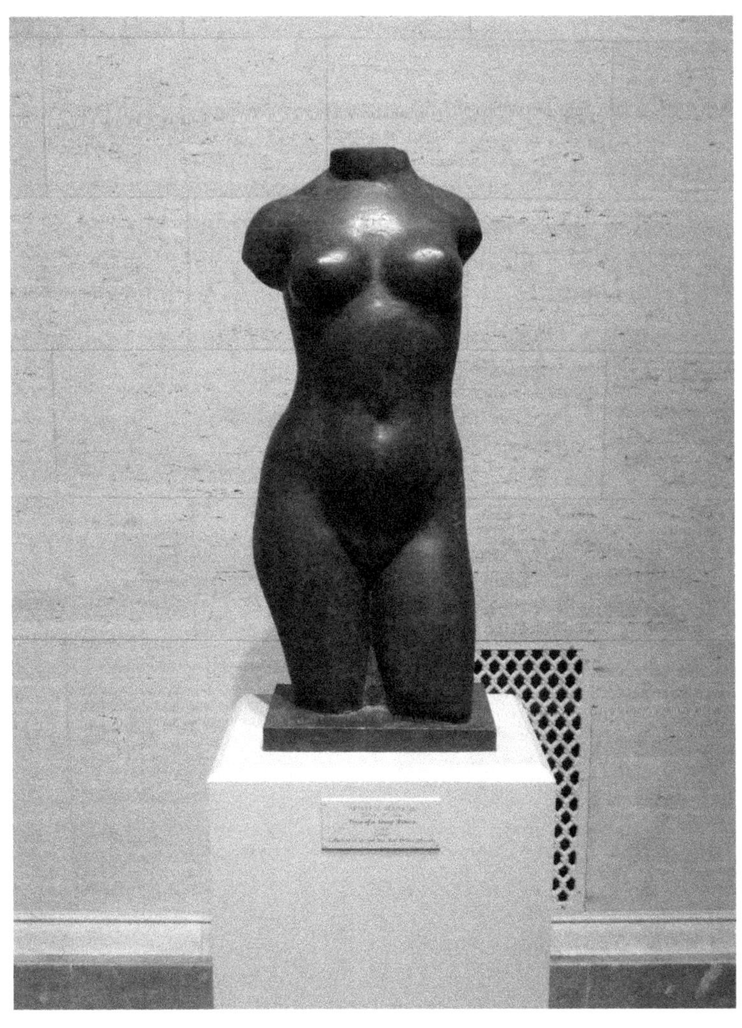

ANIMA

In the Jungian system, Beatrice, Laura, Cleopatra, Isolde, Eurydice, Ariadne and all those women of myth, poetry and legend, are incarnations of the *anima,* which is, as Carl Jung explains, something all males possess: '[e]very man carries with him the eternal image of woman, not the image of this or that particular woman, but a definitive feminine image.'[1] The *anima* is 'a personification of the unconscious in a man, which appears as a woman or a goddess in dreams, visions and creative fantasies', write Emma Jung and Marie-Louise von Franz, glossing Jung's *anima* concept.[2]

Male painters throughout history have depicted their version of the *anima,* it seems. Each (male) painter has a version of the 'inner feminine figure', as Carl Jung calls it.[3] For painters, this idealized *anima* figure seems to be another manifestation of that obscure object of desire, the eroticized woman, a mirror for male lust. The equation is: the more sublime and voluptuous the woman is painted, the more sublime and voluptuous is the artist's desire. The artist's model, then, can be seen as a Jungian *anima,* heavily eroticized, a Lacanian phallic mirror.

---

1 C. Jung: *The Development of Personality,* vol. 17, Routledge, 1954, 198; Marie-Louise von Franz: *The Psychological Meaning of Redemption Motifs in Fairy Tales,* Inner City Books, Toronto 1980, 39f

2 Emma Jung & Marie-Louise von Franz: *The Grail Legend, tr.* Andrea Dykes, Sigo Press, Boston, Mass., 1980, 64

3 C. Jung: *Memories, Dreams, Reflections,* Collins 1967, 210-1

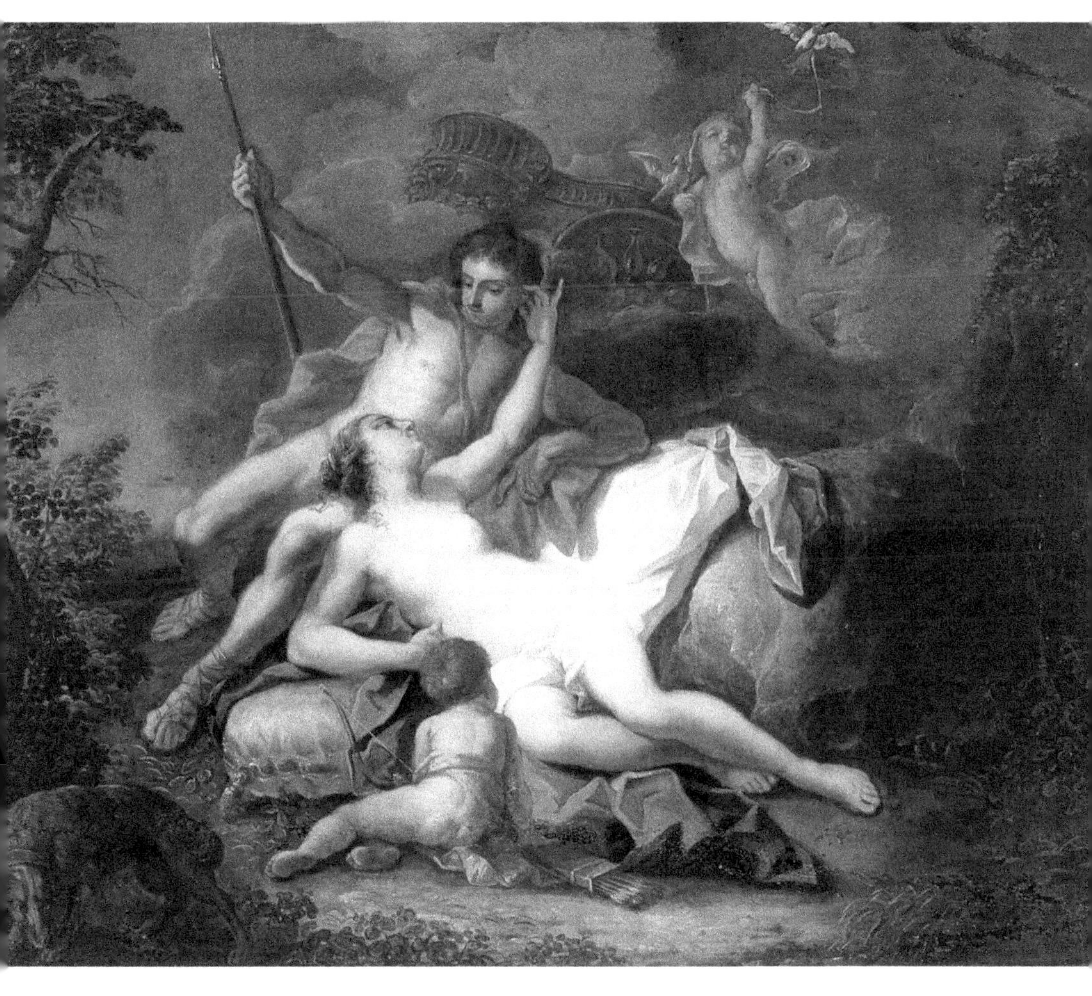

Louis de Silvestre (circle of), Venus and Adonis, 18th century.

ARTISTS AND MODELS

Seen in Lacanian theory, the female model becomes the 'obscure object of desire' feared and desired, ever unreachable, the manifestation of eternal loss.[1] We can see elements of the Lacanian lack, desire, repression, mirror stage, Symbolic Order and œdipal anxiety in the modern artists who create specifically erotic images. In the output of artists such as Pierre Renoir, Henri Matisse, Jules Pascin, Aristide Maillol, Auguste Rodin, Gustav Klimt, Amedeo Modigliani and Pablo Picasso, one finds loss, desire, repression and anxiety quite clearly. The art they produced is fiercely heterosexual, glorifying women, even as, in some cases (Picasso) the paintings seem to denigrate women. Renoir, in paintings such as *Bather Arranging Her Hair*, Pascin in *The Prodigal Son*, and Lawrence Alma-Tadema in *In the Tepidarium*, produced works that exalt women as sexual objects. The soft flesh is available but also distinctly not available; there is acres of skin, especially in Pascin's painting, but it is not touchable either.[2] These nude paintings remain chimeras, never to be possessed, always to be yearned for. As Nicolas Poussin wrote of painting: '[p]ainting is nothing but an imitation of human actions, which alone are, properly speaking, inimitable'.[3] Poussin recognizes that painting is always an imitation, a mirror; the real thing can never be possessed in art. It is the same in erotic art - indeed, it is most dramatically expressed in erotic art - this paradoxical fear and desire, this simultaneous desire and loss, this ambiguous conflict between possession and dispossession.

---

1 Toril Moi: *Sexual Textual Politics*, 99f; Anika Lemaire: *Jacques Lacan*, Routledge & Kegan Paul 1977; Elizabeth Wright: *Psychoanalytic Criticism*, Methuen 1984

2 Pierre Renoir: *Bather Arranging Her Hair*, 1885, canvas, 92 x 73cm, Sterling and Francis Clark Institute, Williamstown, Mass.; Lawrence Alma-Tadema: *In the Tepidarium*, 1881, wood, 24 x 33cm, Lady Lever Art Gallery, Port Sunlight; Jules Pascin: *The Prodigal Son*, 1928, oil on board, 15 x 18in, private collection, Switzerland

3 In R. Goldwater, 154.

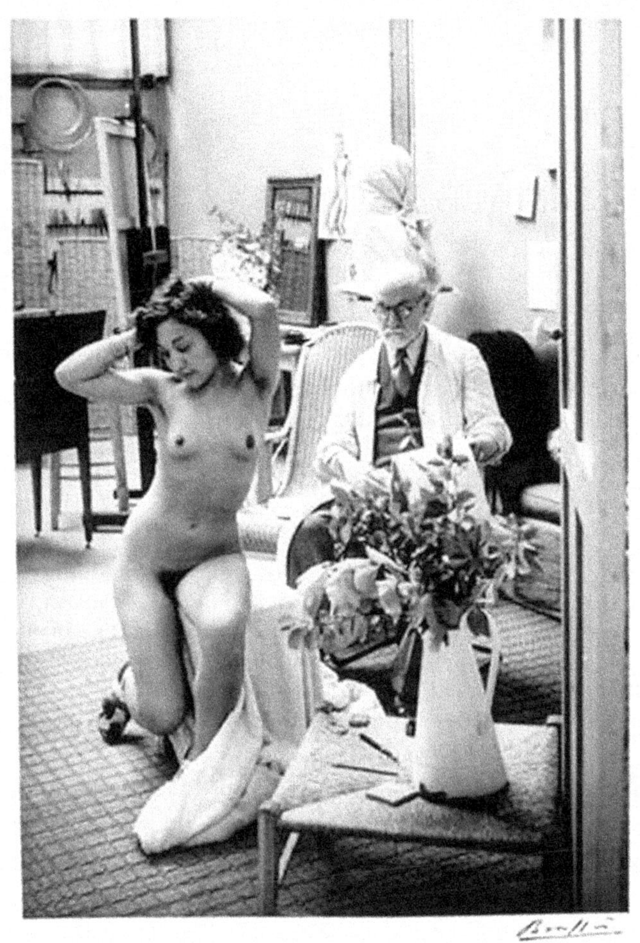

Brassai's photographs of artists and models,
including Henri Matisse (above).

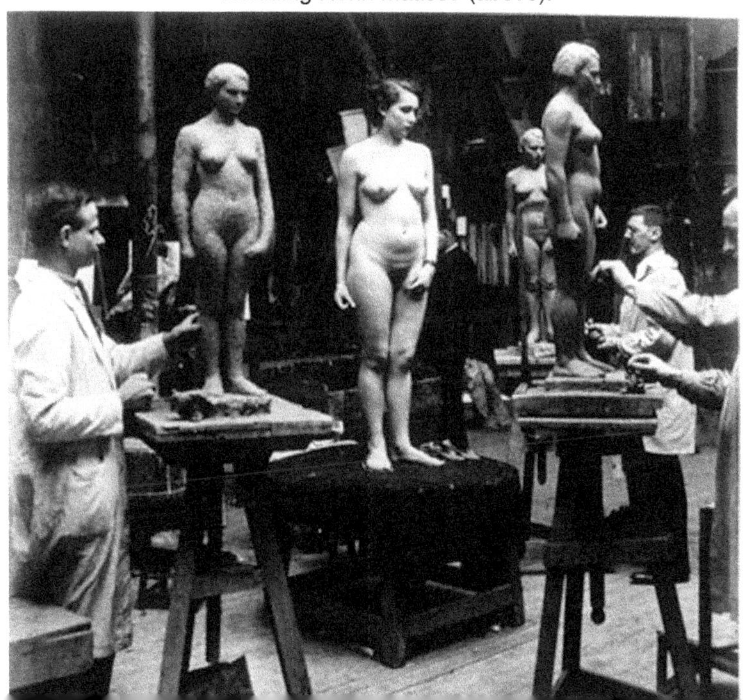

THE FEMALE NUDE - 20TH CENTURY

The female nude is the apotheosis of 'high art', yet it constantly wavers around the borderline between art and pornography. The female nude is erotic *and* obscene, in the male system, both desired and loathed, both representable and un-representable.

Lynda Nead writes in *The Female Nude* (71):

> The body is, therefore, central in the formation of individual identity and is the site of the subject's desires and fantasies, actions and behaviour. Once one rejects the perception of the body as a biologically determined and pre-cultural given and moves towards the conception of 'embodied' subjects, the way is opened for feminist interventions within the definition of the female body.

The 18th century developed the portrayals of nudes in painting of the post-Renaissance period, particularly linked to the emerging academies and art schools. This rise in nude painting reflected the social changes of the 18th century, which exploded in the 19th century with a huge increase in population, the rise of mercantile capitalism, the increase in prostitution, the decline of authoritarian institutions such as organized religion, and the increasing dependence on technology,

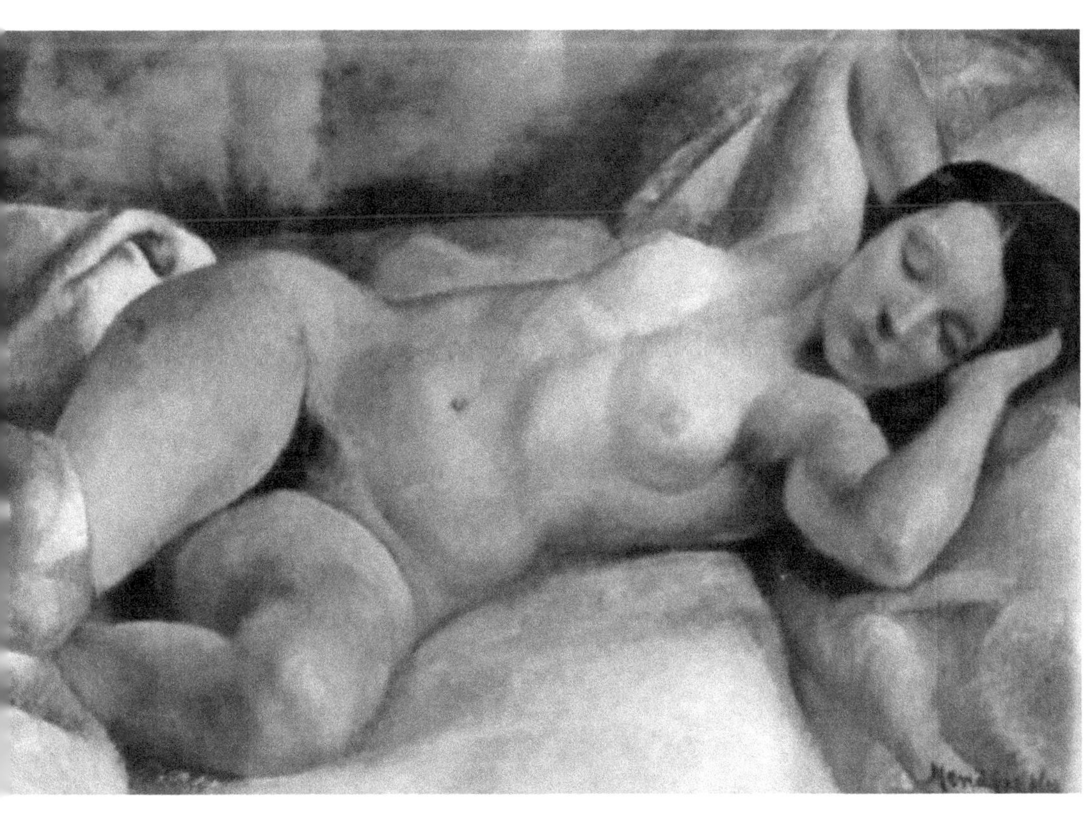

Maurice Medjinsky, Kiki, 1921

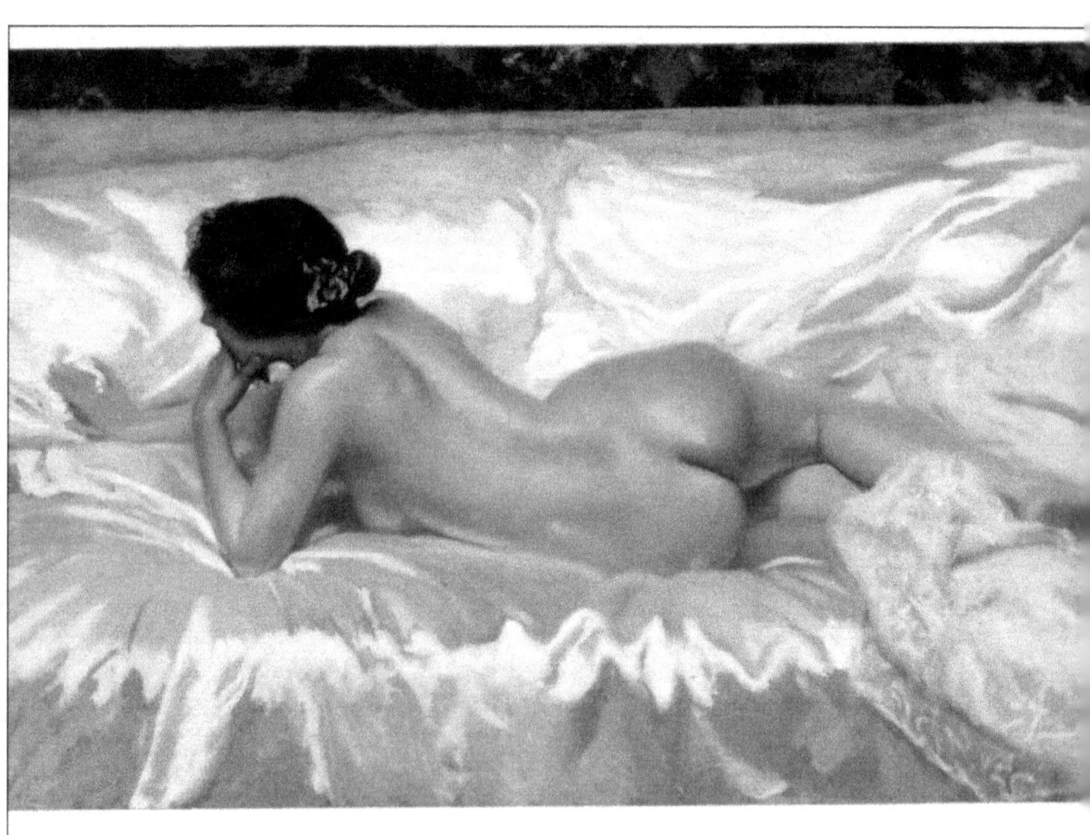

Joaquin Sorolla, Female Nude, 1902

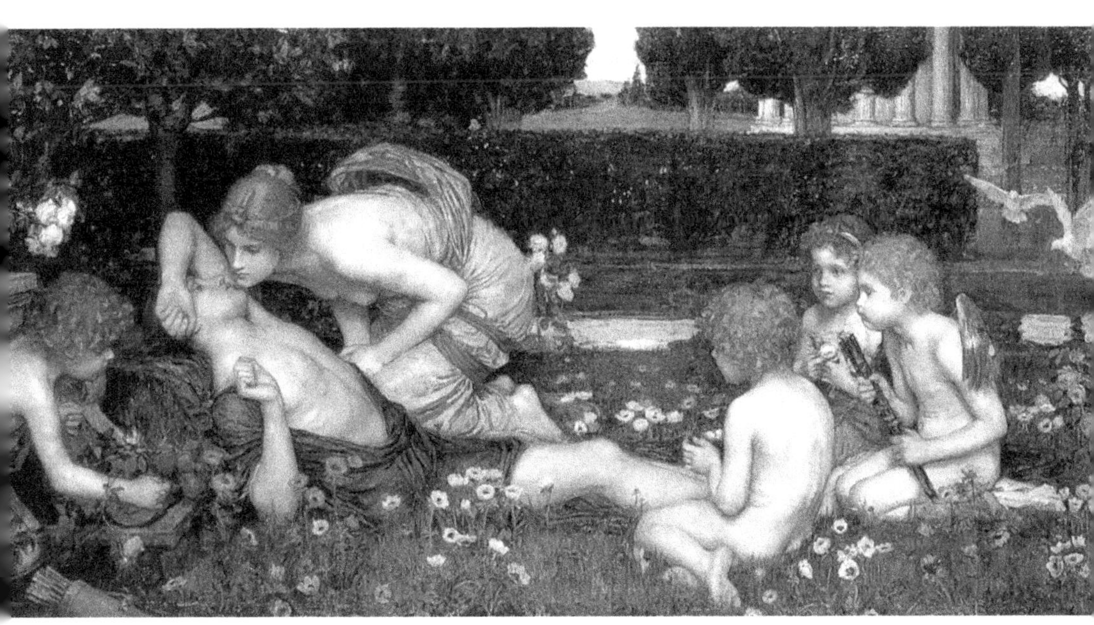

John William Waterhouse, The Awakening of Adonis, 1899

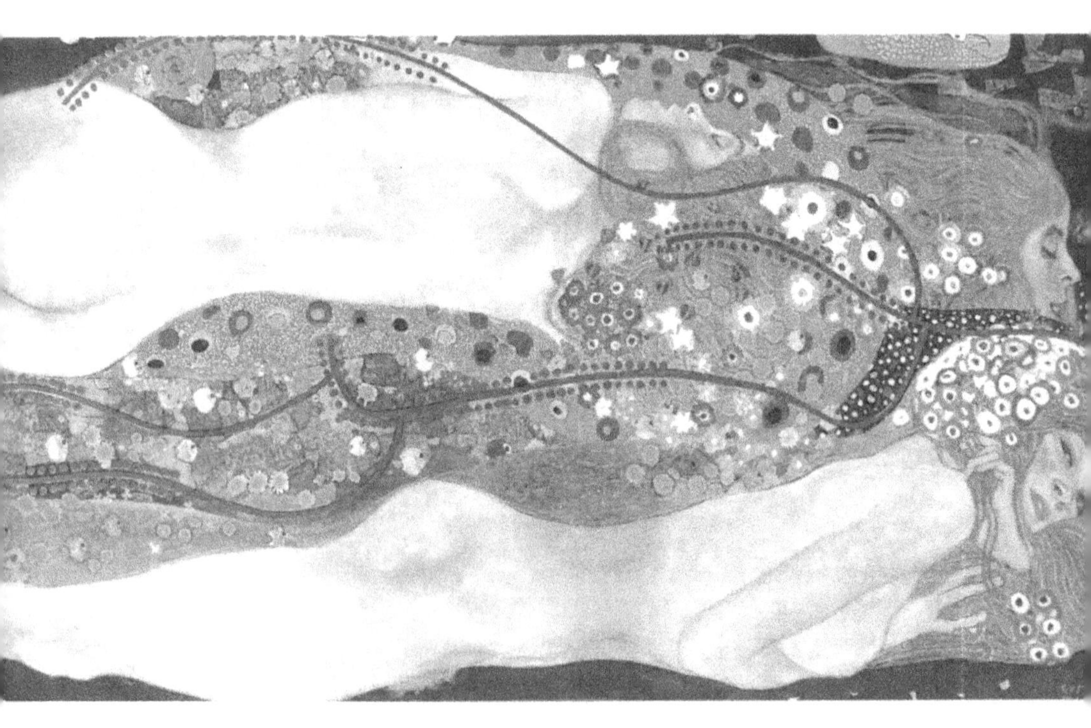

Gustav Klimt

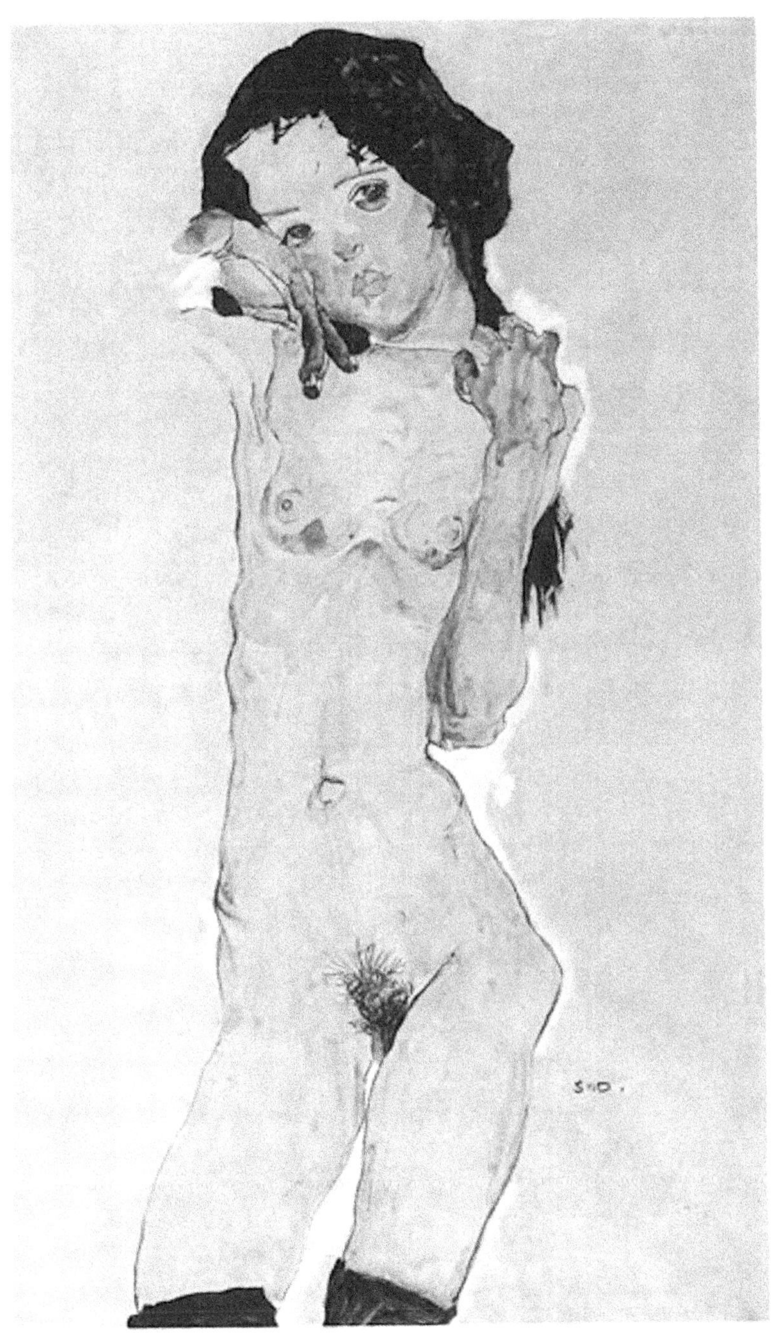

Egon Schiele, Black Haired Nude Woman, Standing, 1910, Vienna

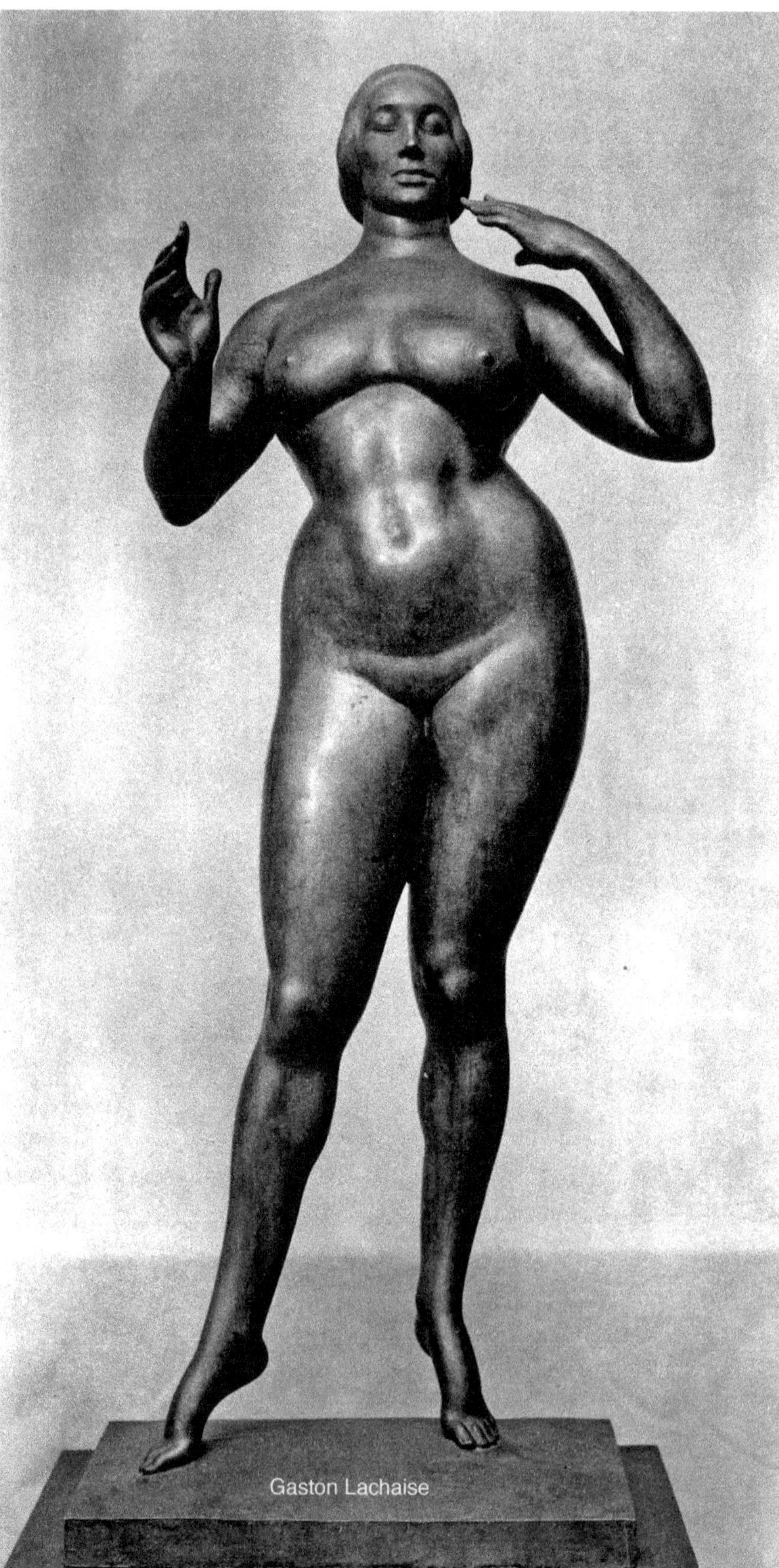

Gaston Lachaise

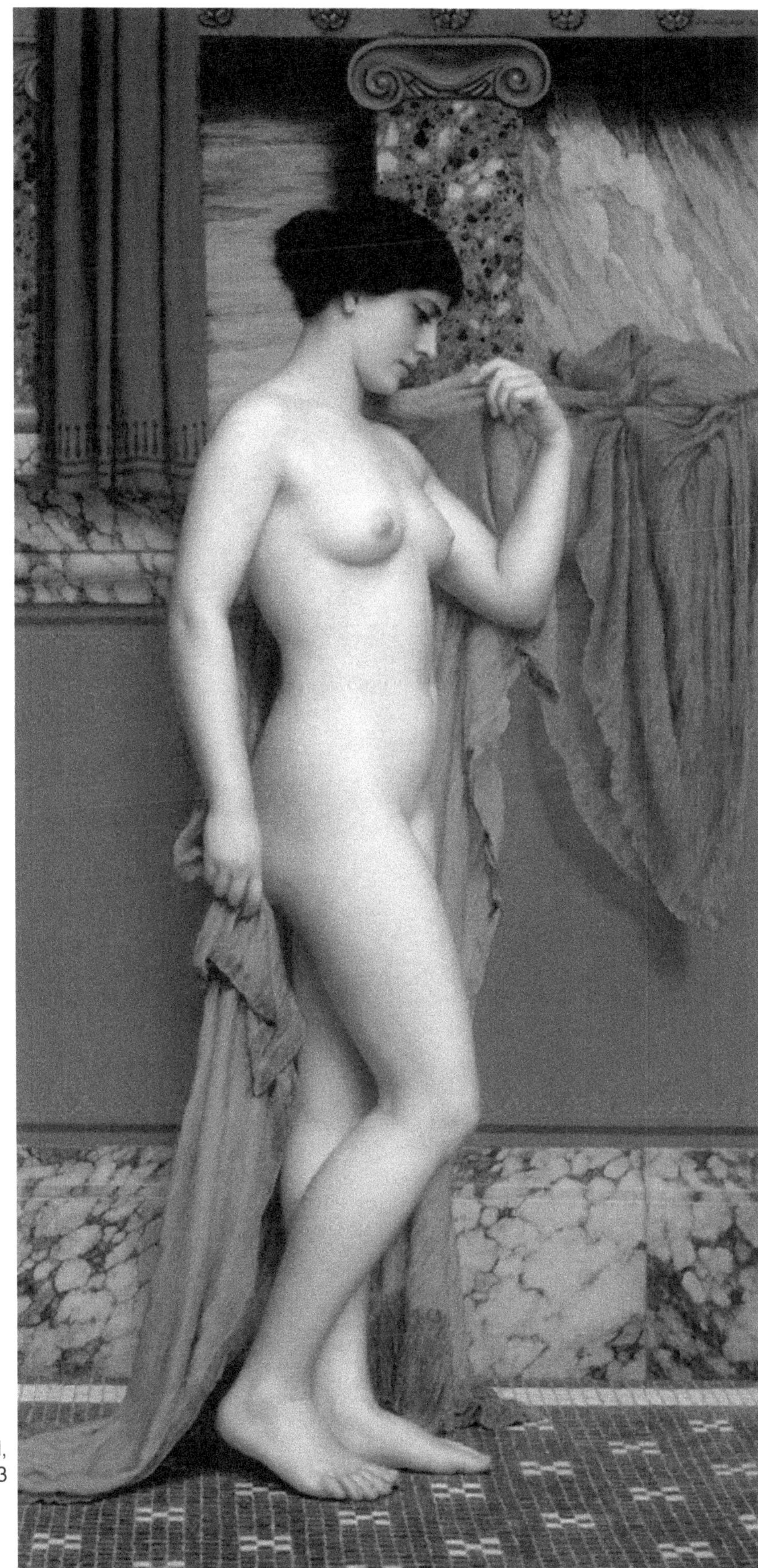

ın William Godward,
he Tepidarium, 1913

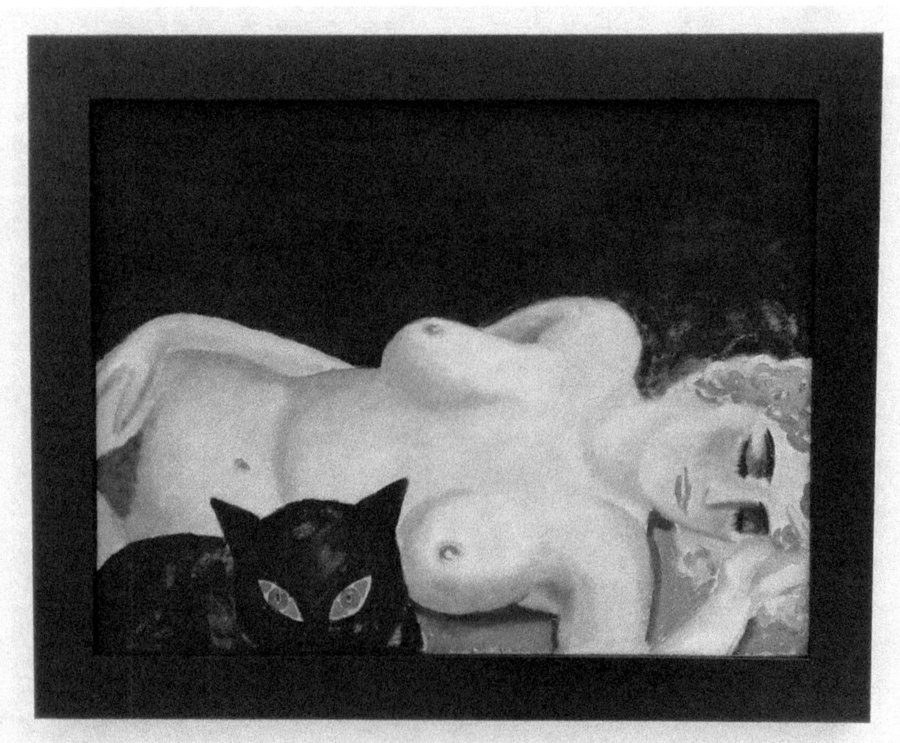

Frans Masereel, Nude With Black Cat, 1920, Heidelberg

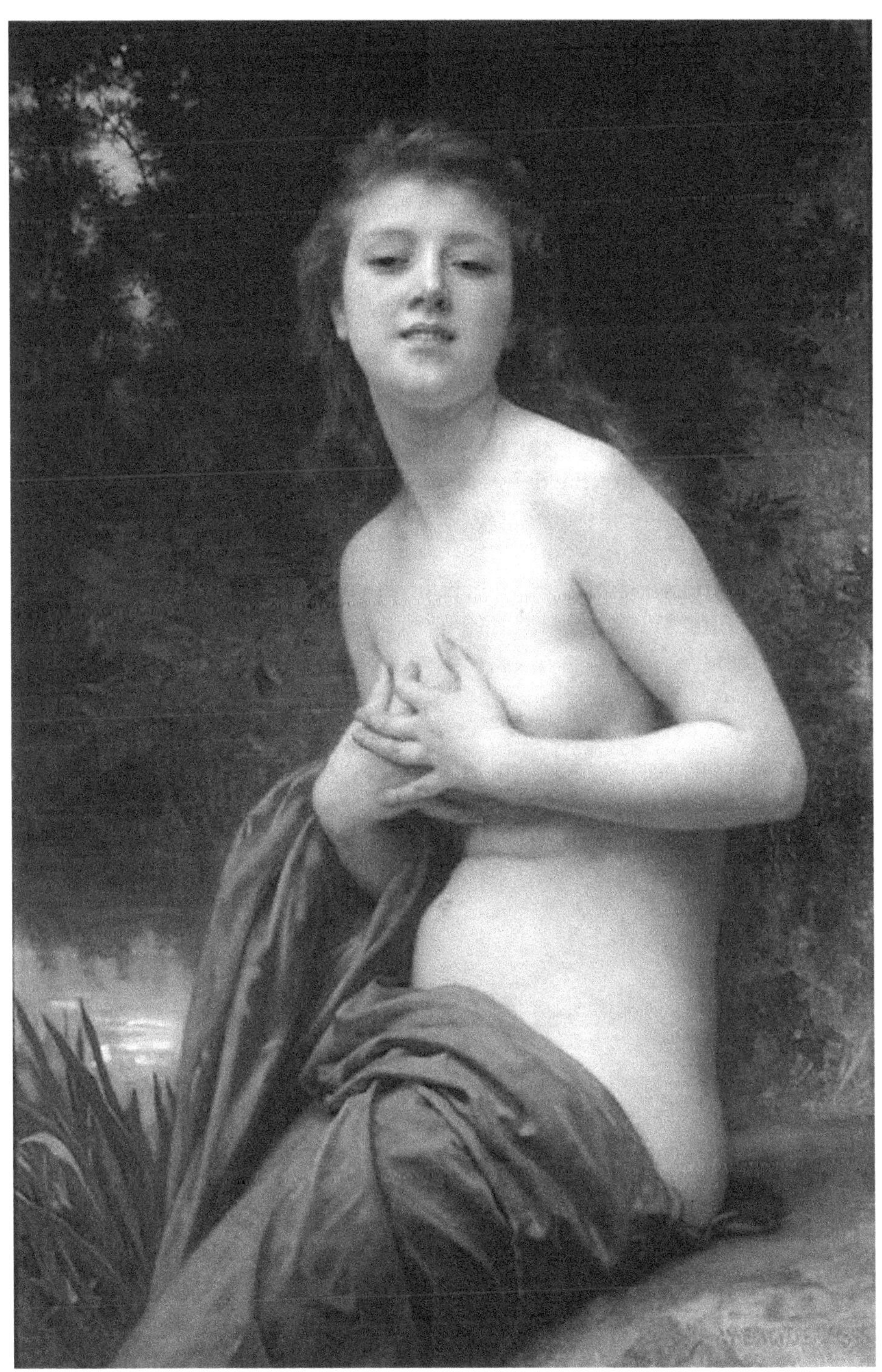

William Bouguereau, Spring Breeze, 1895

MERMAIDS

There is deep sexism in the Judæo-Christian Fall, for it is the woman who picks the apple and offers it to Adam. From the beginning, in the Judæo-Christian tradition, it is the woman who makes men 'fall'. In some depictions, the sexism is doubled, by having the serpent shown as a snake-woman - the torso of a woman, the legs, like those of a mermaid, as in Michelangelo Buonarroti's *Temptation and Expulsion* (1508-12).[1]

The symbol of the half-woman/ half-fish, still in use today,[2] is another manifestation of patriarchal people's projection of their sexual fears onto women, so that what lies 'below the waist' is feared and objectified as something slimy and fishlike, something dark, from the depths of the unconscious, which is the sea. The mermaid appears sculpted on mediæval churches, some of the mermaids expose their genitals, like the *sheila-na-gig* figure, which again fuses sacred and profane, spiritual and sexual, desire and fear.[3] The mermaid appears in much of Victorian art, as an image of men's ambivalent views of female sexuality - in E.M. Hale's *Mermaid's Rock* (1894), for instance, or John William Waterhouse's Pre-Raphaelite *A Mermaid* (1901).[4]

1 Michelangelo: *Temptation and Expulsion*, 1508-12, fresco, Sistine Chapel, Vatican, Rome
2 See the depiction of the Mary Magdalene in the wilderness sequence of Universal's film *The Last Temptation of Christ* (1988, USA)
3 See Anthony Weir & James Jerman: *Images of Lust: Sexual Carvings on Mediæval Churches*, B. T. Batsford, 1986, 48ff
4 John William Waterhouse: *A Mermaid*, 1901, 38.5 x 36.3in, Royal Academy of Arts, London; Edward Matthew Hale: *Mermaid's Rock*, 1894, 48 x 78in, City Art Gallery, Leeds

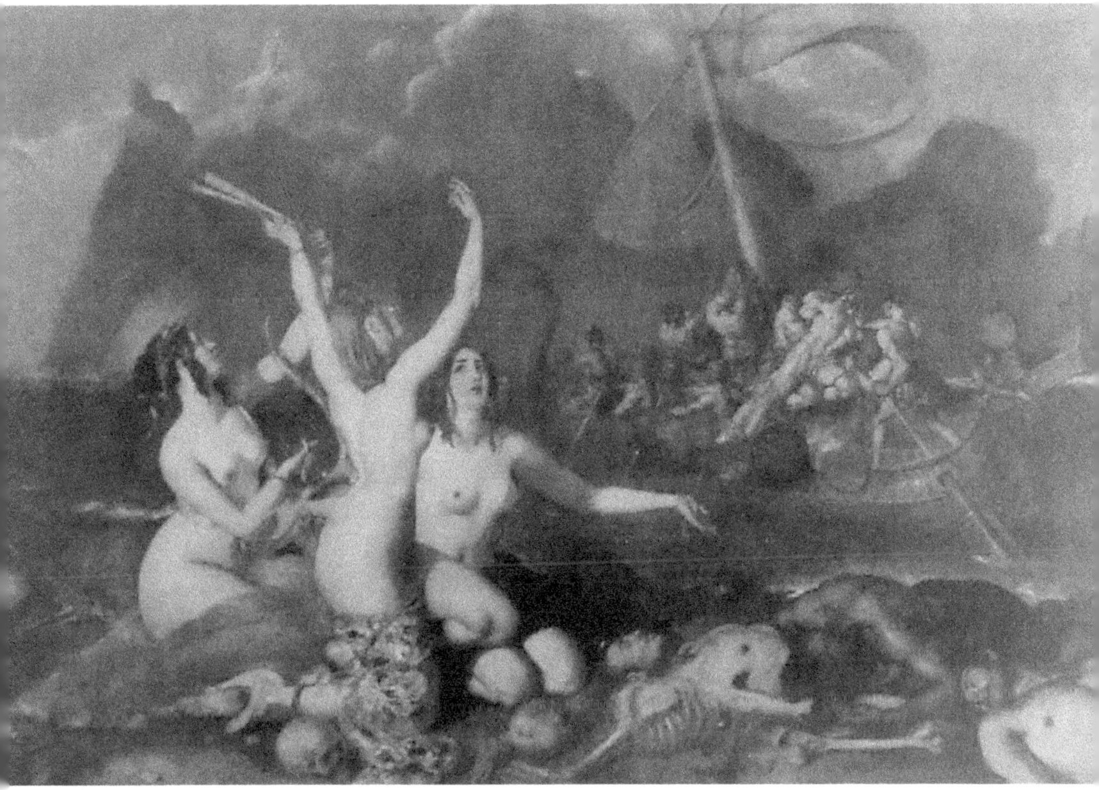

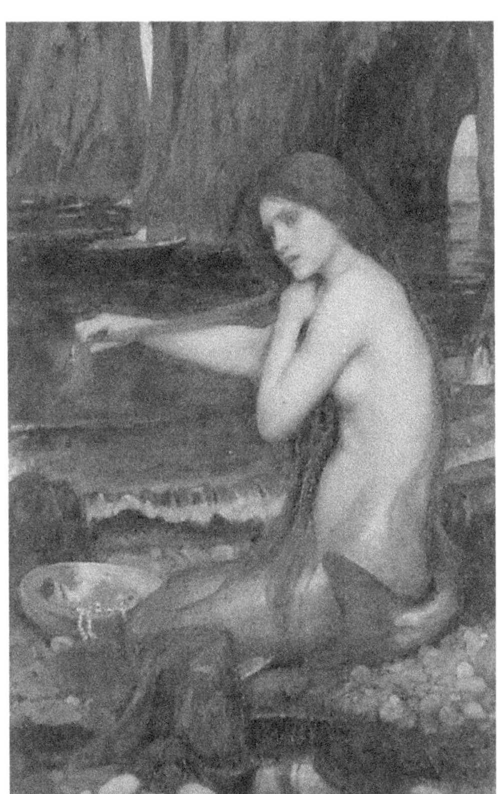

A favourite theme in 19th century painting: sex, death, nudity and the sea.
William Etty's The Sirens and Ulysses, 1837, Manchester. above.

J.W. Waterhouse,
A Mermaid, 1901, Royal Academy, London, below.

LEDA AND THE SWAN

Like Michelangelo Buonarroti, Leonardo da Vinci produced an erotic version of *Leda and the Swan*. Both Michelangelo's and Leonardo's images are lost. We know both, though, because they were copied.[1] Michelangelo's picture is explicitly erotic: the huge swan lies between the deity's legs, the feathers of his wing over her vulva, a touch that expresses male 'possession' of the woman's sexuality.

Leonardo da Vinci made his *Leda and the Swan* as erotica is made; at the request of a (male) client: 'I executed the painting... for a lover. He wished to see the features of his goddess mirrored so that he might kiss them without arousing suspicion', Leonardo wrote.[2] In Antoine Coypel's (?) picture of *Leda and the Swan*, Jupiter's genitals are again the focus of the image, as the woman sits astride his legs.[3]

1 After Michelangelo: *Leda and the Swan*, 16th century, Royal Academy, London
2 quoted in Peter Webb, 112
3 Antoine Coypel (?): *Jupiter with Leda and the Swan*, from *Histoire Universelle*, c. 1750, British Museum

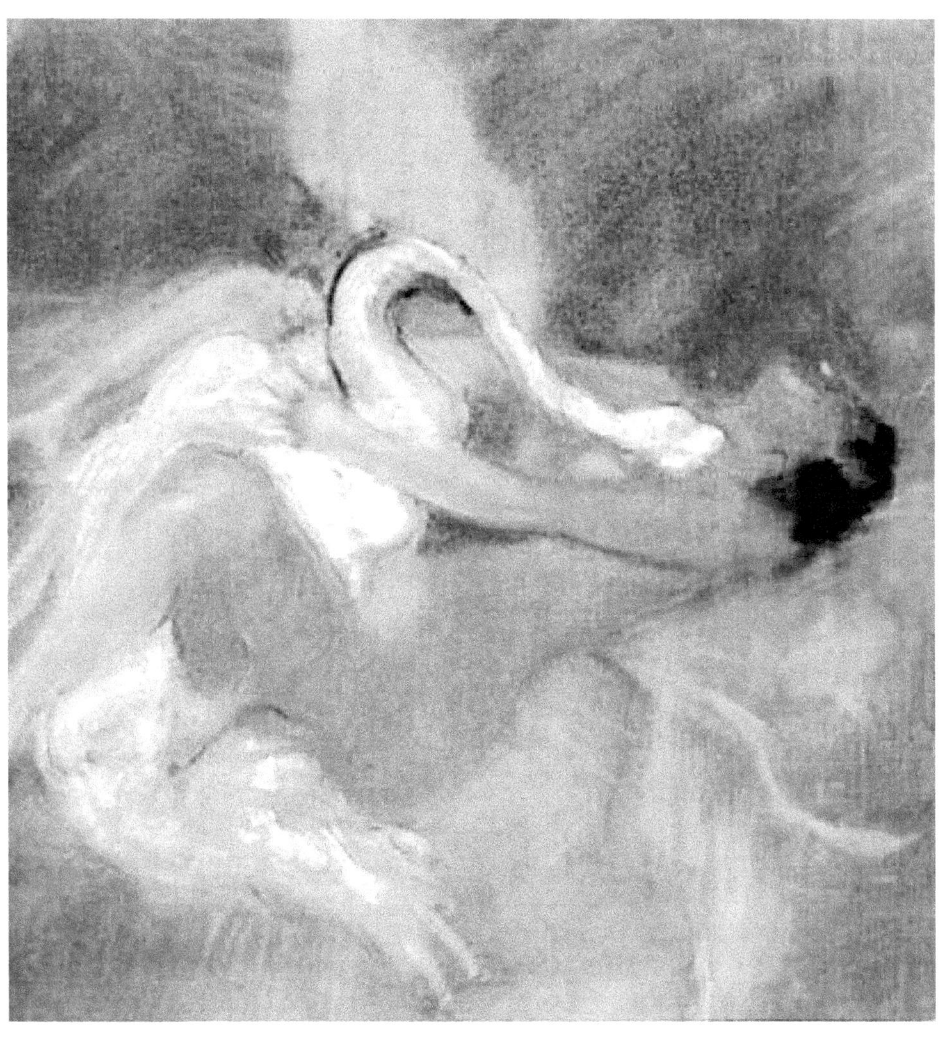

Giovanni Boldoni (1842-1931), Leda and the Swan

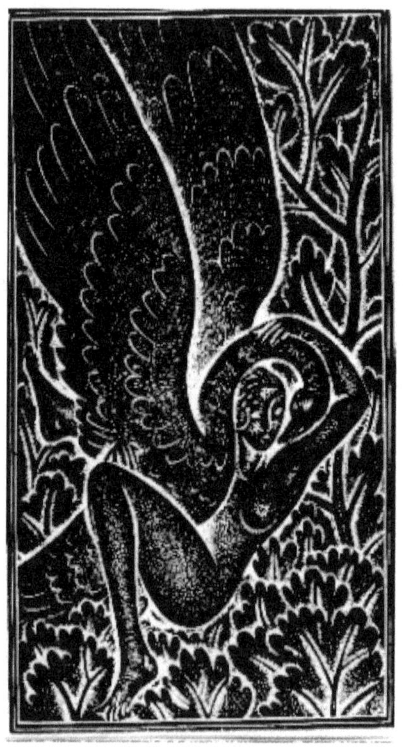

Eric Gill, Leda Loved, 1931

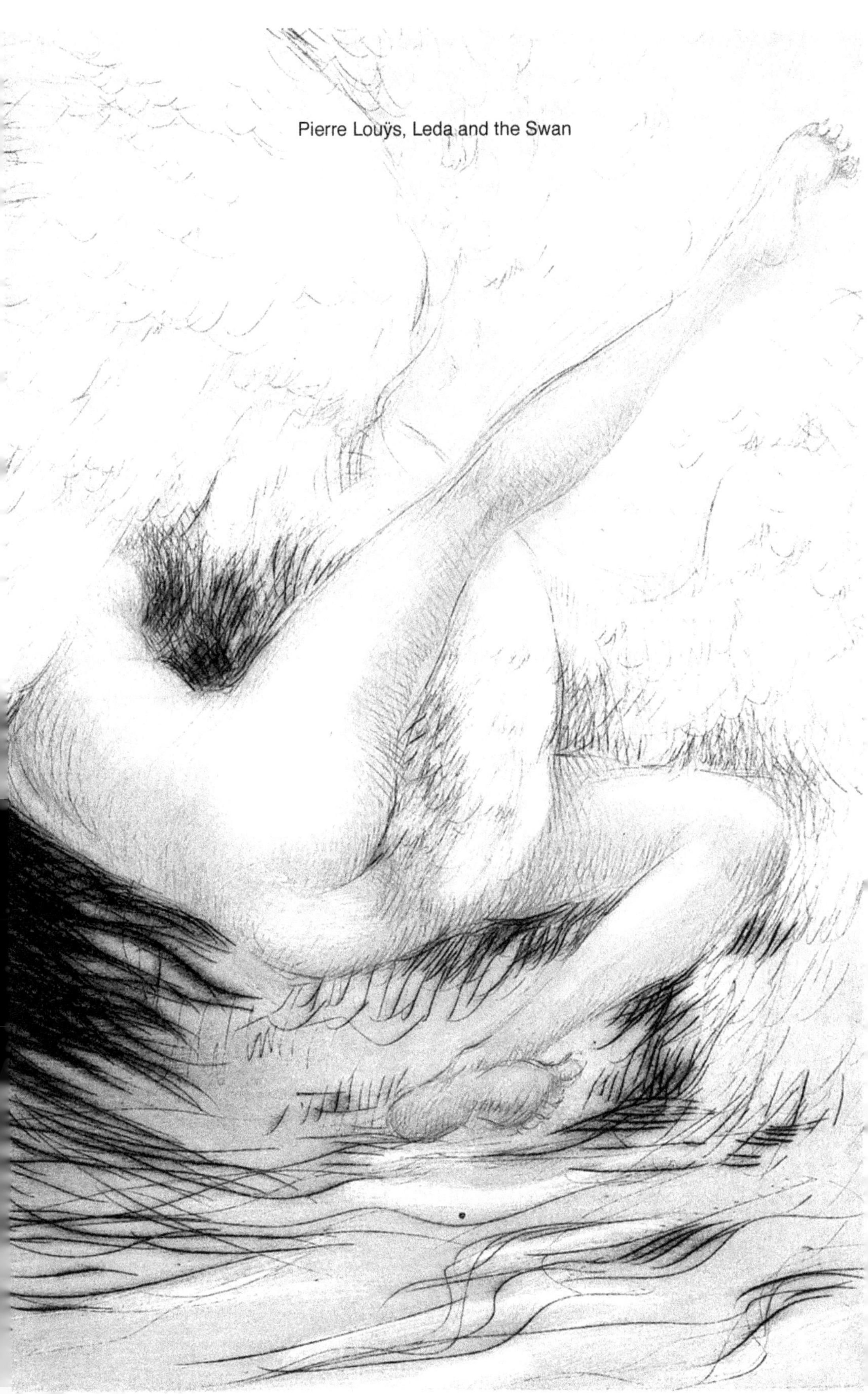

Pierre Louÿs, Leda and the Swan

CHRISTIANITY AND PORNOGRAPHY

Pornography subverts the laws of Christianity, but it is based on the same laws. Porn comes out of the same world, the same politics, the same culture, as Christianity. Not only is there much of Christianity in pornography, there is much of pornography in Christianity. For instance, Christian history is a catalogue of sadomasochistic events and acts, some really horrific scenes of torture and oppression. More acts of terror have been carried out in the name of God than in the name of 'freedom' or 'truth' or 'honour'.

Painters throughout Western history have reflected the violent acts of Christianity, portraying them as heroic gestures: Sandro Botticelli painted the massacre of the Innocents; Nicolas Poussin depicted St Erasmus having his entrails pulled out by a winch, many painters portrayed St Sebastian full of arrows (Andrea Mantegna, Antonella da Messina, Pietro Perugino, Henrick Terbruggen, and, more recently, Eric Gill and Egon Schiele), Francisco de Zurbarán painted a saint being crucified upside down (1629).[1]

1 Nicolas Poussin: *The Martyrdom of St Erasmus*, 1628, Pinacoteca Vaticana, Vatican, Rome; Hendrick Terbrugghen: *St Sebastian Tended by St Irene and the Maid*, 1625, Allen Memorial Art Museum, Oberlin College, Oberlin, Ohio; Antonello da Messina: *St Sebastian*, c. 1475, oil on panel, 67.4 x 33.5in, State Picture Gallery, Dresden; Andrea Mantegna: *St Sebastian*, c. 1470, tempera on canvas, 101.2 x 55.8in, Louvre, Paris, Pietro Perugino: *St Sebastian*, c. 1495, panel, 170 x 117cm, Louvre, Paris; Francisco de Zurbarán: *The Apostle Peter Appearing to St Peter Nolasco*, 1629, oil on canvas, 5ft 11 x 7ft 4in, Prado, Madrid

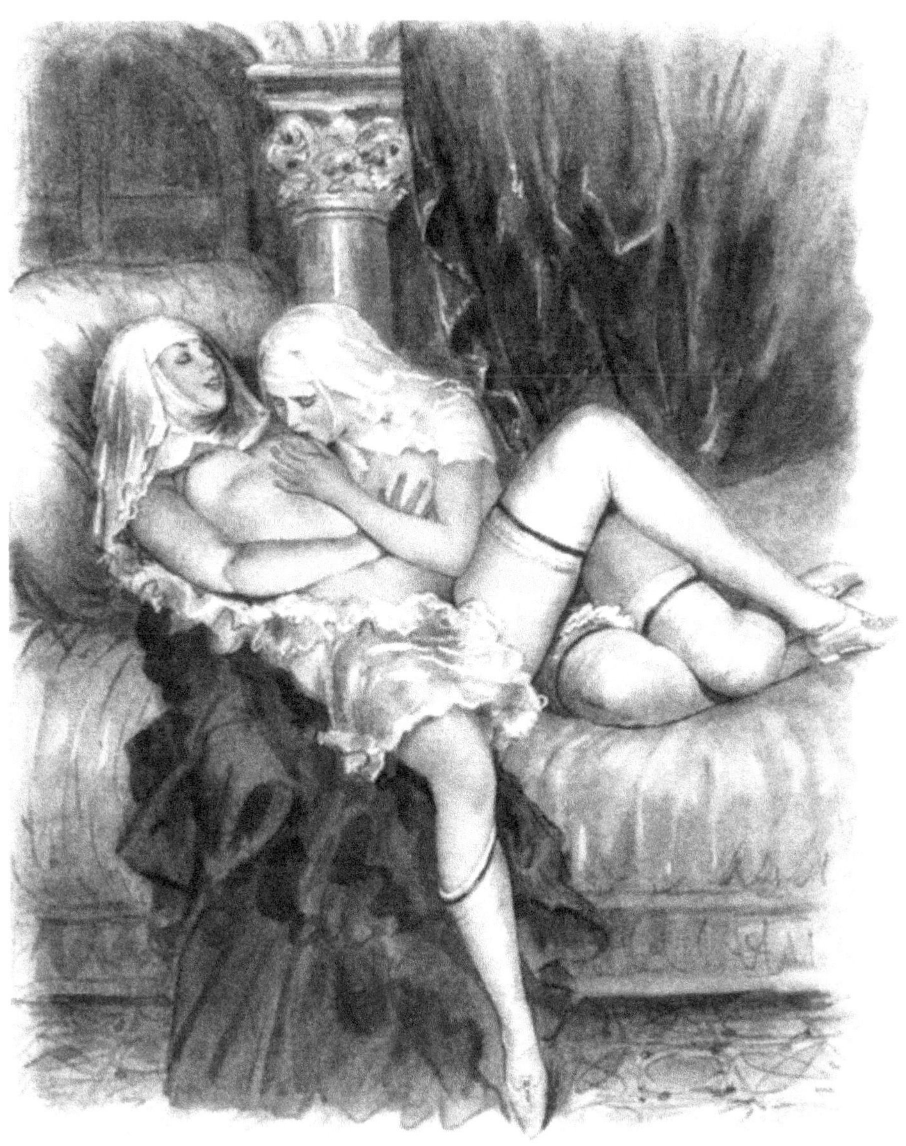

Paul-Émile Bécat,illustration for
Les Ragionamenti by Pietro Arentino (1534)

CHRISTIANITY AND PORNOGRAPHY

A good bout of flagellation goes down well with Christians too, and many Renaissance painters painted Christ being whipped or tortured by the guards, and being crowned with thorns. Examples include Titian's two *Christ Crowned with Thorns* paintings, which make suffering a sublime, heroic experience,[1] or the ritualized whipping in Piero della Francesca's *The Flagellation of Christ*, a much-discussed Renaissance painting, or Luca Signorelli's more staid approach to the torture.[2]

Not to be out-done, Vittore Carpaccio painted a bizarre picture: the crucified Jesus sitting on a throne, dead, with his eyes closed, with two semi-naked old men sitting on either side of him. The title is *Meditation On the Passion of Christ*.[3] There's the Saviour, looking very dead, on a throne, in a ruined landscape, while two old men sit right next to him and muse upon his death. Bizarre.

Sebastiano del Piombo goes even further: his *The Martyrdom of St Agatha* depicts the saint, nude of course, being tortured by a bunch of men, fully clothed of course.[4] They are applying gigantic metal pliers to her nipples. This is a depiction of sadism (in Christianity the euphemism is 'martyrdom'). Naturally, it seems, this is *sexual* torture, painted in such a straightforward fashion, the woman centre frame, the men surrounding her intent on brutalizing her. The rape, which must follow this torture, is not shown, and it is never shown in Renaissance art, and rarely in Western art. When rape occurs, as it must have done millions of times through the Christian era, men dragging away women are depicted, or Jupiter as a swan screwing Leda, but not the rape itself.

---

1 Titian: *Christ Crowned with Thorns*, mid-1450s, panel, 303 x 180cm, Louvre, Paris; *Christ Crowned with Thorns*, c. 1570-6, canvas, 280 x 181cm, Alte Pinakothek, Munich

2 Piero della Francesca: *The Flagellation of Christ*, c. 1450, panel, 59 x 81.5cm, Ducal, Urbino; Signoreli: *Flagellation*, c. 1480, canvas, 80 x 60cm, Brera, Milan

3 Carpaccio: *Meditation on the Passion of Christ*, c. 1505, panel, 70 x 86cm, Metropolitan Museum of Art, New York

4 Sebastiano del Piombo: *The Martyrdom of St Agatha*, 1520, 31 x 175cm, Pitti Palace, Florence

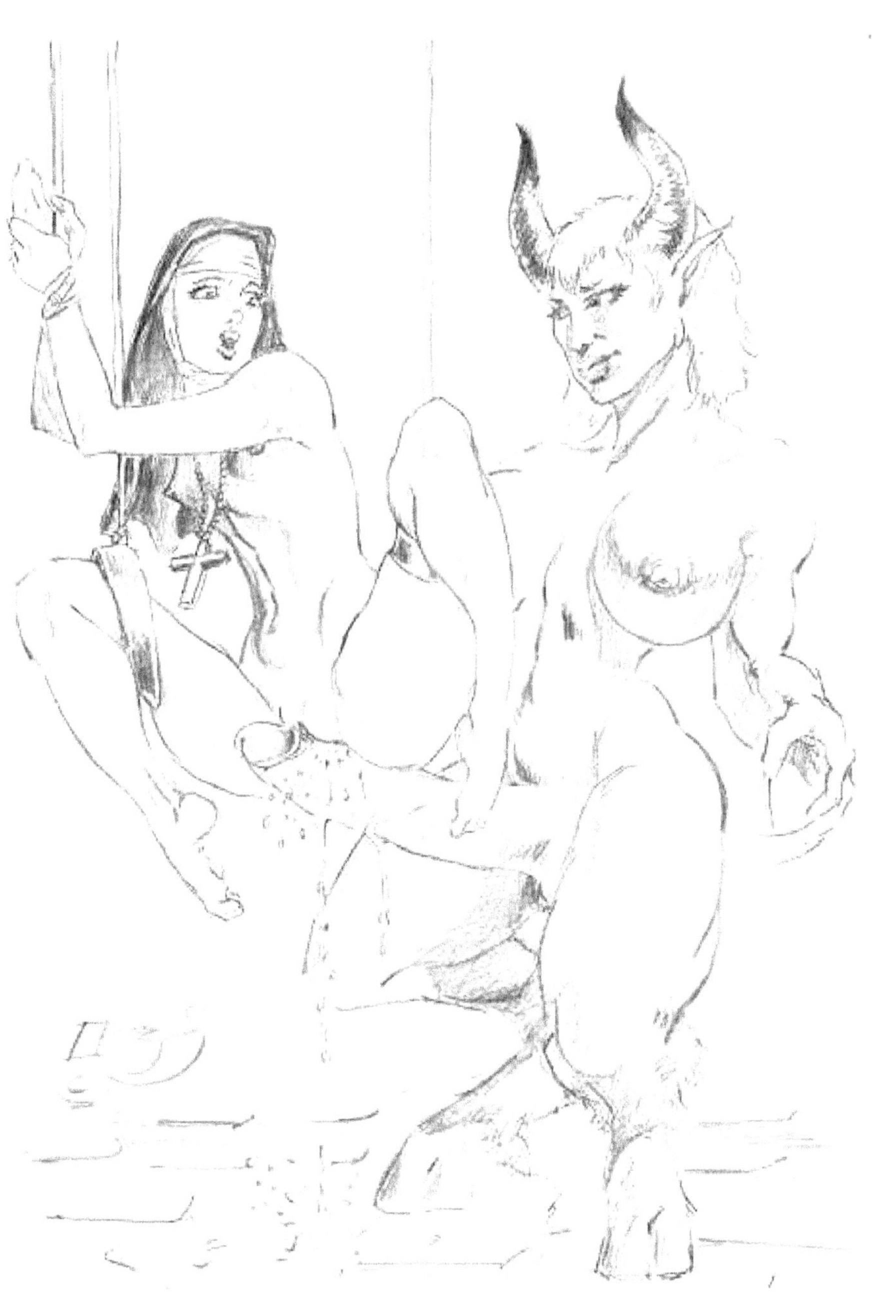

Anonymous, early 20th century

EROTIC ART AND PORNOGRAPHY

The establishment art historical view of erotic art and pornography is that true erotic or high art engenders quiet contemplation, a detached ravishing of the senses, a meditation on Platonic, Aristotlean and Kantian ideas of 'beauty' and æsthetics. 'High art', which is legitimate art, art which justifies itself by its 'genius' or obvious 'greatness', is about distance and disinterested pleasure. The high art nude, in painting or sculpture, in the patriarchal view, justifies its existence by the brilliance of its production, the sumptuousness of its colour and form, the marvel of its human touches, the grandeur of its design, the loftiness of its ambition, the dynamism of its structures, and so on. As that producer of exquisite bodies, French Neo-Classical artist J.A.D. Ingres, wrote:

> There are not two arts, there is only one: it is the one which has as its foundation the beautiful, which is eternal and natural.[1]

1 Ingres, quoted in Goldwater, 216

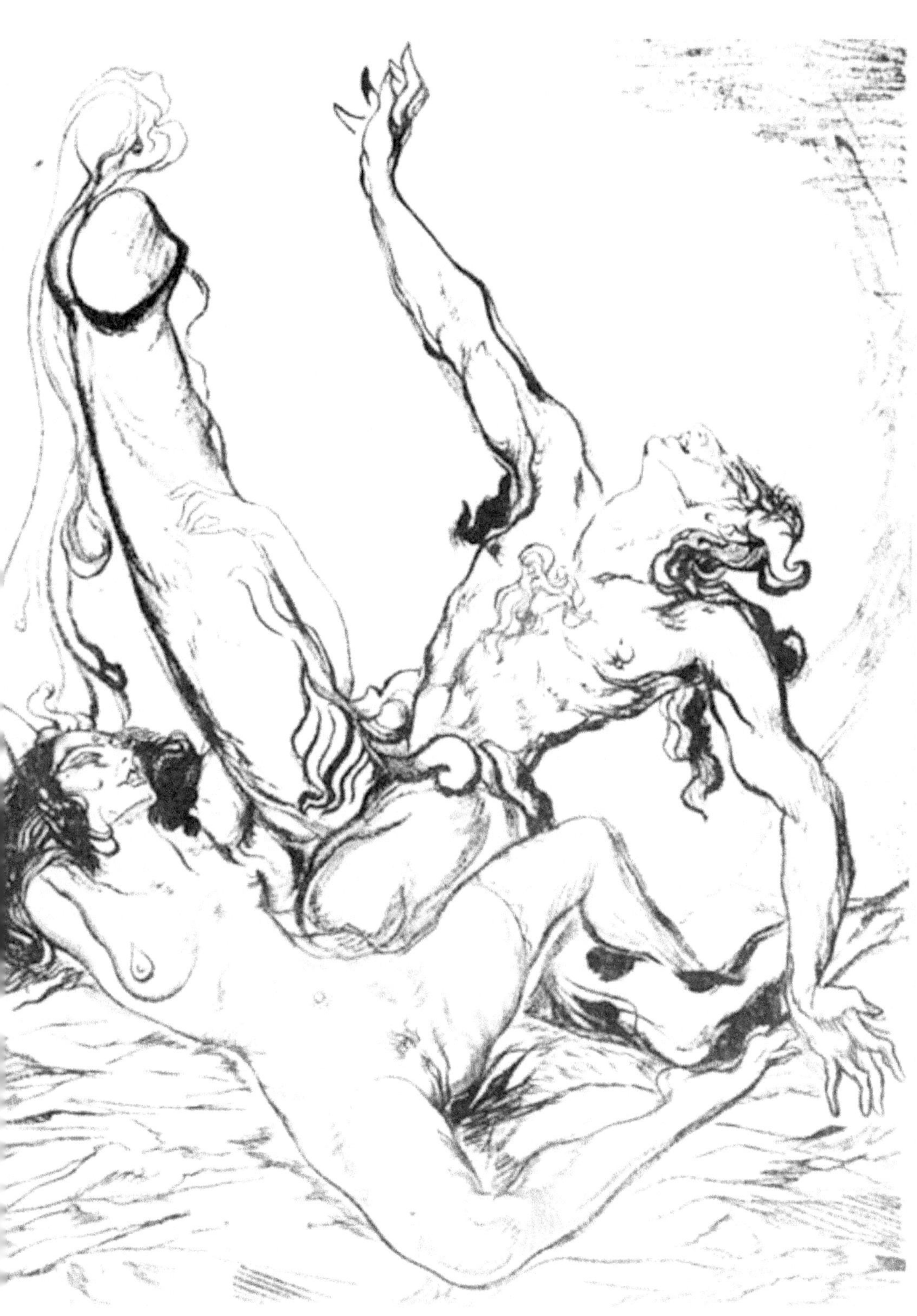

Nicolas Sternberg, from Les orfe vres a la Saint-Éloi (1430), Paris, 1930

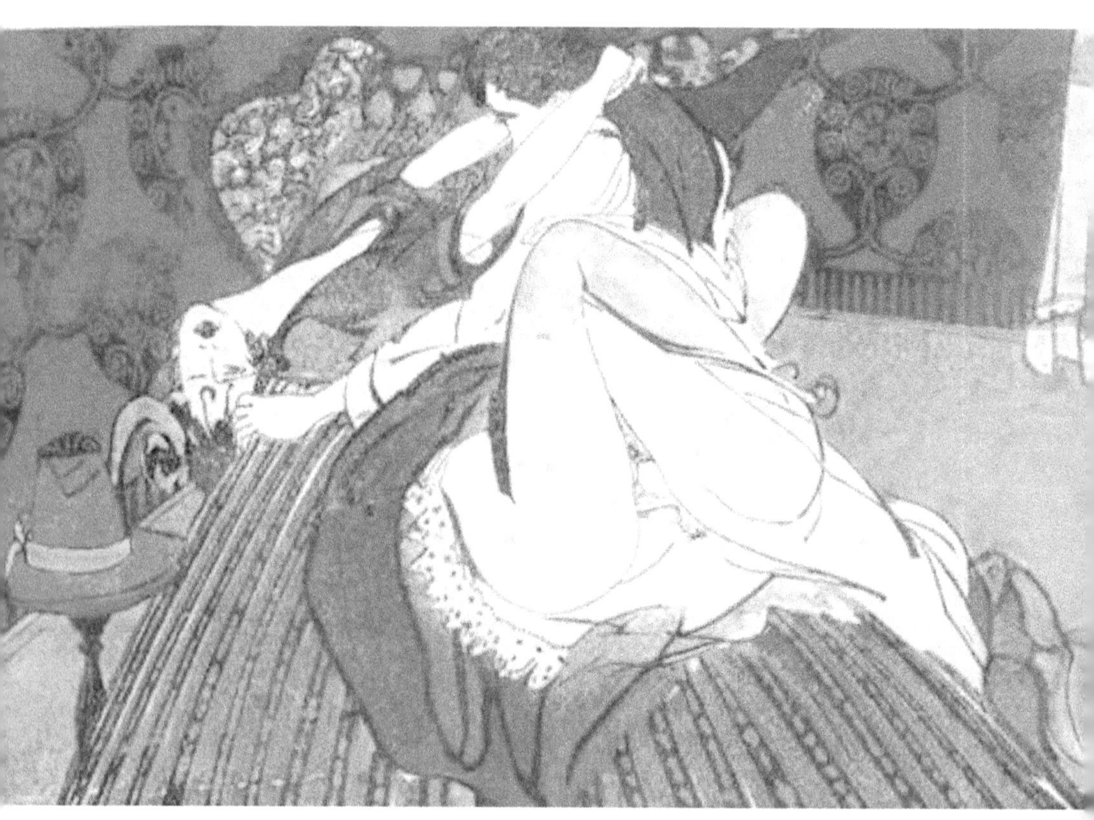

Albert Weisgerber (1878-1915), Passion

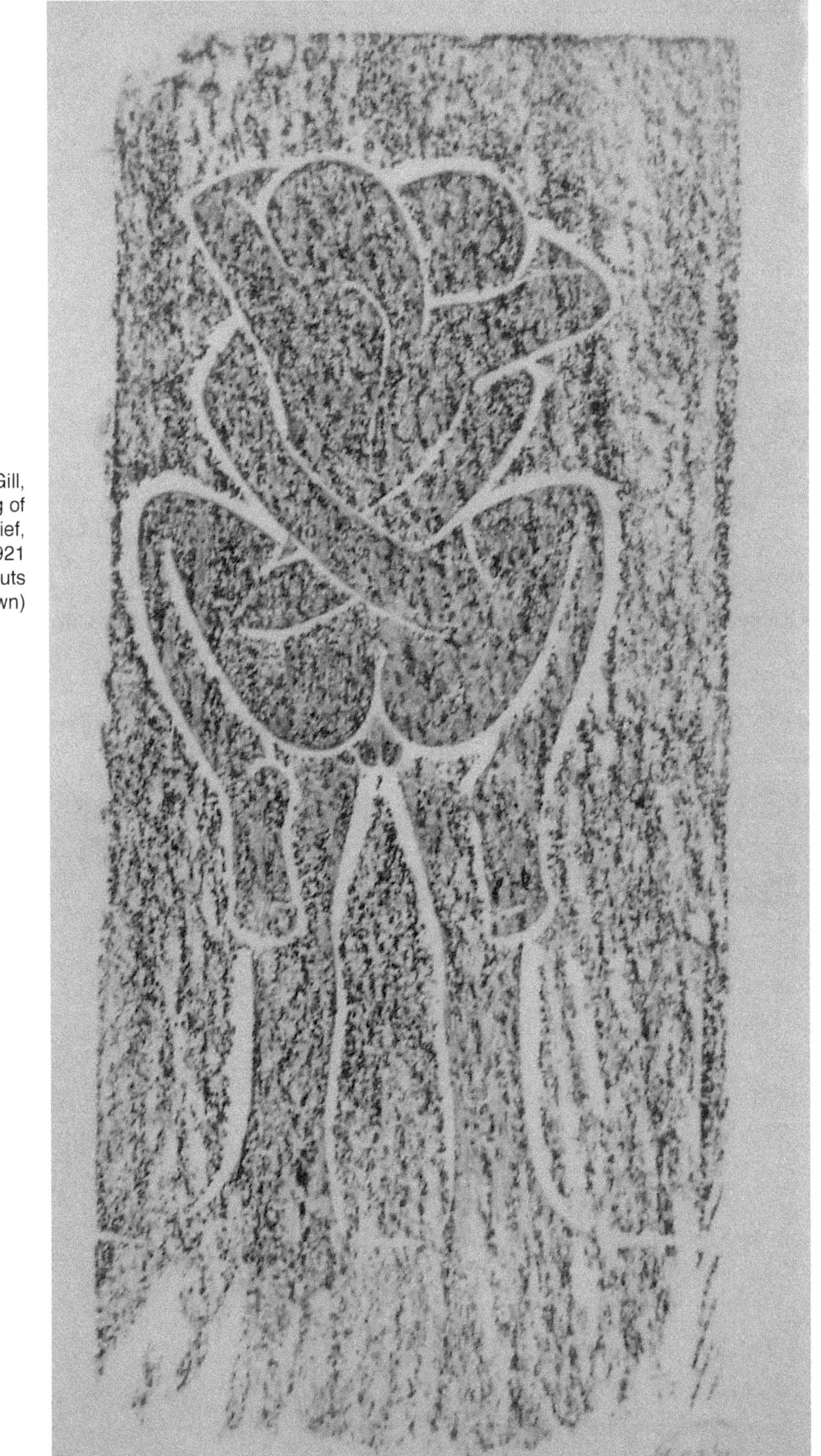

Eric Gill,
rubbing of
Lovers Relief,
1921
(whereabouts
unknown)

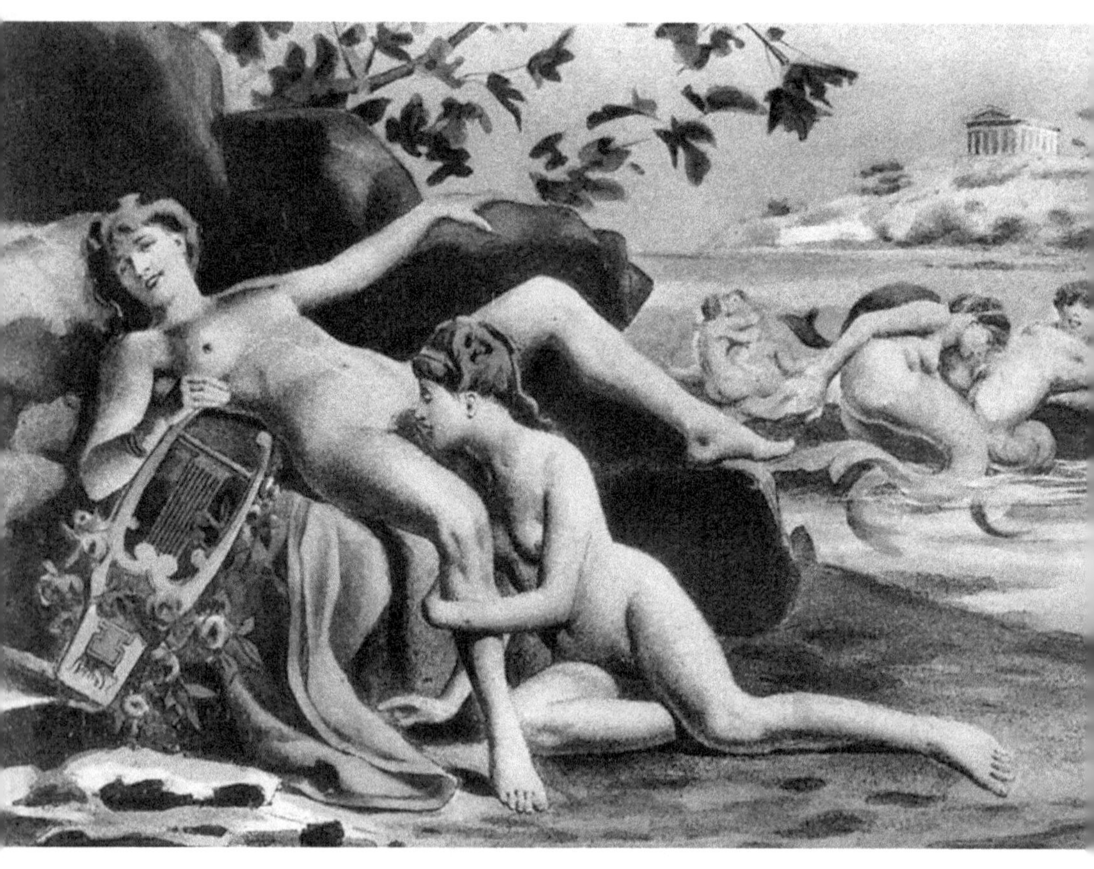

Paul Avril, Sappho and Her Girlfriends

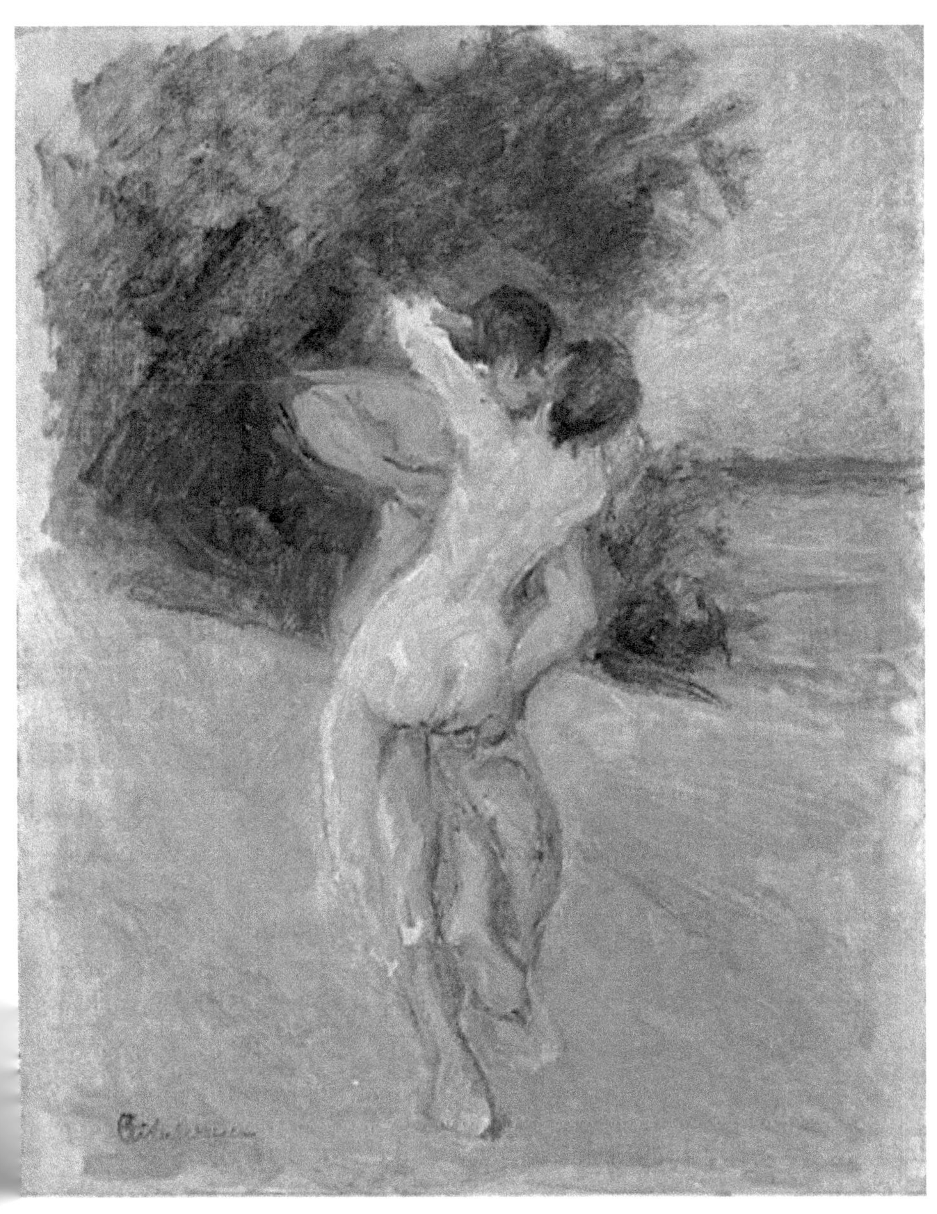

Max Lieberman

FEMME FATALES

The *femme fatale* type neatly melds sex and death, desire and fear, contact and loss, for the (male) artist. She appears in Medusa, Salomé, Delilah, Jezebel, Judith, Lilith, Ninuë (the lover of Merlin), Venus, Helen of Troy, La Belle Dame Sans Merci, and Cleopatra. These female 'types' combined beauty with death, immense power and all manner of sadistic, masochistic and fetishistic fantasies. These are the women who will whip you to death, if you wish, as in Leopold Sacher-Masoch's *Venus in Furs*. Figures such as Cleopatra provided the longed for combination of socio-political, religious sovereignty, wild eroticism, intrigue, magnificent settings and gory love-deaths. As Max Lake informs us:

> The amatory skills of Cleopatra passed into legend while she lived. Apart from the rapid seduction of both Julius Caesar and Mark Antony, she is reported to have fellated one hundred noblemen in a single evening. Her Greek nickname was *meriochane*, 'she who parts wide for a thousand men.'[1]

1 Max Lake: *Scents and Sensuality: The Essence of Excitement*, John Murray 1989, 58

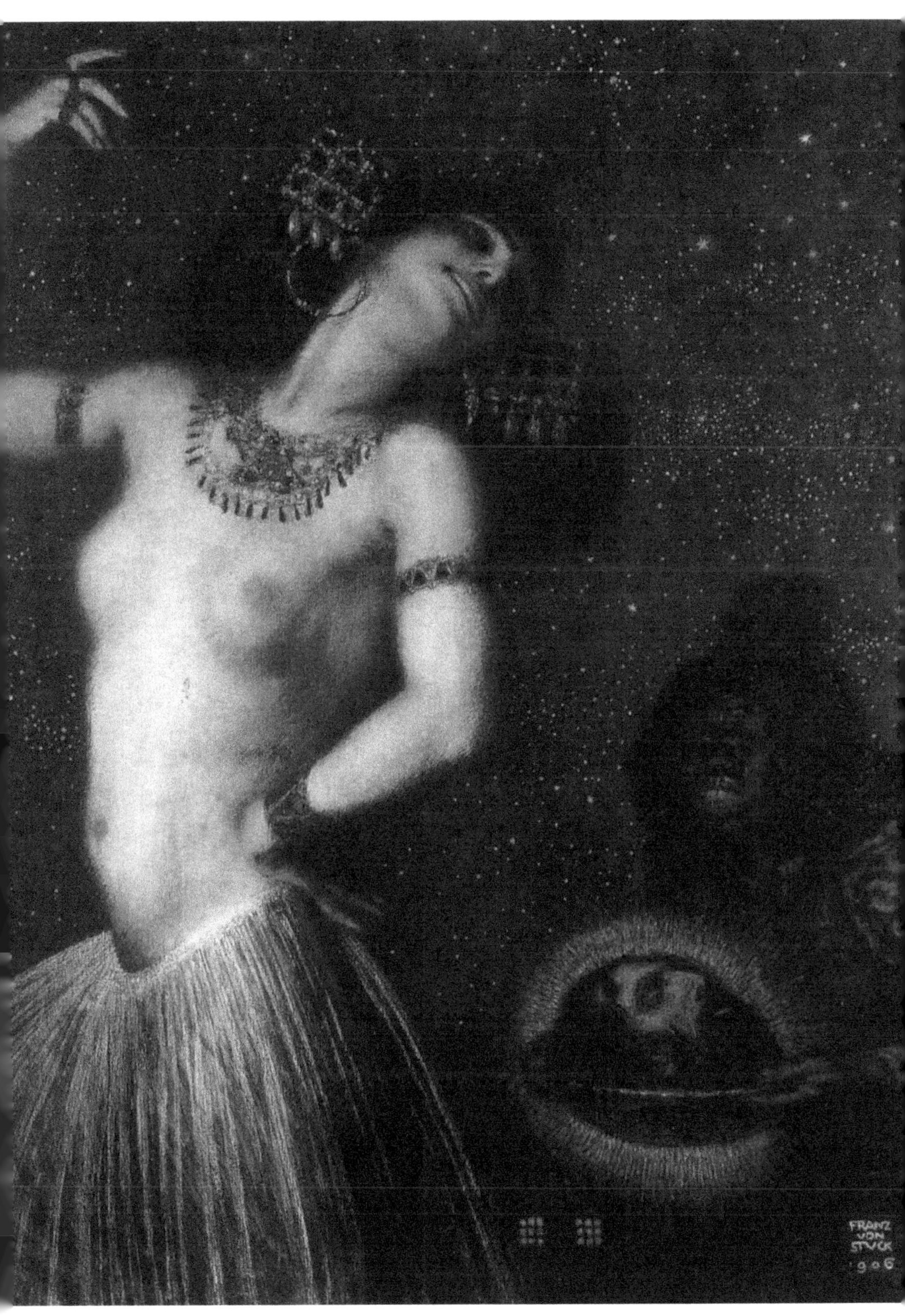

Franz von Stuck, Salomé, 1906

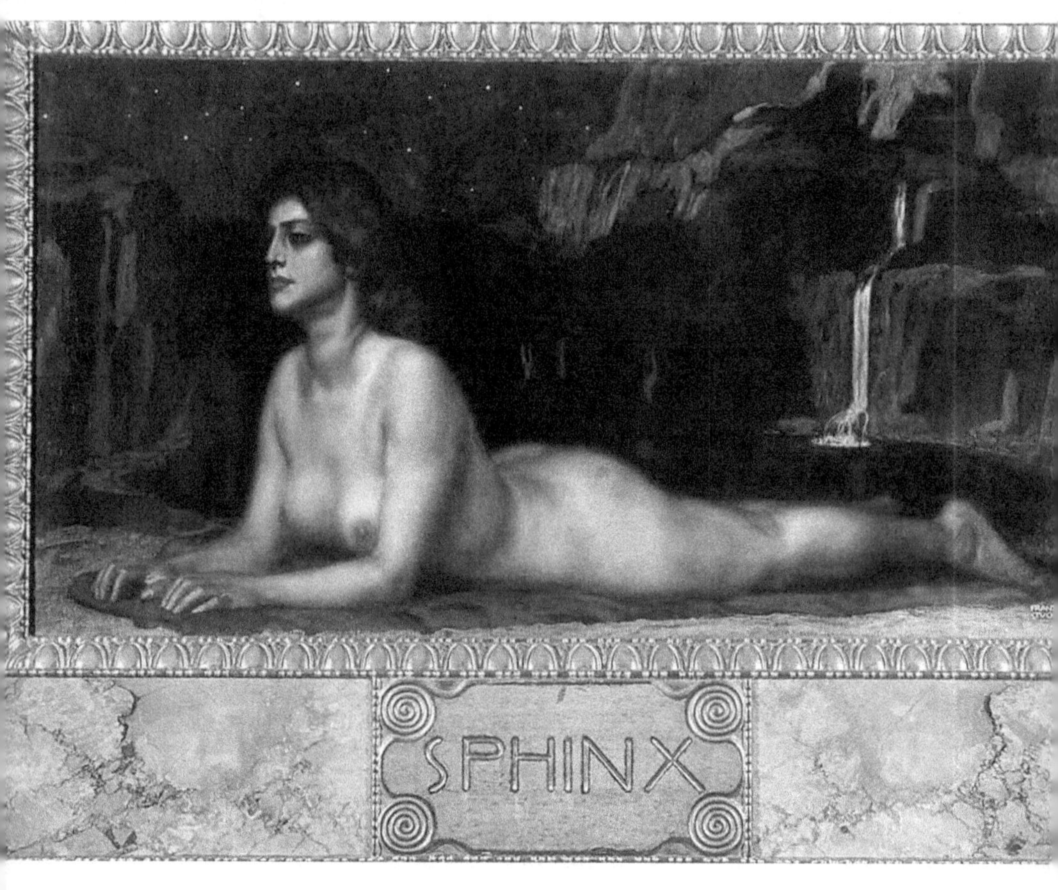

Franz von Stuck, Sphinx

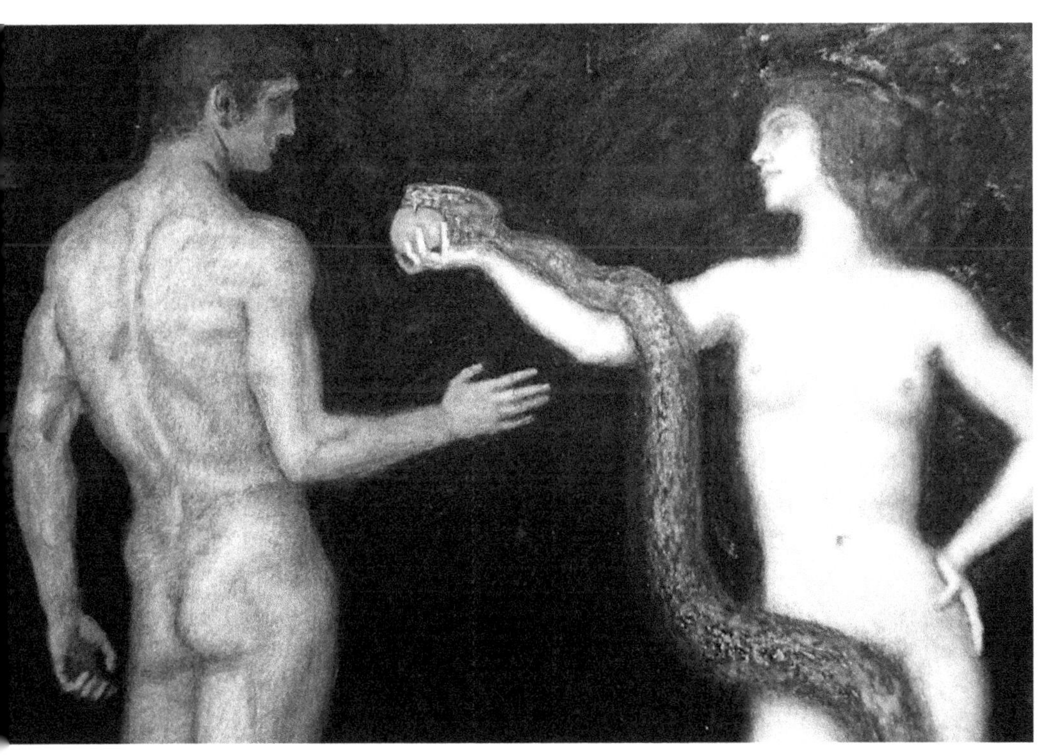

Franz von Stuck, Adam and Eve, 1920

THE MARQUIS DE SADE

Donatien-Alphonse-François de Sade, a.k.a. the Marquis de Sade (1740-1814), was the controversial author of 4 novels, short stories, plays, dialogues, letters, journals and pamphlets (including *Justine, Philosophy of the Bedroom, The Story of Juliette* and *Les Cent Vingt Journés de Sodome*). De Sade's was a notorious life, leading to a number of spells in prison (prostitutes, attempts on his life, run-ins with the police, accused of poisoning Marseilles hookers, etc).[1] He apparently indulged in some of the sadomasochistic practices described in his fiction (some of which led to his imprisonment); that's part of the Sadean Legend, of course.[2]

1 According to Gérard Zwang, 'it is because of excessive imprisonment and vindictive and cowardly censorship that Sade has been put on a pedestal and consecrated a martyr, great philosopher, major writer and specialist in eroticism' (quoted in B. Groult: "Les portiers de nuit", in *Ainsi soit-elle*, Grasset, Paris, 1975, and in E. Marks, 69).

2 We want to believe that notorious writers are *really* notorious! And not like everybody else.

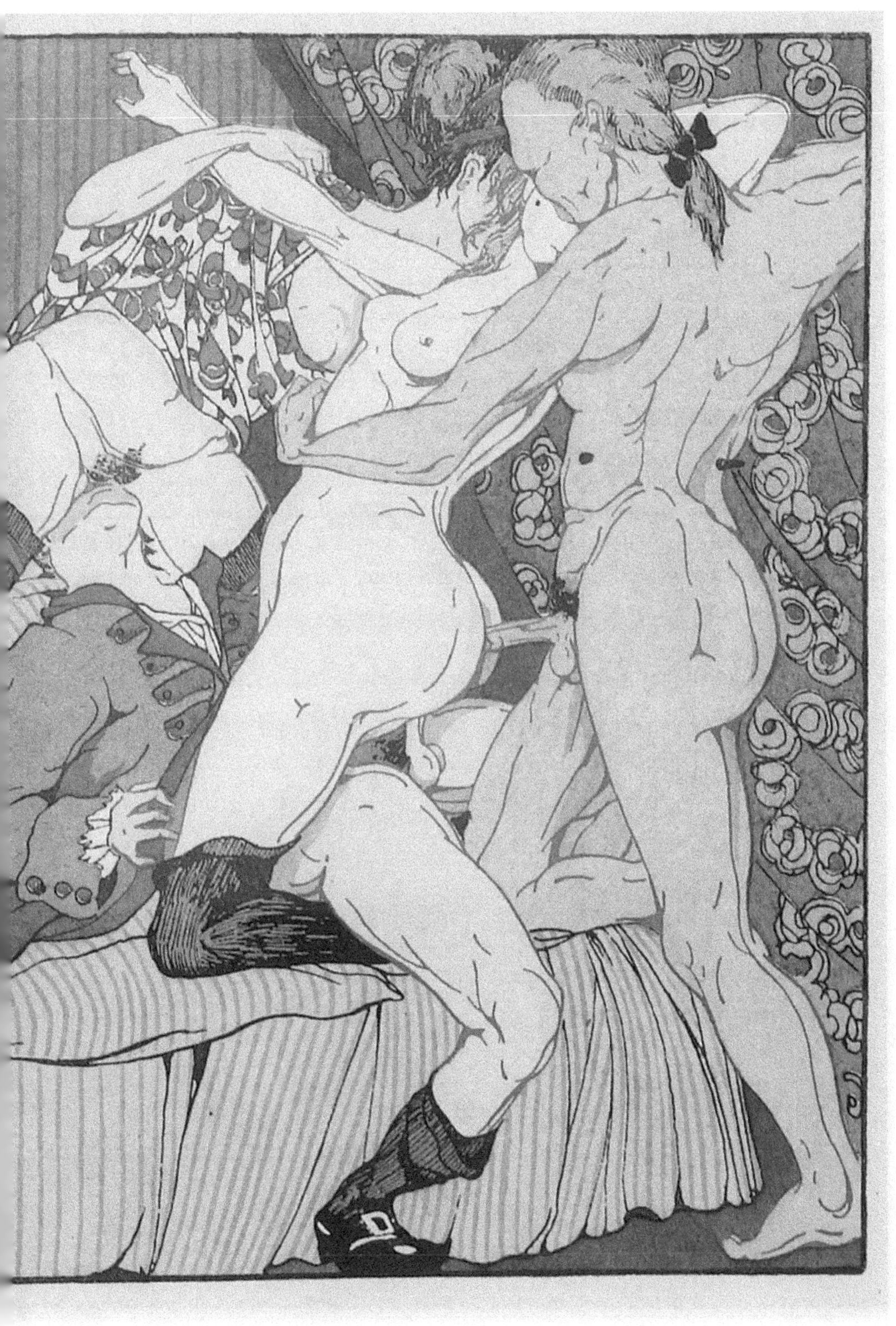

Illustration for the Marquis de Sade,
Le Bordel de Venise, 1921,
by Couperyn (a.k.a. George A. Drains), Paris

THE ANTI-JUSTINE

Nicolas-Edme Rétif de la Bretonne (1734-1806) wrote *The Anti-Justine, or The Joys of Eros* (*Le Anti-Justine, ou les Délices de l'amour,* 1798) in opposition to the Marquis de Sade's *Justine*. However, de la Bretonne's *Anti-Justine* ended up as pornographic as de Sade's own *Justine.*

The early 20th century saw the publication of numerous erotic novels and stories, including *Lady Chatterley's Lover* by D.H. Lawrence, *The Story of the Eye* by Georges Bataille, and the erotica of Anaïs Nin, Colette, Violette Leduc, Frank Harris and André Gide.

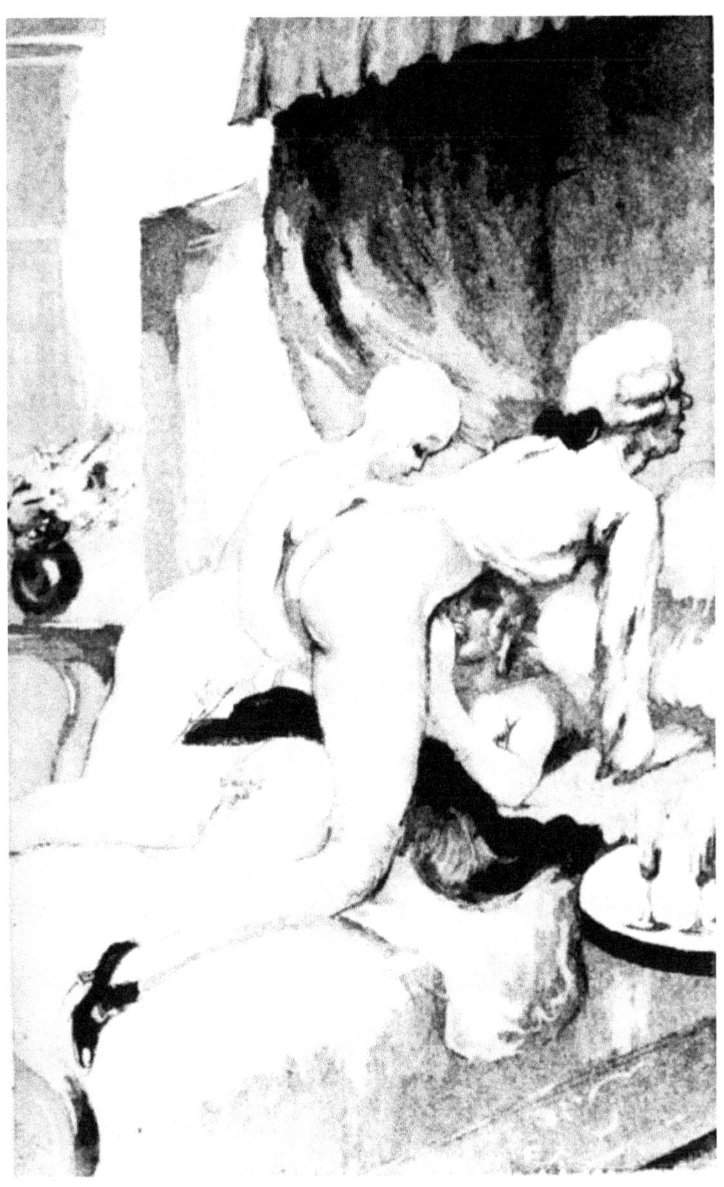

Le Loup, L'Anti-Justine, 1930
(this page and following pages)

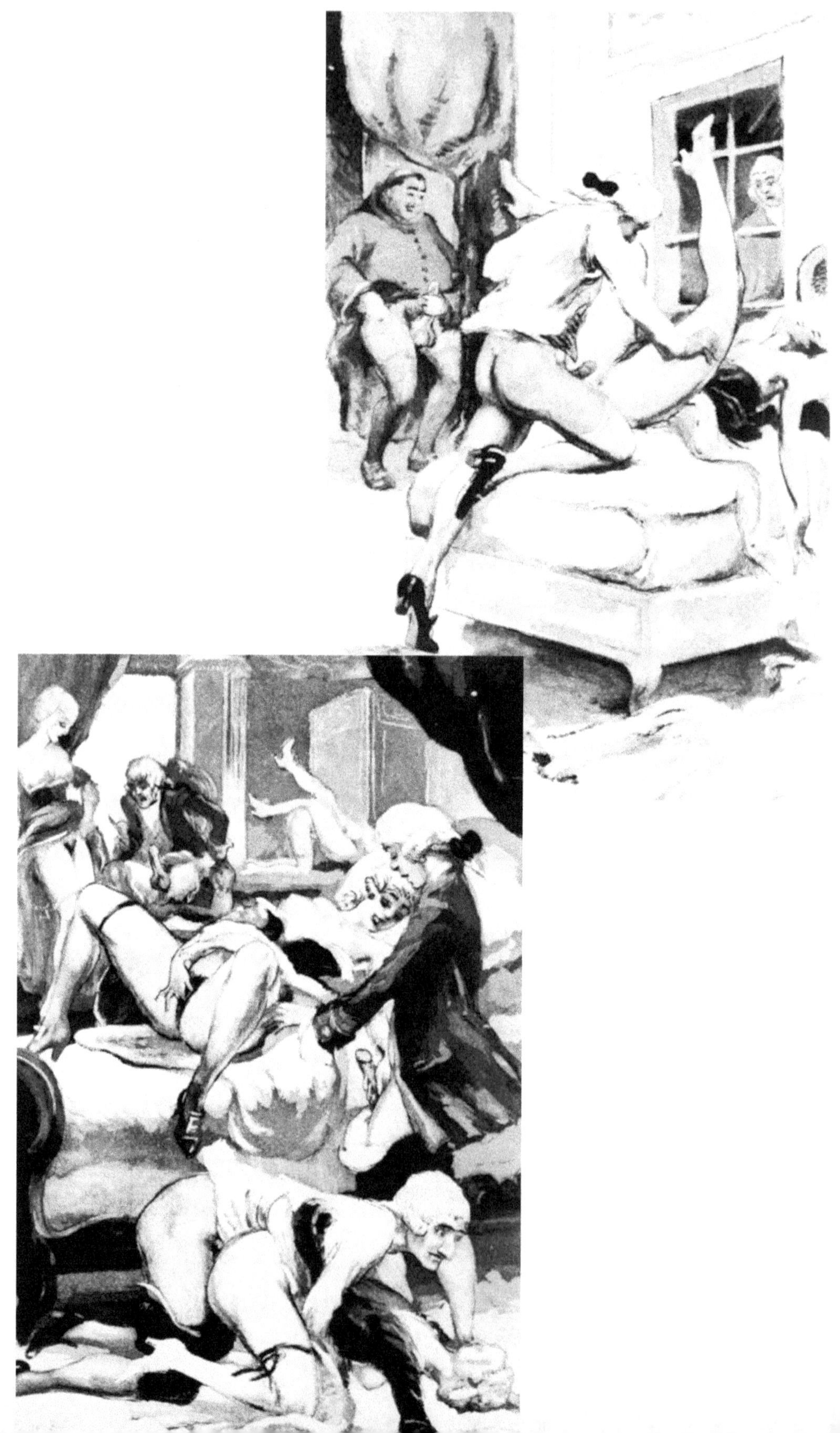

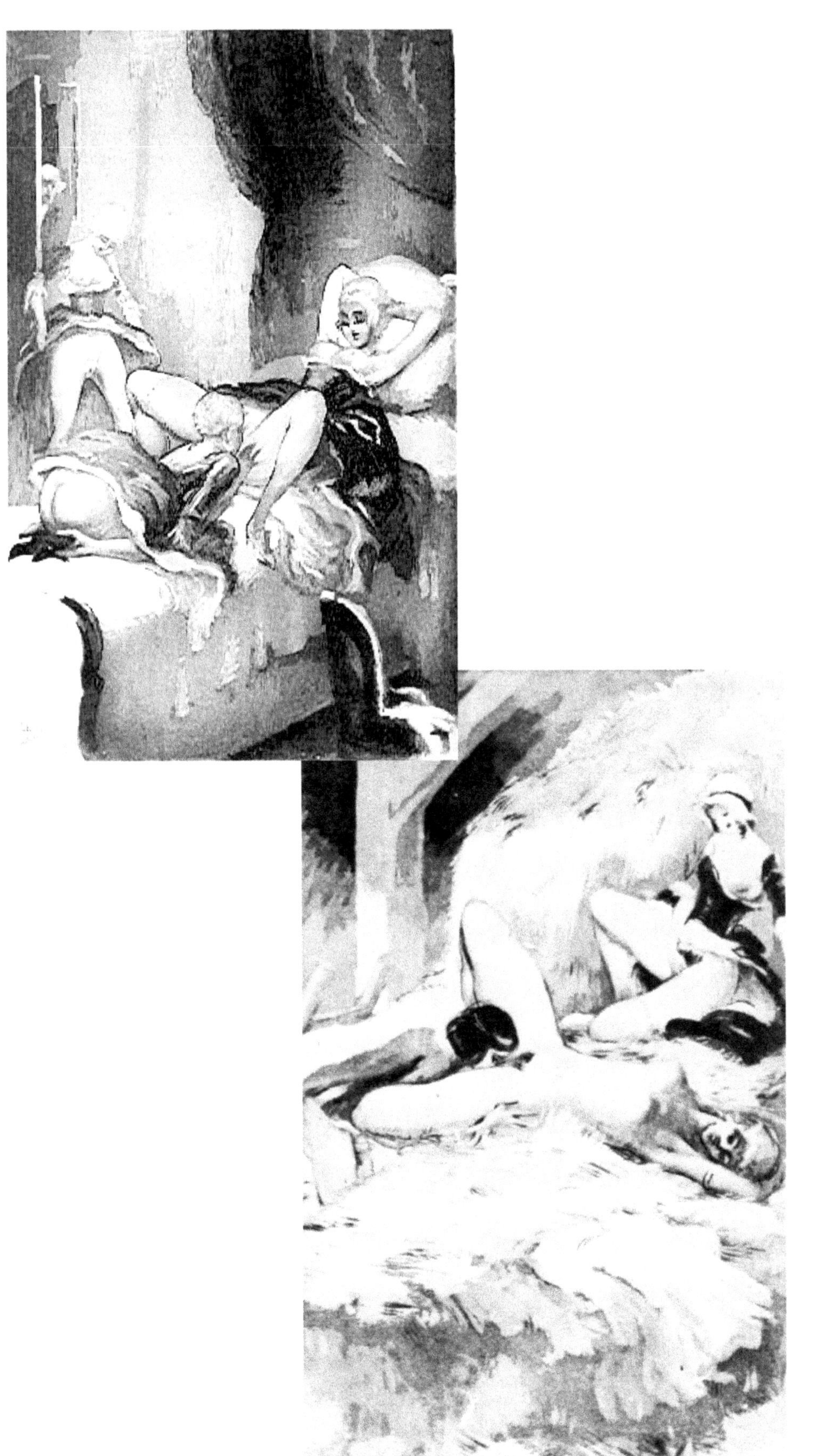

FRANZ CHRISTOPHE

Franz Christophe (1875-1946) was a German artist who illustrated *Die Verfuhrung* in 1925. Born in Vienna, Christophe worked in Munich and in Berlin (from 1910).

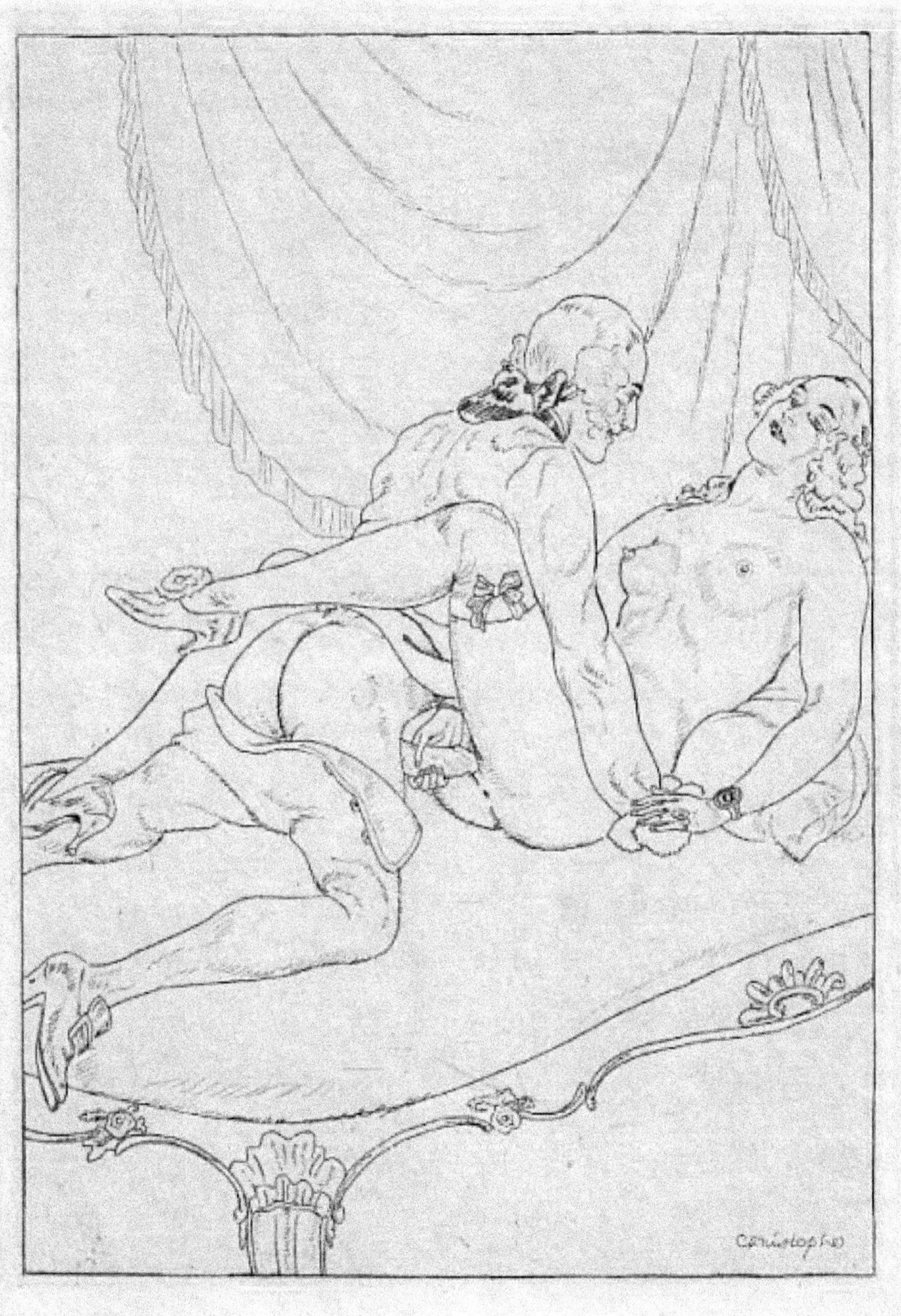

F. Christophe, from Die Verfuhrung,
this page and following pages

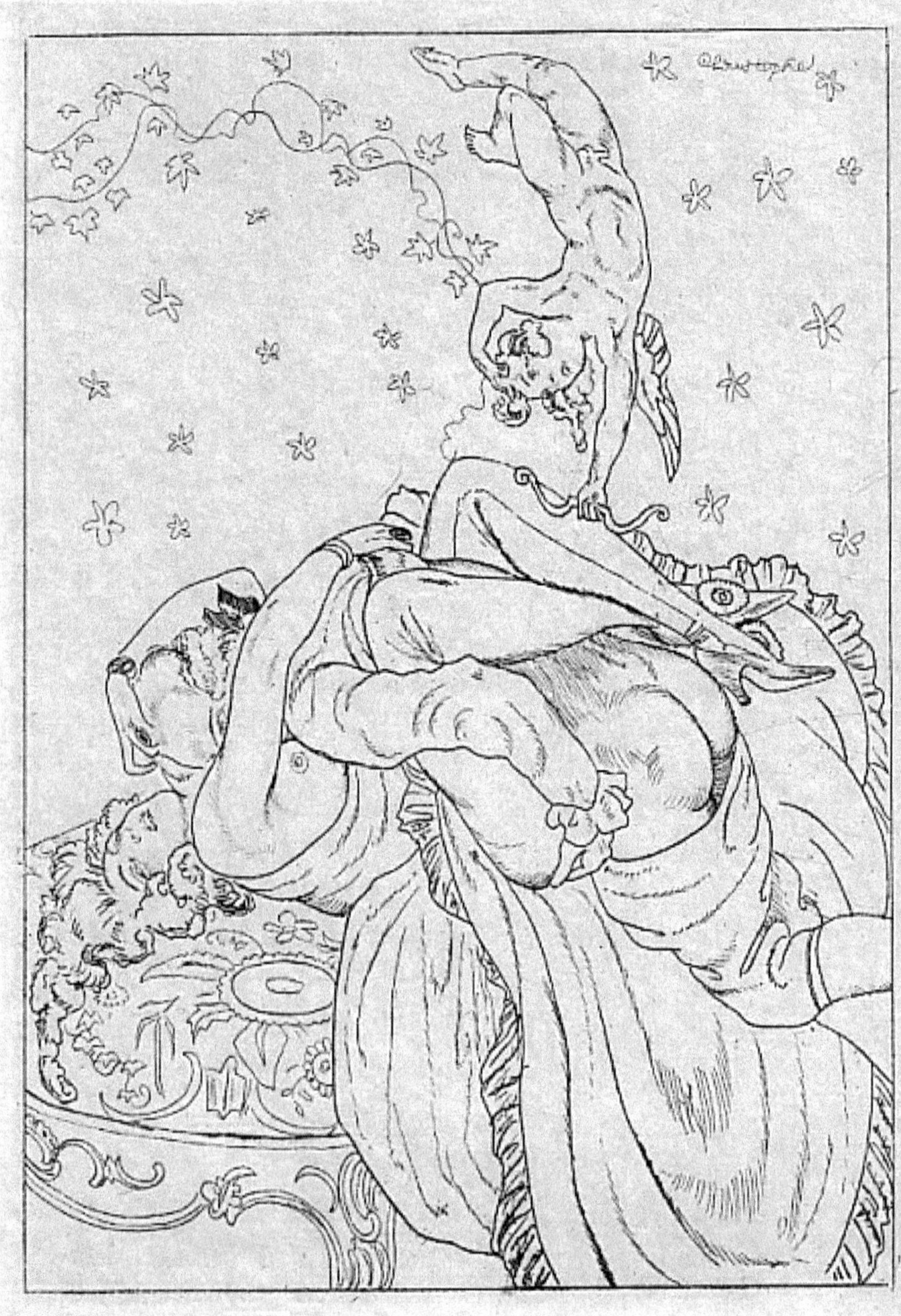

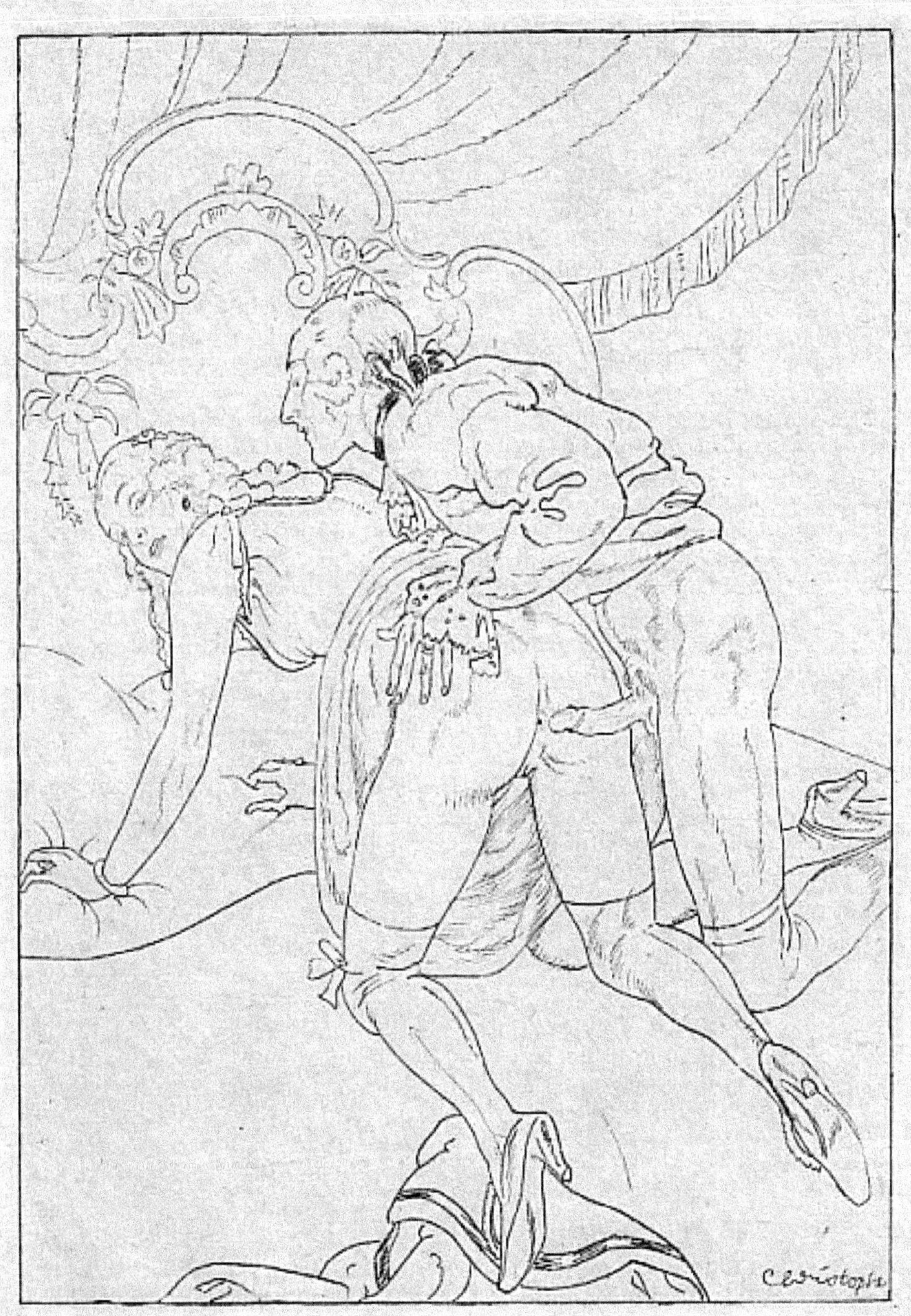
Christoph

PAUL AVRIL - *FANNY HILL*

Fanny Hill: Memoirs of a Woman of Pleasure (1748) by John Cleland (1709-89), is one of the classics texts in the history of erotica, along with *Moll Flanders, The Romance of Lust, The Perfumed Garden,* and of course *The Kama Sutra*. Paul Avril was one of the key modern erotic artists. This is an extract from *Fanny Hill:*

> He threw up my petticoat and shift, whilst my thighs were, by an instinct of nature, unfolded to their best; and my desires had so thoroughly destroyed all modesty in me, that even their being now naked and all laid open to him, was part of the prelude that pleasure deepened my blushes at, more than same. But when his hand, and touches, naturally attracted to their center, made me feel all their wantonness and warmth in, and round it, oh! how immensely different a sense of things, did I perceive there, than when under my own insipid handling! And now his waistcoat was unbuttoned, and the confinement of the breeches burst through, when out started to view the amazing, pleasing object of all my wishes, all my dreams, all my love, the king member indeed! I gazed at, I devoured it, at length and breadth, with my eyes intently directed to it, till his; getting upon me, and placing between my thighs, took from me the enjoyment of its sight, to give me a far more grateful one, in its touch, in that part where its touch is so exquisitely affecting.

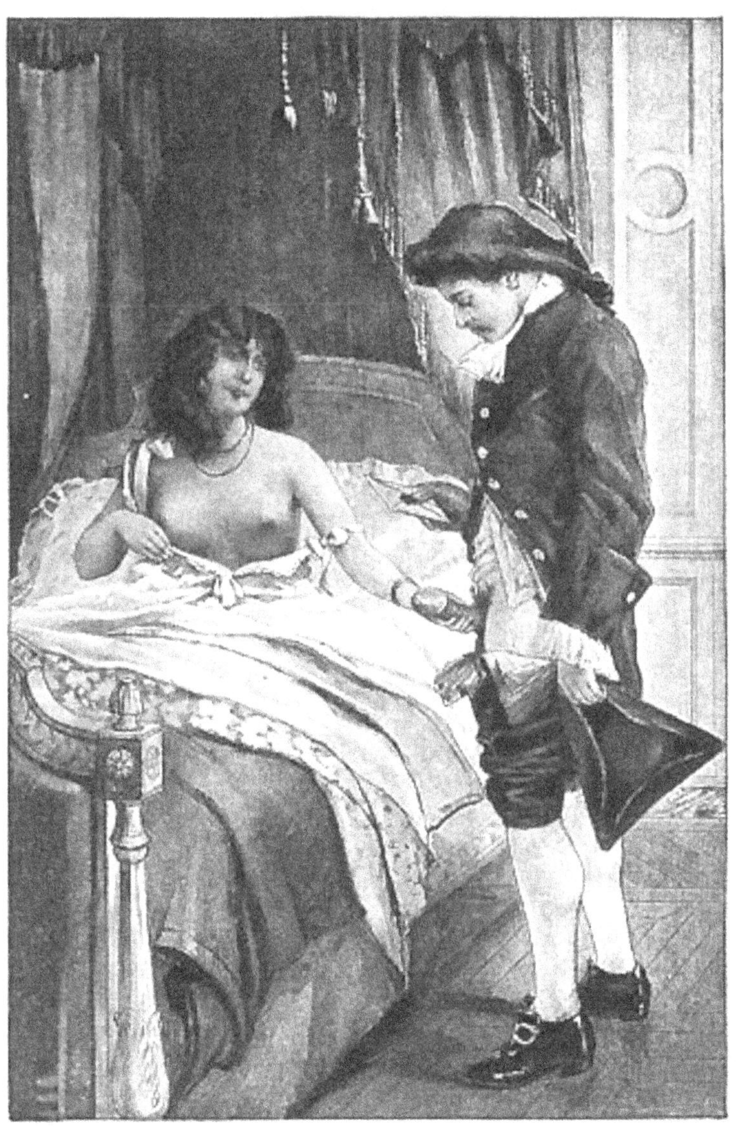

Paul Avril, from Fanny Hill (1908), this page and over,
followed by images from De Figuris Veneris (1906).

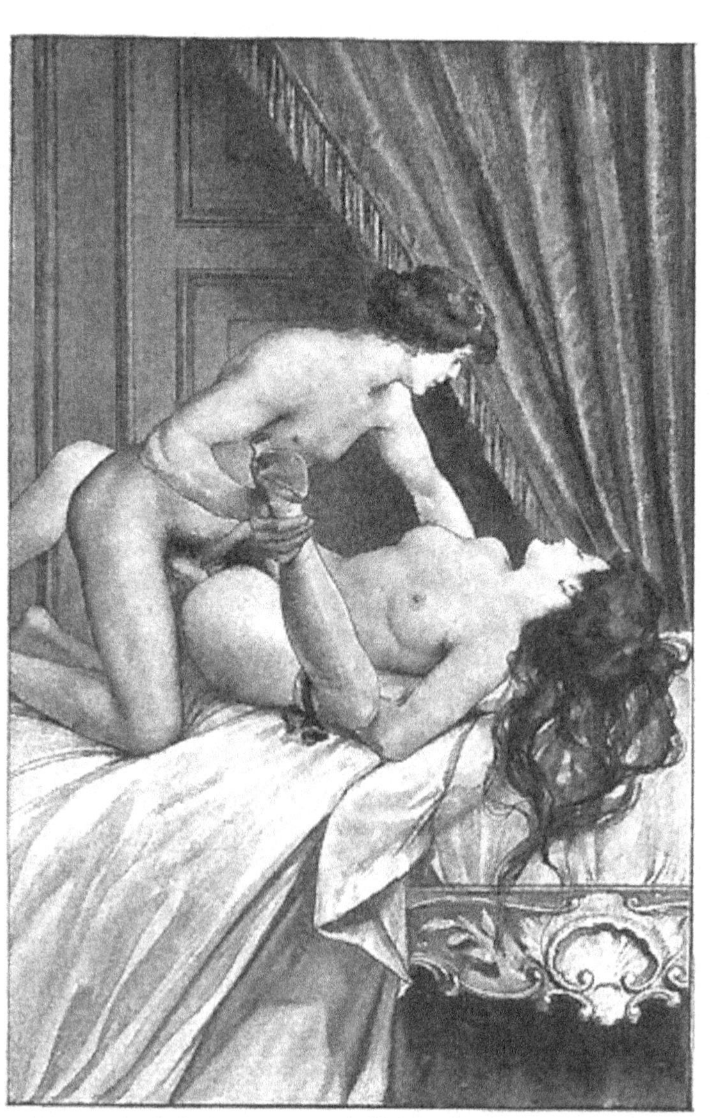

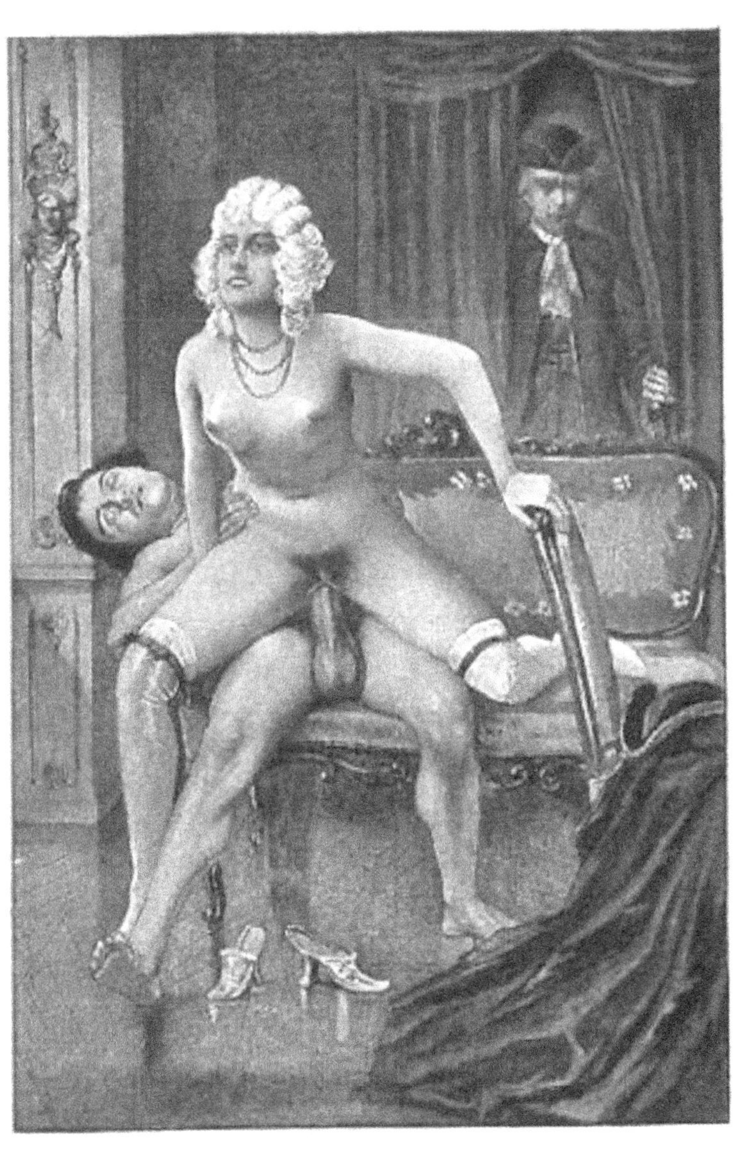

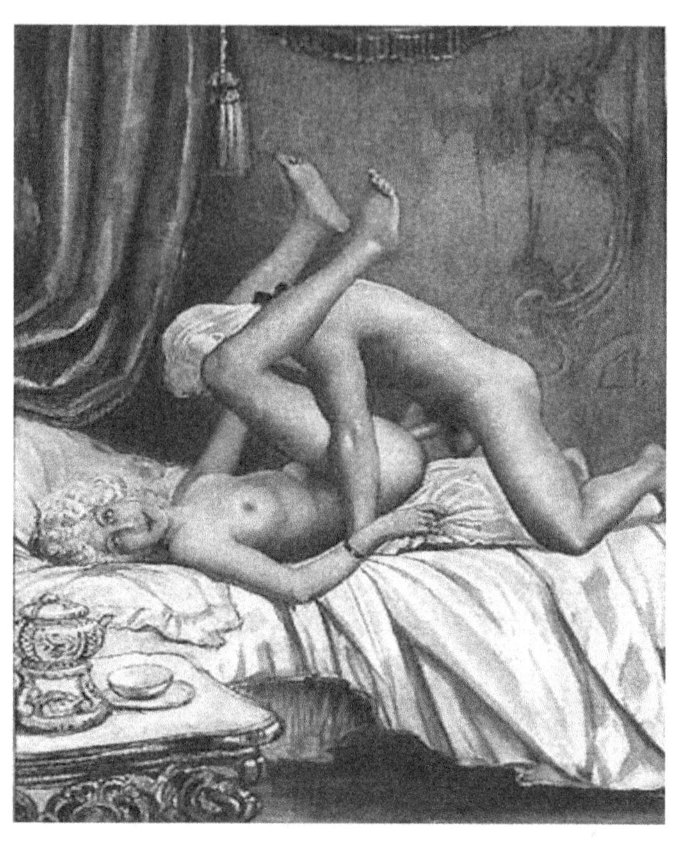

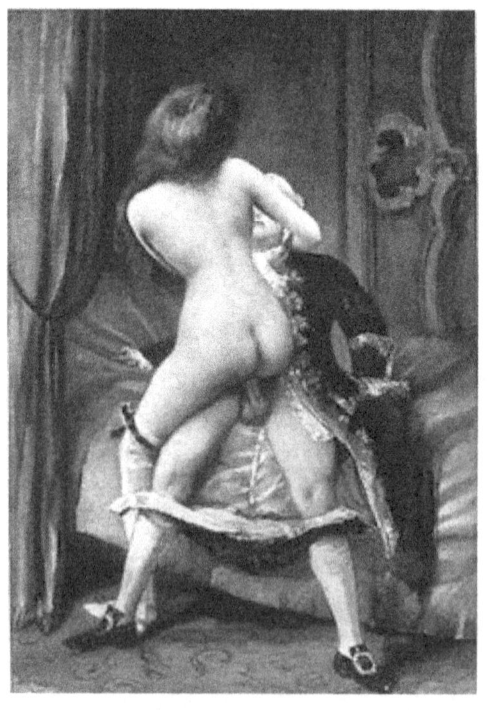

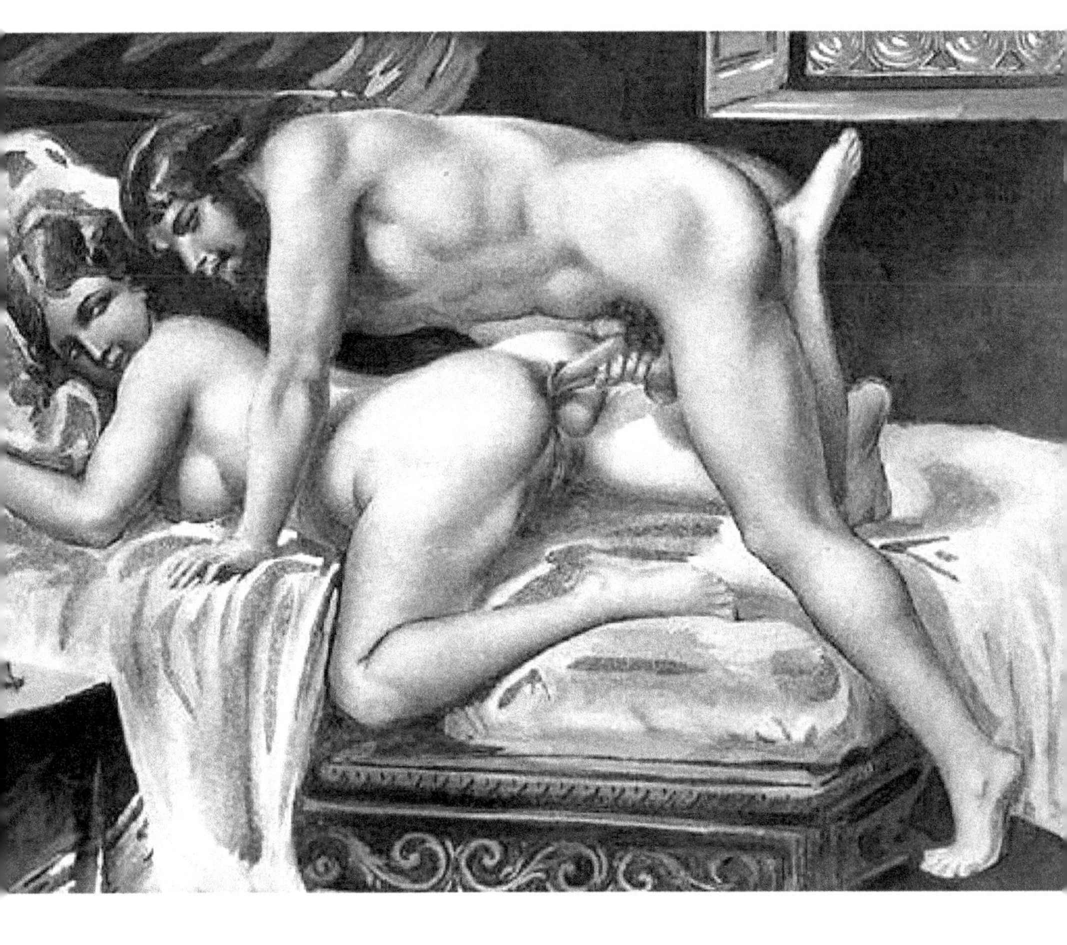

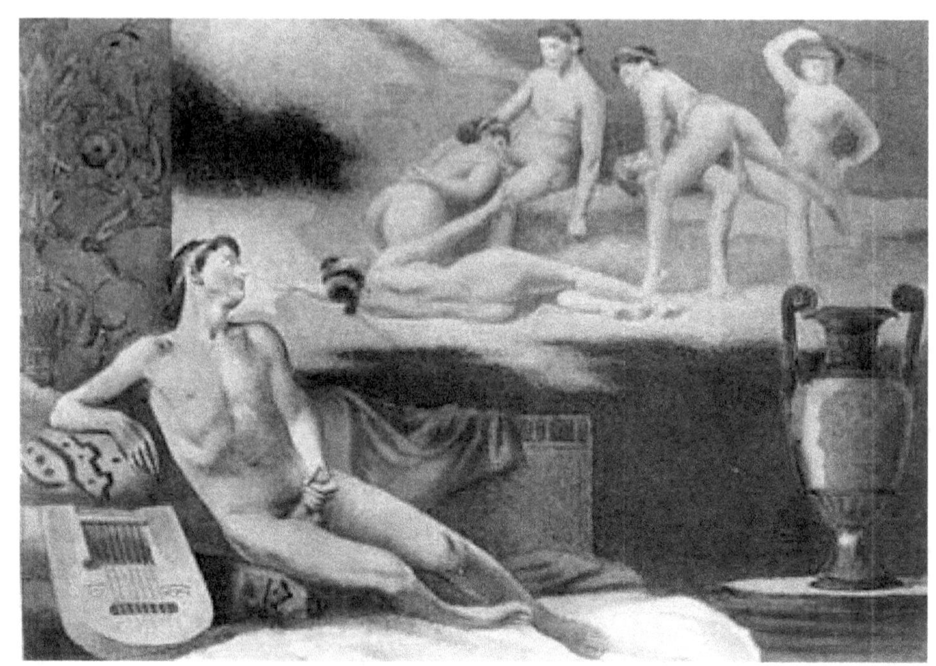

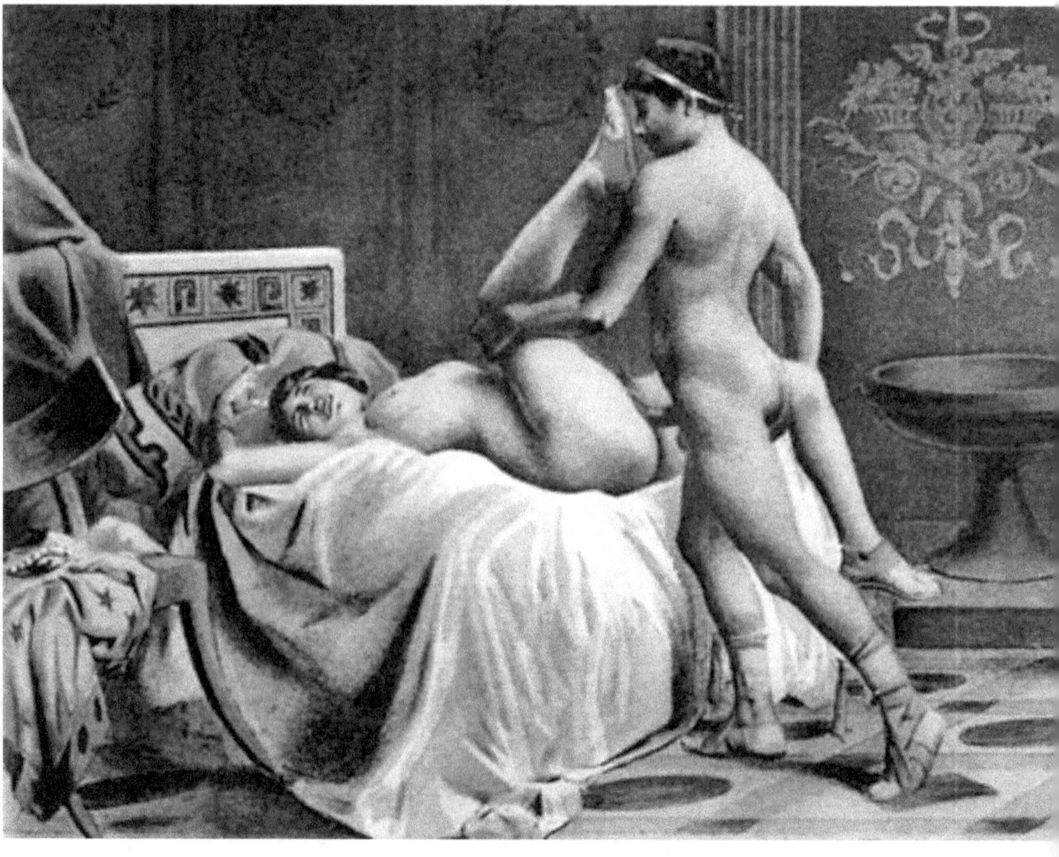

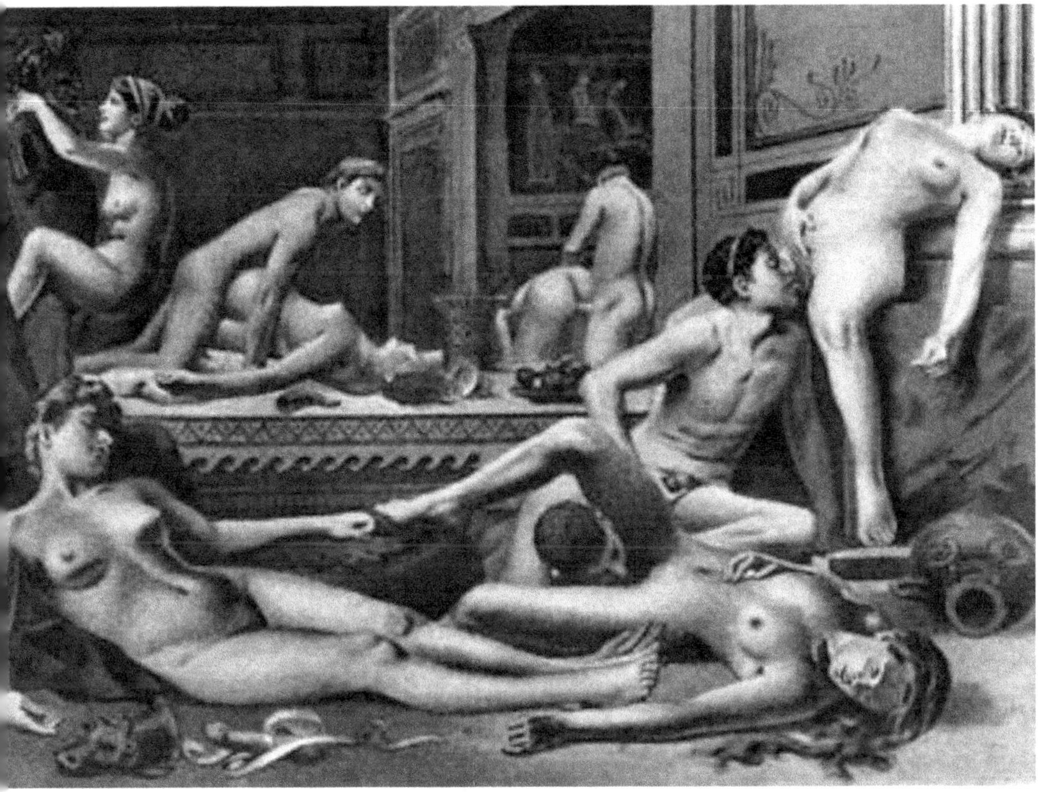

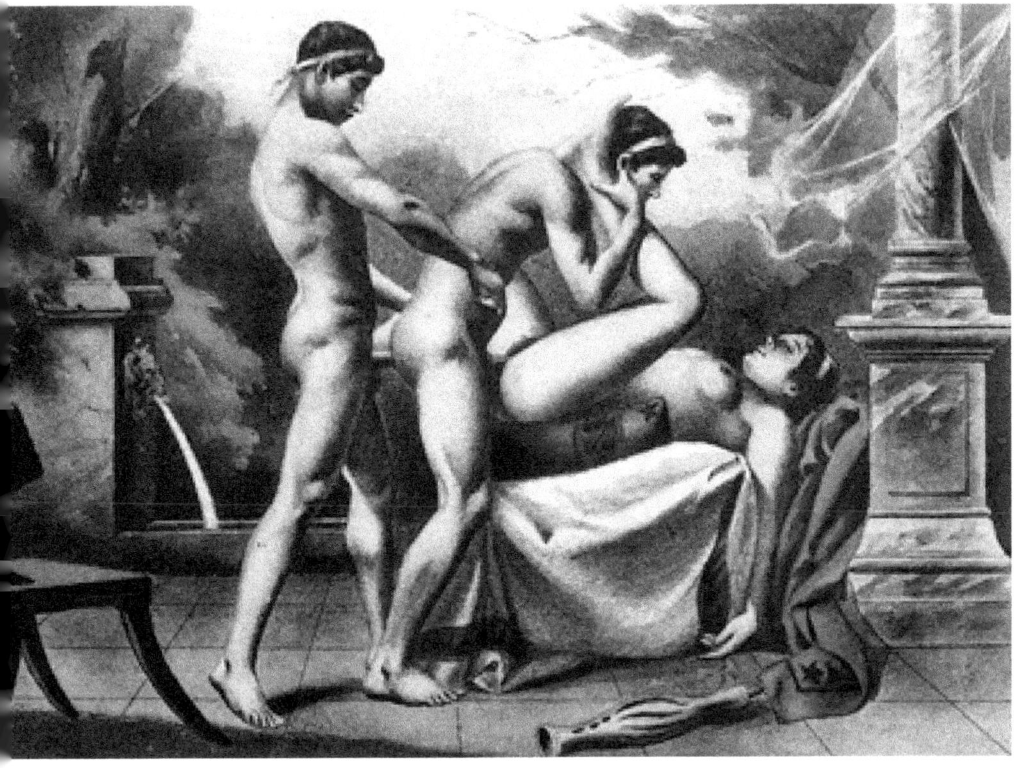

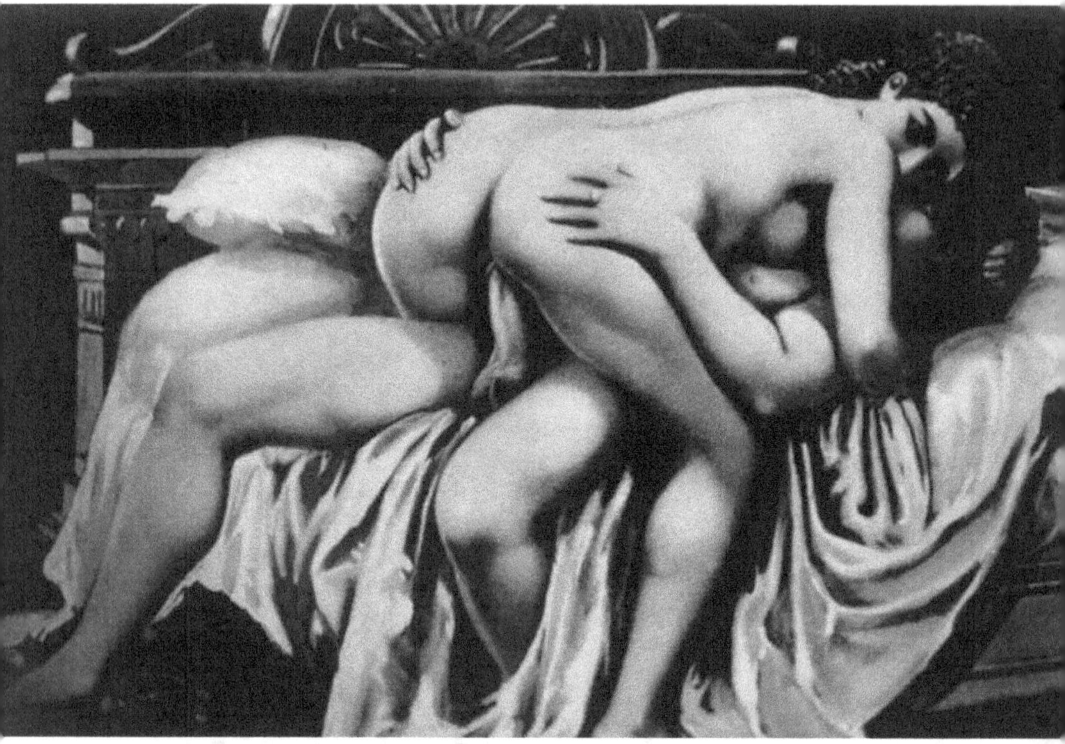

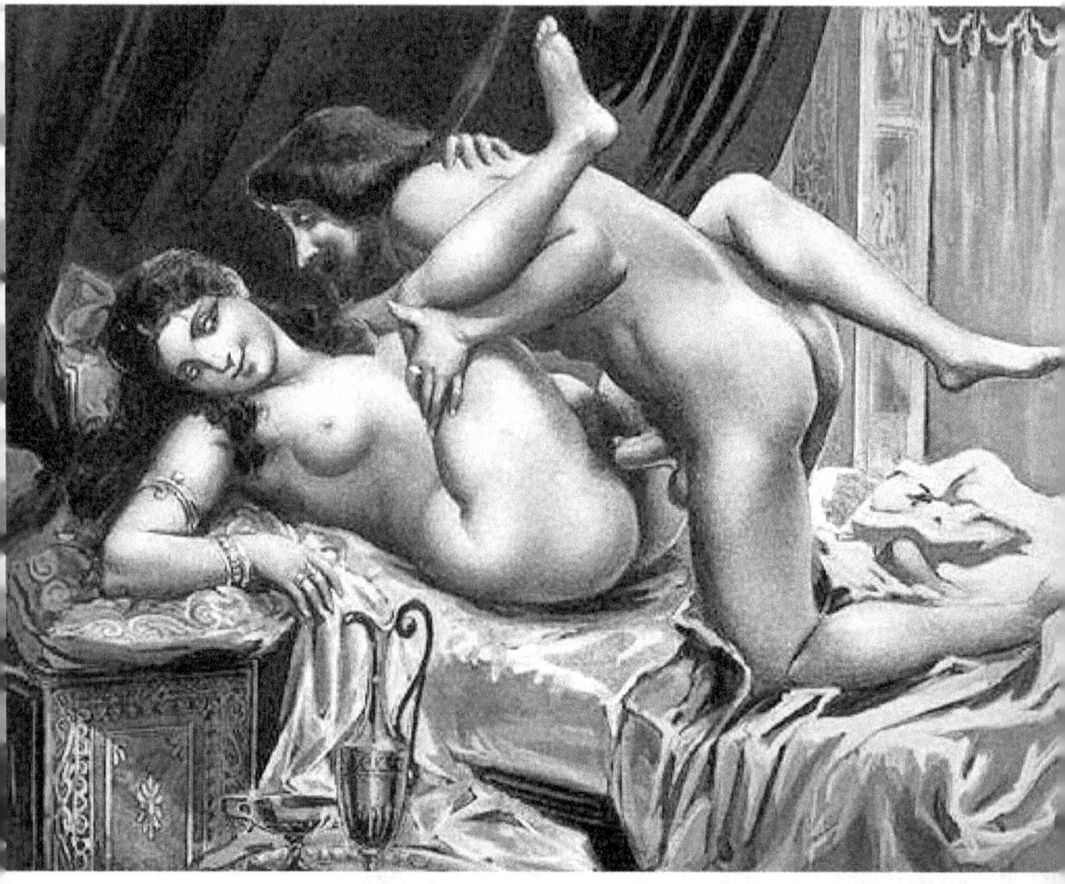

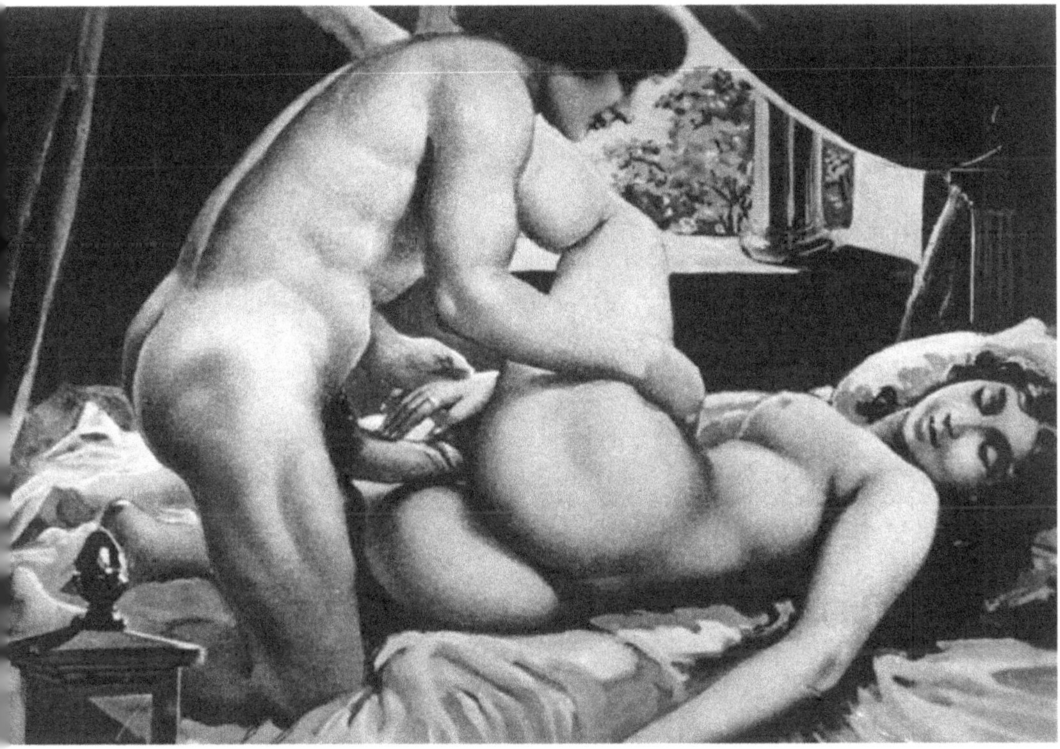

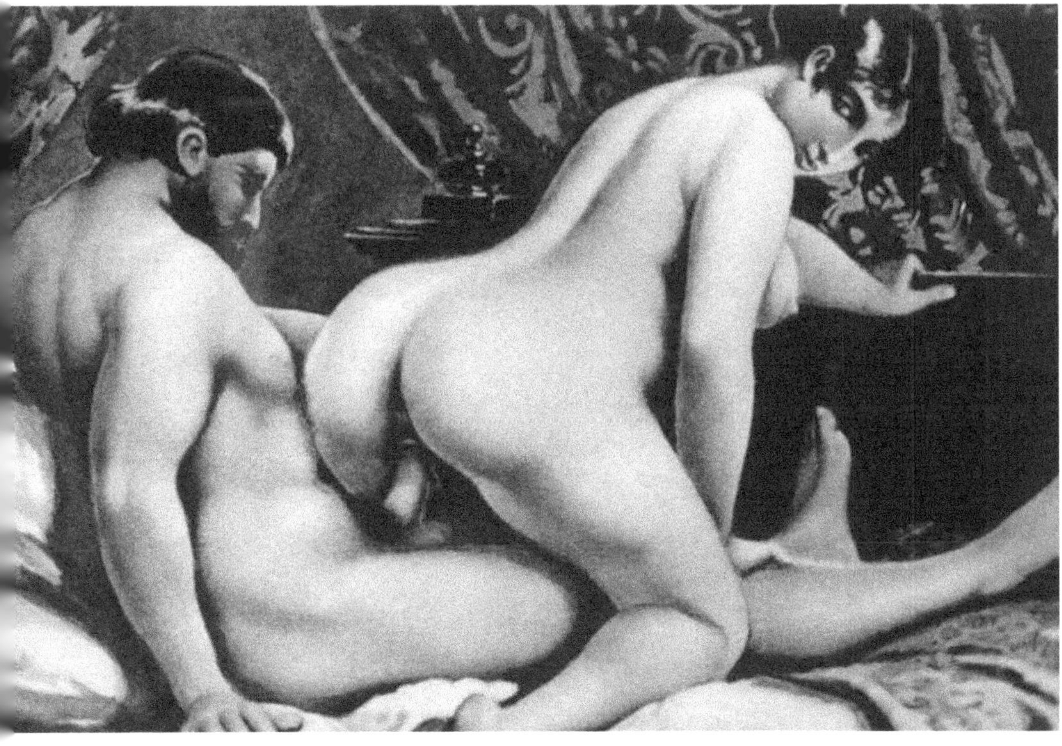

OTTO SCHOFF

Otto Schoff (1888-1938) was a German artist (born in Bremen) who lived in Berlin. Schoff portrayed erotic acts (including homosexuality), and illustrated books by Pierre Louys, Tibullus, Ernest Wenger, Gottfried Keller and August von Platen.

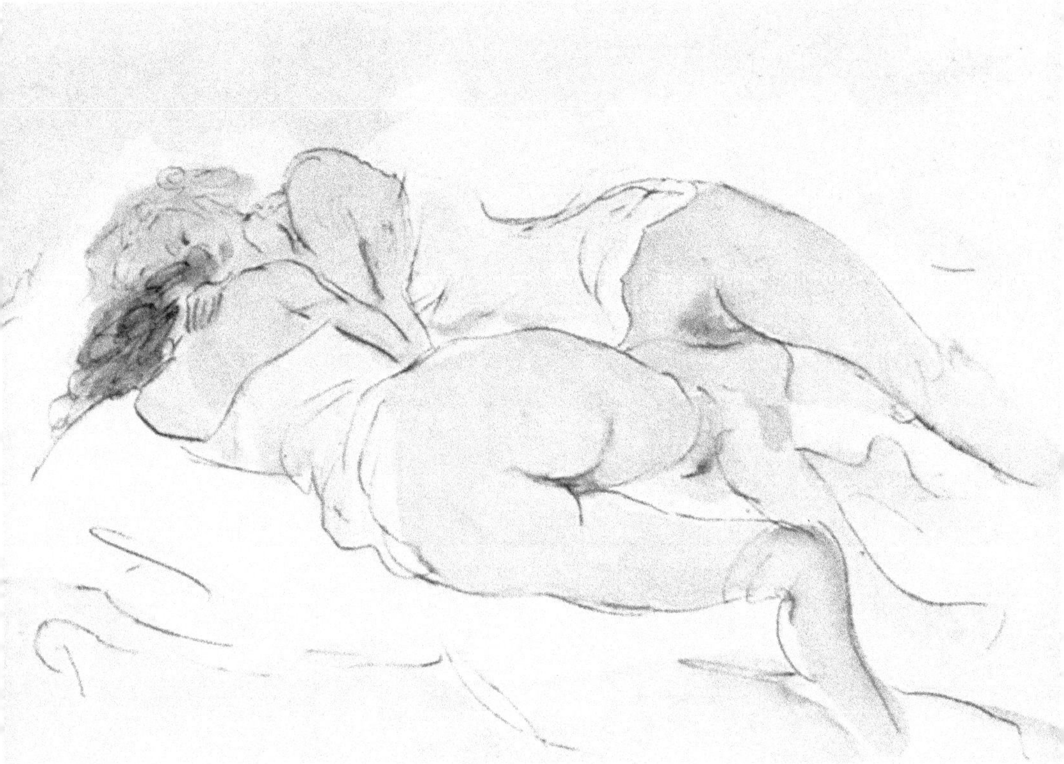

Otto Schoff, this page and following pages

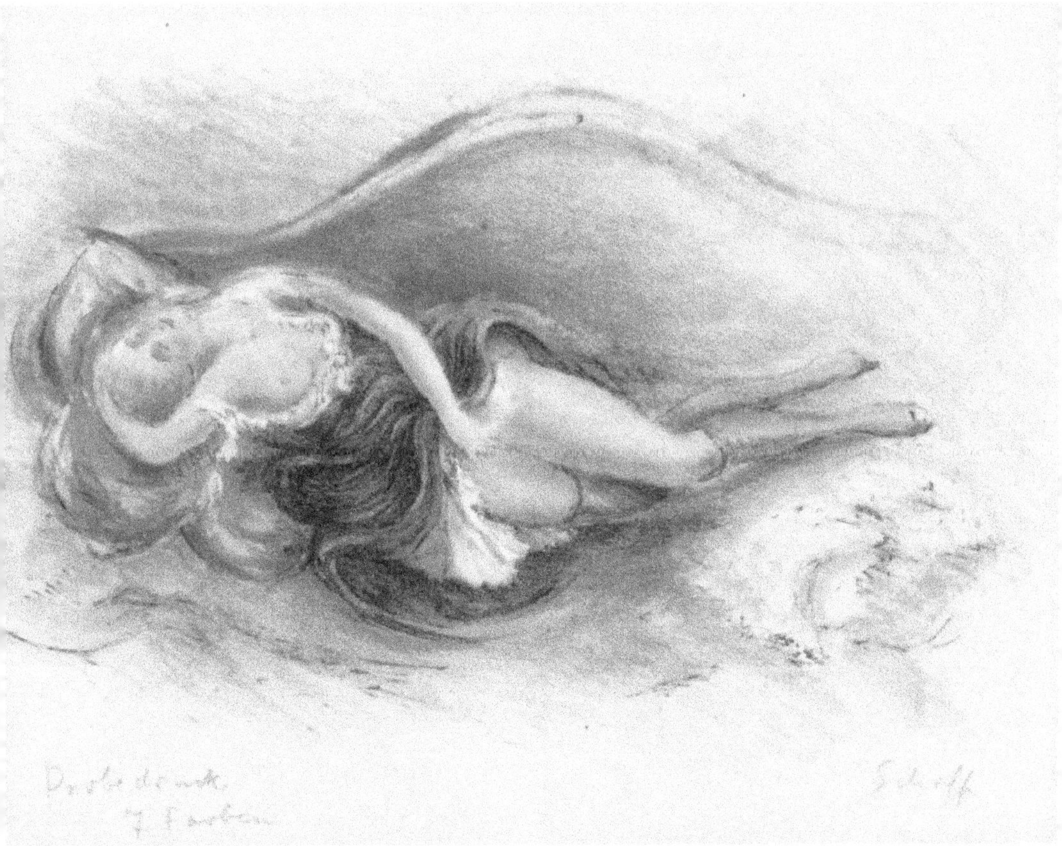

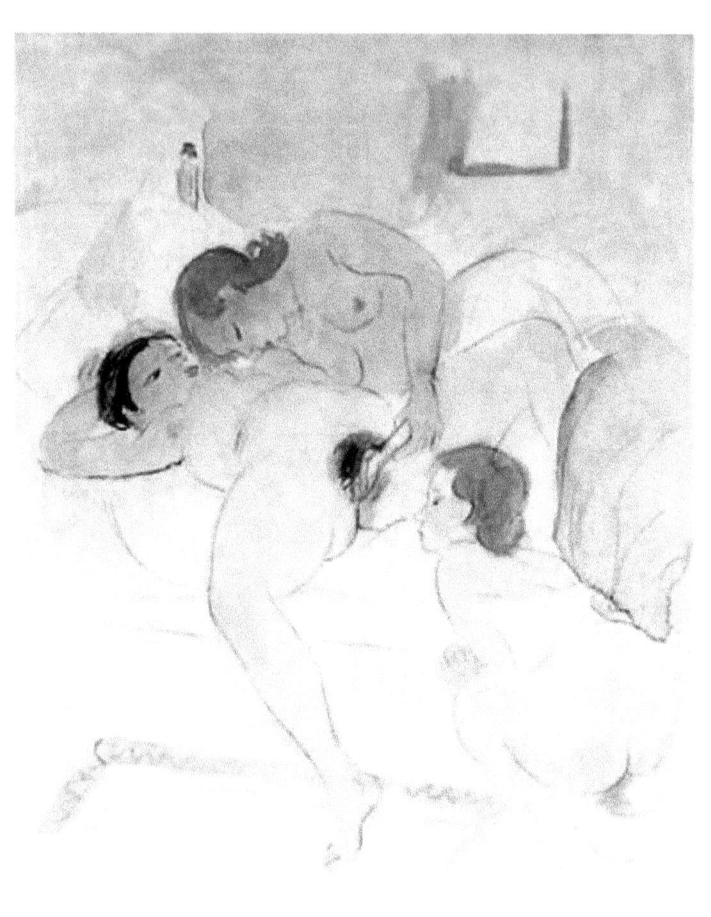

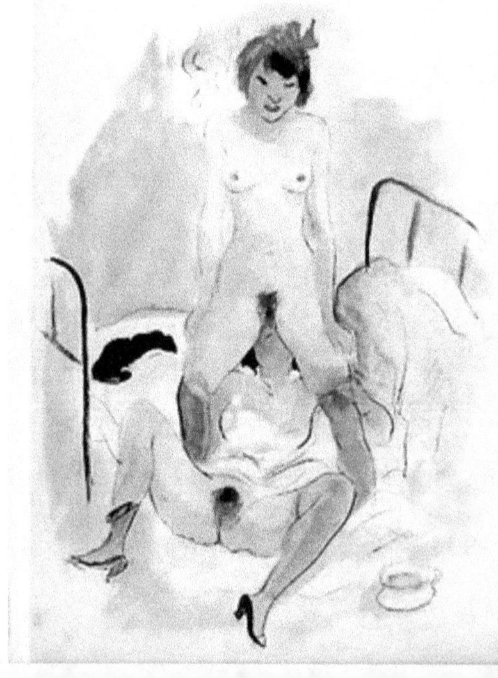

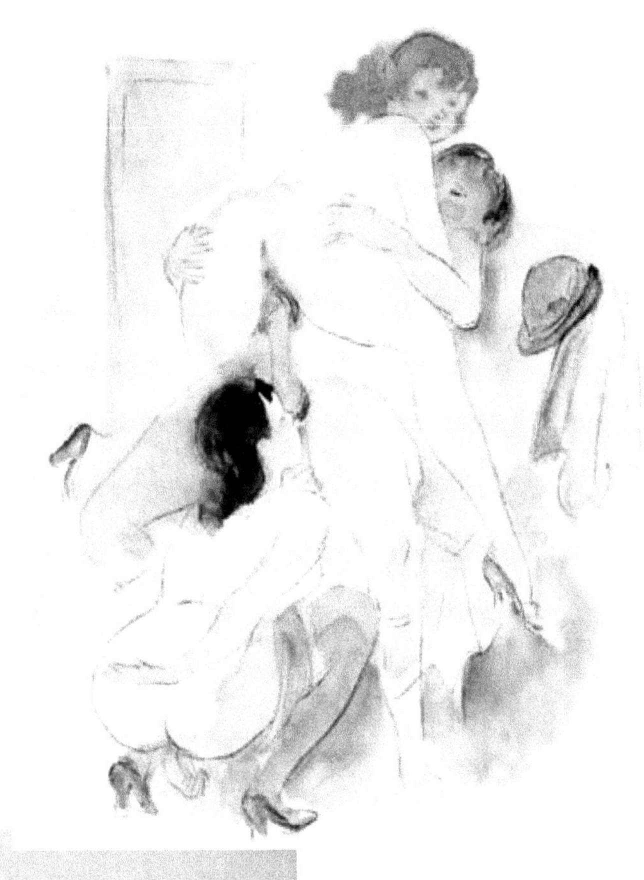

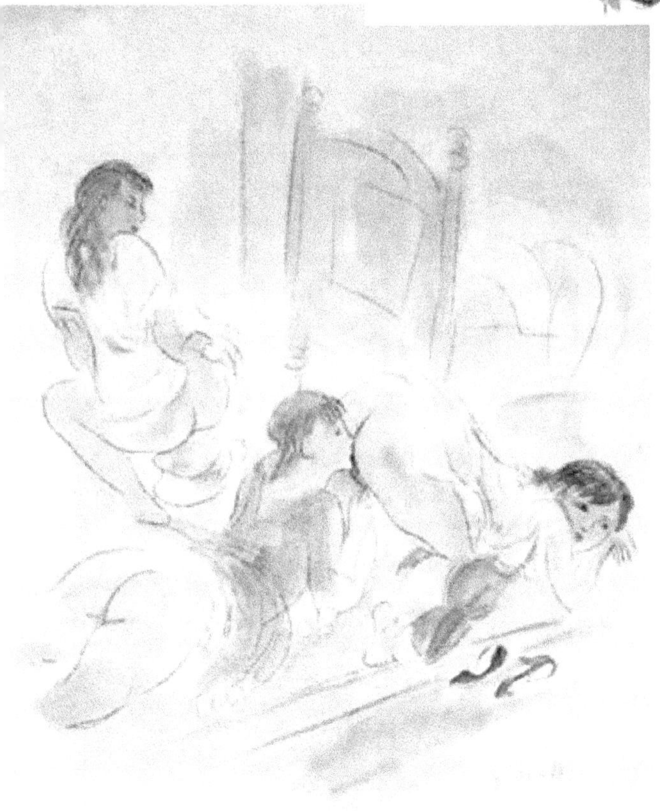

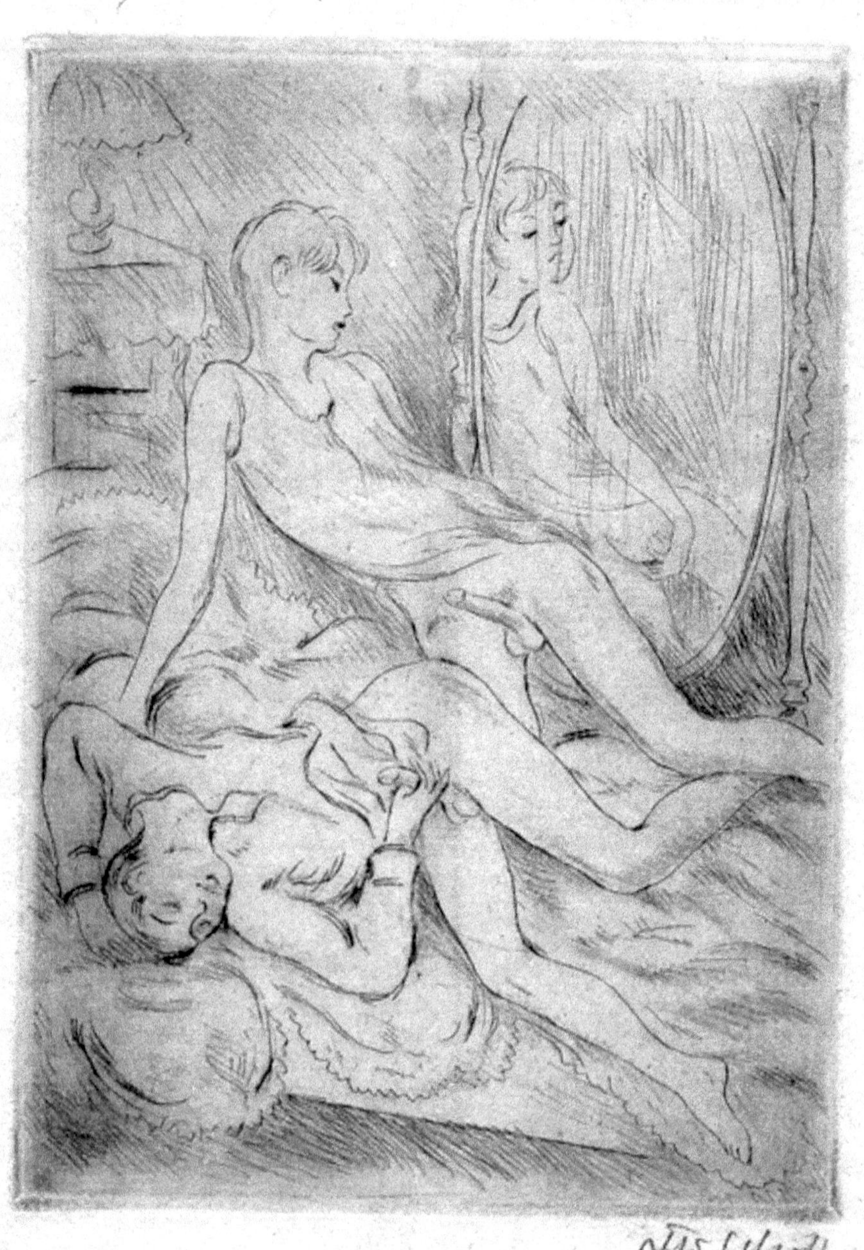

Otto Schoff

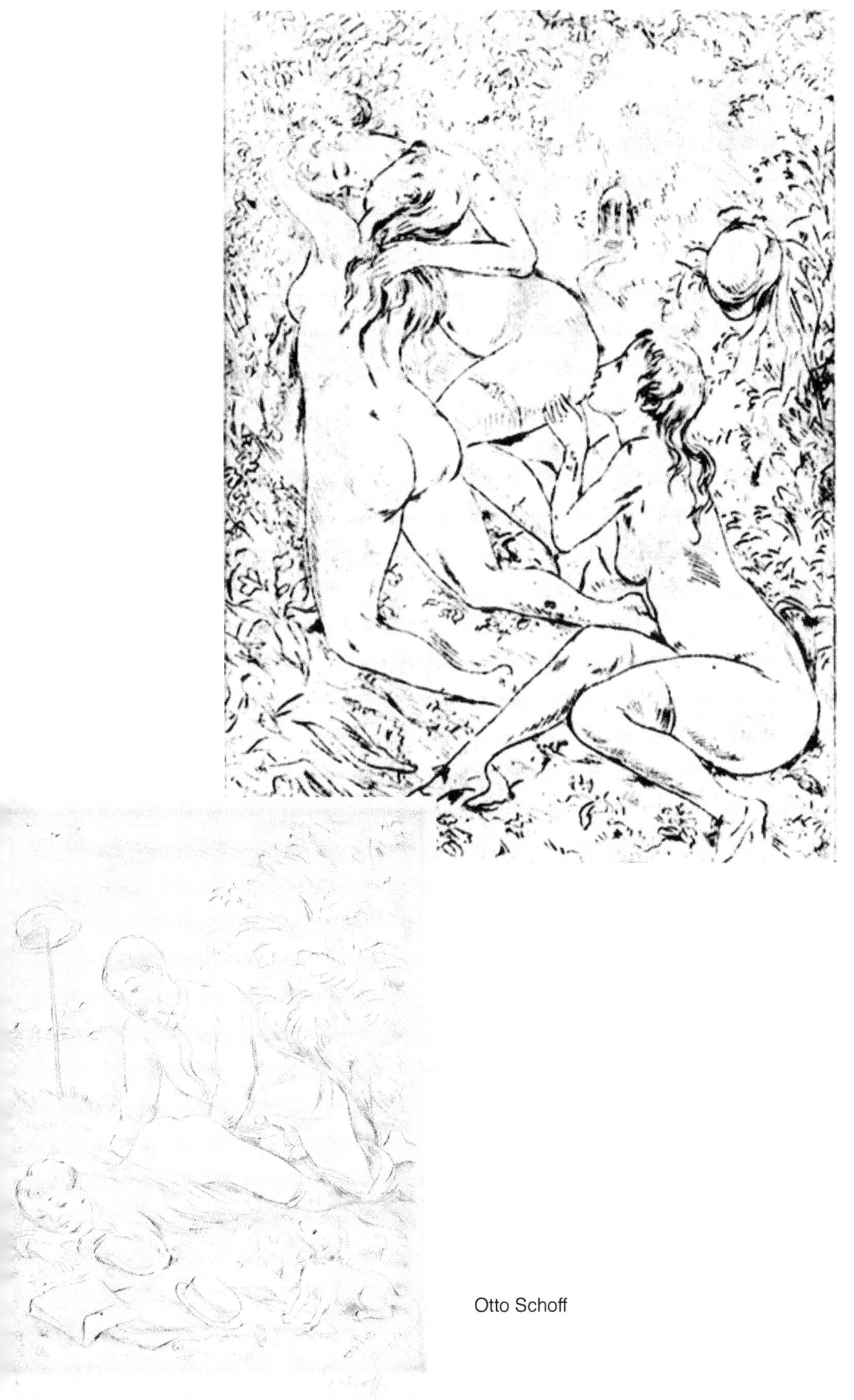

Otto Schoff

MIHÁLY ZICHY

Mihály Zichy (1827-1906) was a Hungarian-born artist who produced a sophisticated form of erotic art in his *Liebe* (published in 1911). Zichy worked mainly in St Petersburg (where he taught art) and Paris.

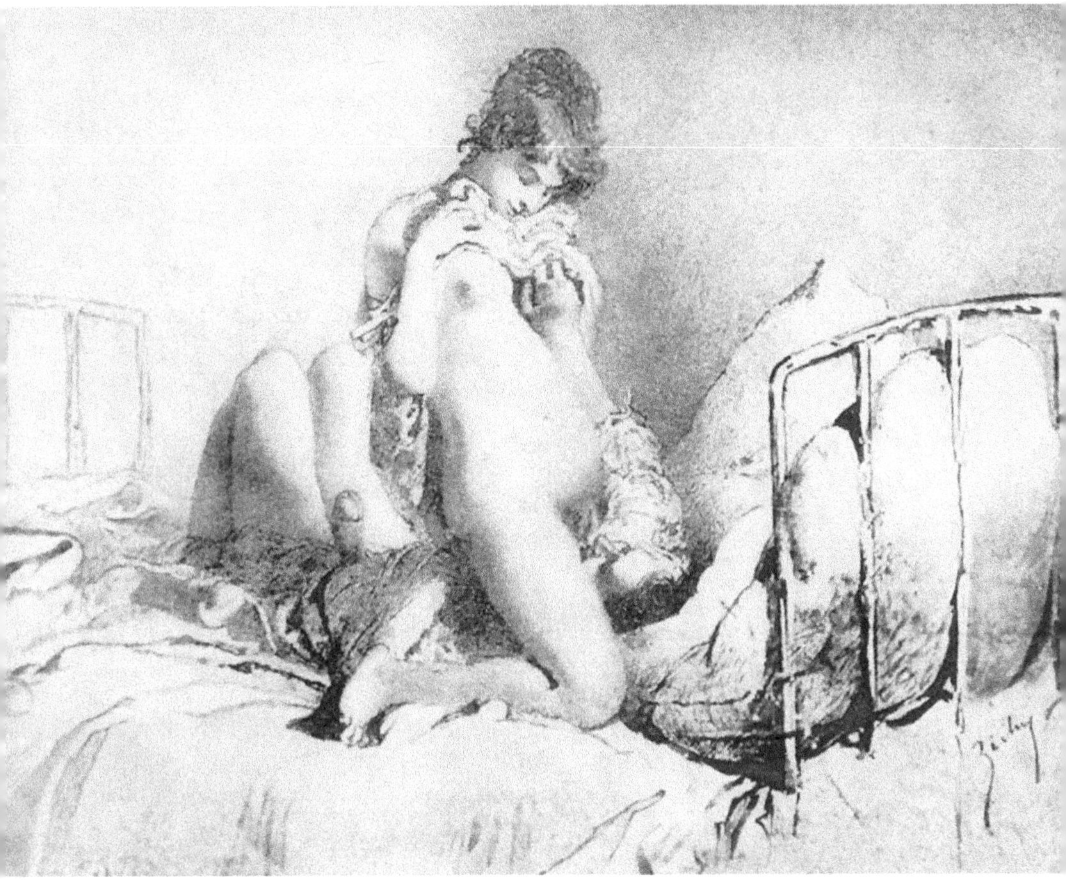

Mihály Zichy (1827-1906), from Liebe, 1911. This page and following pages

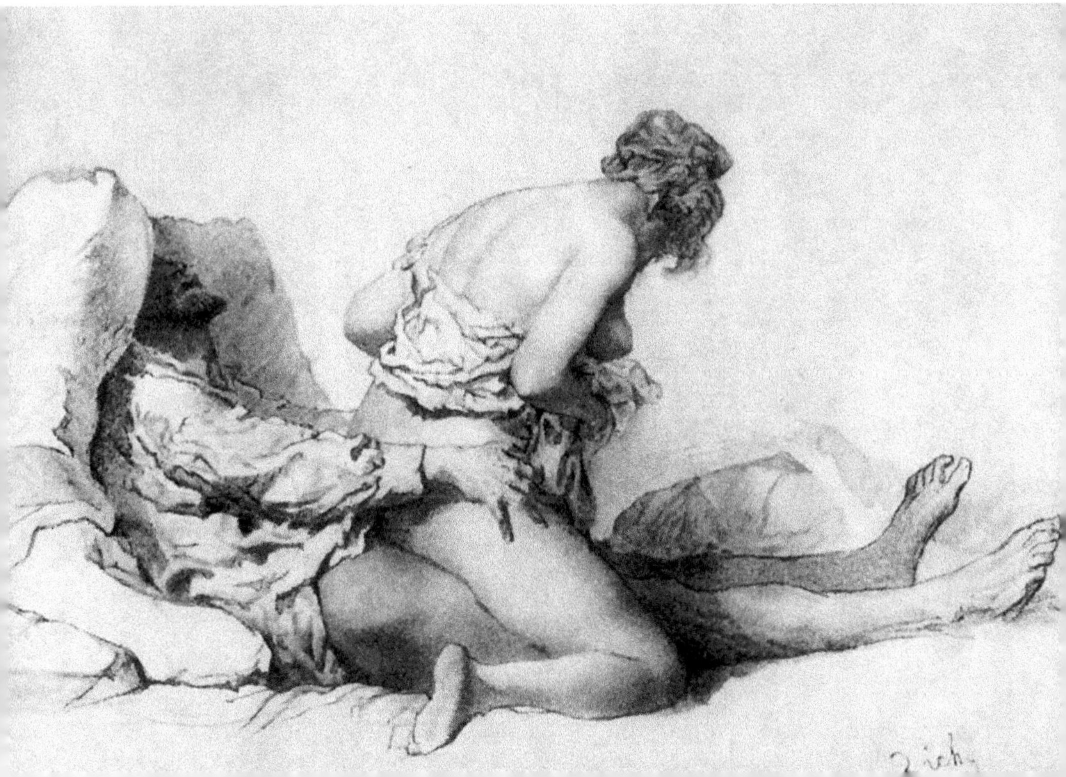

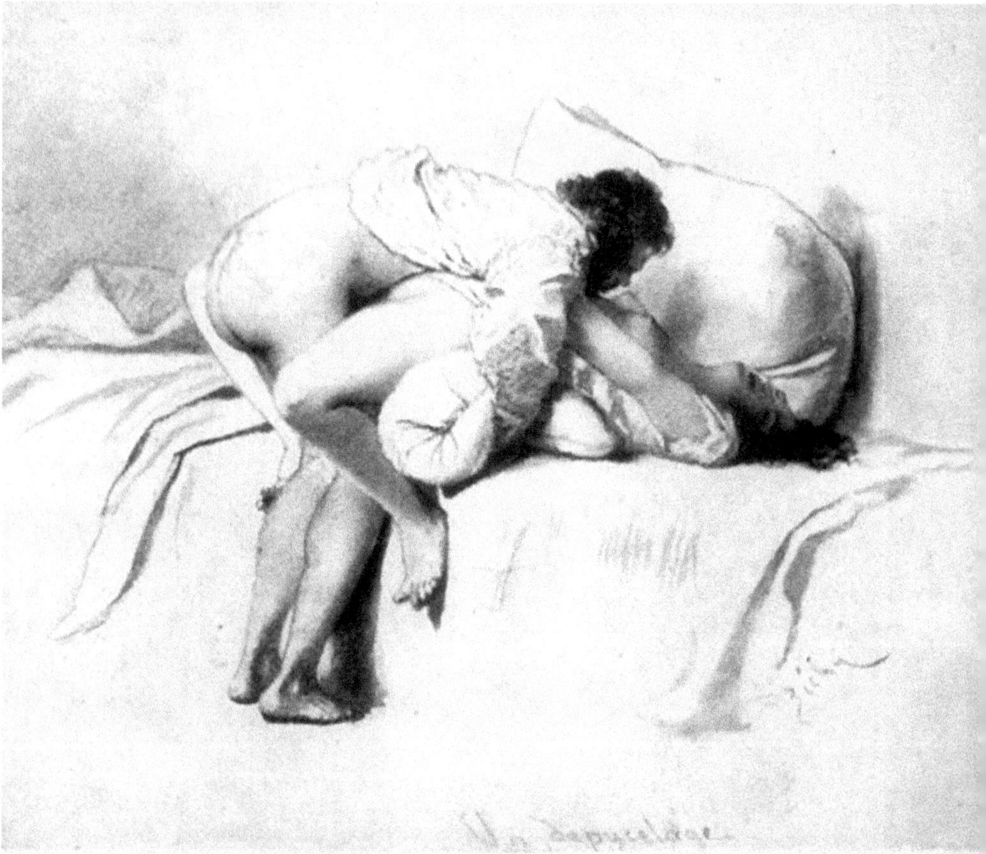

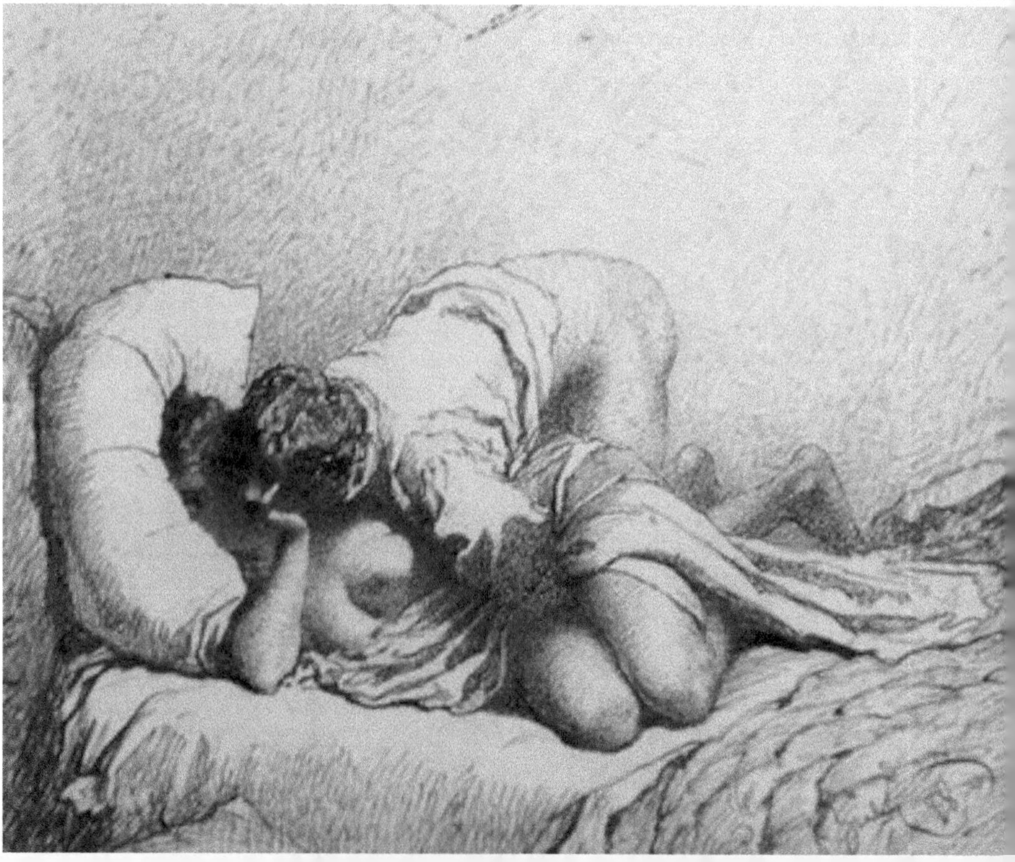

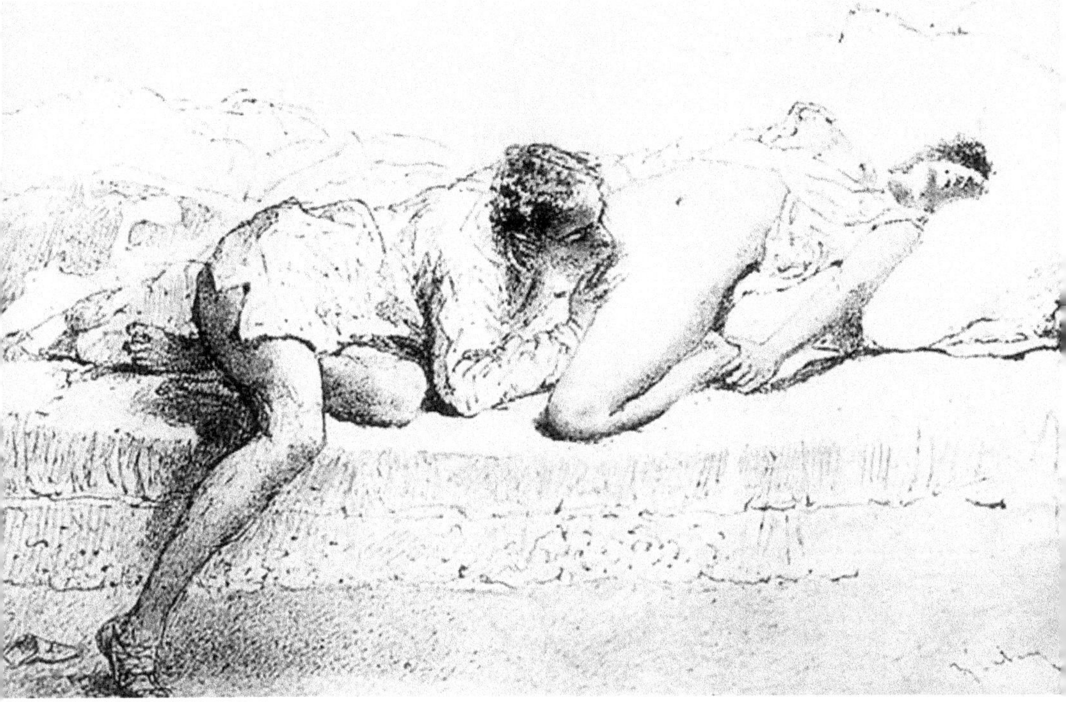

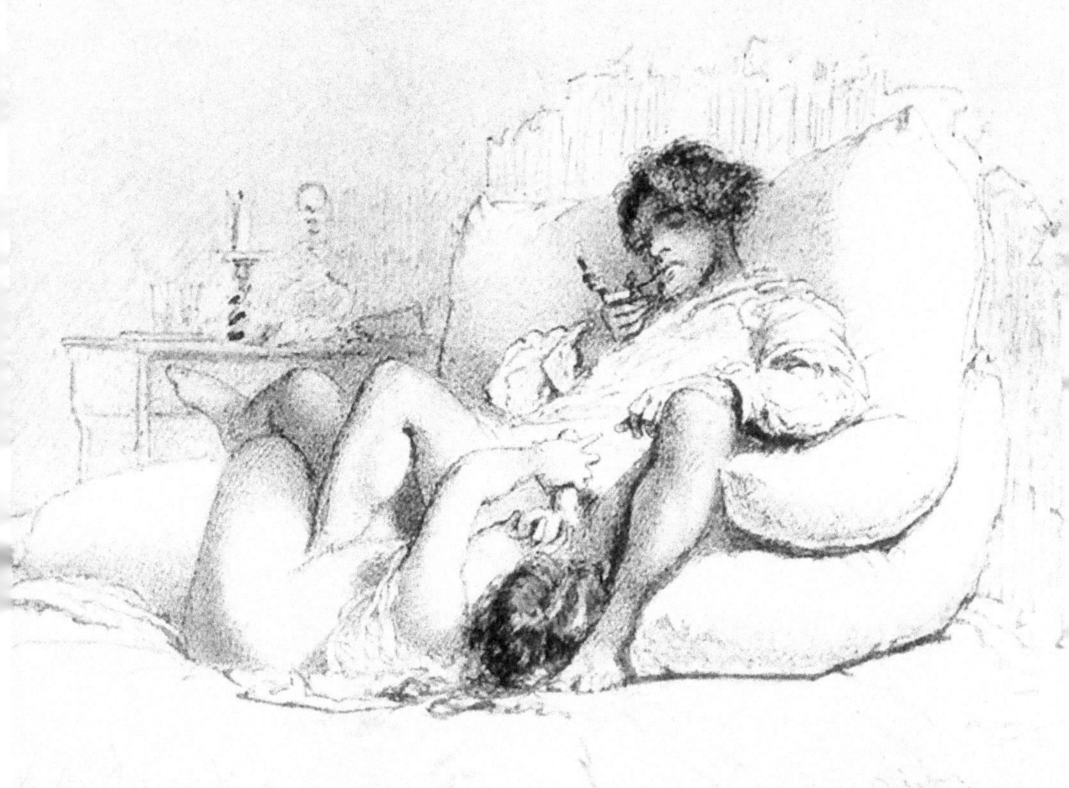

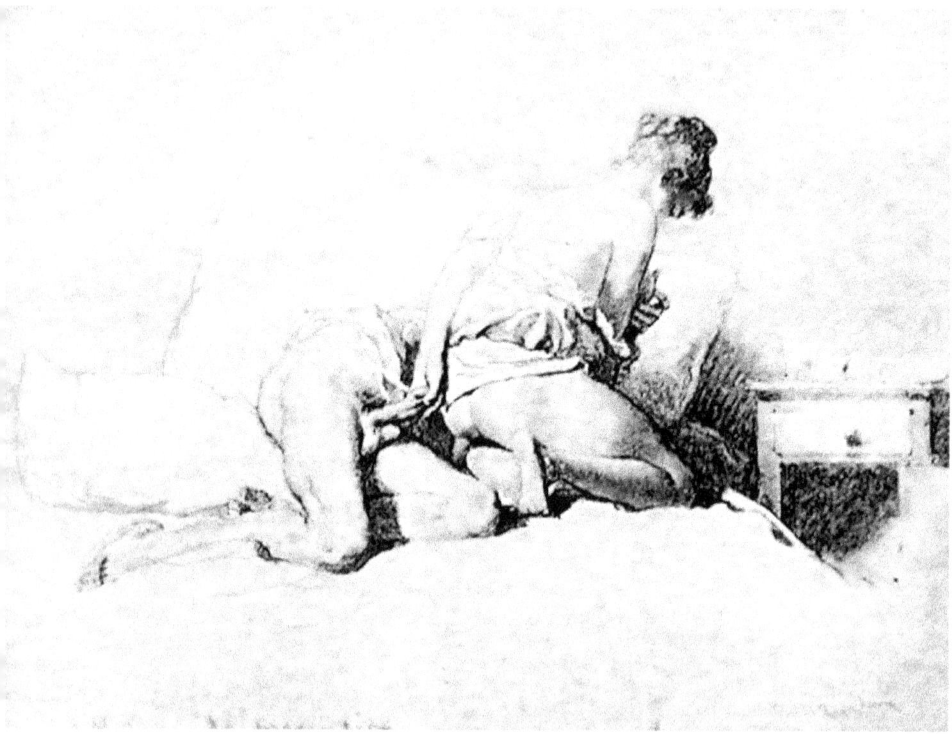

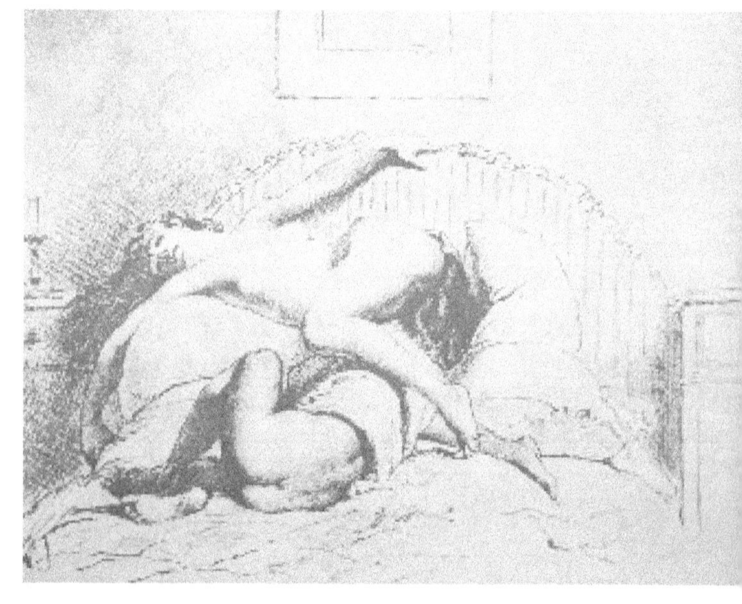

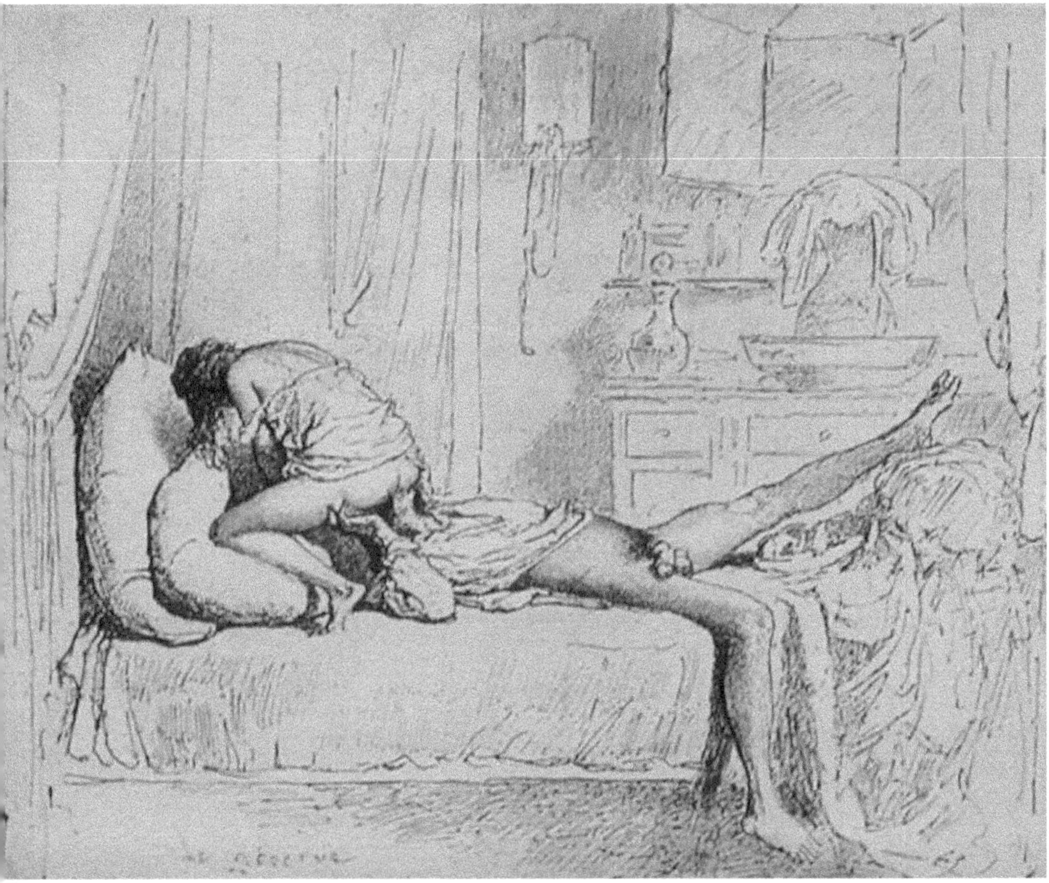

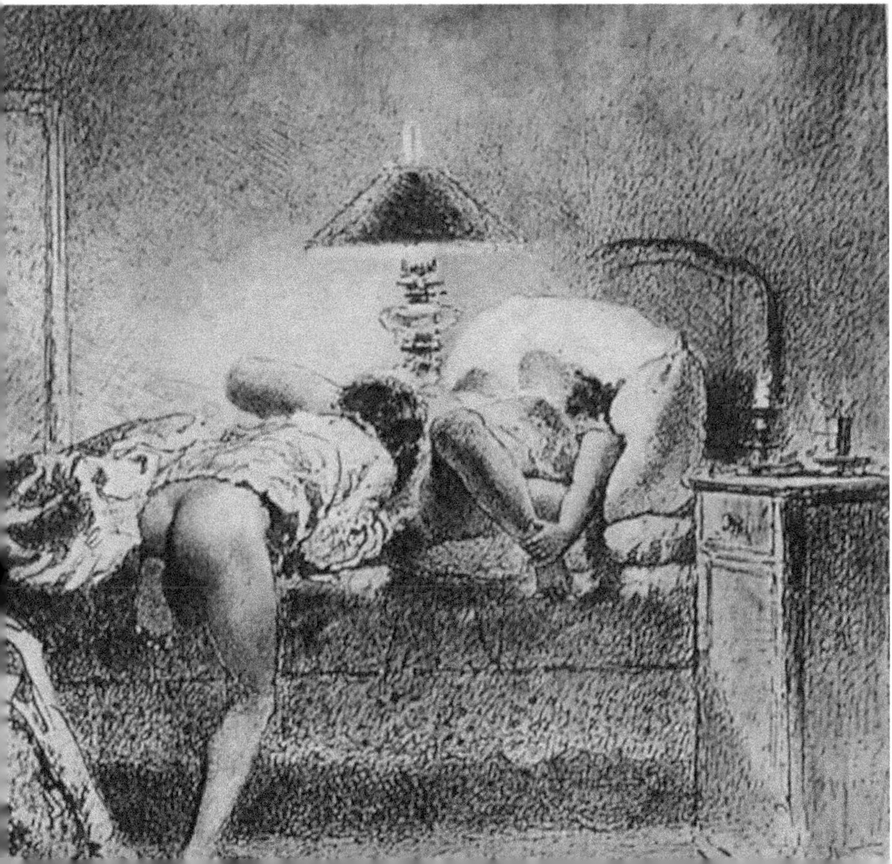

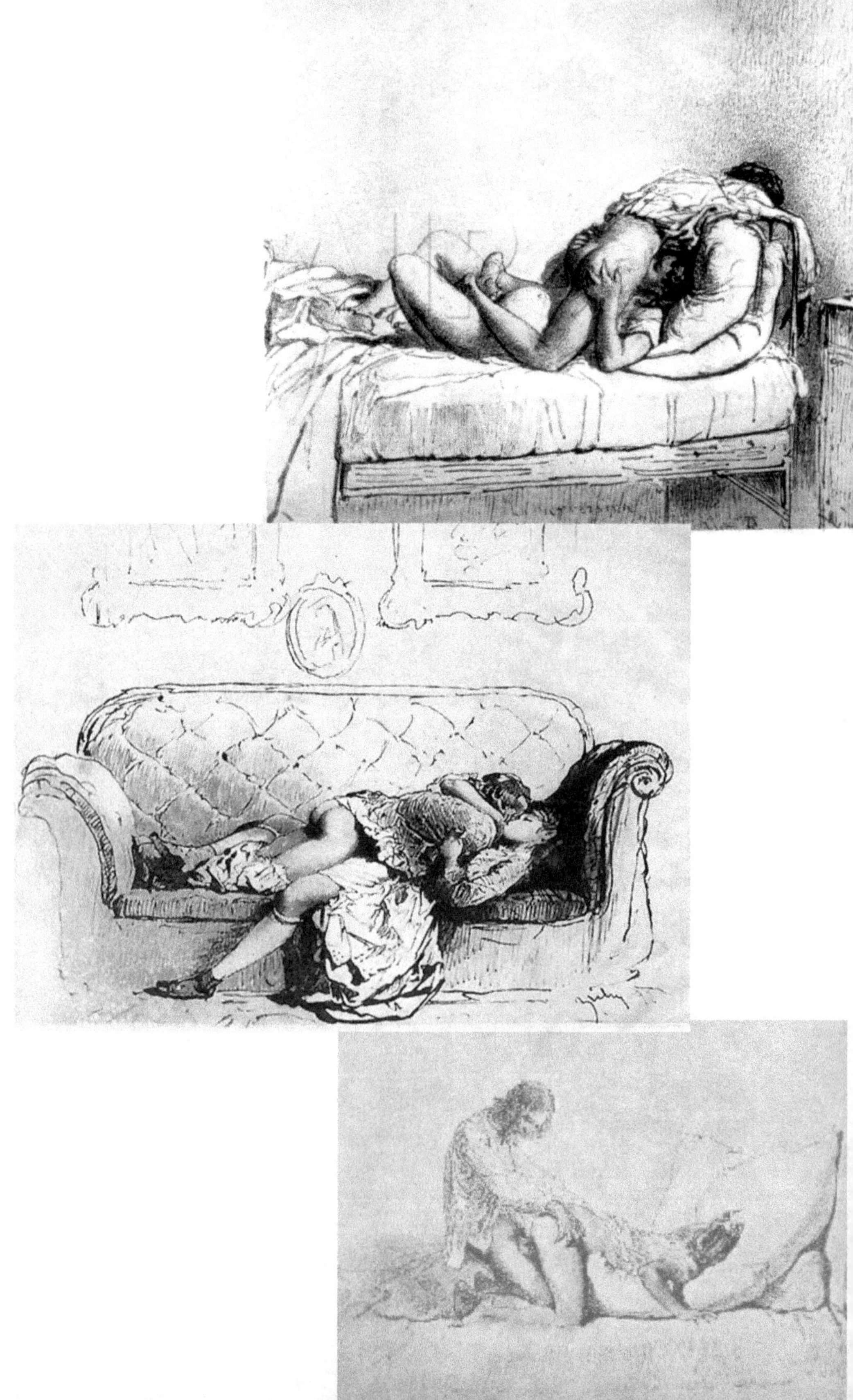

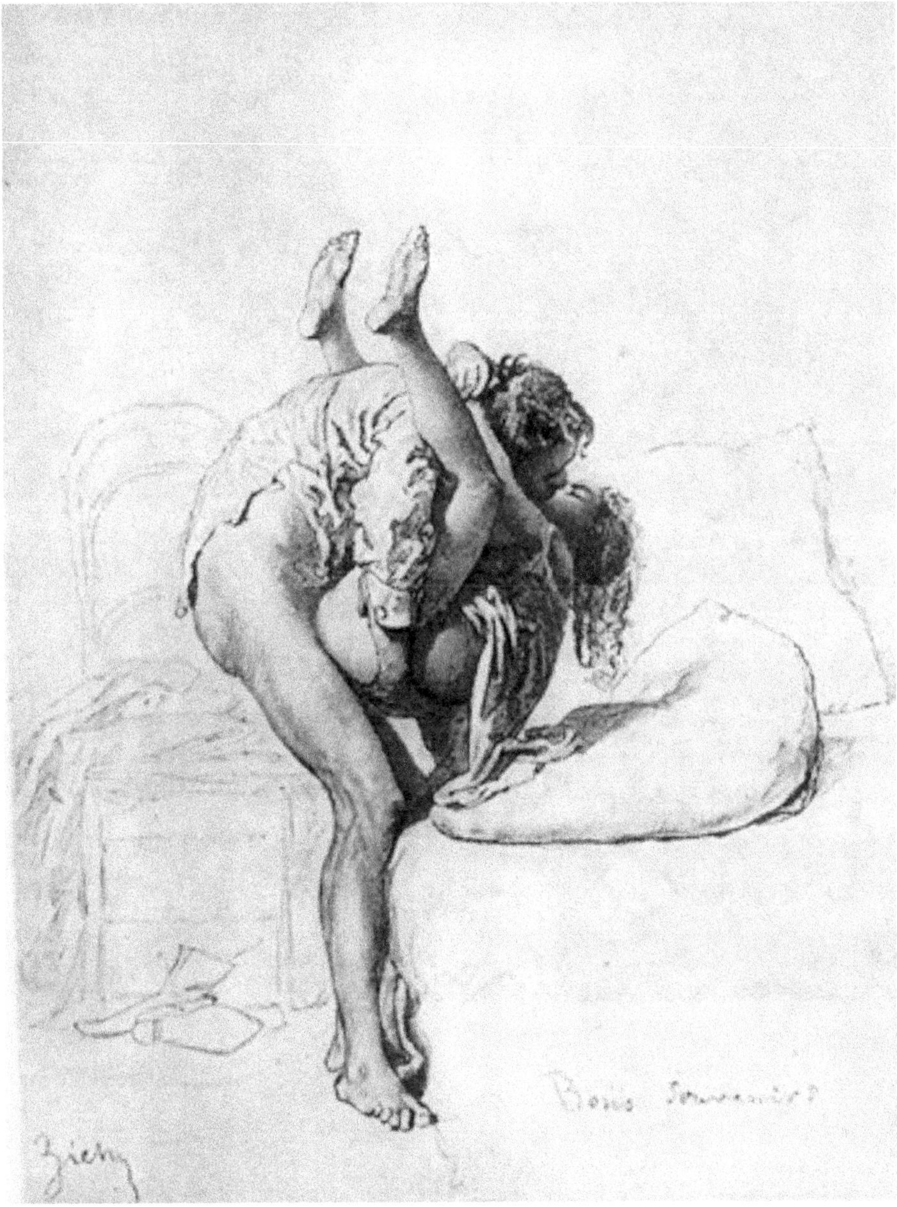

Bons souvenirs?
Zichy

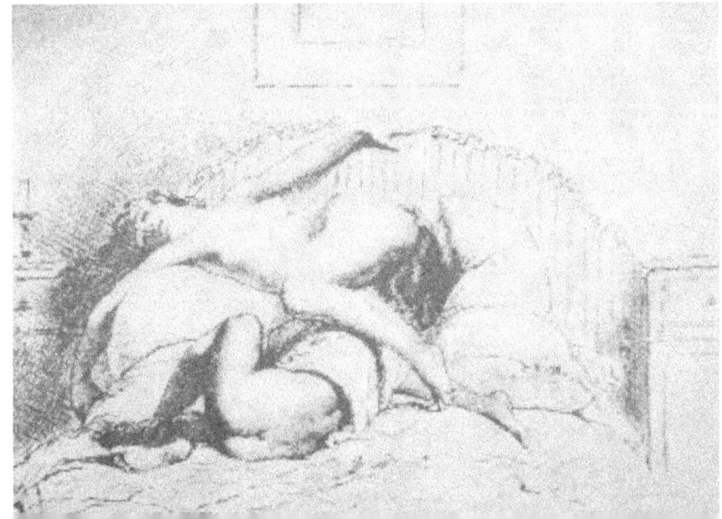

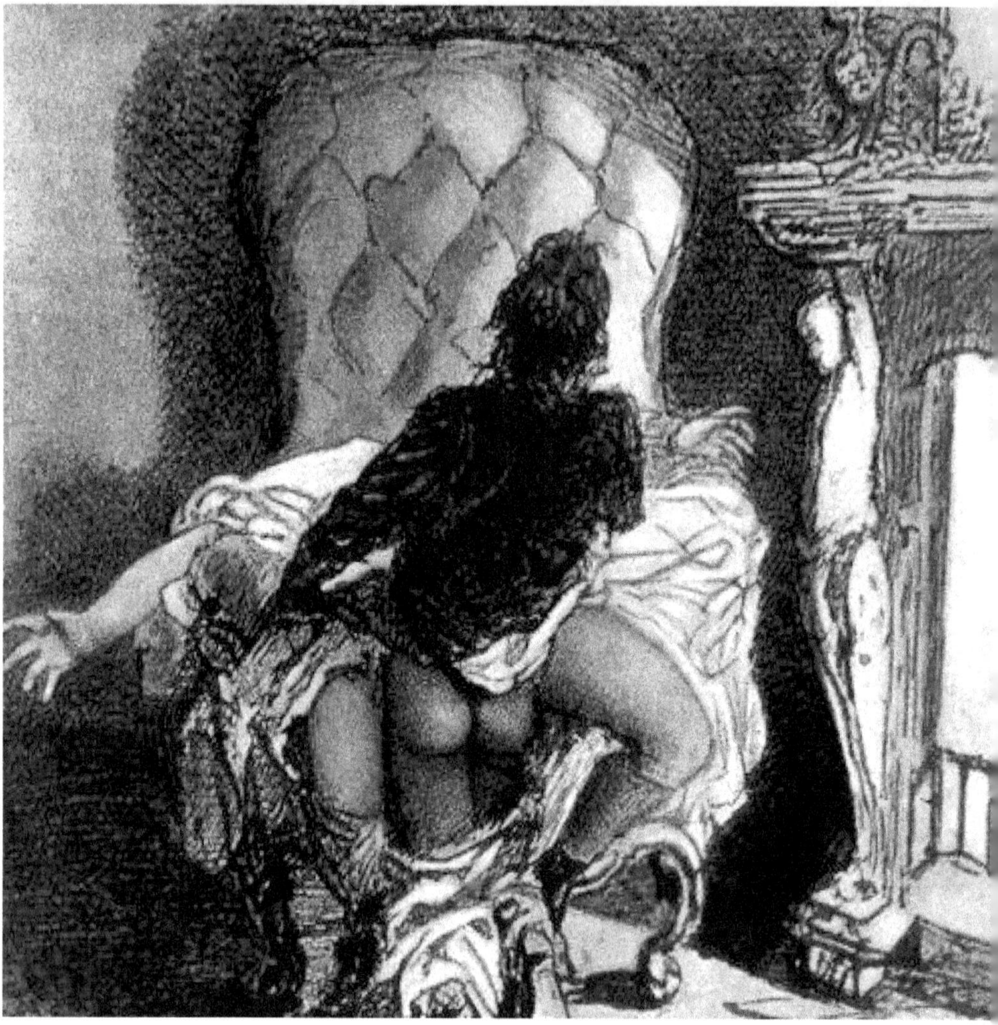

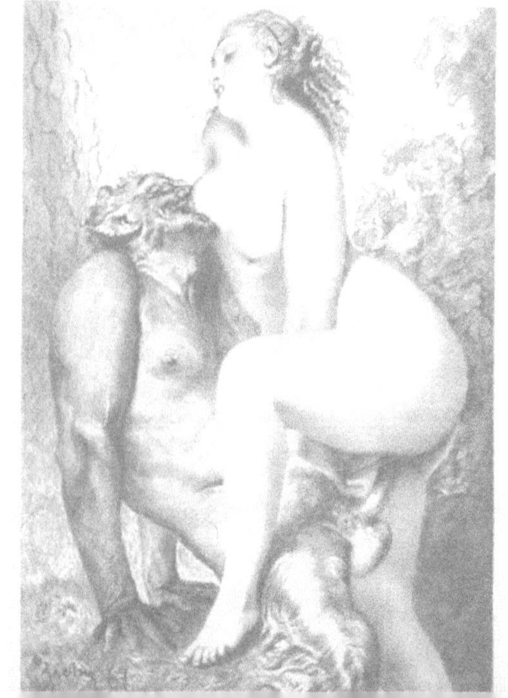

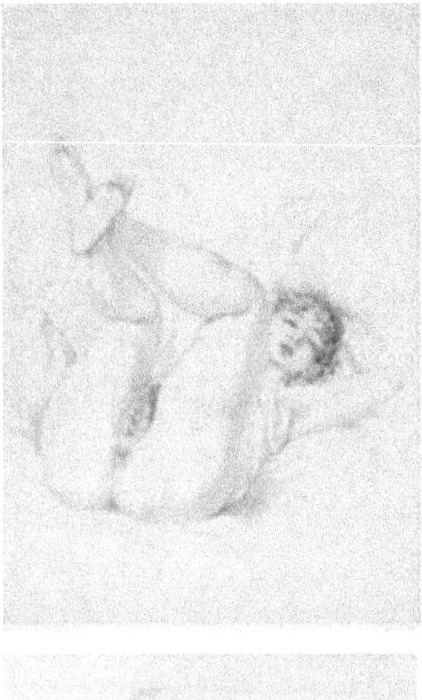

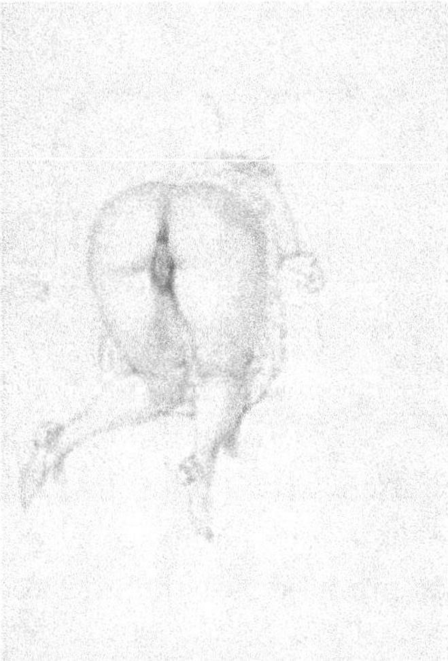

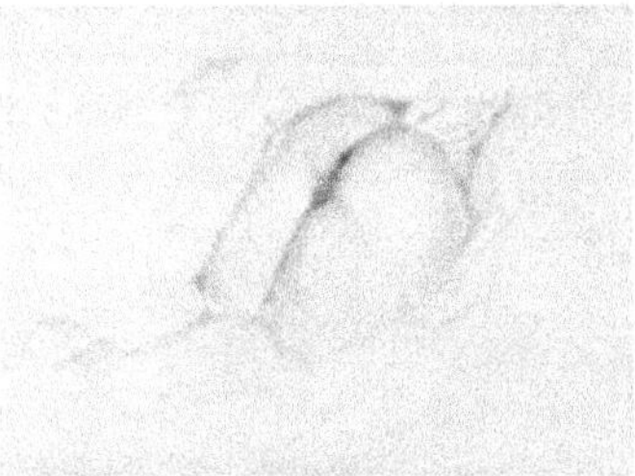

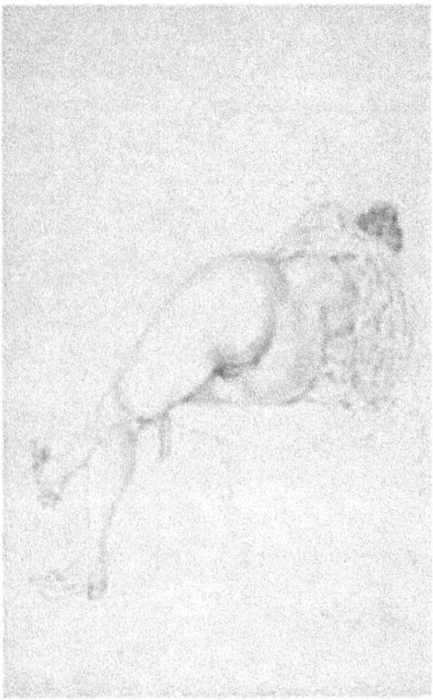

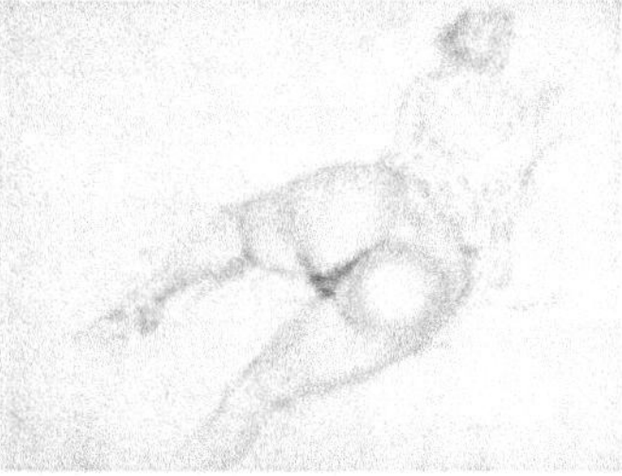

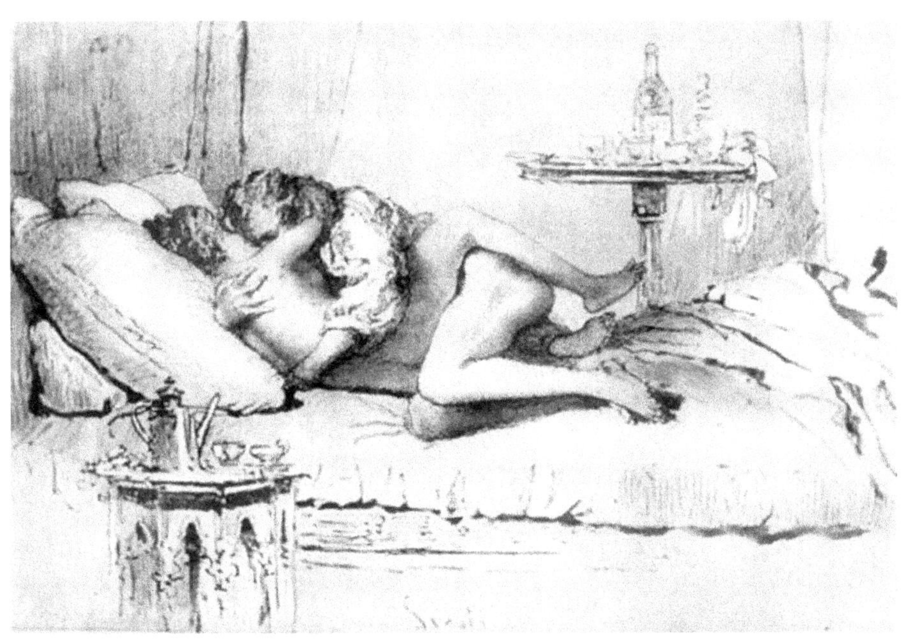

JULES PASCIN

Jules Pascin (born Julius Mordecai Pincas, 1885 - 1930) was a Bulgarian artist who lived in Paris. He was known for his drawings and paintings of young women, including prostitutes. He committed suicide in 1930.

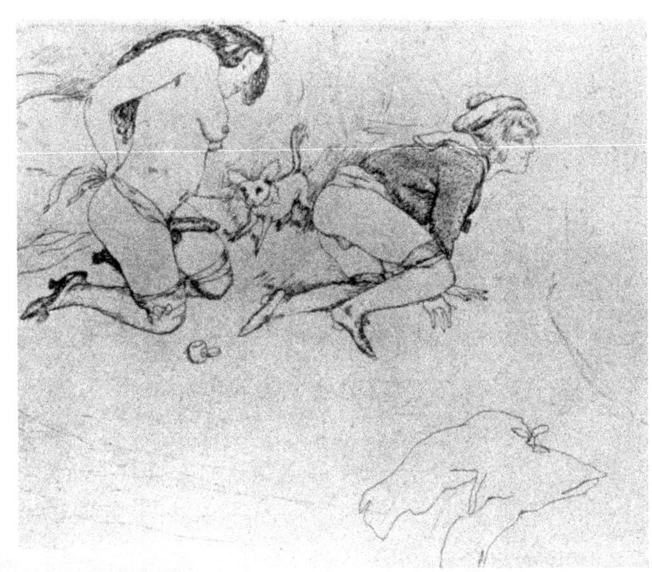

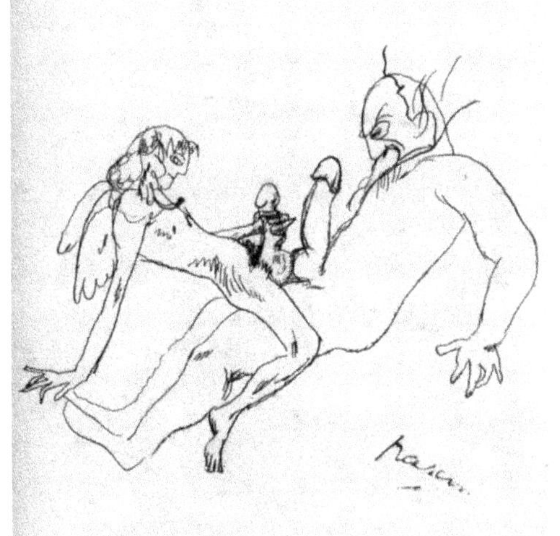

Jules Pascin

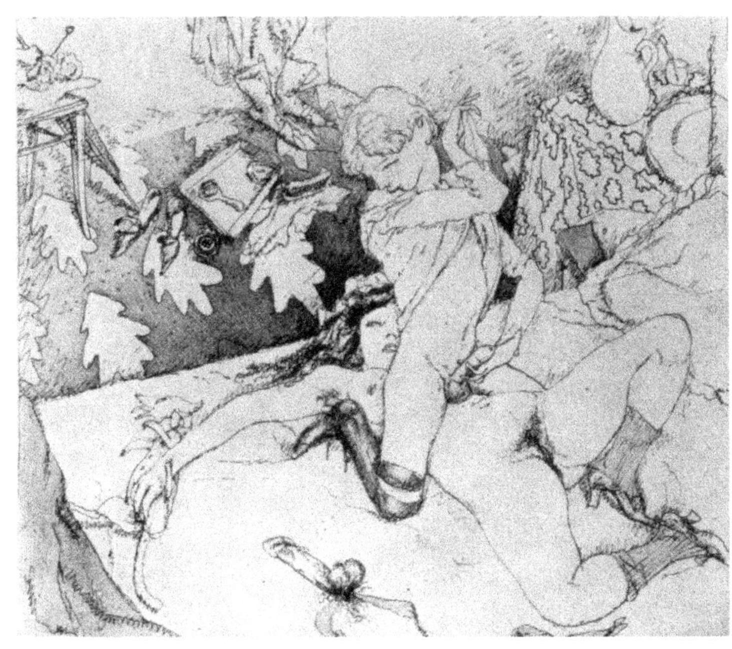

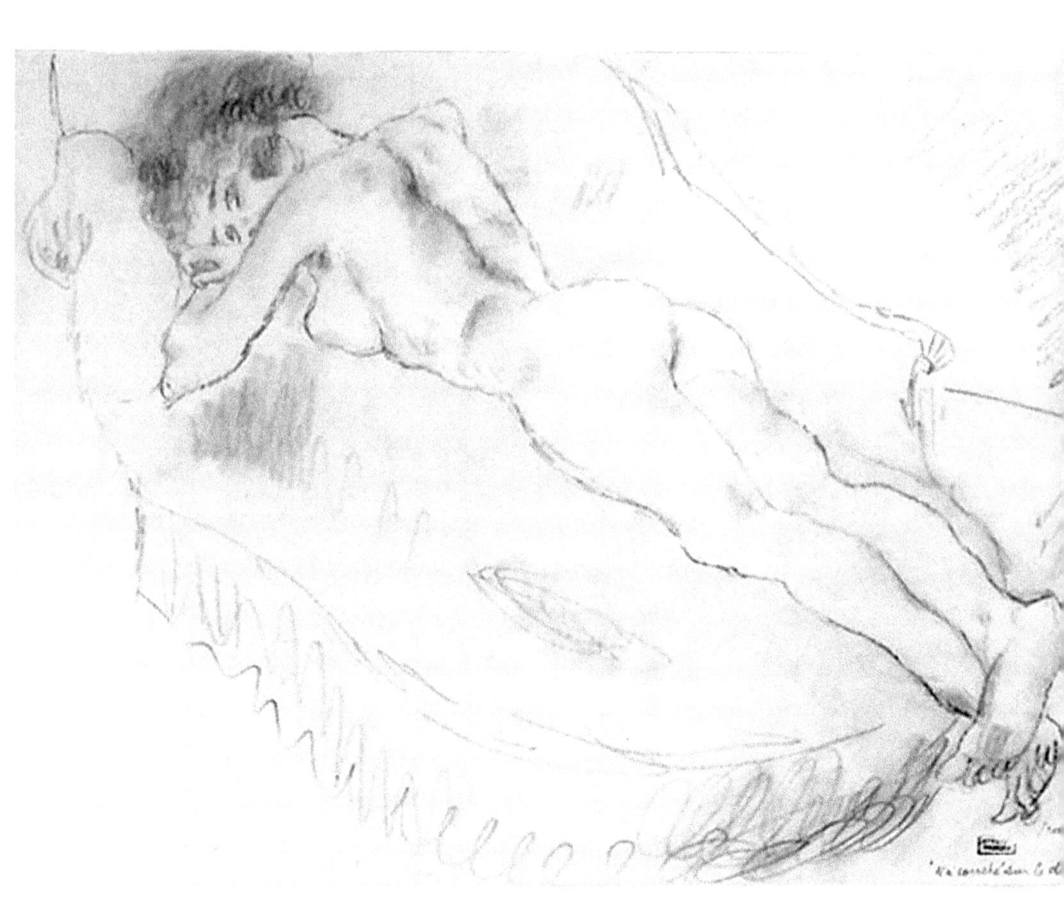

Jules Pascin

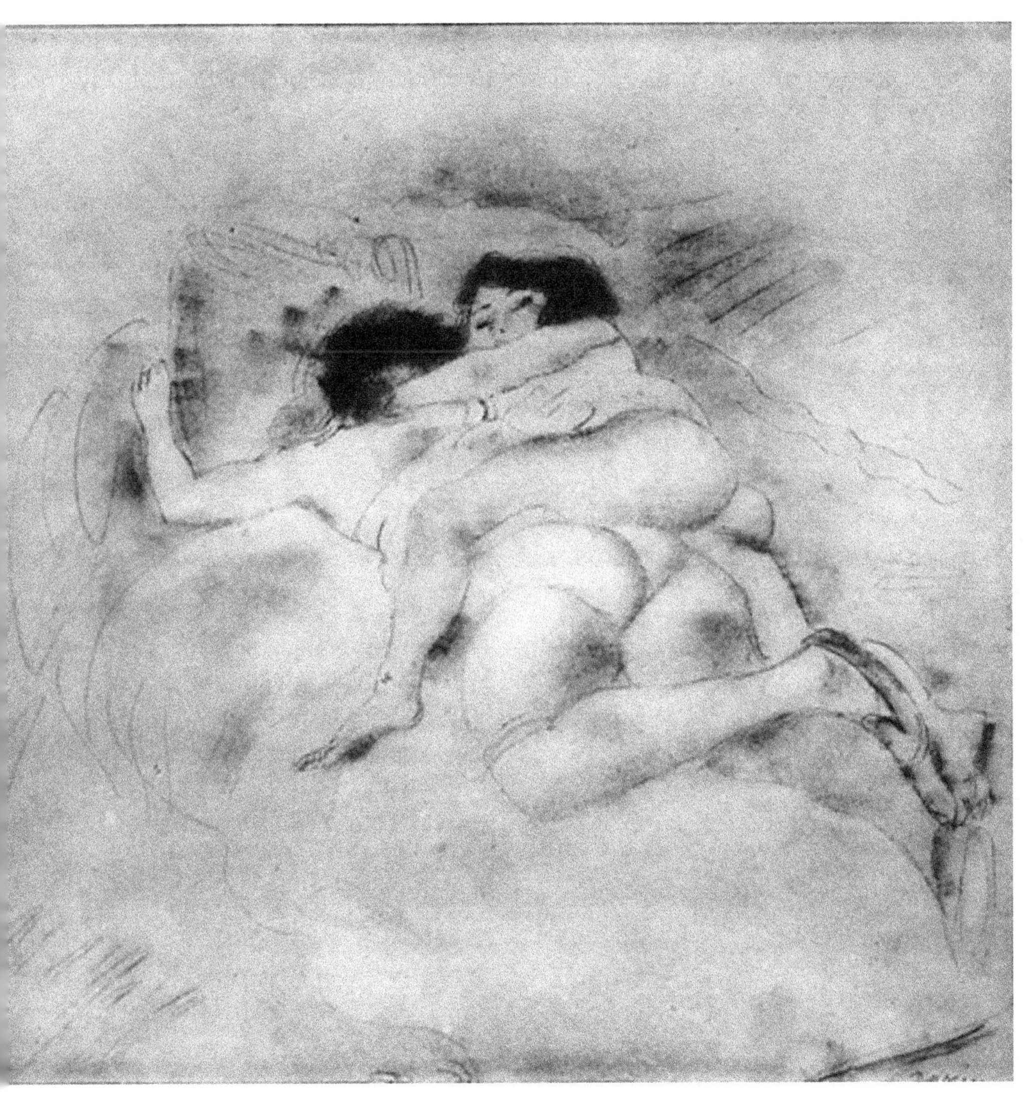

Jules Pascin

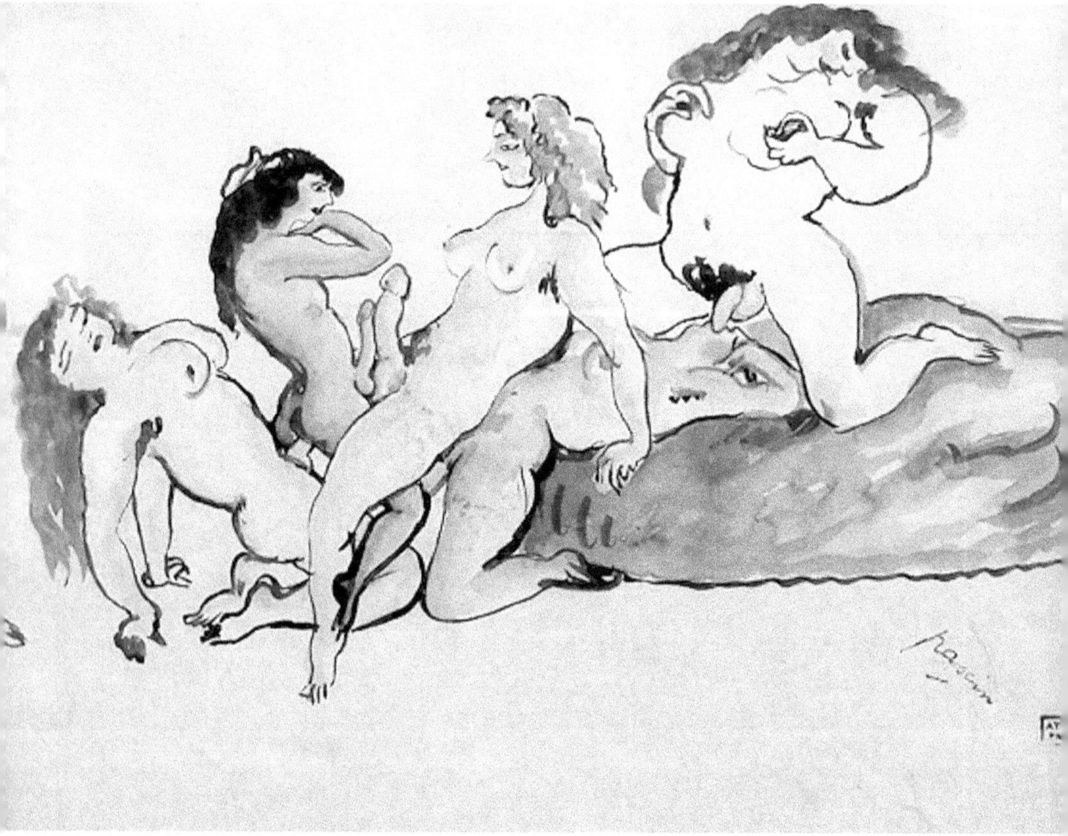

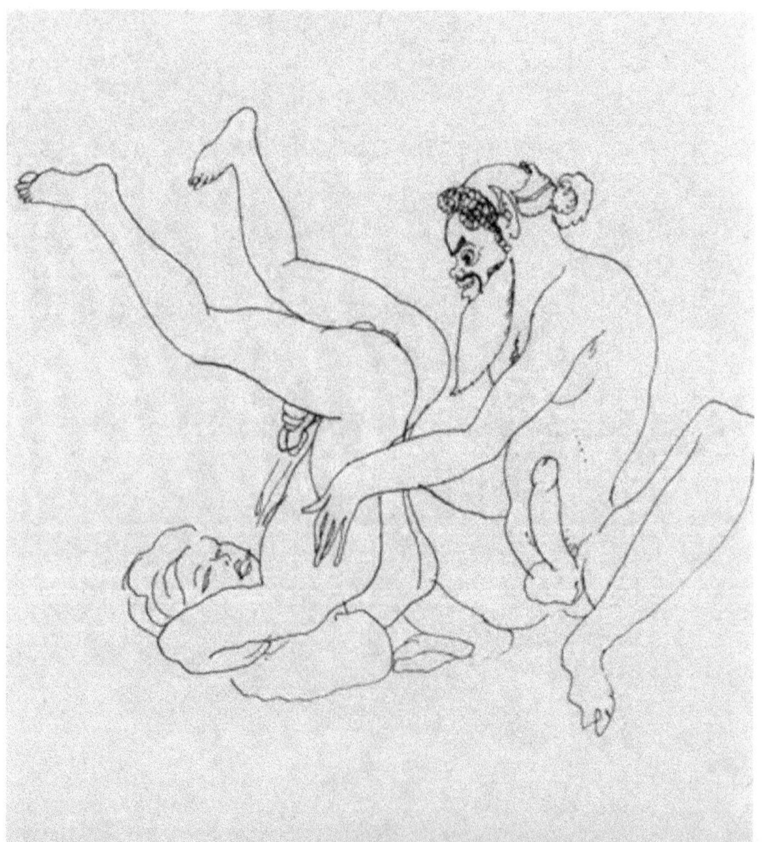

Jules Pascin

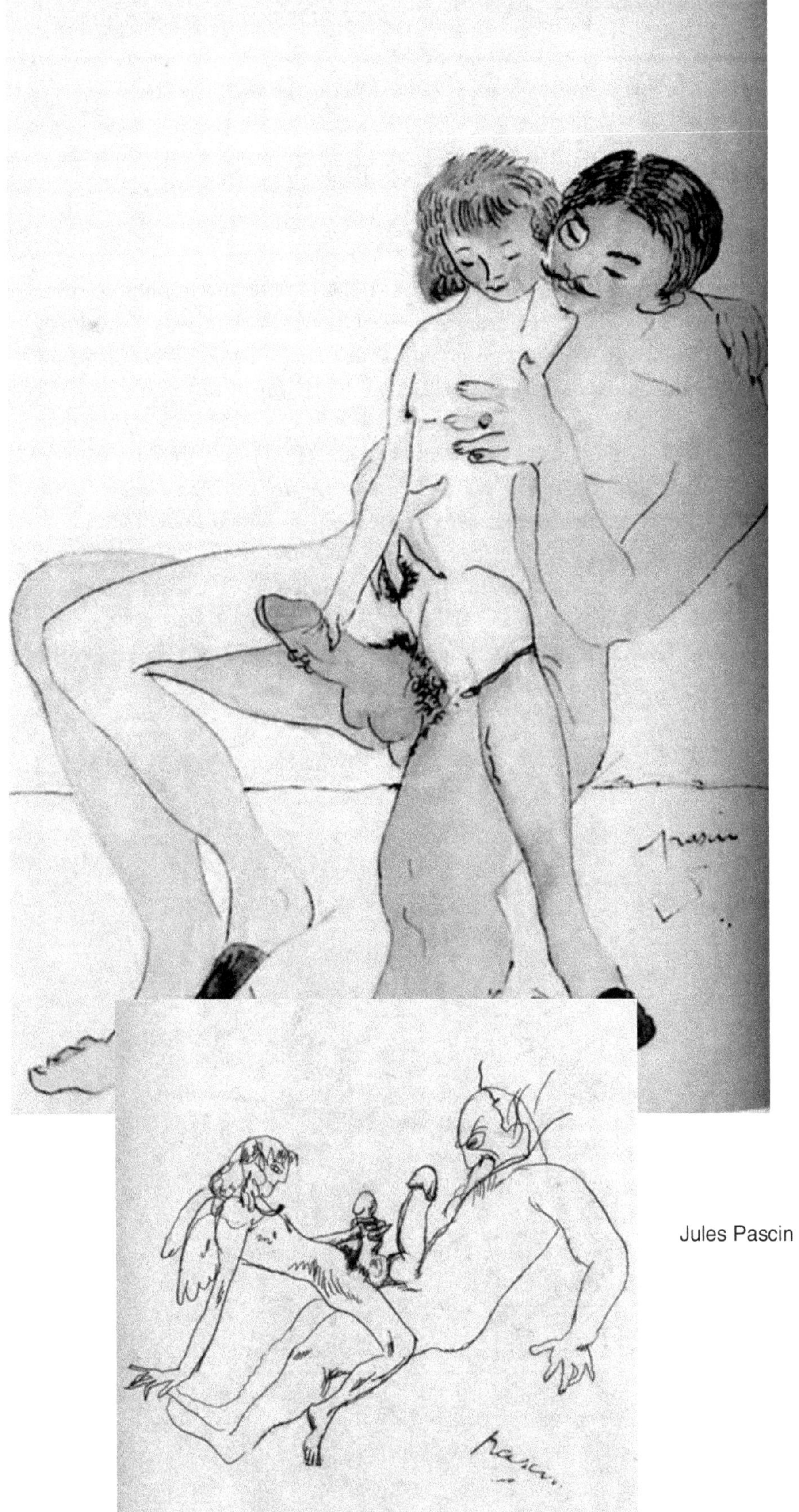

Jules Pascin

PIERRE LOUŸS

The works of Pierre Louÿs (1870-1925) include many photographs, including plenty of erotica (one of Louÿs' books was a study of women's asses, entitled *La cul de la femme*). Some classic, revered movies have been based on Louÿs' work: for instance, his book *La femme et le pantin* was adapted as the Josef von Sternberg-Marlene Dietrich movie *The Devil Is a Woman* (1935) and the last film of Luis Buñuel, *That Obscure Object of Desire* (1977). *La femme et le pantin* was also the basis of a 1992 TV movie, a 2007 TV movie, and movies in 1920, 1929 and 1946.[1]

Pierre Louÿs' erotic poetry included *Astarte* and *Songs of Bilitis*,[2] novels such as *Aphrodite* (1896) and *La femme et le pantin* (1898), and erotic works such as *Les Aventures du roi Pausole* (1901), *Pervigilium Mortis* (1916), and *Manuel de civilité pour les petites filles à l'usage des maisons d'éducation* (1917).

1 Other movies based on Pierre Louÿs' work include: *Bilitis* (1977), *A Woman Like Satan* (1959), *Aphrodite* (1982), *Les filles de leur mère* (1985), *The Adventures of King Pausole* (1933), *Take Me Naked* (1966) and *The Merry Monarch* (1933).
2 Claude Debussy set some of the *Chansons de Bilitis* to music in 1898.

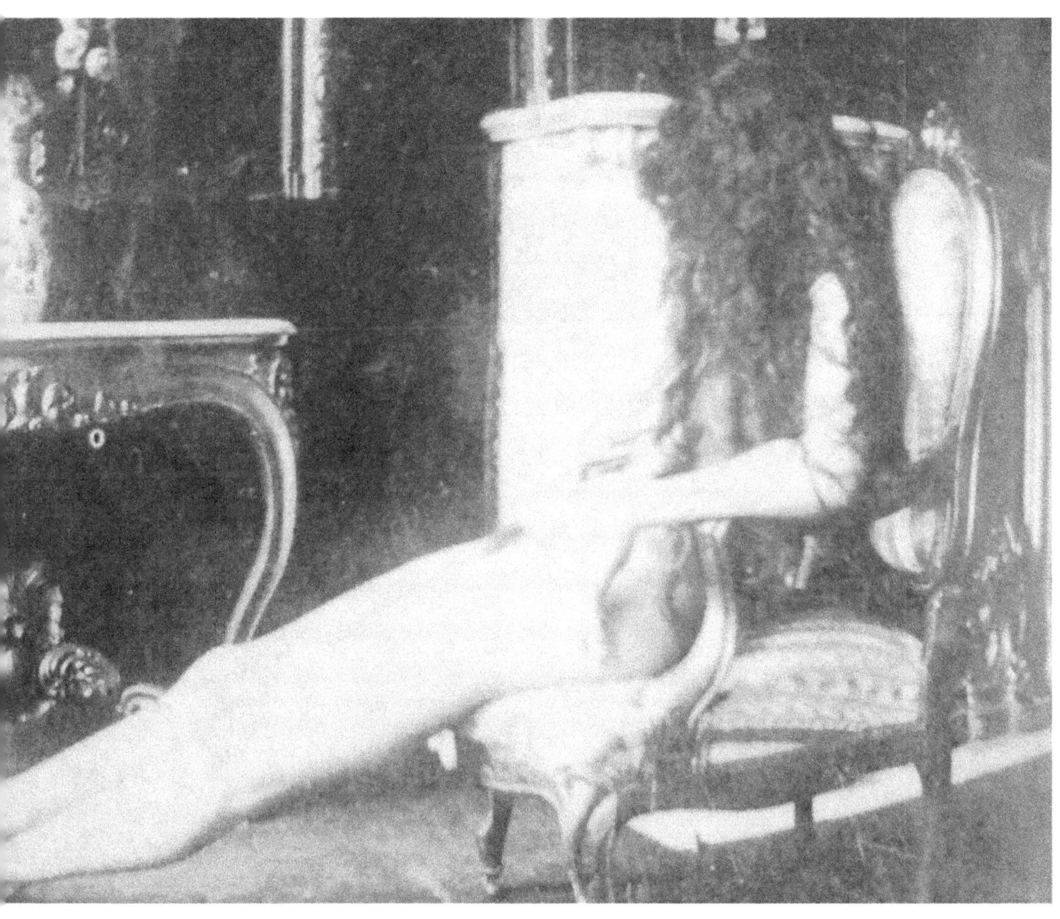

Pierre Loüys on this page and the following pages.
One of the great erotic artists of the modern era,
Louÿs wrote erotica and took many erotic photos.

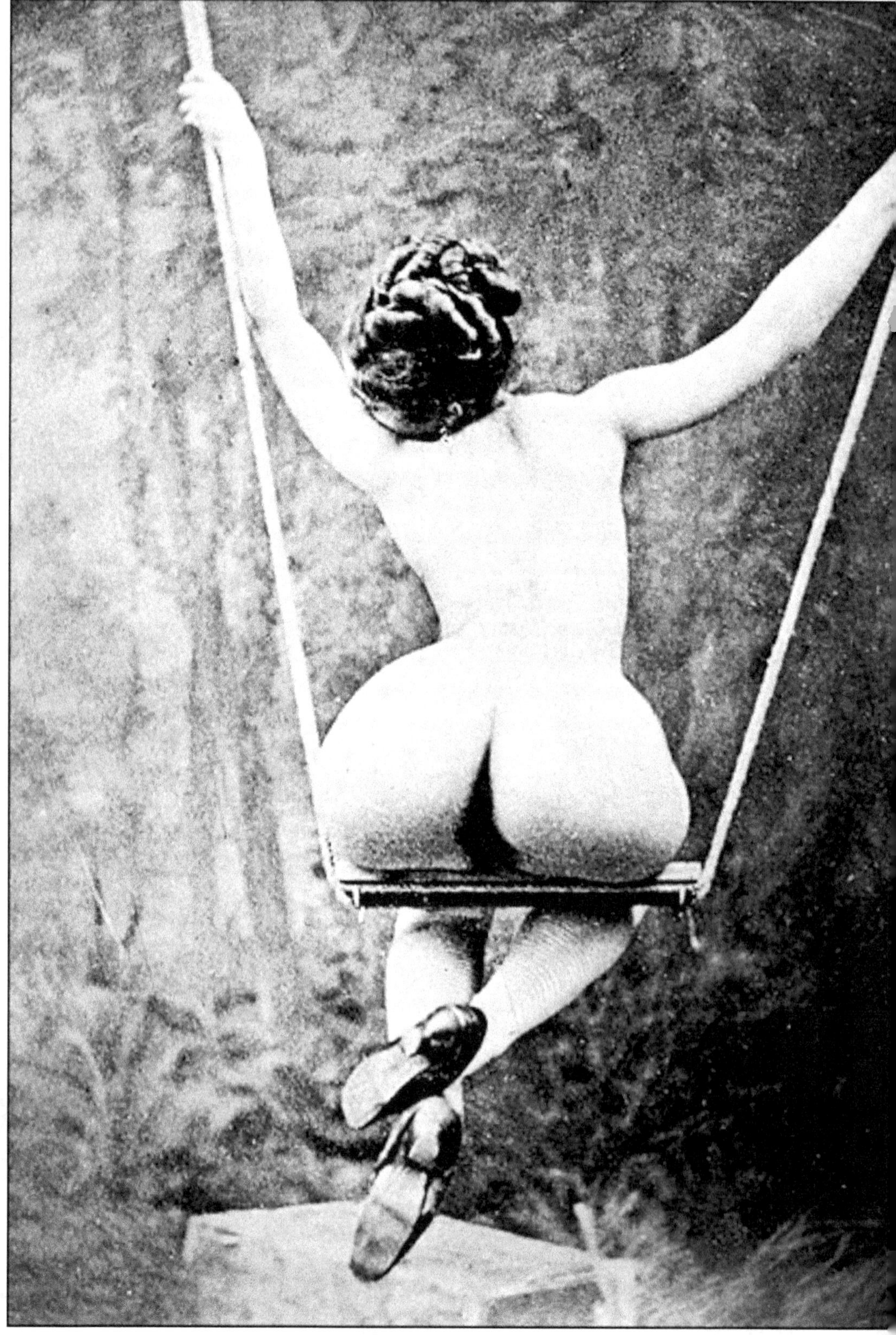

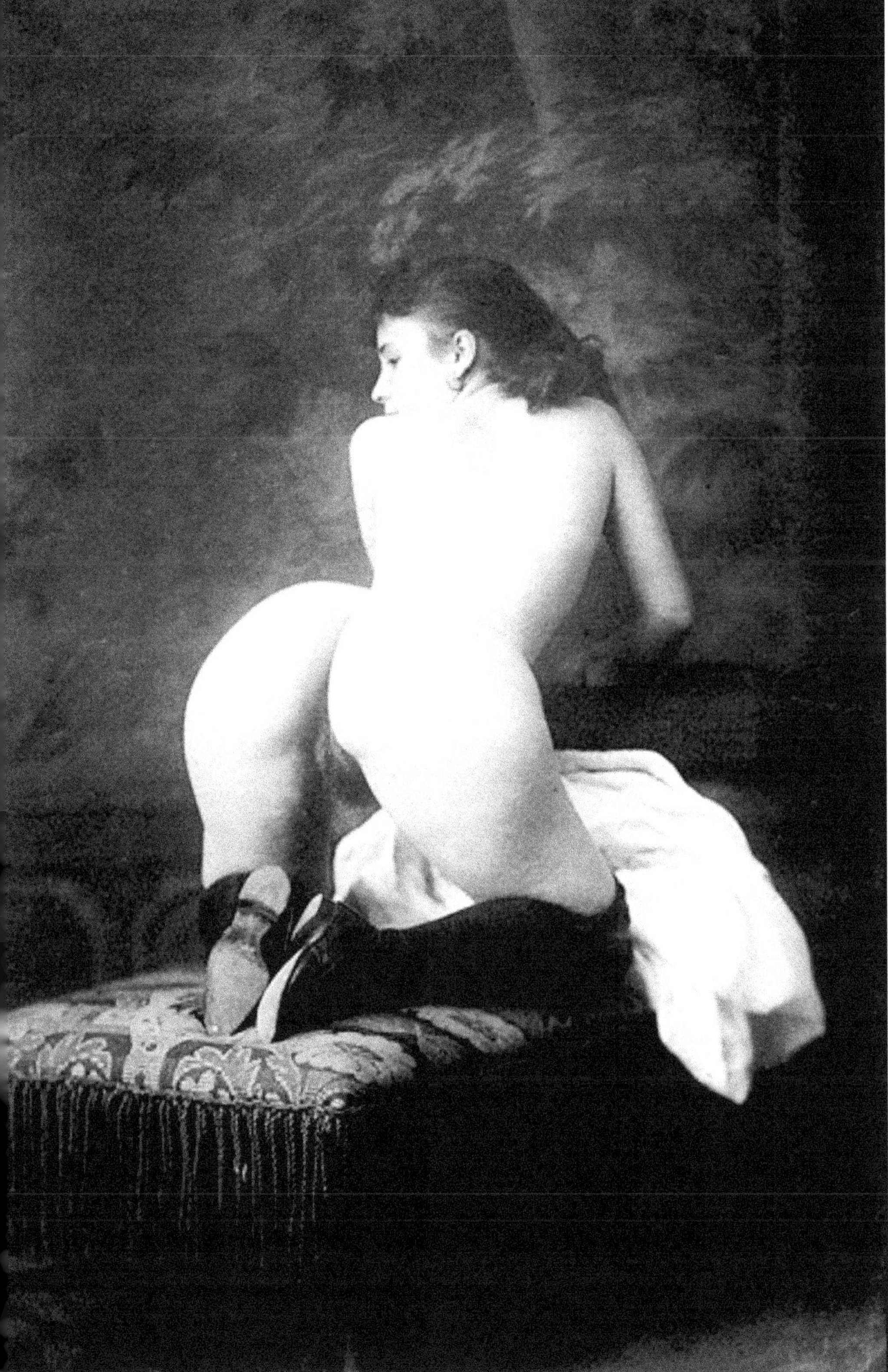

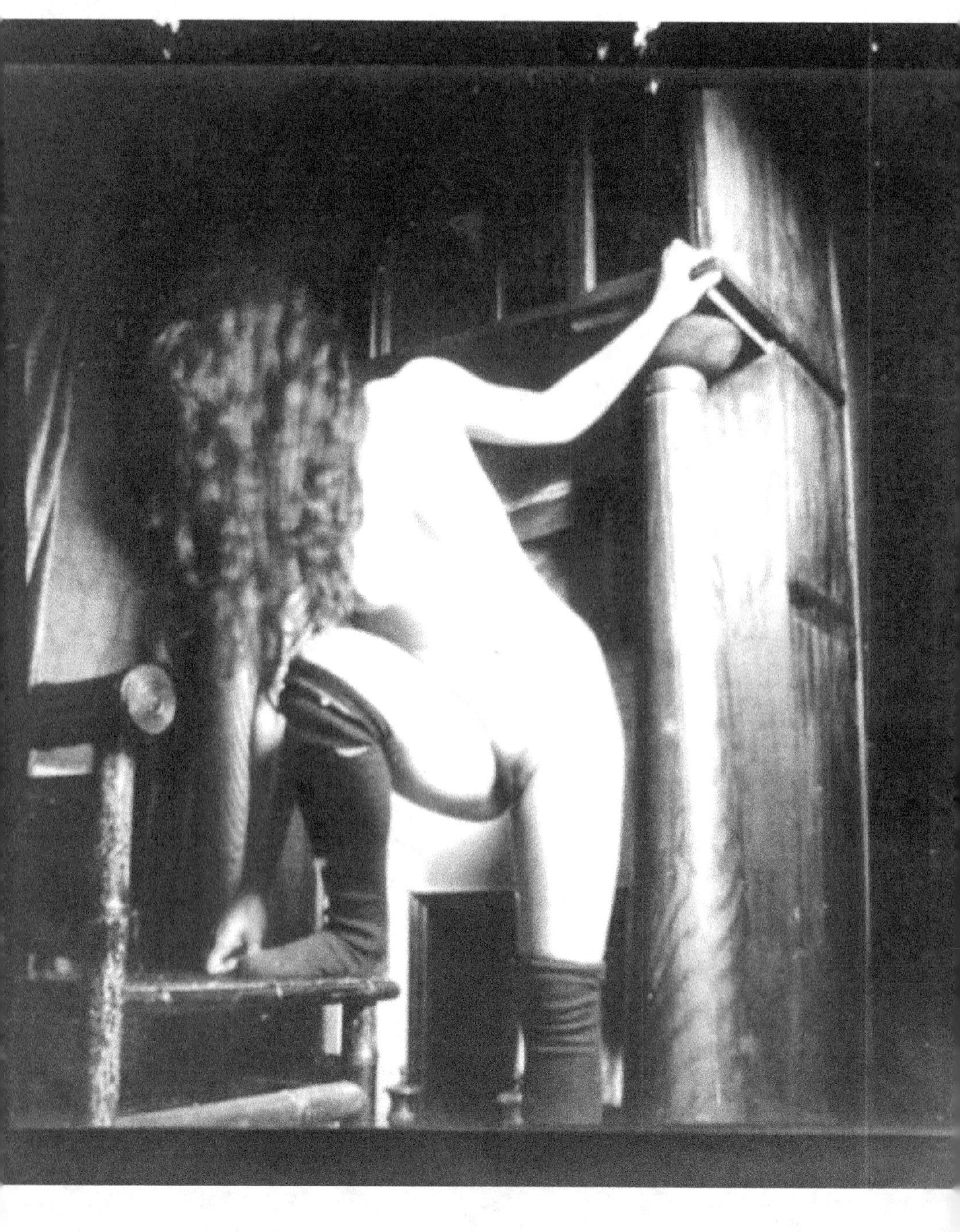

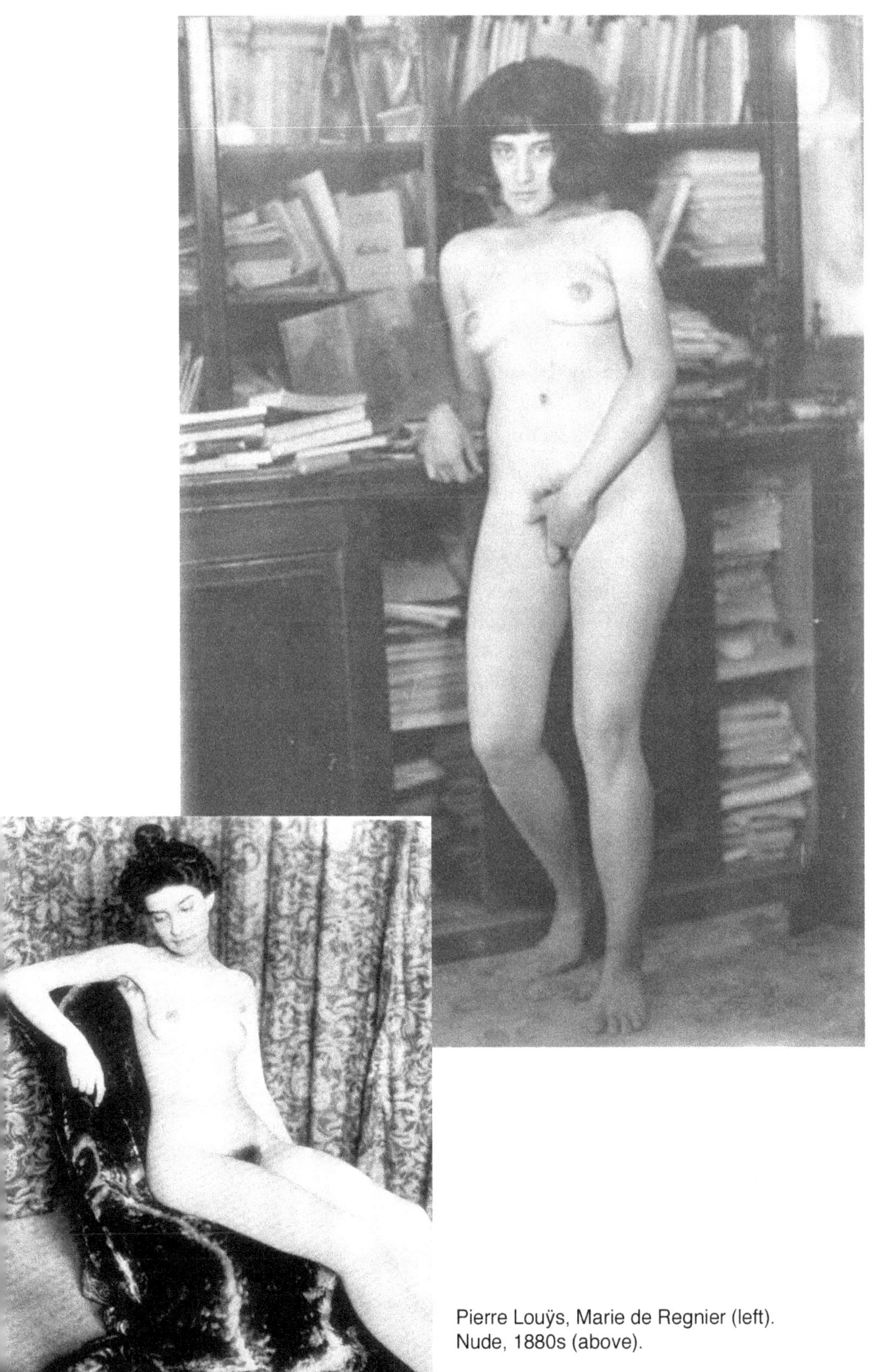

Pierre Louÿs, Marie de Regnier (left).
Nude, 1880s (above).

PHOTOGRAPHY

Eroticism in photography follows the same æsthetic and moral patterns as those found in painting. There are countless nudes in photography, ranging from 'high art' to pornography. Images such as those by US photographer Harry Callahan of his wife Eleanor seem to be distanced and formal, like the pastel nude drawings of Edgar Degas.[1] But the cool approach, of 'high art' photography, as in the art of Degas (who himself used photography), masks the age-old pornographic objectification of women.

Many erotic photographs have been marketed in the same way that erotica has always been marketed – as images of desire for consumption by devotees. One of the differences is that photographs can be reproduced in huge quantities – far more than the woodblock printing mechanisms of the early 19th century, for instance.

1 H. Callahan: *Eleanor, Port Huron,* 1954, 17 x 16.5cm, Museum of Modern Art, New York

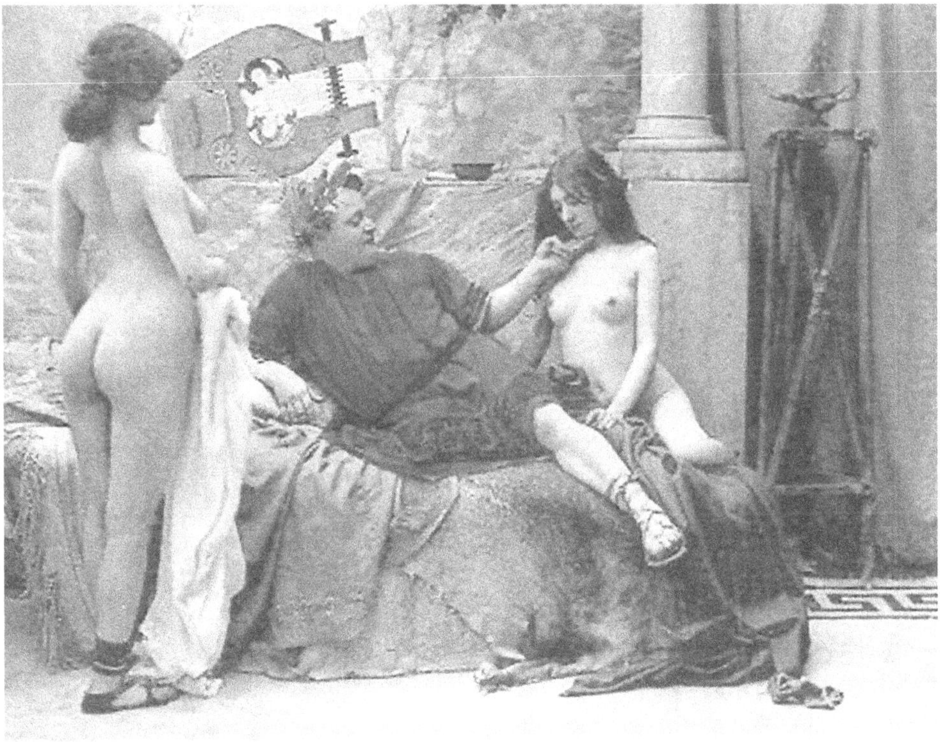

French Postcards, c. 1910 (above), c. 1920 (below).

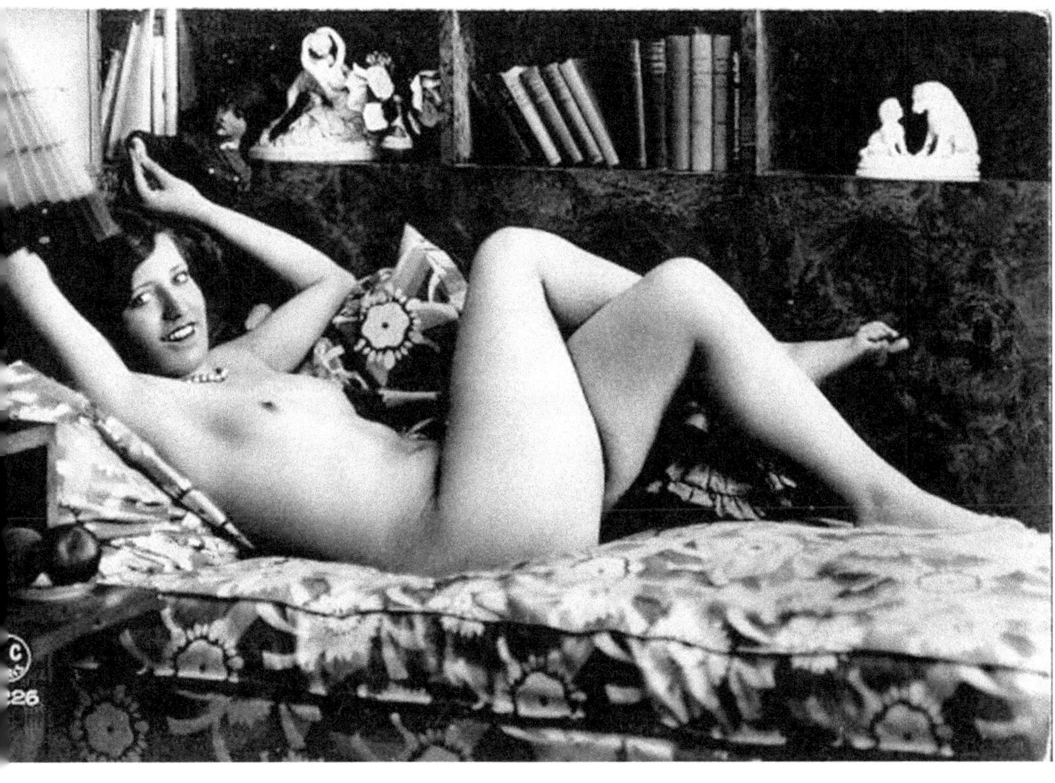

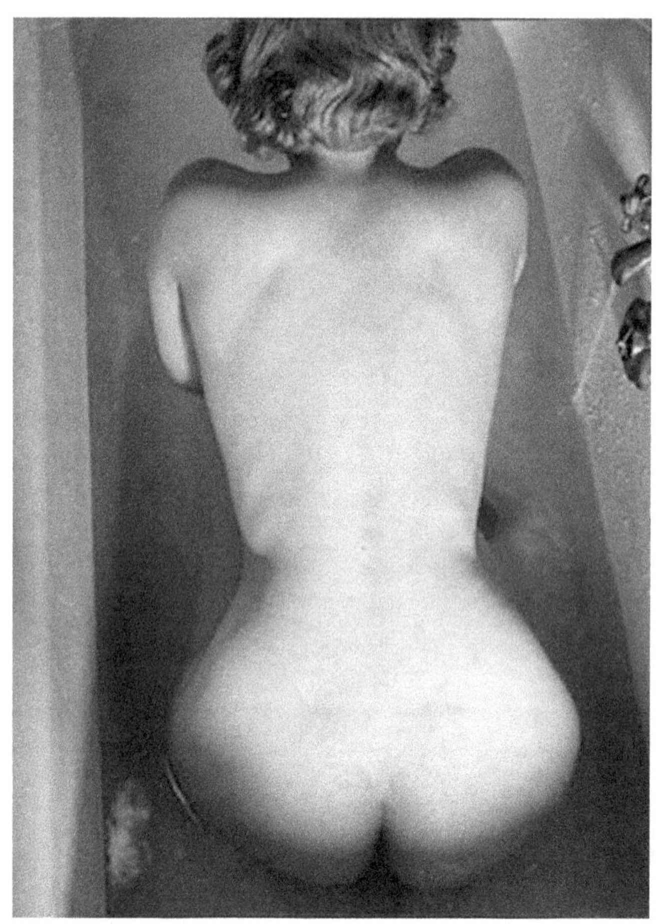

Brassai

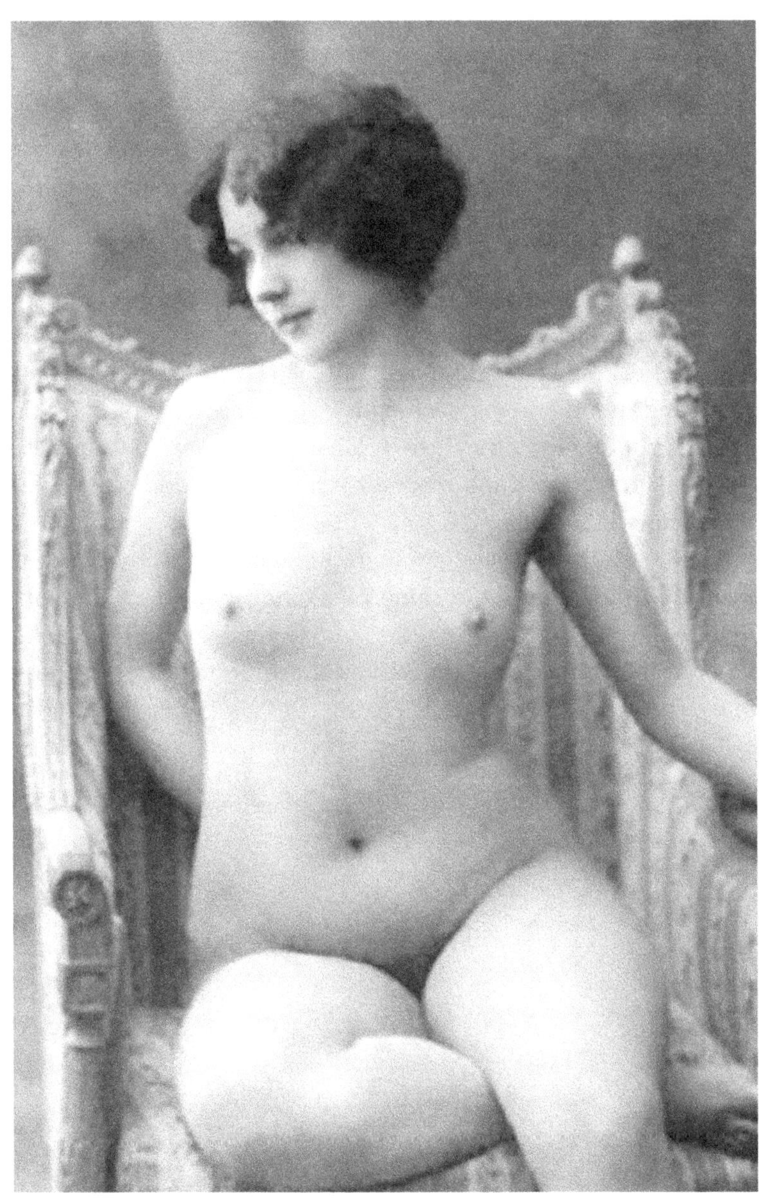

Jean Agélou, c. 1910s

PHOTOGRAPHY

Many photographic nudes are fetishized or eroticized as in pornography. A lot of photography beloved of amateur photographers is essentially soft porn, where 'models' are depicted in swimsuits or topless, against coloured backgrounds and the 'models' have glamorous hairstyles and glossy make-up. These pictures are featured on the covers of amateur photography and digital art magazines. These magazines are full of copy on computer art, digital and photographic techniques, but the examples of the genres of photography they use to illustrate their technical articles - sport, nature, landscape, portrait - are used side-by-side with erotic images of women.

And in many of these photographs included here, many of which are anonymous, the same conflicting issues are at work: desire and pleasure on one side, and technology and the mass media on the other; self-expression and art on one side, and taste and censorship on the other.

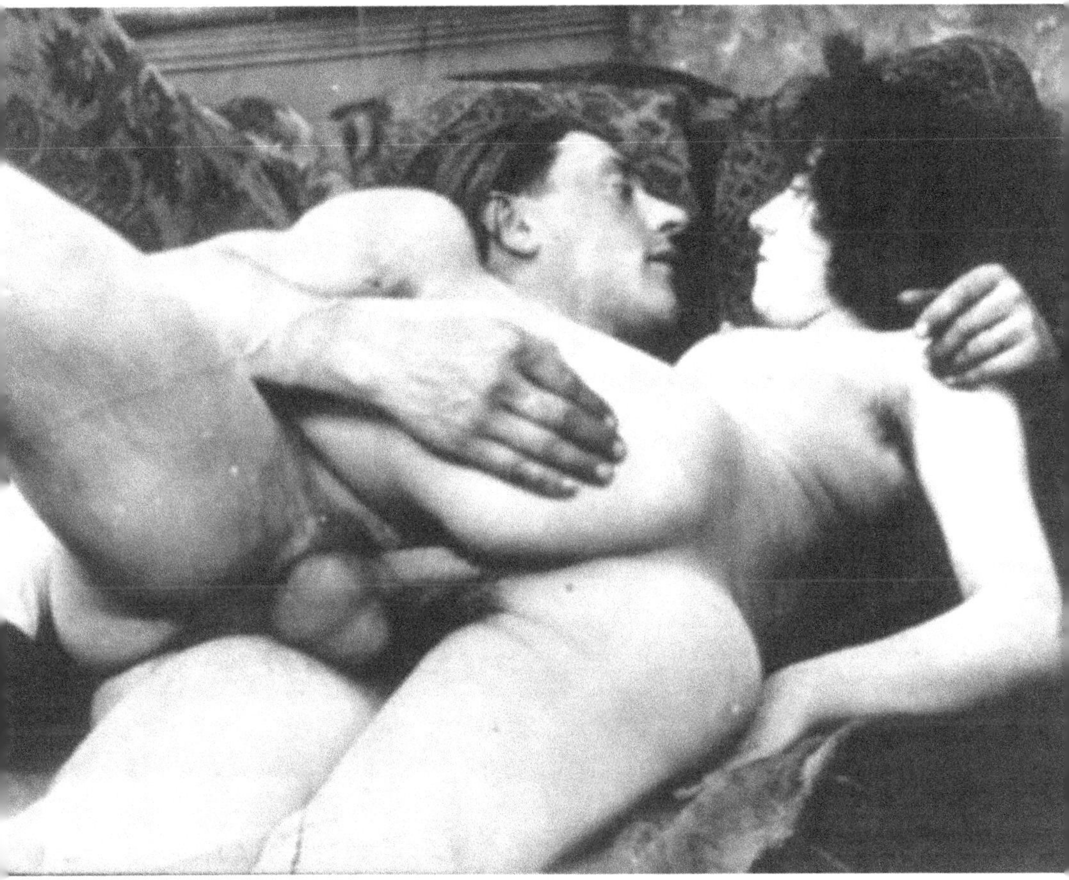

Anonymous, early 20th century

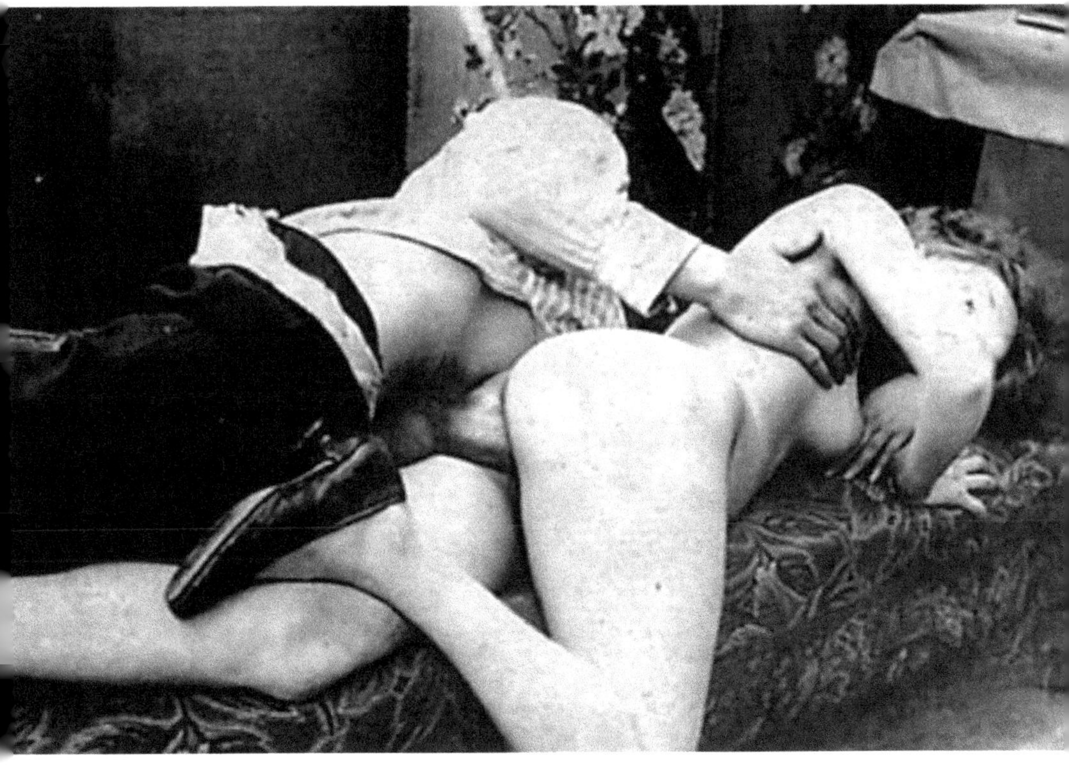

ALMERY LOBEL-RICHE

Almery Lobel-Riche (1880-1950) was a Swiss artist (born in Geneva), who created several erotic works, as well as illustrating books by Charles Baudelaire, Oscar Wilde, Pierre Louys and Paul Valéry.

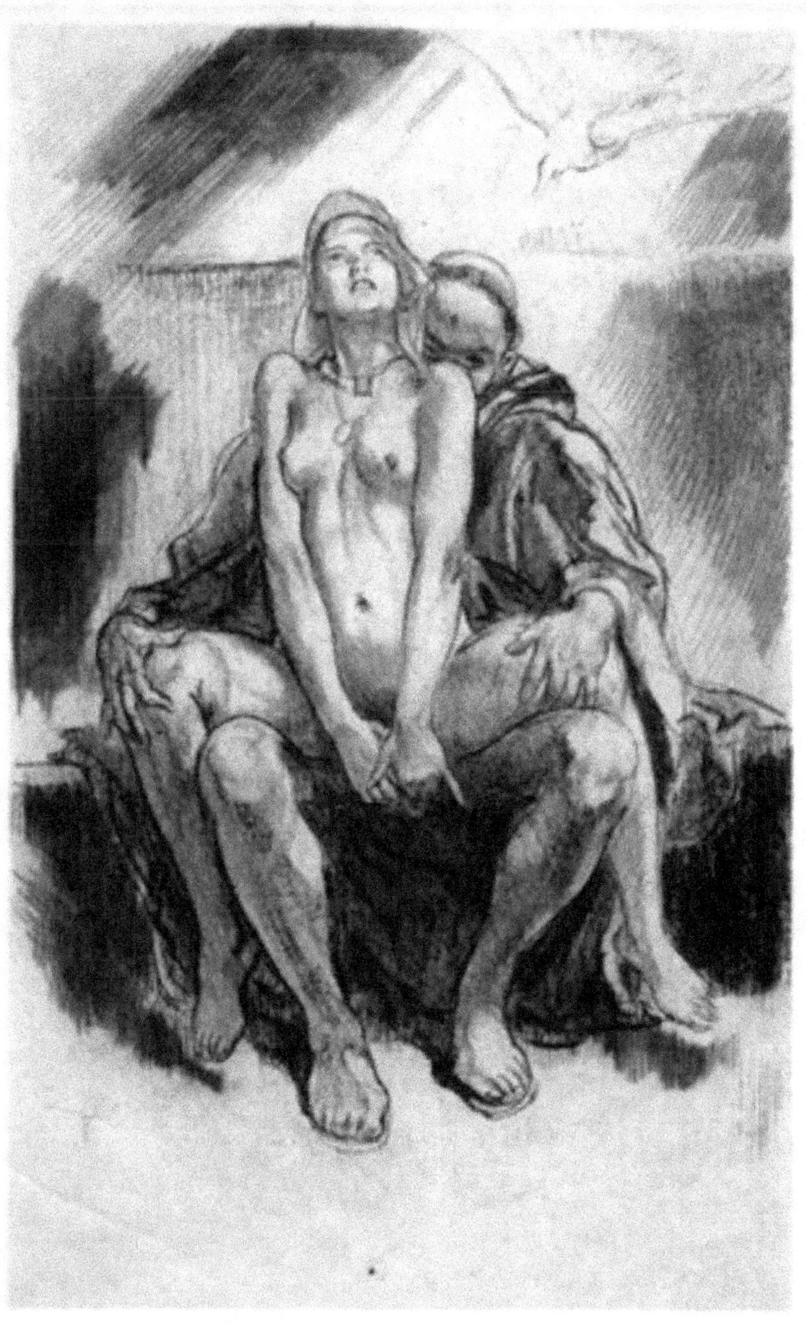

Almery Lobel Riche
(this page and following pages)

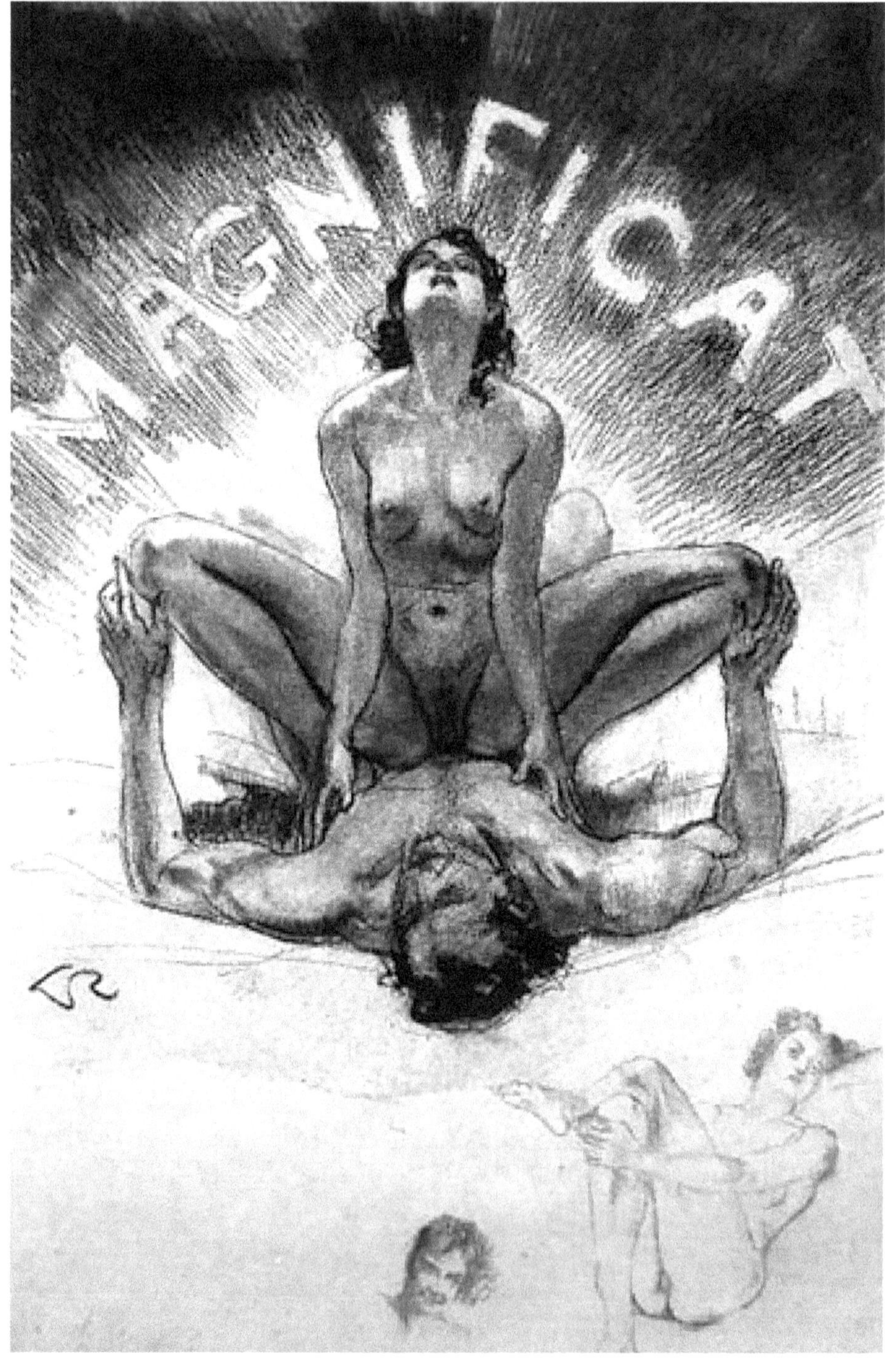
MAGNIFICAT

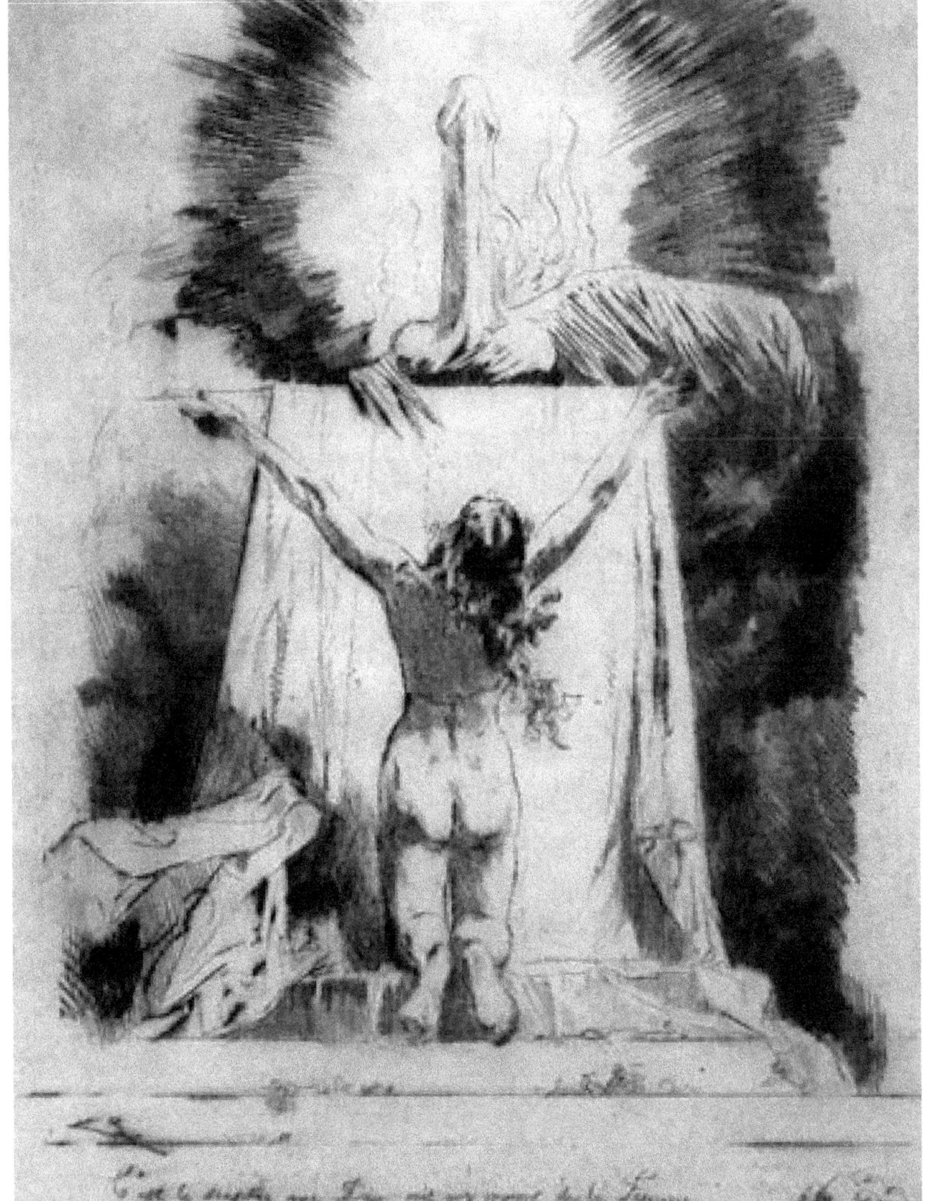

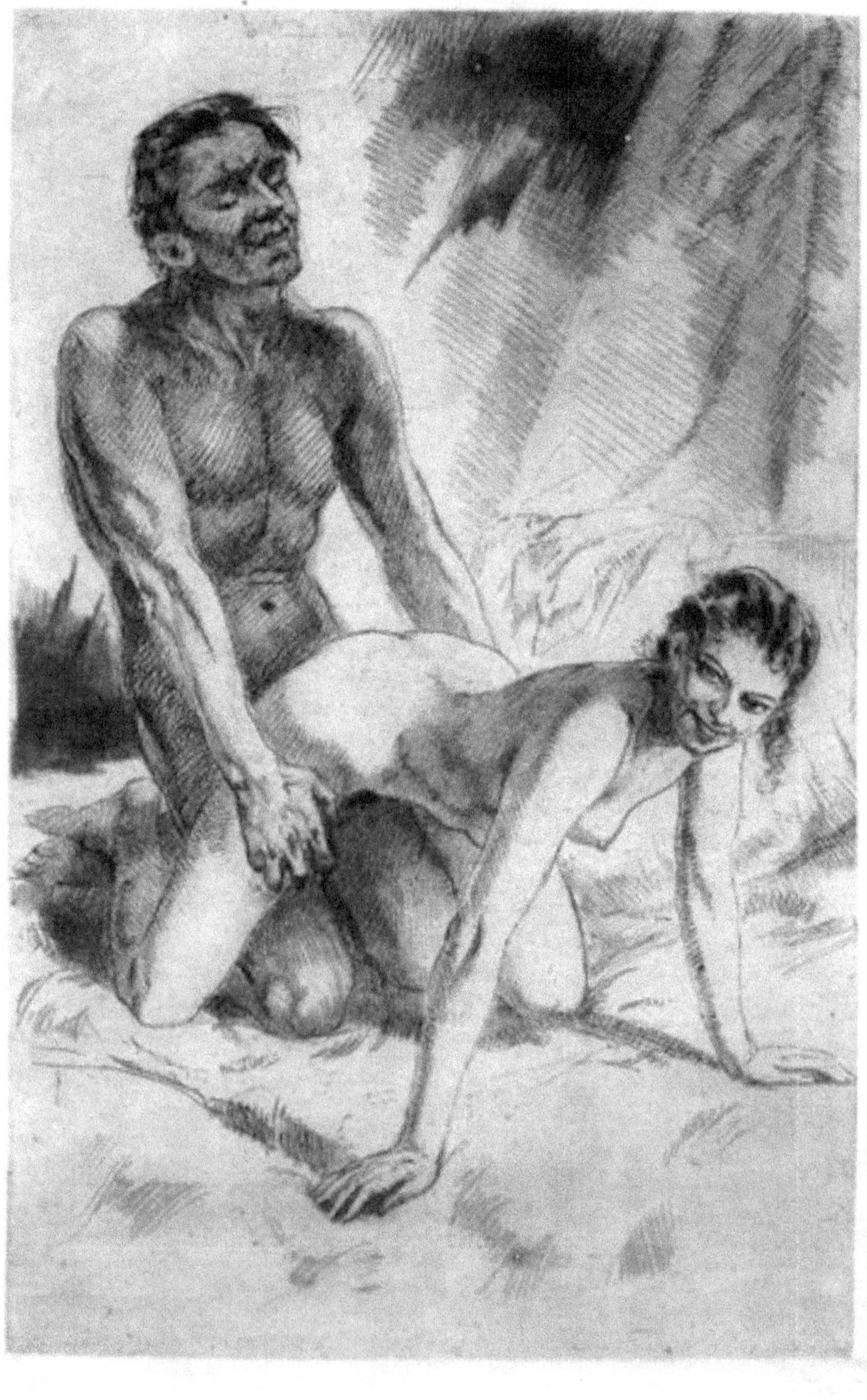

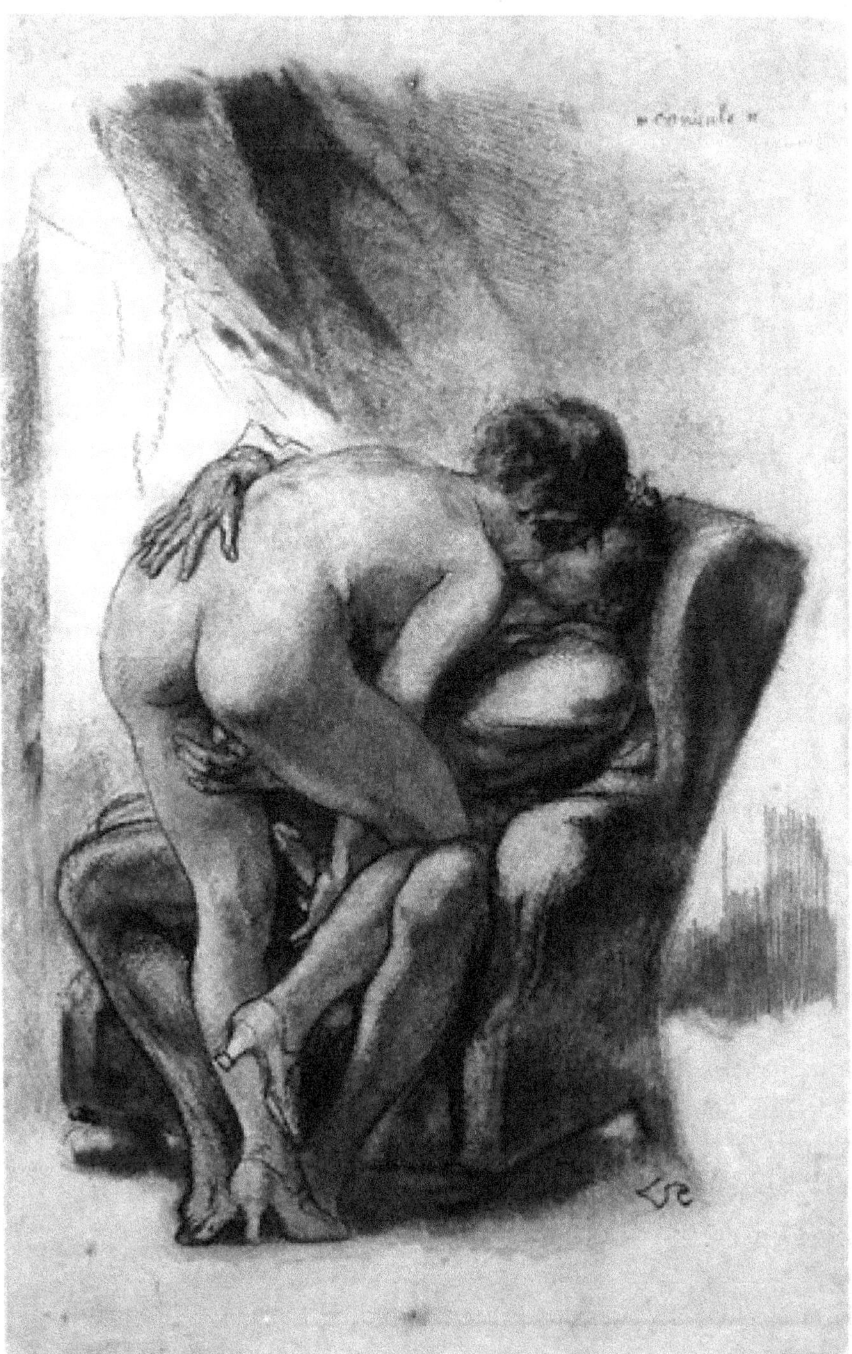

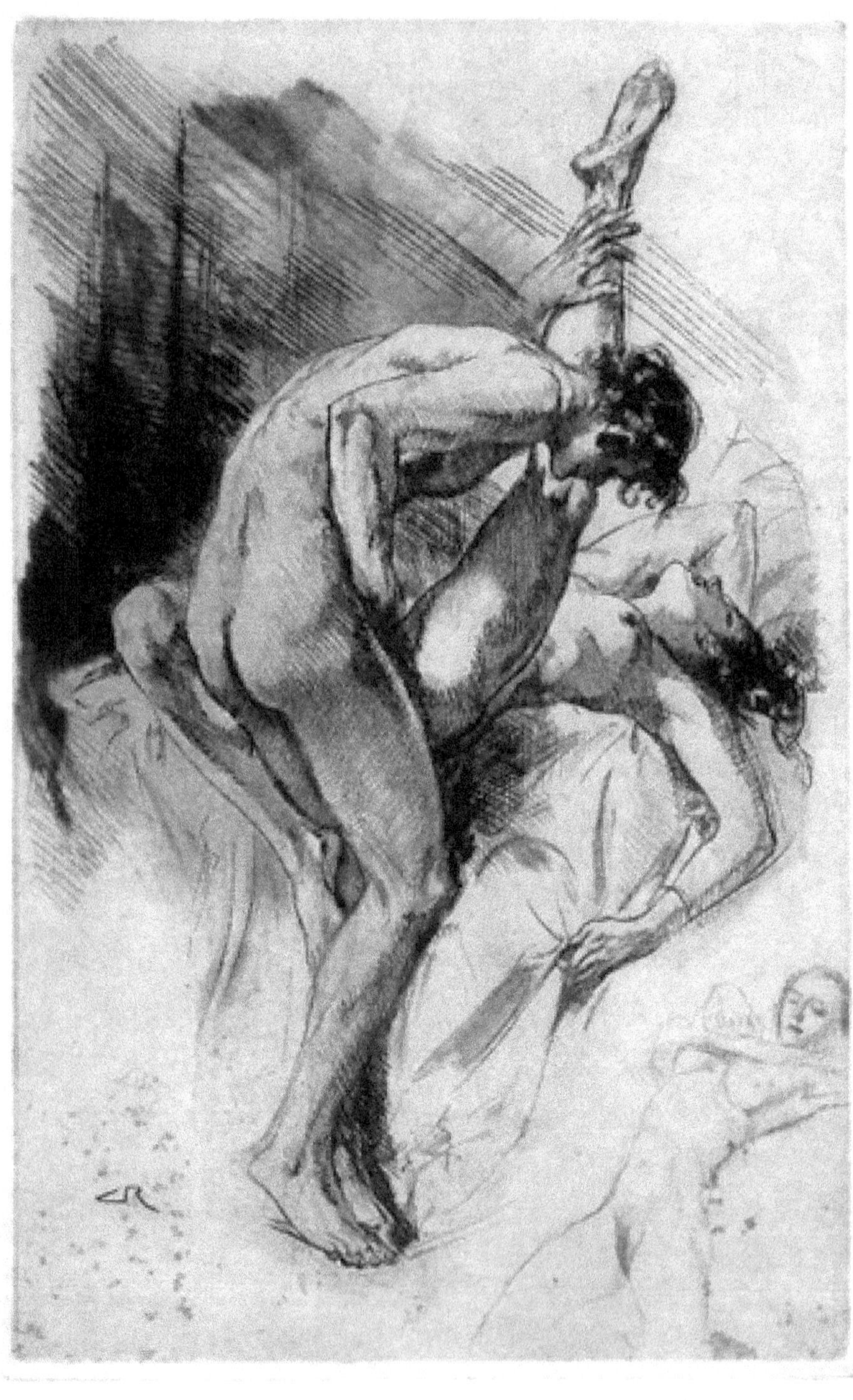

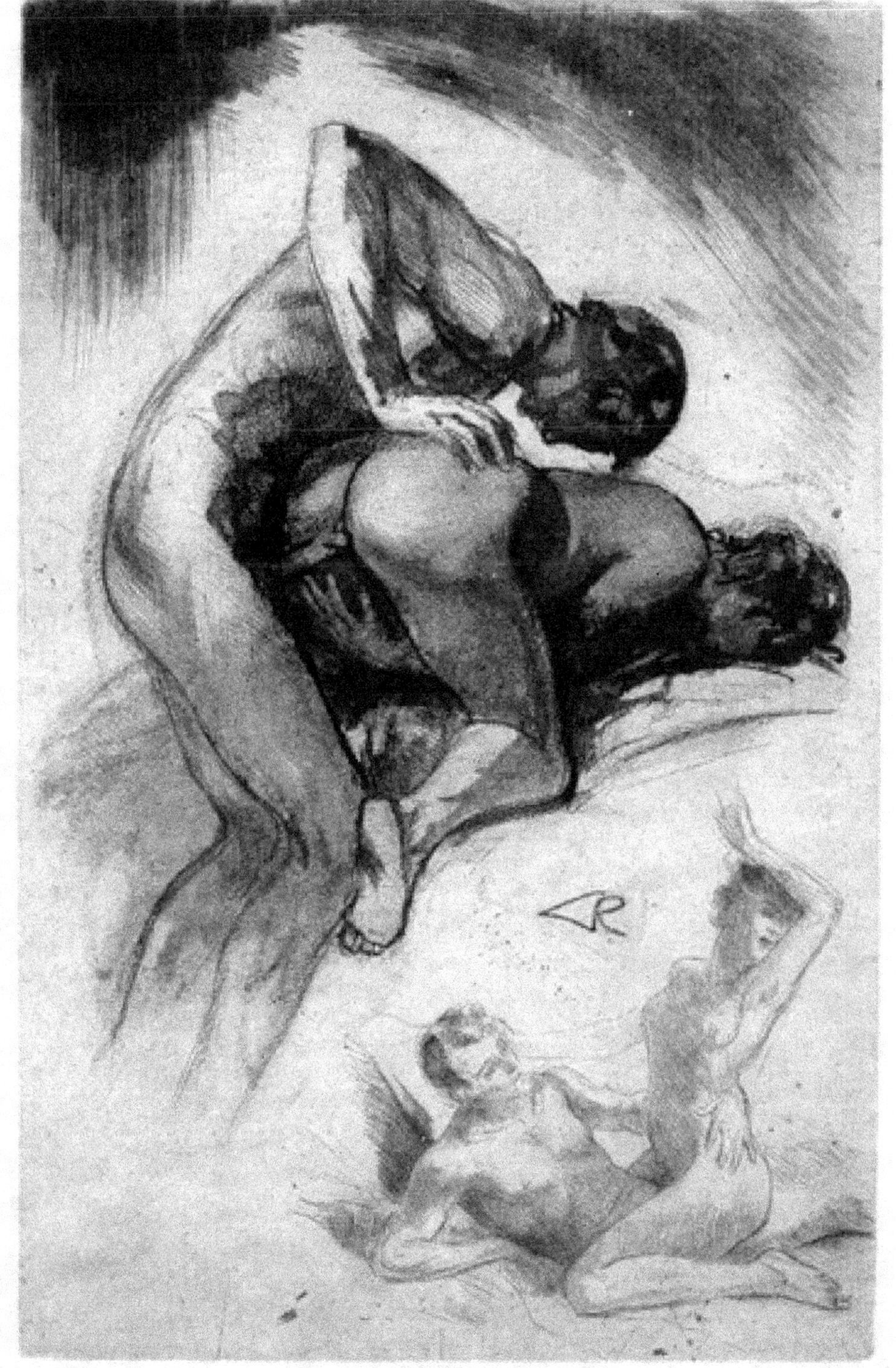

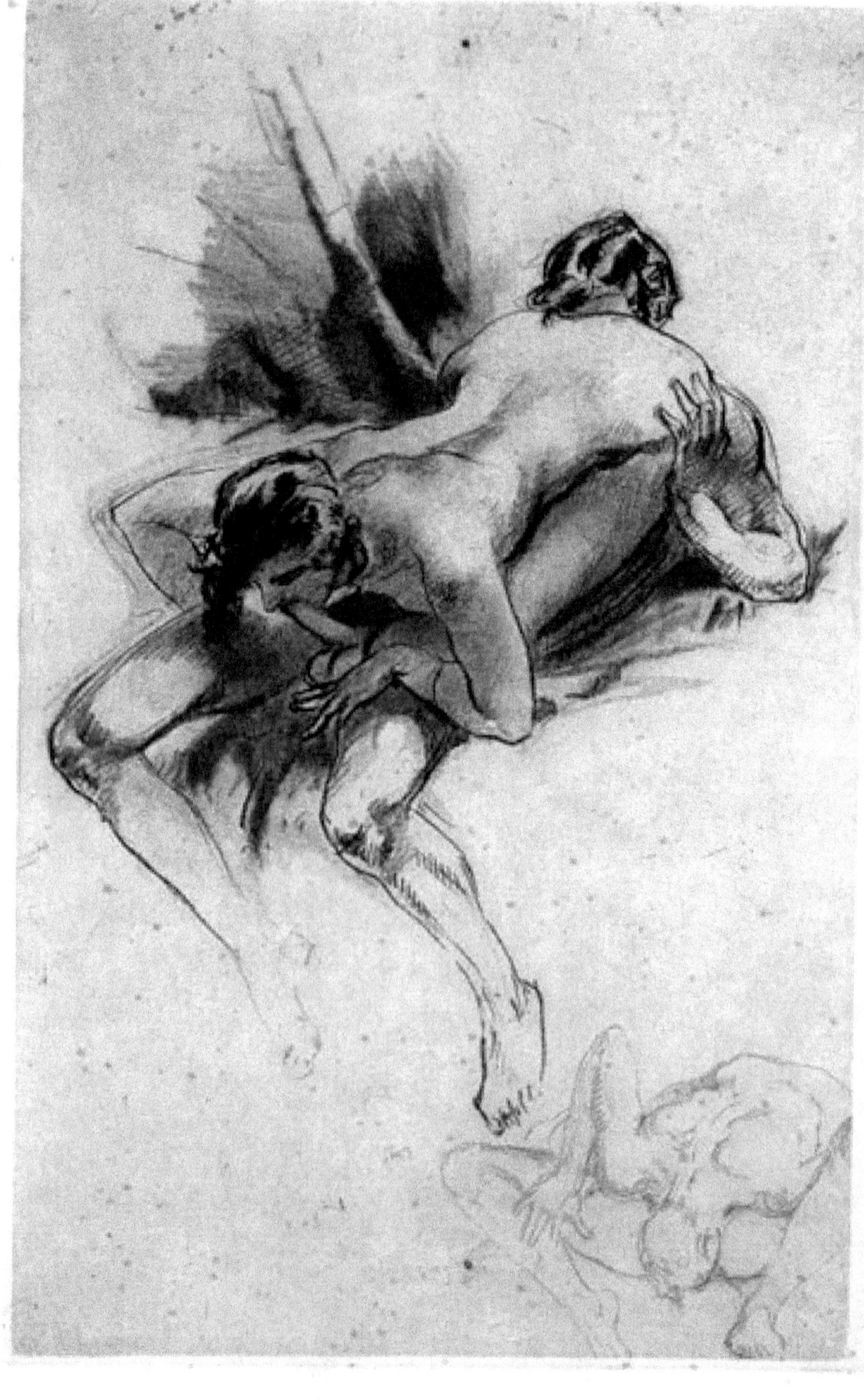

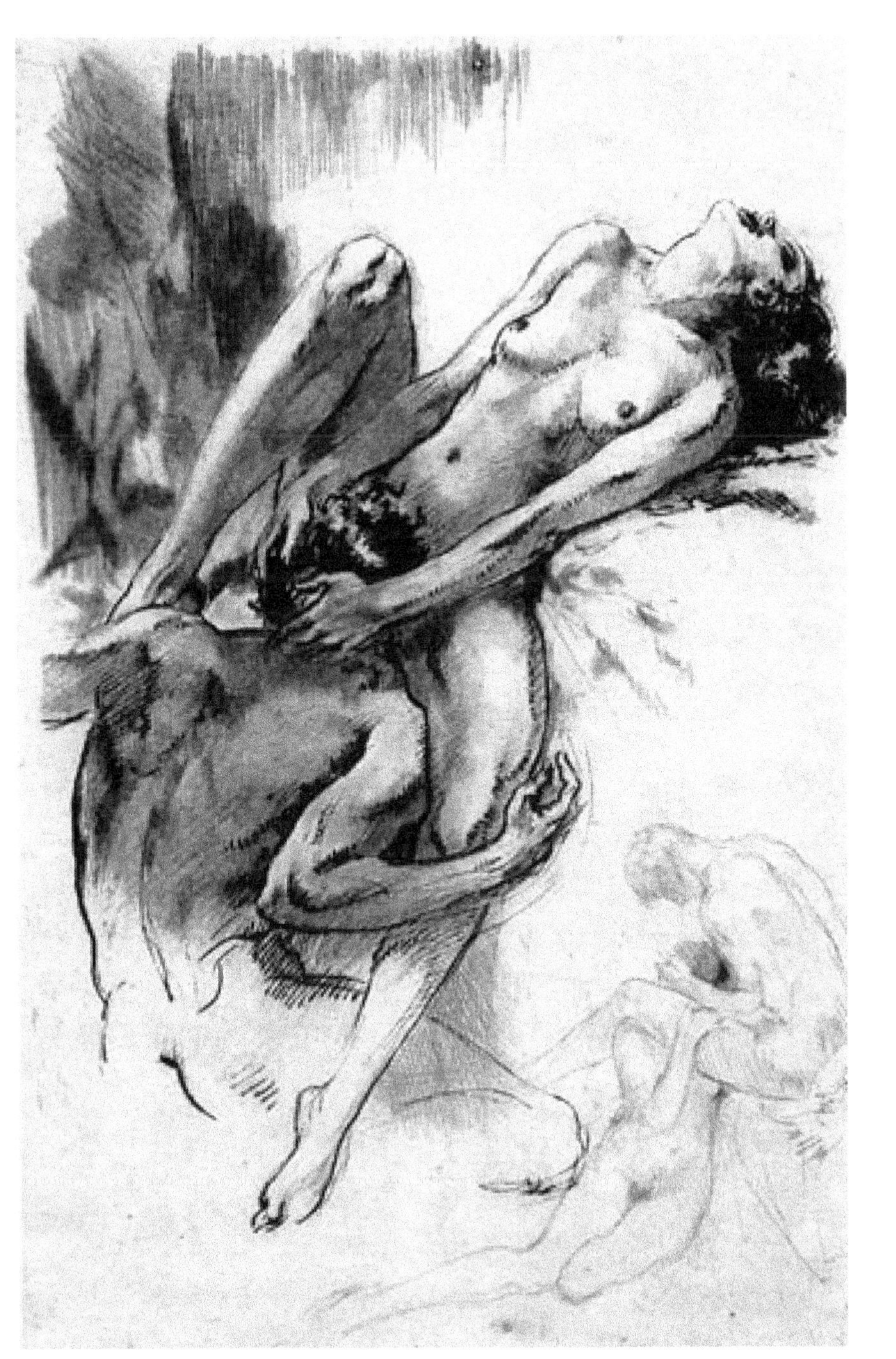

ERNEST GERHARD

Ernest Gerhard (1867-1948) was a German artist who illustrated *The Lantern* (*Die Laterne*) in 1925. Gerhard's work comprised 10 etchings (13.5 x 9 cm). They are, like many works of the early 20th century, collector's items.

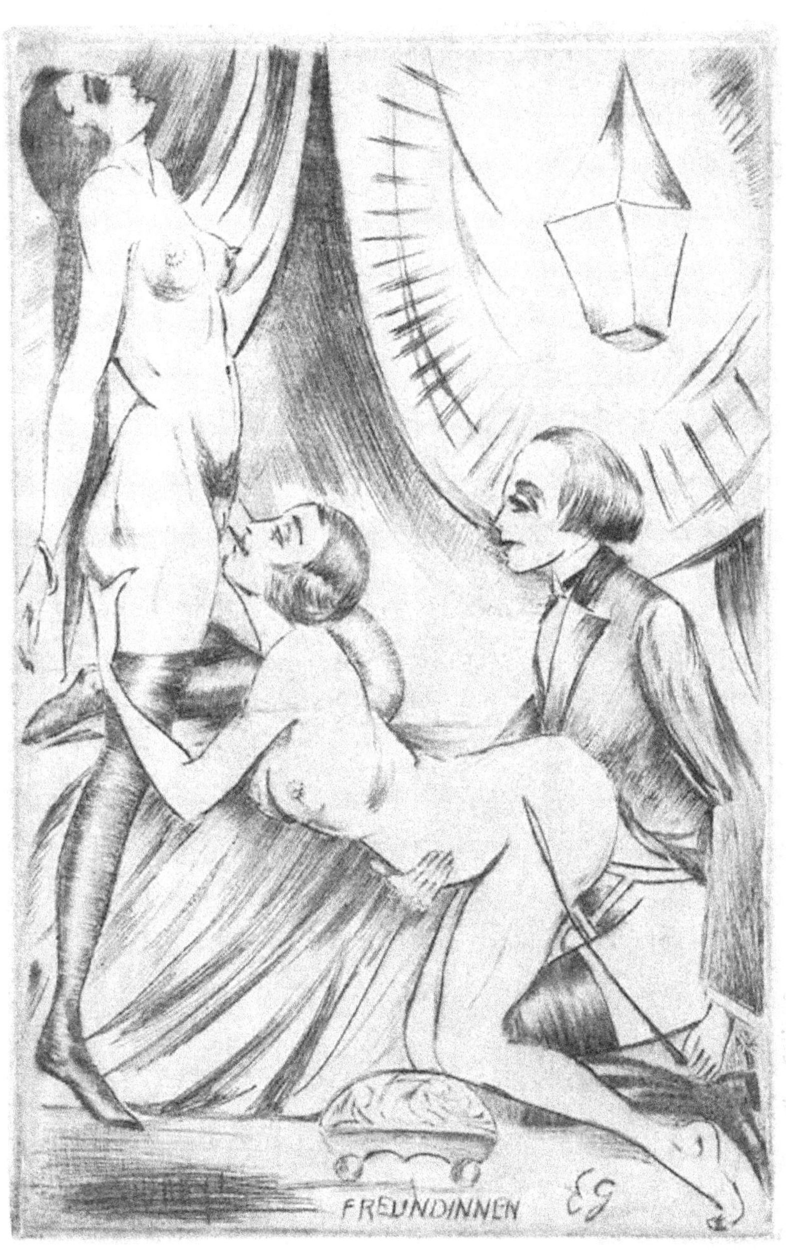

Ernest Gerhard, from Die Laterne (1925).

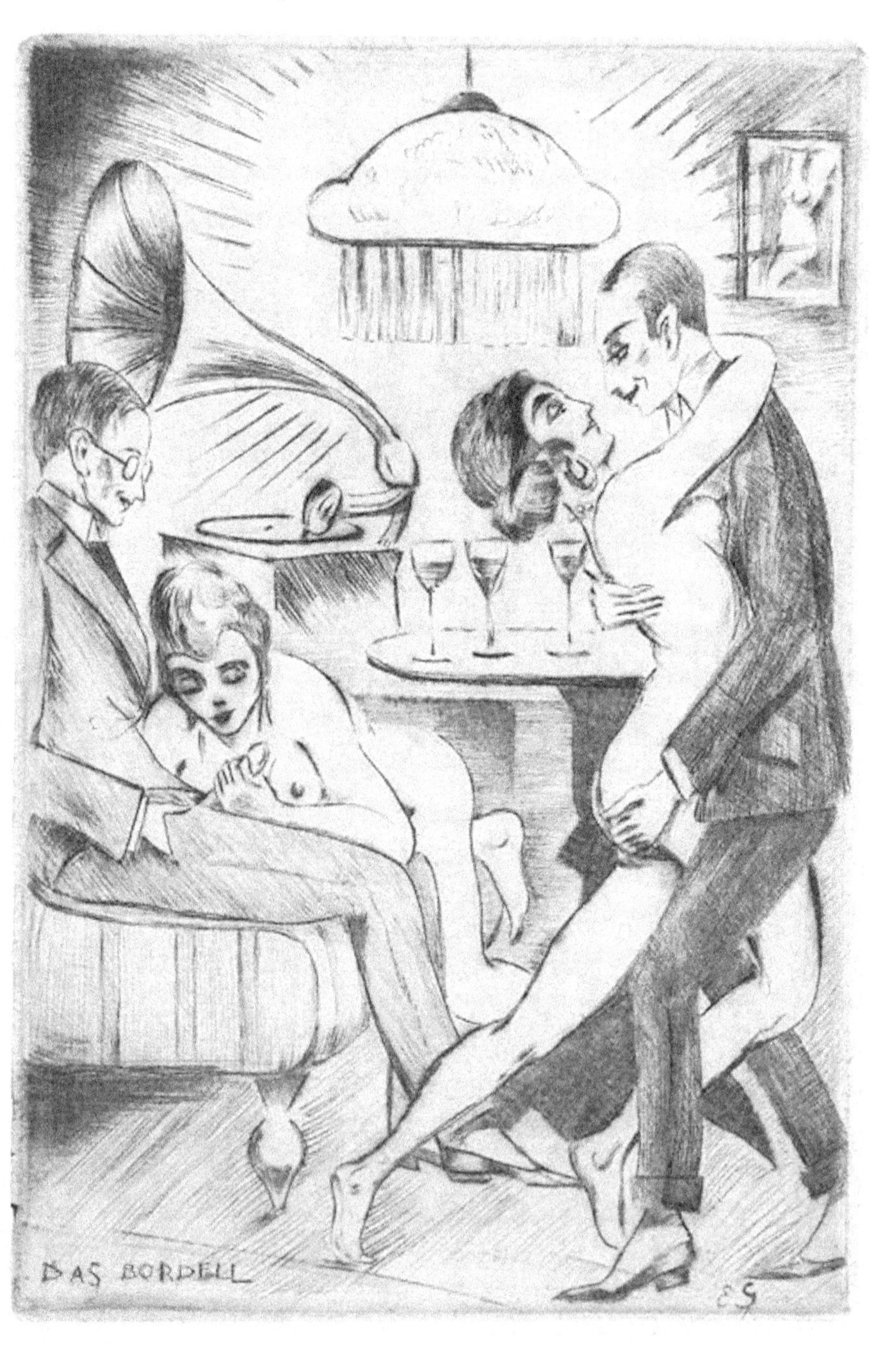
DAS BORDELL
ES

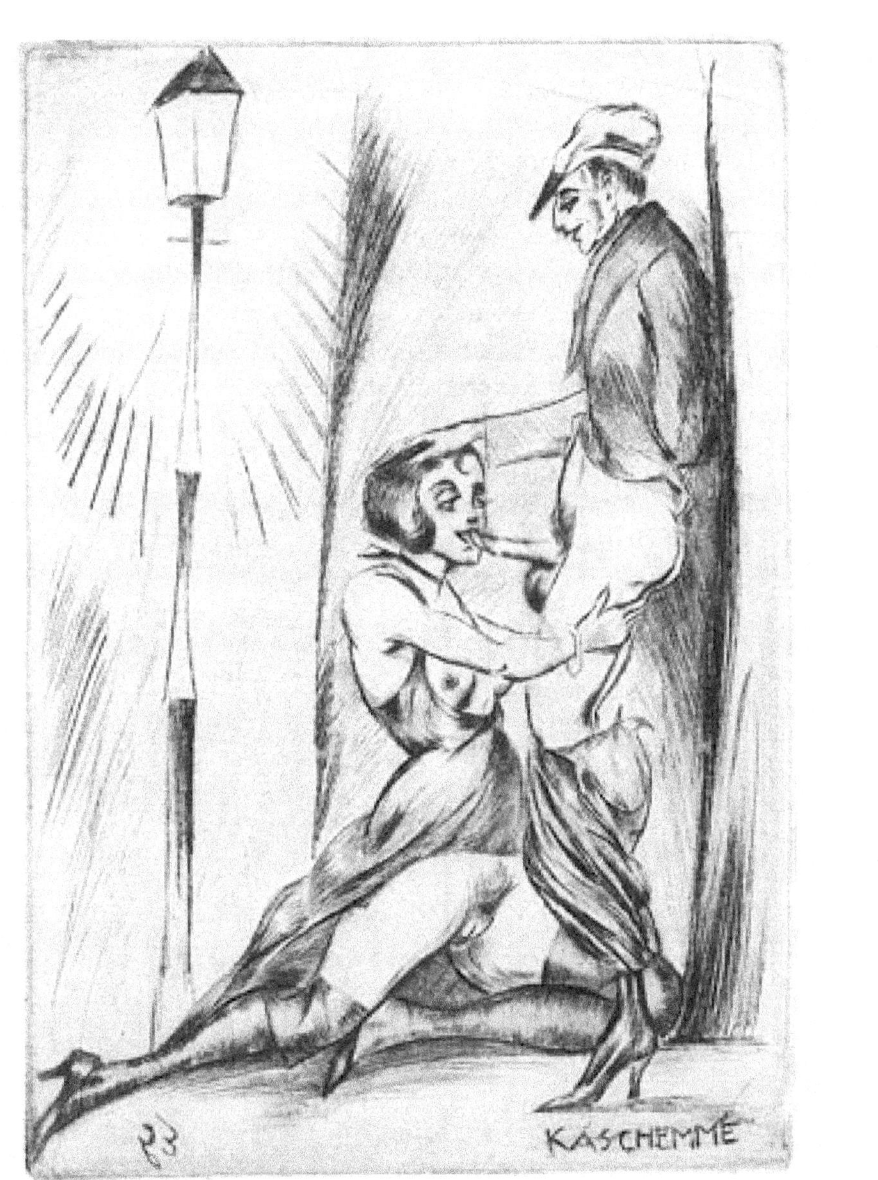
KASCHEMME

ODILON REDON

Odilon Redon (1840-1916) was associated with the Symbolist and the Decadent artists of Paris in the *fin-de-siècle* period (he was friends with J.K. Huysmans and Stéphane Mallarmé, for example). But Redon went on beyond the end-of-the-century Decadence to develop his own, unique approach to mythological and religious art seen from the perspective of dreams and hallucinations. Redon worked in pastels, forging his distinctive colours, and became a forerunner of the Surrealists.

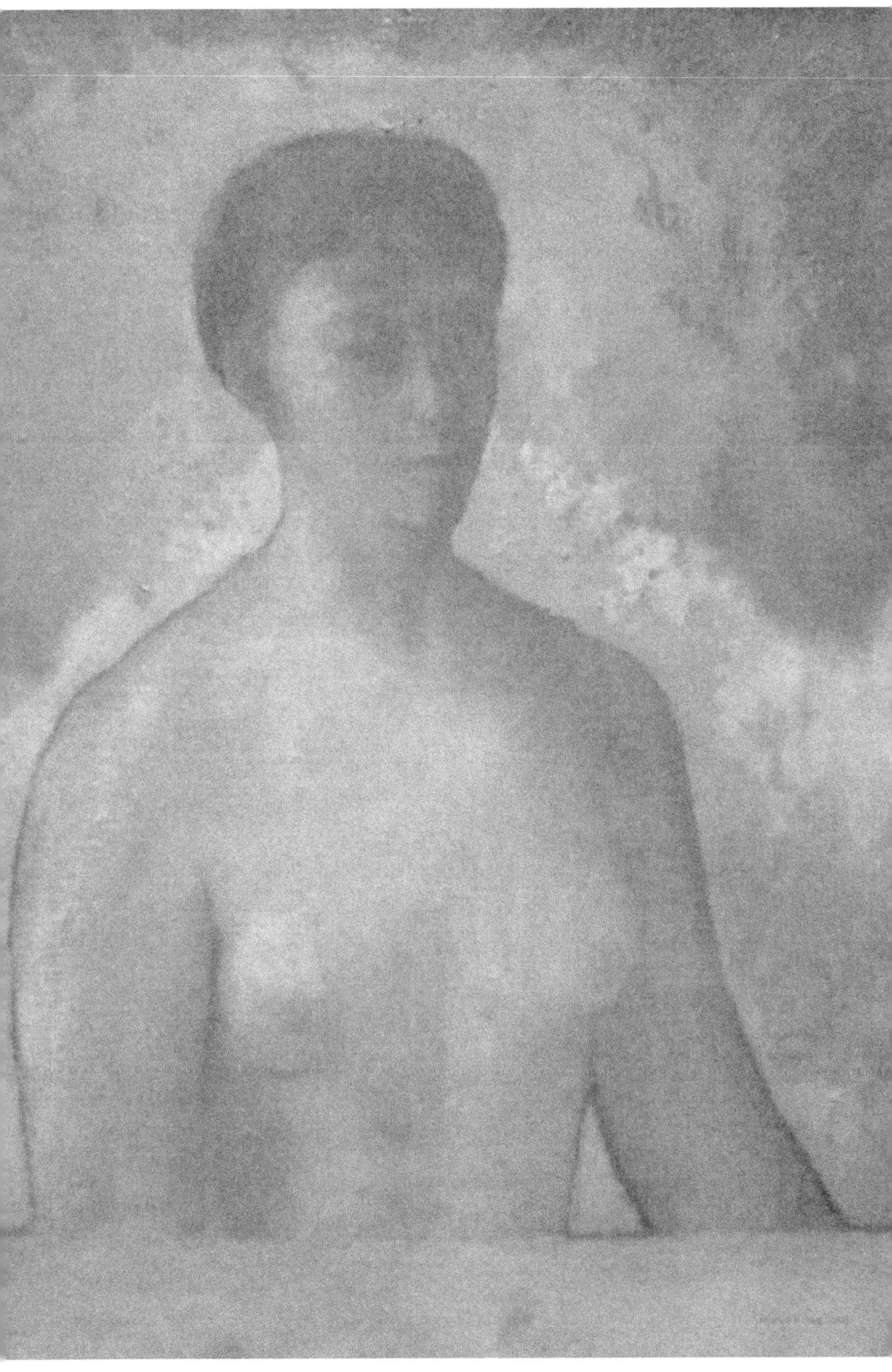

EXPRESSIONISM

The Expressionists' worldview seems more authentic, closer to real life than, say, that of the Impressionists or the Neo-Classicists. In Expressionism we get a sharp sense of the harshness of existence. There are few smiles or laughs in Expressionist art - think of the art of Karl Schmidt-Rottluff, Max Pechstein or Alexander Kanoldt - yet their view of life seems closer to the real thing than that of many other artists. But in amongst the apparently sombre or dour images there are many wild colours and much exuberance - especially in the art of Ernest Kirchner, Alexei von Jawlensky, Kees van Dongen and Gabriele Münter.

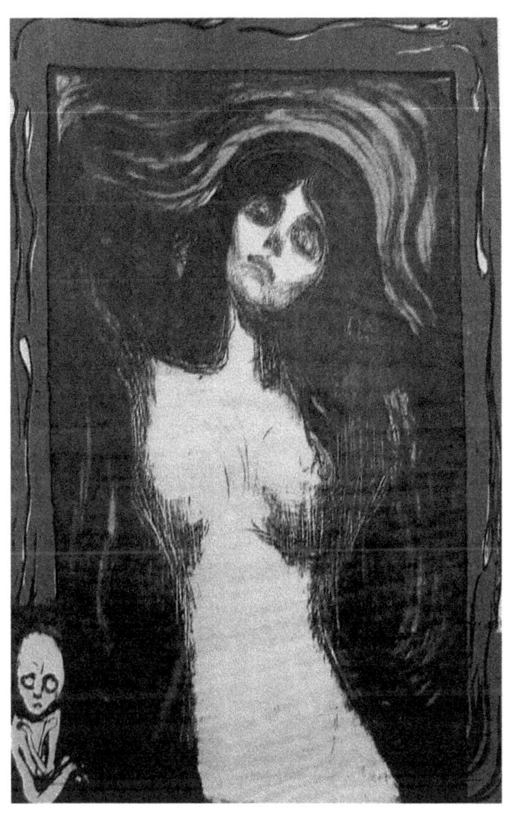

Sexuality in the tortured Scandinavian manner:
Edvard Munch's The Kiss and The Madonna

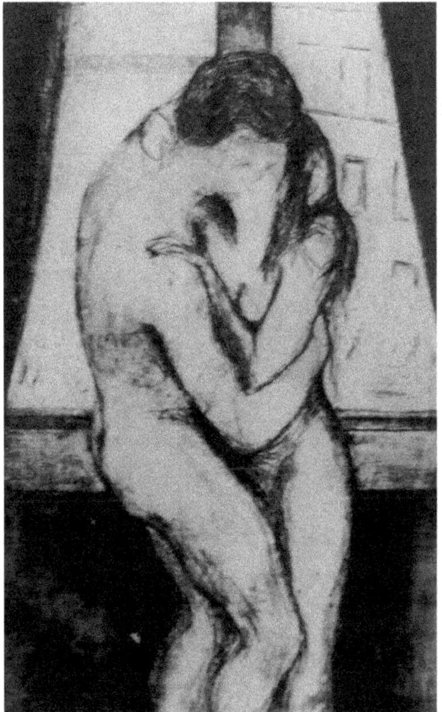

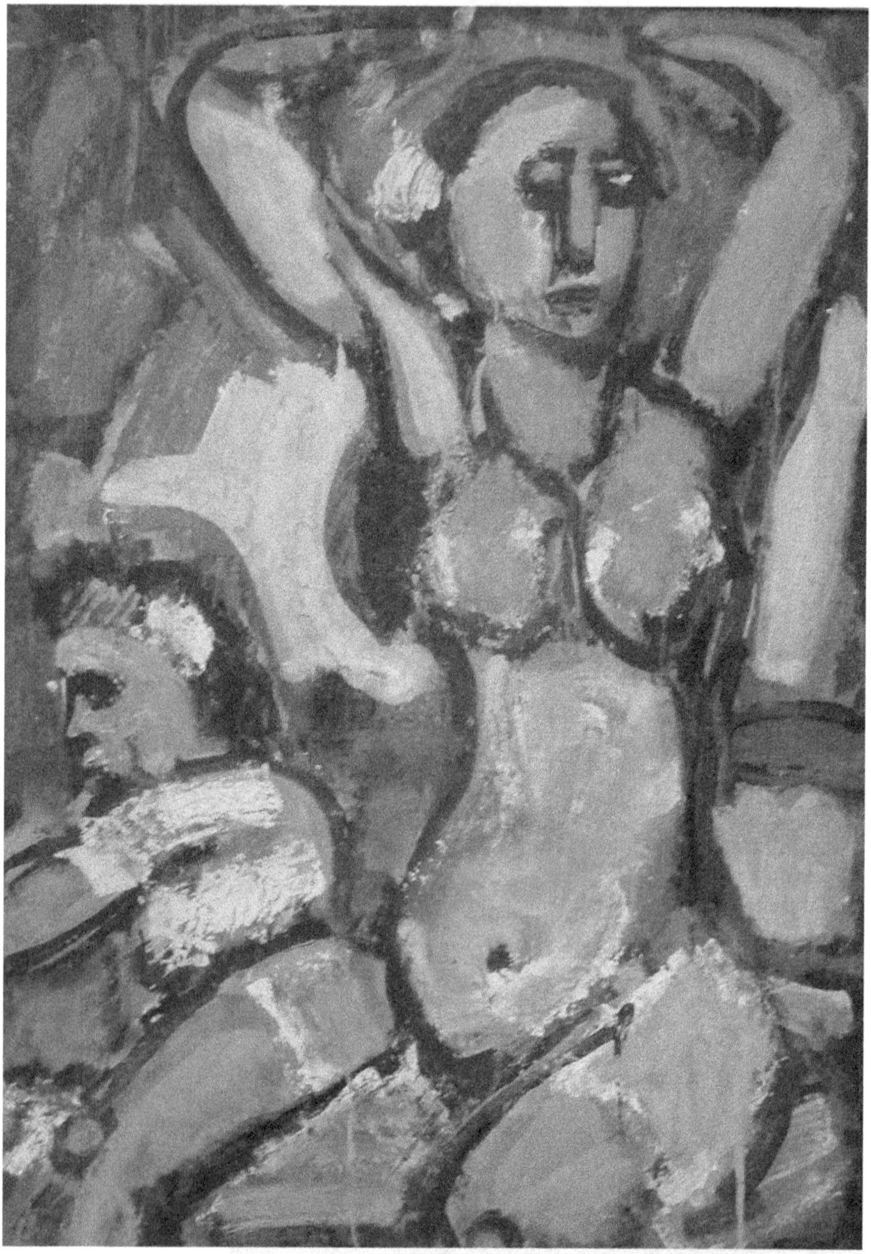

Georges Rouault, Acrobat, 1932, Paris.

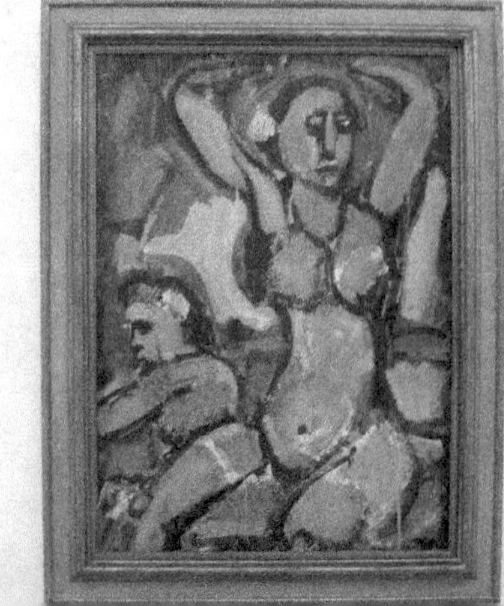

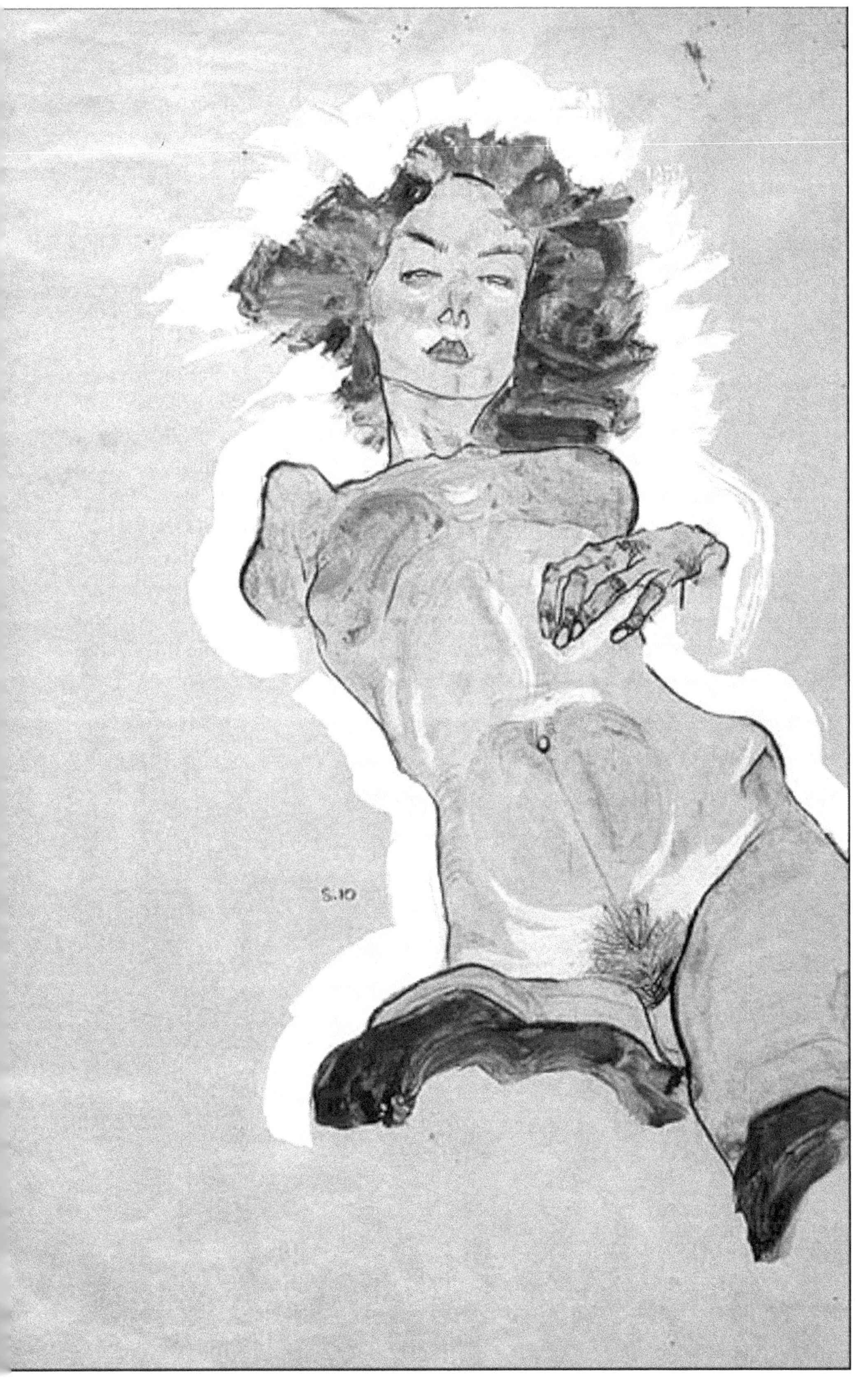

Egon Schiele, Nude

EXPRESSIONISM

Other Expressionists employ a similar approach to erotic art. Like Egon Schiele, artists such as Ernest Ludwig Kirchner, Max Beckmann, Erich Heckel and Emil Nolde employ the thick black outline to define the body in space. Expressionist art - the term 'Expressionist' is used in its widest sense here, to include many different artists - is characterized by its emotional intensity brought into focus by the black line. Instead of softening everything into pure light and colour as the Impressionists had done, the Expressionists made art jagged, restless, urban and anguished. The Expressionists are deeply unhappy artists. As Henri Matisse wrote: 'I too have said one wouldn't paint if one were happy. I'm in agreement with Picasso on that one. We have to live over a volcano.'[1]

1 Matisse, quoted in Pierre Schneider: *Matisse*, Rizzoli, New York 1984, 734

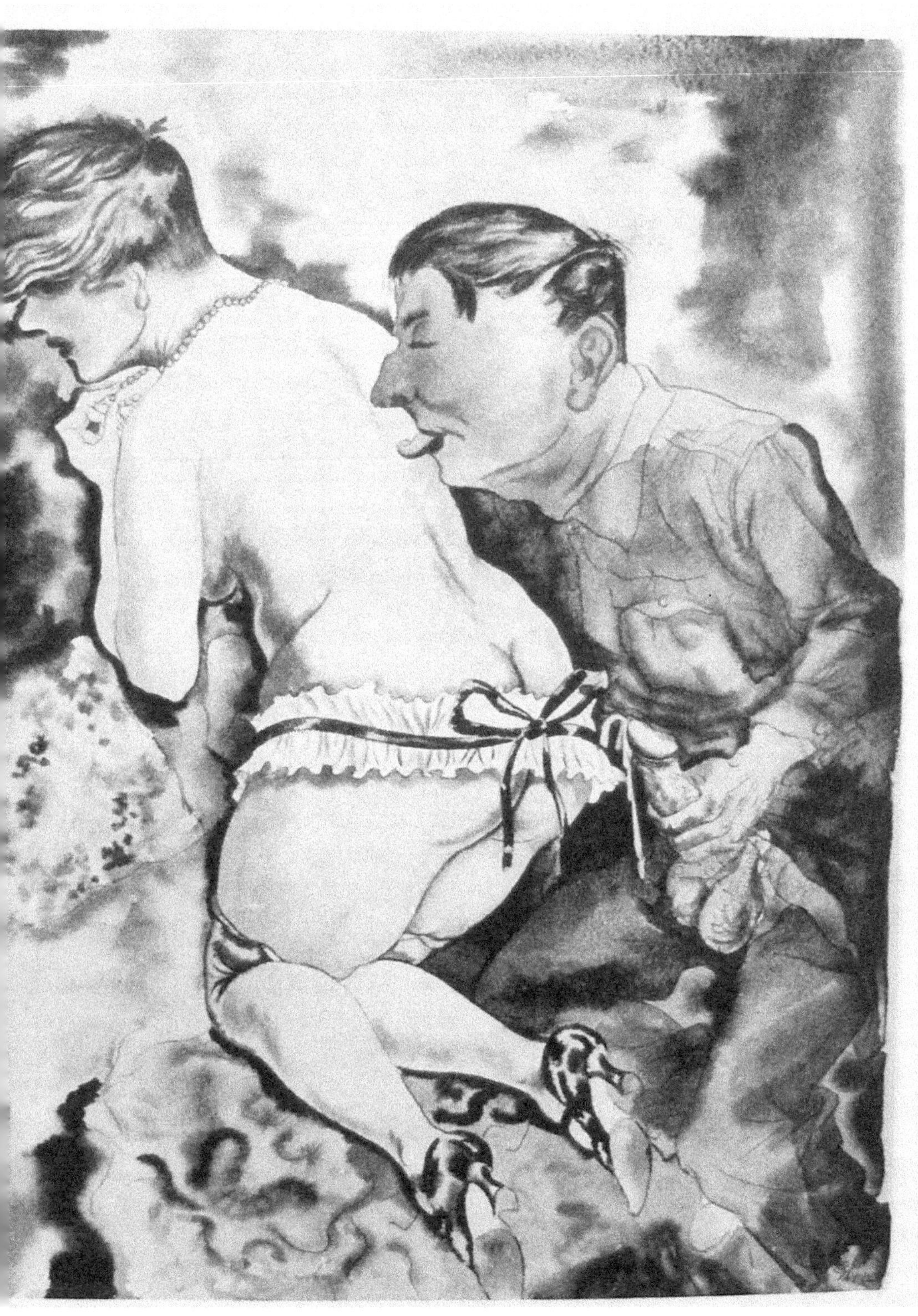

Georg Grosz, Man With Two Prostitutes, 1920

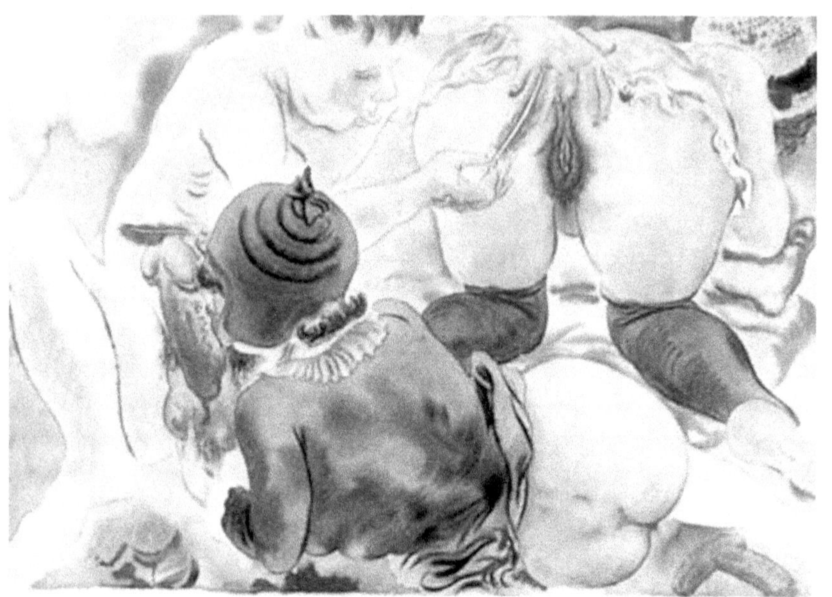

George Grosz

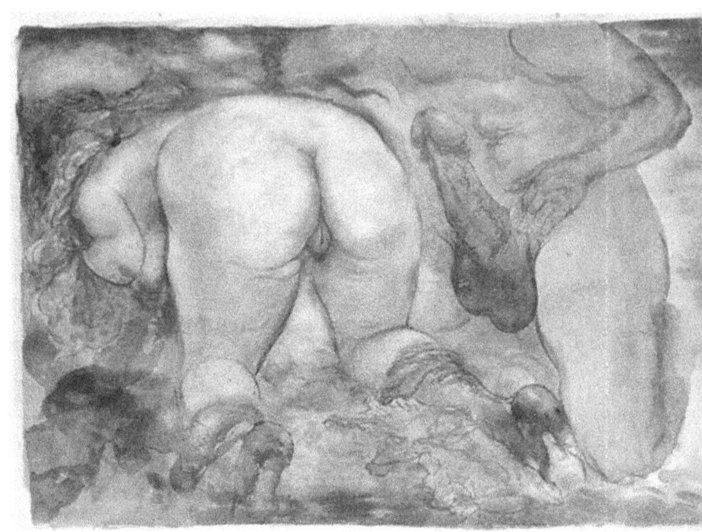

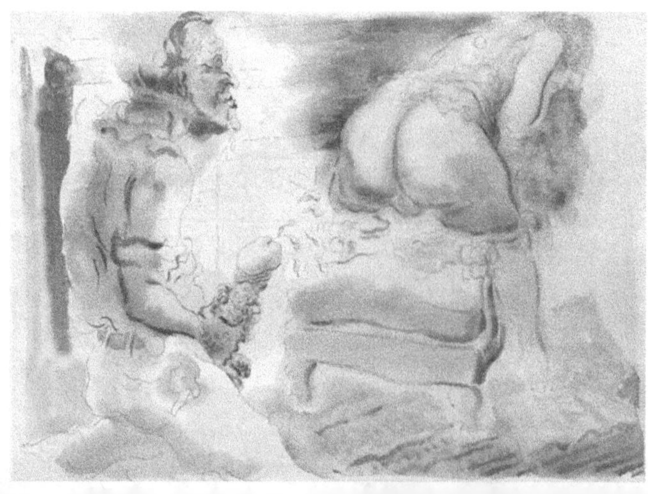

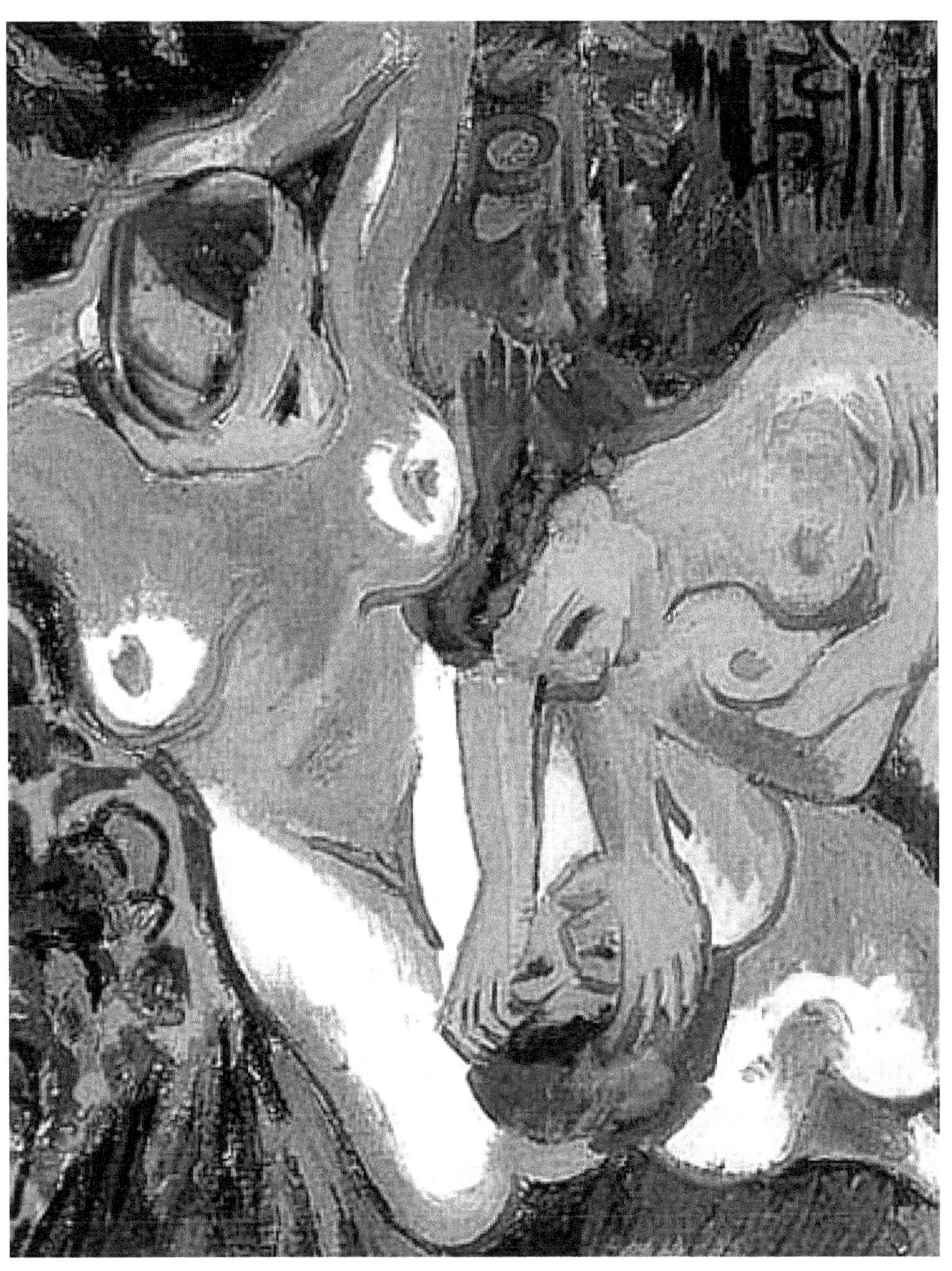

Ernest Ludwig Kirchner, Bathers On the Lawn, 1919

ERNEST LUDWIG KIRCHNER

Agony is one of the hallmark of Expressionist art, and this is true in the depictions of sexuality. Again, it is women who dominate the sexual discourse of the Expressionists. As with the Symbolists and the Viennese Secessionists and New Artists, the Expressionists use women as subjects and sexual objects, as sites of fears and desires about sexuality and life, as vehicles of lust and despair. The emotional and moral ambiguity is apparent in so much of Expressionist art. In Ernest Kirchner's art, for instance, we find simultaneous love and hate of his subjects, which he communicates with his vigorous descriptive lines and his offbeat use of colour, such as in *Five Women In the Street.*[1] Kirchner's portrait of a woman with her blouse pulled down to show her breasts is essentially no different from softcore pornographic images.[2] For art historians, Kirchner's eroticization of his subject is redeemed because of its 'artistic merit'. But no amount of art historical discussion of Kirchner's innovative colouration[3] obscures the fact that his painting objectifies women sexually.

1 Ernest Ludwig Kirchner: *Five Women in the Street*, 1913, 120 x 90cm, Wallraf-Richartz Museum, Cologne
2 E. Kirchner: *Semi-nude Woman With Hat*, 1911, 76 x 70cm, Wallraf-Richartz Museum, Cologne
3 See Wolf-Dieter Dube: *The Expressionists*, 42f

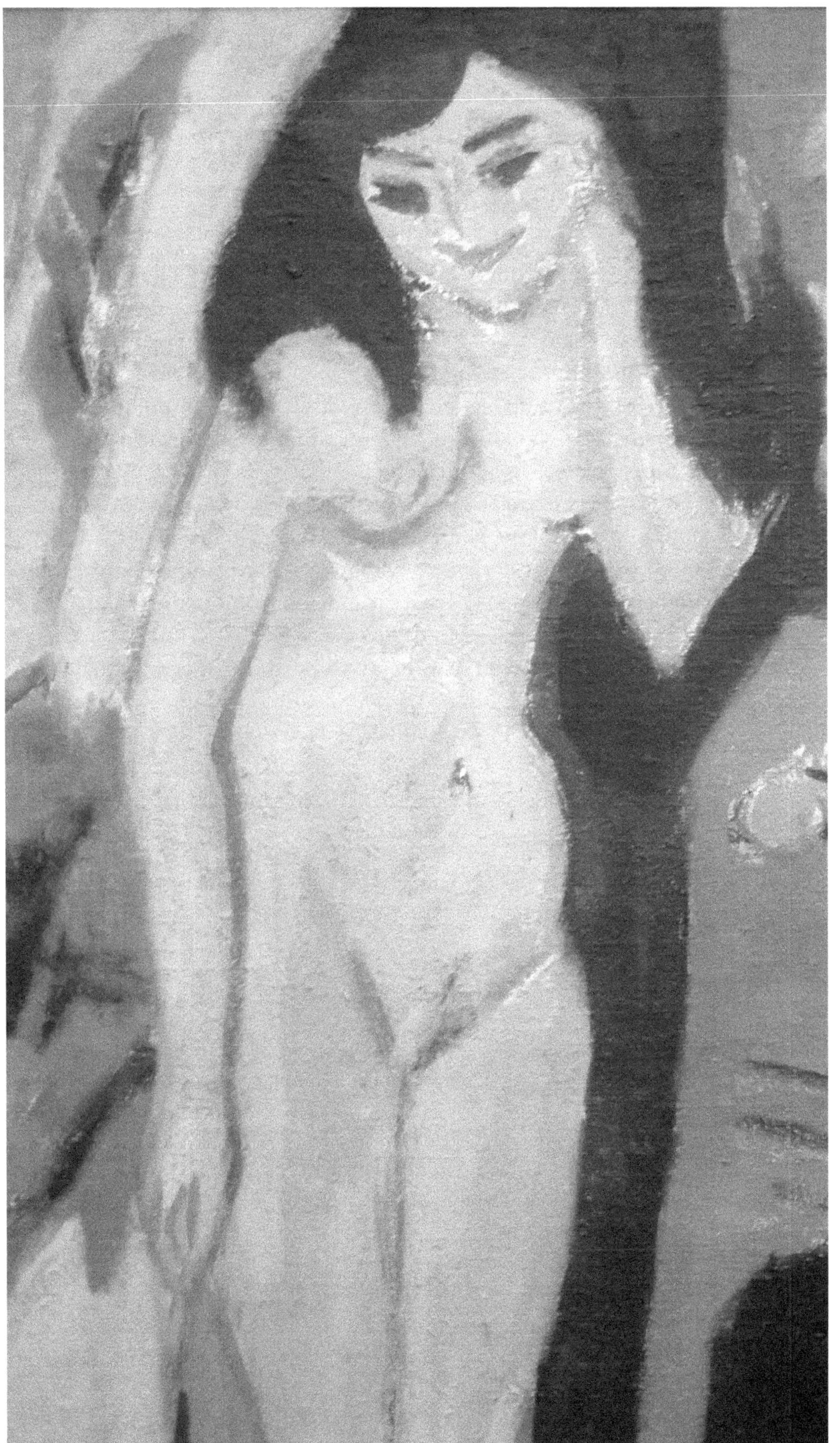

EMIL NOLDE

Eroticism in the art of Emil Nolde, as in Georges Rouault's output, is subsumed into a really intense exploration of religious imagery. Rouault and Nolde are two of the best of modern figurative religious artists. In their work, as in that of Max Beckmann and Marc Chagall, the full pain and ecstasy of the human condition is brilliantly depicted. Nolde is rarely erotic in the way of the art of Ernest Kirchner or Egon Schiele. In his *Golden Calf Dance*, however, Nolde captured some of the wildness of wild dancing.[1] It is a depiction of ecstasy and celebration that is far wilder than, say, Henri Matisse's *The Dance*.[2] While Matisse's painting exudes joy, Nolde's Old Testament dance exudes a wild abandon that comes close to the fervour of lovemaking. Like Paul Klee's *Blossoming*,[3] Nolde's *Golden Calf Dance* is a portrayal of ecstasy that goes beyond sex or religion. It is a non-institutionalized ecstasy, a bliss transcending gender or politics. As Nolde wrote in 1909, he worked in a state close to religious bliss as he painted: '[t]hen again I went down to the mystical depth of human divine existence'.[4]

1 Nolde; *Golden Calf Dance*, 1910, 88 x 105cm, Staatsgalerie, Munich
2 Matisse: *The Dance*, 1910, oil, 260 x 391cm, Hermitage Museum, St Petersburg
3 Klee: *Blossoming*, 1934, oil, 91 x 80cm, Kunst Museum, Winterhur
4 Nolde: *Jahre der Kampfe*, Rembrandt, Berlin 1934, 103f

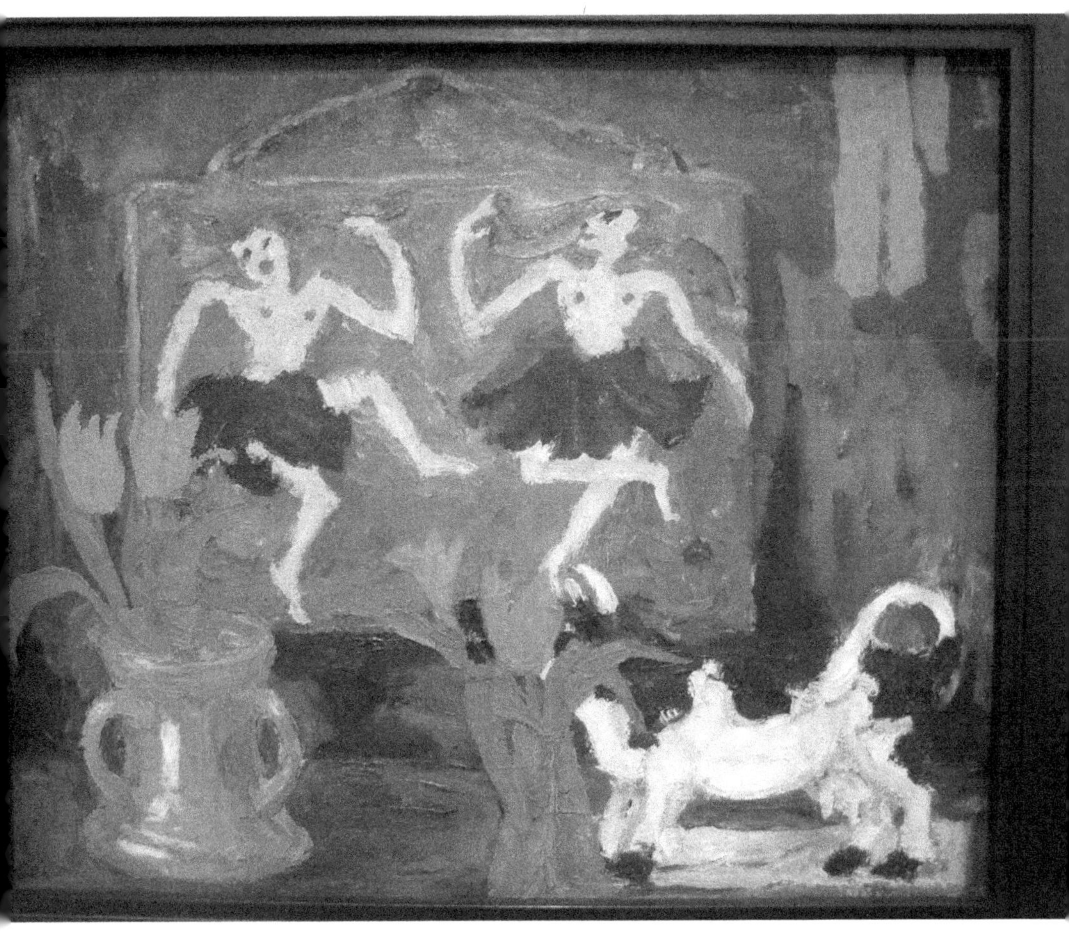

Emil Nolde, Nature morte aux danseuses, 1914, Pompidou, Paris.

OTTO MUELLER

Otto Mueller's motif is a group of young women sitting in long grass. He painted variations on this theme many times.[1] The women are nude, have sallow eyes but no individual personality. They are 'types', with their pointed knees and elbows. They are made up of straight lines, and painted in a style that is deliberately 'primitive' or crude. Mueller's nude women are clearly erotic for him, though they are anonymous, abstracted, curiously bland, as if, once he had painted them, Mueller was scared by what he had created. So he takes all the individuality out of them, and turns them into a series of shapes. Pablo Picasso did this with his Avignon women, though they have more personality, more of a sense of self than Mueller's nude women.[2]

1 Otto Mueller: *Two Girls in the Grass*, 1905, tempera, 141 x 110cm, Staatsgalerie, Munich
2 Pablo Picasso: *Les Demoisels d'Avignon*, 1907, MOMA, New York

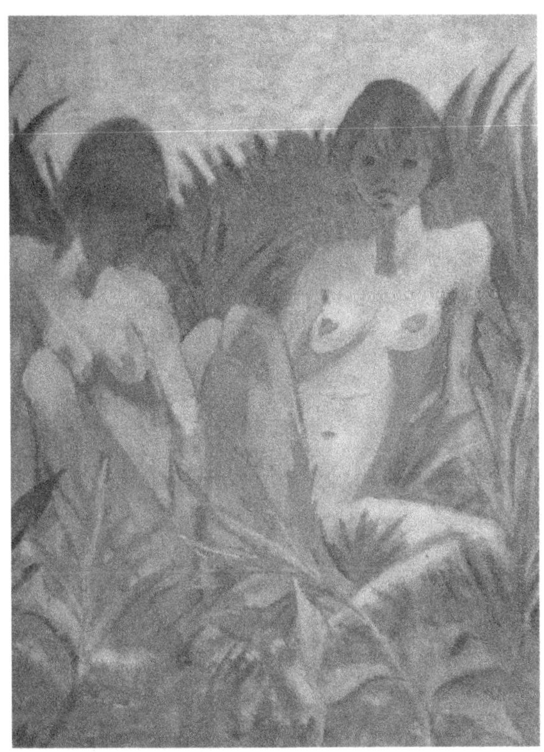

Expressionist sex: Otto Mueller, Two Girls In the Grass, above.
Ernest Ludwig Kirchner, Semi-Nude Woman With Hat, below.

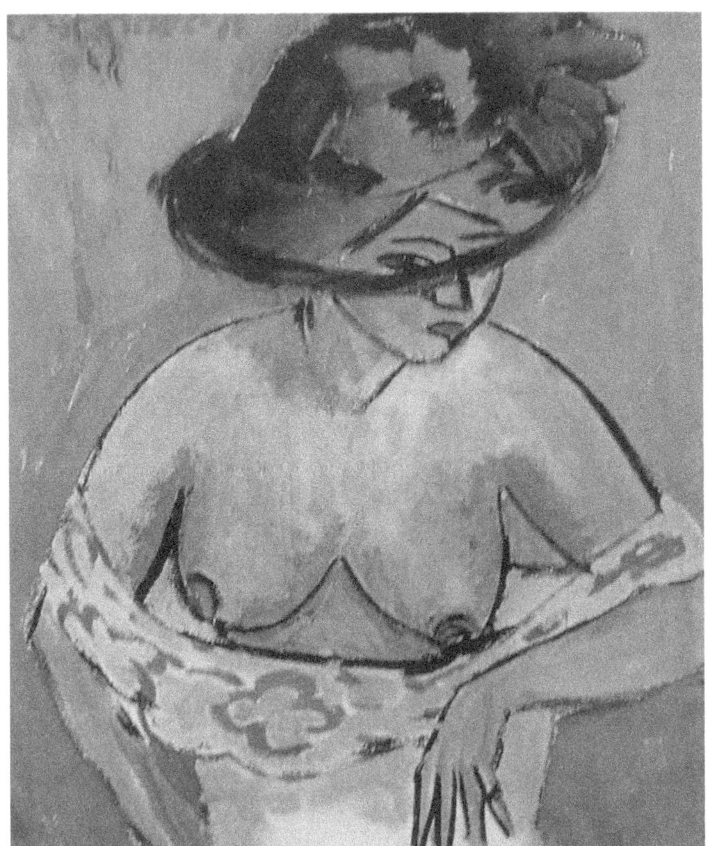

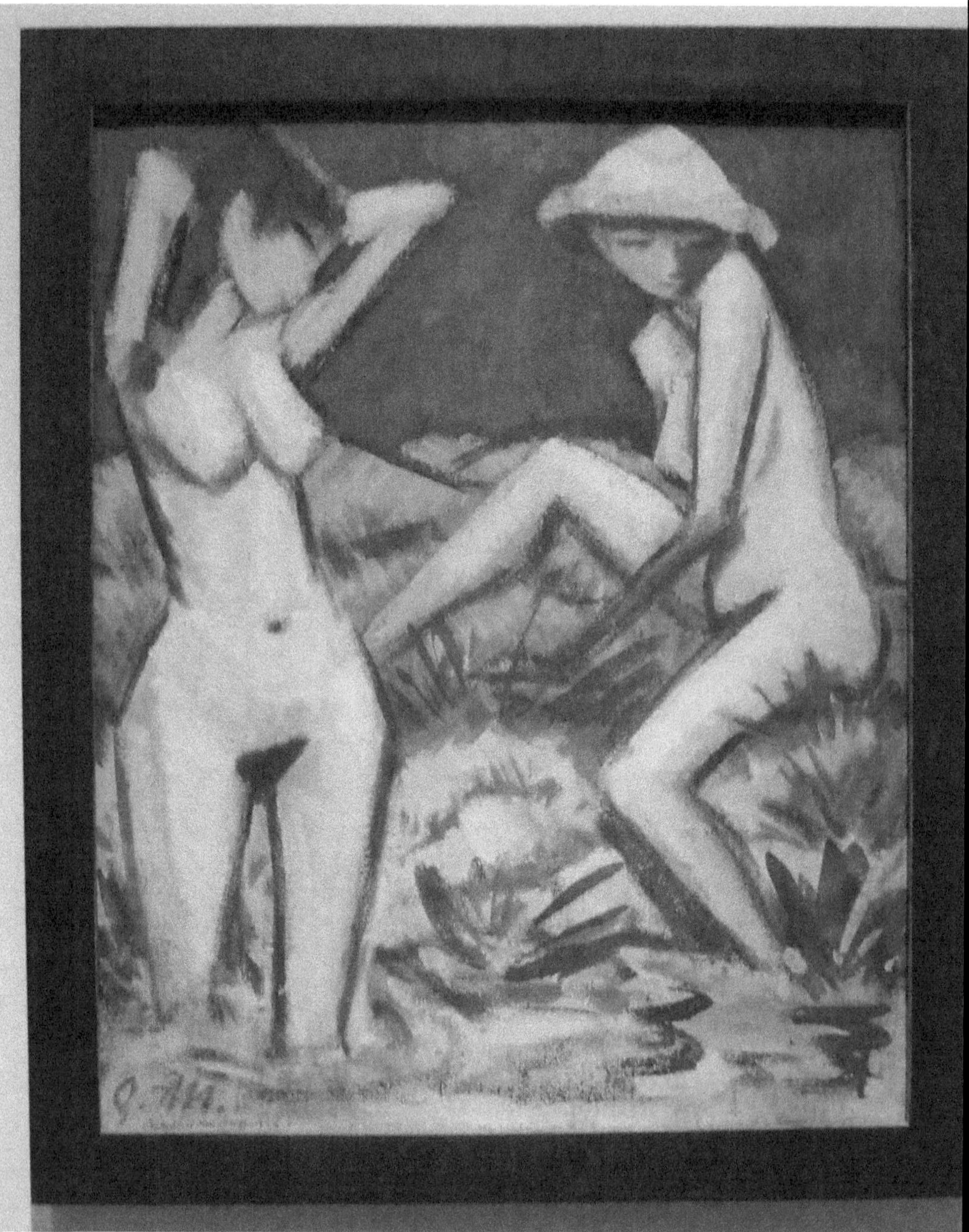

Otto Mueller, Los Angeles.

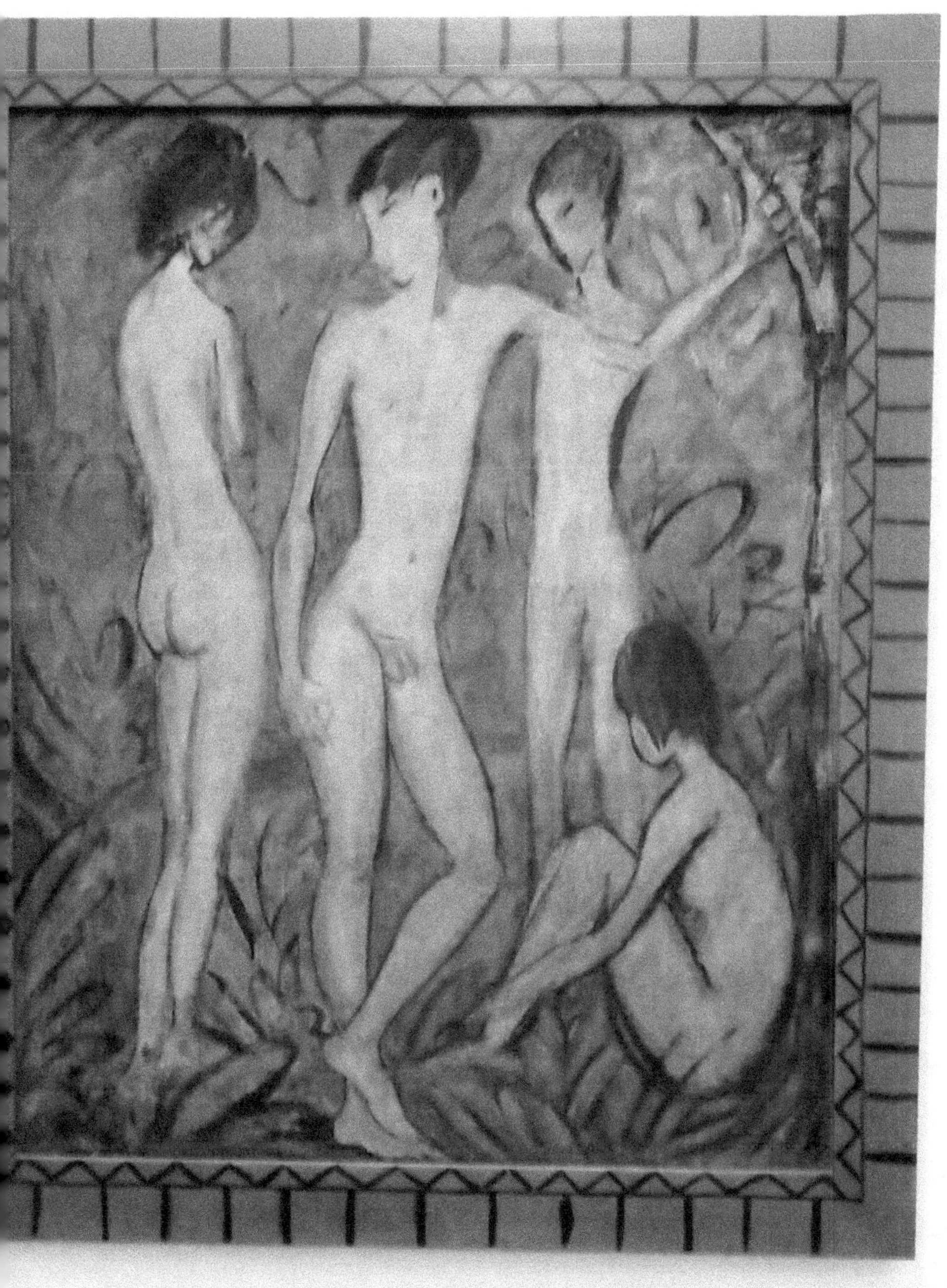

Otto Mueller, Amsterdam

EGON SCHIELE

Egon Schiele (1890-1918), Gustav Klimt's disciple, is the embodiment of *fin-de-siècle* Vienna, the decadent *zeitgeist* of the 'city of dreams' which was obsessed with itself, which psychoanalyzed itself endlessly, which simultaneously celebrated and suppressed eroticism.

Egon Schiele, like Pablo Picasso or Eric Gill, is one of the 'great' modern erotic artists.[1] He is daemonic compared to Gustav Klimt.[2] His view of sex is the usual masculinist, bourgeois one that sex = pain and pain = being truly alive. He said: 'I am a human being. I love death and I love life.'[3] Schiele wrote from prison in 1912: 'I believe that man must suffer from sexual torture as long as he is capable of sexual feelings.' Schiele's poetry is a mass of Expressionist meditations on the painful moments of life - sex, death, birth, violence:

> An eternal dreaming
> full of the sweetest overabundance of life -
> restless - with heavy pangs within, in the soul. -
> It blazes, burns, yearns for battle, -
> spasm in the heart
> Calculating - and madly alert with excited lust.
> (from 'Self-Portrait')[4]

1 See Alessandra Comini: *Egon Schiele*, Braziller, New York 1976; Jane Kallir: *Gustav Klimt, Egon Schiele*, Galerie St Etienne, Crown, New York 1980; Rudolf Leopold: *Egon Schiele*, Phaidon 1973; Peter Selz: "Egon Schiele", *Art International*, 4, no. 10, 1960, 39f
2 Otto Benesch: *Egon Schiele als Zeichner*, Vienna 1950, "Egon Schiele", *Art International*, II, 1958-9, no. S 9-10
3 Quoted in F. Whitford, 193
4 Quoted in E. Schiele: *I, Eternal Child*, 44

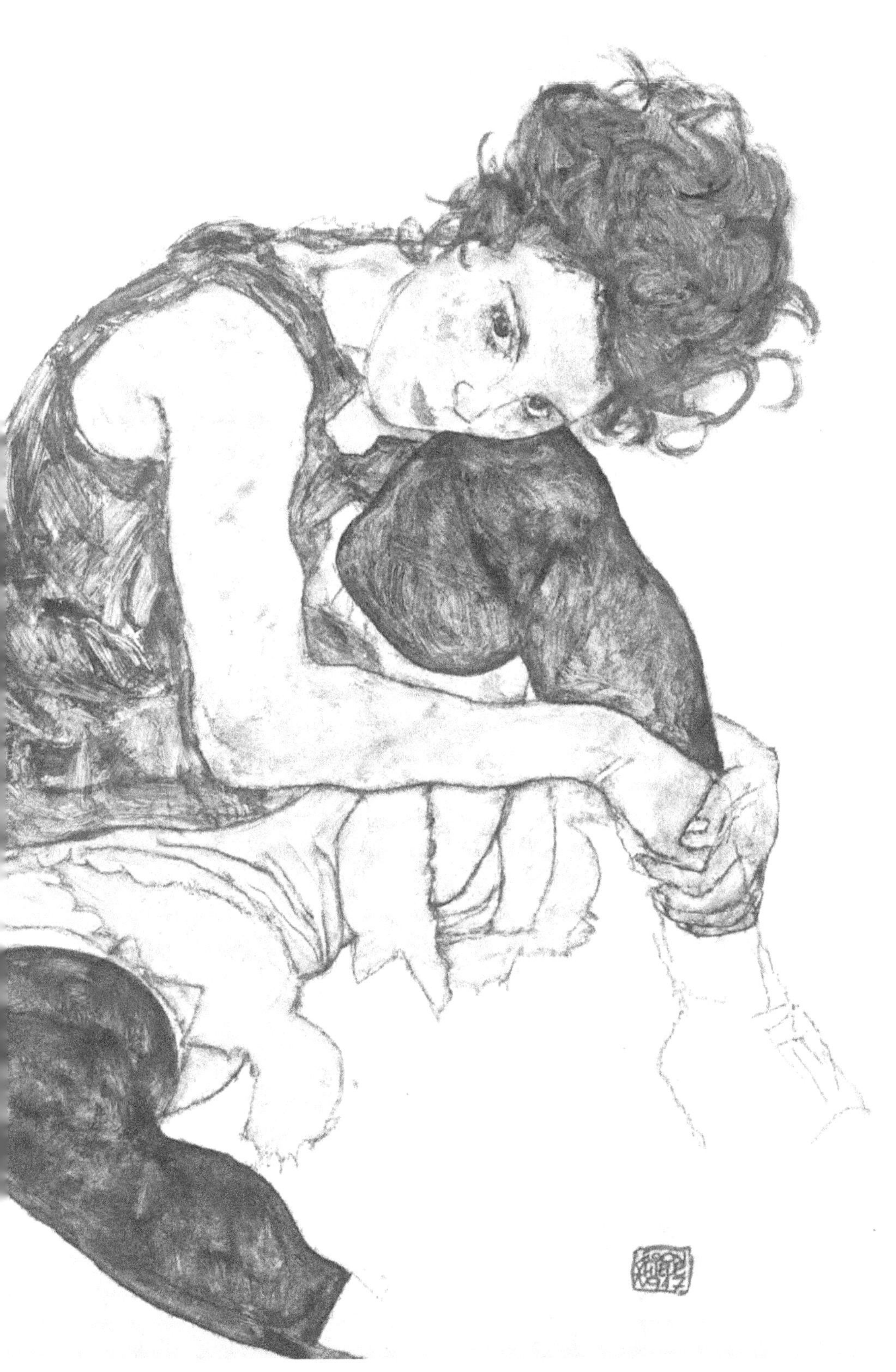

Egon Schiele, Edith, the Artist's Wife, 1917

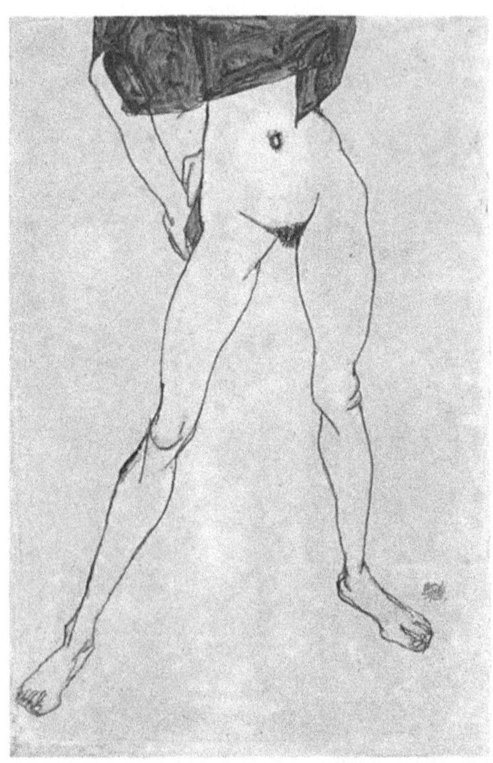

Egon Schiele, Torso, 1913
(left)

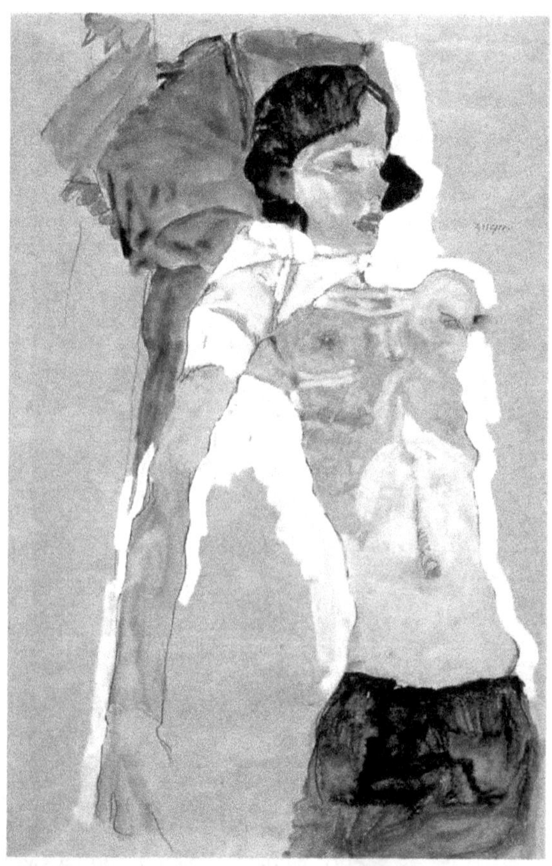

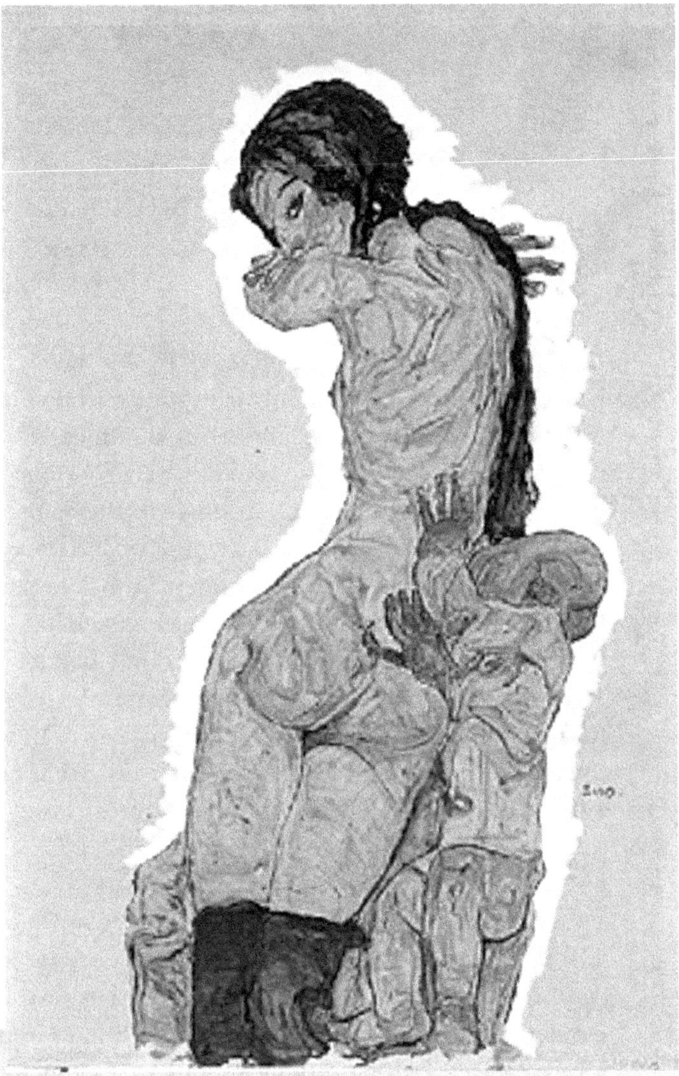

Egon Schiele,
Nude, 1914 (below)

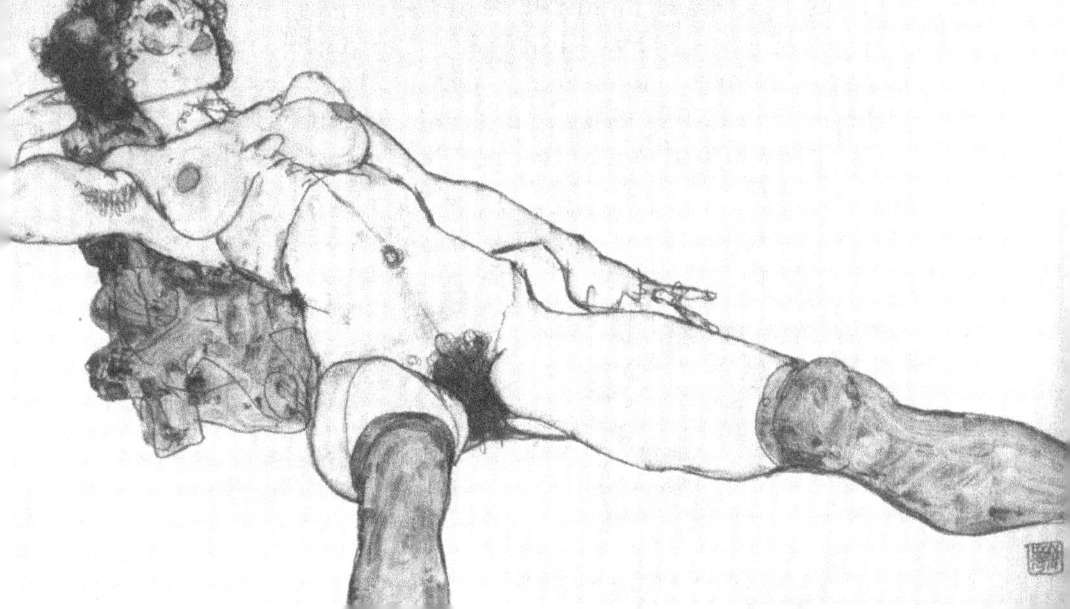

EGON SCHIELE

Egon Schiele's art is characterized by his nervy, stark line. He was not a painter in the richly sensuous tradition of Peter Rubens or Eugène Delacroix. Schiele's oil paintings are like coloured drawings. His drawings, though, are viciously realist and incisive. He does not miss a single blemish or irregularity of bone, skin, muscle or hair. Drawings such as *Recumbent Woman* are ruthless realistic: the sagging flesh of the woman, the blemishes on the skin, the hairy armpit and the indifference of the model are all recorded with a forensic, pathological intensity.[1] This sort of picture is a far cry from the chaste images of traditional, male, academic art. Schiele's' drawings do not romanticize or soften the subject, as Gustav Klimt or Georges de la Tour do. Schiele's thin, spindly figures have something in common with those of Alberto Giacometti (in the latter's *Diego*, for instance).[2]

There are a number of elements in Egon Schiele's art which are the hallmarks of erotic art. Firstly, there is the massive emphasis on sexuality. Always the observer's aware not only of the body, but of the erotic nature of the figure in Schiele's work. Like Gustav Klimt, he produced endless drawings of women in a variety of poses, most of them characterized by twisted limbs, spread legs, heads thrown to one side, hands splayed across thighs or torsos. While Klimt's recline in comfort, luxuriantly, Schiele's women are distinctly uncomfortable, restless, itchy, twitchy, dissatisfied. Schiele did produce erotic drawings that were seemingly direct copies of Klimt, such as the *Reclining Woman* of 1911.[3]

---

1 Egon Schiele: *Recumbent Woman*, 1914, pencil and gouache, 30.4 x 47cm, Graphische Sammlung Albertina, Vienna
2 A. Giacometti: *Diego*, 1953, oil, 100 x 81in, Guggenheim Museum, New York
3 Egon Schiele: *Reclining Woman*, 1911, pencil and gouache, 31.5 x 44cm, Fischer Fine Art, London

gon Schiele, Girl With
ack Hair, 1911 (right).

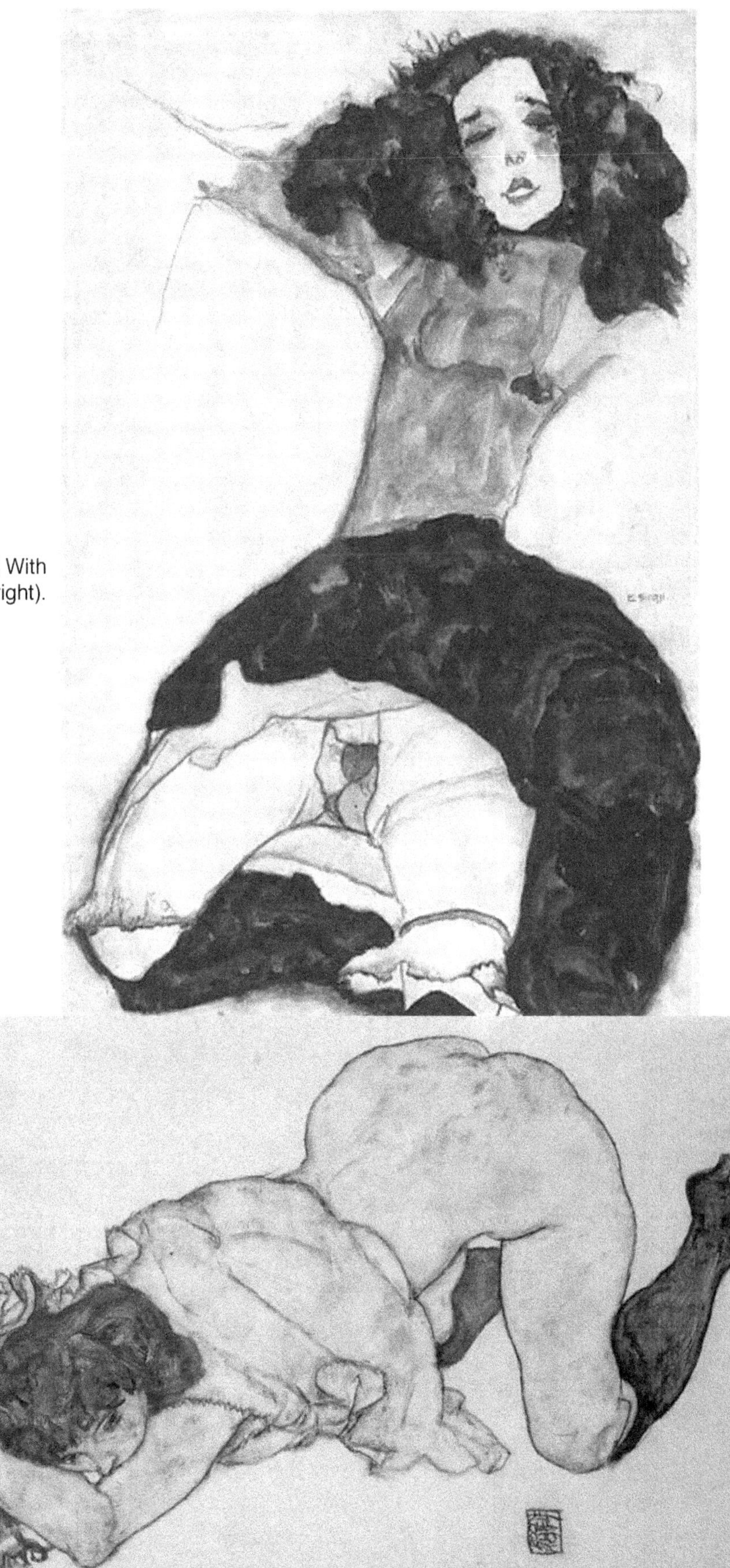

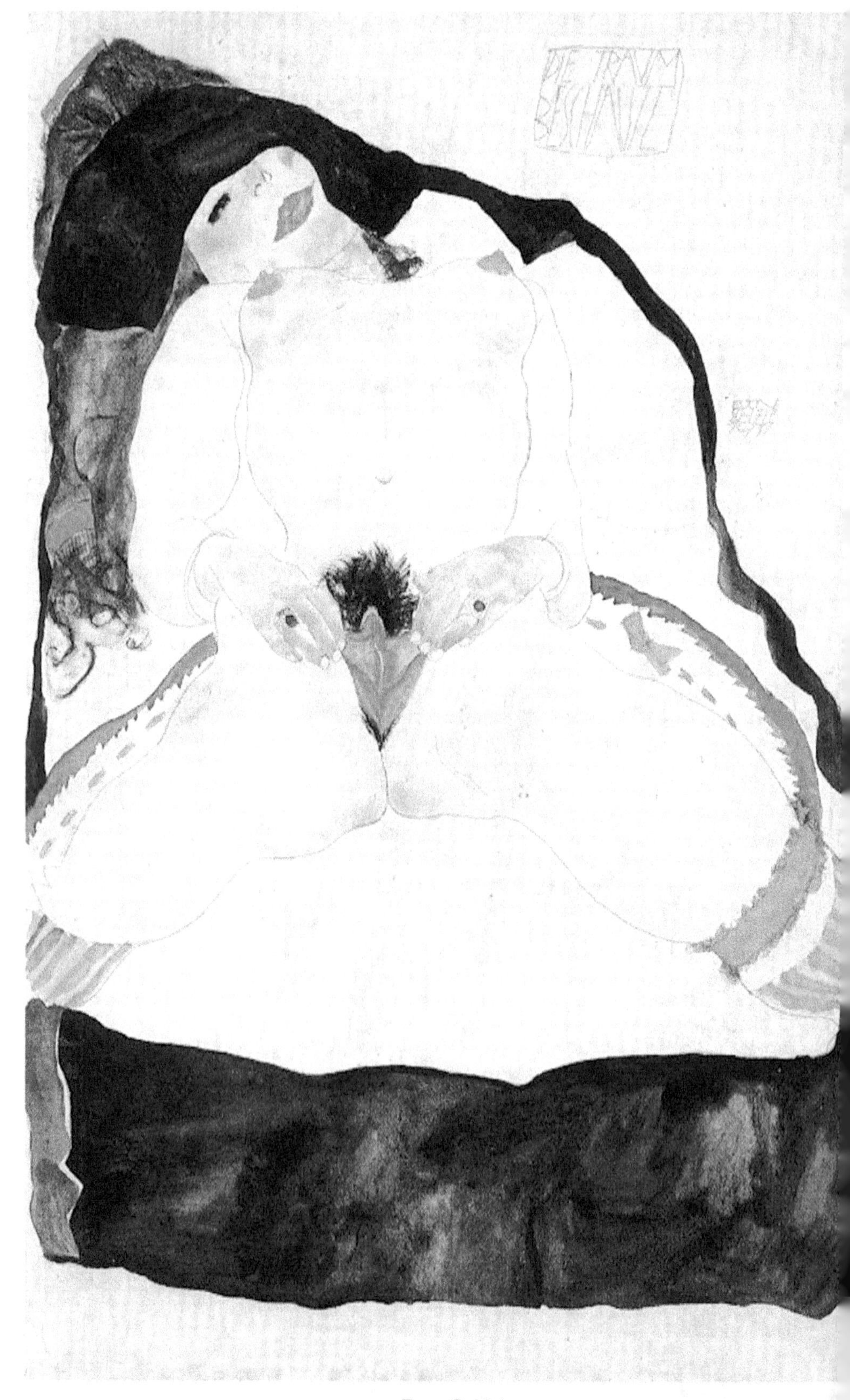

Egon Schiele

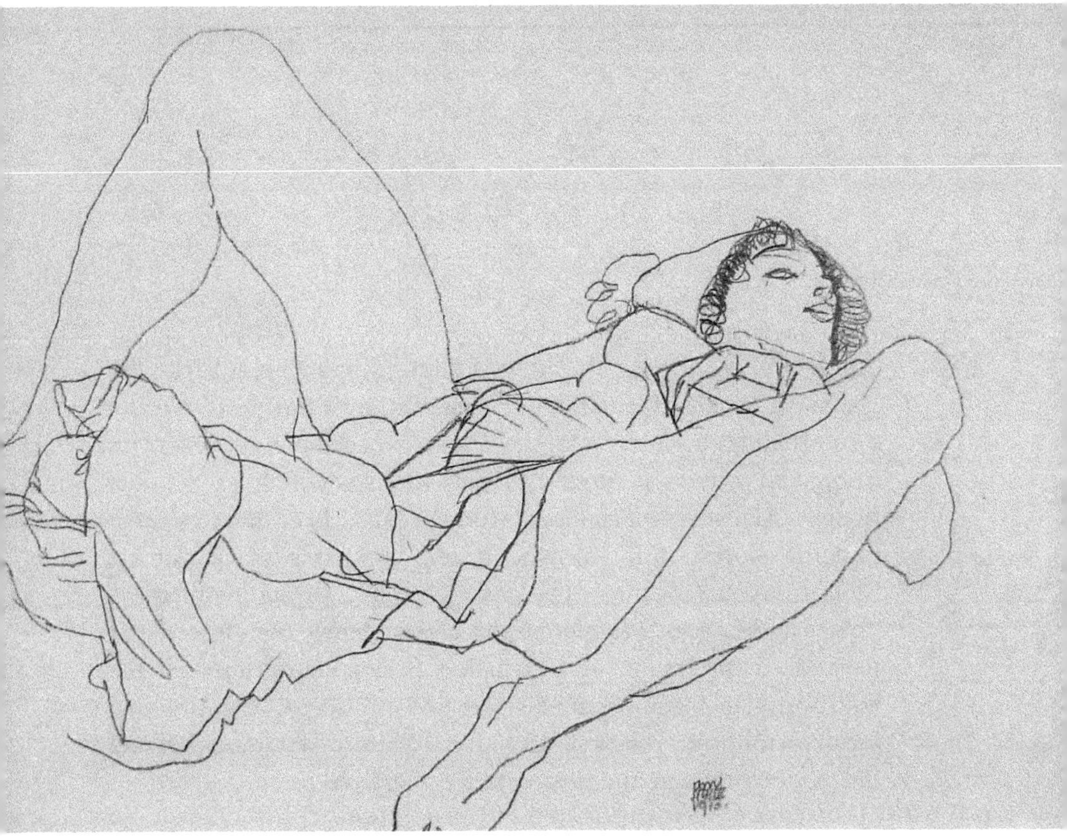

Egon Schiele, Reclining Nude With Spread Legs, 1913 (above).
Reclining Nude With Raised Chemise, 1914 (below).

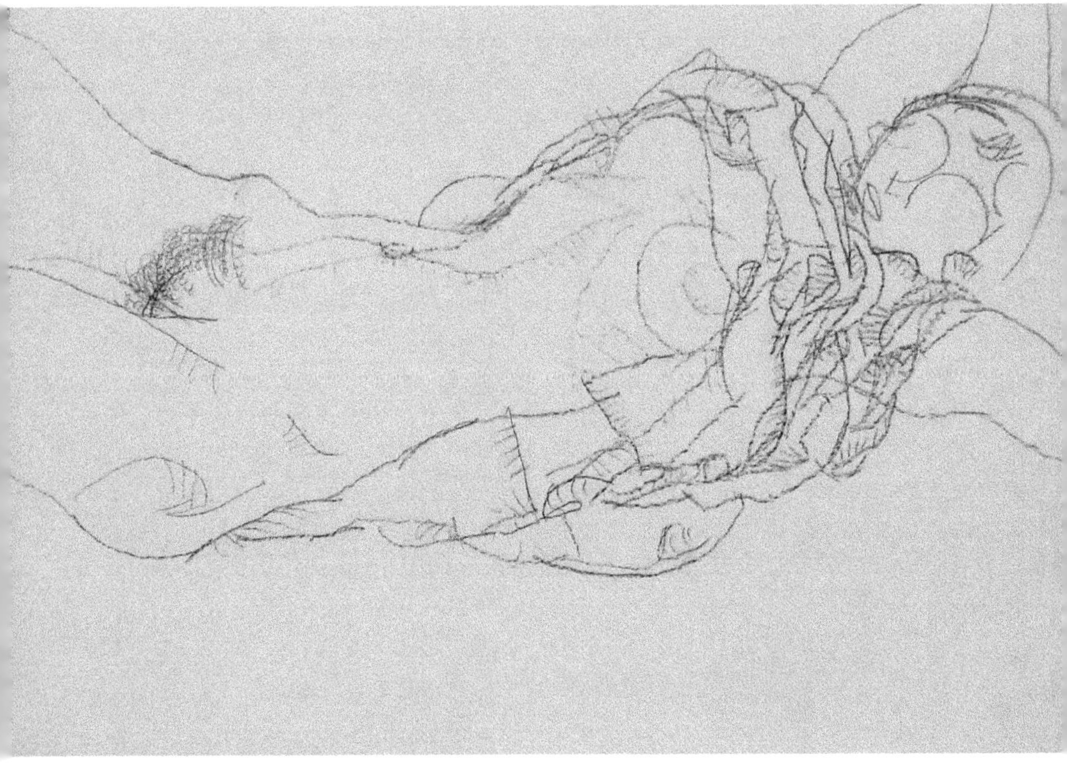

EGON SCHIELE

The *Reclining Girl*[1] of 1910 shows a young woman lying back with her finger on her clit, emulating Gustav Klimt's images of woman masturbating. Egon Schiele plays with expectations however, for his model is young, underage perhaps, something of a Lolita figure. Many of Schiele's women are like this: young, underdeveloped, thin, boyish, to use the terms of patriarchy. Schiele favours women that are 'boyish', yet he emphasizes vulvas and breasts. His models are androgynous, both feared and desired, both male and female. Schiele appropriates the androgyny theme in Symbolist art and infuses it with his own tortured form of eroticism. As Frank Whitford writes, expressing the paradoxical fear and desire theme of art and porn:

> Physically immature, thin, wide-eyed, full-mouthed, innocent and lascivious at the same time, these Lolitas from the proletarian districts of Vienna arouse the kind of thoughts best not admitted before a judge and jury. (82)

---

1 Egon Schiele: *Reclining Girl*, 1910, pencil, 55.7 x 37cm, Neue Galerie am Landesmuseum Joanneum, Graz

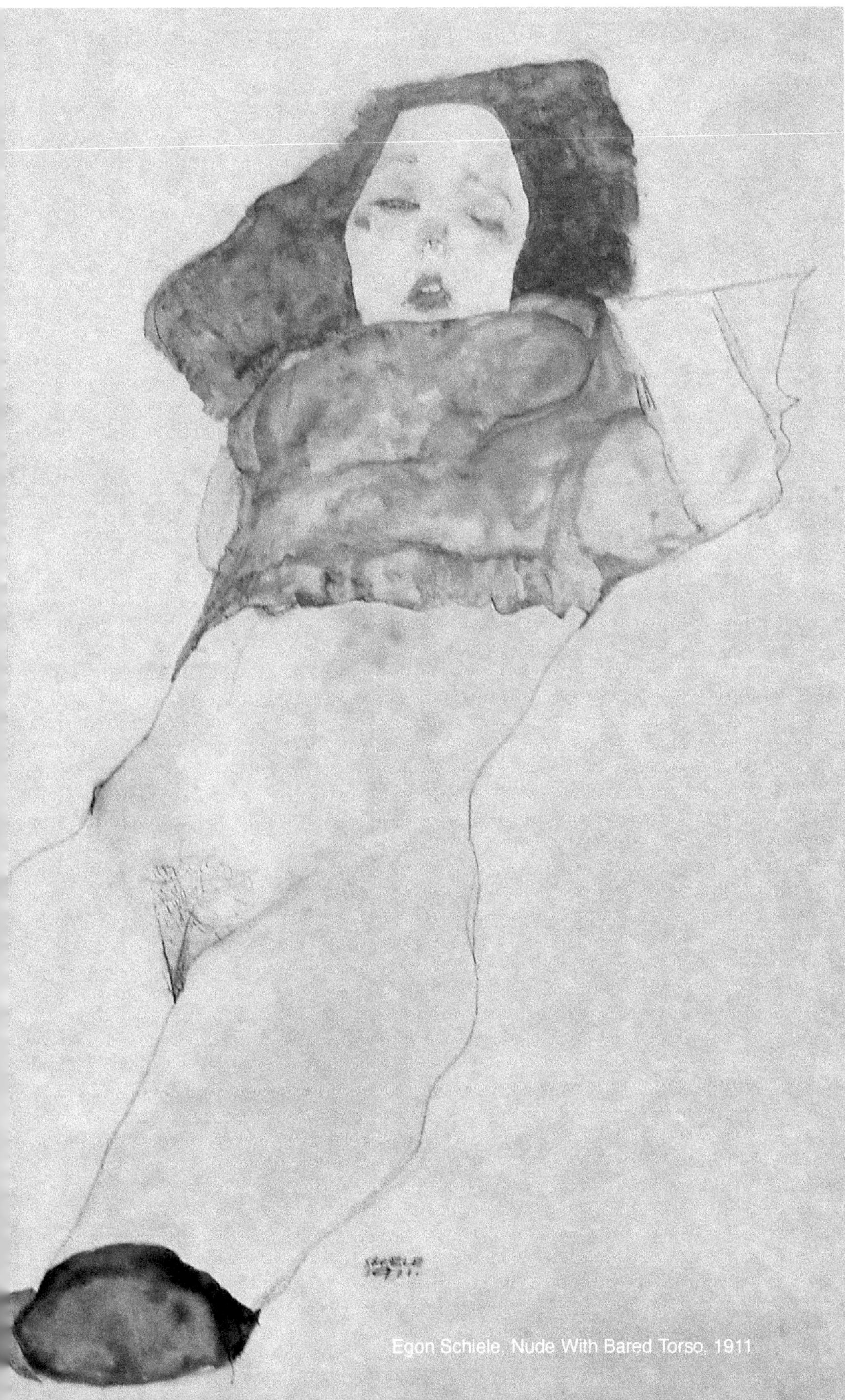

Egon Schiele, Nude With Bared Torso, 1911

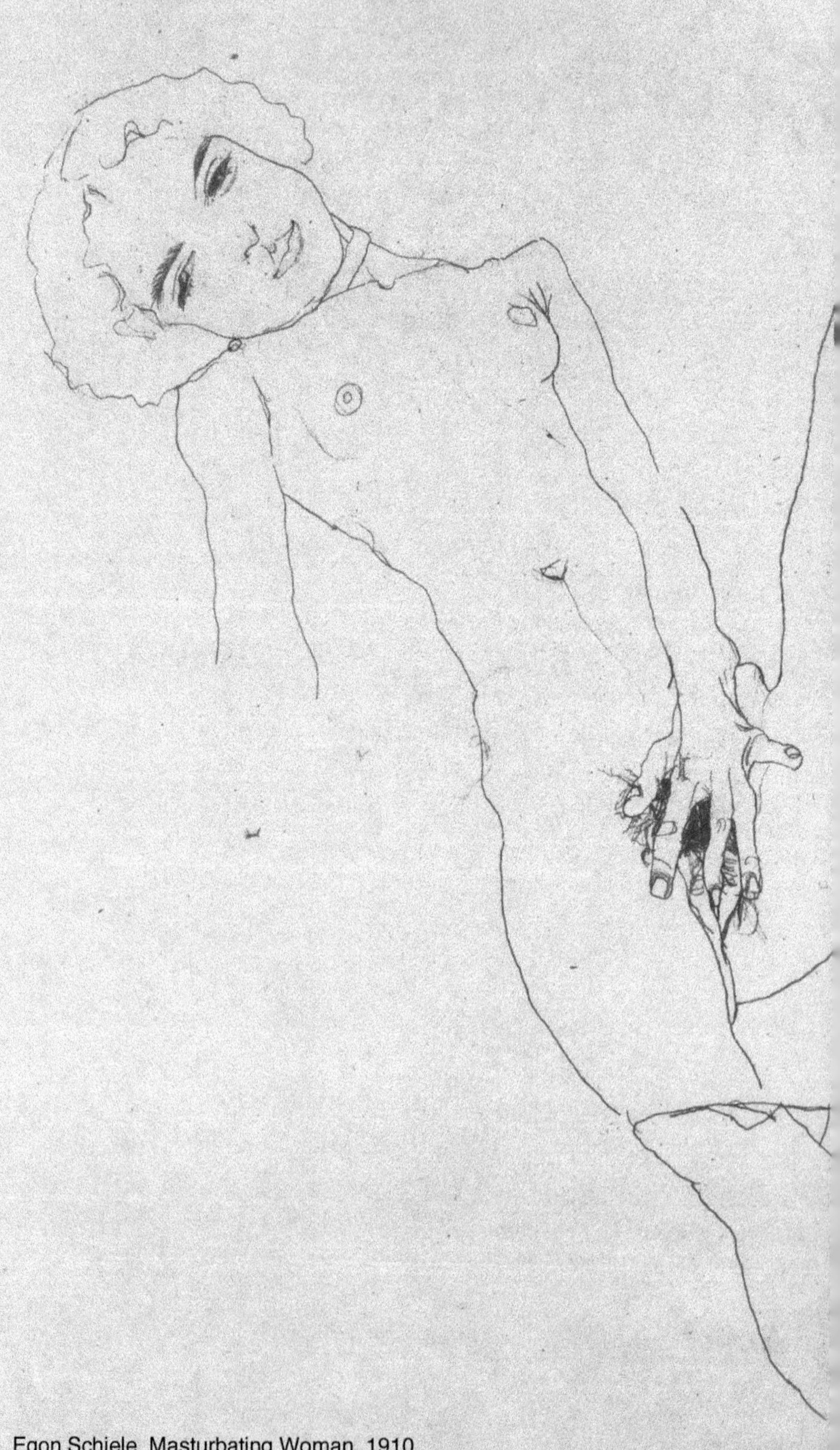

Egon Schiele, Masturbating Woman, 1910

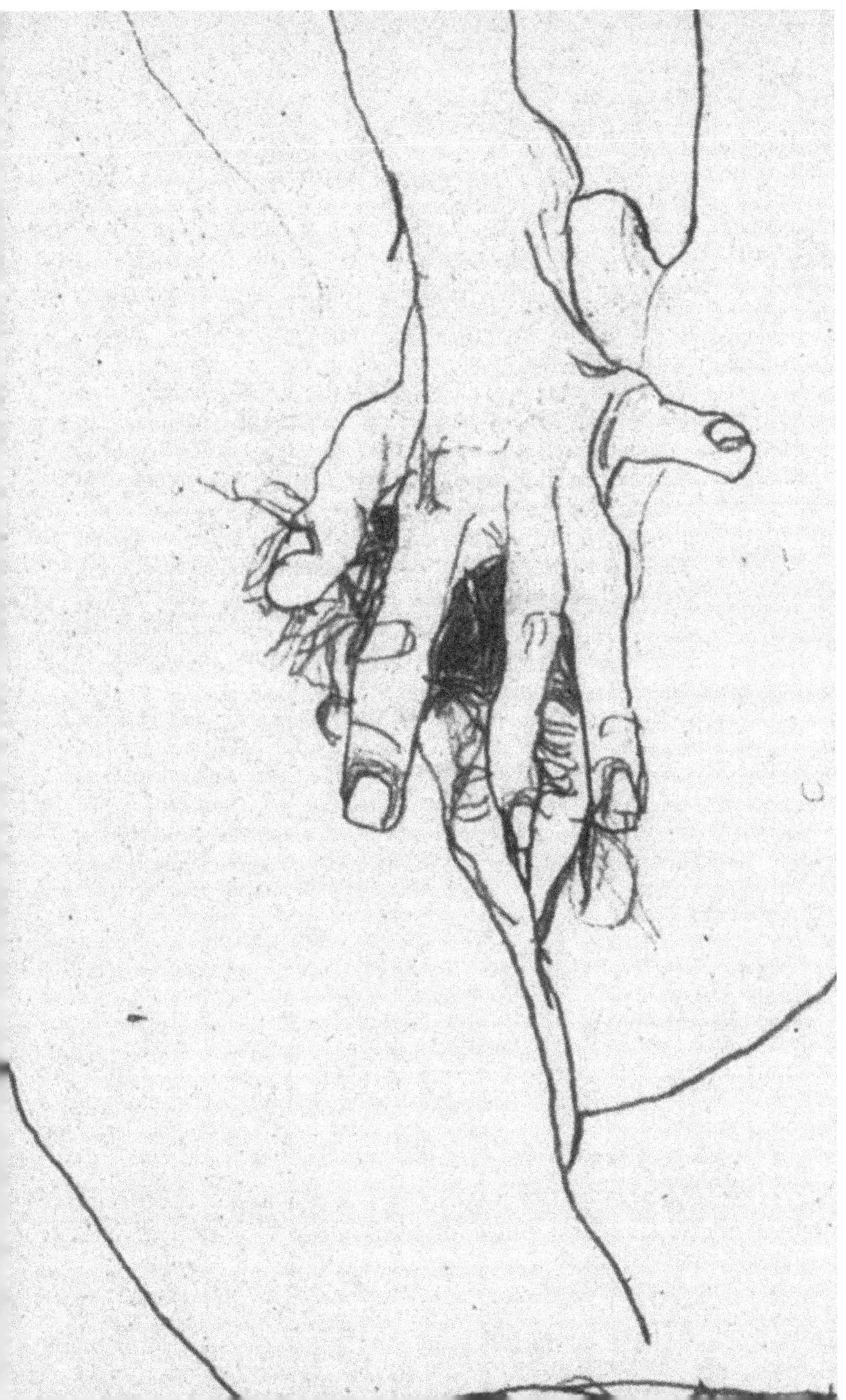

EGON SCHIELE

Another aspect of Egon Schiele's art that is found in both erotica and art is fetishism. So many of Schiele's models wear stockings – striped stockings or purple stockings.[1] Schiele has one of the sharpest eyes for a startling graphic image. All of his art is very *stylish*, very fashionable. It always *looks good*, as fashion can. The dresses and stockings are part of the stylistic design, integrated as ornament, as in the work of Gustav Klimt, and are as crucial as the angular limbs or looks of complicity.

The 1911 drawing of a semi-nude woman lying on her front is typical of Egon Schiele's stylish erotica.[2] She lies with eyes closed, her legs are apart, to reveal her vulva, which Schiele has, as usual, coloured red with watercolour over his pencil drawing. This is usual enough in erotica and pornography, and in Schiele's art, this focusing on the woman's genitals. What is unusual, perhaps, is the fashionable items that Schiele clothes his model in: a stripey skirt, the stripes are very colourful: light blue, red, dark blue, orange, black, purple. She wears a check shirt, the colours here again are bright: green, red, orange, black and white squares. The overall effect is a combination of erotica and fashion. In Schiele's drawings, everything in the picture is fetishized, not just the model.

1 Egon Schiele: *Girl with Striped Stockings*, 1910, gouache, 31.5x 44cm, private collection; *Nude with Purple Stockings*, 1911, watercolour, 45 x 31.4cm, private collection
2 Egon Schiele: *Reclining Nude, Half Length*, 1911, pencil & watercolour, 18.8 x 12.4in, private collection, New York

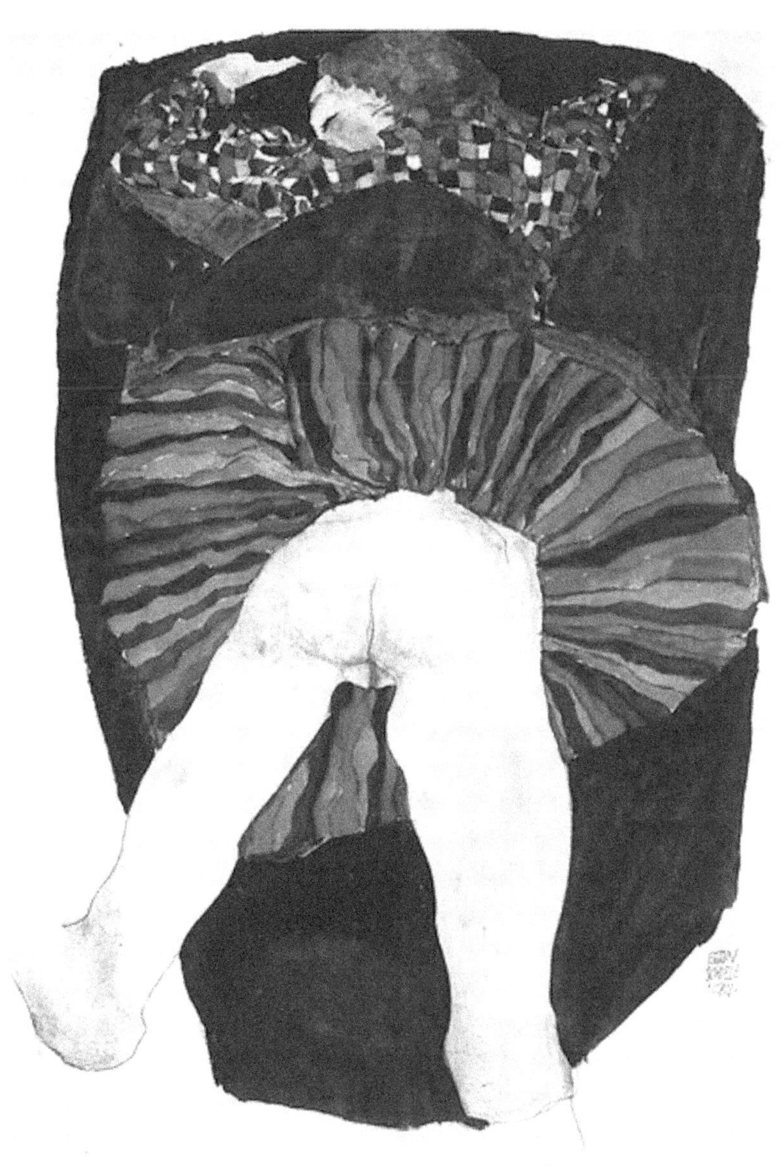

Egon Schiele, Nude, 1911

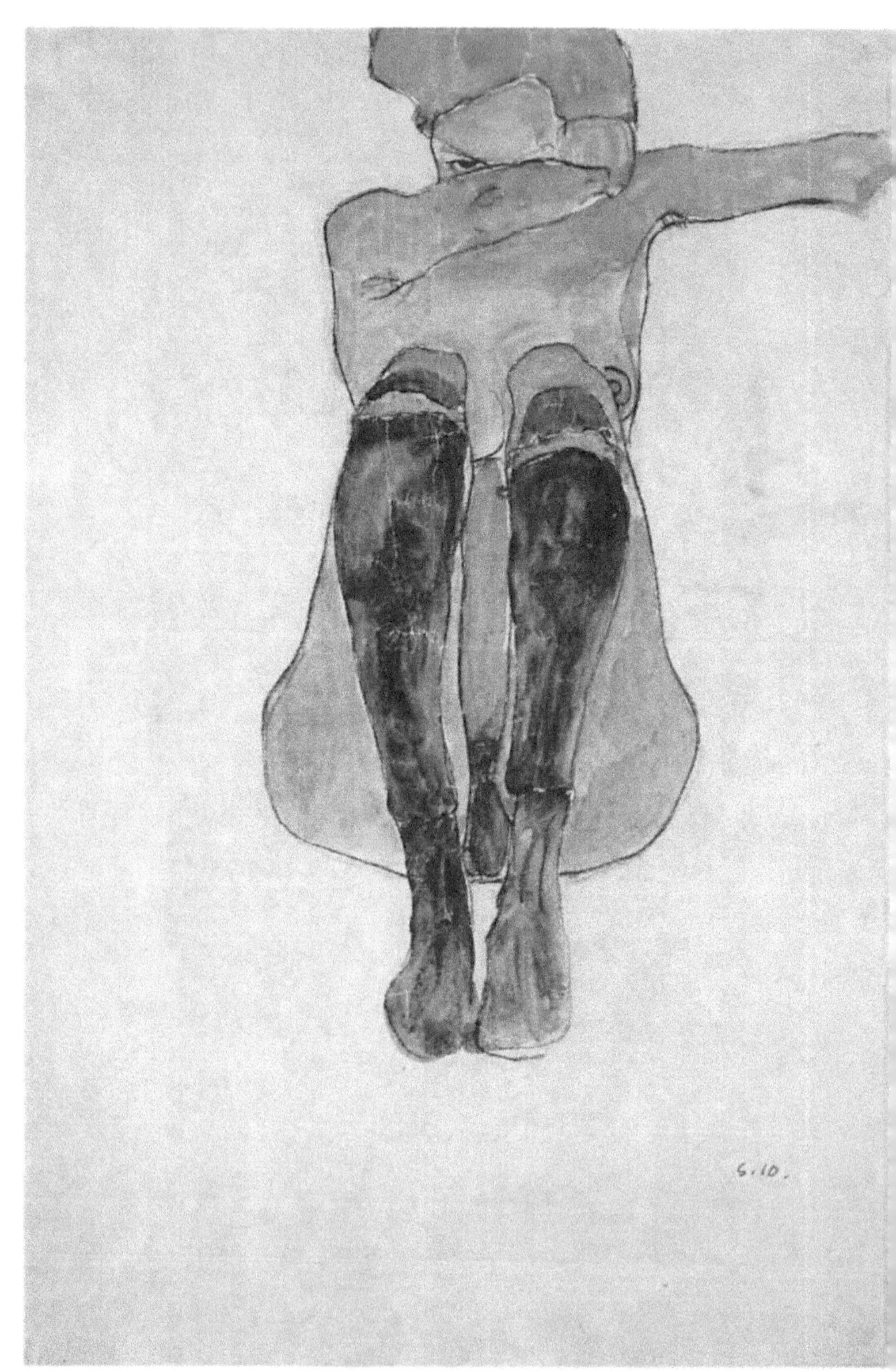

Egon Schiele, Nude, 1910

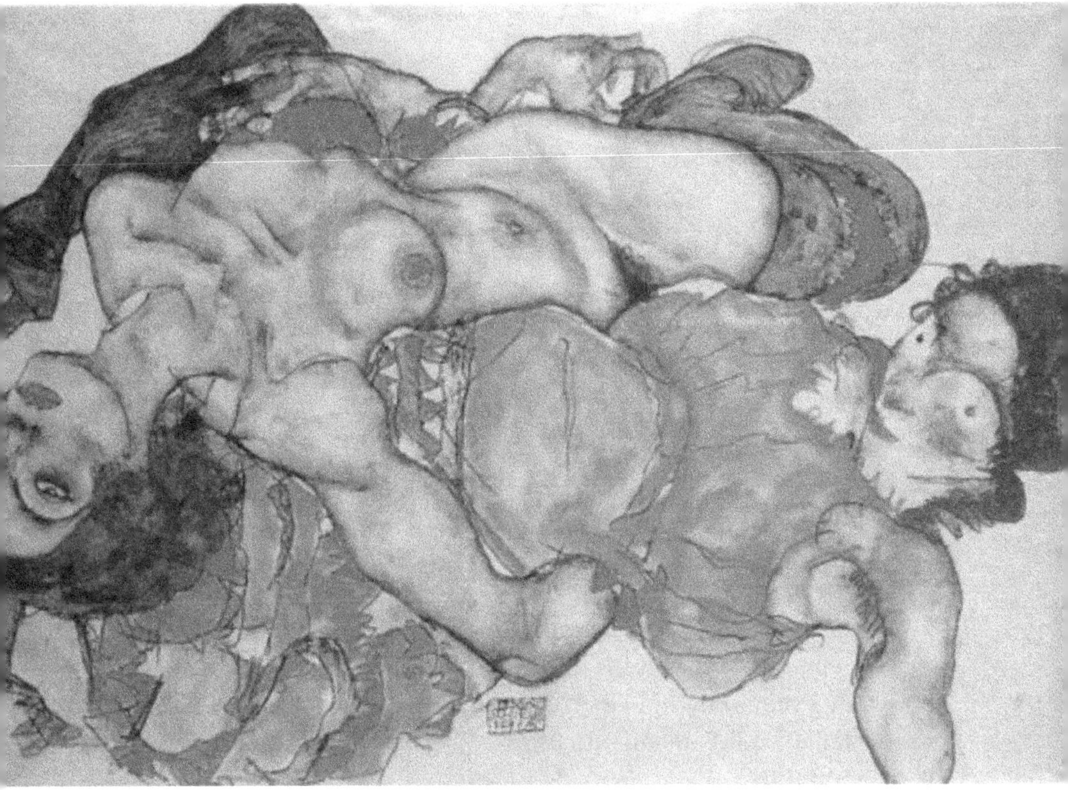

Egon Schiele, Two Women Lying Entwined, 1915, Vienna (above).

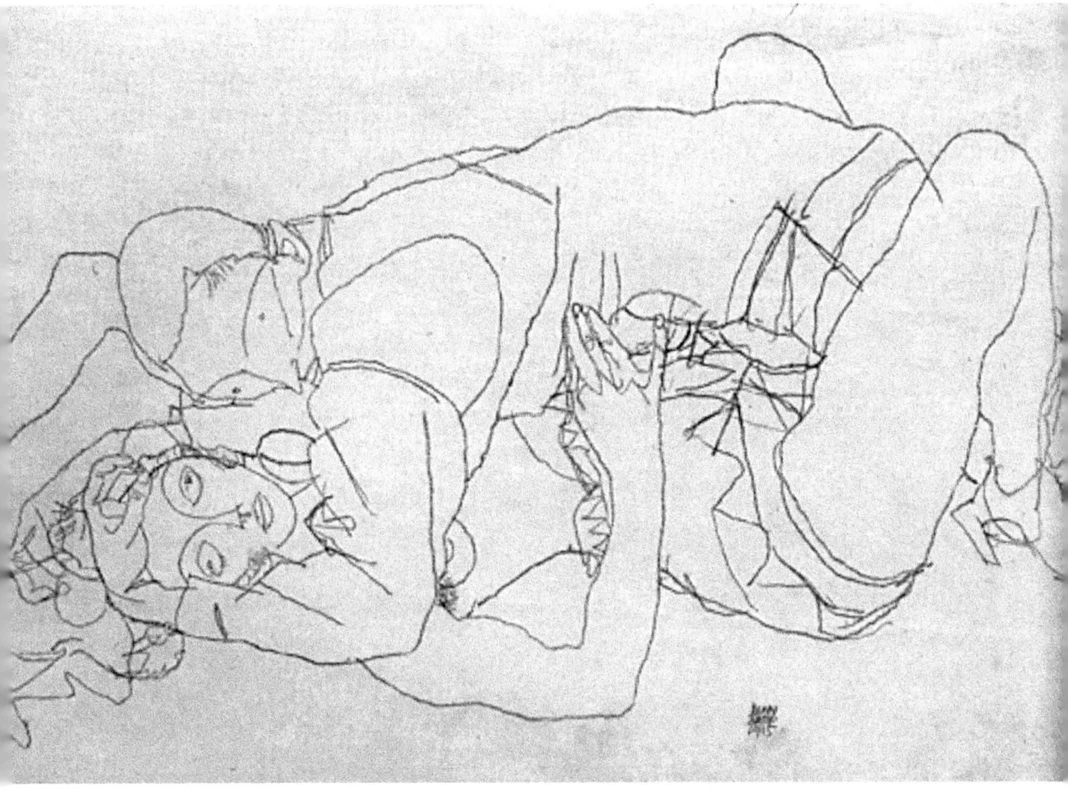

AUGUSTE RODIN

There are a number of renowned modern artists who are unrestrained in their exaltation of women. Auguste Rodin is a typical example. Of the *Venus de'Medici,* Auguste Rodin wrote:

> Notice all the voluptuous curvings of the hip... And now, here, the adorable dimples along the loins... It is truly flesh... You would think it moulded by caresses!

Auguste Rodin is the classic womanizer artist, who made love to his models physically as well as psychologically and æsthetically. His models became his mistresses (such as Camille Claudel). Like many artists, he produced erotica for private consumption.

But enthusiastic eroticism infuses everything Auguste Rodin created. Sculptures such as *The Metamorphoses of Ovid* is typical - it depicts two lovers embracing.[1] The sculpture *Christ and the Magdalene* is more controversial, for it depicts Mary Magdalene sexually embracing the crucified Christ.[2] The image is blasphemous, fusing sex and religion in that age-old fashion. This eroticization of Mary Magdalene occurs also in the art of Félicien Rops and Eric Gill.

1 A. Rodin: *The Metamorphoses of Ovid*, plaster, height 13in
2 A. Rodin: *Christ and the Magdalene*, 1894

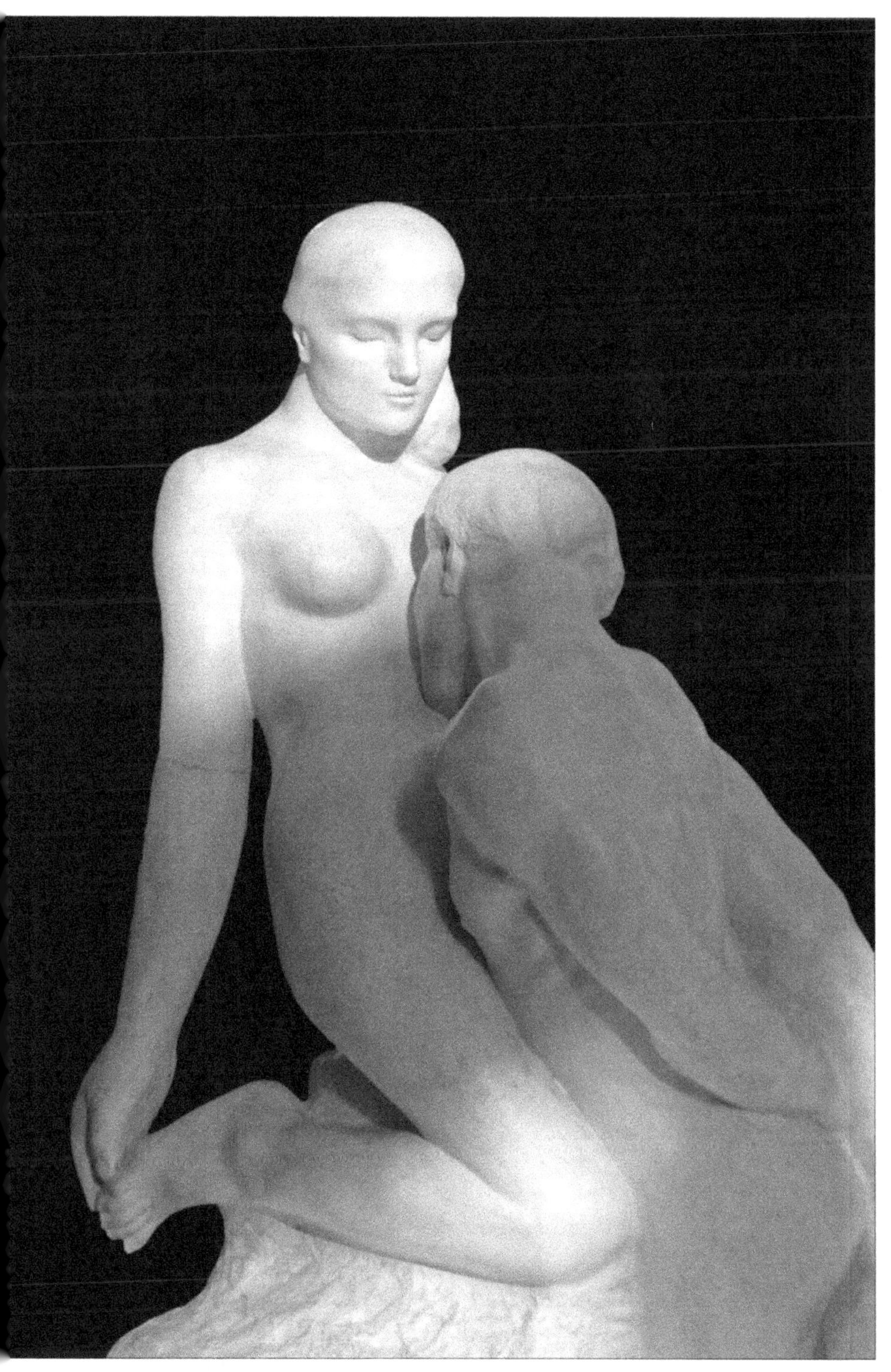

Auguste Rodin, L'Eternelle Idole, Museé Rodin

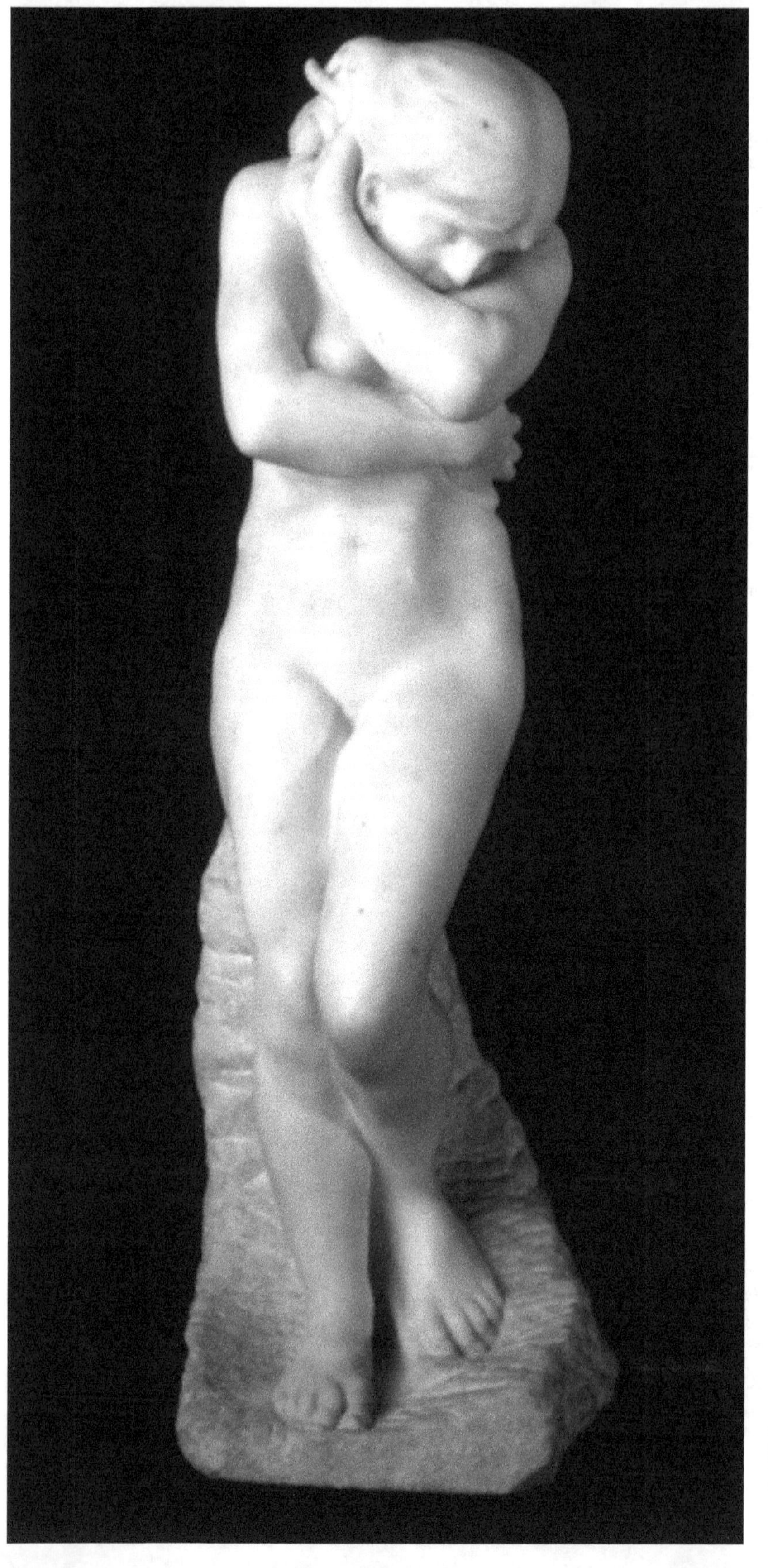

Auguste Ro
Eve, 1892,
Mexico

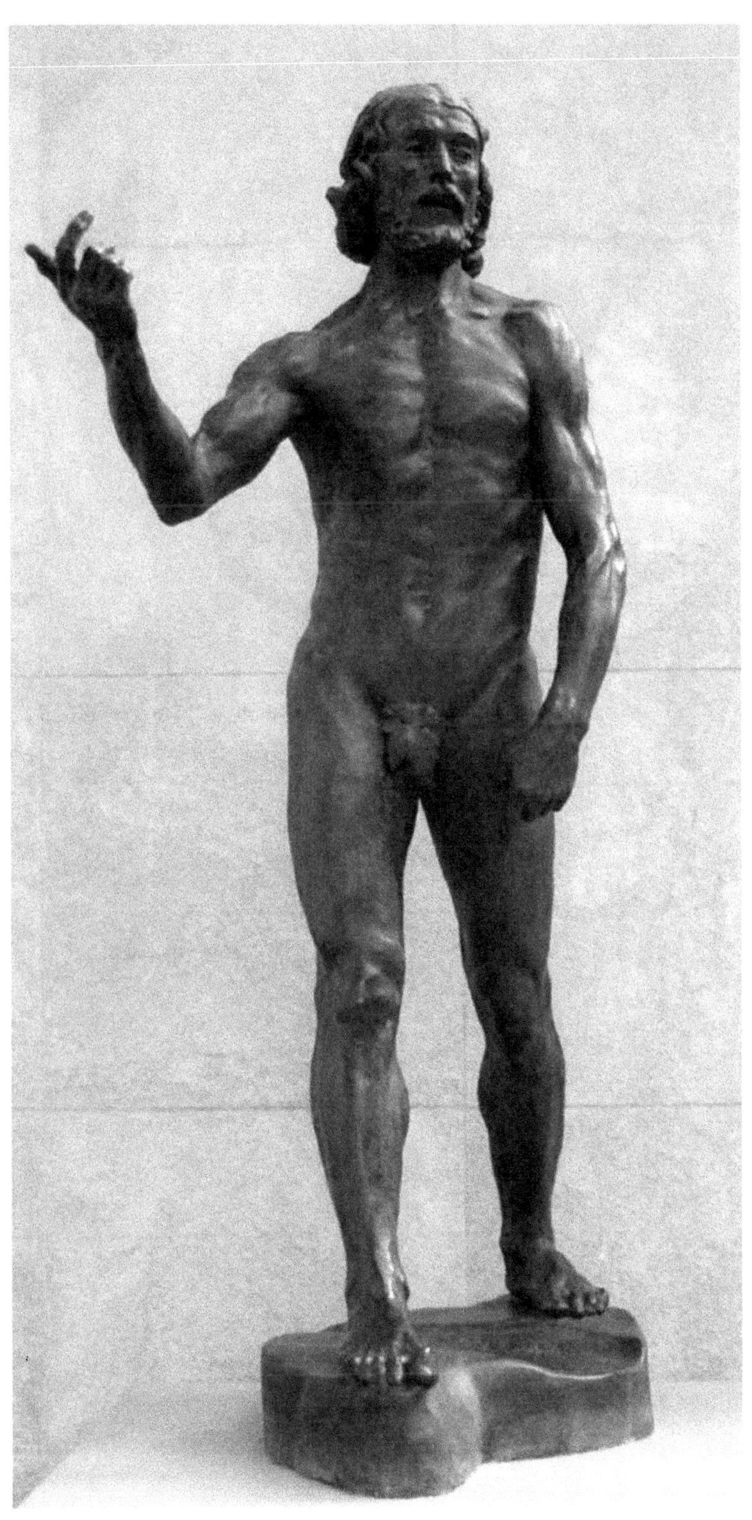

Auguste Rodin, St John the Baptist Preaching

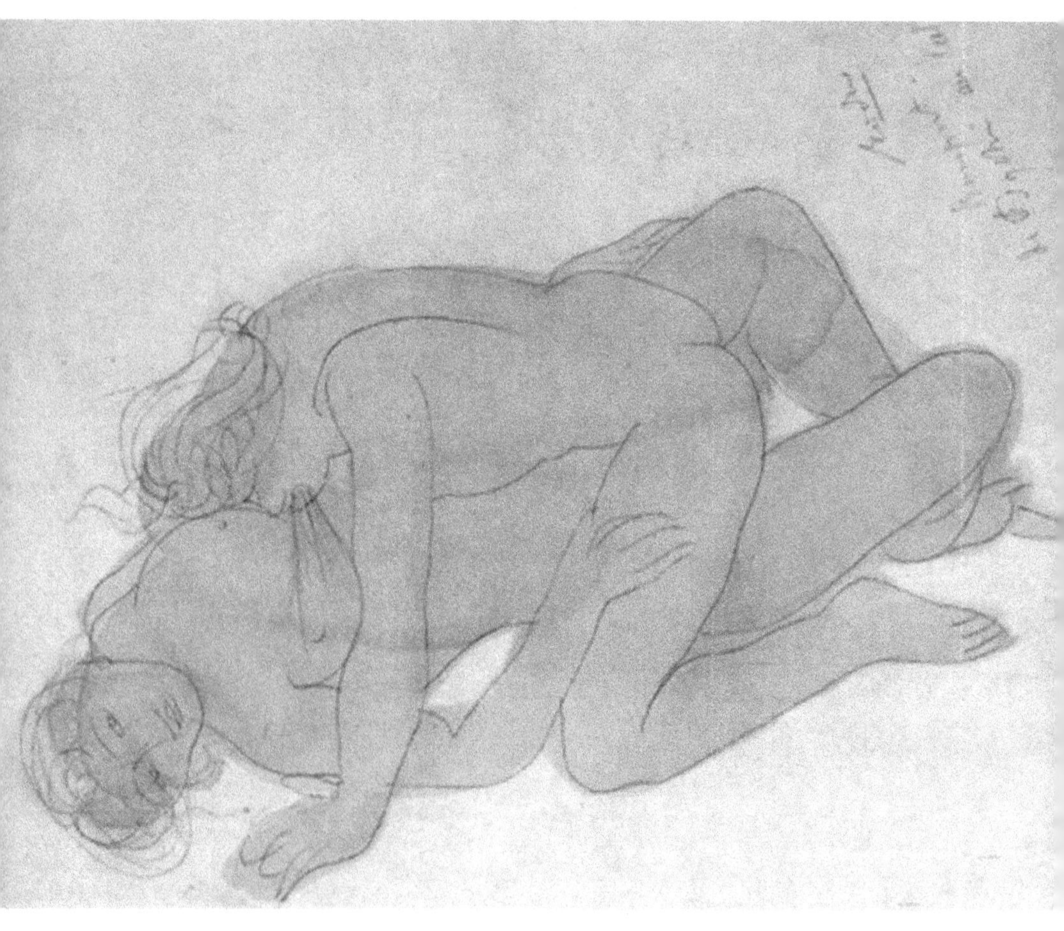

Auguste Rodin, nude drawings (this page and following)

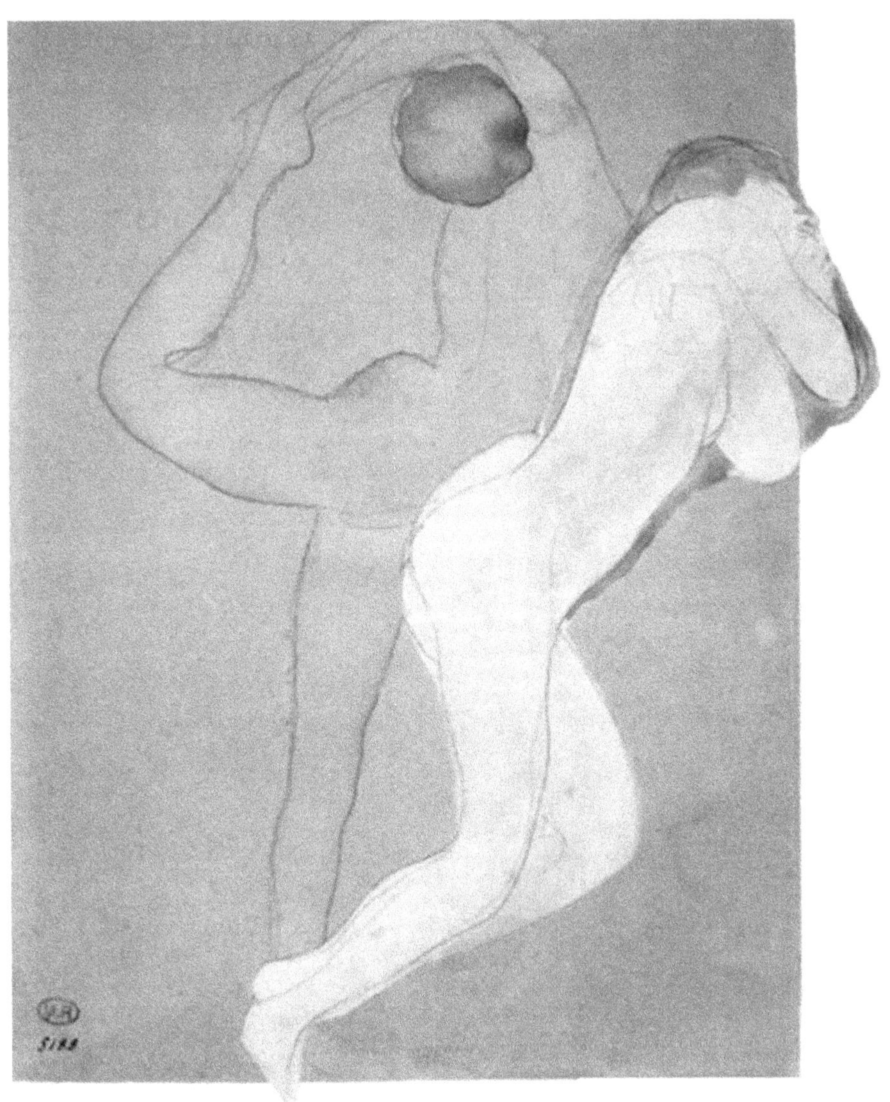

Auguste Rodin, Female Couple

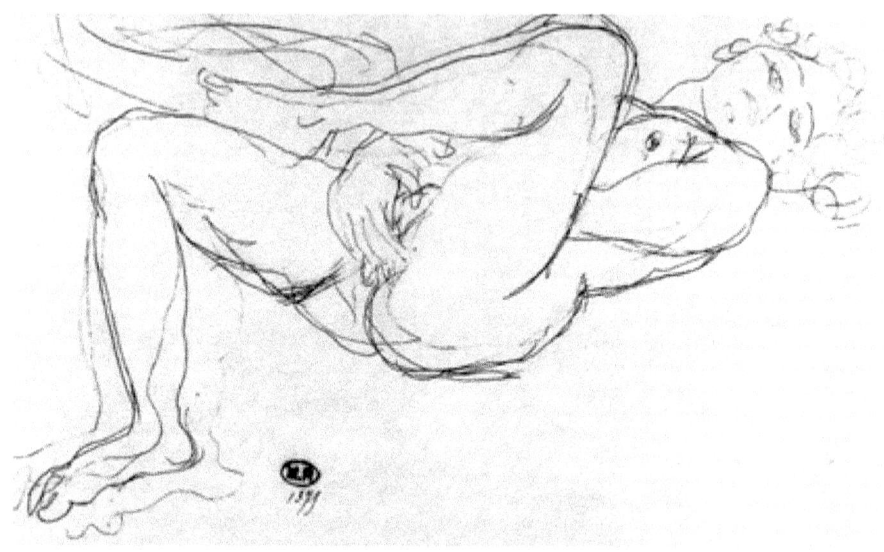

Auguste Rodin, drawings

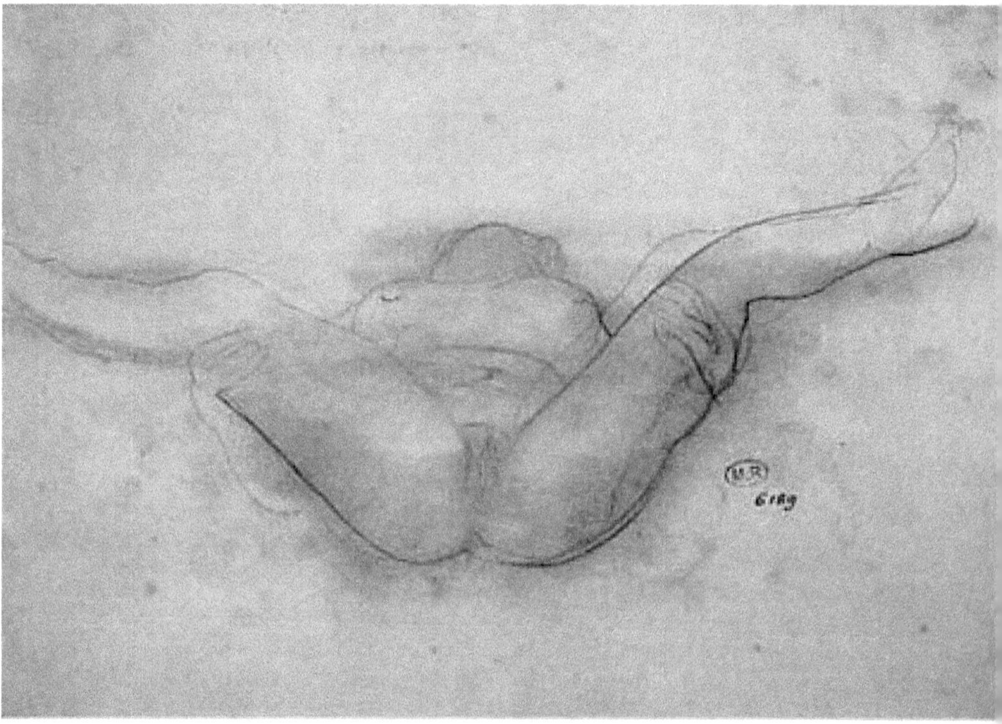

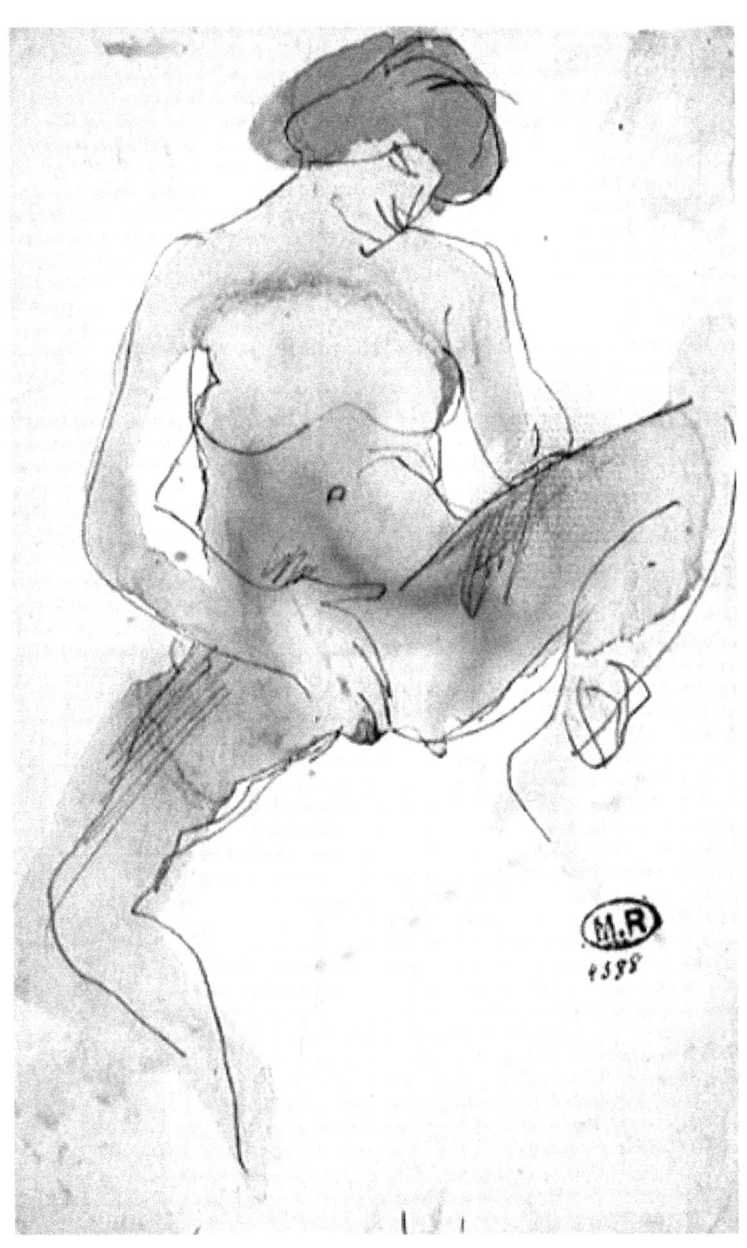

Auguste Rodin

GUSTAV KLIMT

Gustav Klimt is one of those 'acceptable' erotic artists, whose art is consumed these days as mild erotica, regularly appearing in prints and posters and calendars, next to Henri Matisse, Claude Monet and Vincent van Gogh. Klimt never strays from the heterosexist norm of soft-core pornographic consumption. Klimt is ruthlessly, vigorously heterosexual in his art. He passionately adores women, and is a modern summary of all male artists who have loved and painted women. In paintings such as *Danae*, *The Kiss* and *Woman*, Klimt produced luxuriant, post-Symbolist, post-Byzantine icons of femininity in that Art Nouveau style of Vienna termed 'Secessionstil'.[1] Decadence or over-indulgence is one of Klimt's hallmarks. At times, only Gustave Moreau seems more luxuriant. Klimt depicts naked or half-naked bodies flowing over each other, entwined and writhing but also half-asleep, their eyes closed or half-open, as in stuck in some slow motion opium orgy.[2]

Gustav Klimt flattens every element of his representations onto one picture plane, and turns the image into pure ornamentation and decoration. He is supremely stylish, and rarely allows any evil serpent to slither in and spoil his basically tame nostalgic paradise. In his friezes, one sees the epic grandeur asserting itself.

1 G. Klimt: *Danae*, c. 1905, 77 x 80cm, Galerie Weltz, Salzburg; *The Kiss*, 1907-8, 180 x 180cm, Österreichische Galerie, Vienna; *Woman*, 1913, pencil 56 x 35cm, Vicktor Fogarassy Collection,

2 See, for instance, Gustav Klimt's *The Virgin*, 1912-3, Narodny Galerie, Prague

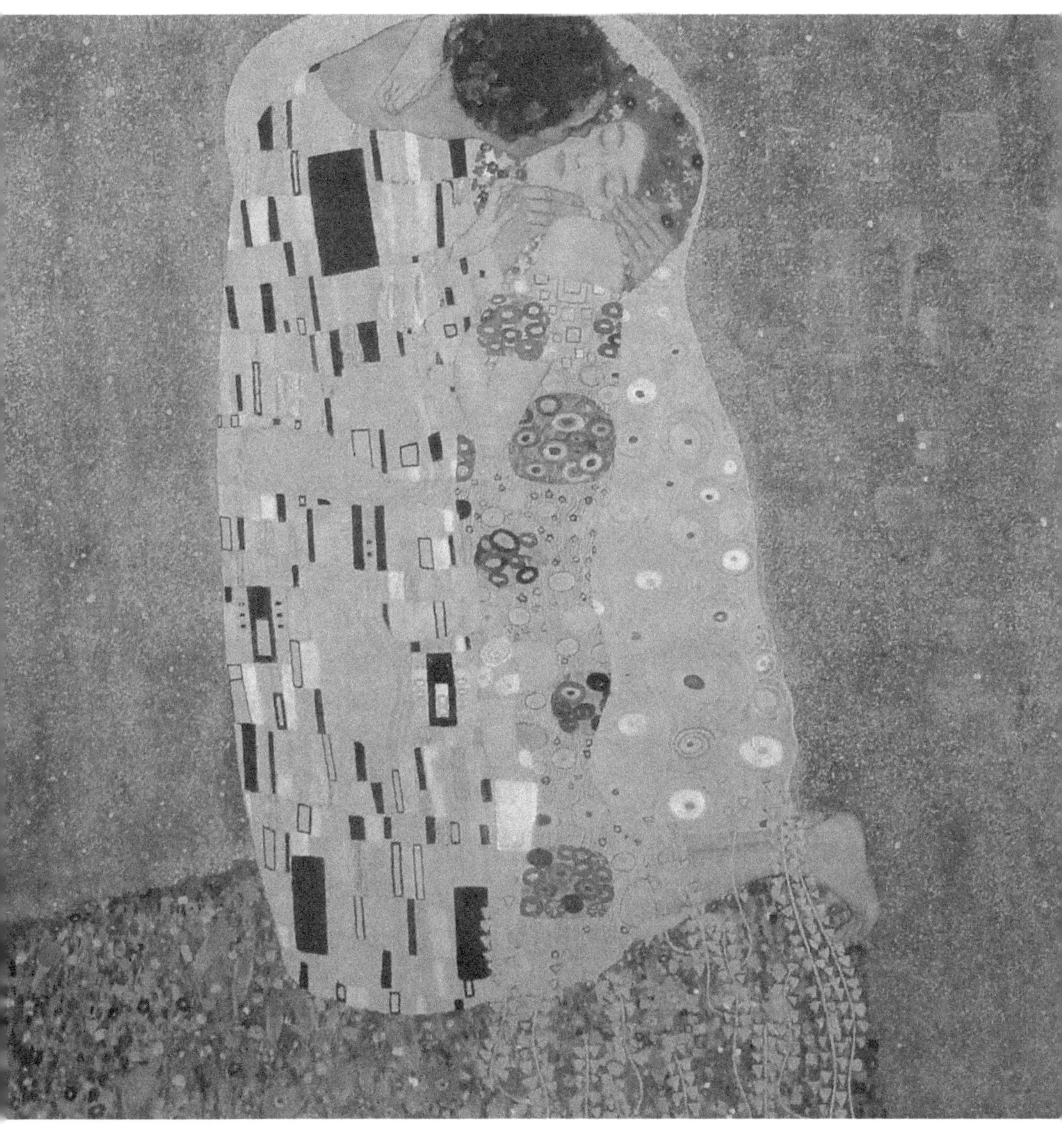

Gustav Klimt, The Kiss

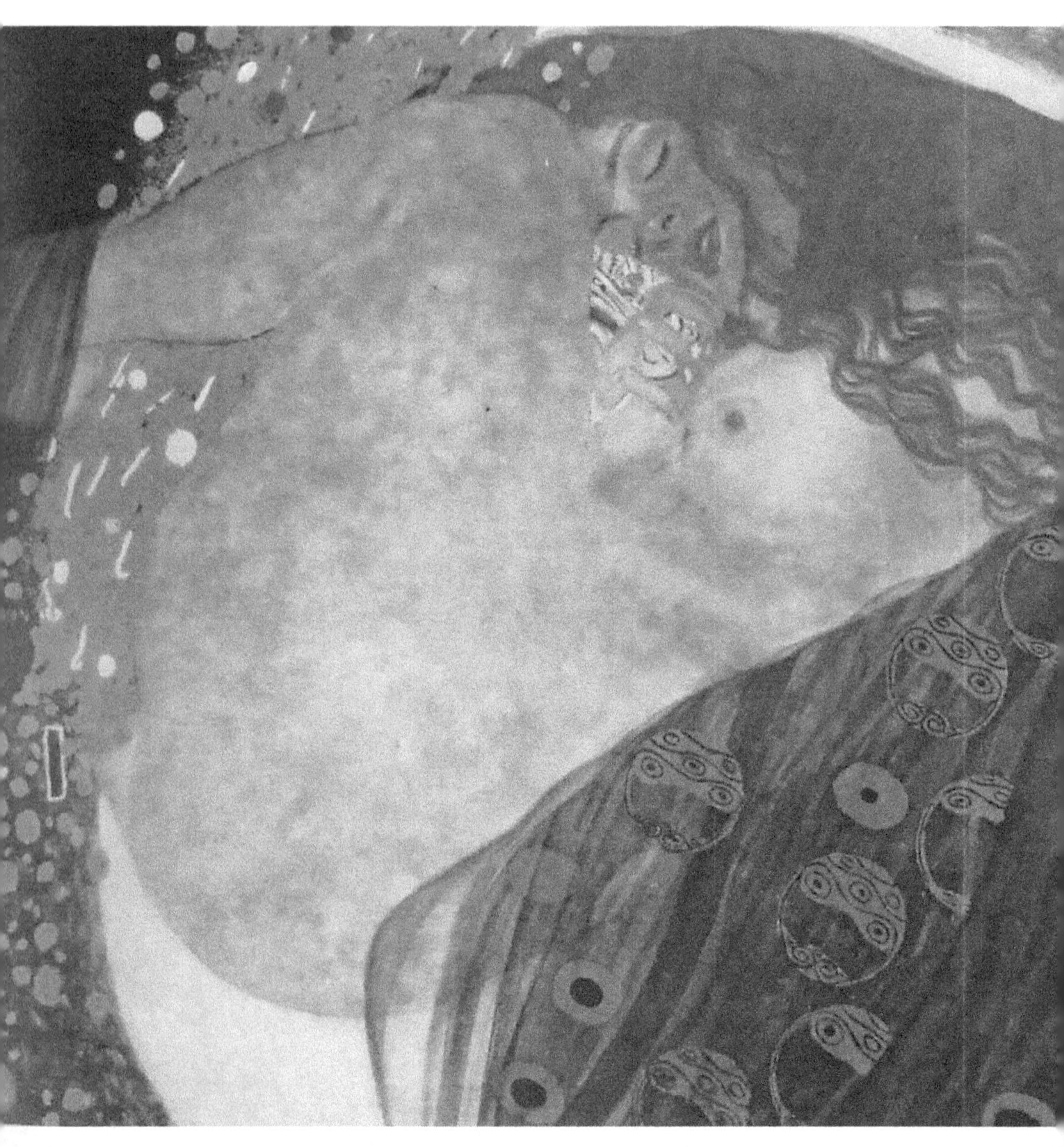

Gustav Klimt, Danaë

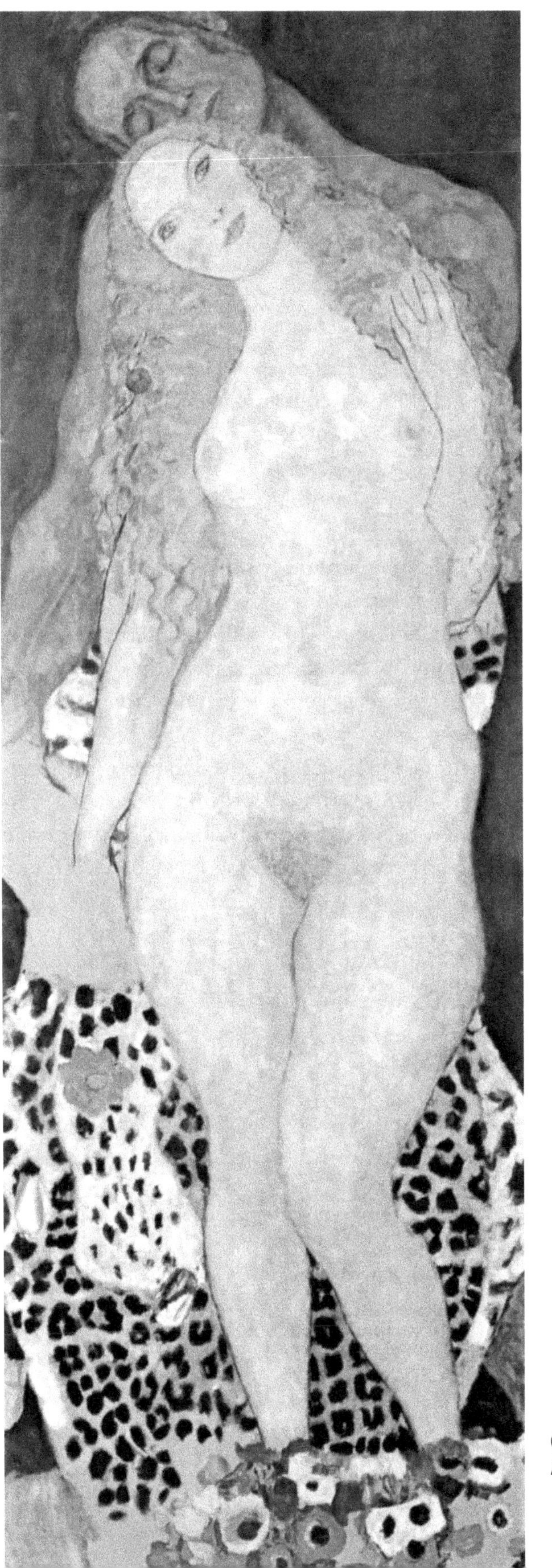

Gustav Klimt,
Adam and Eve

GUSTAV KLIMT

The drawings of women lying back with their legs spread are pure pornography – the *Seated Nude*, for example.[1] *Goldfish* depicts in oil a woman, nude of course, squatting, buttocks prominent.[2] Women are seen as water, that symbolic 'feminine' element, in *Flowing Water.*[3] *Water Serpents I* is the usual Gustav Klimt offering,[4] a semi-nude woman sliding down the picture, eyes closed, dreamy, asleep perhaps, or in bliss, blissed-out, her hair, long of course, flowing around her. So many of Klimt's figures are elongated, slipping vertically down the painting, caught in a cascade of ornamentation. This is the standard Klimtesque scenario, this dreamy nude slipping past the viewer, as in his university pictures and large-scale paintings: *Philosophy, Medicine, Jurisprudence.*[5]

Gustav Klimt's depictions of women are archetypical, absolutely at the centre of mainstream Western art. His lesbian imagery, for instance, is, essentially, that of pornography. When he paints pregnant women, as in the great *Beethoven Frieze*, or in *Hope II*, he uses a much censored image in Western art.[6] The nude, pregnant woman still provokes controversy when it is displayed in the popular media or in art today. Klimt's pregnant women, though, are simply part of his overall exaltation of women.

1 G. Klimt: *Seated Nude with Closed Eyes*, 1913, pencil, 57 x 37cm; *Reclining Semi-Nude Woman*, 1913, pencil, 56 x 36cm, both Historical Museum, Vienna

2 G. Klimt: *Goldfish*, 1901/2, oil on canvas, 150 x 46cm, Dübi-Miller Foundation, Kunstmuseum, Solothurn

3 G. Klimt: *Flowing Water*, 1898, oil, 52 x 65cm, St Etienne Gallery, New York

4 G. Klimt: *Water Serpents I*, 1904-7, oil, gold leaf, mixed media on parchment, 19.6 x 7.8in, Österreichische Galerie, Vienna

5 G. Klimt: *Philosophy*, 1899-1907, oil on canvas, 430 x 300cm, destroyed; *Medicine*, 1900-7, oil on canvas, 430 x 300cm, destroyed; *Jurisprudence*, 1903-7, oil on canvas, 430 x 300cm, destroyed

6 G. Klimt: *Beethoven Frieze*, 1902, casein, gold leaf, semiprecious stones, mother-of-pearl, gypsum, charcoal, pastel and pencil on plaster, 216 x 636cm, Österreichische Galerie, Vienna; *Hope II*, 1907-8, oil and gold on canvas, 110.5 x 110.5cm, Museum of Modern Art, New York. See Marian Bisanz-Prakken: "The Beethoven Exhibition of the Vienna Secession", in Erika Nielsen, ed: *Focus on Vienna 1900*, Houston German Studies, no. 4, Fink, Munich 1982; Peter Vergo: "Gustav Klimt's Beethoven Frieze", *Burlington Magazine*, 115, no. 839, 1973, 109f

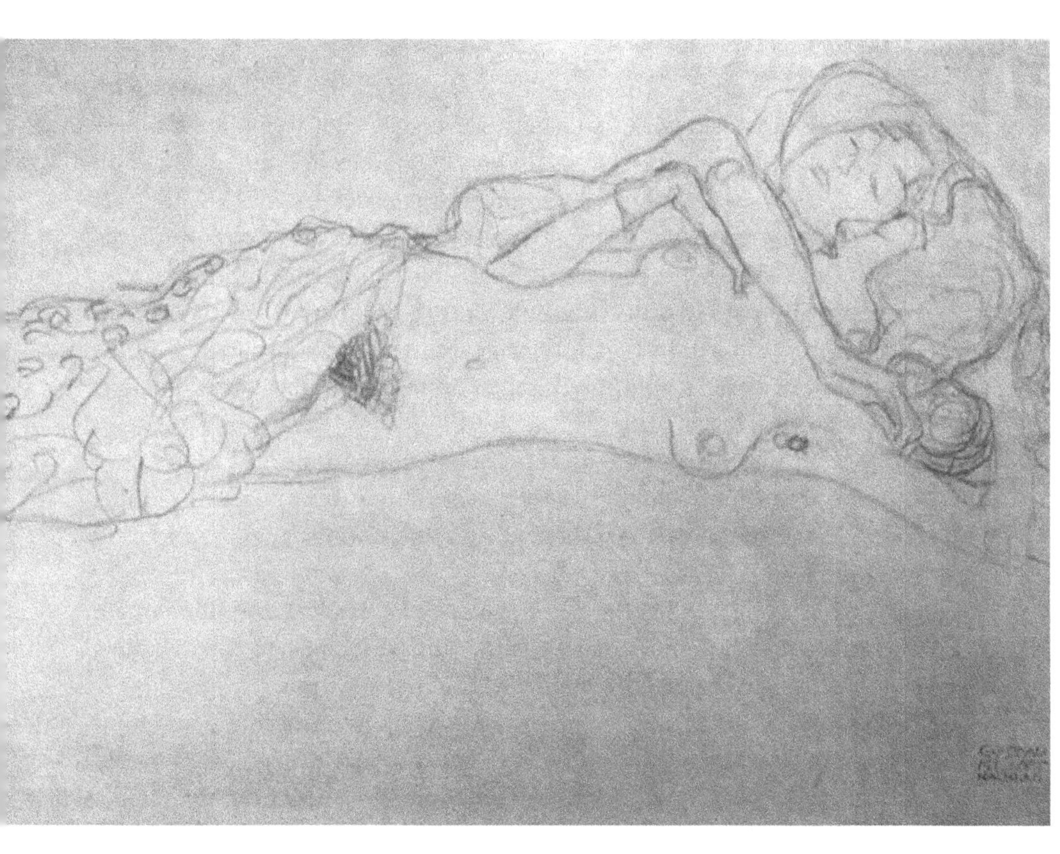

Gustav Klimt

GUSTAV KLIMT

Gustav Klimt's art is relentlessly ornamental. He dispenses with three dimensionality, and goes for an abstract flatness, as in *The Fulfilment* – which features an erotic embrace like that depicted in *The Kiss* – where the background is a mosaic of swirls.[1] Klimt's art is utterly sensual, in its intent, and the signals it gives off: the lush colours, the profuse use of gold, the swirling shapes, the intricate patterns, flowing lines and the exaltations of the human form. In portraits such as that of Adele Bloch-Bauer, Klimt's paintings are as voluptuous as paintings get, with their profusions of gold, acres of gold, walls of gold.[2]

In the drawings the eroticism is more specific: Gustav Klimt drew women reclining, legs drawn up, masturbating, their hands moving dreamily over their vulvas and clitorises as they look at the viewer. They have titles such as *Reclining Woman,* or *Seated Woman, with Open Legs.*[3] Auguste Rodin was the immediate precursor of Klimt's masturbating nudes: Klimt had seen Rodin's erotic drawings,and they inspired him.[4]

As with the images of erotica and some porn, these are anonymous women, any women, with faces but no names, no characters.[5] These are orgasmic images, celebrating female orgasm. This form of eroticism is not confined to the 'private' drawings, drawings which can be seen as a private form of pornography: Gustav Klimt's famous *Judith* stares voluptuously at the viewer with her eyes half-closed, in a orgasmic state.[6] It is a pose cultivated by Hollywood stars, the seductive, luscious look to camera.

1 G. Klimt: *The Fulfilment*, c. 1905-9, Musée des Beaux Arts, Strasbourg
2 G. Klimt: *Adele Bloch-Bauer,* 1907, Österreichische Galerie, Vienna
3 G. Klimt: *Reclining Woman*, 1912-8, pencil, 37 x 56cm, Grapische Sammlung Albertina, Vienna
4 A. Rodin: *Reclining Female Nude*, c. 1900, pencil, 12.2 x 8in, Musée Rodin, Paris
5 G. Klimt: *Seated Woman, with Open Legs*, 1916/7, pencil, 57 x 38cm; *Recumbent Semi-Nude,* 1914/5, blue crayon, 37 x 56cm, Historical Museum, Vienna
6 G. Klimt: *Judith I*, 1901, Österreichische Galerie, Vienna

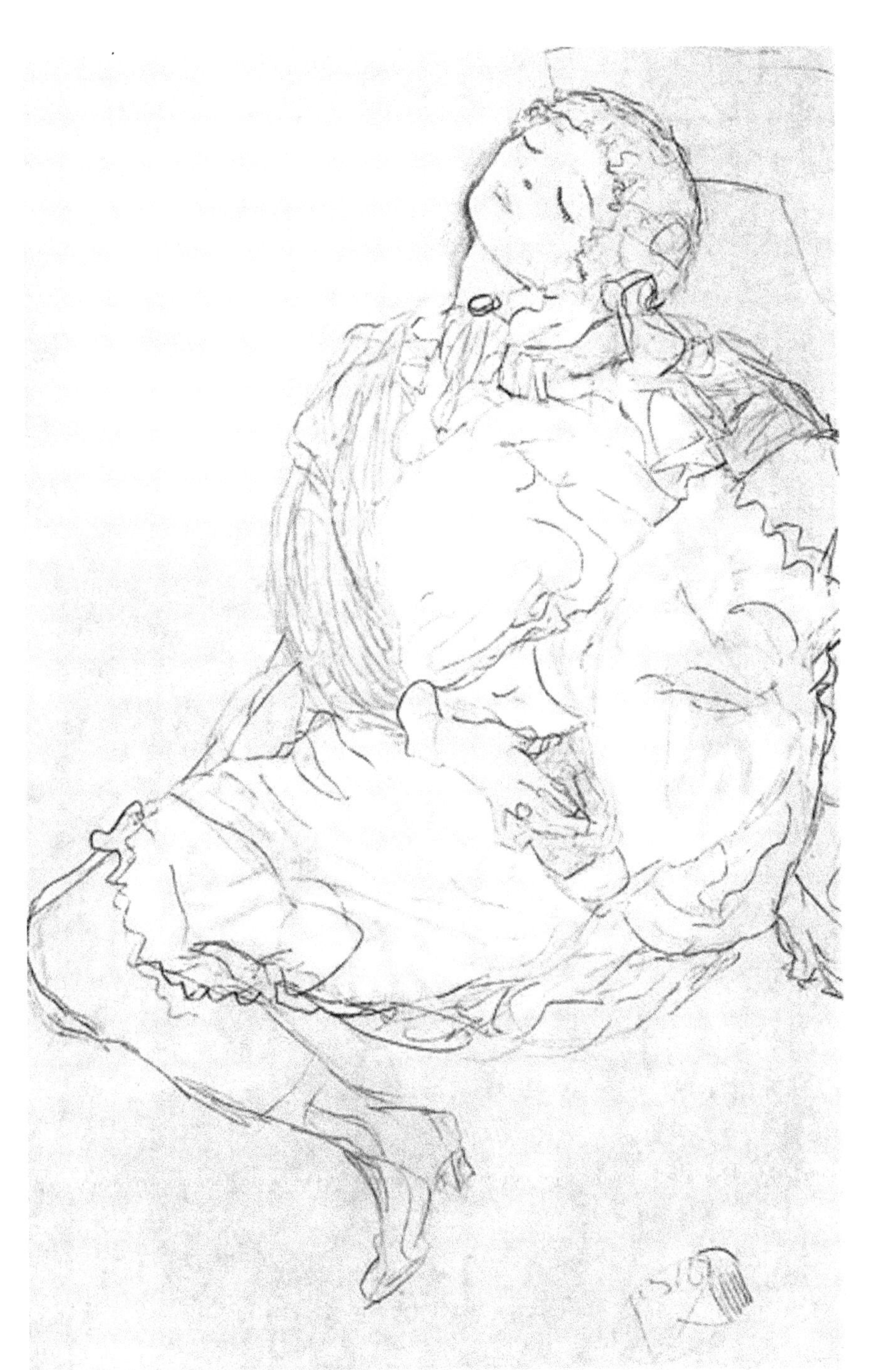

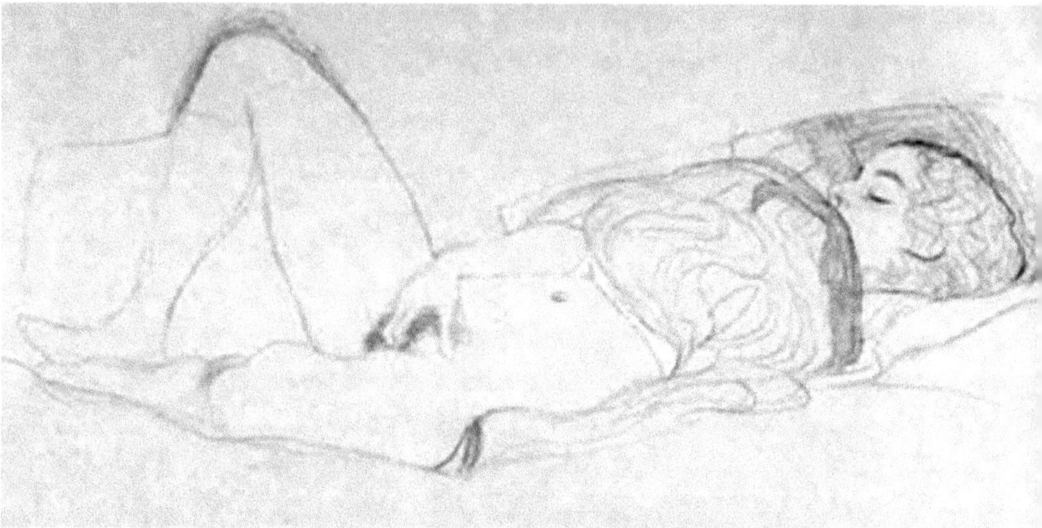

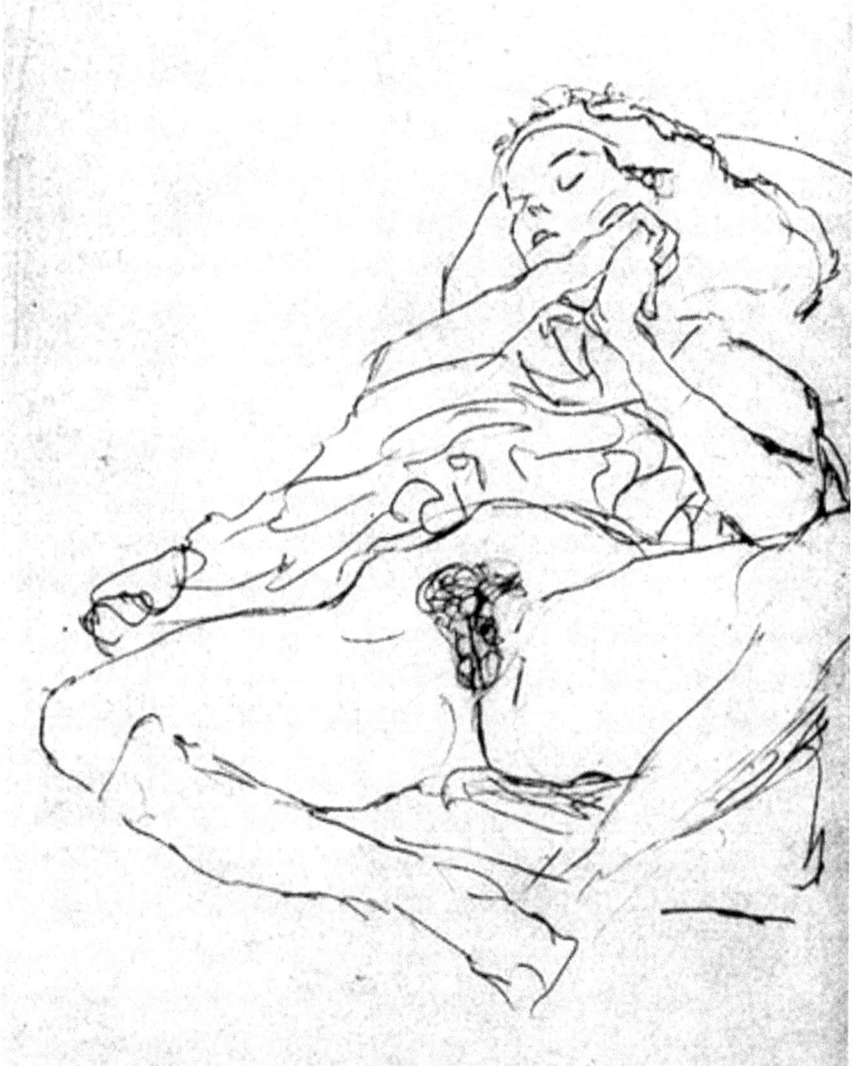

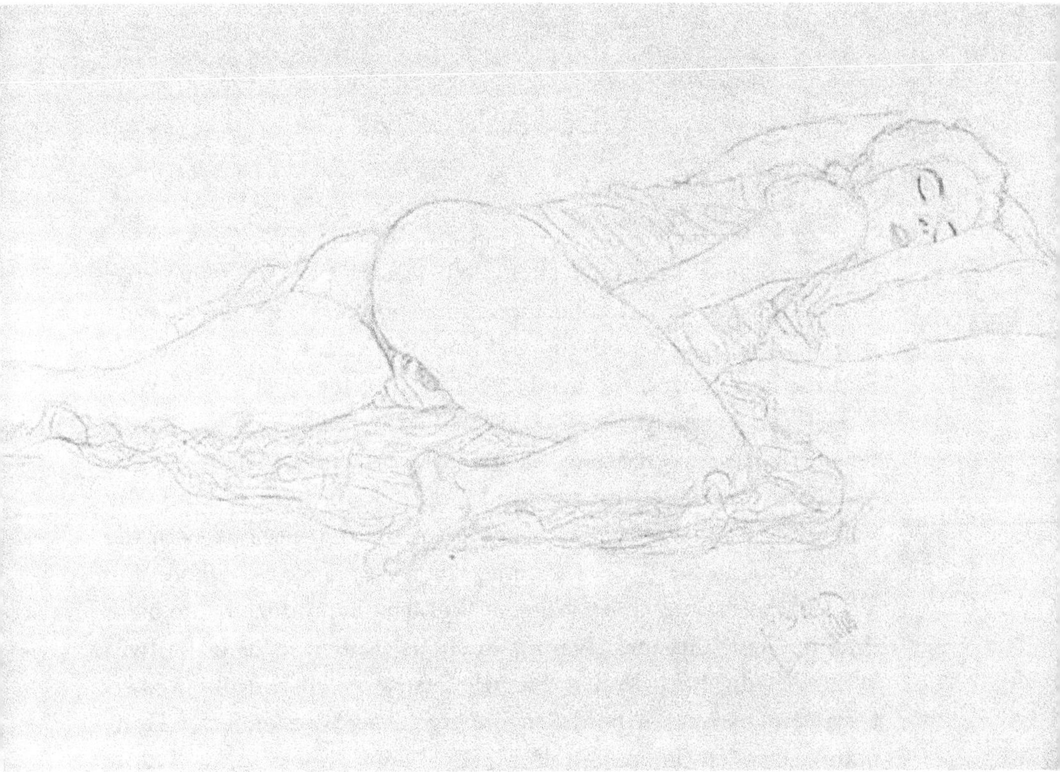

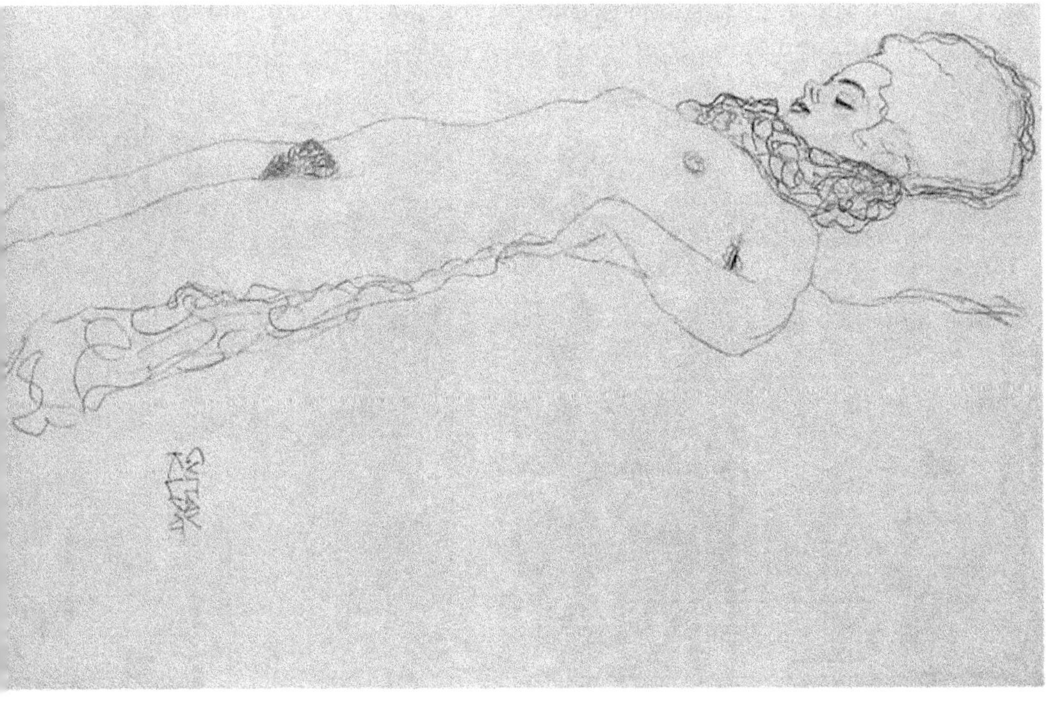

GUSTAV KLIMT

Gustav Klimt's drawings circulated as soft porn in *fin-de-siècle* Vienna among the art collectors and *cogniscenti*. The city is often marketed now as a seething cauldron of decadence and style, the End of the Empires, the heady years before the First World War, like Berlin before the Second World War, when Vienna was a fevered mass of eroticism, death, art and culture. This mythic Vienna is the over-romanticized *mittel European* city, the city where Sigmund Freud was opening up the unconscious with the publication in 1899 of *The Interpretation of Dreams*, where the Vienna Secession and Wiener Werkstäte produced amazing graphic and fine art. Names such as Robert Musil, Ludwig Wittgenstein, Karl Kraus, Freud, Gustav Mahler, Kolo Moser, Oscar Kokoschka, Arnold Schoenberg, Otto Wagner, Josef Hoffmann, JosePH Stalin, Adolf Hitler, Leon Trotsky and Arthur Schnitzler are all associated with the Vienna of the turn-of-the-century era, making it a cultural centre to rival the best. Vienna was the city of sex and death, of pornography and prostitution, as critics attest.[1]

1 See Frank Whitford: *Egon Schiele*, Thames & Hudson 1981, 92f

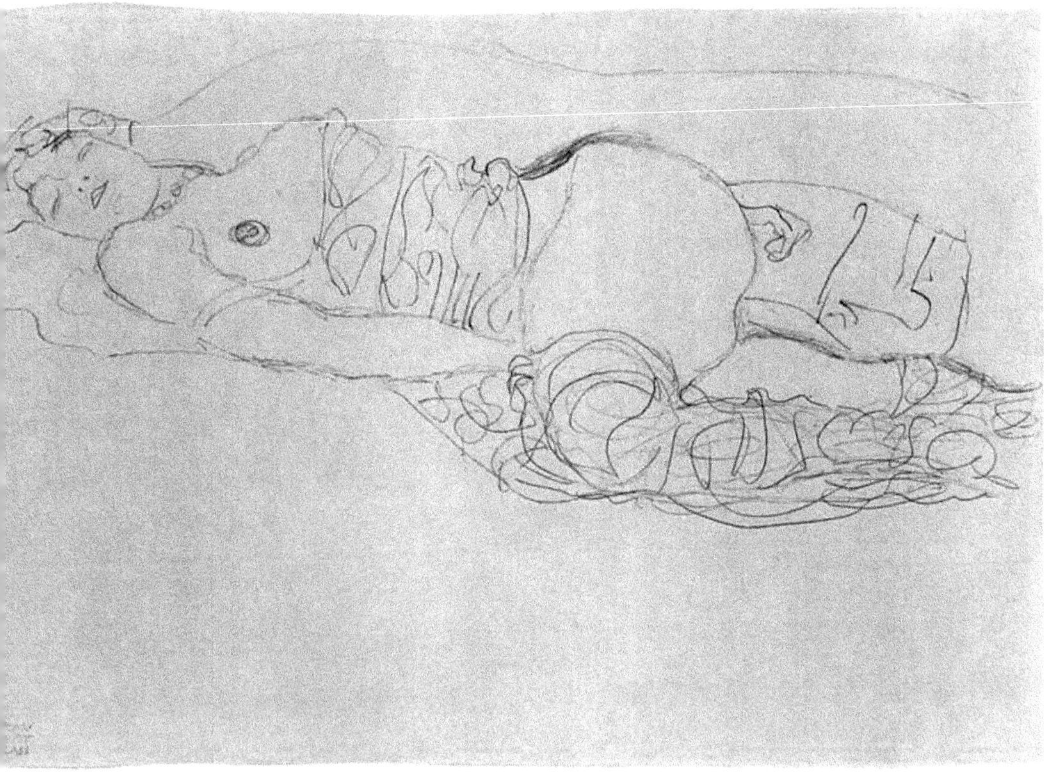

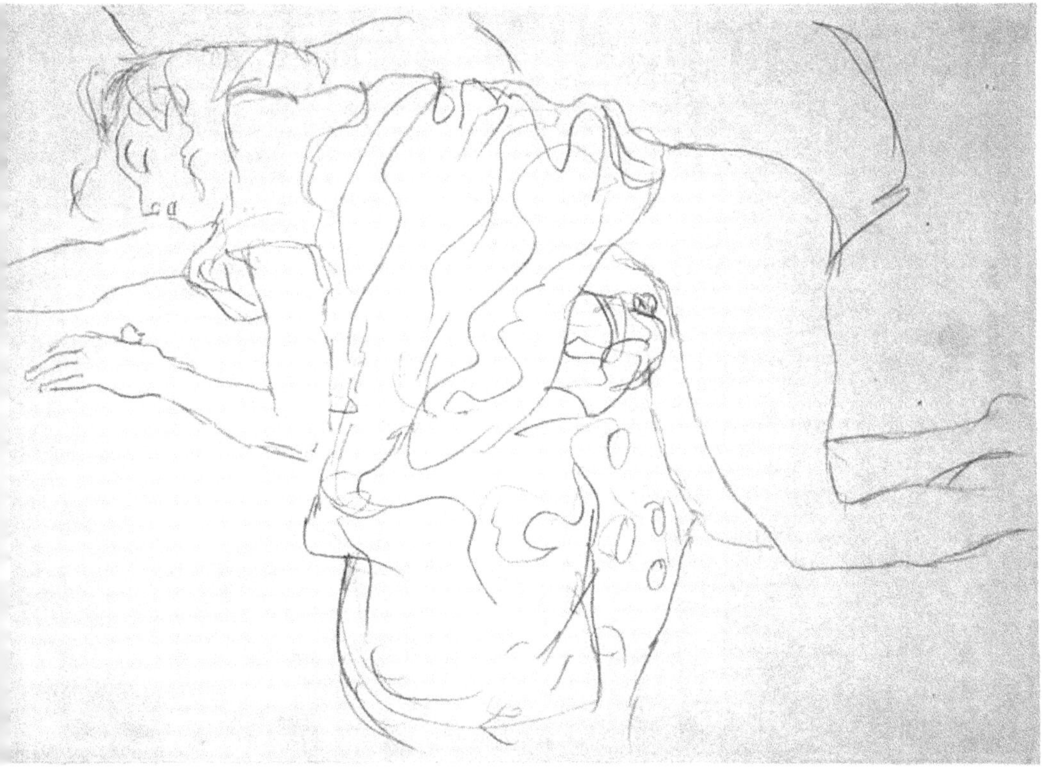

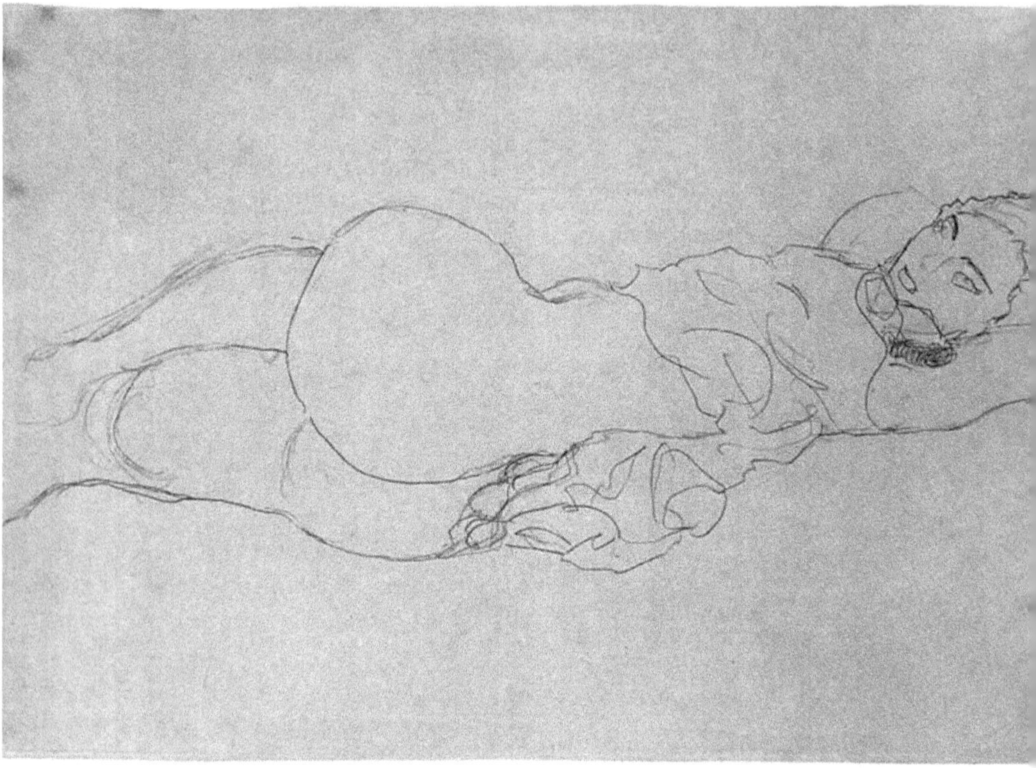

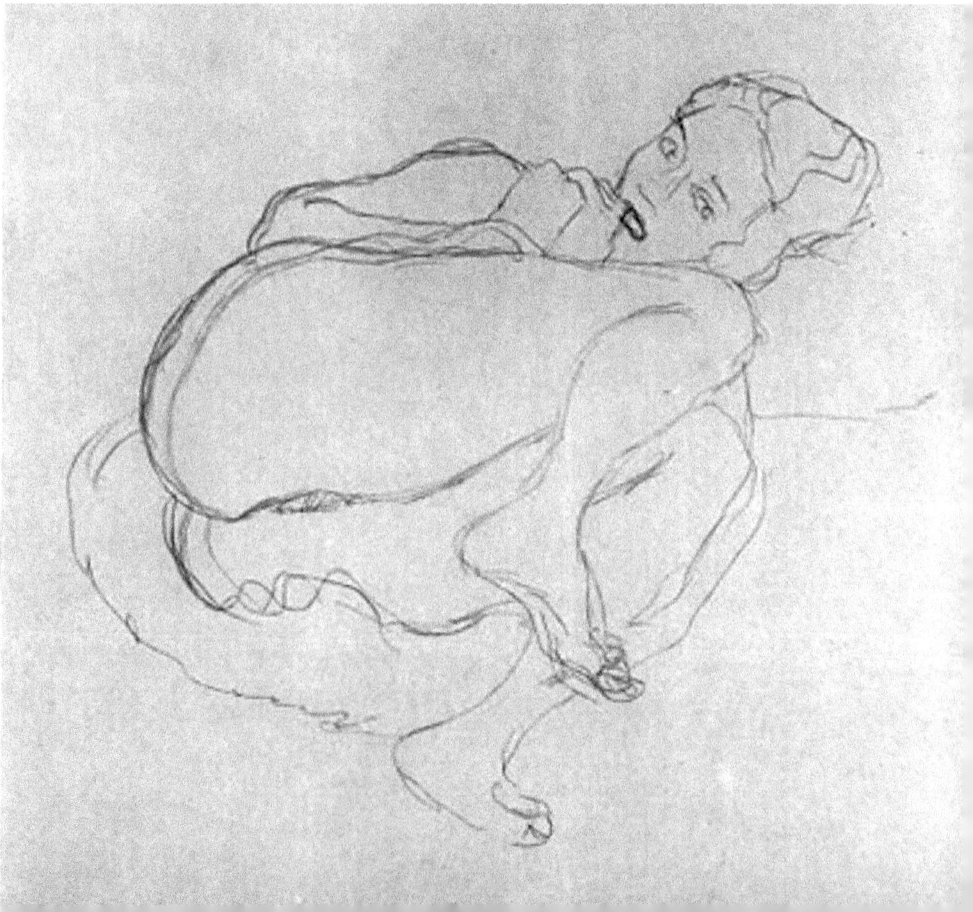

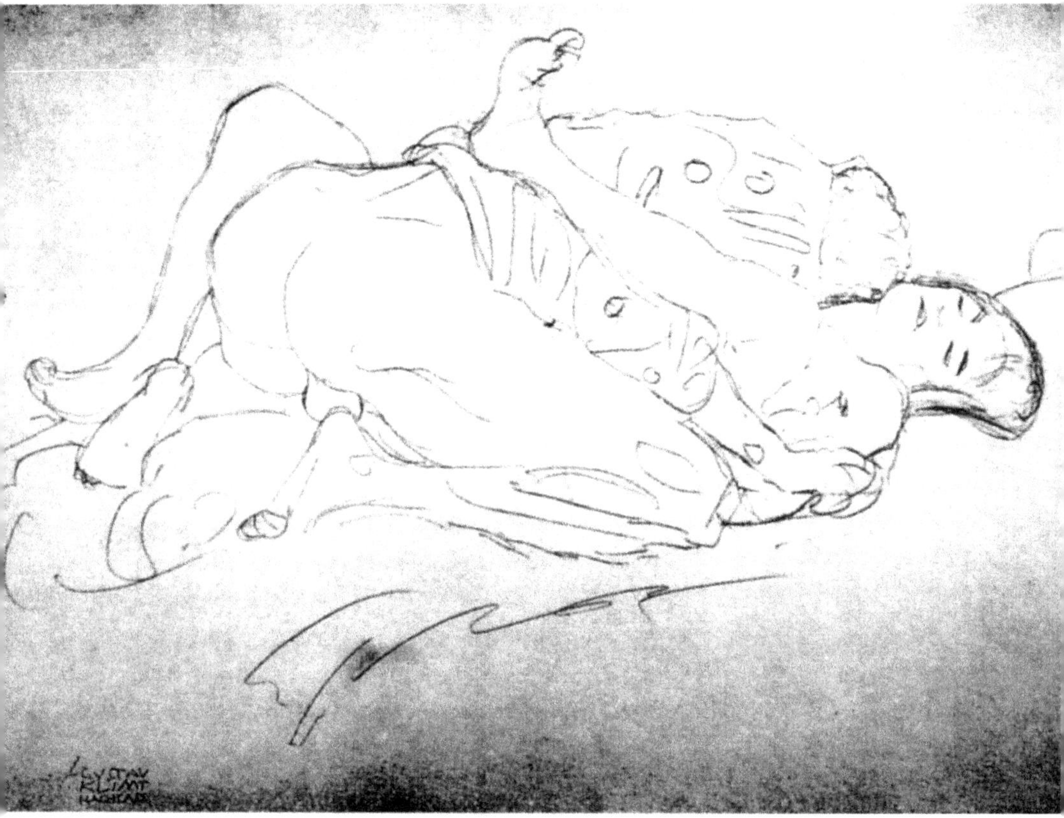

GUSTAV
KLIMT
NACHLASS

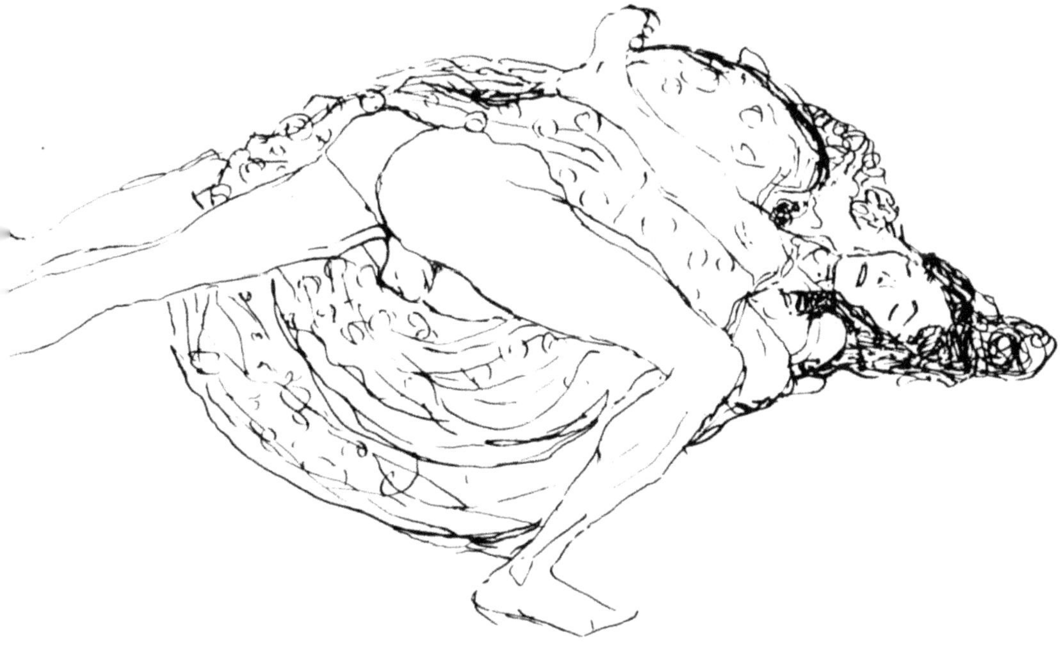

ERIC GILL

Eric Gill (1882-1940) is one of the major erotic artists of the 20th century. For him, eroticism was a vital part of life, and should be openly displayed in art. He moved from nudes to Madonnas easily and simply in his art: sex and religion were part of the same mystery for him. He built eroticism into most of his depictions of people. He continually drew attention to a figure's genitals. He was obsessed, for instance, by pubic hair. He was also fascinated by the penis, particularly his own.

Despite being open about sexuality, Eric Gill did keep some of his art secret. There are private drawings in the collections of the Victoria and Albert Museum and the British Museum in London, which depict, for instance, some seventy drawings of penises. The drawings are careful anatomical studies, complete with measurements. Some of the phallic drawings show Gill masturbating, or on a bed, or in a mirror. Sometimes the drawings of penises enter the critically acceptable arena, as in the prints entitled *The 'Most Precious Ornament'*.[1]

Eric Gill was meticulous in his recording of sexual activities. His private writings reveal a secret code for 'acts' such as anal intercourse. He also 'experimented' with dogs, incest and group sex.[2] So many male artists have drawn, painted or sculpted their penises: Jasper Johns, Egon Schiele, Pablo Picasso, Hans Bellmer, Robert Rauschenberg, Salvador Dali, and Tom of Finland. Men love their dicks. As did the ancients: from the Cerne Giant in Dorset, with its 30-foot long dick, to ithyphallic cave paintings of the palæolithic era.

1 Eric Gill: *The 'Most Precious Ornament'*, 1937, print, Victoria & Albert Museum
2 See Fiona MacCarthy: *Eric Gill*, Faber 1989

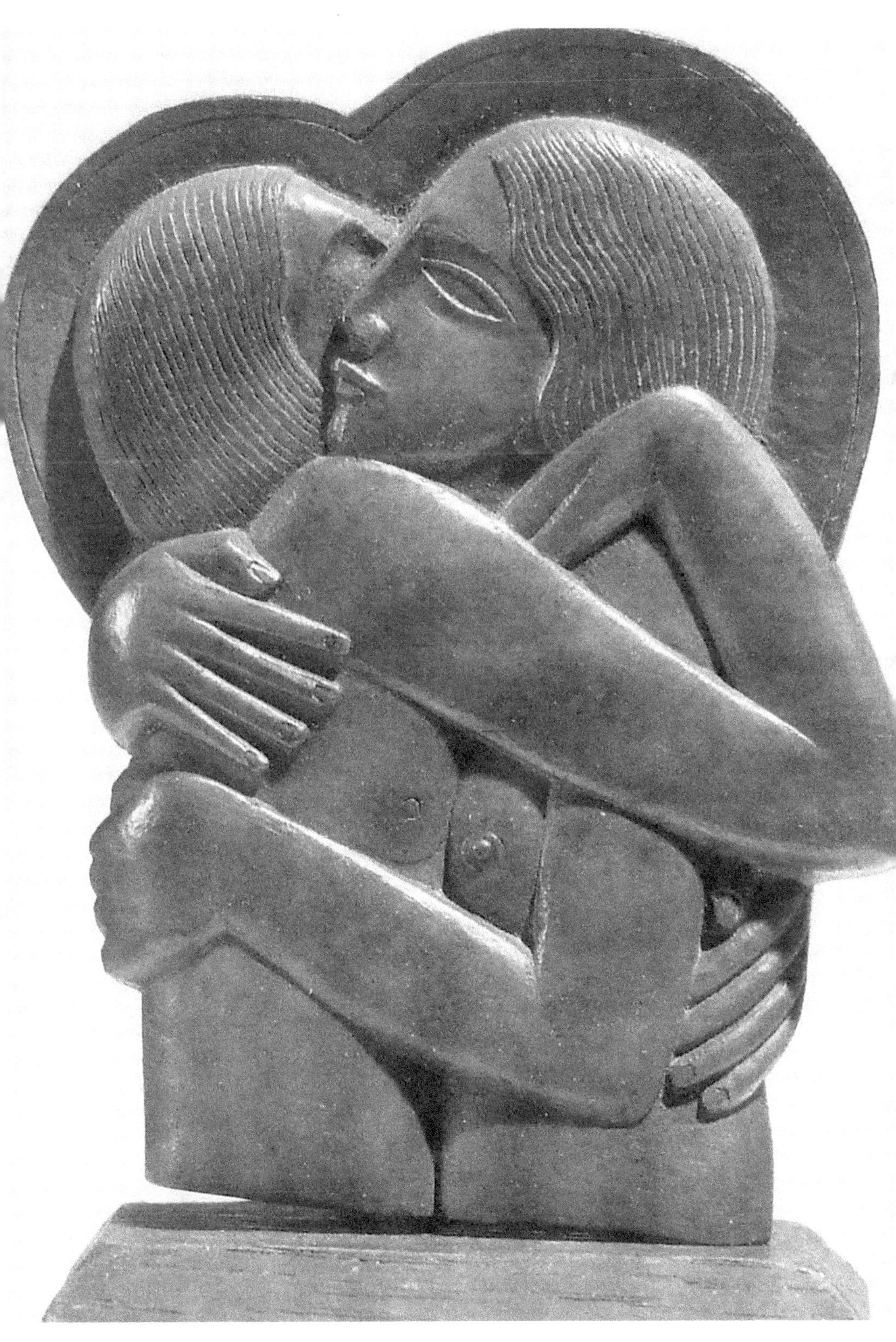

Eric Gill, Divine Lovers, 1922, Fogg Art Museum, Cambridge, MA

ERIC GILL

In Eric Gill's art one finds all the usual tensions of Western art: the relation between women and fertility, agriculture, nature and nurture; the constant eroticization of people, the reduction to sexual identities; and the idea that sex can instigate a social and spiritual renewal or revolution.

Eric Gill's sense of sexuality is distinctly heterosexual, as with other campaigners for sexual liberty, such as D.H. Lawrence. Like Lawrence, Gill exalted women and the idea of 'woman'; like Lawrence, Gill secretly admired the male form: in both Gill and Lawrence there is an emphasis on the phallus, the symbolic erect phallus, which meant religious rebirth, as Lawrence showed in *The Escaped Cock,* a novella of the 'phallic' man, the new Adam. Lawrence's testament of erotic revolution, *Lady Chatterley's Lover,* was admired by Gill, and Gill illustrated it, depicting Mellors and Connie making love, kneeling on grass.[1] (There is also a bisexuality, or multi-sexuality, in Gill's art - or in his life, rather, than in his art. And he also experimented with sex with animals).

1 Eric Gill: *Lady C,* 1931, print, 2nd state, Victoria & Albert Museum

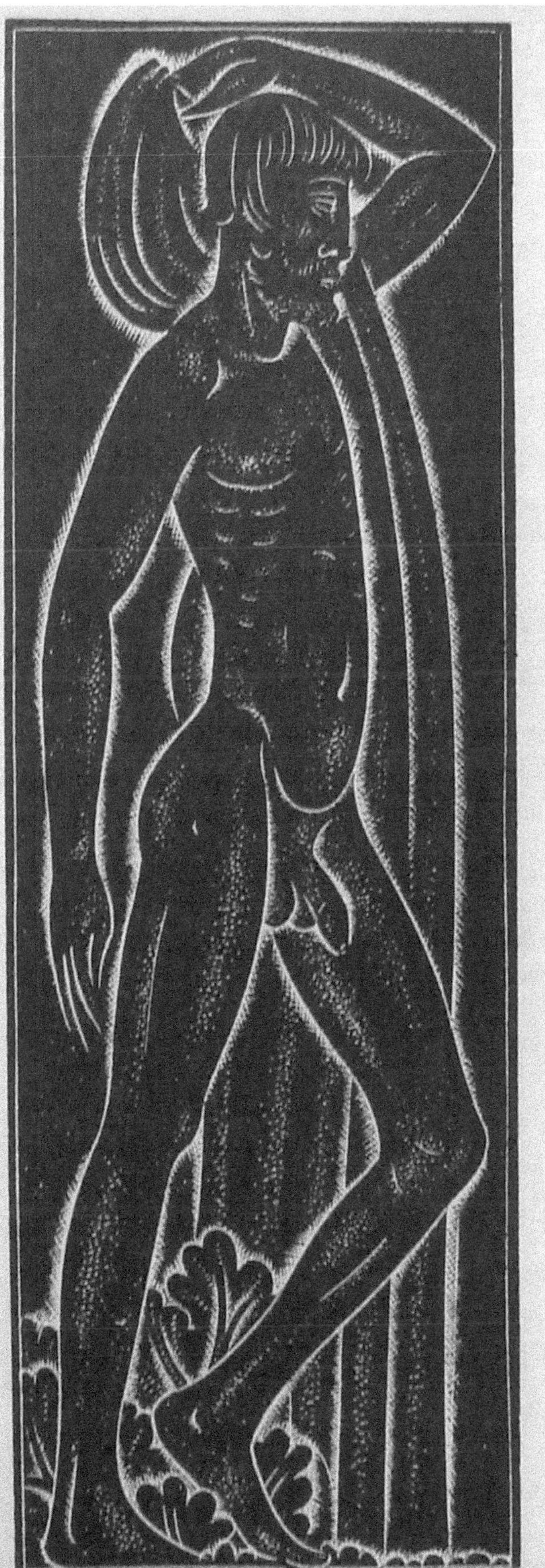

Eric Gill,
Mellors, 1930

ERIC GILL

Like D.H. Lawrence, Eric Gill believed in the holiness of sex and the holiness of art. Sex, art and religion were a continuum for Gill, as for Lawrence and others, such as Gustav Klimt, Michelangelo Buonarroti and Pablo Picasso. For Gill, as for so many artists, making art was a holy activity. Gill espoused the tenets of William Morris and the Arts and Crafts movement, maintaining that craftsmanship was sacred. 'The point is that human works should be holy, for holiness is properly their criterion', wrote Gill in a late essay. The Word of God was the first creative act, Gill said, and writers such as André Gide concur with this view. Gill wrote:

> What is a work of art? A word made flesh. That is the truth, in the clearest sense of the text. A word, that which emanates from the mind. Made flesh; a thing, a thing seen, a thing known, the immeasurable translated into terms of the measurable.[1]

In many images, Eric Gill depicted sex in sacred ways, either by giving his pictures of copulating couples a religious context – a title, perhaps, as in *Earth Wrestling*, or he puts the hand of God above the lovers, and rays of light emanate from the hand, blessing the sex act, as in *Earth Receiving*.[2] The image of the couple making love below the hand of God perfectly summarizes Gill's view of sex, of sex as a religious experience.

---

1 Eric Gill: "The Priesthood of Craftsmanship", *Blackfriars*, in Goldwater, 456-7
2 Eric Gill: *Earth Wrestling*, 1926, engraving on copper, Victoria & Albert Museum; *Earth Receiving*, 1926, engraving on copper, 12.4 x 8.8cm, University of Texas, Austin

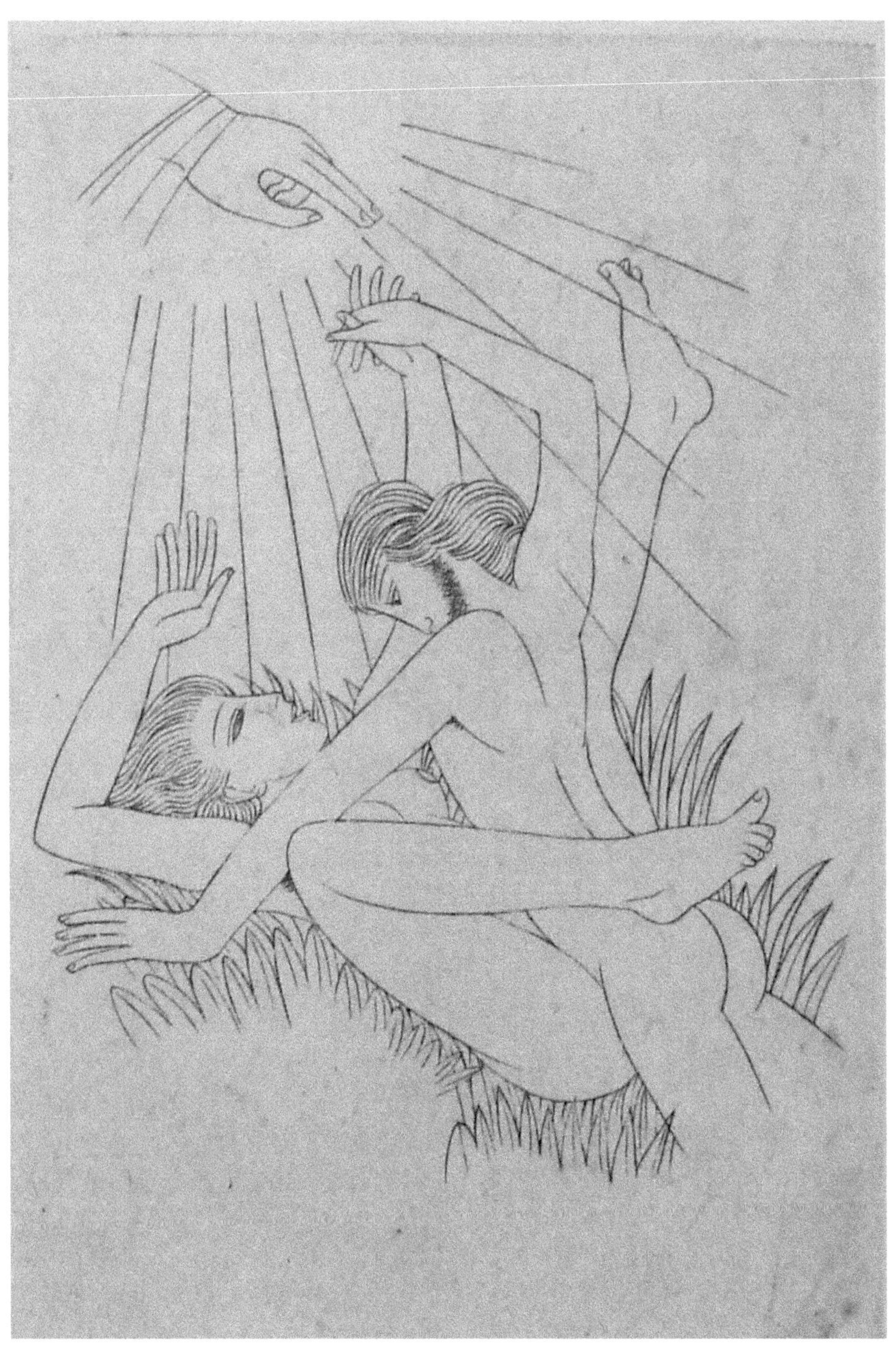

Eric Gill, Earth Receiving, 1926

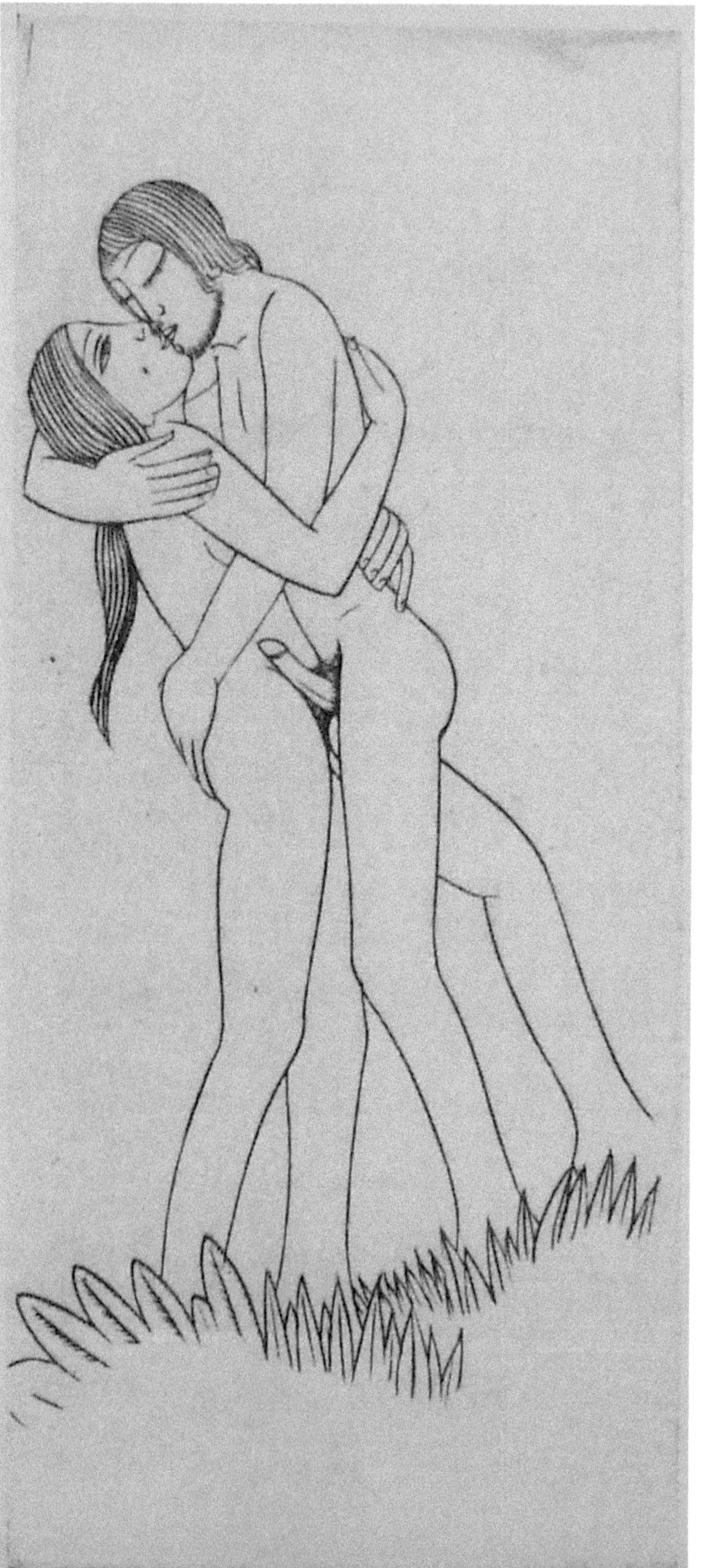

Eric Gill,
Earth Wre
1926

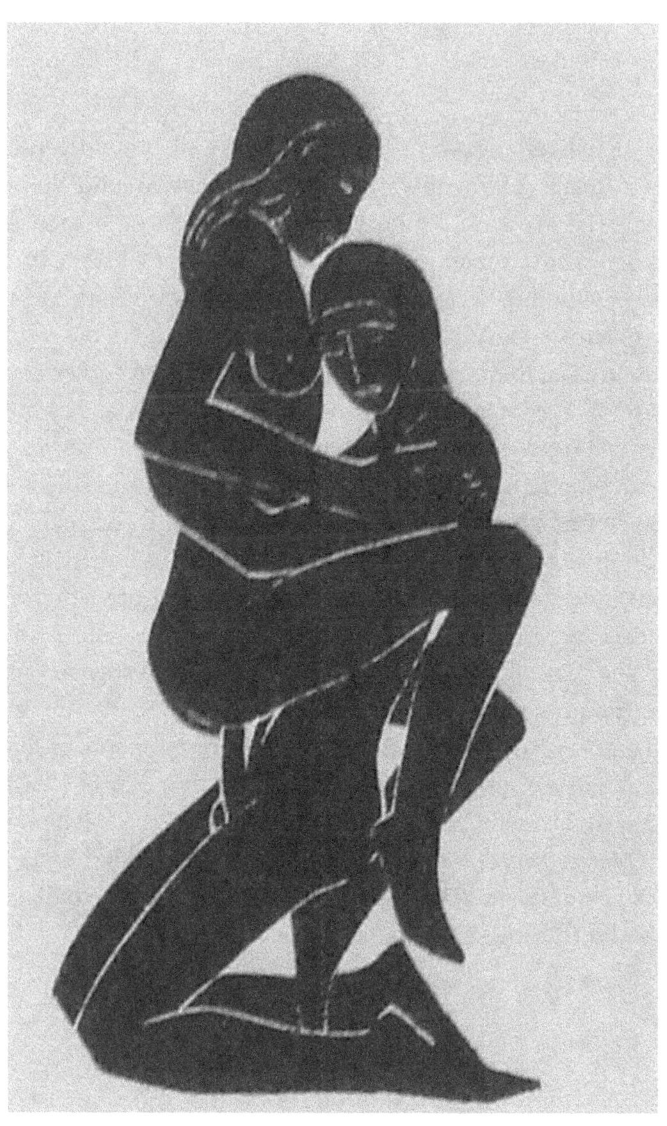

Eric Gill, Lovers, Kneeling, 1920

ERIC GILL

In most of his religious-erotic images, Eric Gill is wildly phallic and heterosexual. The woman is definitely 'passive' and the male is 'active'. The woman, as Earth, 'receives', while the man does the fucking. The woman 'gives' herself, gives of herself, in Eric Gill's art, as in his series of erotic prints illustrating the most sensual poem in the *Bible*, the *Song of Songs*, where the woman offers her breasts to the man.[1] According to Marina Warner (*Alone*, 126), the *Song of Songs* is immensely erotic: '[t]here has never been a more intense communication of the experience of desire.' The *Cantia Canticarum* allows for depictions of unbridled sensuality. The nuptial imagery allows for artists to be as sensual as they dare in a religious setting. Gill's merging of eroticism with Catholicism operates within the mystical tradition of Catholicism, as espoused by St Bernard, Jan van Ruysbroeck, St Theresa and St John of the Cross. It is a wild and ecstatic mysticism which describes religious bliss in very sensual terms.

In the art of Eric Gill, eroticism veers from moments of tender affection, as in *Approaching Dawn*, from an illustration of Geoffrey Chaucer's *Troilus and Creseyde*, to undiluted erotica, such as in *The Chinese Maidservant*, which shows a woman bending over, revealing her buttocks. The aim of such images is to sexualize the female body, to make it available to the (male) gaze.

1 Eric Gill: *Ibi Dabo Tibi*, 1925, Victoria & Albert Museum

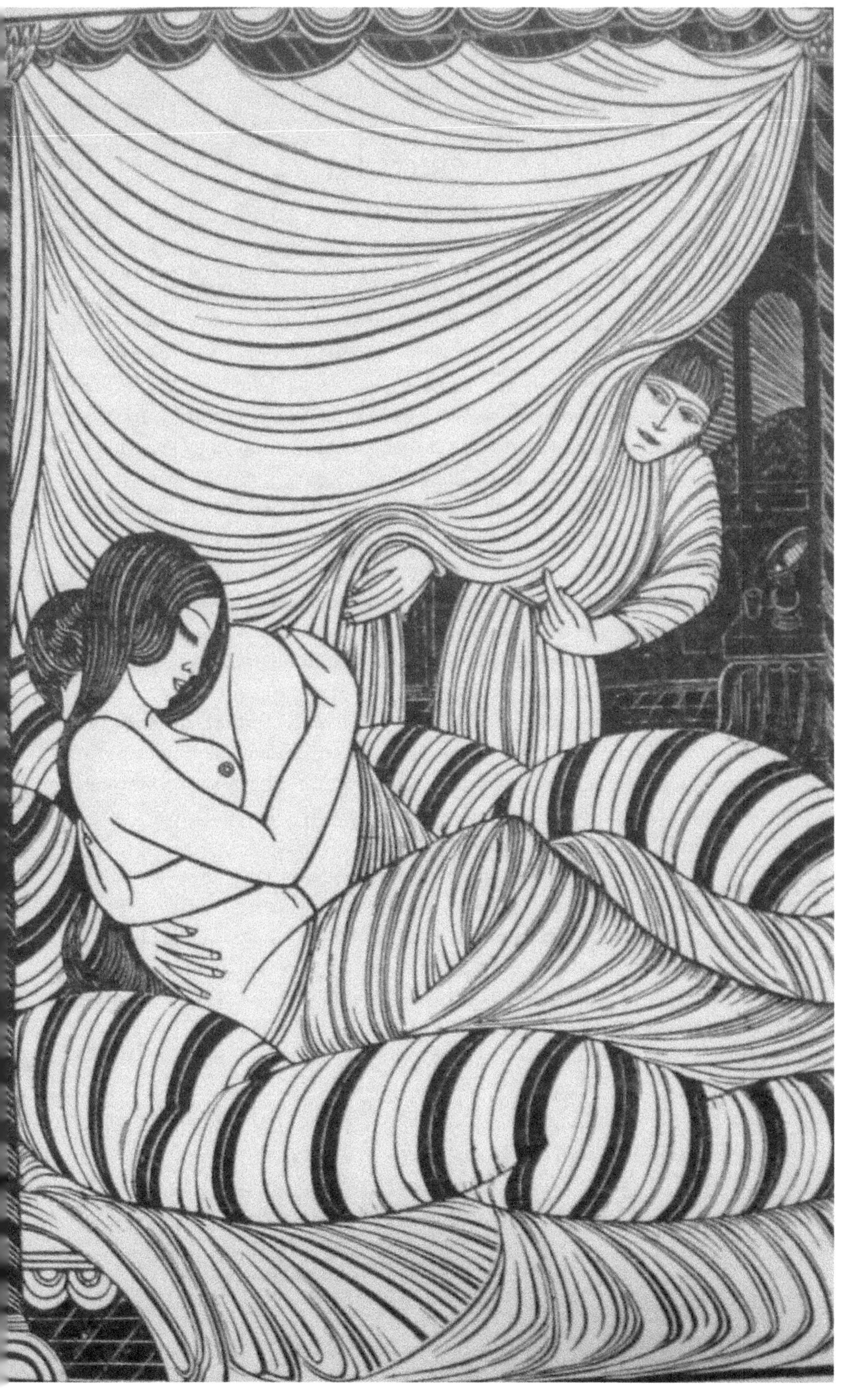

Eric Gill, Approaching Dawn, 1927

ERIC GILL

In other images, such as *Lot's Daughter*, Eric Gill depicts two people making love in a picture employing plain, unadorned marks,[1] as found in Taoist sex manuals,[2] or in the 'acrobatic' fucking of *Lovers in Tent* or *Lovers, the Raised Bottom*, which depicts two people making love,[3] and, as so often in pornography, focuses on the penis and vagina, as if that was all there was to sex. This is clearly the case in Eric Gill's works, where the phallus is at the centre of pleasure and power. Sex in his works means penile thrusting. The man is on top, the woman is underneath, accepting everything. Gill's art reveals the same power relations as depicted in high art, low art, pornography, advertizing, TV and the media: male power is dominant, and sex revolves around the phallus.

There is no clitoris in Eric Gill's art. Similarly, D.H. Lawrence condemned those 'cocksure' women who took control and employed 'clitoral sex', as in his *The Plumed Serpent*. It's only the vulva. For Gill, the phallus is the 'transcendent signifier', as in the print *Eve* which shows a female nude with a snake between her legs, curling towards her groin, clearly the snake here is the penis, as so often in patriarchal art.[4]

Often, Eric Gill's ithyphallic imagery is laughable, as in his *God Sending*, which shows Jesus flying towards the Earth with an erection, his head beaming with light, God's hand behind him, in Heaven, sending Christ on his way.[5] Here is that most blasphemous of images: not only an erotic Christ, but Christ with an erection!

1 Eric Gill: *Lot's Daughter*, 1926, pencil and watercolour, 13.5 x 1.6cm, University of Texas, Austin
2 *The Leaping White Tiger*, album leaf in ink and colours on silk, Chinese K'ang-hsi period 91622-1722), C. T. Loa collection, Texas
3 Eric Gill: *Approaching Dawn*, 1927, in *Troilus and Cresseyde*, Golden Cockerel Press; *Lovers, the Raised Bottom*, 1934, Victoria & Albert Museum
4 Eric Gill: *Eve*, 1926, print, Victoria & Albert Museum
5 Eric Gill: *God Sending*, 1926, engraving on copper, Victoria & Albert Museum

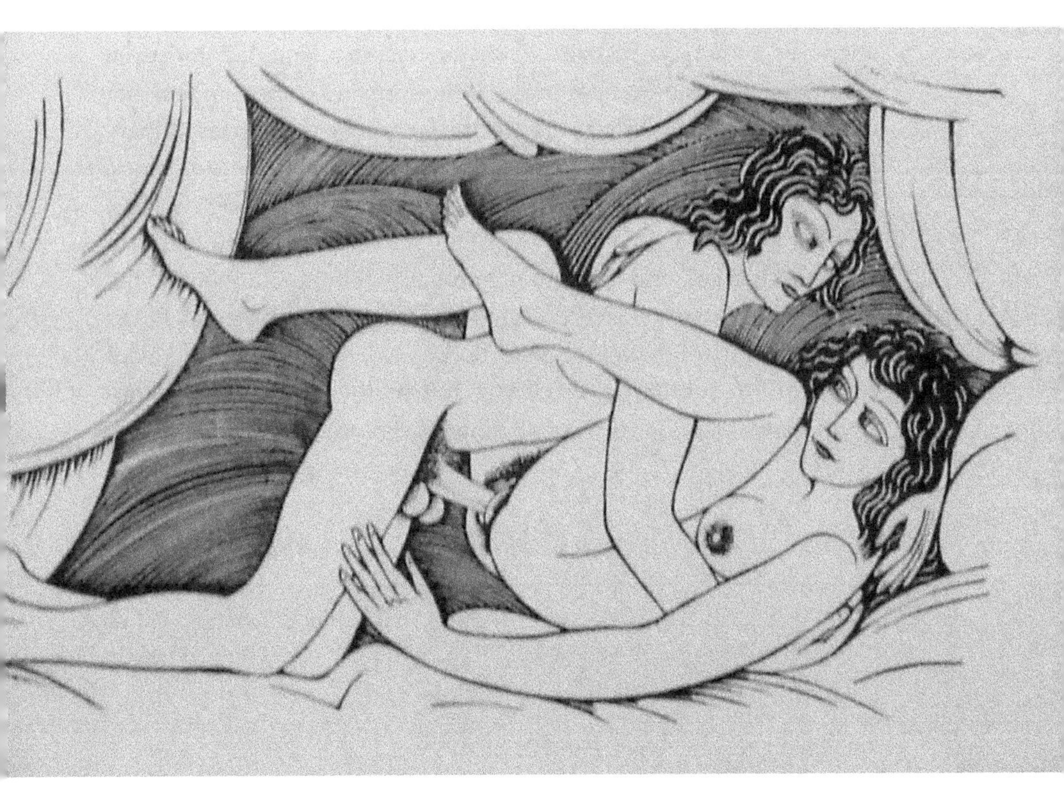

Eric Gill, Lovers (The Raised Bottom), 1934

ARISTIDE MAILLOL

Love infuses every gesture Aristide Maillol makes. There are no blemishes, no irregularities, no awkward poses in Maillol's city of women. Each figure is softly rounded, softly drawn or sculpted. It seems as if make artists have loved creating rounded forms in women since time immemorial - large-hipped women appear not only throughout Western art (in the art of Peter Rubens, Titian, Rembrandt van Rijn, and Henri Matisse), but also in prehistoric imagery, in those faceless, stone "Venuses". These 'large' women are less like potential lovers than mothers. They seem to conform to the Freudian and Lacanian emphasis on the mother as the male's first lover. The 'large' women in the works of Pablo Picasso, Henri Matisse, Auguste Rodin, Aristide Maillol and Paul Gauguin are motherly, so clearly the mother figure of psycho-analysis, and the Goddess of ancient mythology.

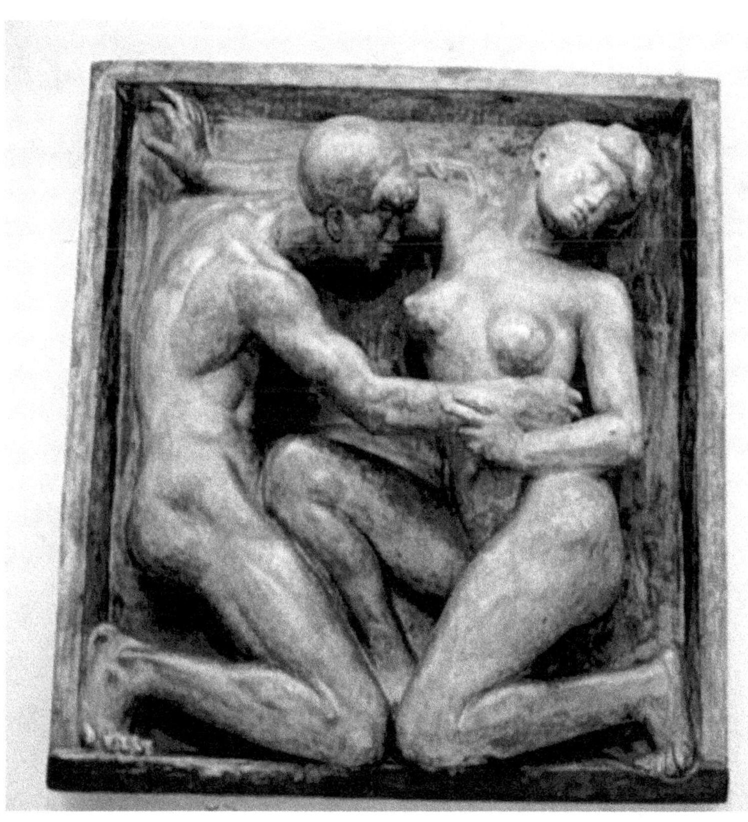

Aristide Maillol, Desire, 1908

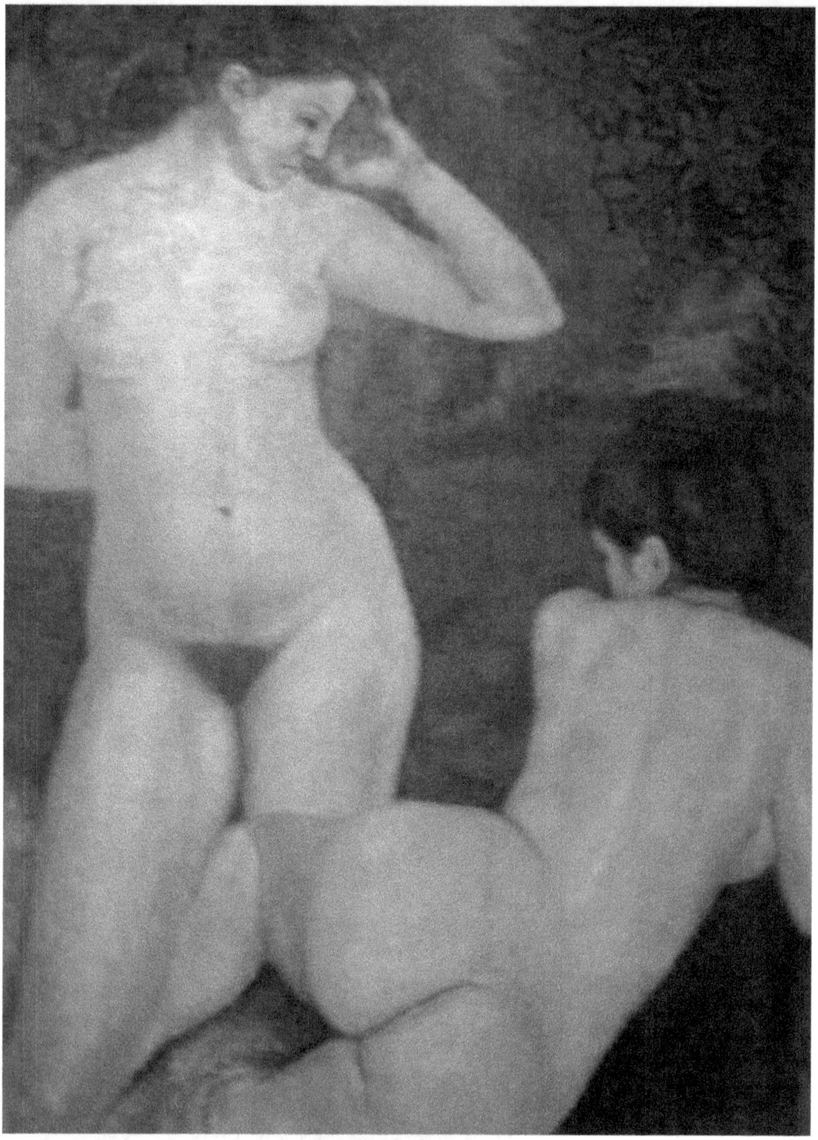

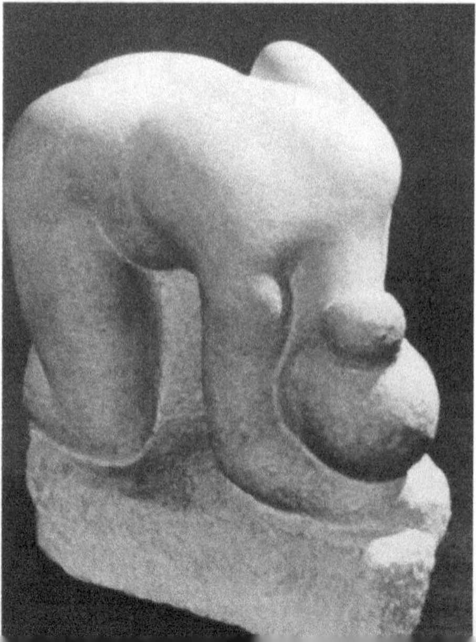

Aristide Maillol, Nudes (above).
Kneeling Bather (left).

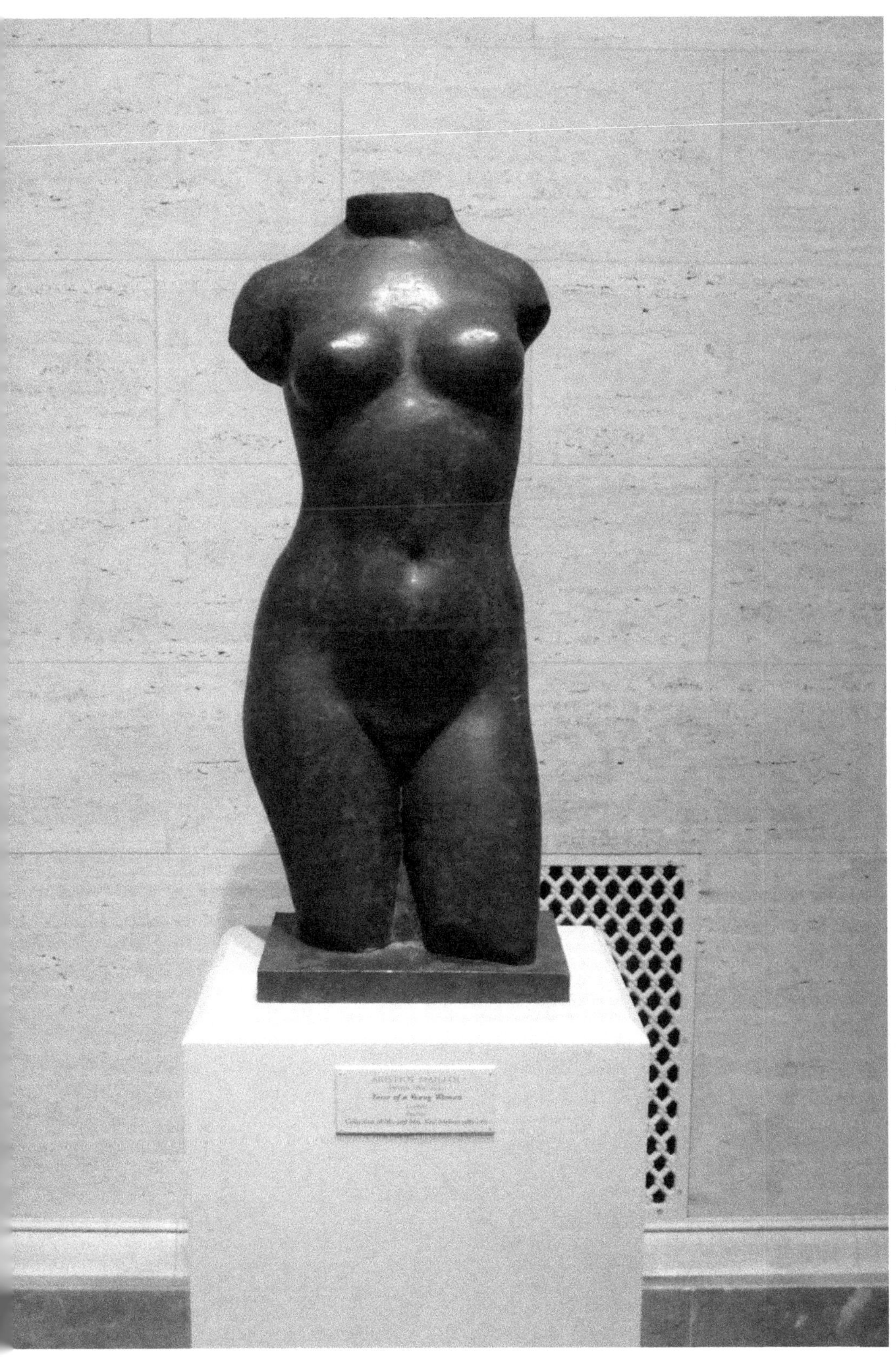

Aristide Maillol, Torse of a Young Woman, 1930, Washington

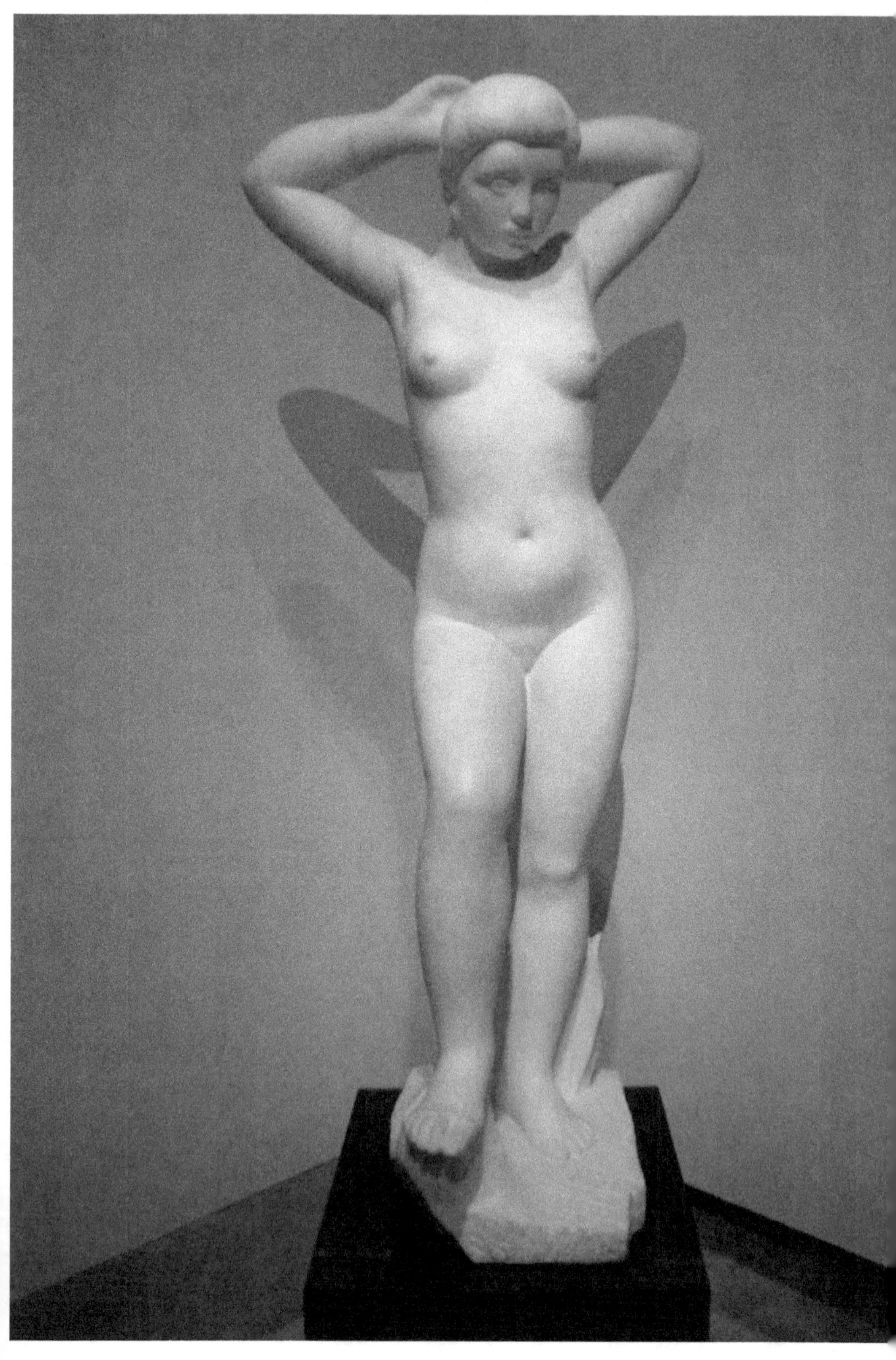

Aristide Maillol, Los Angeles

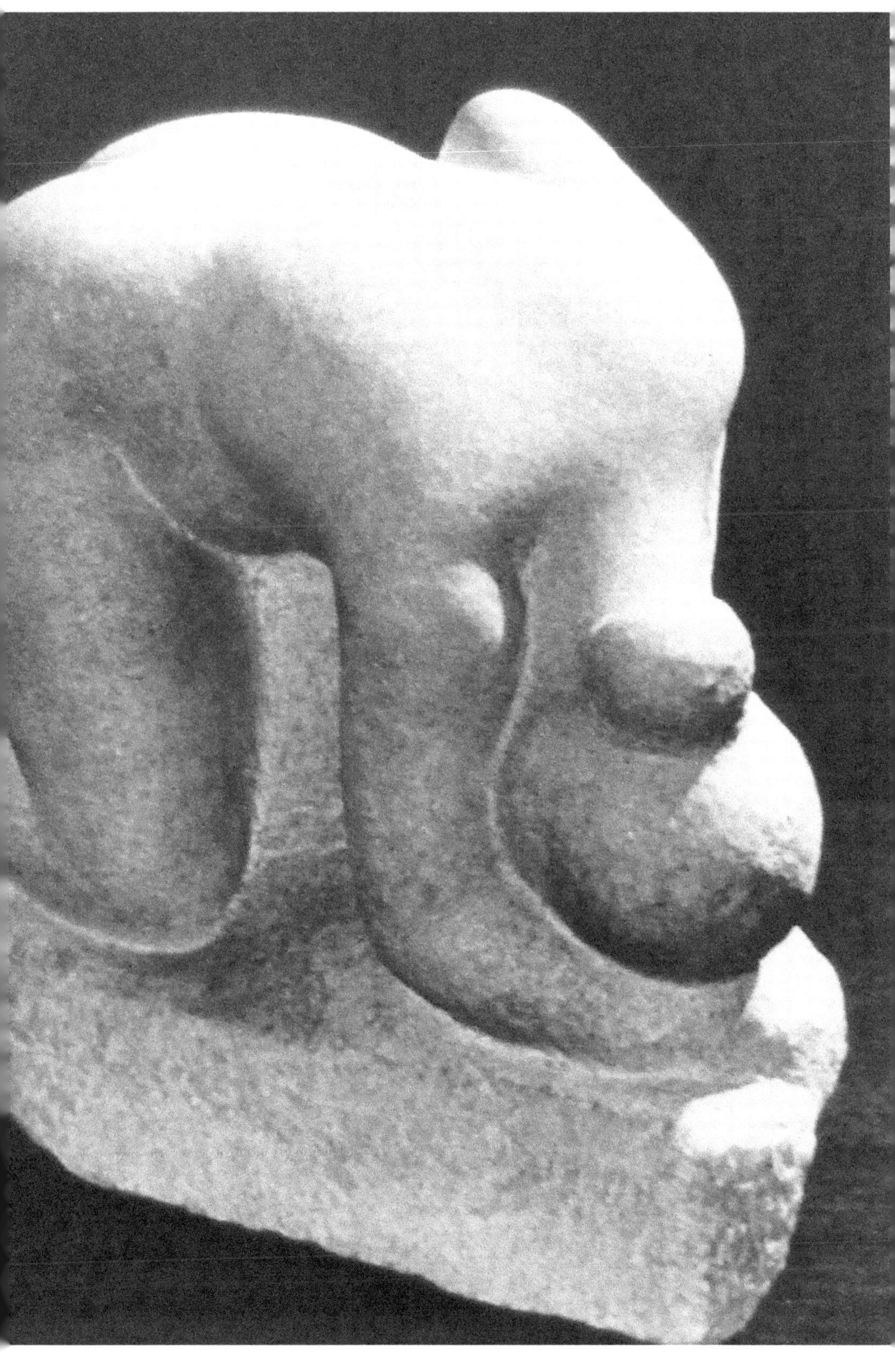

Aristide Maillol, Kneeling Bather, 1910-30.

CONSTANTIN BRANCUSI

Constantin Brancusi (1876-1957) is the key sculptor of the modern period – not Auguste Rodin, Henry Moore, Pablo Picasso, Barbara Hepworth, Naum Gabo, Marcel Duchamp, Alberto Giacometti, Jean Arp or other candidates. Brancusi's art endures: it doesn't look dated at all, it can easily hold its own when set beside contemporary sculpture, it looks as if it were created yesterday. And it's very much apart from academy sculpture, or the 19th century sculpture that preceded it.

Constantin Brancusi's most obviously erotic sculpture was one of his early pieces, which turned up in several forms: *The Kiss* (for example, 1907-08, stone, Museum of Art, Craiova, Romania and *The Kiss II*, *c.* 1908, private collection). Unlike Auguste Rodin's *tour-de-force* depiction of erotic passion, *The Kiss* (1886, Musée Rodin, Paris), Brancusi's *The Kiss* is a 'primitive', non-naturalistic square block of stone, very far indeed from the sculpture of Michelangelo Buonarroti, Gianlorenzo Bernini or Monsieur Rodin. For Brancusi *The Kiss* was his 'road to Damascus', a key work.

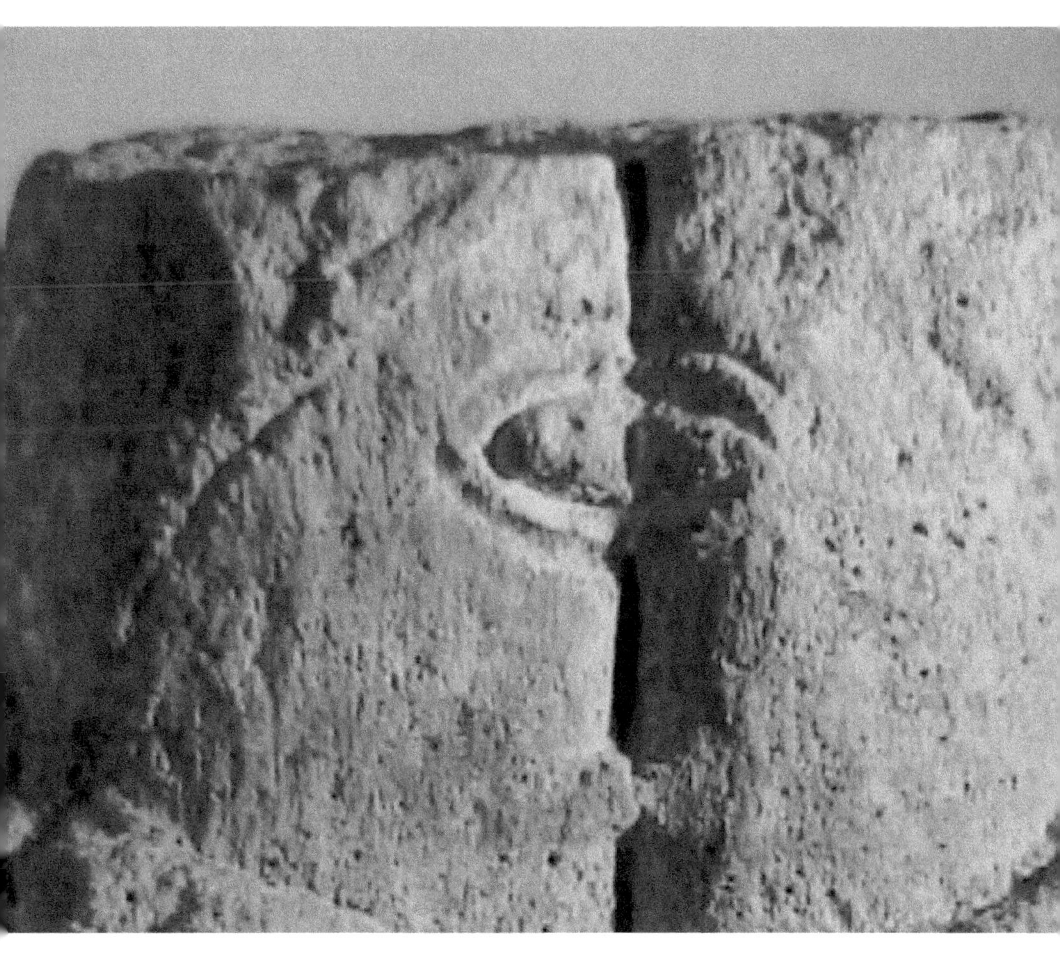

Constantin Brancusi, The Kiss 2, 1908, private collection

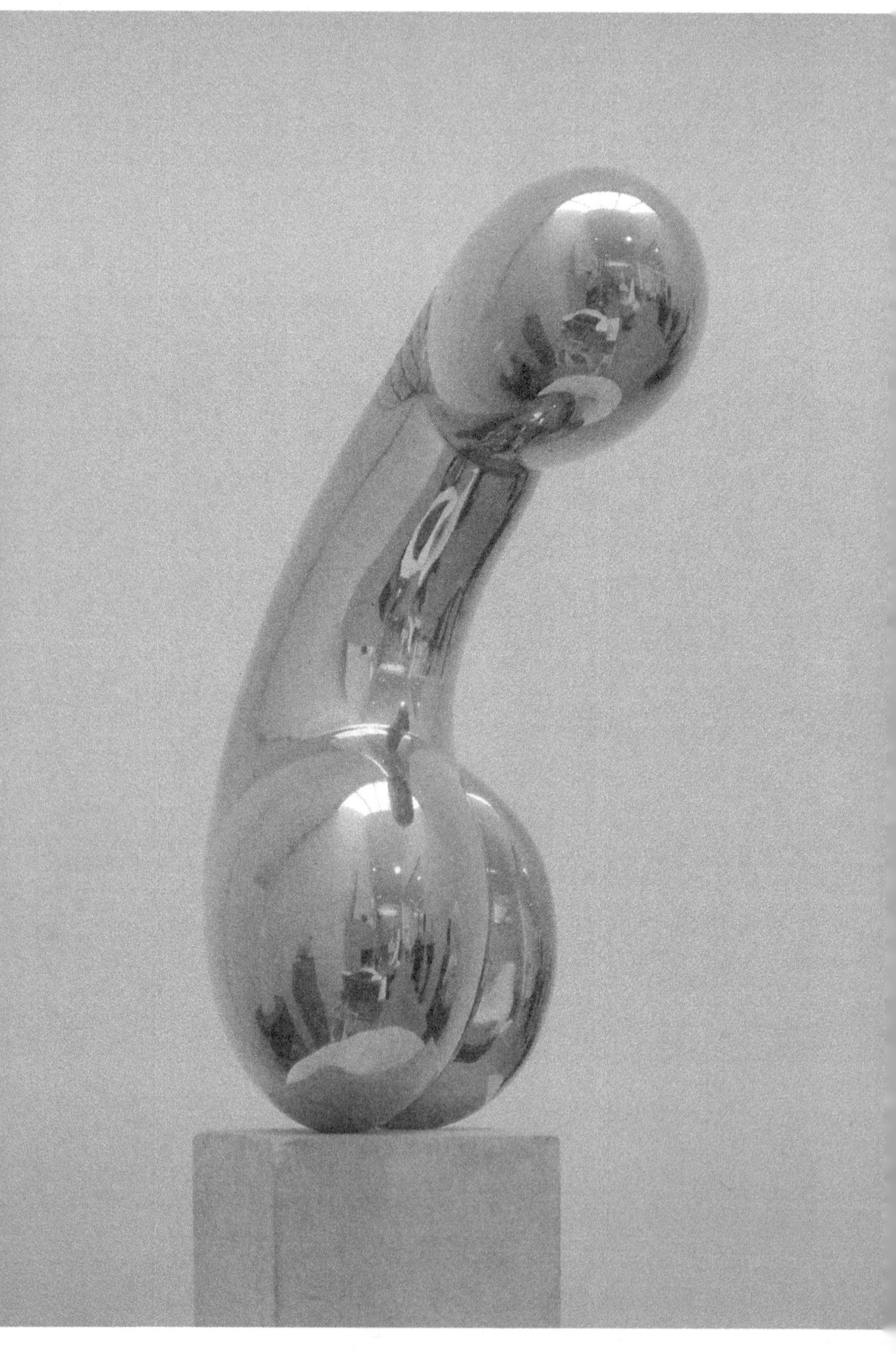

Constantin Brancusi in the Pompidou Centre (this page and over).

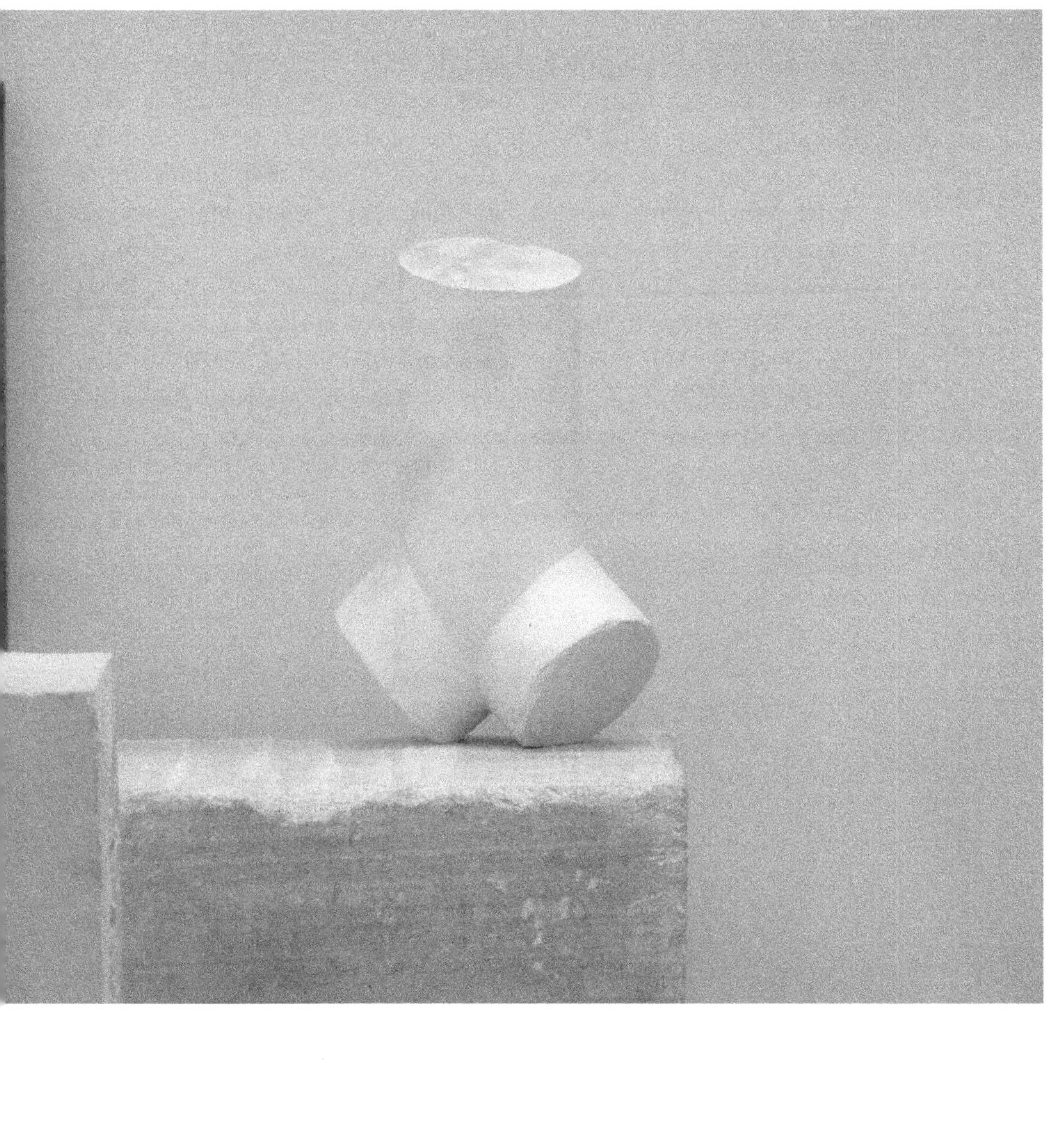

AMEDEO MODIGLIANI

Amedeo Modigliani's nudes seem to be the archetypical 'modern master' nudes, with their sleek bodies at once 'pure', like Classical sculpture or the colder-than-cold lines of J.A.D. Ingres, yet also quite definitely sensual-sexual. Modigliani's nudes are – apart from being women (of course) – 'available', passive, relaxing back for the viewer's enjoyment, just like women in pornography.[1] Their eyes are closed, their arms are open, they show their bodies to the viewer, not always sad, but often smiling mysteriously. The *connection* between viewer and subject in the art of Modigliani, as in the art of Picasso, Matisse, Bonnard, Degas, Schiele, Klimt, Titian, Ingres, Boucher, and other 'high art' painters, is erotic.

1 Amedeo Modigliani: *Recumbent Nude*, 1917-8, private collection; *Seated Nude*, c. 1917, Courtauld Institute of Art, London

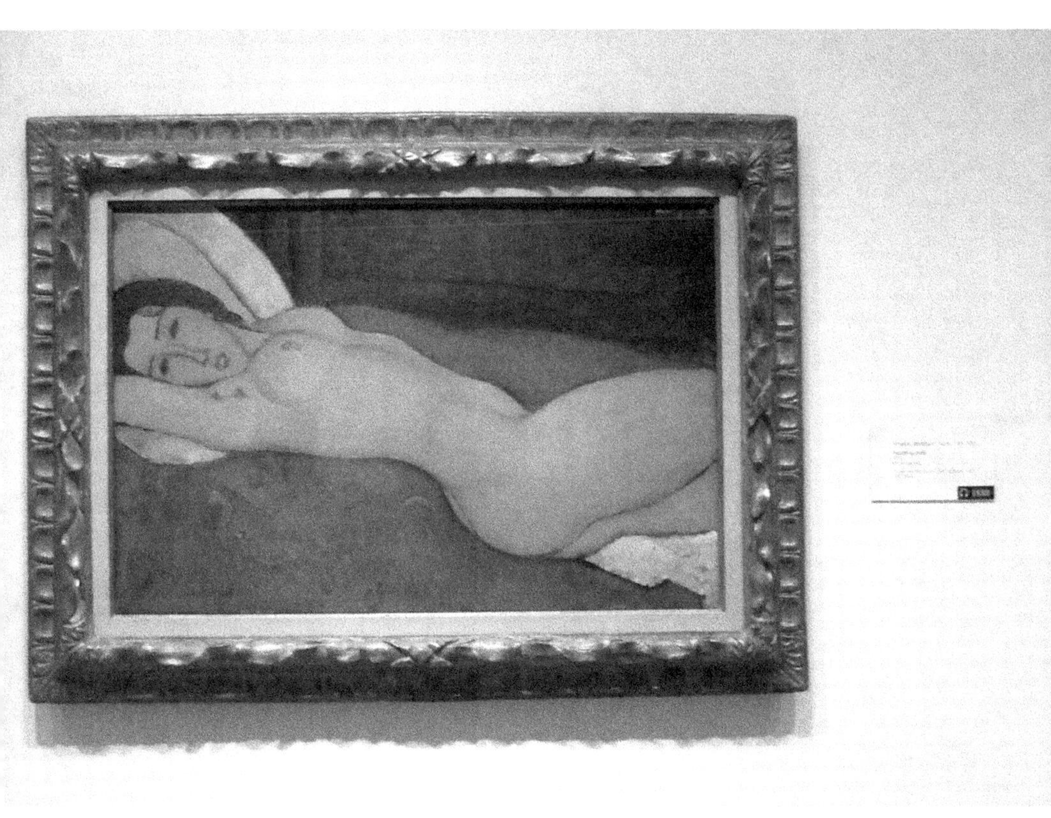

Amedeo Modigliani in New York's Metropolitan Museum of Art

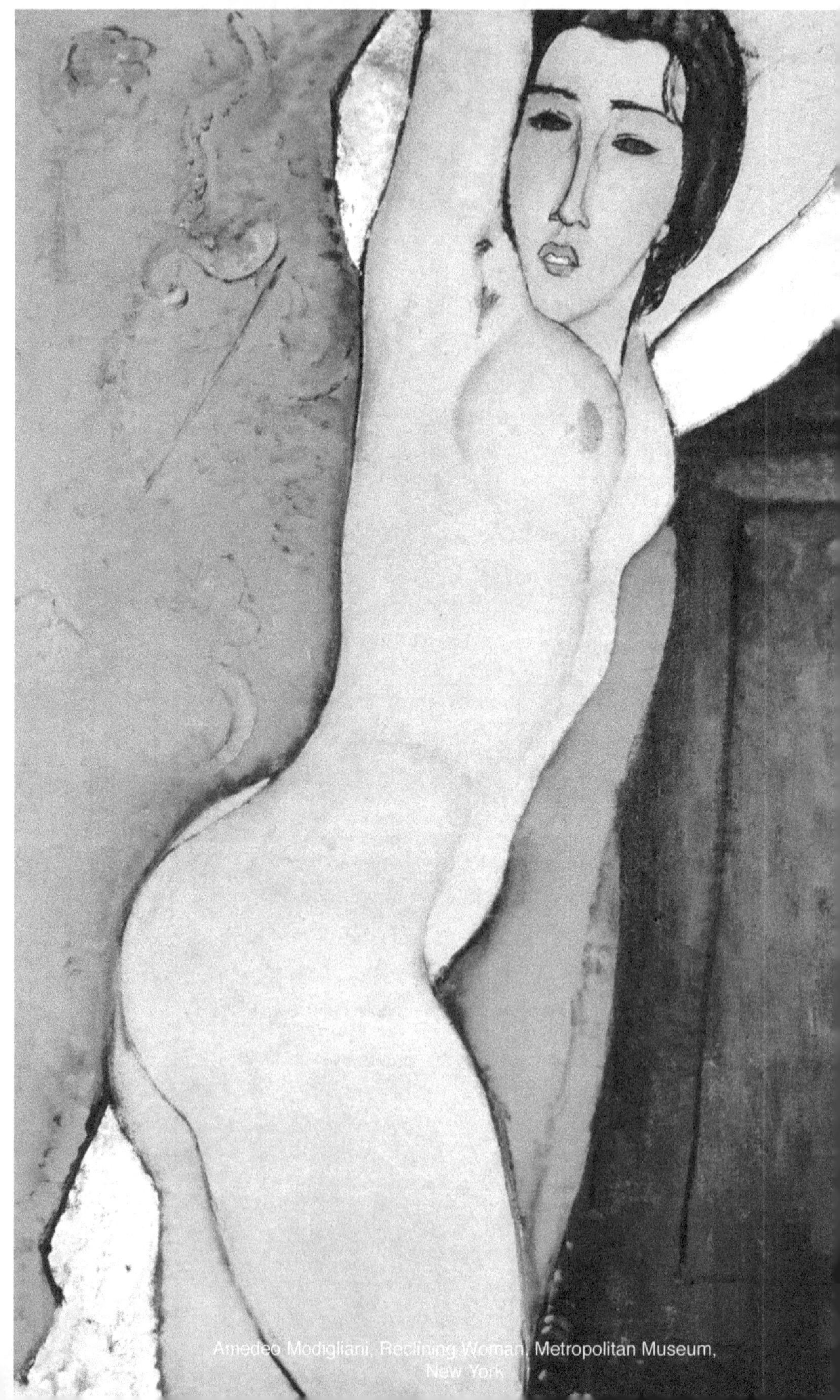

Amedeo Modigliani, Reclining Woman, Metropolitan Museum, New York

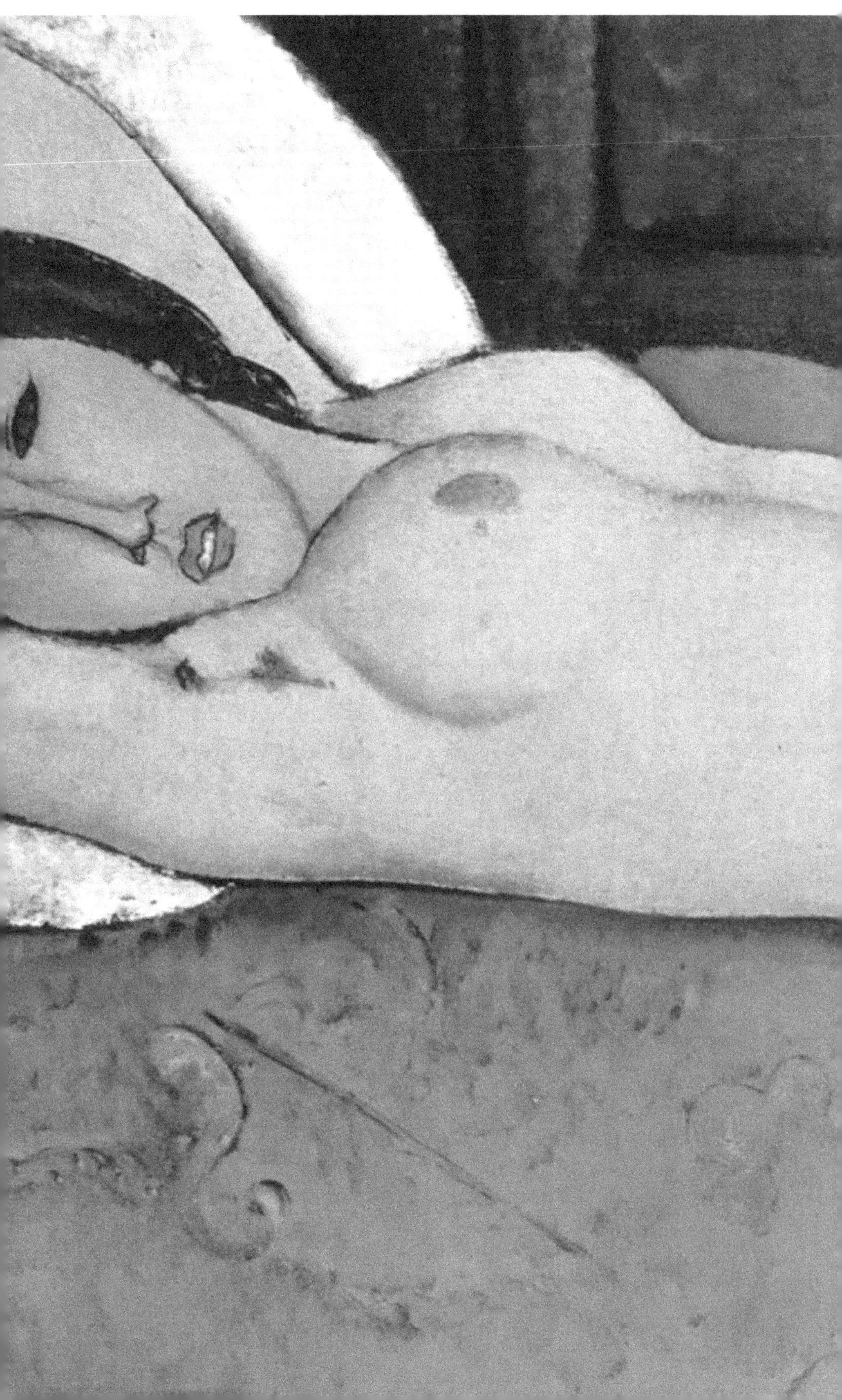

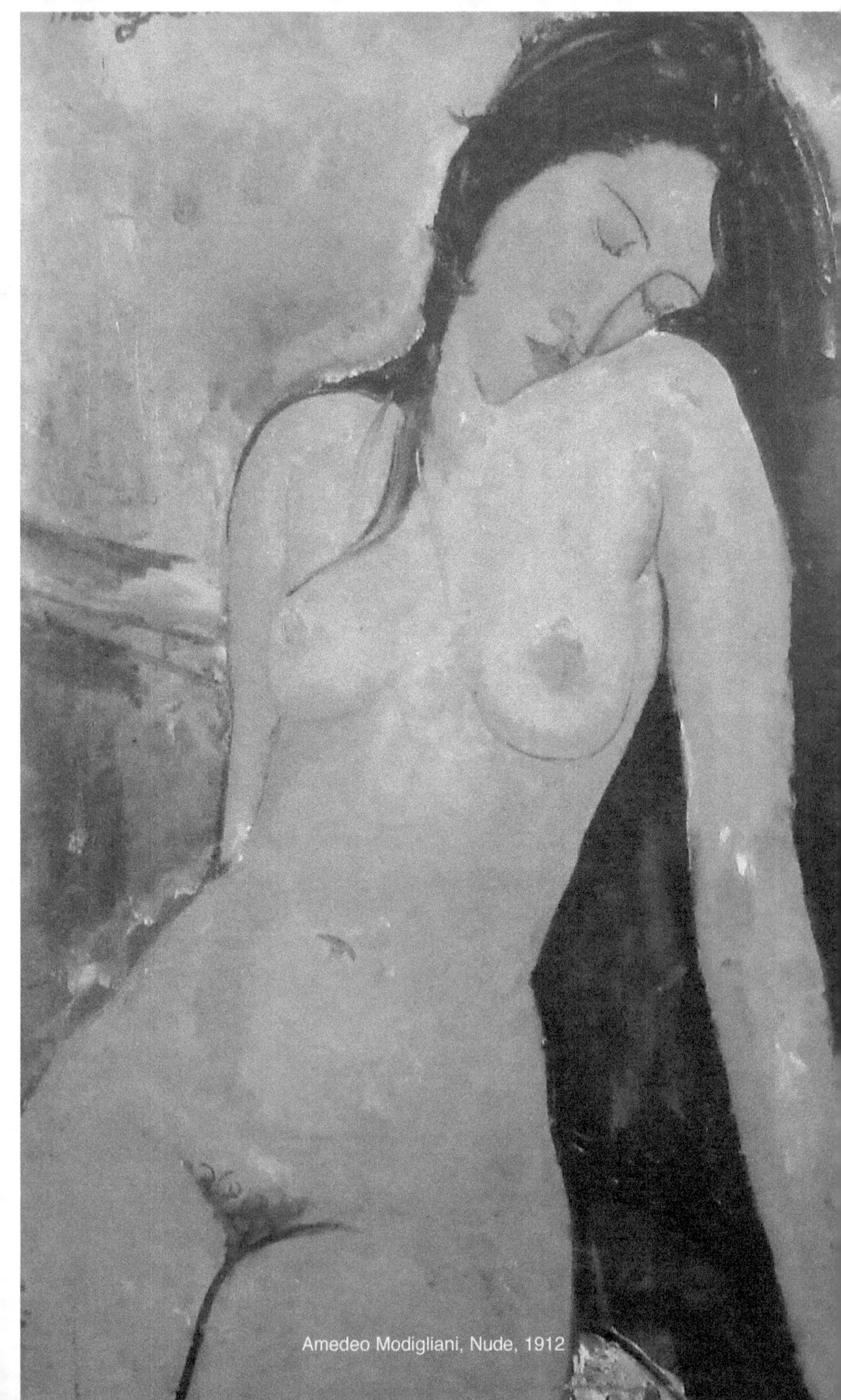

Amedeo Modigliani, Nude, 1912

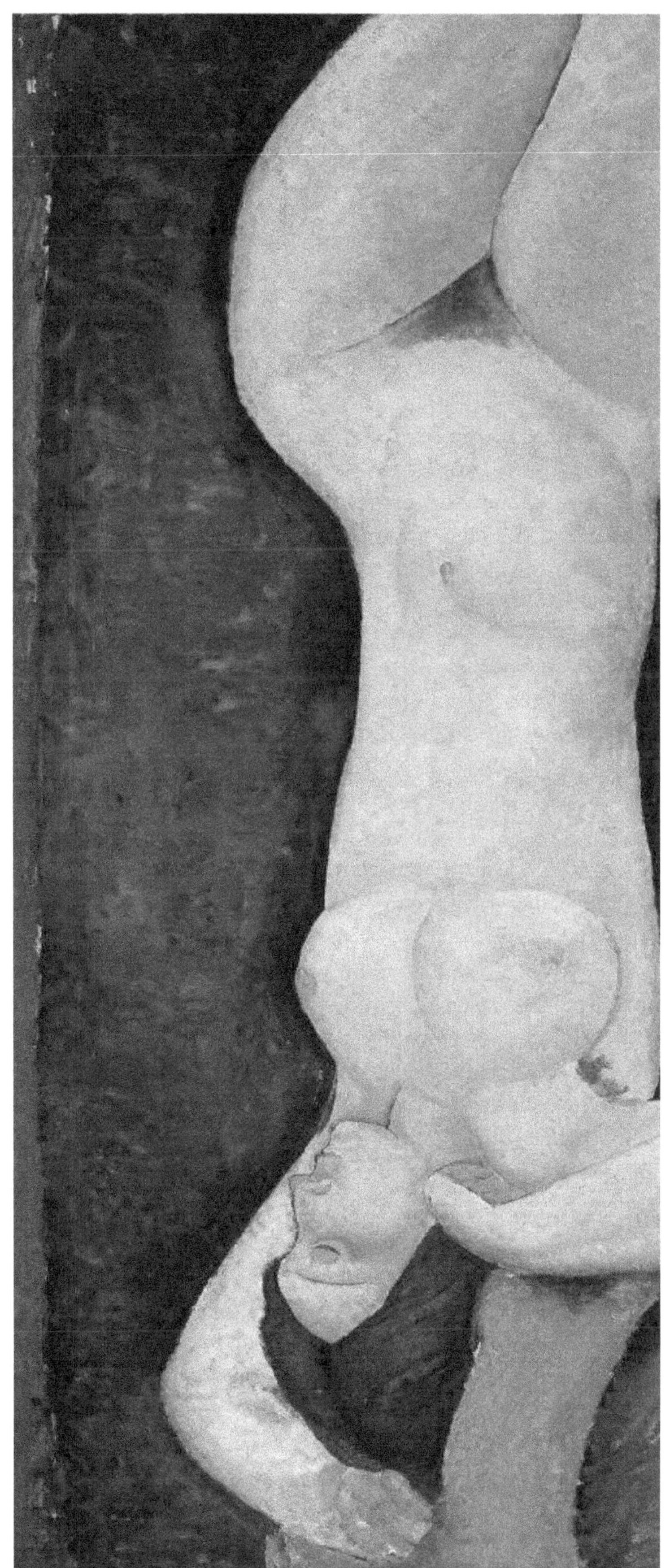

Amedeo Modigliani, Reclining Nude, 1919

THE SURREALISTS

The Surrealists seemed to approach sexuality in a new way, but their concepts of *l'amour fou*, of sex and death, of æsthetics and poetry, turn out to be as patriarchal, as sexist and routinely heterosexual as the rest of Western art. As André Masson wrote, 'eroticism and death are always coexistent.'[1] Typical among Surrealist images and philosophies is Salvador Dali's *Phenomenon of Ecstasy*, showing various photos of women (supposedly) in orgasm, a collage that targets the main areas of Surrealist discourse which are always connected: eroticism, death and 'the feminine'.[2]

The Surrealist artists did not seriously alter notions of sexuality, although they did question them. Indeed, Surrealism focused on sex obsessively, as obsessive as Symbolism, from which it derives much. If a book prints a still from the key Surrealist film, Luis Buñuel's and Salvador Dali's *Un Chien Andalou*, it is always the image of the man's hands pressed against the woman's breasts (or maybe it was just that someone from the film's distributors thought that was the best image to sum up the film).

Nearly all the major Surrealist artists made erotic art, or included erotic elements in their art: René Magritte produced the *Rape*, showing a woman's body as a face, with breasts for eyes and the vagina for the mouth,[3] Salvador Dali drew many erotic pictures, including bizarre moustachioed men being sucked off by prepubescent girls entitled *Choice Treats for Children* (child abuse images which are distinctly un-PC), and Man Ray produced films that evoked pornography.

---

1 André Masson: *Entriens avec Georges Charbonnier*, Paris 1958, 138
2 Dali: *Phenomenon of Ecstasy*, in *Minotaure*, nos. 3-4, 1933, 77
3 Magritte: *The Rape*, 1934, pencil drawing, 14 x 9.5in, Menil Foundation Collection, Houston, Texas

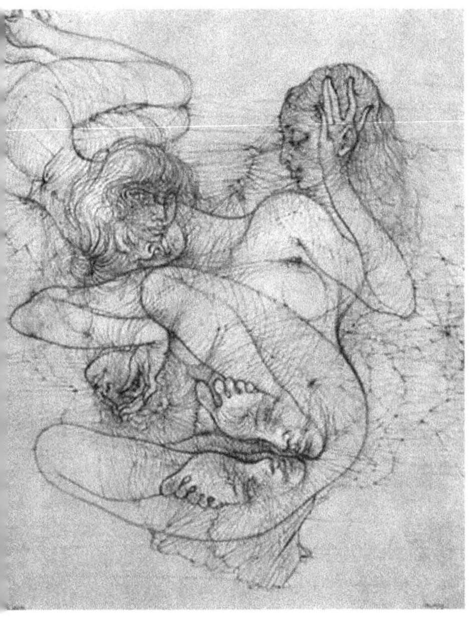

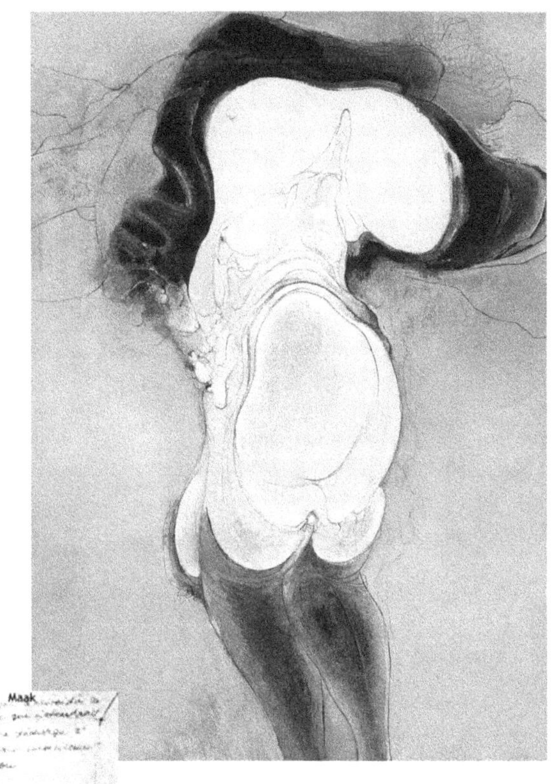

Hans Bellmer, 1930s.

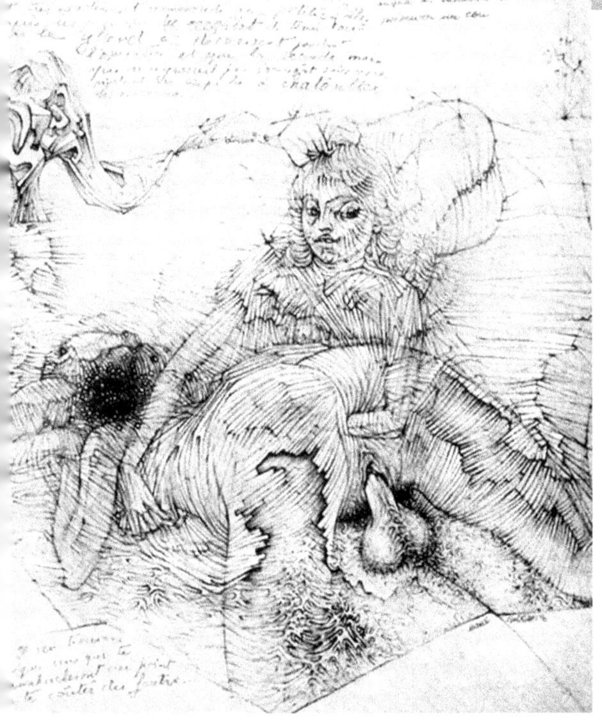

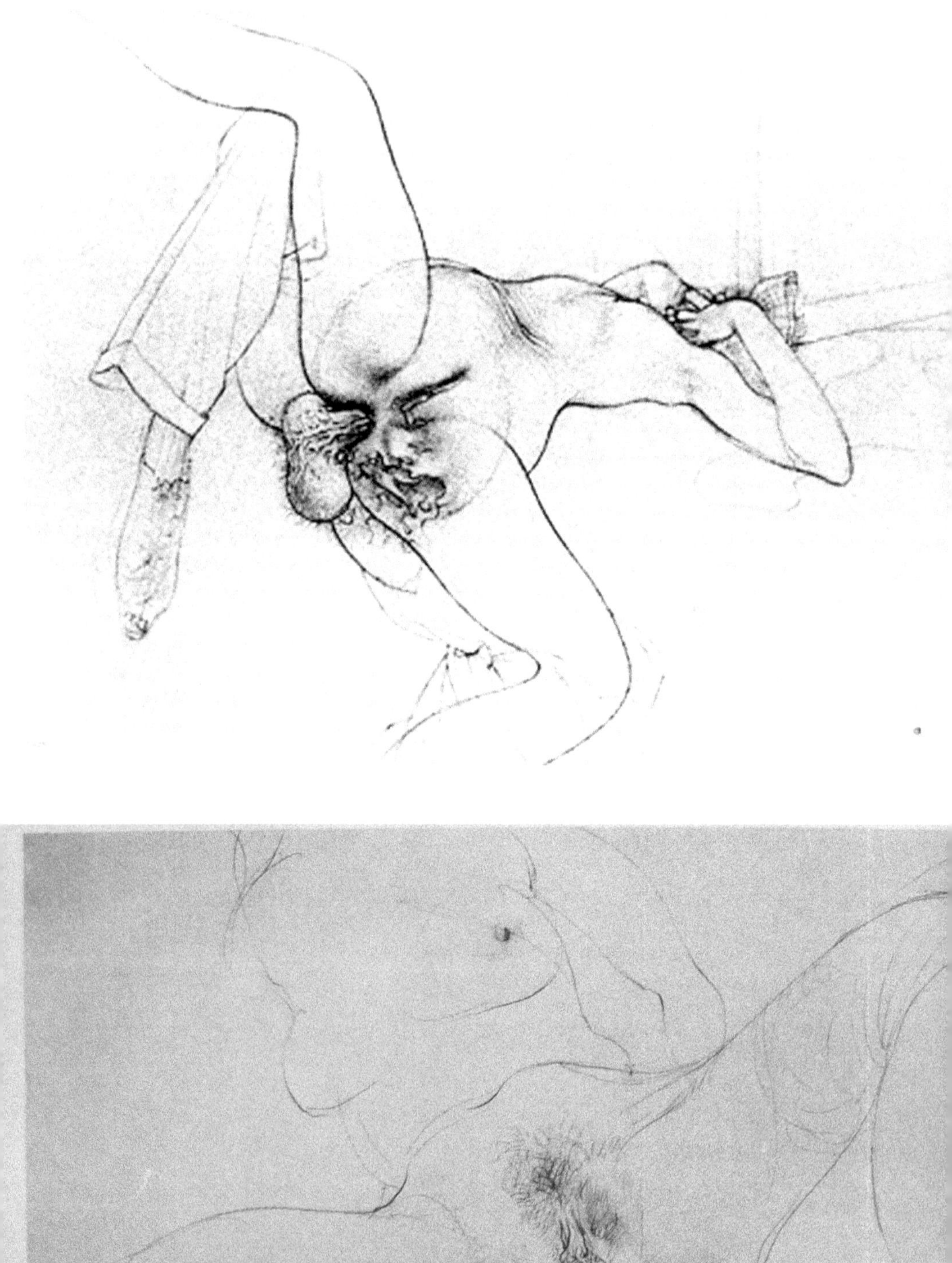

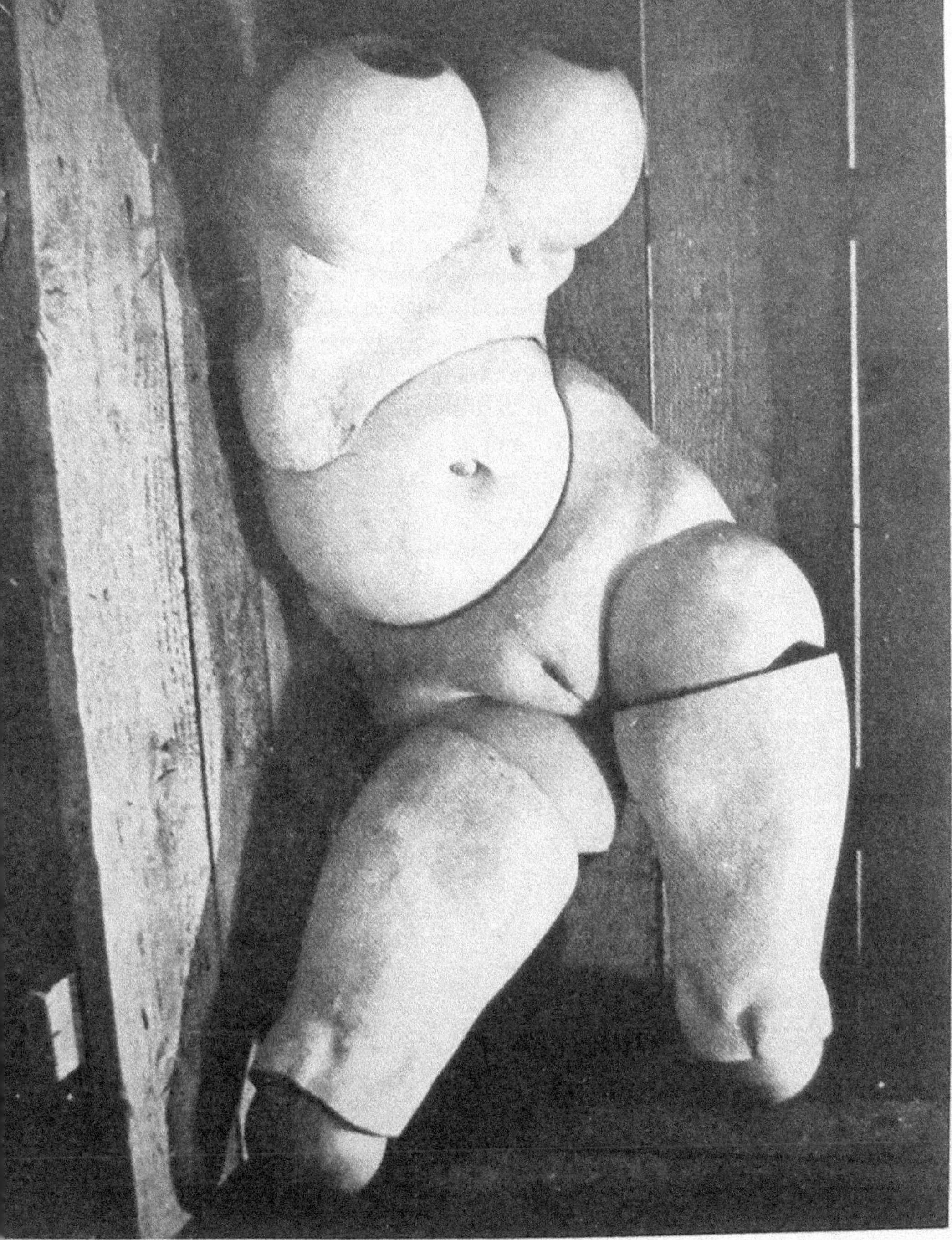

THE GREAT MODERNISTS

Eroticism in the great painters of the modern era, those artists who command millions of dollars when their major works appear at international auctions, is thoroughly conventional, according to the rules and structures of patriarchal culture. From the mid-19th century onwards, the nude becomes increasingly eroticized. Nudes are always in part erotic. Even in nudes which consciously negate any inkling of eroticism – as in the mediæval images of Death and the Maiden, or Adam and Eve – there is always an element of eroticism. In the modern era, an emphasis on the sexuality of the body becomes more and more apparent.

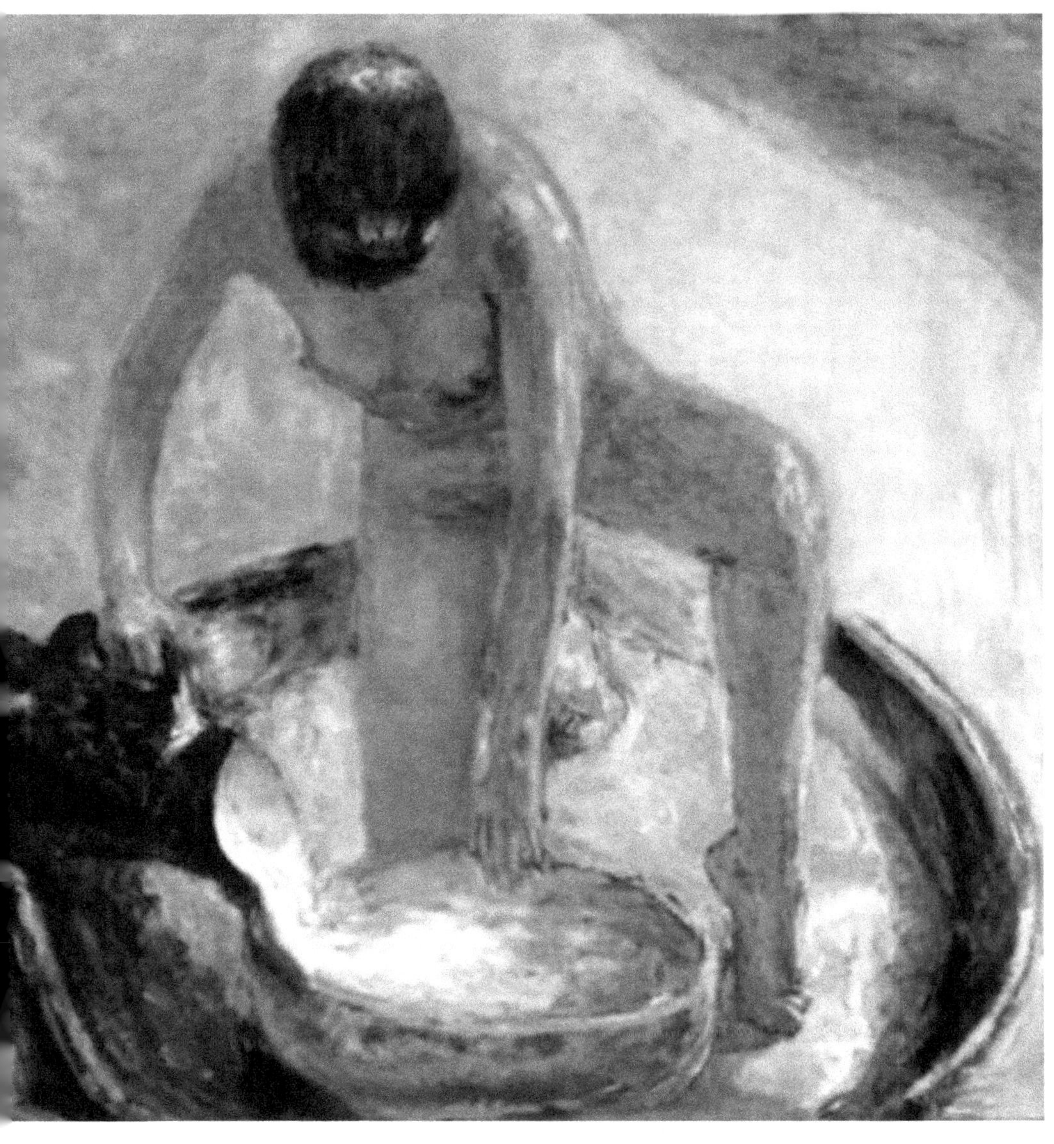

Pierre Bonnard, Nude Crouching In a Tub

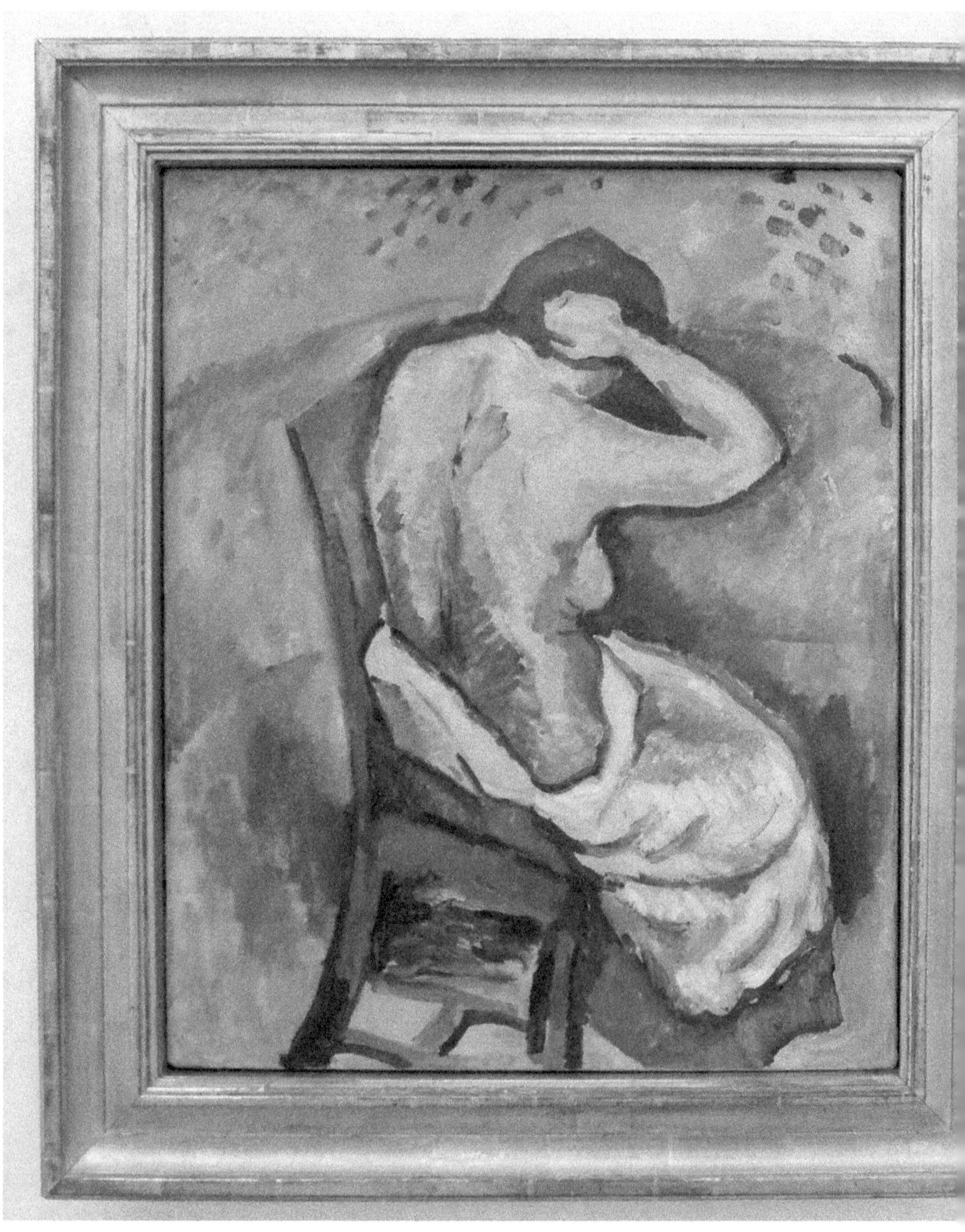

Georges Braque, Nude Sitting, 1907, Pompidou Centre, Paris.

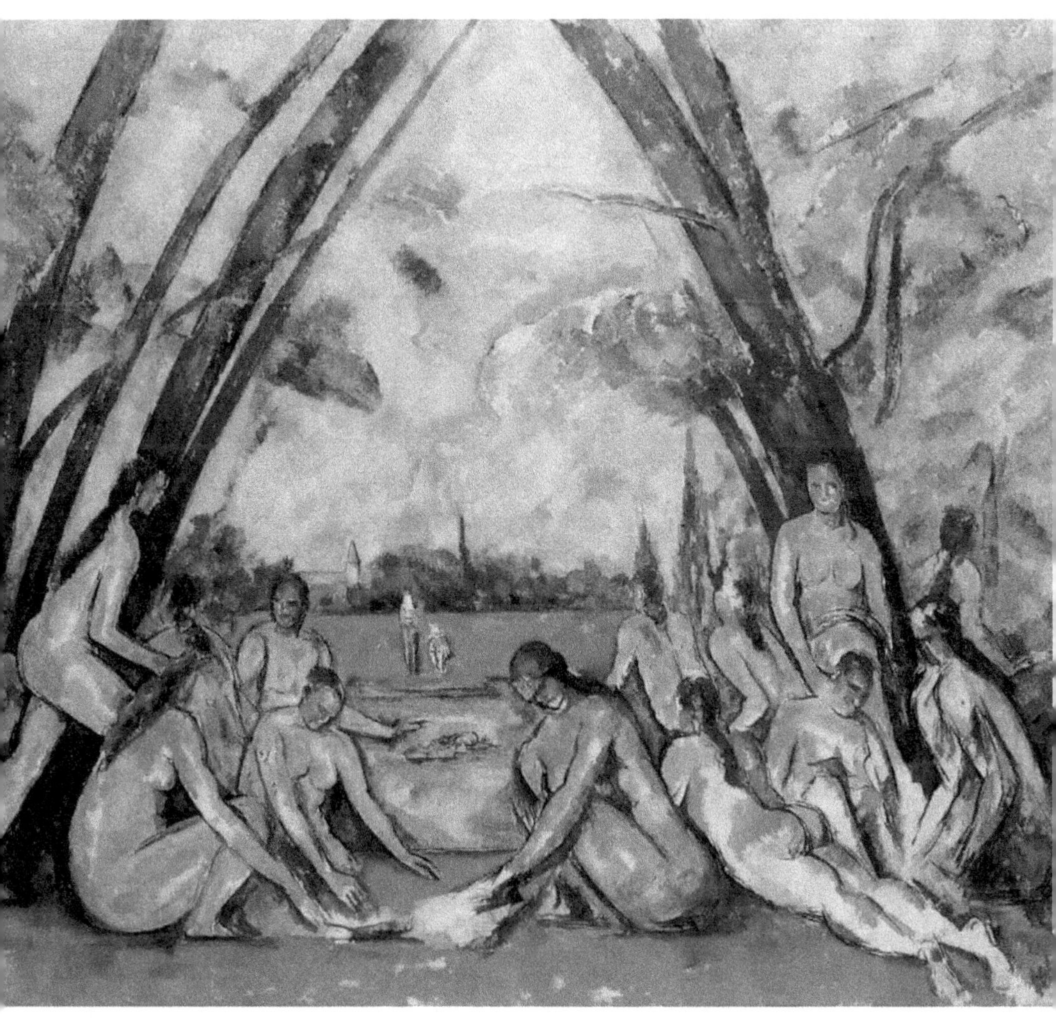

Paul Cézanne, Large Bathers, 1906,
Philadelphia Museum of Art

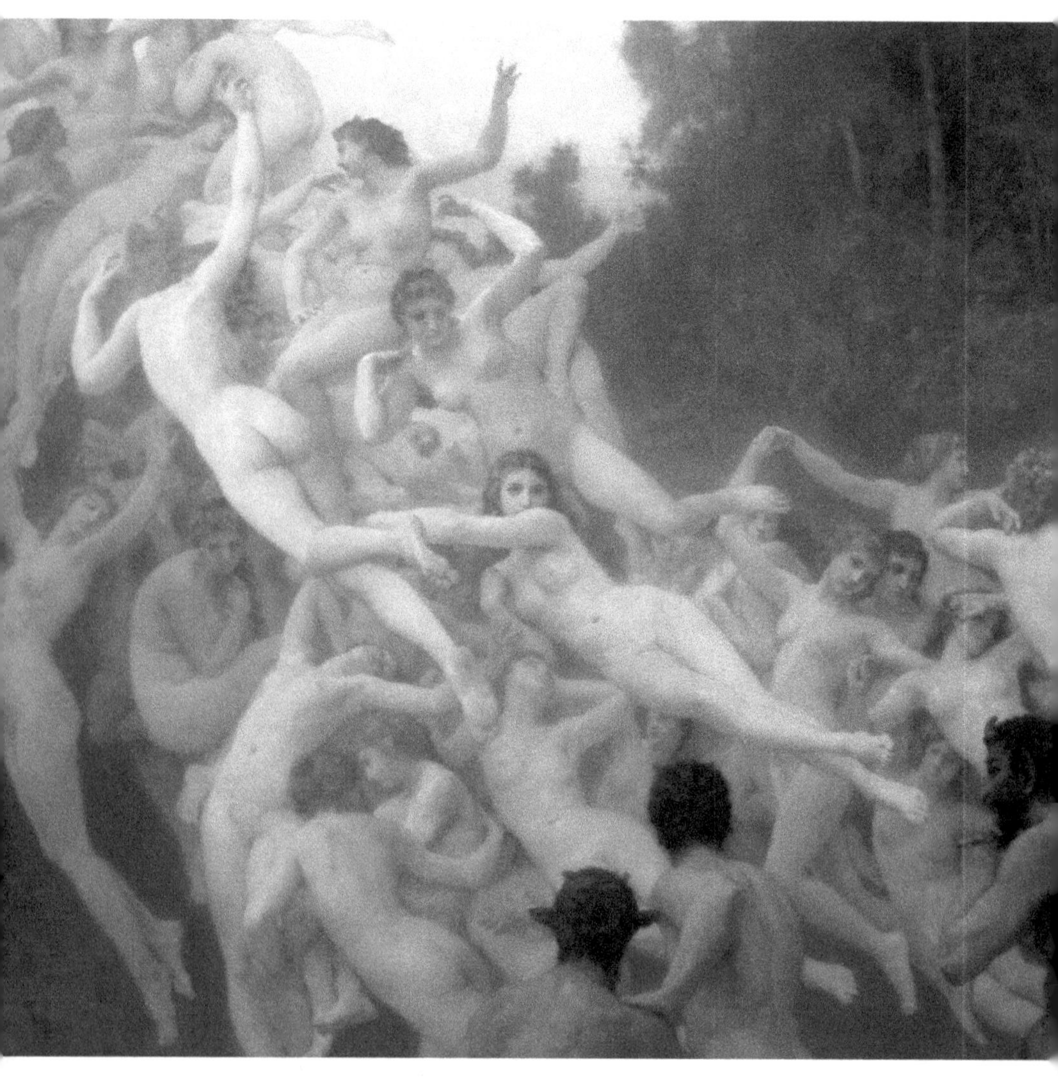

William Bouguereau, Oréades, 1902, Orsay Museum, Paris

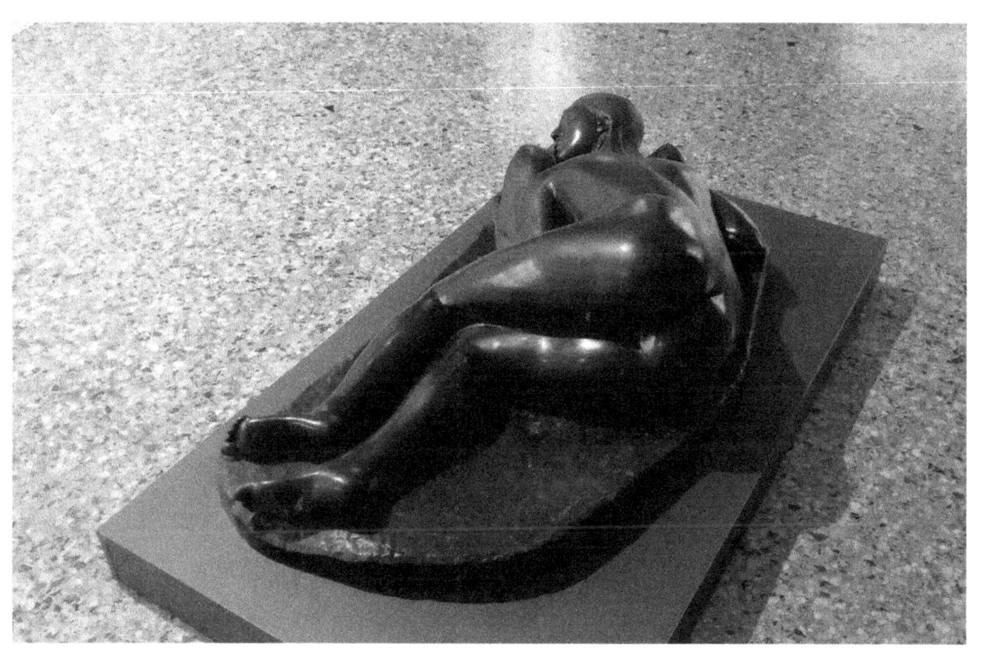

Arturo Martini, La Pisana, 1928.

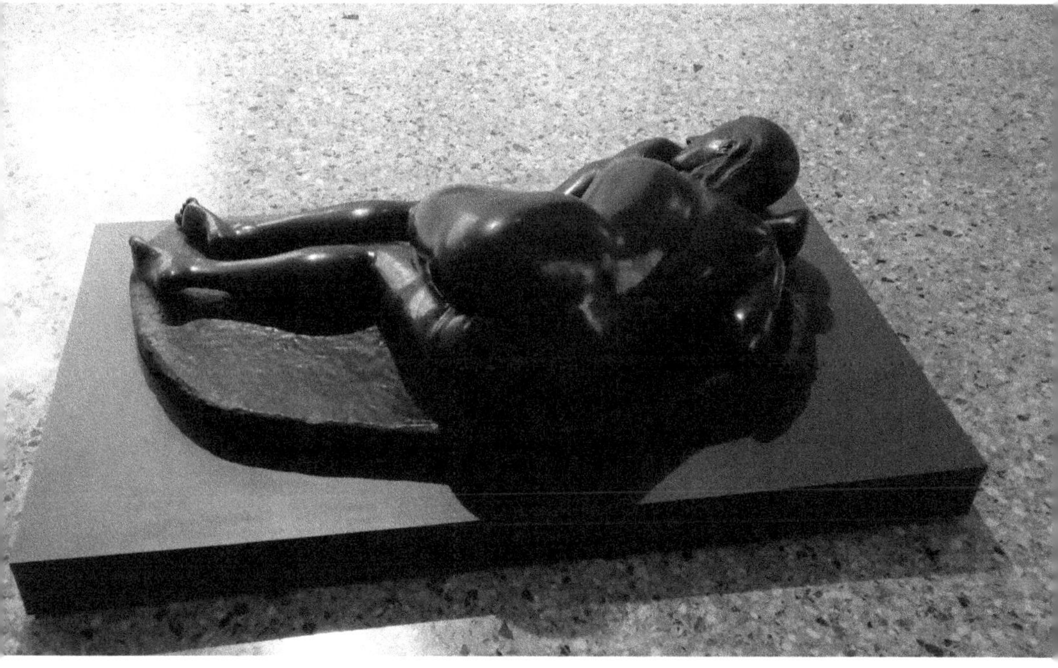

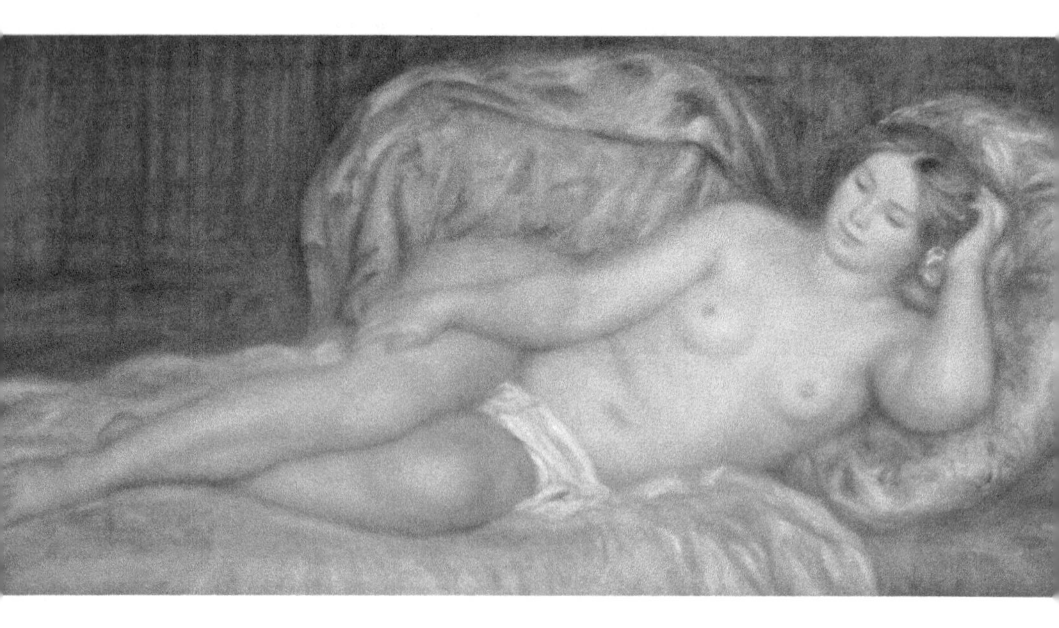

Pierre Renoir, Nude, 1907, Orsay Museum, Paris.

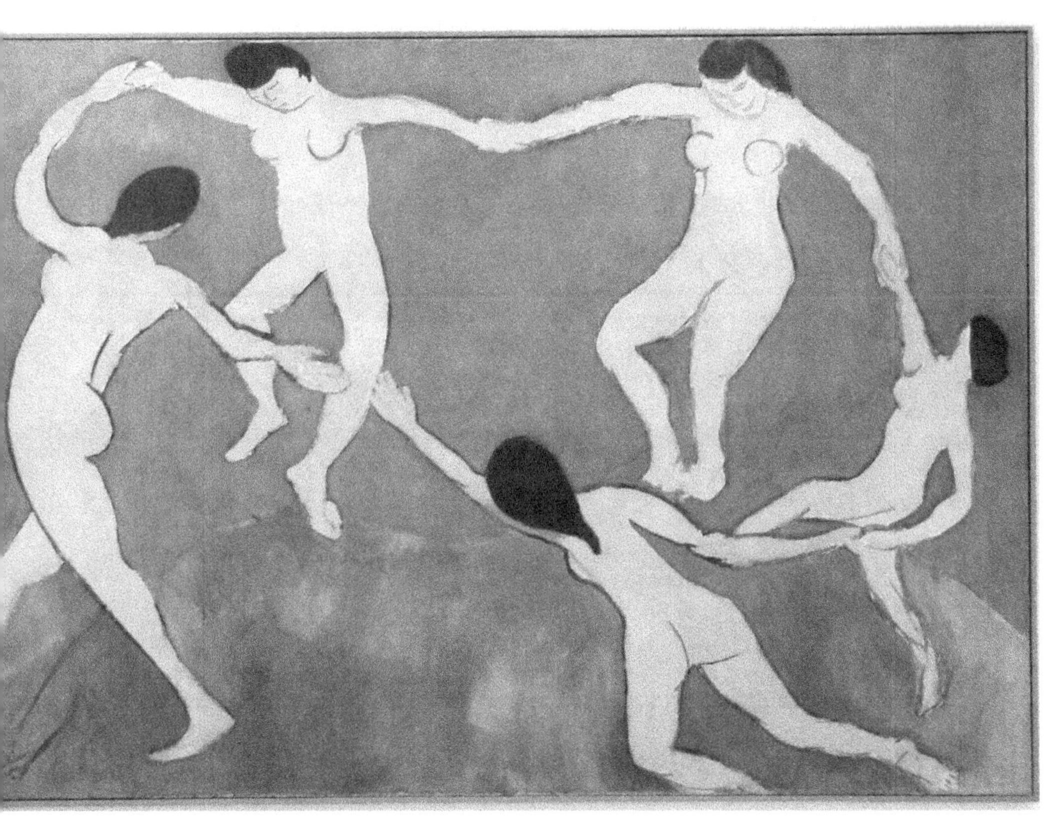

Henri Matisse, The Dance, New York City

BIBLIOGRAPHY

E. de Antonio & M. Tuchman: *Painters Painting,* Abbeville Press, New York, NY, 1984

C.G. Argan: *The Renaissance,* Thames & Hudson, London, 1969

I. Armstrong, ed. *New Feminist Discourses: Critical Essays on Theories and Texts,* Routledge, London, 1992

J. Atkins: *Sex in Literature,* volume 2: *The Classical Experience of the Sexual Impulse,* Calder & Boyars, London, 1973

P. Bade: *Femme Fatale: Images of evil and fascinating women,* Ash & Grant 1979

M. Baxandall: *Painting and Experience in 15th Century Italy,* Oxford University Press 1988

—. *Patterns of Intention: On the Historical Explanation of Pictures,* Yale University Press 1985

G. Bazin: *A Concise History of World Sculpture,* David & Charles, Newton Abbot 1981

J. Beck: *Italian Renaissance Painting,* Harper & Row, New York, NY, 1981

B. Berenson: *The Italian Painters of the Renaissance,* Phaidon, London, 1952

—. *Looking at Pictures with Bernard Berenson*, selected by Hann Kiel, Abrahams, New York, NY, 1974

B. Bernard: *The Queen of Heaven: A Selection of Painting the Virgin from the Twelfth to the Eighteenth Centuries,* Macdonald/ Orbis, London, 1987

—. *The Bible and Its Painters,* Orbis, London, 1983

F. Bonner *et al*, eds. *Imagining Women Cultural Representations and Gender,* Polity Press, Cambridge 1992

S. Bramly: *Leonardo: The Artist and the Man,* Michael Joseph 1992

A. Brahama: *Italian Renaissance Painters of the Sixteenth Century,* National Gallery 1985

J. Burckhardt: *The Altarpiece in Renaissance Italy,* Phaidon, London, 1988

T. Burckhardt: *Sacred Art in East and West,* Perennial Book, Middlesex 1967

W. Chadwick: *Women, Art, and Society,* Thames & Hudson, London, 1990

—. *Women Artists and the Surrealist Movement,* Thames & Hudson, London, 1991

A. Chastel: *Art of the Italian Renaissance,* tr. P. & L. Murray, Alpine Fine Arts Collection, London, 1985

—. *The Studios and Styles of the Renaissance, Italy 1460-1500,* tr. Griffin, Thames & Hudson, London, 1966

G. Chester & J. Dickey, ed. *Feminism and Censorship: The Current Debate,* Prism Press, Bridport, Dorset 1988

H.B. Chipp, ed. *Theories of Modern Art,* University Press of California, Los Angeles, 1968
J.E. Cirlot: *A Dictionary of Symbols,* Routledge, London, 1981
Kenneth Clark. *The Nude,* Pantheon Books, 1957
B. Cole: *The Renaissance Artist at Work,* John Murray, London, 1983
J.C. Cooper: *An Illustrated Dictionary of Traditional Symbols,* Thames & Hudson, London, 1978
L. Dresen-Coenders, ed. *Saints and She-Devils: Images of Women in the 15th and 16th Centuries,* Rubicon Press 1987
W. Dube: *The Expressionists,* Thames & Hudson, London, 1972
S.C. Dubin: *Arresting Images: Impolitic Art and Uncivil Actions,* Routledge, London, 1992
G. Duby & M. Perrot: *Power and Beauty: Images of Women in Art,* Tauris Parke Books,
A. Dworkin. *Intercourse,* Arrow, London, 1988
—. *Pornography: Men Possessing Women,* Women's Press, London, 1984
C. Eisler: *Early Netherlandish Painting: The Thyssen-Bornemisza Collection,* Sotheby's Publications, London, 1989
A. Elsen: *Modern European Sculpture 1918-45,* New York, NY, 1979
J. Evans, ed. *The Flowering of the Middle Ages,* Thames & Hudson, London, 1966
J. Evola: *The Metaphysics of Sex,* East-West Publications, London, 1985
M. Foucault: *The History of Sexuality,* Penguin, London, 1981
—. *The Use of Pleasure: The History of Sexuality,* vol. 2, Penguin, London, 1987
S.J. Freedberg: *Painting of the High Renaissance in Rome and Florence,* Harper & Row, New York, NY, 1972
S. Freud: *Leonardo da Vinci,* tr. A. Tyson, Penguin, London, 1963
E. Gadon: *The Once and Future Goddess,* Aquarian Press 1990
Fred Gettings: *The Hidden Art: A Study of the Occult Symbolism in Art,* Studio Vista, London, 1978
P. Gibson & R. Gibson, ed. *Dirty Looks: Women, Pornography, Power,* British Film Institute, London, 1993
M. Gimbutas: *The Language of the Goddess,* Thames & Hudson, London, 1989
R. Goldwater & M. Treves, eds. *Artists On Art,* John Murray, London, 1975
E.H. Gombrich: *Norm and Form: Studies in the Renaissance I,* Phaidon, London, 1985
—. *Symbolic Images, Renaissance Studies II,* Phaidon, London, 1985
S. Griffin: *Pornography and Silence: Culture's Revenge Against Nature,* Women's Press, London, 1981
J. Hale: *Italian Renaissance Painting,* Phaidon, London, 1977
J. Hall: *A Dictionary of Subjects and Symbols in Art,* John Murray, London, 1984
M. Esther Harding: *Women's Mysteries,* Rider, London, 1989
F. Hartt: *History of Italian Renaissance Art: Painting, Sculpture, Architecture,* Thames & Hudson, London, 1987
N.G. Heller: *Women Artists: An Illustrated History,* Virago, London, 1987
J. Hobhouse: *The Bride Stripped Bare: The Artist and the Nude in the Twentieth Century,* Cape, London, 1988

A. Hollander: *Seeing Through Clothes*, Viking Press, New York, NY, 1980
M. Humm: *Feminisms: A Reader*, Harvester Wheatsheaf, 1992
—. ed. *The Dictionary of Feminist Theory*, Harvester Wheatsheaf 1989
M. Jacobs: *A Guide to European Painting*, David & Charles 1980
—. *Mythological Painting*, Phaidon 1979
P. Julian: *Dreamers of Decadence: Symbolist Painters of the 1890s*, tr. R. Baldick, Pall Mall Press, London, 1971
S. Kappeler: *The Pornography of Representation*, Polity Press, Cambridge 1986
D. Kelder: *Pageant of the Renaissance*, Pall Mall Press, London, 1969
J.A. Kestner: *Mythology and Misogyny: The Social Discourse of Nineteenth-Century British Classical-Subject Painting*, University of Wisconsin Press, Madison 1989
C. Kramarae & P.A. Treichler, eds. *A Feminist Dictionary*, Pandora Press, London, 1987
J. Kristeva: *The Kristeva Reader*, ed. Toril Moi, Blackwell 1986
—. *Desire in Language: A Semiotic Approach to Literature and Art*, ed. L. Roudiez, tr. T. Gora *et al*, Blackwell 1982
J. Lacan and the *Ecole Freudienne: Feminine Sexuality*, eds. J. Mitchell and J. Rose, Macmillan, London, 1982
A. Le Normand-Romain *et al. Sculpture: The Adventure of Modern Sculpture in the Nineteenth and Twentieth Centuries*, Skira, Geneva, 1986
L. da Vinci: *The Drawings of Leonardo da Vinci*, introduction A.E. Popham, Cape, London, 1964
M. Levey: *High Renaissance*, Penguin, London, 1975
—. *Early Renaissance*, Penguin, London, 1967
F. Licht: *Sculpture, 19th and 20th Centuries*, Michael Joseph, London, 1967
L. Lippard: *From the Center: feminist essays on women's art*, Dutton, New York, NY, 1976
—. *Six Years: The Dematerialization of the Art Object from 1966 to 1972*, Praeger, New York, NY, 1973
E. Lucie-Smith: *Symbolist Art*, Thames & Hudson, London, 1972
—. *Sexuality in Western Art*, Thames & Hudson, London, 1991
F. MacCarthy: *Eric Gill*, Faber, London, 1989
E. Marks & I. de Courtivron, eds. *New French Feminisms: an Anthology*, Harvester Wheatsheaf 1981
J.C.J. Metford: *Dictionary of Christian Lore and Legend*, Thames & Hudson, London, 1983
Michelangelo: *The Complete Paintings*, Granada, London, 1980
E. Mitsch: *The Art of Egon Schiele*, Phaidon 1975
T. Moi: *Sexual/Textual Politics: Feminist Literary Theory*, Routledge, London, 1988
E. Mullins: *The Painted Witch: Female Body, Male Art*, Secker & Warburg, London, 1985
L. Mulvey: *Visual and Other Pleasures*, Macmillan, London, 1989
S. Munt, ed. *New Lesbian Criticism: Literary and Cultural Readings*, Harvester Wheatsheaf, London, 1992

P. & L. Murray: *The Penguin Dictionary of Art and Artists,* Penguin, London, 1976
L. Murray: *High Renaissance*, Thames & Hudson, London, 1977
L. Nead: *Female Nude: Art, Obscenity and Sexuality*, Routledge, London, 1992
E. Neumann: *The Great Mother*, Princeton University Press, NJ 1972
S. Nicholson, ed. *The Goddess Re-awakening: The Goddess Principle Today,* Theosophical Publishing House, New York, NY, 1989
J. Paladilhe. *Gustave Moreau*, Thames & Hudson, London,1972
E. Panofsky: *Studies in Iconology,* Harper & Row, New York, NY, 1972
—. *Early Netherlandish Painting*, Harvard University Press, Mass., 1953
R. Parker & G. Pollock. *Old Mistresses: Women, Art an Ideology*, Routledge & Kegan Paul, London, 1981
W. Pater: *The Renaissance*, Oxford University Press 1980
R. Payne: *Leonardo da Vinci*, Robert Hale, London, 1979
K. Petersen & J.J. Wilson: *Women Artists: Recognition and Reappraisal from the Early Middle Ages to the Twentieth Century* Women's Press, London, 1978
G. Pollock: *Vision and Difference: femininity, feminism and histories of art,* Routledge, London, 1988
M. Praz: *The Romantic Agony,* tr. Davidson, Oxford University Press 1933
Peter Redgrove. *The Black Goddess and the Sixth Sense, Bloomsbury, London, 1987*
F. Roh: *German Art in the Twentieth Century: Painting, Sculpture, Architecture*, Thames & Hudson, London, 1968
M. Roskill: *What is Art History?*, Thames & Hudson, London, 1976
G. Saunders. *The Nude: a new perspective*, Herbert Press, London, 1989
P. Selz. *German Expressionist Painting*, University of California Press, Berkely, CA, 1974
—. *Art in Our Times: A Pictorial History 1890-1980*, Thames & Hudson, London, 1982
E. Showalter, ed. *The New Feminist Criticism*, Virago, London, 1986
Penelope Shuttle & Peter Redgrove. *The Wise Wound,* Paladin/ Grafton, 1978/86
M. Sjöo & B. Mor: *The Great Cosmic Mother*, Harper & Row, San Francisco 1987
F. Stella. *Working Space*, Harvard University Press, Cambridge, MA, 1986
—. *Frank Stella*, Madrid, 1995
K. Stiles & P. Selz, eds. *Theories & Documents of Contemporary Art: A Sourcebook of Artists' Writings*, University of California Press, Berkeley, CA, 1996
V.I. Stoichita: *Leonardo da Vinci*, Abbey Library, London, 1978
S. Rubin Suleiman, ed. *The Female Body in Western Culture: Contemporary Perspectives*, Harvard University Press, Cambridge, Mass., 1986
William Thompson. *The Time Falling Bodies Take to Light: Mythology, Sexuality and the Origins of Culture,* St Martin's Press, New York, NY, 1981
A. Tilly: *Erotic Drawings*, Phaidon 1986
P. Trevor-Roper: *The world blunted through sight: An inquiry into the influence of defective vision on art and character*, Thames & Hudson, London, 1970
W. Tucker. *The Language of Sculpture*, Thames & Hudson, London, 1974
L. Venturi: *Renaissance Painting, from Leonardo to Dürer,* Skira/ Macmillan 1979
—. *Italian Paintings,* Zwemmer, London, 1950

P. Vergo: *Art in Vienna: 1898-1918: Klimt, Kokoschka, Schiele and Their Contemporaries*, Phaidon 1975

G. de Vries, ed. *On Art: Artists' Writings on the Changed Notion of Art After, 1965*, Cologne, 1974

B. Walker: *Body Magic*, Paladin, London, 1979

—. *Tantrism: Its Secret Principles and Practices*, Aquarian Press, Wellingborough 1982

Marina Warner. *Alone Of All Her Sex: The Myth and Cult of the Virgin Mary*, Picador, London, 1985

—. *Monuments and Maidens*, Weidenfeld & Nicolson, London, 1985

Valerie Wayne, ed. *The Matter of Difference: Materialist Feminist Criticism of Shakespeare*, Harvester Wheatsheaf, Hemel Hempstead, 1991

P. Webb: *The Erotic Arts*, Secker & Warburg, London, 1983

D. Wheeler: *Art Since Mid-Century: 1945 to the Present*, Thames & Hudson, London, 1991

F. Whitford: *Egon Schiele*, Thames & Hudson, London, 1981

L. Williams: *Hard Core*: Power, *Pleasure, and the 'Frenzy of the Visible'*, Pandora, London, 1990

C. Wilson: *The Sexual Misfits: A Study of Sexual Outsiders*, Collins, London, 1989

H. Wolfflin: *Classic Art*, Phaidon 1952/80

M. Wudram: *Art of the Renaissance*, Weidenfeld & Nicolson, London, 1985

WEBSITES

eroticbibliophile.com
eroti-cart.com
deltaofvenus.com
erotomane.org

CRESCENT MOON PUBLISHING

web: www.crmoon.com e-mail: cresmopub@yahoo.co.uk

ARTS, PAINTING, SCULPTURE

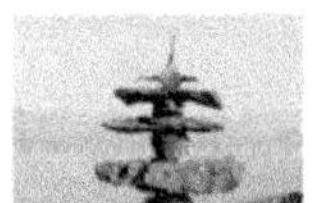

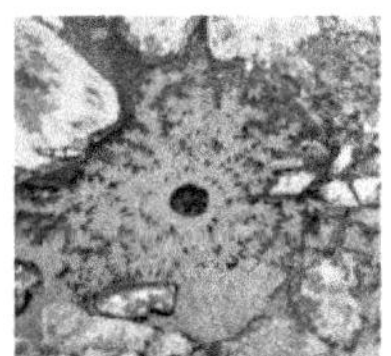

The Art of Andy Goldsworthy
Andy Goldsworthy: Touching Nature
Andy Goldsworthy in Close-Up
Andy Goldsworthy: Pocket Guide
Andy Goldsworthy In America

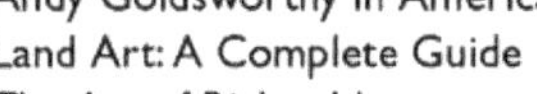

Land Art: A Complete Guide
The Art of Richard Long
Richard Long: Pocket Guide
Land Art In the UK
Land Art in Close-Up
Land Art In the U.S.A.
Land Art: Pocket Guide

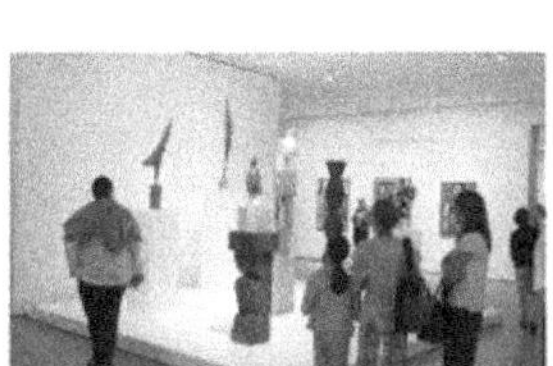

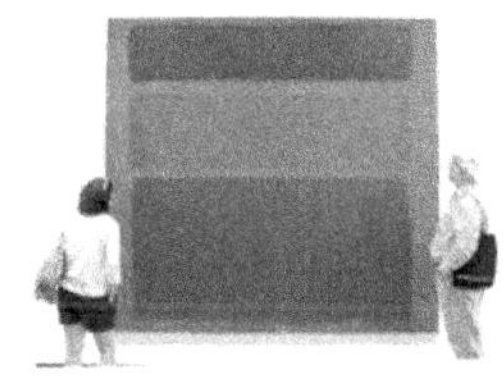

Installation Art in Close-Up
Minimal Art and Artists In the 1960s and After
Colourfield Painting
Land Art DVD, TV documentary
Andy Goldsworthy DVD, TV documentary
The Erotic Object: Sexuality in Sculpture From Prehistory to the Present Day
Sex in Art: Pornography and Pleasure in Painting and Sculpture
Postwar Art
Sacred Gardens: The Garden in Myth, Religion and Art
Glorification: Religious Abstraction in Renaissance and 20th Century Art

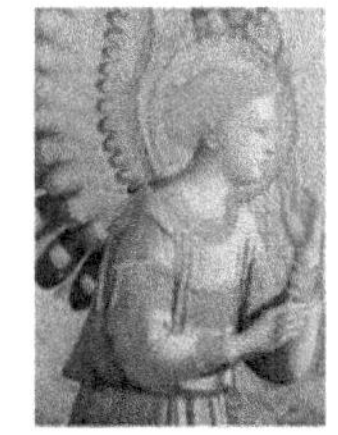

Early Netherlandish Painting
Leonardo da Vinci
Piero della Francesca
Giovanni Bellini
Fra Angelico: Art and Religion in the Renaissance
Mark Rothko: The Art of Transcendence
Frank Stella: American Abstract Artist

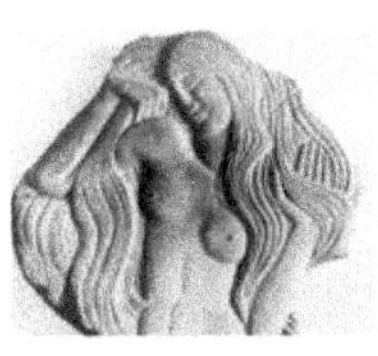

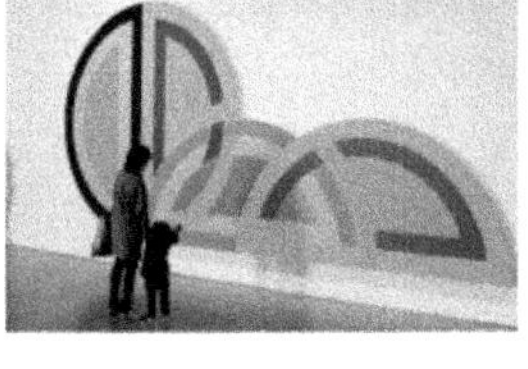

Jasper Johns
Brice Marden
Alison Wilding: The Embrace of Sculpture
Vincent van Gogh: Visionary Landscapes
Eric Gill: Nuptials of God
Constantin Brancusi: Sculpting the Essence of Things
Max Beckmann
Caravaggio
Gustave Moreau

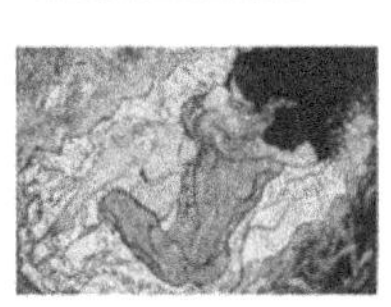

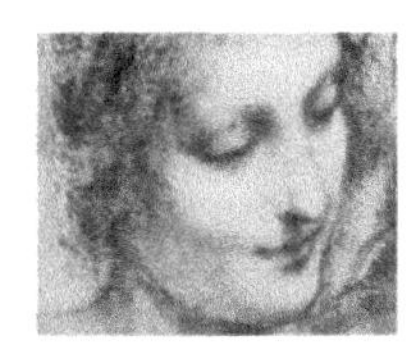

Egon Schiele: Sex and Death In Purple Stockings
Delizioso Fotografico Fervore: Works In Process 1
Sacro Cuore: Works In Process 2
The Light Eternal: J.M.W. Turner
The Madonna Glorified: Karen Arthurs

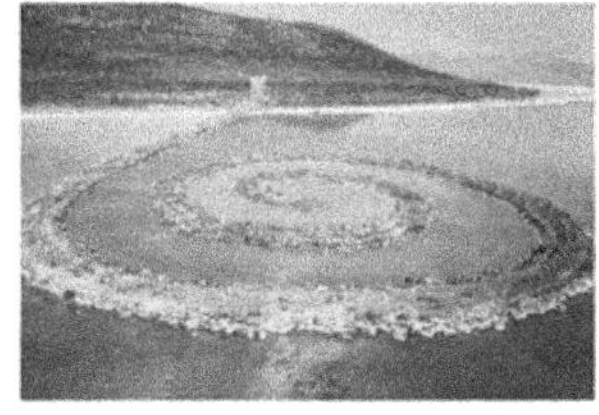

www.ingramcontent.com/pod-product-compliance
Lightning Source LLC
LaVergne TN
LVHW010939100826
845153LV00001B/98
* 9 7 8 1 8 6 1 7 1 1 8 1 6 *